The Encyclopedia of Christian Marriage

The
Encyclopedia
of Christian
Marriage

Edited by

Cecil B. Murphey

Fleming H. Revell
A Division of Baker Book House Co
Grand Rapids, Michigan 49516

Published by Fleming H. Revell
a division of Baker Book House Company
P.O. Box 6287, Grand Rapids, MI 49516-6287

First paperback edition 1994

Printed in the United States of America

Library of Congress Cataloging-in-Publication Data

Main entry under title:
The Encyclopedia of Christian Marriage
    Includes bibliographies and index.
        1. Marriage—Religious aspects—Christianity—Dictionaries.
HQ734.E645 1984 646.7'8   83-13780
ISBN 0-8007-5541-3

Scripture references identified RSV are taken from the Revised Standard Version of the Bible, copyright 1946, 1952, 1971, and 1973 by the Division of Christian Education of the National Council of Churches of Christ in the United States of America.

Acknowledgments for the use of copyrighted material continued on page 9.

Contents

5 FAMILY LIFE AND PARENTING

6 FINANCES

7 DIVORCE

Foreword

Good marriages don't just happen—they require attention, thought, and serious effort. This is a point on which writers and counselors agree. This volume represents some of the best writing on marriage, gleaned from various sources, as well as original material by its compiler, Cecil Murphey.

The Encyclopedia of Christian Marriage covers all the stages of married life—engagement and wedding, the relationship of husband and wife, child rearing, the middle-age years, and retirement. Within these general areas, however, the articles focus on the critical issues, those for which husbands and wives continually seek helpful answers.

In our fast-moving society, the best-informed men and women are the ones most able to make the adjustments necessary to create and maintain healthy, stable marital and family relationships. This book, representing the writings of highly regarded experts in their fields, is a valuable tool for Christian husbands and wives who are seeking guidance in achieving a rewarding life together.

THE PUBLISHER

Acknowledgments

We are grateful to Cecil Murphey, who did the compilation of the material in this volume. Minister of the Riverdale (Georgia) Presbyterian Church since 1974, he is the author of fifteen books, including *Getting There From Here* and *Seven Deadly Sins,* and hundreds of articles, which have appeared in *Christianity Today, New Covenant, Faith and Inspiration,* and other publications.

Acknowledgment is made to the following for permission to reprint copyrighted material:

ABINGDON: Excerpts from ABINGDON MARRIAGE MANUAL by Perry H. Biddle. Copyright © 1974 by Abingdon Press. Used by permission. Excerpts from THE BOOK OF WORSHIP FOR CHURCH AND HOME. Copyright © 1964, 1965 by The Board of Publication of The Methodist Church. Used by permission. Excerpts from LETTERS TO KAREN by Charlie W. Shedd. Copyright © 1965 by Abingdon Press. Used by permission.

ANDREWS AND MCMEEL, INC.: Excerpts from THE BEST DAD IS A GOOD LOVER by Charlie W. Shedd. Copyright © 1977 by Universal Press Syndicate. Used by permission.

ARGUS COMMUNICATIONS: Excerpts from WHY AM I AFRAID TO TELL YOU WHO I AM by John Powell, S.J., copyright © 1969 Argus Communications.

AUGSBURG PUBLISHING HOUSE: Excerpts reprinted from LUTHERAN BOOK OF WORSHIP, copyright © 1978, by permission of Augsburg Publishing House.

NATALIA M. BELTING AND JAMES R. HINE: Excerpts from Interstate Printers and Publishers; Belting and Hine, YOUR WEDDING WORKBOOK. Copyright 1977. Used by permission from the authors.

BOBBS-MERRILL COMPANY, INC.: Excerpts from YOUR WEDDING, copyright © 1960 by Marjorie Binford Woods, used with permission of the publisher, The Bobbs-Merrill Company, Inc.

BROADMAN PRESS: Excerpts from Roger H. Crook, AN OPEN BOOK TO THE CHRISTIAN DIVORCEE (Nashville: Broadman Press 1974) pp. 103–108. All rights reserved. Used by permission. Excerpts from James Randolph Hobbs, THE PASTOR'S MANUAL (Nashville: Broadman Press, 1934, Renewal 1962) pp. 151–56. All rights reserved. Used by permission.

ANDRE BUSTANOBY: For "When the feeling's gone . . . Is the marriage over?"

CONCORDIA PUBLISHING HOUSE: Excerpts from THE LUTHERAN AGENDA authorized by the Synods constituting the Evangelical Lutheran Synodical Conference of North America. Published by Concordia Publishing House.

CONDÉ NAST PUBLICATIONS INC.: Excerpts from VOGUE'S BOOK OF ETIQUETTE are copyright © 1969 by the Condé Nast Publications Inc.

CAROLE B. DAVIS: For "Bonding—The Bridge From Womb to World."

DOUBLEDAY & COMPANY, INC.: Excerpts from TO LIVE AS A FAMILY by Joseph W. Bird and Lois Bird. Copyright © 1982 by Joseph W. Bird Psychotherapy, Inc. Reprinted by permission of Doubleday & Company, Inc. Excerpts from LETTERS TO PHILIP by Charlie W. Shedd. Copyright © 1968 by Charlie W. Shedd and the Abundance Foundation. Reprinted by permission of Doubleday & Company, Inc. Excerpts from MARRYING WELL by Evelyn Eaton Whitehead and James D. Whitehead. Copyright © 1981 by Evelyn Eaton Whitehead and James D. Whitehead. Reprinted by permission of Doubleday & Company, Inc. Excerpts from AMY VANDERBILT'S COMPLETE BOOK OF ETIQUETTE by Amy Vanderbilt, revised by Letitia Baldridge. Copyright © 1978 by Curtis B. Kellar and Lincoln G. Clark, Executors of the Estate of Amy Vanderbilt Kellar and Doubleday & Company, Inc. Copyright 1952, © 1954, 1955, 1956, 1958, 1963, 1967, 1972 by Curtis B. Kellar and Lincoln G. Clark, Executors of the Estate of Amy Vanderbilt Kellar. Reprinted by permission of Doubleday & Company, Inc. Excerpts from EVERYWOMAN'S HEALTH by 17 Women Doctors and D. S. Thompson, M.D., as Consulting Editor. Copyright © 1980 by Nelson Doubleday, Inc. Reprinted by permission of Doubleday & Company, Inc.

JOHN M. DRESCHER: For "The Perils of Middle Age." Copyright © 1982.

E. P. DUTTON, INC.: Excerpts from PREGNANCY AFTER 35 by Carole Spearin McCauley copyright © 1976. Used by permission of E. P. Dutton, Inc.

FORTRESS PRESS: Excerpts from MAN AND WOMAN by Karl Wrage, M.D. Copyright © 1969.

BARBARA FRIED: Excerpts from THE MIDDLE-AGE CRISIS by Barbara Fried copyright © 1967, 1976 by Barbara R. Fried.

DOROTHY J. GISH: For "Caring for Your Aging Parents."

WINIFRED GRAY: Excerpts from YOU AND YOUR WEDDING by Winifred Gray, copyright © 1965.

GROSSET & DUNLAP, INC. Excerpts reprinted by permission of Grosset & Dunlap, Inc. from THE NEW BRIDE'S BOOK OF ETIQUETTE, © 1973, 1981 by The Condé Nast Publications, Inc.

GEORGE AND MARGARET HARDISTY: Excerpts from SUCCESSFUL FINANCIAL PLANNING by George and Margaret Hardisty, copyright © 1978 by George and Margaret Hardisty.

HARPER & ROW, PUBLISHERS, INC.: Excerpts from LOVE AND SEX IN PLAIN LANGUAGE, Third Revised Edition, by Eric W. Johnson (J.B. Lippincott, Publishers). Copyright © 1965, 1967, 1973, 1977 by Eric W. Johnson. Reprinted by permission of Harper & Row, Publishers, Inc. Excerpts from EMILY POST'S COMPLETE BOOK OF WEDDING ETIQUETTE by Elizabeth Post copyright © 1982 by the Emily Post Institute. Reprinted by permission of Harper & Row, Publishers, Inc.

HARVEST HOUSE PUBLISHERS: Excerpts taken from GROWING THROUGH DIVORCE by Jim Smoke. Copyright © 1976, Harvest House Publishers, 1075 Arrowsmith, Eugene, Oregon, 17402.

HERALD PRESS: Excerpts from DIVORCE AND THE FAITHFUL CHURCH by G. Edwin Bontrager copyright © 1978.

INTERSTATE PRINTERS & PUBLISHERS, INC.: Excerpts from ALTAR BOUND by Betty Stuart Rodgers and Elizabeth Connelly Pearce copyright © 1973 (out of print).

JUDSON PRESS: Excerpts from THE NEO-MARRIED by Howard Hovde copyright © 1968. Used by permission of Judson Press.

MARLENE LEFEVER: For "Come Over to My House."

MACMILLAN PUBLISHING COMPANY: From ON DEATH AND DYING by Elisabeth Kübler-Ross.

MOODY PRESS: Excerpts from HOPE FOR THE SEPARATED by Gary Chapman copyright © 1982, Moody Bible Institute, Moody Press, pp. 73–74, 76–77, 98–99, 99–100. Excerpts from TOWARD A GROWING MARRIAGE by Gary Chapman copyright © 1979, Moody Bible Institute, Moody Press, pp. 23–31, 61–63.

ANITA M. MORELAND: For "A Quick Guide to Finding . . . The Church of Your Choice," and "Forbidden Friendships."

MORGAN-PACIFIC PRESS INC.: Excerpts from 49 AND HOLDING by Richard Knox Smith copyright © 1975. (Available through Palos Verdes Book Company, P. O. Box 456, Lomita, CA 90717.)

ELOF G. NELSON: Excerpts from YOUR LIFE TOGETHER by Elof G. Nelson copyright © 1967.

NEW CENTURY PUBLISHERS: Excerpts reprinted from SINGLE PARENTS ARE PEOPLE, TOO! by Carol V. Murdock © 1980. By permission of New Century Publishers, Inc., Piscataway, N.J.

W. W. NORTON & COMPANY, INC.: Excerpts from THE MIRAGES OF MARRIAGE by William J. Lederer and Don D. Jackson copyright © 1968.

PRESBYTERIAN PUBLISHING HOUSE: Excerpts from HOW TO CHOOSE THE WRONG MARRIAGE PARTNER AND LIVE UNHAPPILY EVER AFTER by Robert L. Mason, Jr., and Caroline L. Jacobs copyright © 1979, published by John Knox Press. Excerpts from COMFORTING THOSE WHO GRIEVE by Cecil Murphey copyright © 1979, published by John Knox Press.

READER'S DIGEST ASSOCIATION, INC.: Excerpts from FAMILY HEALTH GUIDE AND MEDICAL ENCYCLOPEDIA (prepared in association with Benjamin F. Miller, M.D.) Reader's Digest Association, Inc., copyright © 1970.

REGAL BOOKS: Excerpts from SEX BEGINS IN THE KITCHEN by Dr. Kevin Leman. Copyright © 1981, Regal Books, Ventura, CA 93006. Used by permission. Excerpts from COMMUNICATION: KEY TO YOUR MARRIAGE by H. Norman Wright. Copyright © 1974, Regal Books, Ventura, CA 93006.

FLEMING H. REVELL COMPANY: Excerpts from BUILDING HAPPY MEMORIES AND FAMILY TRADITIONS by Verna Birkey and Jeanette Turnquist copyright © 1980 by Verna Birkey and Jeanette Turnquist. Excerpts from THE MINISTER'S MARRIAGE HANDBOOK by James L. Christensen copyright © 1966 by Fleming H. Revell Company. Excerpts from HIDE OR SEEK by James Dobson, Ph.D., copyright © 1974, 1979 by Fleming H. Revell Company. Excerpts from YOU CAN BEAT THE MONEY SQUEEZE by George and Marjean Fooshee, copyright © 1980 by George and Marjean Fooshee. Excerpts from THE FOREVER PRINCIPLE by Maxine Hancock, copyright © 1980 by Maxine Hancock. Excerpts from THE PEOPLE YOU LIVE WITH by O. Quentin Hyder, M.D., copyright © 1975 by Fleming H. Revell Company. Excerpts from THE COMPLETE BOOK OF BABY AND CHILD CARE FOR CHRISTIAN PARENTS by Grace H. Ketterman, M.D., and Herbert L. Ketterman,

M.D., copyright © 1982 by Grace H. Ketterman, M.D., and Herbert L. Ketterman, M.D. Excerpts from HOW TO TEACH YOUR CHILD ABOUT SEX by Grace H. Ketterman, M.D., copyright © 1981 by Grace H. Ketterman, M.D. Excerpts from YOU AND YOUR CHILD'S PROBLEMS by Grace H. Ketterman, M.D., copyright © 1983 by Grace H. Ketterman, M.D. Excerpts from I AM A WOMAN BY GOD'S DESIGN by Beverly LaHaye copyright © 1980 by Beverly LaHaye. Excerpts from SPIRIT-CONTROLLED FAMILY LIVING by Tim and Bev LaHaye, copyright © 1978 by Tim and Bev LaHaye.

Excerpts from THE CHRISTIAN WEDDING HANDBOOK by Kay Oliver Lewis, copyright © 1981 by Kay Oliver Lewis. Excerpts from DEVOTIONS FOR CALORIE COUNTERS by Cecil B. Murphey copyright © 1982 by Fleming H. Revell Company. Excerpts from ADOLESCENCE IS NOT AN ILLNESS by Bruce Narramore, Ph.D., copyright © 1980 by S. Bruce Narramore. Excerpts from FAMILY PLANNING THE NATURAL WAY by Josef Roetzer, M.D., copyright © 1981 by Josef Roetzer, M.D. Excerpts from DESIGN FOR CHRISTIAN MARRIAGE by Dwight Hervey Small, copyright © 1959 by Fleming H. Revell Company. Excerpts from YOUR MARRIAGE IS GOD'S AFFAIR by Dwight Hervey Small, copyright © 1979 by Dwight Hervey Small. Excerpts from SUDDENLY SINGLE by Jim Smoke, copyright © 1982 by Jim Smoke. Excerpts from GOD, THE ROD, AND YOUR CHILD'S BOD by Larry Tomczak, copyright © 1981, 1982 by Larry and Doris Tomczak. Excerpts from AN EXPERIENCE OF LOVE by Ingrid Trobisch and Elisabeth Roetzer, copyright © 1981 by Ingrid Trobisch and Elisabeth Roetzer. Excerpts from INTENDED FOR PLEASURE, Rev. ed., by Ed Wheat, M.D., and Gaye Wheat, copyright © 1977 by Fleming H. Revell Company, © 1981 by Ed Wheat, M.D., and Gaye Wheat. Excerpts from HARMONY IN MARRIAGE by Leland Foster Wood, copyright © 1979 by Fleming H. Revell Company.

WAYNE RICKERSON: Excerpts from GOOD TIMES FOR YOUR FAMILY by Wayne Rickerson. Copyright © 1976.

JACK R. RISLEY: For "Steal a Little Time or Two," copyright © Jack R. Risley. Used by permission.

CHARLES SCRIBNER'S SONS: Excerpts from Sex Information and Education Council, SEXUALITY AND MAN. Copyright © 1970 Sex Information and Education Council of the U.S. Inc. Reprinted with the permission of Charles Scribner's Sons.

SEABURY PRESS: Excerpts from THE BOOK OF COMMON PRAYER OF THE PROTESTANT EPISCOPAL CHURCH. The Church Hymnal Corporation and The Seabury Press, 1979, pages 423–432. Excerpts from THE WEDDING BOOK by Howard Kirschenbaum and Rockwell Stensrud. Copyright © 1974 by The Seabury Press, Inc. Used by permission.

SERVANT PUBLICATIONS: Excerpts from FATHERS: A FRESH START FOR THE CHRISTIAN FAMILY by Robert L. Latesta, copyright © 1980. Excerpts from HUSBANDS, WIVES, PARENTS, CHILDREN by Ralph Martin, copyright © 1978.

SIMON & SCHUSTER: Excerpts from SEXUAL PLEASURE IN MARRIAGE by Jerome and Julia Rainer copyright © 1959, 1969 by Jerome and Julia Rainer. Reprinted by permission of Simon & Schuster, a Division of Gulf & Western Corporation. Excerpts from MAN'S BODY by The Diagram Group copyright © 1981 by Simon & Schuster, Inc. Reprinted by permission of Wallaby Books, a Simon & Schuster division of Gulf &

Western Corporation. Excerpts from WOMAN'S BODY by The Diagram Group copyright © 1981 by Simon & Schuster, Inc. Reprinted by permission of Wallaby Books, a Simon & Schuster division of Gulf & Western Corporation.

RICHARD L. STRAUSS: Excerpts from CONFIDENT CHILDREN AND HOW THEY GROW by Richard L. Strauss, Th.D. Copyright © 1975.

TODAY'S CHRISTIAN WOMAN: "Back to Work," by Kesley Menehan (Summer 1981) copyright © 1981 by Fleming H. Revell Company; "Our Spiritual Life Together" (Fall 1981) copyright © 1981 by Fleming H. Revell Company.

TYNDALE HOUSE PUBLISHERS: Excerpts from YOUR MONEY: FRUSTRATION OR FREEDOM? by Howard L. Dayton, Jr. Published by Tyndale House Publishers, Inc., © 1979 by Howard L. Dayton, Jr. Used by permission. Excerpts from WHAT WIVES WISH THEIR HUSBANDS KNEW ABOUT WOMEN by James Dobson. Published by Tyndale House Publishers, Inc., © 1975. Used by permission. Excerpts from THE RIGHT TO LIVE, THE RIGHT TO DIE by C. Everett Koop. Published by Tyndale House Publishers, Inc., © 1976. Used by permission. Excerpts from THE EFFECTIVE FATHER by Gordon MacDonald. Published by Tyndale House Publishers, Inc., © 1977. Used by permission. Excerpts from MAGNIFICENT MARRIAGE by Gordon MacDonald. Published by Tyndale House Publishers, Inc., © 1976. Used by permission. Excerpts from THE CHRISTIAN HUSBAND by Fred Renich. Published by Tyndale House Publishers, Inc., © 1976. Used by permission.

VICTOR BOOKS: Excerpts from LIFE IN THE BALANCE by James C. Hefley copyright © 1980. Excerpts from THE FAMILY THAT LISTENS by H. Norman Wright, copyright © 1978.

VISION HOUSE: Excerpts from CHARACTERISTICS OF A CARING HOME by H. Norman Wright and Rex Johnson, copyright © 1978, Vision House, Ventura, CA 93006. Used by permission.

WESTMINSTER PRESS: Excerpts reprinted from THE WORSHIPBOOK—SERVICES. Copyright © MCMLXX The Westminster Press. Reprinted by permission.

NYLA JANE WITMORE: For "Time Out for Two: What You Really Need Is a Second Honeymoon."

WORD BOOKS: Excerpts from IS THERE A FAMILY IN THE HOUSE? by Kenneth Chafin, copyright © 1978; used by permission of Word Books, Publisher, Waco, Texas 76796. Excerpts from FAMILY LIFE by Ray C. Stedman, David H. Roper, et al., copyright © 1976; used by permission of Word Books, Publisher, Waco, Texas 76796. Excerpts from LIVING AND GROWING TOGETHER, Gary R. Collins, ed., copyright © 1976; used by permission of Word Books, Publisher, Waco, Texas 76796. Excerpts from THE GIFT OF SEX by Clifford and Joyce Penner, copyright © 1981; used by permission of Word Books, Publisher, Waco, Texas 76796. Excerpts from THE BEST HALF OF LIFE by Ray and Anne Ortlund copyright © 1976; used by permission of Word Books, Publisher, Waco, Texas 76796.

ZONDERVAN CORPORATION: Excerpts taken from THE ESSENCE OF MARRIAGE by Julius A. Fritze copyright © 1969 by Zondervan Publishing House. Used by permission. Excerpts taken from HUSBAND

AND WIFE: THE SEXES IN SCRIPTURE AND SOCIETY by Peter DeJong and Donald R. Wilson. Copyright © 1979 by Peter DeJong and Donald R. Wilson. Used by permission of The Zondervan Corporation. Excerpts taken from HOW TO KEEP YOUR FAMILY TOGETHER AND STILL HAVE FUN by Marion Leach Jacobsen. Copyright © 1969 by Zondervan Publishing House. Used by permission. Excerpts taken from THE ACT OF MARRIAGE by Tim and Beverly LaHaye copyright © 1976 by The Zondervan Corporation. Used by permission. Excerpts taken from SEXUAL HAPPINESS IN MARRIAGE by Herbert J. Miles copyright © 1967, 1976, 1982 by Zondervan Publishing House. Used by permission. Excerpts taken from EVERYTHING YOU NEED TO KNOW TO STAY MARRIED AND LIKE IT by Bennard R. Wiese and Urban G. Steinmetz copyright © 1972 by Bennard R. Wiese. Used by permission of Zondervan Publishing House.

The
Encyclopedia
of Christian
Marriage

1

Premarriage and Engagement

DATING

Concerns

Purposeful dating is not without dangers. Chuckholes are marked by barriers and detour signs. Many have disregarded these, however, and have ended up with a badly damaged vehicle. If we are aware of the dangers, we can avoid them. To pinpoint some of these dangers is the purpose of this section.

Perhaps the most common danger in dating is to allow the physical aspect of the relationship to predominate. This seems to be the pattern for far too many Christian couples. Long hours are spent in close, physically charged activity, all of which was designed as a prelude for sexual intercourse. Since this conclusion is forbidden by Scripture, the Christian couple seeks to stop short of this point and ends the evening in tremendous frustration. When the physical aspect is the major part of the relationship, the personal growth of the individuals involved is stymied.

Often the question is raised by conscientious young people, "When should physical expression become a part of the dating relationship?" Any specific answer to that question would be arbitrary, but perhaps there is a principle that will give guidance. I believe that the physical side of the relationship ought to be reserved for the time when both partners agree that there is interest in a long-term relationship with marriage as a possibility.

What I am suggesting is that we may have a ministry-centered relationship designed for mutual self-improvement that would never include sexually motivated physical activity. There may be wholesome nonsexually motivated behavior as a normal part of the ministering relationship, such as a warm embrace expressing joy or genuine sympathetic concern in a time of sorrow. The sexually motivated physical activity, however, ought to wait until some degree of maturity has been reached in the relationship. Some will find such a suggestion objectionable, but I believe that this principle will enhance greatly the ministry aspect of dating.

Assuming that you have followed this principle and are now dating someone whom you view as a potential mate, what part should the physical aspect play in the relationship? I believe that here we move on a continuum from little to much depending upon the degree of commitment and the date of the wedding. The key word is *bal-*

ance. We must not allow the physical to predominate over the spiritual, social, and intellectual.

The couple themselves must regularly evaluate their relationship. When they see the physical aspect getting out of balance, they must discuss the problem and decide upon ways and means of bringing balance. This may mean radically changing the type of date they are having, moving away from long periods alone, planning more social activities, and involving other couples more often.

A couple can avoid this danger if they choose to avoid it. We cannot blame our sexual drive nor our circumstances for failure in this area. We are masters of our own fate.

A second danger is to misread the interest of others. A quiet, withdrawn fellow may well jump to the wrong conclusion when a Christian girl expresses an interest in getting to know him. She may be thinking of ministry, but he reads matrimony.

"I want to help," she says, "but how can I keep from hurting him?" Most likely, she cannot! But then, being hurt is not the worst thing in the world. In fact, most growth is accompanied by pain. Better to have suffered and grown, than never to have suffered at all. God can use heartache as well as headache to help us grow.

We must not sit back and fail to minister to those of the opposite sex because we fear hurting them. We should, however, not seek to hurt. Perhaps the best answer to this problem is open communication early in the relationship. I do not mean that the girl should walk up to the fellow and say, "Now, I don't have any romantic interest in you, but I do want to help you. Would you have ice cream with me after the meeting tonight?"

But somehow we must communicate our real motives to each other. This is the surest way to avoid the misreading of interests. We cannot read each other's mind. Communication alone can reveal our thoughts and intentions. Some have found it helpful to talk of "brother-sister relationships" or of "friendships" rather than "dating." If we cannot rid "dating" of its romantic connotations, then perhaps we can call our get-togethers "friendship appointments."

A third danger, born most often of insecurity, is the danger of limiting our dating experience to one individual. Most of the purposes for dating that we have discussed will find minimal fulfillment if this becomes the pattern. By such action, we short-cut the process and arrive at our destination too soon, void of many of life's most enriching experiences.

I know that there are notable exceptions, and I am happy for every exception. That is, there are couples who have dated only each other from a very early age and have a happy marriage. I am not suggesting they go back and "make up for lost time." This is impossible and undesirable.

What I am saying is that if you are still unmarried and have followed this pattern, I feel that you would do yourself a great service to broaden your base of friendships by developing brother–sister relationships with other individuals. This can be done without undue jealousy in your present relationship if you both understand the purpose.

A fourth danger is that of romantic color blindness. I often confuse green and brown, pink and beige, and certain other color combinations. Many couples do the same in their dating relationships. Because they are caught up in the excitement of romance, they fail to see things as they really are. When we like someone, we are inclined to see only their strengths. We overlook their weaknesses. The truth is that we all have strong points and weak points in our personality and behavior characteristics.

Usually in my premarital counseling program, I will ask the girl to list all the things she likes about her fiancé. I ask the fellow to do the same. With some thought, they can usually give a rather impressive list. Then I ask them to list the weaknesses of their potential partner—the things they do not particularly like or things they see as potential problems. Unless the couple can list at least some traits in this category, I tell them that they are not ready for marriage.

A mature relationship, one that is ready for marriage, will always be realistic enough to admit weakness in the other person. You will not marry a perfect person. We must understand this, not only theoretically, but personally. Spelling out these weaknesses helps us face reality.

A couple will find great profit in discussing openly the weaknesses that they perceive in each other. Can these weaknesses be changed? (Most can if the individual chooses to change.) If there is no change, what problem is this likely to cause in the marriage? Realistic discussion of these questions should be a part of the decision-making process regarding marriage.

Still another danger is the "in love illusion." Some time ago, I had a call from a young man who asked if I would perform his wedding ceremony. I inquired as to when he wanted to get married and found that the wedding date was less than a week away. I explained that I usually have from four to six counseling sessions with those who desire to be married.

His response was classic. "Well, to be honest with you, I don't think that we will need any counseling. We really love each other, and I don't think we will have any problems." I smiled and then wept inwardly. Another victim of the "in love illusion."

Most couples do not get married unless they think they are in love. And most feel the basis for marriage is being in love. I often ask

couples who come for premarital counseling, "Why do you want to get married?" After looking at each other, giggling, and smiling, they say in their own way, "We love each other!"

But when I press to find out what they mean by "love," I find that few are able to describe it. Most end up by saying something about a deep feeling that they have for each other. It has persisted for some time and is in some nebulous way different from what they have felt for other dating partners.

I am reminded of the African animal hunt. A hole is dug in the midst of the animal's path to the water hole, then camouflaged with branches and leaves. The poor animal runs along, minding his own business, then all of a sudden falls into the pit and is trapped.

This is the manner in which we speak of love. We are walking along doing our normal duties when all of a sudden one day we look across the room or down the hall and there she/he is—*wham-o*, we "fall in love." There is nothing we can do about it. It is completely beyond our control. Only one course of action is considered. Get married! The sooner the better. So we tell our friends, and because they operate upon the same principle they agree that if we are "in love," we may as well get married.

No one considers the fact that our social, spiritual, and intellectual interests are miles apart. Our value systems and goals are contradictory, but we are "in love." The great tragedy stemming from this illusion is that six months later we sit in the counselor's office and say, "We don't love each other anymore." Therefore, we are ready to separate. After all, if "love" is gone, then we cannot stay together.

I have a word for the above described emotional experience, but it is not "love." I call it the "tingles." Now I think the tingles are important. They are real, and I am in favor of their survival, but they are not the basis for a satisfactory marriage. . . . we must not allow our culture to squeeze us into the mold of believing that the tingles are all we need for a happy marriage.

I am not suggesting that one should marry without the tingles. That warm excited feeling, the chill bumps, that sense of acceptance, the excitement of the touch, and so on, that make up the tingles, serve as the cherry on top of the sundae, but you cannot have a sundae with only the cherry. Many other factors must be a vital consideration in making a decision about marriage.

We may have the tingles with many people of the opposite sex before we meet the one whom we should marry. Many Christians would testify that it is also possible to feel the tingles for someone other than your mate even after you are married. That does not mean that we follow the tingles and get involved with someone else.

On the contrary, we admit our feelings, but thank God that we do not have to follow our feelings. In His power, we commit ourselves to our partner and go on developing our relationship. The tingles are temporary and should never be dictators of our actions.

Genuine love is a vital factor in deciding upon marriage. This kind of love is observed by actions rather than by feelings. Love is kind, patient, considerate, courteous, never demanding its own way, says the apostle (1 Corinthians 13:4-8). You can tell if your partner loves you by the way he/she treats you. You do not always know your partner's feelings, but you can always observe his actions. Yes, love should be a prerequisite for marriage, but it should be love in action, not emotions only. This reminds me of the little verse:

He held me close—
a chill ran down my spine.
I thought it was love,
but it was just his Popsicle melting.

Lest I be misunderstood, let me clearly state that I believe there ought to be a strong, warm, emotional feeling toward the one you marry. We are emotional creatures, and our emotions ought to be involved in any decision as meaningful as marriage. Yes, we ought to have the "tingles," but we must not make a decision for marriage based only upon the tingles. Marriage ought to be a rational decision as well as an emotional decision. Emotion alone is a poor instructor. Emotion and reason give us the insight we need.

The last danger that I would like to mention is the danger of attempting the impossible. Dreaming is great, but unrealistic dreaming is folly. God has warned us that we are not to try to blend light and darkness. That is impossible, and God wants to spare us the wasted energy. As stated by Paul in 2 Corinthians 6:14-15, the principle reads, "Be ye not unequally yoked together with unbelievers: for what fellowship hath righteousness with unrighteousness? and what communion hath light with darkness? and what concord hath Christ with Belial? or what part hath he that believeth with an infidel?"

Someone will object, "But I know a Christian girl who married a non-Christian fellow, and after they were married he became a Christian, and they are extremely happy." Thank God! We must know, however, that that girl has experienced the exceptional. That is not the rule, as many would testify. Do not count on being the exception.

Others would object, "But I know a Christian who is married to a non-Christian, and they have a happy marriage." Thank God! I am in favor of happy marriages wherever they are found. As we will discuss later, however, the essence of marriage is oneness— that deep sense of being one in every area of life, that sense of freely sharing all life's experiences. A Christian and a non-Christian cannot share in the deepest of life's experiences—personal fellowship with the living God. One entire area of life goes unshared, and because this area is so important, it affects other areas.

No, a Christian/non-Christian alliance cannot experience all that God intended in marriage. It is not that this oneness is difficult to obtain; it is impossible to obtain. God's prohibitions are designed for our benefit.

A common question raised by conscientious Christian young people is, "Should I date a non-Christian?" Some would answer with a strong and definite no! Those who hold this position usually emphasize that dating leads to marriage. "Never date a non-Christian, and you will not marry a non-Christian," they sometimes say.

It would be difficult to argue with the truth of that statement. The surest way to avoid "attempting the impossible" would be to refuse to date a non-Christian.

However, if we take the ministry aspect of dating seriously, and if we believe that non-Christians need Christ, we may minister to non-Christians in the dating context. We may be God's instruments to bring them to Christ. Many Christians would testify that they came to Christ through the loving witness of a Christian dating partner.

The biblical principle is "Be not unequally yoked together with unbelievers." I do not see ministry-centered dating as a yoke. A yoke involves commitment. The initial stages of dating require no commitment. A date is only an agreement to spend a specified amount of time in conversation with another person, perhaps accompanied by some other social activity such as eating or bowling. If this is commitment, it is very minimal commitment.

The danger for the single Christian is to rationalize that the date is ministry-centered when in reality it is not. If Christ is not presented, and spiritual issues are not discussed on the first or second date, you are fooling yourself. If you express your faith in Christ, and there is no interest in further discussion of the matter, you are foolish to go on developing other aspects of the relationship. To allow thoughts and feelings of a long-term relationship with this person to reside in your heart is to court disaster. For the Christian, the spiritual aspect of life is central and all pervasive. This truth must be faced realistically in dating relationships.

Why not evaluate your own dating record? Do you agree with the purposes presented in this chapter? What purposes would you add? Do you understand the dangers discussed? Are you presently involved in any of these dangers? What could you do about it?

—From Gary Chapman, *Toward a Growing Marriage.* Copyright © 1979, Moody Bible Institute, Moody Press, pp. 23–31.

Motives

In some parts of the world, parents have everything to say about selecting a mate for their son or daughter. In American culture, parents have very little or nothing to say.

You have nearly perfect freedom in choosing whom you will marry. Through the process of dating you have both a learning and a searching opportunity to find your marriage partner.

Not all dating, however, is motivated by serious mate selection. For some, dating is an end in itself where casual interest in the person is sought primarily for an evening of social activity. Sometimes we call this "playing the field" to differentiate it from more serious involvement in the social interacting of persons. Casual dating has value in that it helps you to develop early skills in interpersonal relationships and aids you in building a knowledge of the opposite sex. It

21

further serves to sever emotional ties to parents, giving encouragement to the person to begin making his own way in life.

Whether you plan your date for a night or for a lifetime depends most of all on your goals and your values. Dating as an end in itself will primarily be influenced by temporary attitudes of a limited good time. If you see your dating as a chance to get acquainted, to make friends, to develop interpersonal skills, to grow as a person, or to become involved in the process that leads to marriage, your choice of a dating partner will reflect the goals you have foremost in mind.

Some casual dating is done for the purpose of sexual exploitation of women. Men who engage in this degenerate "game" are emotionally immature and spiritually bankrupt. Girls who allow themselves to be exploited usually have poor opinions of themselves and act impulsively. Occasionally girls will feel that this is the way to hold a boy, only to experience that this attitude produces disastrous consequences.

Repeatedly, people who bring me their deepest problems relate how they are still being haunted by the shame and guilt of past mistakes. While they know they are forgiven by God, there seems to be no surgery for the removal of personal emotional scars. We need, therefore, to remind ourselves that we live in daily forgiveness, understanding that we are justified by grace through faith in God. Past mistakes are forgiven by a gracious God, and the personal recognition of forgiveness can be appropriated by renewed faith in ourselves. Christian life is sustained by the fact of forgiveness, for the reality of forgiveness is the foundation of Christian life.

Dating is the process of mate selection. Responsibility and mutual respect of persons on dates adds to the enjoyment of getting to know each other. The most significant way of determining whether you move from casual to serious dating, from serious steady dating to engagement and then marriage, is in the evaluation of all conduct and experiences during courtship. The longer you know each other the more comfortable you feel in each other's presence. You move in courtship from testing each other to trusting each other. As you trust each other more, flashing insights about the possibility of marriage give encouragement to the person you are dating as well as to yourself. Therefore, the conduct and experiences of courtship have very real significance in the decision you are about to make.

—From Elof G. Nelson, *Your Life Together*. Atlanta: John Knox, 1967.

MATE SELECTION

IN REAL LIFE, men and women gradually discover each other as potential marriage partners. Discovery comes at the most unexpected moments of courtship. On a pretest questionnaire in a class on marriage, one young man put it this way: "I know she's the girl for me because we have really grown to know each other. During the past eighteen months we have faced many situations together, including the tragic death of my mother. We have discussed and at times respectfully argued politics, religion, sexuality, attitudes toward children, and I guess the whole field of domestic marriage relations. Throughout our courtship we gradually grew together until there was no thought of ever wanting to separate."

My own clinical observations indicate that couples who move through courtship long enough to get to test each other out tend to select each other on the basis of complementary needs. If you look carefully at married couples, you will note that one is the leader (hopefully the husband) and the other a follower. One is more verbal, the other more reserved. One is more daring, the other more wise; one is more athletic, the other less so inclined. The complementation of each other appears to be basic to the success of a new family, and it may be we select each other through unconscious factors as well as conscious ones.

Our young man, so sure he had the right girl, had used realistic standards in looking for the conscious essentials in his dating partner. No one should make the decision to marry without looking long and seriously at individual differences between persons. These essentials are:

1. How do you get along with people?
2. Do you make wise decisions?
3. Can people trust you?
4. What about your motivation and meaning of values?
5. Can you love someone deeply?
6. Are you free from parental "apron strings"?
7. Are you serious about your life's work?
8. How practical are you about matters around the house?

When you have tested these carefully together, something deep within you will give you the "green light" to go ahead. Chances are that it is at this point that you will begin to realize how you also complement each other, and the realization will grow with each succeeding year of marriage.

—From Elof G. Nelson, *Your Life Together*. Atlanta: John Knox, 1967.

Early Marriage

Teenagers usually resent their parents' referring to their relationships with other boys and girls as "puppy love" or "infatuation."

To be told that they are just going through a stage and that their feelings for that special person will someday wane is equally unacceptable.

While older people can make such comments with reasonable confidence that they are correct because of their personal experiences, young people have no reservoir of experience from which to reach such a conclusion. During adolescence they are the victims of some of the most intense feelings they will ever have. Their feelings are *now*. They have no desire or inclination to be patient or to postpone gratification. Why look for something better or spend long hours analyzing and exploring a relationship when each moment with that special someone is pure ecstasy? Never mind that their concept of love and marriage is straight out of Hollywood or that their range of sexual and romantic encounters has been colored to a large degree by what they have been exposed to in books, magazines, and television.

While such romantic fantasies can provide pleasant interludes from the more mundane and realistic world in which human beings live out their existence, it is important that the concept of love and marriage held by most teenagers not be internalized to the point that they rid themselves of any reasonable chance to build a good marriage based on more realistic views of life with another person.

Unfortunately, most teenagers do enter marriage with many unrealistic and artificial expectations regarding love, sex, marriage, and family. While playing house or living in a make-believe world of rose-covered cottages and sexual wonderlands can be a most pleasant pastime for teenagers, they need to be confronted with the harsh reality that life is seldom what it is painted to be in Hollywood and on television. Despite all their dreams of "living happily ever after," we are confronted with the cold hard statistics which suggest that the prognosis for teen-agers to marry is a rather dismal one. While the odds against the survival of marriage at any age are increasing, those for teenage marriages are much worse.

When a person makes a decision to marry at a young age, he or she makes one of life's most important decisions on the basis of an extremely meager pool of information and experience. No matter how hard teenagers try to convince themselves otherwise, there is no substitute for experience in interpersonal relationships. While people continue to change and grow as long as they live, more mature couples have at least made some progress and achieved some stability in regard to their values and goals in life. Most have been involved in a number of relationships with other human beings and have an accumulation of knowledge and experience on which a more intelligent decision can be made.

The problems encountered in early marriages are too numerous to be detailed here. Suffice it to say that they may include such feelings and difficulties as disillusionment, resentment, jealousy, sexual conflicts, problems with communication, going in separate directions in regard to goals, interests, and values as they grow older, financial woes, educational and career differences, and the hardship of trying to be parents while still in many ways children themselves.

—From Robert L. Mason, Jr., and Caroline L. Jacobs, *How to Choose the Wrong Marriage Partner and Live Unhappily Ever After.* Atlanta: John Knox, 1979.

Unequally Yoked

It is not difficult to see why Scripture admonishes strongly: "Be not unequally yoked together with unbelievers." A believer and an unbeliever could never achieve oneness in marriage, only togetherness. Their marriage might appear very successful and as having a high degree of personal happiness, but it would never reach the potentialities of fulfillment that would be possible if God's blessing were upon it, and it fulfilled the purposes of God. As it has been quaintly put: "For a child of God to marry a child of the Devil is to have Satan for his father-in-law!" What a complication of the in-law problem that is!

The real as well as symbolic oneness of the marriage relation was purposed for man from the very beginning. It was within the realm of perfect realization for our first parents. Such personal intimacy as they originally enjoyed with God was theirs to enjoy with each other. In the beginning there was one will, God's will. But sin introduced another will into the universe that God had willed into being. That sinful will destroyed the basis of union and the unbroken experience of intimacy between man and his Creator-Sovereign. The direct consequence was the cessation of full personal intimacy between the man and his wife. The will that separates man from God is the will that separates man from his wife. The objective reality of union which marriage was to symbolize was shattered, the divine purpose in marriage obscured, and its fulfillment rendered impossible.

—From Dwight Hervey Small, *Design for Christian Marriage.* Old Tappan, N.J.: Revell, 1959.

ENGAGEMENT

Engagement Period

One of the most exciting moments in the life of a serious couple in love is the time of engagement. It is an opportunity to announce to parents, relatives, and friends that you have declared your intention to live your whole life with the one whom you love. Everyone will be happy for you.

Your own love for each other will consist of a mature and healthy idealization confined, of course, to reality. Feelings of self-esteem, mutual trust, and acceptance of virtues and defects in each other's personality, an awareness of the effect each has on the other, and sexual frustration will tend to dominate your waking moments. You have thought through the responsibilities of married living and you love your fiancée as a whole person. You feel ready and you are relatively convinced that the time for marriage is at hand.

The engagement period is usually symbolized by giving the girl a ring. The ring is a symbol of intention and declaration of the couple to marry in the near future. The ring may be a simple band or a costly diamond; there is as much status in one as there is in the other. During engagement, compatibility testing continues as couples preview and resolve some differences that have arisen earlier and may arise again during early marriage. Romantic love, intellectual interests, spiritual depths, social compatibility, and emotional readiness become more alive as the engagement progresses. Both partners near the point where they are convinced they wish to give themselves to each other. As said earlier, even now, occasionally doubting your decision is a perfectly normal reaction. If you discuss doubt openly with a trusted friend, it will help "clear the air" and bring in fresh insights. You have everything to gain by being honest with your feelings. Secret doubt or fear covered up now may eventually loom into serious problems after you are married. Never attempt to "pull the wool over" your own eyes before or after marriage. More emotional and physical illnesses occur in people because they are afraid to reveal their true feelings. Be open and honest to your true self and you will

open the doors to wholeness of body and soul.

In general, engagements should be long enough to make the necessary plans for marriage and to feel greater assurance about each other. The length of time may vary depending on variables such as age, college completion, financial needs, and the like. Research summaries show that marriages rate higher on the happiness scale when engagements have lasted six months or longer. So give yourself a little time for final preparations for your wedding.

Decisions should be reached during engagement about domestic and economic affairs anticipated during early marriage. How much will it cost to live—who will handle the money—will the wife work—if so, for how long? Does she plan to have a career rather than stay at home to raise a family or will she have several careers? It's becoming traditional in our culture for the young wife to work outside the home early in marriage, then mother a family, and years later again assume work outside the home. Will either one continue in school during early marriage? If so, how will they meet their expenses? Where will they live? Should young married couples take allowances from families when they are just starting out—what relationship will this create between the young married couple and their parents? Is the young husband going to be dependent or will both feel they should definitely sever all financial ties with parents?

—From Elof G. Nelson, *Your Life Together*. Atlanta: John Knox, 1967.

Engagement Ring

Contrary to the general belief, presenting a girl with an engagement ring is a fairly recent custom and not at all a binding tradition. Furthermore, diamonds are not the only acceptable stones for engagement rings.

Many girls prefer their birthstones or some other precious or semiprecious stone. Unlike the wedding ring, which is an integral part of the wedding ceremony, the engagement ring serves no other purpose than as a visible token that the girl has accepted the man as her intended husband. Old family jewelry such as a pin, earrings, or a pearl necklace can very properly be substituted for the more usual ring. And many girls choose to go without an engagement ring in favor of using the money for something more practical, such as furniture.

If the man does give his fiancée a ring, it is sensible for them to visit the jeweler together, so she can choose a ring that appeals to her. The man can avoid embarrassment by conferring with the jeweler ahead of time and asking him to choose an assortment of rings within the range the man can afford and that he thinks the girl will like. The jeweler can then show her these when the couple call on him together.

With either a precious or semiprecious stone, the setting should be of precious metal such as platinum, or white or yellow gold. The wedding ring should be of the same metal as the engagement ring and can be chosen at the same time or later. Traditionally, the fiancée does not see it again until it is placed on her finger at the wedding ceremony. Since she will wear both rings after the wedding, it is common sense to choose designs that fit comfortably together on her finger.

Whether the engagement ring is large or small, or with precious or semiprecious stones, expensive or modestly priced, what it signifies, and not the ring itself, is what matters. Unfavorable comment or speculation as to its cost is in very bad taste.

Engagement Presents

The only people, besides her fiancé, who usually give engagement presents to the bride are the couple's parents and immediate families and sometimes a bride's dearest friends. Such presents are purely a matter of inclination and are not obligatory. An affectionate note to the bride from the groom's mother is indispensable if she lives at any distance from the bride and cannot see her often, but nothing else is absolutely necessary.

Announcing the Engagement

The prospective bride's parents announce the engagement in their local newspapers if they want to, and perhaps in the newspapers of other places where they, the groom, and his parents, have strong affiliations. As most newspapers have definite rules for publication of engagement announcements and photographs, it is always a good idea to check with them. There is no charge for publishing such items, but neither is there any guarantee of publication.

Society editors of many papers supply forms to be filled in with the pertinent information. When they do not, a press release must be prepared and sent to the society editor. An announcement recently published in the particular newspaper may be used as a guide.

Essential information is: full names of the bride and groom and the parents of each; the places where the parents live (with or without the street address of the bride's parents); the season or month for which the wedding is planned. Additional facts give the editor a chance to assess the news value of the announcement and save her the trouble of having to ask for more complete information should she want it, but the family should not feel compelled to include them. They usually consist of: the full names of the couple's grandparents and the places where they live; the couple's schools and colleges (with or without the dates of graduation); the place and year of the bride's debut, if any; clubs to which each of the couple belongs; professional affiliations of each and of their fathers.

The wording should be brief, accurate, and to the point. It should be typed, double-spaced, on a plain sheet of paper. The name, address, and telephone number of the bride's mother and the desired release date should be put at the top of the page. The release may be prepared and sent by anyone who is familiar with all the facts. Sometimes it is helpful if the secretary of the bride's father is listed as the person to question (known as the "contact"), since she is in a position to get additional details as needed and can be reached by telephone during business hours.

Following is a sample form:

For release
Monday, June 5

> *To:*   *Society Editor*
>   *News-Tribune*
> *From:*   *Mrs. Eugene F. Sykes*
>   *14 Sweetbriar Road*
>   *Valley Stream, Ohio*
>   *Telephone: 672-8117*
> *Contact:*   *Miss Stephanie Nichols*
>   *Telephone: 543-6161*

Mr. and Mrs. Eugene Foster Sykes of Sweetbriar Road announce the engagement of their daughter, Miss Helen Mathews Sykes, to Charles Sargent Bennett, son of Mr. and Mrs. Warren Rorimer Bennett of Boston.

Miss Sykes was graduated from the Country Day School in 1966, and the Cincinnati Conservatory of Music in 1970, and was presented at the Bachelors Ball. She is the granddaughter of Mr. Henry R. Mathews of New York and the late Mrs. Mathews, and of Mr. and Mrs. Philmore T. Sykes of Milwaukee.

Mr. Bennett, who was graduated from Columbia University in 1968, is in the management training program of United Industries. His grandparents are Mr. and Mrs. R. Sargent Bennett of Boston and Mr. and Mrs. Charles S. Hering of Providence, Rhode Island.

The wedding is planned for August.

This example gives only the street address of the bride's parents since the announcement is intended for local papers. When an engagement announcement is run in out-of-town newspapers, they print a date line at the head of the column identifying the city or town, and state of the announcement's origin.

THE RELEASE DATE

Dating the announcement is important for a number of reasons. It must, of course, arrive at the papers in time for the editor to include it in the space allotted to her; usually about a week in advance is adequate, but it may be as many as three weeks. When it is sent to more than one local paper, the release date must be the same on all, so one paper will not run it before another. Weekly papers should be called to determine the deadline for such items. When an engagement party is planned, the release date should be the following day or as soon after that as possible.

Frequently the society editor simply does not have enough space to include all the announcements dated for release on a certain day. When this happens, she may run the item after, but never before, the specified date.

NEWSPAPER PHOTOGRAPHS

A photograph of a prospective bride may be included with the release announcing her engagement. The picture must be printed on glossy paper and should be the standard eight-inch by ten-inch size. The girl's name should be typed on a separate piece of plain paper which is taped or glued to the picture. Identification should not be written on the back of the photograph because the impression left by a pen or pencil can interfere with reproduction.

When photographs are sent to more than

one paper in a community, it is preferable to choose slightly different poses for each from the photographer's proofs, since many newspapers prefer not to run pictures identical to those appearing in a rival paper. Newspapers are not obligated to run photographs that are voluntarily submitted, but if a newspaper specifically requests a photograph, it invariably runs it.

When the groom and his family live in another community, the engagement announcement and the prospective bride's photograph may also be sent to the newspapers there, but the groom's picture is never submitted. The family of the groom never makes the newspaper announcement.

—From *Vogue's Book of Etiquette*. New York: Simon and Schuster, 1969.

Fiancé, Fiancée

Both words come from the French and mean "a promise." *Fiancé* (fee ahn say, with equal emphasis on all three syllables) refers to the man who promises to marry. *Fiancée*, although spelled with two "e's" is pronounced exactly the same, and refers to the female.

—CECIL MURPHEY

LOVE

MARRIAGE FAILURES, generally speaking, are failures of one or both persons to love deeply.

The active character of love is giving rather than receiving. Beyond the elements of giving, the active characteristics of love always imply certain basic elements common to all forms of love. These are: care, responsibility, respect, and knowledge. . . .

Care, responsibility, respect, and knowledge are a syndrome of attitudes which are found in the mature person. Persons who are mature are ready to give themselves and pledge in marriage to be caring persons, giving attention to the spouse as a whole person. The immature marries for more self-interest reasons, such as sexual stimulation, physical attractiveness, idealization, and personal recognition, and is not ready to commit himself to that love so necessary for a lasting marriage.

When we speak of marital love we must distinguish between three different aspects of it. These aspects correspond to the four qualities of man. . . . as a physical being, emotional being, spiritual being, and social being. In our discussion of love we will consider the spiritual and social needs of married love as one. So we will speak of married love in terms of three little words—*sex, eros,* and *agape* which correspond to the physical, emotional, and spiritual-social qualities of man.

SEX

Let me briefly summarize sexuality, or biological love. . . . Sexuality is a self-centered activity. Consisting of the strong impulse to touch and the impulse to sexual release, it focuses on a person of the opposite sex as an object. It is what Freud called the libido and it is innate in both male and female. You frequently hear moralists describing sexuality as evil and dreadful. It would be in error to discredit sexuality since it carries out the task of procreation and is, therefore, a part of creation and willed by God. Bovet, the Swiss physician, speaks further about the need for true sexuality in marriage, stating that normal sexual drive is essential to the sexual stability of a marriage. To some extent it is unaffected by the ebb and flow of psychological moods and helps to hold a marriage together in the face of the storms and stresses of life. But on the other hand, it can compel us so strongly that one may miss the true person of his spouse. It therefore can inhibit marriage. Endowed by God, it is a good and necessary thing; yet, it has demonic possibilities. For example, sexuality can be a force that is misused by people. The New Testament teaches that the true person can be destroyed by his rebellious libido. This makes one subject to the "flesh" and sex becomes lust (Ephesians 5:5; 1 Corinthians 6:9 ff.). It is degenerative and robs one of intrapersonal harmony with God and with one's self.

Marriages based on pure sexual exploitation of either husband or wife are doomed to early failure. They have made of sexuality a toy or a game. They soon become bored with each other and their marriage is hollow and superficial. Anger, resentments, and retaliation become the content of their marriage dialogue. They become like two freezing porcupines, to recall Schopenhauer's fable: when they huddle for warmth, they repel each other by the sharpness of their quills.

It is disturbing to read well-written technical literature in the field of marriage that deals only with the biology of sexuality and techniques of making love. While a proper understanding of sexuality, including techniques, is valid, we must see all aspects of true marital love. There is a great need, therefore, to speak of the whole person in marriage, for love is indeed more than sexuality. Sex is a part of the whole realm of married love. In itself it cannot bring about the true union of persons who live in a deepening, continuing relationship.

EROS

Another aspect of married love is identified by the Greek word *eros*. I am particu-larly indebted to Dr. Theodor Bovet for his clear teaching on the functions of eros in marriage. Eros refers to person-centered love including the art of making love with one's spouse. It is perhaps little understood by man and, therefore, most often neglected in the romantic relationship of husband and wife.

Eros love looks to a person *as a person* for its expression. It creates a safe climate in marriage for both husband and wife to experience the joy and freedom of coming alive to each other. Each looks to the other in a person-centered love with rich and varied expression. As Bovet says, "Eros does all it can to bring out the specifically masculine and feminine characteristics of each other's personality. Grace and kindness, charm and delicacy on the one side; chivalry and courage, gentlemanly behavior and attention on the other side—all are, in the best sense of the word, erotic things."

Eros places feelings and values on personal experiences and expressions and, therefore, is a primary need of women. Men delight in it, too, but not always to the same extent as their wives do. Men often find difficulty expressing themselves patiently in warm, subjective ways that reach the intuitive, feeling feminine soul. Men are richer in their expression of sexuality, where females have greater depth for the ideals of love in eros. In my own counseling experience, this realization has been basic in making or breaking marriages. Eros expresses respect, appreciation, and care. It says, "It's you I deeply love," over and over again and in creative and meaningful ways: in the demonstration of affection, doing little favors, verbal expression of love, small gifts, anniversary celebrations, and the like. Eros is the expression of personal love that never takes a spouse for granted but expresses love in the warmth of personal intimacy during all the years of marriage.

29

If marriage is to be alive and meaningful, men especially need to be educated to the need of eros. They need to realize that sexuality must be disciplined, so that the art of making love does not consider the woman as an object of their interest, but considers the woman as a whole person—body, mind, and spirit. When sexuality is disciplined, then eros can combine with sexual impulses to create a mutual contentment and harmony. This requires skill and time to master—and explains why impulsive, youthful marriages have difficulty enduring the first year of life together. The secret to successful erotic development lies in the training of the husband. If he takes the time to develop necessary attitudes and romantic skills, his wife never needs to feel emotionally disillusioned and, therefore, sexually repelled by her husband. As Bovet says, sexual coldness—frigidity as it is called—in wives is an exact reflection of a nonerotic and merely sexual attitude on the part of their husbands and can only be cured by treating the latter first.

AGAPE

We turn now to our third little word. The word *agape* in Greek, the language of the New Testament, refers to God's love to man, exemplified by Christ's sacrifice on the cross. Agape love, then, is self-giving love. It is love that does not need a stimulus from without to give itself. It is its own stimulus. Agape is Christ's love that ties the church to Christ. The people of God who are the "body of Christ" respond and there is union.

It is the self-giving love of the husband to the wife that ties the wife to him. She responds and there is union. Marriage in truly Christian perspective has a different center of gravity from non-Christian marriage. Agape's center of concern lies beyond the human couple. Respect and responsibility are true ingredients of their life together as person to person, but together they enjoy a further respect and responsibility to a third Person, namely, the Living God. Agape is not a diluted form of ordinary liking or passionate love, as is sometimes sentimentally imagined, but is something altogether unique.

But agape love can be shown from person to person. The love which a person shows to another person is God's agape in him. The Apostle Paul clearly describes this kind of love in the well-known chapter of 1 Corinthians 13: "Love is patient and kind; love is not jealous or boastful; it is not arrogant or rude. Love does not insist on its own way; it is not irritable or resentful; it does not rejoice at wrong, but rejoices in the right. Love bears all things, believes all things, hopes all things, endures all things" (1 Corinthians 13:4-7).

Agape cradles meaning and purpose to life, giving to married living a strong, deep force of loyalty, honesty, honor, and steadfastness. It affords deep spiritual companionship of unique mystery and strength, for agape love is the foundation of marriage. It sustains marriage by its "sacramental significance" in commitment to life together and lived in the grace of God. While agape love is basic to other aspects of love, it should not be thought of as "spiritualizing" marriage. Those who do, deny themselves as persons and dilute sexuality and eros as inferior or at best "necessary evils" in marriage. God expects us to be real persons who see divine purpose in the entire structure of married love, for he has willed that each husband be true male and each wife true female and that their marriage shall make them "one flesh."

So we see that married love is something truly marvelous and unique. It encompasses the characteristic of the love one might have for friend, parents, and children; but it specifically ties into sexual needs, erotic fulfillments, and is given depth by agape. Marriage, then, is a far greater thing than sex and a greater thing than eros or agape. But it is also a greater thing than all three, for the whole is always greater than the sum of all its parts.

—From Elof G. Nelson, *Your Life Together*. Atlanta: John Knox, 1967.

FOR FURTHER READING

Augsburger, David. *Cherishable: Love and Marriage*. Scottdale, Pa.: Herald Press, 1975.

Chapman, Gary. *Toward a Growing Marriage*. Chicago: Moody, 1979.

Duvall, Evelyn Millis. *Why Wait Till Marriage?* New York: Association, 1967.

Hancock, Maxine. *The Forever Principle*. Old Tappan, N.J.: Revell, 1980.

Hurst, Hugo L. *A Search for Meaning in Love, Sex, and Marriage*. Rev. ed. Winona, Minn.: Saint Mary's, 1975.

LaHaye, Tim and Beverly. *The Act of Marriage*. Grand Rapids: Zondervan, 1976.

Lewis, Kay Oliver. *The Christian Wedding Handbook*. Old Tappan, N.J.: Revell, 1981.

Mason, Robert L., Jr., and Caroline L. Jacobs. *How to Choose the Wrong Marriage Partner and Live Unhappily Ever After*. Atlanta: John Knox, 1979.

Miles, Herbert J. *The Dating Game*. Grand Rapids: Zondervan, 1975.

Nelson, Elof G. *Your Life Together*. Atlanta: John Knox, 1967.

The New Bride's Book of Etiquette. New York: Grosset & Dunlap, 1981.

Rodgers, Betty Stuart, and Elizabeth Connelly Pearce. *Altar Bound*. Danville, Ill.: Interstate, 1973 (out of print).

Small, Dwight Hervey. *Your Marriage Is God's Affair*. Old Tappan, N.J.: Revell, 1979.

Wanger, Maurice E. *Put It All Together*. Grand Rapids: Zondervan, 1978.

2

The Wedding

SPIRITUAL SIGNIFICANCE OF THE WEDDING SERVICE

WHAT IS THE SIGNIFICANCE of being married in a church? To be sure, a church wedding is not a show or an entertainment. It is a service to Almighty God.

The minister begins the wedding service with such words as: "Dearly beloved, we are gathered together here in the presence of God to join this man and this woman in holy matrimony, an estate instituted by God, regulated by His commandments, and to be held in honor among all men." The first fact of Christian marriage is that it is undertaken in the presence of God. It is holy matrimony, instituted *by God*, not by man. By marrying in a church, the bride and groom affirm that God joins them together. Central attention is not focused on the bride, but on God, the One "altogether lovely." Hence, marriage "is not to be entered into unadvisably or lightly, but reverently, discreetly, soberly, and in the fear of God." In Christian marriage, it is God who matters most of all. The relationship is to be regulated by His commandments.

Most ceremonies include such words as: "Marriage is to be held in honor among all men," or "If any of you know cause, or just impediment, why these two persons should not be joined in holy matrimony, you are to declare it." One of the main features of the wedding service in the Judaic and Christian tradition is its public character. Though marriage is intensely personal and intimate, it is never a completely private matter. Society is involved "for better or for worse"; family traditions and reputations are implicated. "Who giveth this woman to be joined to this man?"—When the father has identified himself and gives the family's public approval, and the daughter withdraws her hand, the way is open for the new relationship to be established. Marriage is a highly pleasurable undertaking, but it is not primarily a device designed to provide personal pleasures for two people.

The union is likely to produce children, who may be either a burden or a strength to the community. Hence, each marriage is of concern to all. The "family" is a fundamental unit of society, for it is the medium to propagate the human race, to satisfy emotional needs in beneficial ways, and to perpetuate religious experience. The community has a stake in every new union. The "secret" marriage is a contradiction in terms, and a "quickie" marriage indicates failure to appreciate this public character. This public significance of marriage has led to the establishment of laws whereby the marriage intention is acknowledged openly prior to the solemnizing of it.

The religious wedding service, in essence, is the giving of public approval to the union by the family, the church, and the community. Marriage, therefore, is not to be entered into lightly, but "reverently, discreetly, and soberly," and in the presence of those whose approbation and blessing the couple seek.

Furthermore, the religious wedding service is the recognition before God that marriage is a lifelong commitment. It is not a mere contract or bargain which has certain contingencies and escape clauses. The two participants in marriage pledge themselves "for better, for worse; for richer, for poorer; in sickness and in health." It frankly recognizes in advance the possibilities of economic difficulties, illness, sterility, and other dangers and pitfalls. Nonetheless, marriage is not conceived as a temporary arrangement, to be honored only so long as relationships are mutually pleasant; rather, it is a pledge to be respected "so long as we both shall live."

Hence, it is intrinsically a relationship of mutually corresponding obligations. The ceremony includes such thoughts as: "Our Lord through his apostles has instructed those who enter this relation to cherish a mutual esteem and love; to bear with each other's infirmities and weaknesses; to comfort each other in sickness, trouble, and sorrow; in honesty and industry to provide for each other and for their household in temporal things; to pray for and encourage each other in the things that pertain to God; and to live together as heirs of his grace." When a minister says to the man and woman before him, "I therefore require and charge you both," he does not use empty phrases.

Marriage is an arrangement in which each partner gives *all* that he has: "with all my worldly goods I thee endow." A marriage is not a marriage at all if it is partial or entered into with fingers crossed or with the idea that it is but a temporary trial that can be dissolved at the divorce court if unsatisfactory. There must be a mutual outpouring of unlimited love. A truly married person is more interested in his mate's happiness than in his own. The wedding is the sacred service during which a man and a woman make these vows of lifelong fidelity.

Since marriage is a venture of faith, the wedding ceremony is, in reality, the couple's acceptance of the church's faith. The couple speak for themselves while they stand at the foot of the chancel steps. The minister asks the groom, and then the bride: "Will you love, comfort, honor, and keep (him or her) in sickness and in health; and forsaking all others, keep yourself only unto (him or her) so long as you both shall live?" Each responds, "I will." Thus, the gulf is spanned between the faith of the church and the faith of the persons who come to the church to be married. The attitude of the church toward marriage is that it is a holy relationship. It is a life of loving, comforting, honoring, and keeping; there is no wavering in sickness or in health; and, from the day of marriage to the day of death, no other man or woman shall invade the sacred precincts of sexual union. For nineteen centuries this has also been the faith of the church. With the speaking of the words "I will," the faith of the church is accepted by the couple; this is the kind of relationship they intend their marriage to be.

The man and the woman ascend the chancel steps to the altar to make their promises to one another. Looking into each other's eyes, they repeat the words which bind their lives together for the rest of their days on earth: "I, John, take thee, Mary, to be my wedded wife, to have and to hold, from this day forward ... till death do us part." To bring to remembrance the wedding day and to seal the promises, ring symbols are exchanged, "in token and pledge of constant faith and abiding love." The wedding ceremony is the public acceptance of the bond which limits free expression. The possibility of dating or making love with others is ruled out by virtue of the wedding bond. The pledge of fidelity and the dedication to faithfulness are implied in the ring exchange. Marriage is not compatible with absolute freedom, yet the person who binds himself to one life-mate finds the highest level of freedom.

The sacredness of the wedding ring was understood by Carl Sandburg's mother. Said he, "Mama's wedding ring was never lost— was always on that finger, placed there with pledges years ago. It was a sign and seal of something that ran deep and held fast between the two of them. They had chosen each other as partners. . . ." So should it be for all who are joined in holy matrimony.

Speaking as an agent of the living God and as a representative of the whole community, the minister pronounces that the union is indeed a fact: "I pronounce that they are husband and wife. . . . What God, then, has joined together, let no man put asunder."

The basis of unity is the fact that in this bond two persons are joined together so as to become "one flesh." ". . . they are no longer two individuals: they are one flesh" (MATTHEW 19:6, NEB).

This unity of two in one flesh is not just biological, as it is for animals; rather, it also has spiritual and psychic qualities. Marriage brings into play, not just two biological beings, but two personalities. The dialogue is of the spirit; the kiss is of the soul; the spirit's intensity is echoed by the flesh.

Nowhere in Scripture is marriage discussed in terms of sex; instead, it is discussed in terms of knowledge. The closest union that exists between anything in the universe and man himself is possible only through knowledge. When man knows a flower or a tree, he "possesses" these objects within his mind.

Similarly, marriage involves the mind, soul, heart, and will, as well as the reproductive organs. It is one of the closest unions possible, more personal than carnal. The union is something more than the physical union of the two sexes; the union is psychosomatic, affecting the whole person, body and soul. In the moment of "knowing," each partner receives a gift which neither ever knew before. Henceforth, the woman can never return to her virginity; the man can never return to ignorance. Something happens in oneness; and from that oneness comes fidelity.

The ceremony ends, and a great new life begins, hallowed in the spirit of prayer: "The Lord bless, preserve, and keep you; the Lord mercifully with his favor look upon you, and fill you with all spiritual benediction and grace; that you may so live together in this life that in the world to come you may have life everlasting."

—From James L. Christensen, *The Minister's Marriage Handbook*. Old Tappan, N.J.: Revell, 1974.

CHURCH AND CLERGY

Officiating Minister

People should be married by their own minister, if at all possible, in order that there may be a permanent relationship between the officiating minister and the family which he helps to bring into existence. When young people are married by an outsider, the occasion is robbed of some of the intimate values.

It is a matter of ministerial ethics that a minister does not return to a former parish to perform pastoral duties or assume privileges. The rare occasion for acceptance of such participation may be on the condition that he is invited by the local minister to assist. It is quite easy for a minister to say to a family or a prospective bride who asks him to officiate in his former parish: "I am sorry. As much as I would like to participate, I cannot presume upon the privilege of the local minister. With his invitation, I might assist him in the service. You talk with him about it."

Often the church policy can strengthen this position and save the church's minister from such embarrassment by stating that "a staff member of the local church must be a part of all weddings held." Thus, the outside minister would have an assisting role only.

—From James L. Christensen, *The Minister's Marriage Handbook*. Old Tappan, N.J.: Revell, 1974.

QUESTIONS TO ASK YOUR PASTOR

Some questions you will want to ask:

Does the minister have a set form of service that must be followed, or are we allowed to make some modifications?

Does a specific group in the church handle the reception details? If so, what services do they provide? How much advance notice do they need? And how is payment handled?

Are there guidelines for the music?

Are there any restrictions in decorating the sanctuary or church parlors?

Are there any restrictions concerning who may or may not participate in the ceremony?

What supplies are available from the church? Kneeling benches? Candelabra? Aisle runners? Punch bowls? Coffee pots? Is there a fee?

Is there a fee for using the sanctuary? Church parlors?

Are there standard fees paid to the pastor, custodian, organist, and so on?

Are there any rules concerning wedding photography?

Are facilities available for the bridal party to use for changing clothes? Can these rooms be locked?

During this first meeting, set the dates for premarital counseling. These should begin as early in your engagement as possible for two reasons. First, you will have more time to consider thoughtfully your pastor's advice and make any necessary adjustments in your relationship. Second, your calendar will become increasingly busy as your wedding day nears. Setting these counseling dates establishes your priority to place your relationship above the social flurry.

—From Kay Oliver Lewis, *The Christian Wedding Handbook*. Old Tappan, N.J.: Revell, 1981.

HONORARIUM

In most parts of the country it is still customary for the groom to give the minister or ministers performing the ceremony a monetary token of gratitude. Some ministers refuse honoraria for weddings. Others accept honoraria graciously. One minister keeps a record of the amount received and the date of the wedding. He returns the honorarium on the first anniversary of the couple's wedding with a note asking them to use it for an evening out as his guest! Others give the honorarium to their wives or buy a present for the couple with it. If the minister has qualms of conscience about accepting honoraria he might use it for buying several books on marriage and family living to give the couple as they begin a home.

—From Perry H. Biddle, *Abingdon Marriage Manual*. Nashville: Abingdon, 1974.

Church Regulations

Most local churches have specific regulations regarding weddings. Below I give the wedding policy of the church of which I am currently the pastor:

Riverdale (Ga.) Presbyterian Church
Policy Concerning Weddings

The minister cannot ordinarily commit himself to perform the marriage until after at least one interview. It is proper, therefore, to meet with the minister before any public announcement is made of a wedding in our church. Another minister, after approval by the Session, may perform the marriage ceremony.

All details concerning the wedding and related arrangements must conform to such practices as are in accord with Christian and Presbyterian customs. It is expected that the members of the wedding party will refrain from alcoholic beverages immediately prior to both the rehearsal and the wedding. The bride and groom shall be under obligation to make this rule known to all other members of the wedding party. Needless to say, alcoholic beverages are never to be served in the church building.

1. To reserve the Sanctuary or Joy Hall, call the church office.
2. Rehearsals will be supervised by the officiating minister. The Riverdale Presbyterian Church minister under the direction of the Session will be the final authority in all procedures. Please make sure florists and/or bridal consultants understand this.
3. Flowers used in weddings should be tasteful and in keeping with the traditions of public worship.
4. No decorations of any kind may be installed which are fastened to permanent furniture by such means as nails, staples, screws, gummed tape, clamps, etc.
5. No decoration shall be used which will hide from view any of the primary symbols in the Chancel area. That is: Pulpit and Bible, Communion Table, Baptismal Font, and Cross.
6. Caterers and Florist, or those responsible for these services, will be required to remove their equipment and accessories immediately following the wedding and reception.
7. No pictures may be taken during the ceremony. This means: from the time the bridal party enters the Sanctuary until the minister pronounces the benediction. It is urged that pictures be taken either prior to the wedding itself or after the reception. The time lag between the wedding and the reception while the pictures are being taken is burdensome and inconsiderate to those waiting.
8. Adequate mats or cloth must be placed beneath all candelabra to prevent dripping on the carpet.
9. Exits must be left free of decorations because of fire regulations.
10. It is encouraged that the regular organist be used. If, however, another organist is desired, arrangements should be made with the minister. The organist used must be a qualified organist.
11. All wedding parties are asked to refrain from throwing rice (or any other objects) inside the church building. Rice thrown outside must be swept off the sidewalks to prevent accidents.
12. If a flower girl is used during the wedding, there will be no flowers strewn on the carpet.
13. No smoking is permitted in the Sanctuary or Narthex, but is allowed in Joy Hall. Everyone is asked to be mindful of others' feelings about smoking.

14. Wedding receptions are frequently held in the church, and the church welcomes the opportunity to serve in this way. Receptions may be held in Joy Hall or the annex.

15. Normally, no weddings are scheduled for Saturday after 6:00 p.m. if the Joy Hall is used for a reception. (It is estimated that a minimum of four hours is required to clean and set up the Joy Hall for Sunday services.)

16. *Cost:*

> *For members:* There are no charges for members of Riverdale Presbyterian Church for use of the Sanctuary and Joy Hall, although it is expected that they will be responsible to see that the Joy Hall or annex is cleaned. As an alternative, they may pay the custodial of non-members.
>
> *For non-members:* For those who are not members of this church, there is a schedule of charges which covers the cost of the organist; preparation of the Sanctuary; Joy Hall or annex; the cleaning of these after use; along with the necessary upkeep and utilities. The appropriate charges are payable at the time the reservation is made and filed at the church office.
>
> Money received for the use of church facilities is not considered a church donation. These fees are for maintenance and custodian purposes only. The minister makes no charges for his service.

—CECIL MURPHEY

TYPE OF WEDDING

THERE ARE ONLY four basic types of weddings, whether large or small: very formal, formal, semiformal, and informal. Garden weddings, military weddings, and double weddings may be variations of any of these.

A Very Formal Wedding usually includes

A stately dress with a long train and a veil in a complementary length for the bride.

Formal attire (white tie and tails in the evening, cutaways in the daytime) for the groom and all the men in the wedding party.

Four to twelve bridesmaids in floor-length dresses.

Long dresses for the mothers of the bride and groom.

A high noon, late afternoon or evening ceremony.

200 or more guests.

Engraved invitations, usually the large size, with separate reception invitations enclosed.

A large and lavish reception.

A Formal Wedding usually has these characteristics:

A long dress with a chapel or sweep train and a veil for the bride.

Formal clothes (black tie in the evening, stroller jackets with striped trousers in the daytime) for the groom and his attendants.

Two to six bridesmaids, usually in long dresses.

Long or elaborate street-length dresses for the mothers.

Ceremony at any hour of the day.

At least 100 guests.

Engraved invitations, usually with separate reception invitations enclosed.

A festive reception.

A Semiformal Wedding usually means:

An elaborate street-length dress (or a simple floor-length dress) and a hat or short veil for the bride.

Dark suits for the groom and his attendants.

One or two bridal attendants in street-length dresses.

Street-length dresses for the mothers.

A morning or early afternoon ceremony. Fewer than 100 guests.

A single engraved invitation to both ceremony and reception.

A small but charming reception.

An Informal Wedding is usually characterized by:

Street clothes, often a suit, for the bride.

Suits for the groom and best man.

A maid of honor, but no bridesmaids, in street clothes.

A daytime ceremony anywhere, including City Hall.

A guest list including relatives and close friends.

Handwritten or personal invitations to the small ceremony and reception.

In general, the formality of a wedding increases with the size of the guest list. But a wedding before fifty guests in a magnificent church might enjoy all the pomp of formal dress. Or you might invite several hundred guests to a vast and informal ceremony out of doors.

—From *The New Bride's Book of Etiquette*. New York: Grosset & Dunlap, 1981.

The Setting

Think together about your values and your tastes, and plan a celebration that will feel comfortable to you. Keep in mind that weddings do not belong solely to the bride, but also to the families. Therefore, consider the feelings of others. If your plans would offend a close family member, look for a compromise that will strengthen family ties.

Here are some wedding options you might consider:

Home wedding. This intimate setting provides a warm, comfortable atmosphere for a small group of relatives and close friends. You might feel more relaxed, especially if you enjoy small groups more than crowds. And the service can be worshipful and Christ honoring. His presence is not limited to the church sanctuary, for He promises to be wherever "two or three are gathered together" in His name.

A home wedding can be simple, eliminating much of the work associated with larger ceremonies. Costs can be reduced. And the strain on bride and groom is lessened, leaving the two of you more relaxed to begin your honeymoon.

The disadvantage, of course, is that your guest list must be limited to the number that can comfortably fit in the home.

Small chapel wedding. If a church setting is important to you (or your home is too small to accommodate a wedding), but you want only family and close friends, consider getting married in a small chapel or small room of your church decorated for the occasion. You will probably be able to accommodate a few more guests than you would in a home, yet the service will still be intimate. Expense and strain on the bride and groom can be kept to a minimum.

Outdoor wedding. Perhaps you dream of getting married in a garden or other scenic setting. If so, you are in good company. The first wedding, performed by God Himself, took place in a garden.

A garden wedding can be as formal or informal as you wish and floral decorations are already provided. It will take a bit of extra work to arrange seating and to plan the music with either stringed instruments or recorded selections. But your biggest concern will be the weather. Even if you live in a desert where sunny days are nearly guaranteed, make alternate plans just in case.

Church wedding. A church sanctuary provides an impressive background for a wedding ceremony. It has added significance because you associate the sanctuary with corporate worship. And it has other advantages: a quality organ, good acoustics, a longer aisle, a platform that easily accommodates the wedding party and floral arrangements, and more seating for guests.

Before making your decision, consider a few drawbacks. If your guest list is small, the sanctuary could look empty. A larger event will require more preparation and involve more details. And costs, if not watched closely, can soar. Furthermore, if either of you gets tense or keyed up by large events, the escalated excitement of a full-scale church wedding could prove overwhelming. If either time or budget is sharply limited, this type of elaborate ceremony might prove more taxing than enjoyable.

Know yourselves and your values, then plan the setting where you feel most comfortable. This is your day to remember, so plan wisely. If you are satisfied and enjoy your service, your guests will enjoy it also.

Whatever your setting, a wedding should be, first of all, a worship service. You will want it to be a reverent reflection of your faith in Christ and your praise to the Creator who calls men and women together in marriage.

—From Kay Oliver Lewis, *The Christian Wedding Handbook*. Old Tappan, N.J.: Revell, 1981.

Special Weddings

THE MILITARY WEDDING

The extra flourish and splendor of a military wedding appeal to many brides who marry commissioned officers on active duty. The outstanding characteristic of a military wedding is the traditional arch of sabers (swords in the Navy) under which the bride and groom walk at the end of the ceremony. This arch is formed by the ushers—all fellow officers of the groom in full dress uniform.

A groom in any branch of military service—whether he's an officer or not—may be married in uniform, but swords and sabers are carried only by officers in full dress uniform (blue in winter, white in summer). Like the men in any other wedding party, those in a military wedding should be dressed alike. One or two exceptions are sometimes made to allow your brothers to participate in the wedding, but your father is usually the only man in the procession in civilian clothes. Military decorations are worn by men in uniform instead of boutonnières. Swords and sabers are usually carried, rather than worn, so they don't get in the way when the ushers are seating guests.

Full dress military uniforms are formal attire, and are worn only if you wear a long wedding dress. The bridesmaids, mothers, and wedding guests dress as they would for any other formal wedding at the same hour and season.

Most military weddings take place in military chapels—including those at West Point, Annapolis, and the Air Force Academy—but other locations are acceptable. Decorations usually include an American flag and the standards of the groom's own military unit. Floral decorations are optional, but are often included for large weddings. Military rules on these and all other aspects of a military wedding should be verified with the proper authorities.

Invitations and announcements for a military wedding differ only in that the groom's rank and service are indicated. If your fiancé is a junior officer (below the rank of Army or Air Force Captain or Naval Commander), his title appears under his name, followed by the branch of service on the same line. The title of a senior officer precedes his name, and his branch is indicated on the following line, because "Mr." is never used to address or refer to an officer on active duty.

The procession for a military wedding follows standard procedures, but the recessional includes the traditional arch of steel. This may be formed outside the church, in front of the chancel, or both, depending on church rules, the branch of service, and personal preference. The commands are usually issued by the head usher, starting with "Center face," the signal to form two facing lines. When the order "Arch sabers" (or "Draw swords") is given, each usher raises his saber in his right hand with the cutting edge on top. After you and your groom have passed under the arch, the sabers are sheathed or returned to the "carry" position. When the arch is formed inside, the bride and groom wait in the vestibule until the ushers are in place at the chapel door or on the steps.

The reception following a military wedding often features appropriate military decorations and music. These might include miniature flags and the theme song of the groom's branch of the service. At a sitdown reception, military guests, including the groom's commanding officer and immediate superiors, are seated by order of rank. The final military tradition is the use of the groom's saber or sword to cut the wedding cake.

THE DOUBLE WEDDING

Although any good friends or close relatives may have a double wedding, it's usually two sisters near to each other in age who choose to share their day. The main appeal of a double wedding is the saving—emotional as well as financial—it offers to families facing two successive weddings. A girl without such factors to consider is less inclined to share the spotlight on her wedding day.

Invitations to a double wedding are usually issued jointly. If the brides are not sisters, however, separate invitations may be sent. It is customary for each couple in a double wedding to have their own attendants, but the two wedding parties are usually the same size. The brides often serve as each other's maid and matron of honor, but this is optional.

Double weddings are usually formal and follow the same rules of dress as any other formal wedding. Both sets of ushers dress exactly alike, while the bridesmaids wear dresses of the same length and formality. The styles and colors may be different so long as they harmonize. The brides usually wear different dresses, but their trains and veils should be about the same length.

When the two brides are sisters, the older usually takes precedence. Otherwise, the order of the ceremony and the seating arrangements must be worked out carefully in advance. If there are two aisles, the processions and recessionals may take place simultaneously, one on each side. When there is only one aisle, one set of parents must relinquish their right to the front row; or both sets may share this honor.

With a single aisle, the two grooms walk in together behind the clergyman and take their places side by side, each with his own best man behind him. The future husband of the older or first bride stands nearest the aisle. Both sets of ushers, paired by height, lead the procession. The bridesmaids, the maid of honor, and the flower girl of the older bride come next, followed by the first bride on her father's arm. The second set of attendants and the younger bride follow in similar fashion. At a double wedding of sisters, a brother or other male relative may escort the second bride to the altar, but her father gives her away.

On reaching the head of the aisle, the attendants usually separate so that those of the older bride are all on the left, those of the younger on the right. The two couples stand side by side in front of the clergyman with the first bride on the left. In a double wedding of sisters, the father stands behind the older bride until he gives her away, then moves over to give his second daughter away before taking his seat. A joint ceremony is usually divided into segments, with the two couples completing each segment in turn. After the marriage vows are taken, the final blessing may be given to both couples at the same time.

At the close of the service, the two couples may kiss and turn simultaneously to face their guests. The recession is led by the older sister and her husband, followed by the younger couple. The two sets of honor attendants come next, followed by the bridesmaids and ushers in pairs. When each bride acts as the other's honor attendant, the best men escort bridesmaids in the recessional, with the extra ushers bringing up the rear.

A joint reception always follows a double wedding. When the brides are not sisters, each family forms a separate receiving line. Sisters receive in the same line with the older bride and her husband before the younger couple. To keep the line at a manageable length, the fathers seldom participate. If there is a large wedding party, including separate honor attendants, all the bridesmaids may also be excused from the receiving line. The size of the wedding party determines whether it's better to have a joint bridal table or separate ones.

THE SECOND MARRIAGE

A second-time bride may be married in a formal, religious ceremony if her faith permits, but older widows and divorcées often choose simple ceremonies attended only by relatives and a few close friends. A second-time bride never wears stark white or a veil, traditional symbols of chastity; otherwise she follows the usual rules of dress for the degree of formality she chooses.

A second marriage may do without a procession, for the bride is not given away. Attendants may be limited to a maid or matron of honor and a best man, but there may be bridesmaids and as many ushers as are needed to seat the guests. The children of a first marriage may participate in their parents' second weddings if they are old enough to understand the circumstances and are happy about the wedding.

The bride removes the engagement and weddings rings given her by her first husband when she announces her engagement. If her new husband has no objections, she may continue to wear her first engagement ring on her right hand.

The size of the guest list determines what invitations are correct for a second marriage. Handwritten invitations are suitable for a small ceremony, but engraved invitations may be sent for a large reception. Formal announcements are also proper for a second marriage.

A prior marriage of the groom has far less effect upon the size and style of the wedding. A formal church ceremony is proper if it doesn't violate any religious rule.

THE OLDER BRIDE

A mature woman usually does not choose an elaborate train and veil designed for a girl of twenty. She may wear a long white dress if she wishes, but it should be simple and appropriate for her age. A mature bride may have a church wedding with two or three attendants, but she should not ask her own contemporaries to wear youthful bridesmaids' dresses. Junior bridesmaids or flower girls make charming attendants for an older bride. Whether or not she is given away, she may be escorted down the aisle in the standard procession.

A large and festive reception is always in order—no matter how old the bride and groom may be. Mature couples, however, often omit such frivolous touches as throwing the bouquet and garter.

—From *The New Bride's Book of Etiquette.* New York: Grosset & Dunlap, 1981.

PREPARATIONS

Calendar checklist

Twelfth Week Before Wedding
1. Have conference with minister to arrange day and time.
2. Make reservation for church use for both wedding and reception. If reception is not in a church, you may have to make earlier arrangements.
3. Learn the policy of the church regarding costs, decorations, etc.
4. Schedule at least one or two more premarital counseling sessions.
5. Make arrangements with organist, other musicians, and primary attendants.
6. Read through a wedding planning book.

Eleventh Week Before Wedding
1. Make out wedding invitation list.
2. Make out reception list.
3. Make out announcement list.
4. Order invitations and announcements.
5. Have conference with the caterer.

Tenth Week Before Wedding
1. Select and get commitments from members of the wedding party.
2. Choose general color scheme and flowers.

Ninth and Eighth Weeks Before Wedding
1. Order or begin making wedding dress.
2. Arrange date, time, and place of rehearsal dinner.
3. Select china, glassware, and silver patterns.

Seventh Week Before Wedding
1. Make arrangements with florist.
2. Make arrangements with photographer.
3. Order printed napkins, etc., for reception.
4. Have conference with minister.

Sixth Week Before Wedding
1. Pick out gifts for attendants.
2. Arrange for housing of guests from out of town.
3. Read literature recommended by the minister.
4. Buy wedding rings.

Fifth Week Before the Wedding
1. Buy going-away clothes.
2. Make honeymoon trip reservations.

Fourth Week Before Wedding
1. Have conference with physician.
2. Have blood test.
3. Recheck with all attendants to confirm that they will be present.
4. Send out invitations to wedding and to rehearsal dinner.
5. Submit a release to newspaper of announced wedding plans.

Third Week Before Wedding
1. Give a bridesmaids' luncheon or tea.

Second Week Before Wedding
1. Get license.
2. Have conference with minister.
3. Pose a bride's picture for newspaper.

Last Week Before Wedding
1. Remind all participants regarding rehearsal attendance.
2. Have newspaper release ready.
3. Arrange for announcements to be mailed the day of the ceremony.

—From Natalia M. Belting and James R. Hine, *Your Wedding Workbook*, Danville, Ill.: Interstate, 1977.

Expenses

BRIDE

It is sensible to determine at the beginning just how much is available to spend on the wedding. It is not good judgment to outspend one's means. The wedding service itself does not require any elaborateness. In order to compile an adequate budget, it is necessary to consider the following items as the responsibility of the bride's family.

The engagement party (optional).

The engraving, addressing, and mailing of invitations and announcements.

The trousseau of the bride, including the wedding ensemble.

All expenses in connection with the church, including the fees for the organist, soloist, or choir, and sexton. These fees are usually designated amounts and are no longer considered in the category of gifts or tips. The fees should be paid at the time of the rehearsal.

All expenses in connection with the reception—the food, decorations, music, and rental for hotel or club room.

The bride's gift to the groom and the wedding ring (if there is to be a double ring ceremony).

The bride's gifts to her attendants.

The wedding photographs. (Many times the groom's family wish to pay for the pictures they select.)

The flowers for the bridesmaids and floral decorations for the ceremony and reception: also aisle runner, if used.

Hotel accommodations for out-of-town bridesmaids (and husbands).

A canopy, if one is used. (The canopy is used only in case of inclement weather.)

Traffic policemen at the church.

Insurance on wedding gifts.

Luncheon for the bridesmaids (optional).

Transportation for members of the bridal party between home, church, and reception.

GROOM

Wedding tradition has aimed to equalize some of the financial responsibilities between the families of the bride and groom.

The following items are listed for the groom.

Wedding attire and personal wardrobe.

The marriage license (check state laws in advance).

The engagement ring, wedding ring, and wedding gift for the bride.

Flowers: The bride's bouquet and going away corsage, the corsages for the mothers and grandmothers, and the boutonnières for the groom, best man, fathers, and ushers.

The clergyman's fee: The amount is undesignated, but should be between $25 (for a small unrehearsed wedding) and $50 according to the responsibility the minister assumes at the rehearsal and according to the elaborateness of the wedding. This fee, inserted in a white envelope, should be handed to the minister before the ceremony takes place.

Hotel arrangements for out-of-town ushers (and wives).

Wedding ties and gloves for the best man and ushers.

Personal gifts for the best man and ushers.

The Bachelor dinner (optional).

The Rehearsal dinner (frequently sponsored by the parents of the groom.)

All expenses of the wedding trip.

—From Betty Stuart Rodgers and Elizabeth Connelly Pearce, *Altar Bound*. Danville, Ill.: Interstate, 1973 (out of print).

The Marriage License

Every state requires a marriage license before a couple can marry; however, the requirements vary.

In most states, couples first present blood-test results (which can take up to ten days to obtain).

In addition, most states include any or all of the following:

- proof of age
- consent of parents if either/both under age
- proof of residence
- if previously married, proof of death of previous spouse, annulment, or divorce

Some states have a waiting period after issuing the license, although most do not. Each state has its own regulations when bride and groom come from different towns within the same state or from different states. Some states require witnesses at the wedding, although many no longer have such a requirement.

As soon as wedding plans are made, call and ask requirements of the town clerk. If you see a clergyman at least six weeks in advance, he can usually tell you the requirements.

The clergyman must have the license before performing the ceremony. Some prefer that they receive the license at least two days ahead of time, rather than running the risk of having the best man forget it in the press of activities.

Most states hold the person performing the marriage responsible for returning the completed marriage license. In some places, couples receive either (1) a carbon of the official license, which has no legal significance, or (2) they subsequently receive a legal marriage certificate from the state. If at any time you need certified copies, again contact the place where you received your information regarding the license.

—CECIL MURPHEY

Wedding Invitations

The bride's parents pay for the invitations and are responsible for addressing and mailing them. Normally, they also pay for the announcements. If the groom's parents wish to send out a large number, it is correct for them to suggest paying for their share. However, they do not issue the announcements in their own name. The wording remains exactly the same, unless, as is becoming more popular, they send out a joint announcement. This practice has long been popular in Europe and is becoming more so in the United States.

Customarily, however, invitations are issued in the name of the bride's parents, or under certain circumstances, by a close relative, guardian, or even the bride herself. The groom's parents never properly issue the wedding invitation alone, except in the case of a foreign bride with no family in this country.

In the past decade, couples have been choosing more original invitations, sometimes totally writing their own. The articles below, however, give the traditional view of wedding invitations and announcements.

Printers and stationers usually have a large selection of samples to look through, showing the wording and style for formal and informal weddings.

—CECIL MURPHEY

SELECTING THE INVITATIONS

A small wedding does not require engraved invitations. Instead, the mother of the bride (or the bride) may write short notes or telephone relatives and friends who are invited.

For a larger wedding, select invitations from a stationer, either at a stationery store or at a department store. Traditional invitations are engraved in black ink on the first page of a double sheet. The paper is white, ivory, or ecru. However, photoengraving is now available that looks similar to engraving—even with raised letters—and at a third the cost. When used on plain white, ivory, or ecru paper, these invitations maintain formal dignity and simplicity.

Invitations are also available in a wide range of colors, designs, and folds. Some can include a picture of the couple. Others have a message or Scripture verse on the outside, with the invitation inside the card. Although these depart from the tradition, they may express your individuality.

Budget trimmer. If formal invitations are not important to you, you might have your invitations printed. One bride designed invitations to be printed on eight-and-one-half-by-eleven sheets. She folded and addressed these on the outside, eliminating envelopes altogether. Informal? Yes, but her guests got the message, and she held down her wedding costs.

—From Kay Oliver Lewis, *The Christian Wedding Handbook.* Old Tappan, N.J.: Revell, 1981

ADDRESSING INVITATIONS AND ANNOUNCEMENTS

How They Are Addressed. All invitations and announcements are addressed by hand. A blue-black or black ink is used.

Tissues. Tissues that have been inserted in the invitations to keep the ink from smearing are left in the invitations.

Addressing the Invitations. The bride, the bride's mother or guardian, any member of the bride's family, or a friend may help to address the invitations. Writing should be regular and legible; no one who does not write plainly should be asked to help.

Sealing. The inner envelope is left unsealed.

The outer envelope is sealed.

Inserting the Invitation. Several leading engravers recommend that the inner envelope is inserted so that both envelopes face the same way.

A frequently used method is to place the unsealed envelope in the outer envelope so that it faces the flap.

Since there is no conformity regarding the proper method of insertion, the custom used locally might be the guide as to choice.

Postage. All invitations and announcements are sent by first-class mail; a regulation twenty-cent stamp will suffice unless too many heavy enclosure cards are included.

Delivery of Order. Orders of wedding invitations and announcements are delivered to the home of the bride unless specified otherwise.

Inner Envelope—Outer Envelope. All wedding invitations have two envelopes.

The outer envelope is for the name and address of the person to whom it is being sent.

The inner envelope contains the invitation and any enclosure cards. On the inner envelope are written the title and the last name of the person to whom the invitation is being sent. No address is written upon the inner envelope.

Already Stuffed. The inner envelope comes from the engravers already stuffed with the invitation and any enclosure cards.

Outer Envelope Addressed Before Invitations Are Ready. The outer envelopes can be secured before the invitations are ready, making it possible to address them while waiting for the invitations to be engraved.

Return Address. Wedding invitations may be embossed on the back with the return address. It costs very little and is a courtesy to those being invited and to the postal authorities. Announcements carry no return address. "At Home" cards are used with announcements.

When Mailed. Engraved invitations should be mailed four weeks before the ceremony.

Handwritten invitations are mailed two to three weeks before the ceremony.

Printed invitations are mailed four weeks before the ceremony.

Separate the in-town and out-of-town invitations as an aid to the post office employees.

All invitations are mailed at the same time except those going overseas, which may be mailed a few days earlier.

Announcements are mailed as soon as possible after the ceremony.

Abbreviations Allowable. All invited guests' names are written in full, including the full middle name if it is known; if not, a middle initial may be used.

Abbreviations are not permitted except for "Mrs." "Mr." "Messrs.," "Dr.," "Jr.," and "Lt." when combined with Colonel, General, or Commander.

Write Out in Full. The names of all cities, states, and streets.

The names of all invited guests.

All titles such as "Reverend," "Colonel," "Admiral," "Senator."

—From Winifred Gray, *You and Your Wedding.* New York: Bantam, 1965.

RECALLING WEDDING INVITATIONS

If after wedding invitations have been sent out the wedding is called off, guests must be informed as soon as possible. They may be sent notes, telegrams, printed or engraved cards (when there is time for the engraving).

Dr. and Mrs. Grant Kingsley
announce that the marriage
of their daughter
Penelope
to
Mr. George Knapp Carpenter
will not take place

A telegram is signed by those who issued the invitation. It would read, "The marriage of our daughter Penelope to Mr. George Knapp Carpenter will not take place. Dr. and Mrs. Grant Kingsley." A telegram to a close relative would be less formally worded and carry the familiar signature.

Death in the Family. When a death occurs in a family that has issued formal invitations is it necessary to recall the invitations? It certainly used to be, but our ideas have changed very radically on the subject of mourning. Certainly no bride would want to go through an elaborate wedding ceremony followed by the festivity of a large reception within a few days of her mother's or father's death or of the sudden death of the groom's mother, father, sister, or brother. The death of a very old person, a grandmother or grandfather, rarely calls for the postponement of a wedding these days, but it all very much depends on the feelings of all involved.

If after a family conference it is decided to recall a wedding invitation because of a death, the guests are notified by wire, by phone, or, if there is time, by printed cards in the same style as the invitation. They may read:

Mrs. Grant Kingsley
regrets that the death of
Dr. Kingsley
obliges her to recall the invitations
to the wedding of her daughter
(THE NAMES ARE OPTIONAL)
Friday, the eighth of June

Such notification does not mean, of course, that the marriage won't take place. It may, instead, be a quiet family ceremony on the original day planned. The bride may even wear her bridal gown and have one attendant, but without a crowded church the full panoply of bridesmaids and ushers would be senseless.

Postponing Weddings. If a wedding is postponed and a new date has been set guests may be informed by telegram or sent a new *printed* invitation done in the style of the original engraved one. It reads:

> Dr. and Mrs. Grant Kingsley
> announce that the marriage
> of their daughter
> Penelope
> to
> Mr. George Frank Carpenter
> has been postponed from
> Friday, the eighth of June
> until
> Friday, the seventh of September
> at noon
> St. Mary's Church
> San Francisco

—From *Amy Vanderbilt's Complete Book of Etiquette,* revised by Letitia Baldridge. New York: Doubleday, 1978.

Guest Lists

Four lists are combined to make up the master list—those of the bride's parents, the groom's parents, the bride, and the groom. It is up to the bride's mother to discuss with the groom's mother (by phone or letter) the number of invitations available to her. If both families live in the same community, the invitations should be evenly divided. Since some names would surely be dupli-cated, the bride's mother should let the groom's mother know how many extra spaces are available to her. But since Jennifer lives near Chicago, and Michael comes from California, Mrs. Peterson tells Mrs. Burke that only fifty of their relatives and friends will be able to attend. Therefore, although invitations may be sent to many more out-of-towners, Mrs. Burke knows that she may safely add extra names, if she wishes, to her list. Both families may invite a few more than the total allowed them, since there will always be some refusals other than those expected.

It is most important that the two mothers make up their lists *realistically.* The groom's mother must make every effort to stay within the number of places allotted to her, since the limit set by the bride's family is often dictated by necessity. If she feels she simply *must* invite more than the number specified, she and her husband should offer to pay a share of the expenses sufficient to cover the additional costs. The other alternative is for her to plan a reception for the bride and groom after the honeymoon, to which the friends who could not be included at the wedding are invited.

Many people prefer not to send invitations to those acquaintances who cannot possibly attend. They feel it might appear that they are merely inviting those friends to send a gift. Such friends should receive an announcement, or possibly an invitation to the church only, neither of which carries any obligation whatsoever.

When the church is large, the bride's family and the groom's may invite all their personal acquaintances and also their business associates to the church ceremony. Their lists for the reception should be restricted to more intimate friends. Were the wedding in the house or chapel, and the reception limited to relatives and very close friends, announcements would be sent to all those who could not be included at all. Both bride and groom should check carefully with parents and grandparents to be sure that no old family friends are overlooked.

The bride's mother should also send church and reception invitations to the following people:

The person who performs the ceremony, and his or her spouse, if any

The fiancés(ées) of invited guests (When the bride knows the name of the fiancé(e), she sends him or her a separate invitation. If she does not know it, she should try to get the name and address from the one she knows. Should this be very difficult, she may enclose a note with the latter's invitation, saying, "Dear Pamela, we would be delighted if you would bring your fiancé.")

The parents of the bridesmaids (not necessary, but a nice gesture whenever feasible)

The bridal attendants (who enjoy them as mementos of the occasion) and their spouses

The groom's parents—for the same reason (they are not expected to reply, since their attendance is taken for granted, unless they have called or written a personal note to explain their absence)

Small children, even though they cannot be included at the reception (they are usually thrilled with an invitation to the church ceremony)

People in mourning, even though they may not attend

One member of a married couple should never be invited without the other. Also, both members of an unmarried couple living together should be invited.

—From Elizabeth Post, *Emily Post's Complete Book of Wedding Etiquette*. New York: Harper & Row, 1982.

Attendants

BRIDESMAIDS

The bride chooses as many bridesmaids as she wishes. For a formal wedding, usually up to six. For less formal weddings, she may want a maid of honor and one or two bridesmaids. Other friends of the bride may participate by assisting with gifts, serving at the reception, handling the guest book. In some states, witnesses are required, in others no one but the person who officiates. If unsure, ask your pastor or when you buy your license.

—CECIL MURPHEY

MAID (OR MATRON) OF HONOR

The maid of honor is the bride's most important attendant, usually being her sister or closest friend. She should be notified of her selection several months in advance, before invitations are sent, so that the date can be entered into her schedule and necessary adjustments and clothing preparations can be made.

Unless the bride can afford the expense and wants to give her the wedding outfit, the maid of honor buys her own wedding clothes. The flowers which she carries, however, are given to her by the bride.

The duties and responsibilities of the maid of honor are as follows:

1. Attend the rehearsal.
2. Arrange the bride's train as the procession forms in the rear of the church, and again at the altar if necessary, and straighten it behind the bride as she turns for the recessional.
3. Hold the bride's bouquet during the ring exchange.
4. Carry the groom's ring during the ceremony (unless there is a ring-bearer), and

49

give it to the minister at the appropriate time.

5. If the bride wears a veil, the maid of honor helps to lift it back on her head at the end of the ceremony.
6. Stand in the receiving line next to the groom.
7. Assist the bride in changing clothes and packing for her trip.
8. See that no tricks in bad taste are played.

—From James L. Christensen, *The Minister's Marriage Handbook.* Old Tappan, N.J.: Revell, 1974.

FLOWER GIRL

The flower girl, a small child, is related to the bride or groom or the child of a close friend. Traditionally, she walks down the aisle carrying a basket of flower petals, which she strews in the aisle of the church. Some churches prefer that no flower petals be strewn, so consult the minister first.

She walks immediately in front of the bride in the processional. If she is in the recessional, she walks directly behind the bride and groom.

Often she sits down after the processional and does not participate in the recessional. She doesn't stand in the receiving line at the reception. Her parents are responsible for her wedding clothes.

—CECIL MURPHEY

OTHER HELPERS

Those who love you most will want to participate in the joy of your wedding. As you make your plans, think of ways to include others. Although you may be hesitant to ask for assistance, you will find that most people feel honored that you think enough of them to want their help. The more you involve others, the more your community of friends will surround you with the love and support you need.

Think about the abilities of the people you know. Can some sing? Play instruments? Make artistic banners? Print invitations or programs? Invite them to make their contributions.

Do you know someone who could help with decorating the church or reception site? A cake baker? An organizer to run the reception? Let them share the blessing by giving their abilities. You could invite friends to bring a special dish for the rehearsal buffet or your wedding reception.

Perhaps you could ask close friends or an uncle and aunt to be host and hostess. Assign specific duties to each, such as distributing flowers to the wedding-party, seeing that bridesmaids and ushers enter at the correct time, receiving gifts, greeting guests, and giving directions at the reception.

Think of ways for people to participate in your ceremony. Rather than have your guests be spectators at a pageant, allow them to be worshipers together by singing hymns and reading Scripture. If you think people will feel comfortable, allow a time in the ceremony for guests to offer spontaneous prayers or expressions of love. At your reception have a microphone available and invite guests to say something personal about their relationship with you.

During the ceremony, allow guests to ring bells or light candles. Give each a flower, or invite friends to bring a flower to add to a growing bouquet. For an outdoor wedding, you could have a circle of white fabric where the bride, groom, and minister will stand. Guests could place their flowers around the perimeter to form a wreath.

By involving the larger community of people, you say that you cannot live marriage alone. You need the love and prayers of others.

Attendants' Checklist

Attendant	Attire	Date Fitted	Gift
Maid/Matron of Honor			
Bridesmaids			
Junior Bridesmaid			
Flower Girl			
Ring Bearer			
Best Man			
Ushers			

—From Kay Oliver Lewis, *The Christian Wedding Handbook*. Old Tappan, N.J.: Revell, 1981.

THE BEST MAN

The best man is the groom's primary attendant, and is usually his closest friend or a brother. He is chosen in ample time so that he can make whatever adjustments are necessary to be present.

Among the duties of the best man are:

1. Aid the groom in every possible way in preparation for the wedding. He protects the groom from pranks, and under no circumstance participates in practical jokes played on the bride and groom.
2. Attend the rehearsal; and aid the minister in gaining the cooperation of the male attendants and seeing that they are on time for the wedding.
3. Help the groom dress for the wedding, and go with him to the church at least a half hour before wedding time.
4. Deliver the license and wedding book to the minister for his recording, sign his own signature as one of the witnesses, and deliver the same to the maid of honor for her signature.
5. Give the clergyman his fee, inconspicuously, in a plain, white, sealed envelope.
6. Accompany the groom to the altar, carrying the bride's ring until the time the minister asks for it in the ceremony. If the groom wears gloves, the best man holds them during the ceremony.
7. Stand in the reception line next to the maid of honor. If the reception is at a place other than the church, he gets the hats and coats of the bride and groom and meets them at the front door. He chauffeurs the couple and maid of honor to the place of the reception.
8. Help the groom pack, and take charge of the couple's luggage, seeing that it is placed safely in the going-away car.
9. Keep in safety the keys to the groom's car. When the time comes for the couple's departure, he helps them get away safely.

—From James L. Christensen, *The Minister's Marriage Handbook*. Old Tappan, N.J.: Revell, 1974.

USHERS

The ushers arrive at the church one full hour before the ceremony begins, and each places a boutonnière on the left lapel of his coat. An usher has considerable responsibility in a formal church wedding and cannot be expected to run errands that take him from his duty of graciously meeting and seating the guests.

Guests will arrive beginning one-half hour before the ceremony and should come not later than five minutes before the hour set for the wedding. When seating guests, the ushers extend a friendly greeting and converse only briefly and quietly while escorting guests to their seats.

An usher offers his right arm *always* to a woman guest, the man following. Children under 15 or 16 follow along as their parents are seated. A gentleman guest follows an usher. As an usher seats a guest he pauses at the pew entrance slightly to the back of the pew (if seating a guest on the left facing the front) or in front of the pew (if seating a guest on the right facing the front). In either instance, the guests pass in front of the usher as they take their places in the pew. It is considered most discourteous for an usher to offer his left arm to a woman guest.

The left side of the church facing the altar is reserved for the bride's family and relatives and the right side is reserved for those of the groom. Guests may designate on which side they wish to be seated but custom is gradually suggesting that the ushers equalize the sides to give a balanced effect.

The parents furnish the head usher with special instructions for seating relatives and it is most helpful if these are in writing. If the ushers are to light the candles, this can be done before the guests start arriving.

Just before the processional, two ushers place the aisle ribbons on the pews and draw the aisle runner, if one is used. These ribbons are removed at the end of the ceremony after the parents and those occupying the first pews have been escorted out of the church. The runner remains on the floor. The ushers assist the bridal attendants to the reception, and direct guests to the receiving line.

—From Betty Stuart Rodgers and Elizabeth Connelly Pearce, *Altar Bound.* Danville, Ill.: Interstate, 1973 (out of print).

RING BEARER

The ring bearer, usually a brother or close relative of either the bride or groom, may walk in alone, preceding the flower girl, or he may walk with her.

The ring bearer carries a white satin pillow with the bride's ring (usually not the real one) tied to the center with ribbons. After the ceremony, the ring bearer turns the pillow upside down so that the dummy ring doesn't show. He does not attend prewedding parties and is often excused from the rehearsal.

If the couple use the real ring, the ring bearer must stay with the wedding party until the best man unfastens the ring (held by light stitches of thread) from the pillow. If the real ring is not being used, the ring bearer may leave the wedding party when it reaches the altar and join his mother in her pew.

—CECIL MURPHEY

GIFTS FOR ATTENDANTS

The bride and groom give each of their attendants a gift to express their thanks. These may be given either at the bridesmaids' luncheon and bachelor party, if such are held, or at the rehearsal dinner. Traditionally, brides give gold or silver jewelry, engraved with the wedding date. Grooms give cuff links, pen and pencil sets, paperweights, or letter openers.

Modern trends, however, allow the couple to select any gift they think their attendants would enjoy. These gifts could be other jewelry articles, small totable umbrellas, plants, tickets to a concert or sports event, books, or whatever else you think would please your attendants.

—From Kay Oliver Lewis, *The Christian Wedding Handbook.* Old Tappan, N.J.: Revell, 1981.

Wedding Gifts

BRIDAL REGISTRIES

One of the things you should be sure to do before you send out your invitations is to go to the bridal registries of your local gift and department stores to select and list with them your choices of china, silver, and crystal patterns and indicate which pieces you would like to have. You may also make selections from any of the other articles they have in stock. You should pick out individual items in as wide a range of prices as you possibly can. Then, when someone asks you what you would like as a present, you need only say, "I have listed a number of choices at the X and Y stores. If you'll stop by, they will be glad to show you the things I've chosen." If your friends cannot get to those stores, try to help by suggesting the *type* of gift you would like rather than a specific article. For example, you can say, "I really prefer pewter to silver," or "We're furnishing our living room in Early American," or "We love gardening, so anything for our yard (or terrace) would be great."

—From Elizabeth Post, *Emily Post's Complete Book of Wedding Etiquette.* New York: Harper & Row, 1982.

ACKNOWLEDGMENT OF WEDDING GIFTS

Thank-you Paper. The bride must use a fine quality plain or engraved note paper or informal for her thank-you notes.

If the thank-you paper is engraved or imprinted, it should carry the bride's name or initials only, never Mr. and Mrs.

If the bride is using engraved paper, it should be ordered at the same time as the wedding invitations or very shortly afterwards.

If some of the thank-you notes are to be written before the ceremony, and it is certainly wise to do this, some of the engraved or imprinted note paper should be ordered with the bride's unmarried name or initials, the remainder with her married name or initials.

Written by Hand. All thank-you notes MUST be written by hand. No commercial thank-yous are acceptable.

Written by the Bride. All thank-yous are written by the bride herself, even if the wedding present is addressed to the groom and is from a relative or friend of the groom whom the bride has never met.

When to Acknowledge. All wedding presents must be acknowledged as soon as possible after their arrival. A bride-to-be can usually keep up with her thank-yous until a few days before the ceremony, and it is important that she try to do this.

All wedding presents MUST be acknowledged, and no bride should wait longer than three months to do this, even though the wedding was very large and the gifts numerous.

If it is going to be impossible for a bride to acknowledge her wedding gifts within a reasonable time, a gift receipt card should be sent as soon as the gift is received. (Gift receipt cards will be explained later in this chapter.)

Not Writing Thank-Yous. A bride-to-be should search her soul before deciding on the size of her wedding. Unless she is willing and capable of acknowledging personally the numerous gifts resulting from a large wedding, she should limit herself to the size she will or can handle graciously. Once she has decided to have a large wedding, she has simultaneously accepted the responsibility of personally writing many thank-you notes. It is inexcusable and rude not to write a thank-you note for every wedding gift received, no matter how small.

Wedding Telegrams. A verbal thank-you is all that is necessary for a wedding telegram.

How Does the Bride Sign Her Name? Thank-yous for wedding gifts are signed Cordially, Affectionately, Sincerely, Love, etc.

The bride may sign only her first name if the sender of the gift is well known to her; if not she signs her first name, her maiden name, and her new surname, such as: Mary Jones Smith.

A Thank-You That Was Overlooked. The most careful person may overlook writing a thank-you, especially if the wedding was a large one and many gifts were received. If this happens and the bride hears about it, write or telephone the friend immediately explaining the oversight. Friends will understand and forgive.

Addressing. When a gift has been sent by a married couple, the bride writes to the wife. Within the letter she thanks both the husband and wife.

Return Address. A return address may be embossed or handwritten upon the back of the envelope.

Gift Receipt Card. If the bride and groom are going abroad or on a long trip where it will be impossible to write thank-yous for many months after the wedding, or if the wedding was so large that hundreds of gifts were received, necessitating a delay in completing the thank-yous, a gift receipt card is sent immediately after receiving the gift.

This card may be engraved or printed (engraved for the formal wedding), and it is mailed immediately upon receiving the gift.

This card is sent to inform the sender that her gift has been received and as soon as possible the bride will write a personal thank-you. A gift receipt card does not take the place of a personal thank-you note. Many times this card is used when a bride is absent from her home (at school, etc.) until a few days before the ceremony. In this case they are addressed and mailed by the bride's mother.

A gift card reads:

Miss Doris Townes (before marriage)
or
Mrs. Robert Arthur Bell (after marriage)
acknowledges with thanks
the receipt of your wedding gift
and will take pleasure in writing you
at an early date.

INFORMAL THANK-YOU LETTER

Dear Mrs. Davis:

John and I are delighted with the lovely lamp and know it will be simply perfect in our apartment. We both like brass, as you obviously must have known. The gifts will be shown the day before the wedding. I hope you will be able to come over then, if not before.

Please express our appreciation to Mr. Davis, too.

Affectionately,
Evelyn

FORMAL THANK-YOU LETTER

Dear Mrs. Armstrong:

The tablecloth, which we have just received, is lovely. The color is beautiful and matches our china perfectly. John and I appreciate your thoughtfulness. Please express our appreciation to Mr. Armstrong, too.

John has spoken of you and your husband frequently, and I am looking forward to meeting you at the wedding reception.

Sincerely,

Evelyn Morris

SENDING WEDDING GIFTS

When an invitation to a wedding reception is accepted, a wedding gift is sent.

If an invitation to a wedding reception is declined no gift is necessary, although many times one is sent.

If an invitation is for a wedding ceremony only, there is no gift obligation.

A handwritten or verbal invitation is usually issued when the wedding is quite small and customarily includes a reception or breakfast afterwards. Since this type of invitation is usually issued to a few chosen friends and relatives, whether or not it includes a reception or breakfast afterwards, a gift is ordinarily sent.

An invitation to a home ceremony customarily includes a reception or breakfast afterwards so, unless the invitation is declined, a gift is ordinarily sent.

An announcement does not require a wedding gift.

Gifts of Checks, Bonds, Stocks. If gifts of checks, bonds, or stocks are sent, they are made out in the bride's and groom's names.

To Whom Are Gifts Addressed? All wedding gifts sent before the ceremony are addressed to the bride; after the ceremony they are addressed to the bride and groom.

—From Winifred Gray, *You and Your Wedding.* New York: Bantam, 1965.

DELIVERY OF GIFTS

Gifts are usually sent to the bride's house before the day of the wedding, addressed to her maiden name. When they are sent after the wedding takes place, they go to Mr. and Mrs. Newlywed at their new address, or in care of the bride's family.

In some localities and among certain ethnic groups it is customary to take checks or gifts to the wedding reception. When this is done, they are usually given to the bride as the guest goes through the receiving line. Checks are put into a bag or receptacle held by the bride, and gifts are piled on a table nearby. If there is a great quantity of presents, the bride and groom may wait to open them at a later date, so that they can enjoy their dining and dancing at the reception as well as the company of their guests. If there are not too many gifts, they should open them when the receiving line breaks up, asking the help of one or two attendants to dispose of wrappings and keep a careful list.

—From Elizabeth Post, *Emily Post's Complete Book of Wedding Etiquette.* New York: Harper & Row, 1982.

SUITABLE WEDDING GIFTS

The most satisfactory presents are either useful or beautiful, and ideally they are both. Any object that the couple might like and need for their house, however, is suitable. It should have a fairly permanent quality, and it should never be something for the bride's personal use alone, such as a gold compact. Silver, china, and glass are classic wedding presents. Handsome linens are less enduring but very welcome. Household electric appliances (such as toasters and percolators) and decorative accessories are opposite in appeal but most brides like both. Good-looking wastepaper baskets, lamps, small tables, side chairs, and the like are all necessary furnishings. Sometimes something original, perhaps made by the donor or keyed to a particular bride's interests, as an excellent dictionary, is a happy choice. Antiques—an old ornament or an eighteenth-century silver ladle—are cherished by many brides today. Wedding presents need not be expensive, but they should be a little more special than birthday presents, for example. The safest are so classic that they appeal to any taste and are at home in any setting: a simple crystal bowl fits this definition perfectly. Money, in the form of cash, checks, stock certificates, bonds, or a deposit in a new savings account, is also suitable when given by an older friend of the family or a relative. Like other presents, checks or bonds are made out to the bride when sent before the wedding and to the couple if sent later.

The traditional wrappings for wedding presents are all white or white combined with silver or gold. A card should be enclosed on which the donor's name is written or engraved. A short line, such as "A great deal of happiness," can be written above it or not. A married couple always send a joint wedding present, as indicated by the card: "Mr. and Mrs. James Robert Thurston" or "Jim and Anne Thurston" if the relationship is closer. When presents are sent by shops, they are responsible for the packing. When sent by an individual, a present should be insured in case it arrives in poor condition. The donor's name and address should be clearly lettered on the outside of the package so the bride can enter them on her record list for reference when she writes her thank-you letter.

—From *Vogue's Book of Etiquette*. New York: Simon & Schuster, 1969.

DISPLAYING WEDDING GIFTS

The custom of displaying wedding presents may be observed or not, depending on the bride's wishes and the usual procedure in her community or among her friends. In certain circles, there is always the risk of offending people if their presents are not displayed.

Wedding presents may never be exhibited anywhere but in the house of the bride's parents. If the reception is held there, the presents can be on display at that time. Otherwise, friends may be invited to come before the wedding day to see them. They are arranged on tables set against a wall in a convenient but not essential room, such as a library, enclosed porch, or guest room from which the beds have been moved. The tables are covered with white cloths and may be decorated with vases of flowers, ribbon streamers, and bows. Presents should be arranged so that each is shown to the best advantage. Duplicates should be separated; extravagant objects should be far removed from the modest ones which might suffer by comparison; related items, such as table appointments or electric appliances and saucepans, should be grouped together. One place setting only of flat silver should be shown, unless the set is in a chest that is exhibited with the top lifted. If checks are shown, the amount must always be covered up.

The old custom of putting the donor's card beside each present is no longer considered the best idea. Not everyone has the same taste, bank account, or relationship with a bride or groom, and identification invites too many comparisons. The most desirable solution is to omit donors' cards and any checks to assume that people simply enjoy looking at a bride's new acquisitions.

—From *Vogue's Book of Etiquette*. New York: Simon & Schuster, 1969.

EXCHANGING GIFTS

Gifts may be exchanged if a number of the identical article has been received. This must be carefully done to avoid hurting anyone's feelings. Rather than risk hurting a good friend's feelings, it is better to keep the gift even though at the time it seems unlikely that it will ever be used. Only if the gift can be exchanged without the donor having any knowledge of it should this be done.

RECORDING GIFTS

Recording gifts is very simple if ALL gifts are properly recorded in the gift book as soon as they are opened.

It is not a good plan to have too many people opening gifts at one time. This is confusing and mistakes are more easily made.

Purchase of the correct size gift book to suit the wedding should be made. Gift books can be obtained to keep a record of from fifty to one thousand gifts. These books are sold at the bridal gift consultant shop, gift shops, specialty shops, stationery and department stores.

As each present arrives and is opened, the sender's name and address, a description of the gift, the shop where it was purchased, and the date it is received are recorded in the gift book. The date on which the thank-you note is written is also recorded. . . .

All gift cards that come with the wedding presents must be saved: THIS IS IMPORTANT. A special box to hold these cards should be provided. As soon as the gift is opened, the bride should write, on the back of each card, what the gift is, the store where it was purchased, and the number that corresponds to that in the bridal gift book. This gives a second check on all wedding gifts.

RETURNING GIFTS

When the Engagement Is Broken. If an engagement is permanently broken, ALL wedding gifts MUST be returned.

Each gift is accompanied by a note from either the bride or the bride's mother saying that the wedding plans have been terminated and thanking them for their kindness in sending the gift. No explanation of why the wedding plans were changed is necessary.

When the Marriage Is Broken. Even if the marriage lasts only a few days or weeks, the wedding gifts are not returned unless they have been unopened and unused. If they are returned, they are accompanied by a thank-you note. No explanation of why the marriage was terminated is necessary. If a marriage is broken, wedding gifts are divided equally, between the husband and wife.

—From Winifred Gray, *You and Your Wedding.* New York: Bantam, 1965.

Wedding Clothes

Dreams of a long, white gown begin early.

Now it's your turn to translate that dream into reality. No doubt you've already paged through bridal magazines, trying to determine your taste. Taste, budget, and sentimental value will help guide your decision. Before you begin shopping, consider some of the options.

Buy a gown at a bridal salon. These specialty shops have the largest selection of gowns in a wide range of prices. The bridal salon also has a selection of veils, accessories, bridesmaids' dresses, and dresses for mothers. Everything can be conveniently arranged with one shopping trip.

Before entering, determine what you can spend. Ask the salesperson to show only gowns in that range. Gowns purchased in these stores must be specially ordered and will take up to two months for delivery.

Although gowns bought in salons are generally expensive, these stores have substantial off-season and sample sales. If you have plenty of time, ask when the next sale is scheduled.

Buy at a department store. Most large stores have bridal departments, although

Wedding Clothes   Daytime—up to 6 P.M.

	FORMAL	SEMI-FORMAL	INFORMAL
Bride	Long white or pale tint wedding dress, train and veil, gloves or mitts are optional.	Floor length dress, short or no train, and short veil or veil-less.	Floor or street length dress, or suit (not black) or traveling costume, hat and gloves.
Bridesmaids	Formal length or midi-length dresses. Maid of Honor may be in contrasting color.	Same as formal wedding.	Same as Bride.
Groom, Best Man, Ushers and Fathers	Black or oxford gray cutaway coat, gray waistcoat, striped trousers, wing collar, ascot tie, black hose and shoes, gray gloves.	Black or oxford gray jacket, striped trousers, gray striped tie, turn-down collar, black shoes and hose. *Summer*—White linen suit or dark blue or gray jacket with light trousers.	Dark blue or oxford gray business suit. No gloves. *Summer*—White linen or tropical worsted suit.
Mothers	Formal length or midi-length dresses and gloves.	Formal or street length dresses and gloves.	Street length dress and gloves.
Women Guests	Floor length or street length dress and gloves.	Floor length or street length dress and gloves.	Street length dress and gloves.
Men Guests	Same as Groom.	Same as Groom, or dark business suits.	Dark business suits.

they may not have as large a selection as a bridal salon. You'll need an appointment, and the gowns must be ordered with a two-month wait for delivery. Prices are similar to a bridal salon.

Rent a gown. Check your Yellow Pages to see whether your city has a rental service for bridal gowns. These carry a variety of styles and sizes which can be altered. All gowns are cleaned after each use, so they look fresh. You won't have your gown to save, of course, but neither will you have the expense of cleaning and storing it.

Use an heirloom. Does your mother or grandmother still have her wedding dress, her veil? If they are your taste and size, wear them with pride.

Sew your gown. Your groom will think he's marrying a genius. If you have moderate sewing skills, this project isn't as difficult as it might seem. Or you might hire a seamstress. Allow plenty of time. First, make a model at least of the bodice in muslin or an old sheet. Then you can cut into the good fabric confident that it will fit.

Borrow your dress. A good friend (married more than a year) about your size might be delighted to have you wear her dress.

Wedding Clothes Evening—after 6 P.M.

	FORMAL	SEMI-FORMAL	INFORMAL
Bride	Same as daytime.	Same as semi-formal daytime.	Dinner dress, hat or street length dress.
Bridesmaids	Formal evening dresses or midi-length dresses. Gloves or mitts are optional.	Formal length dresses.	Same as Bride.
Groom, Best Man, Ushers and Fathers	Black or midnight blue tail coat, trousers to match, white shirt, white tie, wing collar, dark hose and shoes, gloves.	Dinner jacket or tuxedo, single stripe trousers, matching waistcoat, white shirt. black hat, black hose and shoes. *Summer*—White dinner coat, black tie, black trousers, no gloves.	Dark gray or blue business suit. *Summer*—White suit.
Mothers	Formal evening or dinner dress.	Dinner dresses or midi-length dresses.	Same as Bride.
Women Guests	Formal evening or dinner dress.	Dinner dresses or midi-length dresses.	Same as Bride.
Men Guests	Same as Groom.	Same as Groom.	Same as Groom.

—From Betty Stuart Rodgers and Elizabeth Connelly Pearce, *Altar Bound.* Danville, Ill.; Interstate, 1973 (out of print).

She'll feel honored that you appreciate her taste and glad that her dress can get further use. You'll enjoy the convenience and the savings. Be sure to have the dress professionally cleaned and preserved before returning it.

TROUSSEAU

That quaint word *trousseau* means, quite simply, the clothes you take with you into your new life. It is probably unwise to buy an entire new wardrobe. Your tastes and pattern of living could easily change. And though you detest the thought, many brides do gain weight after marriage. Also, because you'll be changing your name and marital identity, and perhaps be making other changes as well, you may welcome something familiar.

Carefully go through the contents of your closet. Were some items not worn in the past year? Discard or give them away. Check to see that everything is clean and that any necessary mending or alterations have been made.

List any items needed to complete your wardrobe, and plan shopping time for these.

Also make a detailed list of everything you'll need on your honeymoon and complete your shopping before those final weeks.

Plan your going-away outfit. You may want a new dress or suit that will become the mainstay of your wardrobe. Or you may prefer to leave in a pantsuit or comfortable jeans.

—From Kay Oliver Lewis, *The Christian Wedding Handbook*. Old Tappan, N.J.: Revell, 1981.

Prewedding Parties

One of the happiest reasons for giving a party is to celebrate a forthcoming marriage and to honor a bride-to-be. Naturally, entertaining for an engaged couple tends to become more frequent as the wedding date approaches. If a number of the attendants come from out-of-town, and arrive early enough, the final week or last few days are invariably packed with festivities.

Too many parties before a wedding can result in frayed nerves and an exhausted bride and groom when the wedding day arrives. Complications can be avoided and sunny dispositions saved if the bride sets up a social calendar as soon as her engagement is announced. She should also use it to allot time for shopping, fittings, being photographed, and so on. Friends or relatives who wish to entertain for her and her fiancé will naturally consult her in order to plan a party on a convenient date. If the bride finds that too many parties are already planned to sensibly allow time for another, she may courteously thank a prospective host or hostess and regretfully explain that one more round of gaiety is an impossibility.

SHOWERS

The original purpose of the bridal shower was to help a girl equip her new home with some of the necessities. Shower parties are a custom still based on practicality, and they are popular in some sections of the country. They have one distinct drawback, however: every guest is expected to bring a present, which is a mild form of extortion. This need distress no one, if the presents are inexpensive and if the same guests are not invited to several showers, with resultant strain on their generosity and pocketbooks. People who are invited to showers are also invited to the wedding, in most instances, and will give the bride a wedding present, too. It is really the bride's responsibility to insist that shower parties be limited in number, with a different guest list for each, and that the presents be modest.

There are, of course, circumstances when a shower party is exactly what a group of friends wants to give or go to, and when no imposition is involved. If a bride-to-be has been working in a large city some distance from home, for example, and plans to go home to be married, friends she has made in the office may delight in having a shower for her. Most of them will probably not be invited to the wedding or be able to go if they are, and, therefore, need not send wedding presents. A shower gives them the opportunity to honor the bride and celebrate the coming marriage on their own ground and in their own way.

The Procedure. When showers are given for the bride, and only women are invited, the party is usually a luncheon or tea unless most of the people involved are working, in which case it is a dinner or evening party. If both the bride and her fiancé are to be honored, there should be men guests as well as women—at a party given in the evening or on a weekend.

A shower is customarily given by a close friend and contemporary of the bride who may well be her maid or matron of honor or one of her bridesmaids. Since all guests are expected to bring presents, only the bride's closest friends and, perhaps, a few members of her family are included. In some areas, guests are limited to friends in the same age group as the bride, but in others they are not. Close members of the bride's and groom's families never give showers for her because the necessity for present giving would make the family look grasping, whereas a shower should have the air of a kindly plot arranged by friends. Relatives may, of course, entertain for the couple in other ways. When a bride has many friends, several may be co-hostesses at one or two showers which all can enjoy without putting too much of a strain on their finances. If someone is invited and cannot come, she should send along a small present to be opened with the others.

A shower may or may not have a theme, but it usually does. Such a party, traditionally, is planned as a "surprise" for the bride, but it is sensible for the hostess to consult her quietly beforehand about a convenient date, the type of shower she wants, what color schemes she has planned for her house, and what she has already acquired. She may prefer that some guests join together to give her one important present.

Invitations may be issued by telephone or sent on informal cards of one sort or another, and of course the theme is mentioned, together with any necessary information about colors, sizes for stockings, gloves, underwear, and so on.

Decorations and menus may be elaborate or simple, according to the inclination of the hostess. As a rule, all the presents are grouped together in some sort of attractive or amusing arrangement. Presents at a pantry shower could be packed into brown paper bags from the grocery store which are then decorated with pasted-on labels; kitchen items might be stowed in a shiny trash can tied up with paper ribbon and a huge bow; linens could be packed in a bag made of decorative dish towels sewn together.

A shower is one party to which the guest of honor often comes after the other guests, so they may enjoy her pleasure when she first sees the presents. The bride (and her fiancé, if he is included) should act delighted and surprised even if everyone is aware that she has known about the party for the last month.

Shower Themes are endless, although some are far more usual than others. When all the guests will be girls, the theme should be one that appeals primarily to women—such as lingerie, linens, or kitchen equipment. Lingerie is always appreciated by *any* bride. Guests should know her sizes in underwear and stockings ahead of time. Kitchen necessities may not be glamorous but they certainly are essential. The hostess should find out what color scheme the bride has chosen and tell the guests to follow it. For more lavish presents, there are marvelous casseroles, kettles, and pots and pans. Linens are among the nicest shower themes, provided the guests know the bride's color schemes and bed sizes. Bathroom accessories are so blithe and well-designed that bathroom showers can be the most colorful of all. Here again, it is essential to know the bride's ideas. The guests should discuss their presents with the hostess ahead of time, because no bride wants three or four shower curtains or tissue boxes! Recipes shower a bride with useful information provided that most of the guests are experienced cooks. Each brings her favorite recipe, together with some of the necessary ingredients or a container in which to cook or serve it. For example, a recipe for coffee mousse might be presented with a pound of coffee or a good-looking mold.

When both the bride and groom are guests of honor, naturally husbands and other men are also invited. Themes for these parties should appeal to both sexes: wines, books, or records are examples.

When guests are thanked in person for their presents, it is not necessary for the bride to write follow-up thank-you notes. Exceptions are those to the hostess and to any guest who could not come but sent a present to be opened at the party.

BRIDESMAIDS' PARTY FOR THE BRIDE

In some communities the bridesmaids collectively honor the bride with a special party other than a shower. It may be a luncheon for girls only, or a tea or cocktail party to which all the members of the wedding party are invited. If the bridesmaids have bought the bride one important wedding present from all of them, they may give it to her at this time. Individual presents should be sent or given privately.

BRIDE'S PARTY FOR THE BRIDESMAIDS

Many brides like to give a luncheon or dinner for their bridesmaids on the day or night of the bachelor dinner. This is a particularly nice gesture if one or more of the attendants is from out-of-town and a stranger to the others; all can meet in an easy, pleasant atmosphere. It also provides an opportunity for a final checkup of their dresses and accessories, although there rarely is time for more than very minor alterations. The bride usually gives her bridesmaids their presents, and she may serve the traditional bride's pink cake in which a symbolic coin, thimble, or ring is baked. According to legend, the girl who is served the slice of cake containing the symbol will be the next bride.

—From *Vogue's Book of Etiquette*. New York: Simon & Schuster, 1969.

Rehearsal

As a general rule, weddings with more than two attendants need a rehearsal, scheduled one or two days before the event, and at the convenience of the clergyman.

The entire wedding party needs to be present, which includes:

- bride and groom
- attendants
- organist and minister
- parents of both the bride and groom

The bride-elect always rehearses her part so she will be at ease during the ceremony.

Even when bridal consultants are hired, the officiating minister is in charge of the rehearsal. Bridal consultants, social secretaries, and photographers should not interfere in the rehearsal or the actual wedding.

Most ministers will explain and practice the ceremony until everyone knows where to stand and what to do.

Here are the most important parts of the rehearsal:

- timing and spacing of the processional practiced with any music played during it
- the passing of the bride's bouquet to her maid of honor
- the procedure of the bride's father when he gives her away (although this is now being omitted from some ceremonies; in those cases, the father escorts the daughter, joins her hand to the groom's, and then sits down)
- the ring ceremony
- the end of the marriage ceremony in which the bride and groom normally kiss
- the return of the bride's bouquet by the maid of honor
- the order and spacing of the recessional together with the accompanying music
- instruction to ushers on seating procedures

and any other duties such as candle light-ing

Generally, the minister does not read the actual service but goes over the main parts so that the bride and groom will know when and how to make their responses.

—CECIL MURPHEY

THE REHEARSAL DINNER

It is becoming more and more popular for the wedding rehearsal to be held in the late afternoon the day before the wedding, fol-lowed by a rehearsal dinner, which may be scheduled for six-thirty or seven o'clock.

In some sections of the country, mainly the South and Midwest, it is customary for the groom's parents to give the rehearsal dinner, which may be formal or buffet. How-ever, a close friend of either family or an-other relative may ask to entertain. The size of the invitation list is, of course, determined by the hostess, but all members of the wed-ding party and the parents of the bride and groom and the clergyman and his wife must be included. It is not necessary, but it would probably make the dinner more enjoyable for those concerned if the spouses of married members of the bridal party were invited. If the dinner is large enough to include them, relatives or wedding guests who have arrived early from out of town might enjoy partici-pating in some of the pre-wedding festivi-ties.

—From *Amy Vanderbilt's Complete Book of Etiquette*, revised by Letitia Baldrige. New York: Doubleday, 1978.

Photographs

Most churches have a policy of no pictures taken during the ceremony itself. Always ask about the church's policy.

Many photographers now arrange to come one or two hours before the wedding to take pictures. Some will include pictures of the ceremony, so that a minimum of pictures are taken afterward.

If the reception is being held on the church grounds, I encourage the bridal party to go immediately from the ceremony to the reception, have pictures taken at the recep-tion, then return to the church for pictures. This procedure shows courtesy for guests who otherwise may have to wait as long as an hour between the end of the ceremony and the beginning of the reception. Being considerate of your guests' time will make them glad they came to your wedding.

—CECIL MURPHEY

THE SANCTUARY

Flowers and Candles

The florist should be acquainted with the sanctuary or chapel and the requests of this church:

In the sanctuary, floral arrangements in the front center must be so arranged that the organist's mirror view of the center aisle and door is unobstructed. The electrical signals are simply an aid of this visual contact with the procession.

If a kneeling bench is desired, the church has one available, or the florist can supply one.

Flowers and candles should enhance the beauty of our sanctuary and chapel rather than hide it.

Candles must be of the nondrip variety and have a protective covering on the floors; proper precautions should be taken for safety. Be sure someone is delegated to see that the candles are lighted and that he knows where the lighting taper is located!

If you desire to leave any flowers for church use or for distribution to the sick, arrangements should be made in the church office. All wedding decorations other than flowers left for such purposes must be removed immediately following the service.

It is expected that NO RICE OR CONFETTI will be thrown within the buildings, please.

—From Perry H. Biddle, *Abingdon Marriage Manual.* Nashville: Abingdon, 1974.

Music

Music forms an integral part of the marriage service. For this reason, couples need to choose their music with care. Couples unaware of appropriate music for a religious service will do best to defer to the minister and/or organist.

Too much music is chosen on the basis of romantic concepts and secular selections which were favorites of the couple during their dating period. Others choose music that they consider entertaining.

Most churches recognize the sanctity of marriage and, therefore, first consideration should be given to music that aids in the dignity, meaning, and spiritual basis of the wedding. Choose music centering on God rather than upon the bride or pageantry.

The most frequently used wedding marches, by Wagner and Mendelssohn, are being omitted in some churches and being replaced by processional hymns.

The bridal chorus from Wagner's *Lohengrin* ("Here Comes the Bride") was not written for church use. In the opera, the music occurs when the bridal couple enter the bridal chamber. Before the scene is over, the bridegroom murders a rival and abandons his wife forever.

Mendelssohn composed his music as an accompaniment to Shakespeare's *A Midsummer Night's Dream* in which a workman named Bottom is transformed into a jackass and courts and bewitches a fairy.

Some couples have congregational singing as part of their service, such as the processional or the recessional. One couple had a hymn played for the couple coming in, and then after the wedding party reached the altar, the congregation sang.

Traditional weddings use the organ for its majestic tones. Pianos are also used. String ensembles, or even the church choir are coming into use. In more contemporary weddings, the guitar has become popular. At some weddings musicians play instruments such as the violin, cello, flute, or trumpet.

When couples select music that the organist or vocalist does not already have, it is expected that the couple will purchase the music.

—CECIL MURPHEY

Seating

As one faces the altar, the bride's section is on the left, the groom's on the right.

Parents occupy the first pews, with the fathers in the aisle seats. Relatives sit with them and in the rows immediately behind.

Divorced parents do not occupy the same pew, even if they have remained on good terms. The bride's mother occupies the first pew with her mother and father or other family members in rows immediately behind her.

If the parents are divorced, the bride's father, after giving the daughter away, takes his place in the pew behind those occupied by his former in-laws. His family sits beside and immediately behind him.

If a bad relationship exists between divorced parents, the bride makes any final decisions, which may be quite painful. Sometimes, because of such family situations, the couple plans a private ceremony with no family members present.

If the parents cannot agree to meet, the father may escort his daughter up the aisle, give her away, sit several rows back, and then depart after the ceremony, not attending the reception.

—CECIL MURPHEY

Aisle Canvas and Pew Ribbons

If an aisle canvas or pew ribbons are used, they are unrolled by a pair of ushers as soon as the bride's mother has been seated. If both are used, the ribbons are put in place first. These are usually wound or folded and waiting in the second or third pew on each side so that the ushers can simply pick up the ends and return down the aisle to the back of the church, stretching the ribbons across the aisle posts and securing them on the last ones. The aisle canvas is generally placed on a spool or in accordion pleats at the steps of the chancel. With one usher holding each corner, they walk in step down the aisle, smoothing the runner into place behind them. Although not necessary in a carpeted church, this white canvas is frequently used to protect the bride's dress and train. The ribbons—a gentle reminder to guests to stay in their places, as well as a pretty device— are removed by the ushers as soon as the wedding party and honored guests have left the church, but the canvas stays in place until all the guests have departed.

—From *Vogue's Book of Etiquette.* New York: Simon & Schuster, 1969.

THE CEREMONY

The Procession

The wedding procession begins immediately after the mothers have been seated and the aisle carpet and pew ribbons, if any, have been put in place. A signal is given to the organist to begin the processional music. The bride's family rises and the guests follow suit as the wedding party appears in this order:

The clergyman enters from a door on one side of the altar, walks to his place on the steps leading to the chancel, and stands facing the congregation.

The groom and the best man enter in that order, directly behind the clergyman, and walk single file to their places at the head of the main aisle on the right. Depending on the location of the side door through which they enter, they stand at the foot or the top of the chancel steps. The best man takes his position one step behind the groom and slightly nearer the congregation, but both stand at an angle so they can watch the procession as it comes up the aisle. Neither wears gloves because these might be cumbersome when the best man must hand the ring to the groom and he must put it on the bride's finger. (The ushers keep their gloves on before and during the ceremony.)

The ushers lead the procession up the aisle. They always walk in pairs by height, with the shortest two first. Starting with their left feet, they walk in step and slowly, leaving a distance of three or four pews between each pair.

The bridesmaids follow at a distance of four or five pews behind the ushers. Four or more bridesmaids usually walk in pairs, but a smaller number may walk single file. If there is an uneven number, the shortest bridesmaid usually goes first alone, followed by the others paired according to height.

The maid of honor follows the last of the bridesmaids. If there are both a maid and a matron of honor, they may walk together or separately. If separately, the one with the most duties follows the other.

The ring bearer (if any) follows the maid of honor.

The flower girl may walk with the ring bearer or with another flower girl, but she is always the last attendant to come up the aisle before the bride.

The bride and her father walk up the aisle together, keeping a distance of about six pews between them and the rest of the procession. Unless religious considerations interfere, the bride always takes her father's right arm. (Since he must sit on the left side of the church, it is much more convenient for him to be on the bride's left.)

The pages (if any) follow the bride, each holding one side of the end of her train.

At the Altar

There are two equally acceptable arrangements for the bridal party in front of the altar. For the first, the ushers walk to the head of the aisle and turn right to form a line behind the groom and best man, the bridesmaids turn left to form a similar line on the opposite side.

The alternate plan is preferable when there is a large wedding party or an unequal number of ushers and bridesmaids. As each pair of attendants reaches the first row of seats, one person turns to the left, the other to the right. The bridesmaids stand either between the ushers or one step in front of them. The identical rows of attendants line up on each side of the main aisle at the foot of the chancel steps or in front of the choir

stalls in the chancel, depending on the size and plan of the church.

The maid of honor does not follow the other bridesmaids to one side, but takes her position at the foot of the chancel steps on the left, opposite the best man, and she faces sideways to the congregation as the bride and her father come up the aisle.

As the bride reaches the spot where the groom is waiting, she drops her father's arm and takes one step forward. The groom and best man move to the bride's right, while the maid of honor takes her place on the bride's left. The bride usually hands her bouquet to the maid of honor at this time, and takes the groom's left arm as they step toward the clergyman.

The bride and groom stand throughout most Protestant wedding ceremonies, but they kneel during parts of other marriage services.

—From *Vogue's Book of Etiquette.* New York: Simon & Schuster, 1969.

Giving the Bride Away

In some wedding ceremonies, the bride is not actually given away. In most Protestant ceremonies, however, the bride's father remains standing a step or two behind her on the left, while the clergyman reads the betrothal part of the ceremony. When he asks, "Who gives this woman to be married?" the bride's father steps forward, places her right hand in the right hand of the clergyman, and replies, "I do." Or he may use the more graceful but less traditional answer: "Her mother and I do." The clergyman places the bride's hand in the bridegroom's, and the bride's father takes his seat in the front pew next to his wife.

—From *Vogue's Book of Etiquette.* New York: Simon & Schuster, 1969.

MARRIAGE SERVICES

Baptist

MARRIAGE CEREMONY

Holy and happy is the sacred hour when two devoted hearts are bound by the enchanting ties of matrimony. And these precious evidences of purity of heart and contentment of mind, for all their future, are made more sure, when the contracting parties enter this glad time, clad in the comely robes of reverence, humility, and faith, that they may then be blessed of our Heavenly Father, Maker of us all—the One who has ordained marriage as the cornerstone of family life and the guarantee of honorable human society.

First and noblest of human contracts, marriage was divinely instituted when Jehovah God spoke the nuptial words to Adam and Eve in the Garden of Eden. Jesus of Nazareth honored its celebration by his presence at the wedding in Cana of Galilee, and chose its beautiful relations as the figure of that benign union between himself and his Church. Paul, militant missionary Apostle, commends it as a worthy institution, alike essential to social order, human efficiency, and well-being while the race inhabits the earth, and tells the husband to love his wife as Christ loved his Church and gave himself for it, and the wife to be faithful to her husband, even as the Church is obedient to Christ in everything. Thus the two, husband and wife, forsaking all others become one flesh, one in thought, intent, and hope, in all the concerns of the present life.

You _____, and You _____, having come to me signifying your desire to be formally united in marriage, and being assured that no legal, moral, or religious barriers hinder this proper union, I command you to join your right hands and give heed to the questions now asked you.

_____ In taking the woman whom you hold by the right hand to be your lawful and wedded wife, I require you to promise to love and cherish her, to honor and sustain her, in sickness as in health, in poverty as in wealth, in the bad that may darken your days, in the good that may light your ways, and to be true to her in all things until death alone shall part you.

Do you so promise?

_____ In taking the man who holds you by the right hand to be your lawful and wedded husband, I require you to promise to love and cherish him, to honor and sustain him, in sickness as in health, in poverty as in wealth, in the bad that may darken your days, in the good that may light your ways, and to be true to him in all things until death alone shall part you.

Do you so promise?

Then are you devoted to each other until death parts you.

(If the ring ceremony is desired, the minister will take the ring from the receptacle of the ring-bearer, or from the groomsman, and read the following):

From time immemorial, the ring has been used to seal important covenants. When the race was young and parliaments unknown, the great seal of State was fixed upon a ring worn by the reigning monarch, and its stamp was the sole sign of imperial authority. Friends often exchanged the simple band of gold as enduring evidence of good will, while many a hero and heroine of immortal song and thrilling tale threaded winding paths of intrigue and adventure, safe and unhurt, bearing as a magic talisman the signet of some great benefactor. From such impressive precedents the golden circlet, most prized of jewels, has come to its loftiest prestige in the symbolic significance it vouches at the hymeneal altar. Here untarnishable

67

material and unique form become the precious tokens of the pure and abiding qualities of the ideal marital state.

(The minister hands the ring to the groom, instructing him to place it upon the third finger of the bride's left hand and to hold it while the minister propounds the following questions):

Do you _____ give this ring to _____ as a token of your love for her?

The man shall answer, I do.

Will you _____ take this ring as a token of _____'s love for you and will you wear it as a token of your love for him?

The woman shall answer, I will.

(Where the double ring ceremony is desired, the minister will take the other ring from the receptacle of the ring-bearer, or from the groomsman and hand it to the bride, instructing her to place it upon the third finger of the groom's left hand and to hold it in place while the minister propounds the following questions):

Do you _____ give this ring to _____ as a token of your love for him?

The woman shall answer, I do.

Will you _____ take this ring as a token of _____'s love for you, and will you wear it as a token of your love for her?

The man shall answer, I will.

(The minister will now instruct the couple to rejoin their right hands, after which he will repeat the following):

Having pledged your faith in, and love to, each other, and having sealed your solemn marital vows by giving and receiving the ring (or rings), acting in the authority vested in me by the laws of this State, and looking to Heaven for divine sanction, I pronounce you husband and wife in the presence of God and these assembled witnesses. Therefore, let all men take care in the sight of God this holy covenant shall ever remain sacred.

Prayer:

Holy, Righteous, and Merciful Father, alike Creator, Preserver, and Redeemer of mankind, fill these thy servants with a deep sense of the solemn obligations which they have just assumed. Guide them to look to thee for grace in their efforts to discharge these obligations with honor to themselves, in thy sight and in the sight of men. Ordain that their love now mutually plighted, may never falter whatever course life may take with them. Crown their lives with lovingkindness and tender mercies, and provide for their protection while they travel the uneven way that leads from now to the end. Give them a rich measure of material prosperity, and lead them into the fulness of spiritual understanding and holy living, that they may have an abundant entrance into the joys everlasting. So we pray through Jesus Christ our Lord.

The Lord bless and keep you. The Lord make his face to shine upon you and be gracious unto you. The Lord lift up his countenance upon you and give you peace, through Jesus Christ our Lord. Amen.

—From James Randolph Hobbs, *The Pastor's Manual.* Nashville: Broadman, 1962.

Episcopal

THE CELEBRATION AND BLESSING
OF A MARRIAGE

At the time appointed, the persons to be married, with their witnesses, assemble in the church or some other appropriate place.

During their entrance, a hymn, psalm, or anthem may be sung, or instrumental music may be played.

Then the Celebrant, facing the people and the persons to be married, with the woman to the right and the man to the left, addresses the congregation and says

Dearly beloved: We have come together in the presence of God to witness and bless the joining together of this man and this woman in Holy Matrimony. The bond and covenant of marriage was established by God in creation, and our Lord Jesus Christ adorned this manner of life by his presence and first miracle at a wedding in Cana of Galilee. It signifies to us the mystery of the union between Christ and his Church, and Holy Scripture commends it to be honored among all people.

The union of husband and wife in heart, body, and mind is intended by God for their mutual joy; for the help and comfort given one another in prosperity and adversity; and, when it is God's will, for the procreation of children and their nurture in the knowledge and love of the Lord. Therefore marriage is not to be entered into unadvisedly or lightly, but reverently, deliberately, and in accordance with the purposes for which it was instituted by God.

Into this holy union *N.N.* and *N.N.* now come to be joined. If any of you can show just cause why they may not lawfully be married, speak now; or else for ever hold your peace.

Then the Celebrant says to the persons to be married

I require and charge you both, here in the presence of God, that if either of you know any reason why you may not be united in marriage lawfully, and in accordance with God's Word, you do now confess it.

THE DECLARATION OF CONSENT

The Celebrant says to the woman

N., will you have this man to be your husband; to live together in the covenant of marriage? Will you love him, comfort him, honor and keep him, in sickness and in health; and, forsaking all others, be faithful to him as long as you both shall live?

The Woman answers

I will.

The Celebrant says to the man

N., will you have this woman to be your wife; to live together in the covenant of marriage? Will you love her, comfort her, honor and keep her, in sickness and in health; and, forsaking all others, be faithful to her as long as you both shall live?

The Man answers

I will.

The Celebrant then addresses the congregation saying

Will all of you witnessing these promises do all in your power to uphold these two persons in their marriage?

People   We will.

If there is to be a presentation or a giving in marriage, it takes place at this time.

A hymn, psalm, or anthem may follow.

THE MINISTRY OF THE WORD

The Celebrant then says to the people

The Lord be with you.
People   And also with you.

Let us pray.

O gracious and everliving God, you have created us male and female in your image:

Look mercifully upon this man and this woman who come to you seeking your blessing, and assist them with your grace, that with true fidelity and steadfast love they may honor and keep the promises and vows they make; through Jesus Christ our Savior, who lives and reigns with you in the unity of the Holy Spirit, one God, for ever and ever. *Amen.*

Then one or more of the following passages from Holy Scripture is read. If there is to be a Communion, a passage from the Gospel always concludes the Readings.

Genesis 1:26-28 (Male and female he created them)

Genesis 2:4-9, 15-24 (A man cleaves to his wife and they become one flesh)

Song of Solomon 2:10-13; 8:6-7 (Many waters cannot quench love)

Tobit 8:5b-8 (*New English Bible*) (That she and I may grow old together)

1 Corinthians 13:1-13 (Love is patient and kind)

Ephesians 3:14-19 (The Father from whom every family is named)

Ephesians 5:1-2, 21-33 (Walk in love, as Christ loved us)

Colossians 3:12-17 (Love which binds everything together in harmony)

1 John 4:7-16 (Let us love one another for love is of God)

Between the Readings, a Psalm, hymn, or anthem may be sung or said. Appropriate Psalms are 67, 127, and 128.

When a passage from the Gospel is to be read, all stand, and the Deacon or Minister appointed says

> The Holy Gospel of our Lord Jesus Christ according to

People Glory to you, Lord Christ.

Matthew 5:1-10 (The Beatitudes)

Matthew 5:13-16 (You are the light . . . Let your light so shine)

Matthew 7:21, 24-29 (Like a wise man who built his house upon the rock)

Mark 10:6-9, 13-16 (They are no longer two but one)

John 15:9-12 (Love one another as I have loved you)

After the Gospel, the Reader says

> The Gospel of the Lord.

People Praise to you, Lord Christ.

A homily or other response to the Readings may follow.

THE MARRIAGE

The Man, facing the woman and taking her right hand in his says

In the Name of God, I. *N.*, take you, *N.*, to be my wife, to have and to hold from this day forward, for better for worse, for richer for poorer, in sickness and in health, to love and to cherish, until we are parted by death. This is my solemn vow.

Then they loose their hands, and the Woman, still facing the man, takes his right hand in hers, and says

In the Name of God, I *N.*, take you, *N.*, to be my husband, to have and to hold from this day forward, for better for worse, for richer for poorer, in sickness and in health, to love and to cherish, until we are parted by death. This is my solemn vow.

They loose their hands.

The Priest may ask God's blessing on a ring or rings as follows

Bless, O Lord, *this ring* to be *a sign* of the vows by which this man and this woman have bound themselves to each other; through Jesus Christ our Lord. *Amen.*

The giver places the ring on the ring-finger of the other's hand and says

N., I give you this ring as a symbol of my vow, and with all that I am, and all that I have, I honor you, in the Name of the Father, and of the Son, and of the Holy Spirit (*or* in the Name of God).

Then the Celebrant joins the right hands of husband and wife and says

Now that N., and N. have given themselves to each other by solemn vows, with the joining of hands and the giving and receiving of *a ring,* I pronounce that they are husband and wife, in the Name of the Father, and of the Son, and of the Holy Spirit.

Those whom God has joined together let no one put asunder.

People Amen.

THE PRAYERS

All standing, the Celebrant says

Let us pray together in the words our Savior taught us.

People and Celebrant

Our Father, who art in heaven,
  hallowed be thy Name,
  thy kingdom come,
  thy will be done,
    on earth as it is in heaven.
Give us this day our daily bread.
And forgive us our trespasses,
  as we forgive those
    who trespass against us.
And lead us not into temptation,
  but deliver us from evil.
For thine is the kingdom,
  and the power, and the glory,
  for ever and ever. Amen.

OR

Our Father in heaven,
  hallowed be your Name,
  your kingdom come,
  your will be done,
    on earth as in heaven.
Give us today our daily bread.
Forgive us our sins
  as we forgive those
    who sin against us.
Save us from the time of trial,
  and deliver us from evil.
For the kingdom, the power,
  and the glory are yours,
  now and for ever. Amen.

If Communion is to follow, the Lord's Prayer may be omitted here.

The Deacon or other person appointed reads the following prayers, to which the People respond, saying, Amen.

If there is not to be a Communion, one or more of the prayers may be omitted.

Let us pray.

Eternal God, creator and preserver of all life, author of salvation, and giver of all grace: Look with favor upon the world you have made, and for which your Son gave his life, and especially upon this man and this woman whom you make one flesh in Holy Matrimony. *Amen.*

Give them wisdom and devotion in the ordering of their common life, that each may be to the other a strength in need, a counselor in perplexity, a comfort in sorrow, and a companion in joy. *Amen.*

Grant that their wills may be so knit together in your will, and their spirits in your Spirit, that they may grow in love and peace with you and one another all the days of their life. *Amen.*

Give them grace, when they hurt each other, to recognize and acknowledge their fault, and to seek each other's forgiveness and yours. *Amen.*

Make their life together a sign of Christ's love to this sinful and broken world, that unity may overcome estrangement, forgiveness heal guilt, and joy conquer despair. *Amen.*

Bestow on them, if it is your will, the gift and heritage of children, and the grace to bring them up to know you, to love you, and to serve you. *Amen.*

Give them such fulfillment of their mutual affection that they may reach out in love and concern for others. *Amen.*

Grant that all married persons who have witnessed these vows may find their lives strengthened and their loyalties confirmed. *Amen.*

Grant that the bonds of our common humanity, by which all your children are united one to another, and the living to the dead, may be so transformed by your grace, that your will may be done on earth as it is in heaven; where, O Father, with your Son and the Holy Spirit, you live and reign in perfect unity, now and for ever. *Amen.*

THE BLESSING OF THE MARRIAGE

The people remain standing. The husband and wife kneel, and the Priest says one of the following prayers

Most gracious God, we give you thanks for your tender love in sending Jesus Christ to come among us, to be born of a human mother, and to make the way of the cross to be the way of life. We thank you, also, for consecrating the union of man and woman in his Name. By the power of your Holy Spirit, pour out the abundance of your blessing upon this man and this woman. Defend them from every enemy. Lead them into all peace. Let their love for each other be a seal upon their hearts, a mantle about their shoulders, and a crown upon their foreheads. Bless them in their work and in their companionship; in their sleeping and in their waking; in their joys and in their sorrows; in their life and in their death. Finally, in your mercy, bring them to that table where your saints feast for ever in your heavenly home; through Jesus Christ our Lord, who with you and the Holy Spirit lives and reigns, one God, for ever and ever. *Amen.*

or this

O God, you have so consecrated the covenant of marriage that in it is represented the spiritual unity between Christ and his Church: Send therefore your blessing upon these your servants, that they may so love, honor, and cherish each other in faithfulness and patience, in wisdom and true godliness, that their home may be a haven of blessing and peace; through Jesus Christ our Lord, who lives and reigns with you and the Holy Spirit, one God, now and for ever. *Amen.*

The husband and wife still kneeling, the Priest adds this blessing

God the Father, God the Son, God the Holy Spirit, bless, preserve and keep you; the Lord mercifully with his favor look upon you, and fill you with all spiritual benediction and grace; that you may faithfully live together in this life, and in the age to come have life everlasting. *Amen.*

THE PEACE

The Celebrant may say to the people

The peace of the Lord be always with you.
People   And also with you.

The newly married couple then greet each other, after which greetings may be exchanged throughout the congregation.

When Communion is not to follow, the wedding party leaves the church. A hymn, psalm, or anthem may be sung, or instrumental music may be played.

AT THE EUCHARIST

The liturgy continues with the Offertory, at which the newly married couple may present the offerings of bread and wine.

PREFACE OF MARRIAGE

At the Communion, it is appropriate that the newly married couple receive Communion first, after the ministers.

In place of the usual postcommunion prayer, the following is said

O God, the giver of all that is true and lovely and gracious: We give you thanks for binding us together in these holy mysteries of the Body and Blood of your Son Jesus Christ. Grant that by your Holy Spirit, *N.* and *N.*, now joined in Holy Matrimony, may become one in heart and soul, live in fidelity and peace, and obtain those eternal joys prepared for all who love you; for the sake of Jesus Christ our Lord. *Amen.*

As the wedding party leaves the church, a hymn, psalm, or anthem may be sung; or instrumental music may be played.

—From *The Book of Common Prayer of the Protestant Episcopal Church.* The Church Hymnal Corp. and the Seabury Press, 1979, pp. 423–432.

Lutheran

MARRIAGE

Stand

1. The bride, groom, and wedding party stand in front of the minister. The parents may stand behind the couple.

[P] The grace of our Lord Jesus Christ, the love of God, and the communion of the Holy Spirit be with you all.

[C] And also with you.

[A] Let us pray.

Eternal God, our creator and redeemer, as you gladdened the wedding at Cana in Galilee by the presence of your Son, so by his presence now bring your joy to this wedding. Look in favor upon ____name____ and ____name____ and grant that they, rejoicing in all your gifts, may at length celebrate with Christ the marriage feast which has no end.

[C] Amen

Sit

2. One or more lessons from the Bible may be read. An address may follow. A hymn may be sung.

73

[A] The Lord God in his goodness created us male and female, and by the gift of marriage founded human community in a joy that begins now and is brought to perfection in the life to come.

Because of sin, our age-old rebellion, the gladness of marriage can be overcast and the gift of the family can become a burden.

But because God, who established marriage, continues still to bless it with his abundant and ever-present support, we can be sustained in our weariness and have our joy restored.

[P] ___name___ and ___name___, if it is your intention to share with each other your joys and sorrows and all that the years will bring, with your promises bind yourselves to each other as husband and wife.

Stand

3. *The bride and groom face each other and join hands. Each, in turn, promises faithfulness to the other in these or similar words:*

I take you, ___name___,
to be my *wife/husband* from this day forward,
to join with you and share all that is to come,
and I promise to be faithful to you
until death parts us.

4. *The bride and groom exchange rings with these words:*

I give you this ring as a sign of my love and faithfulness.

5. *The bride and groom join hands, and the minister announces their marriage by saying*

[P] ___name___ and ___name___, by their promises before God and in the presence of this congregation, have bound themselves to one another as husband and wife.

[C] **Blessed be the Father and the Son and the Holy Spirit now and forever.**

[P] Those whom God has joined together let no one put asunder.

[C] **Amen**

Sit

6. *The bride and groom kneel.*

[P] The Lord God, who created our first parents and established them in marriage, establish and sustain you, that you may find delight in each other and grow in holy love until your life's end.

[C] **Amen**

7. *The parents may add their blessing with these or similar words; the wedding party may join them.*

May you dwell in God's presence forever; may true and constant love preserve you.

8. *The bride and groom stand.*

Stand

[A] Let us bless God for all the gifts in which we rejoice today.

[P] Lord God, constant in mercy, great in faithfulness: With high praise we recall your acts of unfailing love for the human family, for the house of Israel, and for your people the Church.

We bless you for the joy which your servants, ___name___ and ___name___, have found in each other, and pray that you give to us such a sense of your constant love that we may employ all our strength in a life of praise of you, whose work alone holds true and endures forever.

[C] **Amen**

[A] Let us pray for ___name___ and ___name___ in their life together.

[P] Faithful Lord, source of love, pour down your grace upon ___name___ and ___name___, that they may fulfill the vows they have made this day and reflect your steadfast love in their life-long faithfulness to each other. As members with them of the body of Christ, use us to support their life together; and from your great store of strength give them power and patience, affection and understanding, courage, and love toward you, toward each other, and toward the world, that they may continue together in mutual growth according to your will in Jesus Christ our Lord.

[C] **Amen**

Other intercessions may be offered.

[A] Let us pray for all families throughout the world.

[P] Gracious Father, you bless the family and renew your people. Enrich husbands and wives, parents and children more and more with your grace, that, strengthening and supporting each other, they may serve those in need and be a sign of the fulfillment of your perfect kingdom, where, with your Son Jesus Christ and the Holy Spirit, you live and reign, one God through all ages of ages.

[C] **Amen**

9. *When Holy Communion is celebrated, the service continues with the Peace.*

10. *When there is no Communion, the service continues with the Lord's Prayer.*

[C] Our Father in heaven,
    hallowed be your name,
    your kingdom come,
    your will be done,
        on earth as in heaven.
Give us today our daily bread.
Forgive us our sins
    as we forgive those
        who sin against us.
Save us from the time of trial
    and deliver us from evil.
For the kingdom, the power,
    and the glory are yours,
    now and forever. Amen

OR

[C] Our Father, who art in heaven,
    hallowed be thy name,
    thy kingdom come,
    thy will be done,
        on earth as it is in heaven.
Give us this day our daily bread;
and forgive us our trespasses,
    as we forgive those
        who trespass against us;
and lead us not into temptation,
    but deliver us from evil.
For thine is the kingdom,
    and the power, and the glory,
    forever and ever. Amen

[P] Almighty God, Father, ✠ Son, and Holy Spirit, keep you in his light and truth and love now and forever.

[C] **Amen**

—From *Lutheran Book of Worship.* Minneapolis: Augsburg, 1978.

Methodist

A CLASSICAL WEDDING SERVICE

The United Methodist Service
The Order for the Service of Marriage

The minister is enjoined diligently to instruct those requesting his offices for their prospective marriage in the Christian significance of the holy estate into which they seek to enter.

All arrangements pertaining to the service of marriage shall be made in full consultation with the minister.

This service may begin with a prelude, anthem, solo, or hymn. It may include a processional and recessional and be concluded with a postlude.

The congregation shall stand as the wedding procession begins.

The Christian names of the bride and bridegroom may be used in place of "this man and this woman" in the first, third, and fourth paragraphs.

When the Sacrament of the Lord's Supper is requested, this service should be provided at a time other than the service of marriage.

At the time appointed, the persons to be married, having been qualified according to the laws of the state and the standards of the Church, standing together facing the minister, the man at the minister's left hand and the woman at the right hand, the minister shall say,

Dearly beloved, we are gathered together here in the sight of God, and in the presence of these witnesses, to join together *this man and this woman* in holy matrimony; which is an honorable estate, instituted of God, and signifying unto us the mystical union which exists between Christ and his Church; which holy estate Christ adorned and beautified with his presence in Cana of Galilee. It is therefore not to be entered into unadvisedly, but reverently, discreetly, and in the fear of God. Into this holy estate these two persons come now to be joined. If any man can show just cause why they may not lawfully be joined together, let him now speak, or else hereafter forever hold his peace.

Addressing the persons to be married, the minister shall say,

I require and charge you both, as you stand in the presence of God, before whom the secrets of all hearts are disclosed, that, having duly considered the holy covenant you are about to make, you do now declare before this company your pledge of faith, each to the other. Be well assured that if these solemn vows are kept inviolate, as God's Word demands, and if steadfastly you endeavor to do the will of your heavenly Father, God will bless your marriage, will grant you fulfillment in it, and will establish your home in peace.

Then shall the minister say to the man, using his Christian name,

N., wilt thou have this woman to be thy wedded wife, to live together in the holy estate of matrimony? Wilt thou love her, comfort her, honor and keep her, in sickness and in health; and forsaking all others keep thee only unto her so long as ye both shall live?

The man shall answer,

I will.

Then shall the minister say to the woman, using her Christian name,

N., wilt thou have this man to be thy wedded husband, to live together in the holy estate of matrimony? Wilt thou love him, comfort him, honor and keep him, in sickness and in health; and forsaking all others keep thee only unto him so long as ye both shall live?

The woman shall answer,

I will.

Then shall the minister say,

Who giveth this woman to be married to this man?

The father of the woman, or whoever gives her in marriage, shall answer,

I do.

Then, the minister, receiving the hand of the woman from her father or other sponsor, shall cause the man with his right hand to take the woman by her right hand, and say after him,

I, N., take thee, N., to be my wedded wife, to have and to hold, from this day forward, for better, for worse, for richer, for poorer, in sickness and in health, to love and to cherish, till death us do part, according to God's holy ordinance; and thereto I pledge thee my faith.

Then shall they loose their hands; and the woman, with her right hand taking the man by his right hand, shall say after the minister,

I, N., take thee, N., to be my wedded husband, to have and to hold, from this day forward, for better, for worse, for richer, for poorer, in sickness and in health, to love and to cherish, till death us do part, according to God's holy ordinance; and thereto I pledge thee my faith.

Then they may give to each other rings, or the man may give to the woman a ring, in this wise: the minister, taking the ring or rings, shall say,

The wedding ring is the outward and visible sign of an inward and spiritual grace, signifying to all the uniting of this man and woman in holy matrimony, through the Church of Jesus Christ our Lord.

Then the minister may say,

Let us pray.
Bless, O Lord, the giving of these rings, that they who wear them may abide in thy peace, and continue in thy favor; through Jesus Christ our Lord. **Amen.**

Or, if there be but one ring, the minister says,

Bless, O Lord, the giving of this ring, that he who gives it and she who wears it may abide forever in thy peace, and continue in thy favor; through Jesus Christ our Lord. **Amen.**

The minister shall then deliver the proper ring to the man to put upon the third finger of the woman's left hand. The man, holding the ring there, shall say after the minister,

In token and pledge of our constant faith and abiding love, with this ring I thee wed, in the name of the Father, and of the Son, and of the Holy Spirit. **Amen.**

Then, if there is a second ring, the minister shall deliver it to the woman to put upon the third finger of the man's left hand; and the woman, holding the ring there, shall say after the minister,

In token and pledge of our constant faith and abiding love, with this ring I thee wed, in the name of the Father, and of the Son, and of the Holy Spirit. Amen.

Then shall the minister join their right hands together and, with his hand on their united hands, shall say,

Forasmuch as *N.* and *N.* have consented together in holy wedlock, and have witnessed the same before God and this company, and thereto have pledged their faith each to the other, and have declared the same by joining hands and by giving and receiving *rings;* I pronounce that they are husband and wife together, in the name of the Father, and of the Son, and of the Holy Spirit.. Those whom God hath joined together, let not man put asunder. **Amen.**

Then shall the minister say,

Let us pray.

Then shall the husband and wife kneel; the minister shall say,

O eternal God, creator and preserver of all mankind, giver of all spiritual grace, the author of everlasting life: Send thy blessing upon this man and this woman, whom we bless in thy name; that they may surely perform and keep the vow and covenant between them made, and may ever remain in perfect love and peace together, and live according to thy laws.

Look graciously upon them, that they may love, honor, and cherish each other, and so live together in faithfulness and patience, in wisdom and true godliness, that their home may be a haven of blessing and a place of peace; through Jesus Christ our Lord. **Amen.**

Then the husband and wife, still kneeling, shall join with the minister and congregation in the Lord's Prayer, saying,

Our Father, who art in heaven, hallowed be thy name. Thy kingdom come, thy will be done on earth as it is in heaven. Give us this day our daily bread. And forgive us our trespasses, as we forgive those who trespass against us. And lead us not into temptation, but deliver us from evil. For thine is the kingdom, and the power, and the glory, forever. Amen.

Then the minister shall give this blessing,

God the Father, the Son, and the Holy Spirit bless, preserve, and keep you; the Lord graciously with his favor look upon you, and so fill you with all spiritual benediction and love that you may so live together in this life that in the world to come you may have life everlasting. **Amen.**

Suggested music from *The Book of Hymns:*
Processional: "Praise the Lord! ye heavens, adore him"; "For the beauty of the earth"; "Praise to the Lord, the Almighty"; "Praise, my soul, the King of heaven."
Recessional: "Now thank we all our God"; "Joyful, joyful, we adore thee," "God is love; his mercy brightens"; "Love divine, all loves excelling."
Prayers and hymns: "May the grace of Christ our Savior"; "Blessed Jesus, at thy word"; "The King of love my Shepherd is"; "O perfect Love, all human thought transcending."

—From *The Book of Worship for Church and Home.* Copyright © 1964, 1965 by Board of

Publication of The Methodist Church, Inc. Used by permission.

Presbyterian

THE MARRIAGE SERVICE

The man and the woman to be married may be seated together facing the Lord's table, with their families, friends, and members of the congregation seated with them.

When the people have assembled, let the minister say:

Let us worship God.

There was a marriage at Cana in Galilee; Jesus was invited to the marriage, with his disciples.

Friends: Marriage is established by God. In marriage a man and woman willingly bind themselves together in love, and become one even as Christ is one with the church, his body.

> Let marriage be held in honor among all. All may join in a hymn of praise and the following prayer:

Let us confess our sin before God.

> Almighty God, our Father: you created us for life together. We confess that we have turned from your will. We have not loved one another as you commanded. We have been quick to claim our own rights and careless of the rights of others. We have taken much and given little. Forgive our disobedience, O God, and strengthen us in love, so that we may serve you as a faithful people, and live together in your joy; through Jesus Christ our Lord. Amen.

The minister shall declare God's mercy, saying:

Hear and believe the good news of the gospel.

Nothing can separate us from the love of God in Christ Jesus our Lord!

In Jesus Christ, we are forgiven.

> The people may stand to sing a doxology, or some other appropriate response to the good mercy of God.

> The minister may offer a Prayer for Illumination.

> Before the reading of the Old Testament lesson, the minister shall say:

The lesson is . . .

Listen for the word of God.

> The Gloria Patri, or some other response, may be sung.

> Before the reading of the New Testament lesson, the minister shall say:

The lesson is . . .

Listen for the word of God.

> The minister may deliver a brief Sermon on the lessons from Scripture, concluding with an Ascription of Praise.

> Then let the minister address the man and woman, saying:

_____ and _____, you have come together according to God's wonderful plan for creation. Now, before these people, say your vows to each other.

Let the man and the woman stand before the people, facing each other. Then, the minister shall say:

Be subject to one another out of reverence for Christ.

The man shall say to the woman:

_____, *I promise with God's help to be your faithful husband, to love and serve you as Christ commands, as long as we both shall live.*

The woman shall say to the man:

_____, *I promise with God's help to be your faithful wife, to love and serve you as Christ commands, as long as we both shall live.*

A ring, or rings, may be given, with the following words:

I give you this ring as a sign of my promise.

The minister shall address the man and the woman, saying:

As God's picked representatives of the new humanity, purified and beloved of God himself, be merciful in action, kindly in heart, humble in mind. Accept life, and be most patient and tolerant with one another. Forgive as freely as the Lord has forgiven you. And, above everything else, be truly loving. Let the peace of Christ rule in your hearts, remembering that as members of the one body you are called to live in harmony, and never forget to be thankful for what God has done for you.

Or,

Love is slow to lose patience—it looks for a way of being constructive. It is not possessive: it is neither anxious to impress nor does it cherish inflated ideas of its own importance. Love has good manners and does not pursue selfish advantage. It is not touchy. It does not keep account of evil or gloat over the wickedness of other people. On the contrary, it is glad with all good men when truth prevails. Love knows no limit to its endurance, no end to its trust, no fading of its hope; it can outlast anything. It still stands when all else has fallen.

The minister shall call the people to prayer, saying:

Praise the Lord.

The Lord's name be praised.

Life up your hearts.

We lift them to the Lord.

Let us pray.

Eternal God: without your grace no promise is sure. Strengthen _____ and _____ with the gift of your Spirit, so they may fulfill the vows they have taken. Keep them faithful to each other and to you. Fill them with such love and joy that they may build a home where no one is a stranger. And guide them by your word to serve you all the days of their lives; through Jesus Christ our Lord, to whom be honor and glory forever and ever. **Amen.**

The Lord's Prayer shall be said.

Then, the man and the woman having joined hands, the minister shall say:

_____ and _____, you are now husband and wife according to the witness of the holy catholic church, and the law of the state.

Become one. Fulfill your promises. Love and serve the Lord.

What God has united, man must not divide.

Here may be sung a hymn of thanksgiving. Then, let the people be dismissed:

Glory be to him who can keep you from falling and bring you safe to his glorious presence, innocent and happy. To God, the only God, who saves us through Jesus Christ our Lord, be the glory, majesty, authority, and power, which he had before time began, now and forever. **Amen.**

Or,

The grace of the Lord Jesus Christ, the love of God, and the fellowship of the Holy Spirit, be with you all. **Amen.**

—From *The Worshipbook—Services*. Philadelphia: Westminster, 1970.

Service for the Recognition of a Marriage (Presbyterian)

This service may be used to recognize a civil marriage; or with the deletion of the first paragraph, it may be used as a brief marriage service.

The service may be conducted during public worship on the Lord's Day, when the Sacrament is not celebrated, immediately after the preaching of a sermon; or it may be used at other times. Members of the congregation should be present, in addition to the minister.

Let the minister or an elder say:

_____ and _____ have been married by the law of the state, and they have spoken vows pledging loyalty and love. Now, in faith, they come before the witness of the church to acknowledge their marriage covenant and to tell their common purpose in the Lord.

Then, the minister shall say:

Friends: Marriage is God's gift. In marriage a man and a woman bind themselves in love and become one, even as Christ is one with the church, his body.

_____ and _____, be subject to one another out of reverence for Christ.

The man shall say to the woman:

_____, *you are my wife. With God's help I promise to be your faithful husband, to love and serve you as Christ commands, as long as we both shall live.*

The woman shall say to the man:

_____, *you are my husband. With God's help I promise to be your faithful wife, to love and serve you as Christ commands, as long as we both shall live.*

A ring, or rings, may be given, with the following words:

I give you this ring as a sign of my promise.

Then, let the minister say:

Hear the words of our Lord Jesus Christ:

Remain in my love. If you keep my commandments you will remain in my love, just as I have kept my Father's commandments and remain in his love. I have told you this so that my own joy may be in you and your joy be complete. This is my commandment: love one another, as I have loved you.

Let us pray.

Eternal God: without your grace no promise is sure. Strengthen _____ and _____ with the gift of your Spirit, so they may fulfill the vows they have taken. Keep them faithful to each other and to you. Fill them with such love and joy that they may build a home where no one is a stranger. And guide them by your word to serve you all the days of their lives: through Jesus Christ our Lord, to whom be honor and glory, forever and ever. **Amen.**

> The man and the woman having joined hands, the minister shall say:

_____ and _____, you are husband and wife according to the witness of the holy catholic church. Help each other. Be united: live in peace, and the God of love and peace will be with you.

> What God has united, man must not divide.

> The following benediction may be said:

The grace of the Lord Jesus Christ, the love of God, and the fellowship of the Holy Spirit, be with you all. **Amen.**

—From *The Worshipbook—Services.* Philadelphia: Westminster, 1970.

The Consecration of a Civil Marriage

(Lutheran)

If this Order is used in the public church service, it may follow the Offertory in the Order of Morning Service or the Canticle in the Matins and Vespers, and the Lesson should be read at the proper time.

The persons having presented themselves in the church, a suitable Hymn may be sung.

> The Minister shall say:

> In the Name of the Father and of the Son and of the Holy Ghost.

> The Congregation shall say or chant:

> *Amen.*

The Minister shall read Psalm 67 or Psalm 128.

> The Congregation shall chant the Gloria Patri.

The Minister, standing before the married pair, who have come to the entrance of the chancel, shall give the Address, or

> The Minister shall say:

> Dearly Beloved: Whereas you have been duly united in wedlock by an official of the civil State and have presented yourselves here to have your marriage consecrated by the Church of Jesus Christ, it behooveth you to hear what the Word of God teacheth concerning marriage.
>
> The Lord God saith: It is not good that the man should be alone; I will make him an help meet for him.
>
> Our Lord Jesus Christ saith: Have ye not read that He which made them at the beginning, made them male and female, and said, For this cause shall a man leave father and mother, and shall cleave to his wife; and they twain shall be one flesh? Wherefore they are no

more twain, but one flesh. What therefore God hath joined together, let not man put asunder.

The Apostle Paul, speaking by the Holy Ghost, saith: Husbands, love your wives, even as Christ also loved the Church and gave Himself for it. So ought men to love their wives as their own bodies. He that loveth his wife loveth himself. For no man ever yet hated his own flesh, but nourisheth and cherisheth it, even as the Lord the Church. Wives, submit yourselves unto your own husbands as unto the Lord. For the husband is the head of the wife, even as Christ is the Head of the Church; and He is the Savior of the body. Therefore as the Church is subject unto Christ, so let the wives be to their own husbands in everything.

And although, by reason of sin, many a cross hath been laid upon this estate, nevertheless our gracious Father in heaven doth not forsake His children in an estate so holy and acceptable to Him, but is ever present with His bountiful blessings.

For thus saith the Lord in the Psalm: Blessed is everyone that feareth the Lord, that walketh in His ways. For thou shalt eat the labor of thine hands. Happy shalt thou be, and it shall be well with thee. Thy wife shall be as a fruitful vine by the sides of thine house; thy children like olive plants round about thy table. Behold, that thus shall the man be blessed that feareth the Lord. The Lord shall bless thee out of Zion; and thou shalt see the good of Jerusalem all the days of thy life. Yea, thou shalt see thy children's children and peace upon Israel.

Thus hath our heavenly Father sanctified the estate of matrimony. He will ever bless therein all who love Him, trust in Him, and live in His fear, for Jesus' sake.

Dearly beloved, as you have united in this holy estate, which consisteth in your mutual consent, sincerely and earnestly given, it is fitting and necessary for you to declare the same before God and these witnesses.

Then shall the Minister say to the man:

N., Hast thou taken this woman to be thy wedded wife, to live with her after God's ordinance in the holy estate of matrimony, to love her, comfort her, honor her, and keep her in sickness and in health, and, forsaking all others, to keep thee only unto her so long as ye both shall live?

The man shall say:
I have.

Then shall the Minister say unto the woman:

N., Hast thou taken this man to be thy wedded husband, to live with him after God's ordinance in the holy estate of matrimony, to love him, comfort him, honor him, and keep him in sickness and in health, and, forsaking all others, to keep thee only unto him so long as ye both shall live?

The woman shall say:
I have.

If the wedding ring be used, the Minister shall now receive it and deliver it to the man to be put on the fourth finger of the woman's left hand.

Then shall the man, facing the woman, say, or if two rings be used, the man and the woman, facing each other, in turn, shall say, after the Minister:

RECEIVE THIS RING / as a pledge and token / of wedded love and faithfulness.

Then shall the Minister say:

MAY THE GIVING and receiving of this ring (these rings) ever be a symbol of the faithful and unselfish community of goods that you as husband and wife, in weal and woe, will cultivate without ceasing, and a reminder of the excellent Christian virtues with which you will adorn your marriage. To this end may God bless you through the heavenly Bridegroom, Jesus Christ, our Lord.

Then shall the Minister say:

JOIN your right hands. What therefore God hath joined together, let not man put asunder.

Then shall they turn to face the altar and kneel, and the Minister shall bless them, saying:

MAY THE ALMIGHTY AND ETERNAL GOD look down from His exalted throne in heaven upon you with His favor and sanctify and bless you with the benediction first spoken to Adam and Eve in Paradise, that you may please Him both in body and soul, and live together in holy love until life's end.

The God of Abraham, the God of Isaac, the God of Jacob, be with you and richly bless you forevermore. Amen.

Then may be sung a Hymn.

Then shall the Minister say or chant:

LET us pray:

Almighty God, our heavenly Father, who hast united this man and this woman in the holy estate of matrimony, grant them the grace to live therein according to Thy holy Word, strengthen them in constant faithfulness and true love toward each other; sustain and defend them amidst all trials and temptations; and help them so to pass through this world in faith towards Thee, in communion with Thy holy Church, and in loving service one of the other, that they may ever enjoy Thy heavenly benediction; through Jesus Christ, Thy Son, our Lord, who liveth and reigneth with Thee and the Holy Ghost, ever one God, world without end.

The Congregation shall say or chant:
Amen.

Then shall all say:
Our Father who art in heaven. Hallowed be Thy name. Thy kingdom come. Thy will be done on earth as it is in heaven. Give us this day our daily bread. And forgive us our trespasses, as we forgive those who trespass against us. And lead us not into temptation. But deliver us from evil. For Thine is the kingdom and the power and the glory forever and ever. Amen.

Then shall the Minister say or chant the Benediction:

THE LORD bless thee and keep thee.

The Lord make His face shine upon thee and be gracious unto thee.

The Lord lift up His countenance upon thee and give thee peace ✠.

Then shall the Congregation say or chant:
Amen.

SILENT PRAYER

—From *The Lutheran Agenda.* St. Louis: Concordia, 1941.

The Order for
The Anniversary of a Marriage
(Lutheran)

If this Order is used in the public church service, it may follow the Offertory in the Order of Morning Service or the Canticle in the Matins and Vespers, and the Lesson should be read at the proper time.

The anniversary couple having presented themselves at the altar, a Hymn of Praise may be sung.

Then shall the Minister say:

OUR HELP is in the name of the Lord, who made heaven and earth.

Beloved in the Lord: These Christian spouses appear this day before the Lord to renew the remembrance of that covenant of matrimony which was made between them _____ years ago, to offer to the Lord the sacrifice of thanksgiving for all the mercies and all the truth which for so many years He hath shown unto them, and to supplicate His gracious aid for the portion that remaineth of their days. Let us pray:

O Thou faithful and merciful God, heavenly Father, who hast instituted the estate of matrimony, hallowed it by the presence of Thy Son at the marriage in Cana of Galilee, and protected and preserved it until this day: we thank Thee for Thy goodness and heartily beseech Thee, Thou wouldst evermore maintain Thine ordinance by Thy gracious and almighty presence, and grant unto these, and all others united in marriage, peace and unity, and comfort and hope in the day of trouble; through Jesus Christ, our Lord. Amen.

Then may another Hymn be sung.

Then shall follow a short Address.

For the Address one of the following texts may be used: Gen. 32:10; 1 Sam. 7:12; 2 Sam. 7:18; Job 10:12; Ps. 9:1-2; Ps. 40:5; Ps. 64:9-10; Ps. 71:17-18; Ps. 92:13; Ps. 115:13, 15; Ps. 128:5; Prov. 16:16; Prov. 17:6; Is. 46:4; Zech. 8:4; 1 Cor. 15:10.

BELOVED IN THE LORD: Inasmuch as God, of His bountiful goodness, hath permitted you to live together in holy wedlock these _____ years, to share with each other both joy and sorrow and to walk together in love and faithfulness that may not be broken so that you are able to celebrate this day of thanksgiving: you heartily desire to commit also the remainder of your days to His gracious care and humbly to implore His blessing. Lift up your hearts, therefore, and offer your thanksgiving unto the Lord and pray:

Now follows the prayer, the celebrating couple kneeling.

LORD GOD, heavenly Father, we give Thee thanks for the fatherly love and grace which Thou has bestowed upon us, Thine unworthy servants, in such rich measure since the days of our youth and especially during these _____ years of holy wedlock. Thou hast accompanied us with loving-kindnesses and tender mercies, visited us with Thy comfort, strengthened us in sorrow and sickness, and hast crowned our life with every blessing. To Thee alone, O most merciful God, belong all honor and praise, for Thou hast helped us to walk in marital love and fidelity without forsaking each other; nor didst Thou forsake us in sickness or health, in weal or woe, in adversity or prosperity, but didst grant us comfort and strength, patience and faithfulness. Be Thou with us in the future, O Lord, until the end of our days. Be Thou our Guide as Thou hast guided us in the past. Be Thou our Light though the light of our eyes begins to dim. Be Thou our Strength though our strength departs. Be Thou our Support though earthly supports fall. Be Thou our Health in sickness and infirmity. Be Thou our Refuge and our Life in the hour of death. When the days of our pilgrimage on earth shall cease, graciously bring us to the marriage supper of Thy Son and our Lord Jesus Christ, that we may dwell with Thee and rejoice in Thy joy forever.

Then may the Minister, turning to the kneeling celebrating couple and laying his right hand upon their hands, say:

MAY THE MERCIFUL GOD AND FATHER, who hath hitherto sustained and blessed you by His grace in your wedded life, grant unto you the continuance of His divine protection and blessing and cause your hearts to remain united in faithful love unto the end ✠. Amen.
Peace be with you.

Then shall the Minister, facing the altar, say or chant:

LET us pray:
O almighty God, most merciful Father, we bless and praise Thee for all Thy loving-kindness and tender mercies which, for so many years, Thou hast bestowed upon these Thy servants, providing for them by Thy bounty, defending them by Thy power, and guiding them by Thy mercy. We beseech Thee, let the sacrifice of thanksgiving which they offer to Thee be acceptable in Thy sight, and give ear to their humble requests. During the days which still remain of their pilgrimage on earth, even to their old age, be Thou their Strength and their Deliverer in every infirmity and peril of body and soul. Let them at all times know the comfort and peace of Thy Holy Spirit. Be Thou with them, and fulfill in them Thy promise that the house of the righteous shall stand and the tabernacle of the upright shall flourish forevermore. And finally, let them depart this life in joy and peace and with rejoicing meet in Thy heavenly kingdom to laud and praise Thee and the Son and the Holy Ghost, world without end. Amen.

Then the Minister, facing the anniversary couple, shall say:

GO YOUR WAY, then, beloved in Christ, whom we have blessed in the name of the Lord and commended to His gracious keeping. May your hearts continue to be united in love and truth and your home to be a dwelling place of the Lord, that, at the end of your sojourning here on earth, you may together see God face to face and enjoy that glory which He hath promised unto all who abide in true faith unto the end. Amen.

Then may another Hymn be sung.

Then shall the Minister say or chant the Benediction.

THE LORD bless thee and keep thee.
The Lord make His face shine upon thee and be gracious unto thee.
The Lord lift up His countenance upon thee and give thee peace ✠.

The Congregation shall say or chant:
Amen.

SILENT PRAYER

—From *The Lutheran Agenda.* St. Louis, Concordia, 1941.

AFTER THE CEREMONY

WHEN THE CEREMONY is concluded and the clergyman has congratulated the new couple, the bride's face veil, if she is wearing one, is lifted by the groom or the maid of honor. If they wish, and the clergyman does not object, the bride and groom may then kiss briefly before turning toward the congregation. The bride takes her bouquet in her right hand and places her left hand through the groom's right arm as the organist begins the recessional music. The maid of honor hands her own bouquet to a bridesmaid, so that both her hands are free to arrange the bride's train. The bride and groom pause long enough for her to do this, then descend the steps to lead the recessional from the church.

The Recessional

The recessional moves at a brisker pace than the processional. The bride and groom lead the way, with other members of the wedding party falling into place behind them. Moving simultaneously from each side of the chancel, the attendants meet in the center and walk down the aisle in pairs. Child attendants come first, followed by the maid of honor on the best man's right arm and each bridesmaid on the right arm of an usher. Any extra ushers bring up the rear.

Another less usual form of recessional simply reverses the order of the processional. The maid of honor alone follows the bride and groom or any child attendants, the bridesmaids come in couples, followed by the paired ushers. The best man does not take part in such a recessional, but goes with the clergyman into the vestry by the side door through which he and the groom entered.

As soon as all members of the wedding party have left the church, the head usher returns to escort the bride's mother down the aisle. She takes his arm, and her husband follows. A second usher escorts the groom's mother in the same way, and sometimes grandmothers are also taken down the aisle, after which other close relatives leave. No guests, however, should ever leave the pews until the immediate members of both families have reached the vestibule of the church. Then, as the wedding party and the couple's parents depart for the reception, two ushers remove the pew ribbons if these are used, so that the rest of the guests may leave the church in any order they wish.

Whether the best man walks in the recessional or not, it is his duty to return to the vestry immediately after the wedding ceremony and give the clergyman his donation. He then collects the groom's hat and gloves and his own (if these were worn to the church) and goes to the wedding reception.

—From *Vogue's Book of Etiquette.* New York: Simon & Schuster, 1969.

Receiving Line

The receiving line is falling into disuse, especially after informal weddings, where the bride and groom prefer to mingle among their guests and friends.

If the couple choose to have a receiving line, it occurs at the reception. A receiving line occurs in the church vestibule only if (1) the wedding is not followed by a reception, or (2) everyone is not included in the reception. In this case, the receiving line is similar to that of any wedding reception:

1. bride's mother
2. father of the groom (optional)
3. the groom's mother
4. father of bride (optional)
5. bridesmaids
6. maid/matron of honor
7. bride
8. groom

At very formal receptions, often fathers stand in line, but this is not obligatory; however, they usually stay near the receiving line. If either father is unknown to most of the people present, it is better for him to stand in line so that he will feel a real part of the proceedings.

The receiving line may vary although the bride stands on the groom's right (except when he's in uniform). The best man (unless he's the groom's father) is never in the receiving line.

—CECIL MURPHEY

Reception

You don't have to have a reception. But if you do, its primary purpose is to give your friends and relatives an opportunity to help you celebrate your happy event.

What kind of reception should you have? It can be as informal and simple as letting one of your talented friends bake a wedding cake. It can be a banquet with full decoration down to place cards. Arrange the reception in your home, the home of a friend, in the garden, a private club, a local restaurant, or in the church's fellowship hall.

You may serve anything from the traditional wedding cake and punch to a five-course dinner. Morning weddings sometimes have breakfast, brunch, a tea, or even lunch.

Receptions follow the ceremony. As a pastor, I urge the bride and groom, out of consideration for their guests, to go immediately to the reception, and come back later for any posed wedding pictures.

—CECIL MURPHEY

MENU SUGGESTIONS

Even though your guests may have an eye on the food as well as on your wedding gown, don't serve too much. The spirit of the party is the main thing, and sustenance secondary.

Climates and seasons should influence you in deciding on your breakfast or supper menus. A wedding in Virginia, for instance, conjures up thoughts of juicy, succulent ham, while out-of-town guests at a New Orleans breakfast will be delighted to find French or Creole dishes.

Chicken is popular everywhere, at any time. Caterers admit that nothing more appropriate has been devised for wedding fare. So, if chicken it is to be, make it a proud, tempting dish. Cooked in white wine with a clove of garlic, then added to sautéed mushrooms and cream sauce, and served in paste puff patties, it is perfect for a stand-up buffet.

Try chicken paprika or chicken in pieces with lemon and sour cream. Substitute fresh green salad for the usual green peas; or baked zucchini, broccoli, or wild rice.

For dessert, ice cream is the wedding favorite. Or an ice (but not if the weather is scorching, as it melts rapidly), and always the delicious rich bride's cake. Then a demitasse, black and steaming.

Sit-Down Breakfast Suggestions
Grapefruit cups
Chicken salad (or chicken patties)
Lattice potatoes
Hot biscuits and marmalade
Mint-ice cream   Bride's cake
Bonbons   Demitasse

o o o

Vichysoisse
Creamed sweetbreads and mushrooms
Avocado salad
Melba toast   Chocolate parfait
Bride's cake
Mints   Demitasse

o o o

Consommé royale
Baby guinea hen with juniper sauce
Broccoli
Small French rolls
Ice cream with spun sugar
Bride's cake
Mints   Demitasse

Buffet Breakfast

Smörgåsbord
Sliced smoked turkey   Mousse of chicken
Tomato aspic salad   Celery   Olives
Croissants
Vanilla ice cream with brandied-cherry
sauce
Bride's cake
Coffee   Mints

Afternoon Reception

Assorted tea sandwiches
Lobster salad
Champagne punch
Bride's cake
Coffee and tea for those
who don't take punch

o o o

Ice cream in molds
Bride's cake
Nuts, mints and bonbons
Coffee and tea

Evening Supper

Fresh fruit supreme
Green turtle soup
Rock Cornish hen   Wild rice
Green peas
Endive salad   Cheese straws
Orange-water ice
Bride's cake
Chocolate-covered mints
Demitasse

—From Marjorie Binford Woods, *Your Wedding.* New York: Bobbs-Merrill, 1960.

THE WEDDING CAKE

The tiered wedding cake may be a caterer's dream or it may be made in the kitchen of the bride and be as simple or as elaborate as the cook can manage. It need not be topped with the miniature of the bride and groom, as is so often seen, but may be covered with charming sugar flowers in pastel colors with pale green leaves. Or it may be decorated with a pastry tube in white and pastel icing or plain white. The most popular cakes are the silver cake, which is made with the egg whites alone and is light and airy, the gold cake, a yellow pound cake which is richer, and the dark, rich fruit cake, most expensive of all. It should have nothing "written" upon it with icing, however. This sort of decoration is reserved for birthday cakes. The occasional exception is the "ring cake"—a wedding cake baked in the shape of the wedding ring and which may have the bride's initials, first, then the groom's to the right, in icing on the "band." Often little bridal favors are baked in the cake to tell fortunes.

Cutting the Wedding Cake.   At the end of the repast the bride rises—and with her all the gentlemen at the table—to cut the cake.

Usually the guests are told that the propitious moment has arrived and gather around.

If the groom is in uniform the cake is cut with his dress sword, undecorated. At a civilian wedding a silver cake knife is used, and it may have its handle decorated with a streamer of white satin ribbons knotted with bridal flowers. The bride cuts only the first slice, with the groom's help, and she and the groom share it. Some member of the family, a knowledgeable friend, or a domestic employee then cuts and apportions the rest of the cake for service to guests, usually with ice cream. The tiered, decorated cake is cut as follows, after the bride and groom's slice has first been taken. A long sharp knife is inserted vertically through the cake at the base of the second tier and a core is cut all around the second tier. Subsequent slices are then taken from the first layer. When the first tier has been completely served, then the second tier of the cake is cored in the same way and then cut. The very top tier, which may or may not have the traditional bride and groom decoration—sometimes pastel icing flowers are used, for example—is gently lifted off, wrapped, and preserved. It can be stored in the freezer, of course (with the icing removed) for the first anniversary of the couple. If it is to be stored without freezing, it may be wrapped in a brandy soaked cloth and stored in an airtight container. The remaining layers after the top tier has been lifted off, will be small but may still be cut in wedge-shaped pieces. In this case, start with the top layer and work down. At second marriages, by the way, wedding cakes may be used but the decorative bride and groom or white bell should not be used at the top. The cake is traditionally a white cake, but it can also be a fruit cake and I know one pretty Northern bride who insisted that it be chocolate. But whatever the interior, the outside is always white, although it may have pastel decorations (usually flowers). One lovely cake put out by a master caterer is literally covered with pastel flowers and leaves, and skips the bride and groom or wedding bell on the top.

—From *Amy Vanderbilt's Complete Book of Etiquette*, revised by Letitia Baldridge. New York: Doubleday, 1978.

Rice

Traditionally, people throw rice at the departing couple. Increasingly, caterers provide the rice in small plastic bags or pastel net tied with satin ribbon. (Confetti and bird seed are sometimes used instead of rice.)

Each guest receives a tiny rice bag just before the couple leaves the place of the reception. Young girls who are friends or relatives of the couple, usually distribute them to guests. The rice (or substitute) is thrown outside the building.

Bridal Bouquet

When the couple has finished the wedding reception and just before they change into their going-away clothes, the bride traditionally throws her bouquet to her assembled bridesmaids. In some areas, the bride hands her special blue garter to the groom and he then tosses it to his ushers and bachelor friends.

—CECIL MURPHEY

Honeymoon

The term "honeymoon," from the French *Lune de Miel* (literally "moon of honey") refers to a time of leisurely adjustment to each other.

According to ancient French custom, for a month after the wedding, the couple drank a special beverage called metheglin, a kind of honey wine.

Today's honeymoons generally run less than a full month because of the expense and

90

because the groom (and often the bride as well) must go back to work shortly afterward. Many couples opt for weekend honeymoons.

—CECIL MURPHEY

Bride's New Name

Today when you become legally linked to your husband, you have several options for your married name.

Use your husband's last name. This, of course, is the traditional way. You'll sign checks and legal papers as first name, maiden name, husband's last name. *Debra Sue Johnson* becomes *Debra Johnson Long.* If you wish, you may retain your middle name: *Debra Sue Long.*

Form a combined last name. You may choose to use a hyphenated name: *Debra Johnson-Long.* Your husband would also legally change his name to include your maiden name: *Thomas Johnson-Long.*

Keep your maiden name. It is now acceptable to retain your maiden name. Thus you would be *Debra Johnson* married to *Thomas Long.* Although legal, this can cause confusion. If you have established your career in your maiden name, you might keep that name professionally but legally and socially take your husband's name. . . .

For monograms, use the first initial of your first name, the initial of your maiden name, and the first initial of your married name—the latter being the largest. Or (more informal) use a large initial of your married name centered between the initials of your first name and your husband's first name.

$$\mathcal{D}\mathcal{L}\mathcal{J} \quad \text{OR} \quad \mathcal{D}\mathcal{J}\mathcal{L} \qquad \mathcal{D}\mathcal{L}\mathcal{T}$$

Establishing Your Identity

Marriage is a joyful celebration. But it is also a legal change of name and status, and that means paperwork. Some legal papers you can care for before the wedding. Others, such as driver's license and social security, may require a certified copy of your marriage certificate. Here are some of the name changes and legal matters to which you must attend.

Bank accounts. You may open joint savings and/or checking accounts with your fiancé a few weeks before the wedding. The account will read: Gerald Allen Long or Phyllis Mosher Morgan (also known as Phyllis Mosher or Mrs. Gerald Long). This arrangement allows you to transact business both before and after the wedding.

Magazine subscriptions. Send notice of your change of name and address six to eight weeks before the wedding.

Charge accounts. Send notice in writing of your new name and address. You can also instruct creditors to add your new husband's signature to your accounts, and he can do the same for you on his accounts.

Postal service. Give a forwarding address (in both your maiden and married names) to begin after the wedding.

Board of voter registration. Send written notice either before or after your wedding. If you move to another community, register to vote there.

Car registration. Send written notice either before or after the wedding.

Employment office. Give notice before the wedding and change your deduction status with the Internal Revenue Service.

School records. Send your new information to any schools from which you have graduated to update records, or to the registration office if you are still in school.

Insurance. Change the name of beneficiaries on all policies to become effective the day of the wedding. If you have no household insurance, take out a policy to cover your wedding gifts and furnishings. Be sure you have adequate health insurance as well.

Wills. No one likes to contemplate death—especially before a wedding! But the wise couple will meet with a lawyer before their wedding and draw up their wills. Should anything happen to either of you, the other would be saved much grief and inconvenience not to mention legal expense if you have a will.

Social Security. You must present a certified copy of your marriage certificate and your Social Security card to make this change.

Driver's license. Check local requirements, but you usually are required to go in person with a certified copy of your marriage certificate.

—From Kay Oliver Lewis, *The Christian Wedding Handbook.* Old Tappan, N.J.: Revell, 1981.

TRADITIONS

Rice. The rituals of wishing luck to the couple are familiar to all of us. One of the oldest and most universal of all celebrative customs is that of throwing *rice*, grain, or nuts at the couple after the wedding. It is still very popular today, yet most people have no idea why they are standing around tossing Uncle Ben's Rice at good friends who were married a few minutes before.

Grains that literally sustain life also symbolically represent life and growth. A good crop is an occasion for much joy. Before our ancestors understood that babies are conceived by a man and woman in sexual intercourse, they made up stories or myths that connected pregnancy with the yearly appearance of crops. Both functions were perceived to be the same—and often blesssed by the same deity. Both were very mysterious occurrences; both brought life into the

world; and both involved risk and possible loss of life.

The custom of throwing rice and grain at newlyweds probably originated to symbolize the close relationship between woman and the life-bearing grain. Just as sowing seeds makes new life grow from the seeds, so might throwing grains increase the bride's fertility. Since in many cultures a barren woman could be divorced or even killed, throwing "life" in the form of grain was thought of as bringing good luck to the new wife.

Other meanings of this rite have also been recorded. Among Indians, throwing rice, the basic food source, symbolized the wish of plenty and prosperity for the couple. Nowadays this is the main sentiment involved in the custom. Throwing rice is a way of saying, "Good Luck!"

But rice is not the only thing that has been thrown at weddings. In many lands eggs also represented fertility and prosperity. Westermarck notes that in Morocco, the groom throws an egg at his new wife in the hope that she will have ease in childbirth. This is a rather messy ritual, but magic is magic. In another case, dates and figs were tossed after the couple in order to make the bride sweeter to her husband. Ancient Hebrews threw barley in front of the couple to express their hopes for numerous progeny. Not just one child—five or ten! Fecundity was a blessed sign for most people until the middle of this century. Children were essential to the growth and power of a family, tribe, city, or nation. The more people, the more help available to bring in the crops or man the battle stations. A woman who could bear and raise ten children was for many centuries a hero.

In these days of great concern about the world's overpopulation, and with many couples deliberately controlling the size of their families or remaining childless, the ritual of rice throwing seems out of date to many people. On the one hand, it really expresses the wish, "Have many children." On the other hand, it would be a shame if the custom were to disappear (especially since it has lost its original meaning and now is simply another means of nonverbal celebration). Perhaps the modern meaning of rice throwing will simply be: "We wish you much happiness and prosperity."

Flowers have long been used to decorate weddings. One tradition we have inherited through the centuries is the use of "flower girls" in a wedding. One or two children may precede the bride down the aisle carrying bouquets of flowers. This is an updated version of the original ritual when children carried bunches of grain to symbolize fertility. Grains and flowers are interchangeable in this ritual because the meaning is clear: nature's "children" are used to bring luck to the humans.

In olden days, the bridal flowers were another way to represent the wish for fertility (although today many claim the bouquet is carried to hide the bride's nervously shaking hands from public view). The ritual of throwing the bouquet goes back many centuries. Numerous objects have been thrown by brides in the past—garters, cakes, wheat, or flowers—with the idea that the person who caught the object would be the next to marry. It was the bride's way of wishing luck to the unmarried girls in the crowd. . . .

Receptions. The reception, or the feast of food, drink and dancing, is the final public custom of weddings the world over. In virtually all societies, some kind of feast accompanies or follows the actual wedding. Wedding feasts can last only a few minutes, or as long as a week. In the Orient, for example, the drinking of wine by the bride and groom constitutes what we call the ceremony—the bond is the feast itself.

In the Western world, we expect a wedding service to be followed by a reception; it is the time to receive and acknowledge the married couple, to toast them, share in their joy, and send them on their way. But in numerous societies in the past, these two celebrations—the nuptial and the social—have been combined. People feasted with a couple as the wedding was taking place. Certainly for primitive people, the wedding *was* the feast. Only much later did the two functions become separate. We have witnessed some movement back to the "open ceremony," or extended feast, in this country recently. Couples who have combined the "wedding services" with the "reception" have tried to achieve a certain casualness and freedom in their marriage ceremony.

Eating and drinking together is one of the oldest signs of love and union. In ancient times, the bride and groom probably shared some bread and drink together and were then considered legally married. No vows, no papers to sign. It was as easy as that. By simple sharing, they were united. There are many old myths about two enemies who become friends by sharing a meal, or about a boy and girl falling in love by drinking from the same cup or goblet. When one comes this close to another, one cannot help but be affected. Jews made the drinking of wine an integral part of their marriage service. This sharing, coming together, is as universal as holding hands, it's understood by anyone in the world.

The sharing between bride and groom also extends to the guests. The communal aspect is very important. The couple, once united, share their happiness with those around them. In old times, a wedding gathering was usually made up of the entire clan, tribe, or village. A wedding day was a time for dancing and singing, often for drunkenness, and always a celebration for everyone. A wedding was truly a feast in numerous societies —laws were relaxed, people could drink

93

openly (an act not usually condoned), and sexual mores were relaxed. In some societies, sexual intercourse was permitted even between strangers, although outlawed during normal times. And the feast wasn't always a short one; sometimes it lasted for days, or until everyone collapsed from exhaustion.

As social customs became more sophisticated and highly regulated, the wedding feast became a "reception" where the bride and groom could meet and feast with friends and relatives. The idea was the same, but the wild activities were somewhat toned down. A receiving line was formed so the couple could greet all the guests in a systematic fashion. Most of the exuberant rituals were either displaced or made acceptable to each culture. But the reception itself remained an important part of the entire wedding ritual.

Many elements of the wedding feast have not changed since our ancestors used them. One of these is dancing. Whether to jungle drums or a rock band, a reception has never been complete without music and dancing. The dance was a central ritual in most primitive cultures, and many wedding ceremonies included ritual dances as expression of emotion. Ritual dance involves the spirits and gods, and calls them to witness and bless the occasion. Dance is a means of having everyone present participate in the celebration. And dance can also be highly erotic—another means of prayer to the gods that the couple will have ease and fruitfulness in their sexual life. Today, dancing is more a way of being social and enjoying others. Even though we no longer perform prayer dances at our friends' weddings, the enjoyment and group unity is the same as it must have been for thousands of years.

The Wedding Cake is another part of the feast that dates back to antiquity. The beautifully frosted, decorated, tall wedding cake we often see today is an updated version of the grain cake that was broken over the bride's head to insure fruitfulness centuries ago. The wedding cake has always been a "special" food, a mixture and shape used only for the feast. It has always been a communal food; everyone ate from it, both as a sign of union and also as a way of wishing luck to the new couple. Today many couples give each guest a small piece of their cake in boxes, to make certain everyone gets a piece to take home. This is their way of sharing their "special" moment with the community of guests.

When we see the bride and groom slicing the first piece of a huge wedding cake and offering it to each other to eat, they are enacting one of the most ancient rituals. And as all the guests join in the festivities, we can sense something very special and unique about the occasion. It is a time of joy, a time when people, many of whom do not know each other, can join together in one common interest: the wish of happiness for a newly married couple.

Veils. Bridal veils have a long and complicated history. The custom of covering the bride's face on her wedding day is widespread, recorded in numerous societies around the world. The first instances of veiling were undoubtedly to protect the vulnerable new bride from the evil eye. Because the woman was regarded as weaker and more prone to danger, she was usually the one to be veiled. The tradition lingered on for centuries until it became an expected practice. Christians changed the custom to a representation of a woman's innocence and purity, and it is in this form that we have inherited the custom.

In Moslem countries, women have always been regarded as servants. Until recently, women kept their faces veiled at most times throughout their whole lives (some still do), since only her husband is supposed to see a woman's face uncovered. In this case the veil is a symbol of submission and servitude, and many anthropologists believe that the wedding veil also had its origins in the same attitude of male domination.

Veils have also been used to protect another kind of secret. When weddings had been arranged by the couple's parents, and the bride and groom had never seen each other, the girl wore a veil throughout the ceremony. These marriages were negotiated in childhood, and when the right time came the couple had no choice but to fulfill their parents' wishes. After the ceremony was completed the husband would lift his new bride's veil and see her face for the first time.

Still other variations on the theme of hiding the bride have been observed. In some Near East lands, a curtain was placed between the couple all through the ceremony so they could not see or touch each other until officially united. This practice is really a more elaborate form of veiling in which the whole body of both bride and groom is hidden from the other. These customs, which were originally intended to save the couple from bad luck or the evil eye, later led to the superstition that bad things would happen to the bride and groom who saw each other on their wedding day before the ceremony. In many countries, the couple was kept from seeing one another for as much as two or three days before the ceremony. Elaborate precautions were carried out to prevent them from laying eyes—or hands—on each other.

Certainly magic isn't the only issue here. Bad luck is one thing, but what all these customs may also indicate is that the bride and groom had to be restrained from seeing each other because their sexual passion was so high. Taboos against seeing or touching a loved one are based on conflicting feelings—desire for and fear of someone close. Thus separating the couple before the wedding, and veiling the bride during it, lessened the possibility that a couple might break a rule or taboo of the society.

—From Howard Kirschenbaum and Rockwell Stensrud, *The Wedding Book*. New York: Seabury, 1974.

The Bride's Shower is said to have originated because of the refusal of a Dutch father to give his daughter her dowry. She, it seems, wished to marry a miller, an exemplary fellow according to his neighbors, who impoverished himself by giving bread and flour to the poor. Her father, who had more ambitious plans, wanted her to marry a farmer whose livestock included one hundred pigs. When the recipients of the miller's generosity heard that his future wife was giving up her dowry in order to marry him, they got together to see what they could do about it and decided, since they could not scrape together much money, that the best thing would be for each to contribute a simple but practical present. This they did, calling on the girl in a group. The resultant showering of presents, we are told, produced a finer dowry than her father had intended to give her. We do not know if he ever relented.

Miscellaneous Wedding Traditions. The popularity of the diamond as an engagement stone stems from the superstition that its sparkle comes from the fires of love ▢▢▢ May is traditionally an unlucky month for marriage, perhaps because in Roman folklore it was the month of old men; June was dedicated to Juno, the goddess of young people ▢▢▢ According to superstition, not fact, the wedding ring is put on the third finger of the left hand because there is a vein or nerve running from that finger to the heart ▢▢▢ Today people tie shoes to a bridal automobile for luck, but once they were thrown by the bride's parents as a symbol that they had renounced their authority over their daughter ▢▢▢ The best man may be a relic of the days when a bridegroom went out, accompanied by a friend, to capture his bride ⬜⬜ In medieval days two little girls, usually sisters, dressed alike and carrying garlands of wheat—a symbol of fertility— walked before the bride in the wedding procession; later, baskets of flowers replaced the wheat, and the blooms were strewn in the bride's path ⬜⬜ The custom of wearing something blue may stem from the wedding dress of the ancient Israelite bride, who put a blue ribbon along the border of her fringed robe; blue was the color of purity, love and fidelity ⬜⬜ Giving the bride away is a relic of the days when parents arranged marriages and sold or gave away their daughters.

—From *Vogue's Book of Etiquette*. New York: Simon & Schuster, 1969.

FOR FURTHER READING

Biddle, Perry H. *Abingdon Marriage Manual*. Nashville: Abingdon, 1974.

Chapman, Gary. *Toward a Growing Marriage*. Chicago: Moody, 1979.

Christensen, James L. *The Minister's Marriage Handbook*. Old Tappan, N.J.: Revell, 1974.

Gray, Winifred. *You and Your Wedding*. New York: Bantam, 1965.

Kirschenbaum, Howard, and Rockwell Stensrud. *The Wedding Book*. New York: Seabury, 1974.

LaHaye, Tim and Beverly. *The Act of Marriage*. Grand Rapids: Zondervan, 1976.

Lewis, Kay Oliver. *The Christian Wedding Handbook*. Old Tappan, N.J.: Revell, 1981.

The New Bride's Book of Etiquette. New York: Grosset & Dunlap, 1981.

Post, Elizabeth. *Emily Post's Complete Book of Wedding Etiquette*. New York: Harper & Row, 1982.

Rodgers, Betty Stuart, and Elizabeth Connelly Pearce. *Altar Bound*. Danville, Ill.: Interstate, 1973 (out of print).

Small, Dwight Hervey. *Your Marriage Is God's Affair*. Old Tappan, N.J.: Revell, 1979.

Amy Vanderbilt's Complete Book of Etiquette, revised by Letitia Baldridge. New York: Doubleday, 1978.

Vogue's Book of Etiquette. New York: Simon & Schuster, 1969.

Woods, Marjorie Binford. *Your Wedding*. New York: Bobbs-Merrill, 1960.

3

Husband and Wife

MARRIAGE—DEFINITIONS AND GOALS

Marriage is an emotional fusion of two personalities into a functional operation yet both retaining their own identities. The Biblical concept is contained in Genesis 2:24—"One flesh."

AN ANALOGY TO THIS can be two pieces of modeling clay, both green. One is a lighter green than the other—here is the commonality. We knead these two pieces of clay until there is one mass of green clay. On closer inspection the lines of demarcation between the light and the darker green can be clearly seen. These two pieces of clay have become "fused," yet they both retain their own identities.

Any kind of vocation requires a period of training, regardless of what it is. We train ourselves for a minimum of 12 years to keep from becoming parasites on society. But the very root of our society, marriage, can be entered into without preparation. (Having a college education does not automatically qualify anyone for marriage.) This is a paradox of the American people. Due to this lack of preparation and training, the root of our society is deteriorating to the point that society itself will deteriorate and in the final end, destroy itself.

Clinical experience has led me to classify marriages into four different kinds. The first I list as the *happy* marriage. This includes the ultimate capability of two mature people to carry out all three aspects of love and establish the real essence of marriage. It produces a happy interrelationship as well as a contentment to each one individually. All of its functioning processes are working because of mature effort and motivation. The various areas of marriage are producing toward a mutual sharing of an ecstatic relationship that can exist between a man and a woman. I estimate that about 5 percent of American marriages belong in this class.

The next type is a *good* marriage. The marks of this marriage are similar to the marks of a happy marriage, only to a lesser degree. It is a more laborious process which does not produce the results that are gained in the happy relationship. It lacks understanding and production on the part of both individuals of what it takes to be married. It also includes a lesser degree of maturity on the part of either one or both spouses. I estimate that about 10 percent of American marriages belong in this class.

The third I have termed the *agreeable* marriage. The greatest mark of this type is struggle. There is difficulty in achieving the art of loving. There is little education, if any, in the concepts of marriage. There is stupidity even though there is knowledge of the tools. There is also a minimum amount of motivation to work at this business of being married. It may also include a major rank of immaturity on the part of one spouse in the relationship. This necessitates struggle because immaturity hinders a full relationship between two people. The immature person cannot relate. This automatically blocks the proper functioning of all the areas of marriage, including love, communication, sex, the handling of finances, stability with in-laws, commonality areas, and social living.

The last is the *tolerable* marriage. The greatest mark of this relationship is that it is purely a legal marriage and it has no "essence." It is fraught with hostility, competition, and purposeful destruction of the mate. It is both ignorant and stupid and lacks motivation for any type of improvement or betterment. Its result is misery in the emotional makeup of both people. Because spouses merely tolerate each other in their relationship, they "put up" with each other for reasons either external or unknown. I estimate that 85 percent of the marriages in our society fall in the category of the *agreeable* and *tolerable*.

—From Julius A. Fritze, *The Essence of Marriage*. Grand Rapids: Zondervan, 1969.

Goals

"Seek ye first the kingdom of God and his righteousness and all these things will be added unto you." Matthew 6:33

A couple's goals will leave their impact on the family. This axiom is true of both short-term and long-term goals. For example, if one of the short-term goals is a college education for the husband, the wife may work and the couple may delay having children to reach their chosen goal. Or if the couple feel a new car is important for them, they may have to wait for items of furniture or a new stereo until the payments on the car are finished. What the couple decide is important will determine how they use their time, resources, and talents.

IMMEDIATE AND LONG-RANGE GOALS

The immediate life goals for neo-marrieds usually revolve around such matters as furnishing the house, completing some educational or vocational training, planning for a family, and saving for the future. Other personal goals for neo-marrieds are: growing intellectually, growing in self-knowledge, growing in knowledge of their mate, and growing in knowledge of God. Forty-nine neo-marrieds answered a Goals of Life Inventory. Nearly all of the above goals were important to some of the neo-marrieds. The choices given first or second place most often were (D) "devotion to God, doing God's will" and (L) "giving love and security to one's family." There are many short-comings to the responses in the Goals of Life Inventory because it is not possible to tell what each person meant by the answers he gave. However, the inventory did give the couples an opportunity to think carefully about their life goals and to see their lives in the light of these goals. . . .

The neo-marrieds who answered the questionnaire were interested in some immediate material goals—house, car, furnishings—but many felt that they wanted to develop their lives and have goals which were more satisfying to them personally. In response to another questionnaire fifty-five neo-marrieds indicated the following things were important to them:

"Wanting to improve myself culturally" (22)

"Not using my leisure time well" (30) Whatever the goals may have been for these neo-marrieds, they felt they were not meeting their own expectations of the life they

RESPONSE TO THE LIFE GOALS INVENTORY BY
FORTY-NINE NEO-MARRIEDS

Life Goals		Number of Times Items Selected by Neo-Married				
		1st	2nd	3rd	4th	5th
A.	Self-sacrifice for the sake of a better world; giving one's self for others.		3	3	2	2
B.	Peace of mind, contentment, quietness of spirit.	2	7	6	2	6
C.	Serving the community of which one is a part.		1	1	3	2
D.	Devotion to God, doing God's will.	17	2	4	5	4
E.	Being genuinely concerned about other people.	1	4	3	6	3
F.	Finding one's place in life and accepting it.	2	2	2	3	4
G.	Achieving personal life after death; going to heaven.	3	1	5	2	2
H.	Discovering a way of personal communion with God.	2	5	5	6	2
I.	Making a place for one's self in the world; getting ahead.	3	2	1		3
J.	Doing one's duty.	3		2	3	2
K.	Being able to "take it"; brave and uncomplaining acceptance of what life brings.	1		2	3	
L.	Giving love and security to one's family.	6	15	5	4	5
M.	Understanding one's self; having a mature outlook.	2	5	5	4	6
N.	Depending on a personal message from God.	1		2		
O.	Disciplining one's self to a wholesome and clean way of life.	4	2	3	4	4
P.	Participating fully in the life and work of the church.	2			2	4
	Totals	49	49	49	49	49

wanted. Even if their evident goals related to the personal comforts and status symbols which are important to all, yet beneath those material things there were goals of a different kind.

CRITERIA FOR A SUCCESSFUL MARRIAGE

The term "good marriage" is difficult if not impossible to define. Perhaps it would be helpful, however, to try to discover what some aspects of a good marriage are and to try to determine some criteria that could be used to assist a couple in evaluating their progress toward the goal of a successful marriage. The following questions may help:

1. To what degree have the lines of communication continued to be open with their mates, with friends, and with inlaws?
2. To what degree has a satisfactory routine been established that includes time with each other, as well as spiritual, social, mental, and physical development?
3. To what degree has the couple worked out means of handling disagreements constructively?
4. To what degree have the neo-marrieds moved closer to fulfilling the commandment of Jesus to love God and one's neighbor, thus fulfilling the primary convenant?
5. To what degree has there developed a clarity of role responsibilities in the home?
6. To what degree have the neo-marrieds worked out a satisfactory arrangement for income and outgo of money?
7. To what degree has each neo-married found ways to handle family and personal tensions?
8. To what degree has the determination to "build" a successful marriage continued to be important for the neo-marrieds?
9. To what degree has the couple worked out a satisfactory sex relationship, including the planning for children?
10. To what degree have some of the short-term goals of the neo-married been achieved?

Through the use of these criteria a couple may be able to see what is happening to their marriage. It will also assist them in knowing whether their goals are "material and competitive or spiritual and cooperative." (Letter from Wayne E. Oates, Southern Baptist Theological Seminary, Louisville, Kentucky, July, 1965.)

GOALS AND THE COVENANT

The neo-married person who is committed to God revealed in Jesus Christ finds a number of goals clearly indicated in the Bible. In the Sermon on the Mount, Jesus speaks to his followers about life goals. Money or clothing and abundance of food or drink may be goals for some, but to his followers Jesus says, "Seek ye first the kingdom of God and his righteousness and all these things shall be added unto you." (Matthew 6:33 KJV.) First, this primary goal could be expressed in terms of obedience to the will of God. When Jesus was asked to tell the people the greatest commandment, he responded: "You shall love the Lord your God with all your heart, and with all your soul, and with all your mind." (Matthew 22:37) If this is the greatest commandment, it should have first place in the heart of one who is seeking to be obedient to God. Second, this primary goal could be expressed in terms of love. The apostle Paul would tell all neo-marrieds to "earnestly desire the higher gifts. And I will show you a still more excellent way" (1 Corinthians 12:31), the way of love. Thus the neo-marrieds might think of this primary goal in terms of growth in their capacity to love and be loved. . . . The neo-married's goal of developing a love in which the mate and others are drawn toward God is a lofty one. If it is achieved, the home becomes an instrument through which this love of God flows to all others.

The early church was characterized by the presence of the love of God. It made the early Christians live such magnificent lives that people began to ask who the Christians were and why they lived as they did, and this questioning gave to the early Christians the opportunity to share with the inquirers the good news about the love of God as it had come to the followers of Christ. The presence of the love of God means that the home will become a place of witness and that the neo-marrieds will become instruments through which his love flows to the world.

Another facet of the presence of the neo-married's goal of love (God's will) is the necessity it places on the couple to be involved in the community. The covenant established between the neo-marrieds when they were married also had the dimension of the community in it. The neo-married couple whose minds and hearts are stayed on God will begin to see their responsibility to give "a cup of cold water" to the needy in their own community. The community is much interested in the strength of the marriage, because the community is affected positively or negatively, depending on the direction the marriage takes. The couple, on the other hand, must also be interested in the positive and negative aspects of their community. This could mean special interest in the schools, community welfare, local politics, and any number of other things in which couples or individuals can become involved in changing the community.

Neo-marrieds are busy; thus, the necessity for clear goals may be even more important for them than for couples who have been married longer. When the neo-marrieds

launch out on a pilgrimage as exciting and magnificent as marriage can be, it would seem wise to look carefully at two things: the direction they are going and their destination. Their direction should be toward God, and their destination should be his eternal presence. If they ultimately seek God in Jesus Christ, Jesus will fulfill his promise: "I came that they might have life, and have it abundantly." (John 10:10.) Is not that the primary goal neo-marrieds are seeking—abundant life, now and forever? The total life of a couple can be pointed toward an abundant life which the Lord of the primary covenant has promised to all who were willing to be his followers. The promise is for this life and the life to come. Thus there is an eternal dimension that can assist the couple in their daily strivings and give them an eternal hope.

—From Howard Hovde, *The Neo-Married.* Valley Forge, Pa.: Judson, 1968.

Marital Unity

Obviously, getting married does not give a couple this kind of unity. There is a difference between "being united" and "unity." As the old country preacher used to say, "When you tie the tails of two cats together and hang them across the fence, you have united them, but then unity is a different matter."

Perhaps the best biblical example of this kind of unity that we have is God Himself. It is interesting that the word used for "one" in Genesis 2:24, where God says, "Therefore shall a man leave his father and his mother, and shall cleave unto his wife: and they shall be *one* flesh," (italics added) is the same Hebrew word used of God Himself in Deuteronomy 6:4 where we read, "Hear, O Israel: The LORD our God is *one* LORD" (italics added).

The word "one" speaks of composite unity as opposed to absolute unity. The Scriptures reveal God to be Father, Son, and Spirit, yet one. We do not have three Gods but one God, triune in nature. Illustrations of the Trinity are many, and all break down at some point, but let me use a very common one to illustrate some of the implications of this unity.

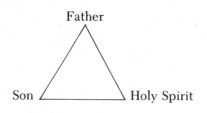

Father

Son — Holy Spirit

The triangle may be placed on any side, and the Father, Son, and Spirit labels moved to any position. It makes no difference, for God is one. What we cannot do is to erase one side or remove one title. It must all stand together. God is triune, and God is one. We cannot fully understand this statement, yet we must speak of God in this manner, because this is the manner in which He has revealed Himself. We would not know that God is triune unless God had revealed Himself as triune. We would not know that the Trinity is a unity except that God has revealed it as such.

God is unity. On the other hand, God is diversity. We cannot rightly say that there are no distinctions among the Trinity. Strictly speaking, the Holy Spirit did not die for us upon the cross. That was the work of the Son. As believers, we are not indwelt by the Father, but by the Spirit. The Members of the Trinity do have varying roles, yet unity. It is unthinkable that members of the Trinity would ever operate as separate entities. From Genesis 1:26 where God said, "Let *us* make man in *our* image" (italics added) to Revelation 22:16-21, we find the Trinity working together as composite unity.

What implications does this divine unity have for marriage? Let me use a second triangle to illustrate.

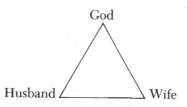

God

Husband — Wife

This time the triangle may not be tilted to rest on another side. God must remain at the apex of a Christian marriage. We can, however, exchange the labels "husband" and "wife," for they are to be one. Their objective is to cooperate with God in developing their unity. This does not mean that the wife will lose her identity as a person any more than the Holy Spirit loses His identity in the Trinity.

Marital unity is not the kind of unity that eradicates personality. Rather, it is the kind of unity that frees you to express your own diversity, yet experience complete oneness with your mate. You are free to be all that God intends you to be, while experiencing all that God intended when He made us male and female. No truth could be more liberating and satisfying.

—From Gary Chapman, *Toward a Growing Marriage*, copyright © 1979, Moody Bible Institute, Moody Press, pp. 61–63.

Roles

In 1982 the Equal Rights Amendment (ERA) was defeated because the needed 36 states didn't ratify the change in our Constitution. Christians argued on both sides of the issue.

Even with the failure of ERA the issue has not been settled. Nor will it be settled for a long time. One thing is clear, however, marriage roles and our view of husband-wife relationships have changed in recent years. Today we have moved toward a more equalitarian position. Even among the most conservative, the theological stance has moderated. For instance, those who point out the apostle Paul's use of *submission* for women and *headship* for men, just as quickly affirm that those words don't mean servitude and suppression for women and autocratic control by men.

Theologians of earlier days took a less-gentle approach.

Martin Luther, in his *Table-Talk* said, "Men have broad and large chests, and small narrow hips, and more understanding than women, who have but small and narrow chests, and broad hips, to the end that they should remain at home, sit still, keep house, and bear and bring up children." (DCCXXV, 1569.)

Charles Hodges, in his commentary on Ephesians (1856), wrote:

"The apostle, therefore, says, wives are to be obedient to their husbands, because the husband is the head of the wife, even as Christ is the head of the church. The ground of the obligation, therefore, as it exists in nature, is the eminency of the husband; his superiority in those attributes which enable and entitle him to command. He is larger, stronger, bolder; has more of those mental and moral qualities which are required in a leader. This is just as plain from history as that iron is heavier than water. . . . This superiority of the man, in the respects mentioned, thus taught in the Scripture, founded in nature, and proved by all experience, cannot be denied or disregarded without destroying society and degrading both men and women; making the one effeminate and the other masculine."

I wonder how many today would agree with the obvious interpretation of male *superiority?*

As in most critical issues, devout Christians have based their arguments on biblical texts. Their interpretations have spanned the spectrum.

In various passages God sets a pattern of authority. He declares the husband head of the wife as Christ is head of the church (*see* especially Ephesians 5:21–33, but also Colossians 3:18–19). Abraham is also Sarah's master (1 Peter 3:1–7). Thus, Scripture says that a wife submits to her husband. The children are the third link in this divine chain of command (*see* Ephesians 6:1), so that human authority in the Christian home, given by God, starts with the husband as the head with the wife submissive to him, and the children submissive to both.

This position further declares that God's chain of command in marriage has no cultural considerations and is based on God's eternal principles.

Today, most conservatives would agree that certain cultural situations existed. After all, women had few rights. But that does not change the principle, they argue.

An often-used illustration involves Paul's injunction to "greet one another with a holy kiss." (*See* Romans 16:16; 1 Corinthians 16:20; 2 Corinthians 13:12.) Today most of us do not kiss upon meeting. That's the cultural aspect. But we do greet each other. A kiss symbolized a warm and affectionate greeting. The principle, then, is to greet each other warmly.

Below is a fairly representative conservative view on the roles of husbands and wives today.

—CECIL MURPHEY

WHAT IS THE BIBLICAL ROLE OF THE WIFE?

Ephesians 5:22-33 contains the clearest

Biblical definition of marriage roles. In Ephesians 5:22-24 Paul speaks particularly to the wife about her responsibilities to her husband:

You wives must submit to your husband's leadership in the same way you submit to the Lord. For a husband is in charge of his wife in the same way Christ is in charge of his body the church. (He gave his very life to take care of it to be its Savior!) So you wives must willingly obey your husbands in everything, just as the church obeys Christ (TLB).

Genesis 2:18-20 teaches that the woman was created to be a "helpmeet," one who is to be a complement to the man and assist him. In a real sense the wife is a fulfillment of the husband's life.

Ephesians 5:22-24 teaches that the wife is to be "subject" or "submissive" to her husband. How are these two concepts wed together? How can the wife be a "completer" of her husband and also be submissive to him? What does this mean in a practical sense?

First, a wife's submission to her husband is from complete freedom and love, not from compulsion or fear. The Church submits to the Lordship of Christ on a voluntary basis—in response to His love. The wife's motivation in submitting to her husband should be the same.

But what does it mean to submit? It does not mean to "be a doormat." The Scriptures say submit, but they do not say "sell out." The wife is *not* to become a nothing, a pawn in her husband's hand. She retains her distinctiveness as an individual with the right to her own ideas and feelings. She is not a servant. She remains a person with a distinct personality and personal needs. She needs to accept responsibility and make decisions as much as her husband does.

The marriage relationship functions smoothly when the Biblical guidelines are followed. Traffic laws enable a driver to reach his destination with the least possible chance of accident or injury. Biblical guidelines help a couple reach their destination of a happy, growing relationship. One of these guidelines is for the wife to submit to her husband as the leader in their relationship. She submits to her husband not because he demands it but because Christ directs her to in His Word. Lack of submission to her husband is as much a spiritual problem as it is a marital problem!

The wife encourages and strengthens her husband's masculine leadership role and *never* tries to destroy, usurp, weaken or eliminate it. A wife is to respect her husband and affirm his leadership.

Dwight Small suggests that "each is an active participant in building the relationship. . . . Precluded forever is any assumption of superiority-inferiority." He (Paul) affirms the principle of "personal interdependency in marriage". . . .

WHAT ABOUT THE HUSBAND'S ROLE?

In Ephesians 5:25–32 Paul deals specifically with the husband's responsibilities:

And you husbands, show the same kind of love to your wives as Christ showed to the church when he died for her, to make her holy and clean, washed by baptism and God's Word; so that he could give her to himself as a glorious church without a single spot or wrinkle or any other blemish, being holy and without a single fault. That is how husbands should treat their wives, loving them as parts of themselves. For since a man and his wife are now one, a man is really doing himself a favor and loving himself when he loves his wife! No one hates his own body but lovingly cares for it, just as Christ cares for his body the church, of which we are parts.

(That the husband and wife are one body is proved by the Scripture which says, "A

man must leave his father and mother when he marries, so that he can be perfectly joined to his wife, and the two shall be one.") *I know this is hard to understand, but it is an illustration of the way we are parts of the body of Christ* (TLB).

In Ephesians 5:23 Paul declares that the husband is the head of his wife. Unfortunately, too many men only read that much of the Scripture and fail to read the rest of the verse—"as Christ is the Head of the church." Authority is given to the man, but Paul did not mean that husbands should be bosses over their wives. Being the head does not mean being the victor in a struggle. The husband sets the pace by being a leader. The authority is there but he is always answerable to God for his use of it.

As the husband submits to Christ, his authority is transformed by Christ into sacrificial care. The basic truth of this passage is *not* control and domination, but sacrificial love for the wife. The husband is nowhere given the prerogative to rule with a rod of iron. He may *not* impose his own selfish will upon his wife and overshadow her feelings. He is not to demand leadership. The Scripture does not emphasize that Jesus Christ dominates or dictates to the Church. Christ gave Himself for the Church. He takes the initiative to love and serve the Church; *this is the pattern that husbands are to follow in caring for their wives.* When a husband does not do this, he has a spiritual problem (disobedience to the Word) as well as a marital problem.

A loving husband is willing to give all that is required to fulfill the life of his wife. His love is ready to make any sacrifice for her good. The man's first responsibility is to his wife. His love for her enables him to give himself to her.

His love is also a purifying love. The husband never asks his wife to do something which would degrade or harm her. His caring love for his wife is compared to his love for his own body. A man certainly cares for and nourishes his own body. A loving husband does not try to extract service from his wife nor does he make sure that his own physical comfort is assured; he does not love her for the sake of convenience. He does not regard his wife as a kind of permanent servant who simply cooks, washes and trains the children. Rather, the loving husband sees his wife as a person whom he is to cherish and strengthen. A caring love is a serving love. A husband's love is to be patterned after the caring love of Christ.

WHERE DO WE GO FROM HERE?

As you study Ephesians 5:22–33 you should remember to apply these truths in a *very personal and specific way.* Do not concern yourself with your partner's role. Concentrate on your *own responsibility* in your marriage, according to what God's Word teaches. We all like to apply the Scriptures to "someone else." Applying it personally often gets too close to home. And in Ephesians 5 Paul is "close to home," indeed.

For example, some wives react to Paul's teaching in Ephesians by saying, "I will submit to my husband if he does his part and loves me the way I want to be loved."

But in Ephesians 5:21–24 Paul doesn't say that. Paul says to wives, in so many words, "Forget what the man is to do and concern yourself with your own responsibility. Don't base your attitudes and actions on the idea that if your husband does one thing you will do another. Your attitudes and actions are to be the result of your commitment and obedience to Christ, who should be at the center of your marriage."

The same thing is true for husbands. Some men take Paul's teaching and deduce that,

"I'm boss in my house. My wife has to obey me. Scripture is on my side."

But notice in Ephesians 5:22–33 Paul does not emphasize the husband's *authority* over his wife. Instead Paul focuses on the husband's *responsibility* to have a self-giving love for his wife. A master illustrator, Paul reminds the husband that he loves his own body; does he love his wife as much? Christ loved His "body," the Church. He set the example that the husband is to follow.

As the husband, you do not demand obedience. You do not order your wife to respect your authority. You do not say, "You be submissive and obedient and *then* I will love you as Scripture tells me to." Instead, you focus on your responsibility to give love. You *give your wife the freedom to decide to submit to you.* Submission, according to Paul, is her responsibility, not yours. And, of course, as she submits, she returns your love freely and joyfully, *because she knows she is loved.*

In Ephesians 5:33 Paul puts his teaching into one capsule statement:

So again I say, a man must love his wife as a part of himself; and the wife must see to it that she deeply respects her husband—obeying, praising and honoring him (TLB). Husband or wife, here is the blueprint for a truly happy marriage. Meet your responsibility and give your mate the freedom to meet his or hers. Then you will build a marriage in which both partners are free to communicate openly and honestly. With good communication, there will be no leadership gap. As husband and wife fulfill their respective Biblical roles, love and submission intertwine. The result is an atmosphere of trust and security where both partners grow and mature as God intends.

—From H. Norman Wright, *Communication: Key to Your Marriage.* Ventura, Calif.: Regal, 1974.

A further modification, again from a conservative viewpoint, is presented below:

A CIRCLE OF LOVE, NOT A CHAIN OF COMMAND

If we men have come to the conclusion that God in His word has given us some sort of authority guide that makes us the last word in all family decisions, then we need to face again what this passage says about how we love our wives. When we do, we will see that our homes would be better described as a circle of love than as a chain of command. I have a problem with the image of a home where the husband is a hammer, the wife is the chisel, and the children are diamonds. You're supposed to be hitting your wife over the head, and that makes changes come about in the lives of the children. That's not the circle-of-love family that I see described in the New Testament. . . .

All of us must reexamine the atmosphere in our homes. Is our relationship with one another based on *roles that we are fulfilling,* or is our relationship with each other based on *love that we are expressing?*

—From H. Norman Wright and Rex Johnson, *Characteristics of a Caring Home.* Ventura, Calif.: Vision House, 1978.

LIBERAL STANCE

The most liberal stance among evangelicals bases its primary position on Galatians 3:28 where the apostle Paul states that in Christ there is no "male or female." This interpretation means the *principle* of New Testament theology finds itself in those words. The other instances are answers by the apostle to troubled churches about specific problems and issues. This position says that true Christianity transcends male-female roles in marriage.

Leadership depends upon individual gifts from God, such as: the wife may be a better administrator and handler of money, the husband may be a better cook. They appeal to passages such as Romans 12:4–8; 1 Corinthians 12–14; 1 Peter 4:10–11.

They buttress their position by pointing out that neither Jesus nor Paul spoke against slavery, yet no one would condone it today. Instead, Paul gave instructions on how slaves and masters were to regard each other. That is, he spoke with divine authority about a particular situation which prevailed in a specific place and time in history.

Whatever view Christians take of the husband-wife relationship, certain things seem clear.

1. *Every home needs leadership.* Whether this is done with the husband as absolute head or through mutual decision making, the family still needs a head. A head assumes leadership, responsibility, and accountability.

2. For harmony and mutual growth, *a good relationship needs mutual dependence.* The rubric over the entire passage of Ephesians 5:21–33 begins, "Be subject to one another out of reverence for Christ" (v. 21 RSV). A truly Christian marriage means two people depend upon and support each other.

3. *There are clearly defined roles within marriage.* Husbands impregnate. Wives conceive. Women give birth. Generally, husbands are larger and physically stronger and can do tasks that require strength.

4. *Each is an individual in the eyes of God.* Both must answer to God for their own salvation, their own faithfulness, and their own growth.

5. *The principle of love binds them together* when a husband and wife are in right relationship to each other. I use *love (agape)* in its biblical sense of caring and acting on behalf of another, and not purely as an emotion.

6. *Both are created in the image of God.* "So God created man in his own image, and in the image of God he created him; male and female he created them" (Genesis 1:27 RSV).

—CECIL MURPHEY

COMMUNICATION FOR HARMONY AND GROWTH

Levels of Communication

Someone has aptly distinguished five levels of communication on which persons can relate to one another. Perhaps it will help our understanding of these levels to visualize a person locked inside of a prison. It is the human being, urged by an inner insistence to go out to others and yet afraid to do so. The five levels of communication, which will be described a little later, represent five degrees of willingness to go outside of himself, to communicate himself to others. . . .

Most of us make only a weak response to the invitation of encounter with others and our world because we feel uncomfortable in exposing our nakedness as persons. Some of us are willing only to pretend this exodus, while others somehow find the courage to go all the way out to freedom. There are various stages in between. These stages are described below, under the headings of the five levels of communication. The fifth level, to be considered first, represents the least willingness to communicate ourselves to others. The successive, descending levels indicate greater and greater success in the adventure.

Level Five: Cliche Conversation. This level represents the weakest response to the human dilemma and the lowest level of self-communication. In fact, there is no communication here at all, unless by accident. On this level, we talk in cliches, such as: "How are you? . . . How is your family? . . . Where

107

have you been?" We say things like: "I like your dress very much." "I hope we can get together again real soon." "It's really good to see you." In fact, we really mean almost nothing of what we are asking or saying. If the other party were to begin answering our question, "How are you?" in detail, we would be astounded. Usually and fortunately the other party senses the superficiality and conventionality of our concern and question, and obliges by simply giving the standard answer, "Just fine, thank you."

This is the conversation, the noncommunication, of the cocktail party, the club meeting, the neighborhood laundromat, etc. There is no sharing of persons at all. Everyone remains safely in the isolation of his pretense, sham, sophistication. The whole group seems to gather to be lonely together. . . .

Level Four: Reporting the facts about others. On this fourth level, we do not step very far outside the prison of our loneliness into real communication because we expose almost nothing of ourselves. We remain contented to tell others what so-and-so has said or done. We offer no personal, self-revelatory commentary on these facts, but simply report them. Just as most of us, at times, hide behind cliches, so we also seek shelter in gossip items, conversation pieces, and little narrations about others. We give nothing of ourselves and invite nothing from others in return.

Level Three: My Ideas and Judgments. On this level, there is some communication of my person. I am willing to take this step out of my solitary confinement. I will take the risk of telling you some of my ideas and reveal some of my judgments and decisions. My communication usually remains under a strict censorship, however. As I communicate my ideas, etc., I will be watching you carefully. I want to test the temperature of the water before I leap in. I want to be sure

that you will accept me with my ideas, judgments, and decisions. If you raise your eyebrow or narrow your eyes, if you yawn or look at your watch, I will probably retreat to safer ground. I will run for the cover of silence, or change the subject of conversation, or worse, I will start to say things I suspect that you want me to say. I will try to be what pleases you.

Someday, perhaps, when I develop the courage and the intensity of desire to grow as a person, I will spill all of the contents of my mind and heart before you. It will be my moment of truth. It may even be that I have already done so, but still you can know only a little about my person, unless I am willing to advance to the next depth-level of self-communication.

Level Two: My Feelings (Emotions). "Gut Level." It might not occur to many of us that, once we have revealed our ideas, judgments, and decisions, there is really much more of our persons to share. Actually, the things that most clearly differentiate and individuate me from others, that make the communication of my person a unique knowledge, are my *feelings* or *emotions.*

If I really want you to know who I am, I must tell you about my stomach (gut-level) as well as my head. My ideas, judgments, and decisions are quite conventional. If I am a Republican or Democrat by persuasion, I have a lot of company. If I am for or against space exploration, there will be others who will support me in my conviction. But the *feelings* that lie under my ideas, judgments and convictions are uniquely mine. No one supports a political party, or has a religious conviction, or is committed to a cause with my exact feelings of fervor or apathy. No one experiences my precise sense of frustration, labors under my fears, feels my passions. Nobody opposes war with my particular indignation or supports patriotism with my unique sense of loyalty.

It is these feelings, on this level of communication, which I must share with you, if I am to tell you who I really am. To illustrate this, I would like to put in the left hand column a judgment, and in the right hand column some of the possible emotional reactions to this judgment. If I tell you only the contents of my mind, I will be withholding a great deal about myself, especially in those areas where I am uniquely personal, most individual, most deeply myself.

Judgment	Some possible emotional reactions
I think that you are intelligent.	. . . and I am jealous.
	. . . and I feel frustrated.
	. . . and I feel proud to be your friend.
	. . . and it makes me ill at ease with you.
	. . . and I feel suspicious of you.
	. . . and I feel inferior to you.
	. . . and I feel impelled to imitate you.
	. . . and I feel like running away from you.
	. . . and I feel the desire to humiliate you.

Most of us feel that others will not tolerate such emotional honesty in communication. We would rather defend our dishonesty on the grounds that it might hurt others, and, having rationalized our phoniness into nobility, we settle for superficial relationships. This occurs not only in the case of casual acquaintances, but even with members of our own families; it destroys authentic communion within marriages. Consequently, we ourselves do not grow, nor do we help anyone else to grow. Meanwhile we have to live with repressed emotions—a dangerous and self-destructive path to follow. Any relationship, which is to have the nature of true personal encounter, must be based on this honest, open, gut-level communication. The alternative is to remain in my prison, to endure inch-by-inch death as a person.

Level One: Peak Communication. All deep and authentic friendships, and especially the union of those who are married, must be based on absolute openness and honesty. At times, gut-level communication will be most difficult, but it is at these precise times that it is most necessary. Among close friends or between partners in marriage there will come from time to time a complete emotional and personal communion.

In our human condition this can never be a permanent experience. There should and will be, however, moments when encounter attains perfect communication. At these times the two persons will feel an almost perfect and mutual empathy. I know that my own reactions are shared completely by my friend; my happiness or my grief is perfectly reduplicated in him. We are like two musical instruments playing exactly the same note, filled with a giving forth precisely the same sound. This is what is meant by level one, peak communication.

—From John Powell, S.J., *Why Am I Afraid to Tell You Who I Am?* Allen, Tex.: Argus, © 1969.

Goals for Communication

1. *We will aim to be "best friends."* Since friendship is built on time spent together we will have no less than one good visit daily with each other. We will arrange

our schedule for this and keep it high on the docket of each day's business.

2. *At least once each week we will go out together.* A dinner, lunch, or any occasion to read each other's souls is time well spent. We will not let the children, or company, or the budget, or a committee meeting, or the tyranny of "the musts" and "the shoulds" crowd out the time for each other.

3. *We make it a goal to be honest all the way.* Since this requires self-honesty first we will spend some time in healthy self-analysis. By reading, studying, and discussion we will seek to understand how our personal histories are affecting our marriage.

4. *As an ideal, forty-eight hours will be our hiding limit.* But since absolute honesty cannot always meet a deadline we agree to this—if we are not yet able to shape our feelings in words, we will keep trying. We will admit that we are struggling inside and ask for continued patience.

5. *We will aim for total mercy and forgiveness.* We may question, but we will not condemn. We will seek a spirit between us where confession is heard with tenderness. We will be thankful for a place where we can face what we are.

6. *We will respect each other's privacy.* We will not crowd or jam the works by over inquisitiveness. Aware that what we hide may be damaging, we nevertheless extend each other the amazing courtesy of inner destruction. Because self-revelation must come from the inside we will not push.

7. *We will remember that mystery is a blessing.* Because it takes a lifetime to close all the gaps in the most perfect relationship we will be gentle. We will love to the fullest what is given today and expectantly wait for tomorrow.

It will be obvious why we call these goals. After that first leap forward, some of the road to heaven is bound to be slow going. To let someone into your heart can be plain awful. Sometimes it is scary. It brings up things we didn't know we had, and one of these is resistance. This is the psychological term for slamming the door, running away fast, and saying "Let's forget the whole business."

This is why so few people have what it takes to make it all the way through to genuine transparency. But you can, and if you do keep it moving with a loving hand you will one day reach those high levels reserved for brave souls who have been to the depths together.

I have known more than a dozen thrilling old couples who reached their fiftieth anniversary and three who went as far as their sixtieth. They represented a wide range of income, employment, status, and influence. But they had one thing in common. Whether it was the weather-beaten farmer in Nebraska or the smooth-faced banker in one of our largest cities; the schoolhouse janitor in a crossroads' town or the president of a great university, whoever he was, he and this woman beside him had learned how to share themselves with each other in total companionship.

That is a great word—companionship. It takes on added significance as the years pass. Sexual desires might fade and the need for excitement diminish. Money worries may subside and so could your other anxieties. But there is one thing that you must be sure is continually on the increase. This is the gradual opening of two hearts to welcome each other at the core of their beings. The surfacing of the real you is the secret to long life, inner health, and total communion.

—From Charlie W. Shedd, *Letters to Philip.* New York: Doubleday, 1968.

Balance

In a marriage, each partner tries to maintain behavioral systems which provide himself with maximum satisfaction. Sometimes the satisfaction assumes neurotic dimensions, such as finding pleasure in illness because it can be used as a weapon against the spouse. When both partners are in a state of satisfaction, there is present an emotional and psychic balance, a homeostasis. That is what they strive for. But human behavior changes frequently and radically, and every action and mood of one spouse begets a reaction from the other. Therefore, to remain in balance, the marriage system always is in a state of flux. The forces in it move this way and then that way, go up and down to various levels, increase and decrease in intensity. The systems concept makes this situation clear and can be used to describe the process mathematically.

When people marry, the first important action which takes place is the attempt of each spouse to determine the nature of the relationship; that is, each wants the system to be satisfying to himself, and would prefer to achieve this end without changing his already established behavioral pattern. Each wants the other partner to make the accommodations. Usually a spouse approves of his own ways of behaving, his own mannerisms, habits, and performances, and finds fault with those of the other. For this reason almost all marriages—at least at first—have friction. And to reduce this friction is difficult, because of "behavioral blindness." The individuals contribute not only their *conscious* behavioral tendencies, tastes, and so on to the joint system, but also the greater part of their total personality—the part about which they know nothing, which is motivated *unconsciously*. Nevertheless, each spouse attempts to shape the relationship, to influence how the joint system will operate, and determine the limits of acceptable behavior. Once a system is established, it tends to remain in homeostasis.

Here is an example of the operation of balance, or homeostasis, in a marital system. Assume that through their interaction up to this time, a newly married man and woman, on their honeymoon, have established an unspoken "rule" that each is to fill the other's needs without being asked. Mary prepares John's favorite meals, compliments him, straightens his clothes; and John buys small gifts for Mary, compliments her cooking, makes all travel arrangements, and so forth. In this interaction neither has to ask the other to fulfill his role according to their mutual expectations.

Now suppose that on the fifth day of the honeymoon, Mary (having already received a number of small gifts from John without asking for them) sees a ring which she would like to own and asks John if he will buy it for her. At this point, one unspoken rule of their relationship has been broken. *Mary has asked for a gift.* The system is temporarily *out of balance.* Now any number of things can happen, depending on John's reaction to Mary's rule breaking.

John may comply cheerfully with Mary's request; in this case the system is in balance again, but a new rule has been established: Mary has the "right" to make requests of John.

But the action may go in another direction. John may agree to purchase the ring, but make it clear by his grumbling that he is not happy about the new turn of events. In this case, balance is reestablished on the basis of a rule which implies that Mary may ask for things, but must pay the price for this privilege by tolerating John's grumbling.

Reactions belonging to a third category are provoked if John refuses to purchase the ring. Now the establishment of homeostasis becomes dependent upon *Mary's* reaction to

John's reaction to her original action. Mary may choose passively to let John define the nature of the relationship, or she may choose to fight.

If Mary accepts John's refusal cheerfully ("You're right, dear, I shouldn't have asked"), the original system is reestablished and the rule of not asking remains in force. If Mary accepts his refusal but is quietly unhappy about it, balance is reestablished, but Mary is learning a new kind of behavior necessary to keep the system operating: she is learning to withdraw in order to avoid rocking the boat. John is learning that the price of his refusal is to be temporarily isolated by Mary's silence. In this case, as in the case of John's grumbling, no real agreement on the ring issue has been reached, but they have temporarily agreed to accept the disagreement without pressing it. The system is in balance again, but the balance is exceedingly precarious.

Another possible reaction of Mary's may lead to what is called a runaway. Suppose Mary refuses to accept John's refusal to buy the ring. She may express anger, stubborn insistence, hurt, at his refusal, casting the responsibility back on John to accept her new definition of the relationship or accept her angry behavior, each of which implies a new rule. She may say something like, "Why can't I have the ring? I made your favorite dinner last night and didn't even ask to go out. You can certainly do this one small thing for me." John may reconsider and agree to buy the ring, thereby reestablishing the balance with a new rule: Mary can ask for what she wants and she will get it. But John may become angered by her anger and lack of appreciation for what he's done for her under the old system (without being asked). He may accuse her of being "a typical woman," "unreasonable," "selfish." If the argument continues to escalate in this fashion, the situation is called a runaway; the balance can be reestablished only when some agreement is reached on a new rule or

rules for the relationship. Balance in a system lasts only until a new challenge to the system is presented. If no agreement is reached and the escalation continues until it is completely out of hand, the runaway eventually ends in divorce, desertion, murder, or suicide—in the complete breakup of the system or relationship.

. . . .

Marriage is an interlocking, self-contained system. The behavior and the attitudes of one partner *always* stimulate some sort of reaction from the other. A slight half-smile, a lifted eyebrow, a quick wrinkling of the forehead, will beget *some* response, though not necessarily a verbal one. Even silence can be a forceful message. Neither spouse may be aware of the action and reaction, for these usually originate at the unconscious level. Much of the interaction between the two consists of what might be considered behavioral reflexes, manifested without conscious knowledge.

In the course of time, as partners experience recurring patterns of behavior in their relationship, certain predictable successions of events are established. The wife's left eyelid may quiver almost imperceptibly when the husband has badgered her too much about how boring her parents are. After this sequence has been repeated a few times, they both "know" that if husband continues nagging, the wife will lose her temper and may walk out. At this point, the husband may say, "Let me make you some coffee," to indicate that he is sorry and will change the subject, yet neither party is consciously aware of the nature of their exchange. In this situation they are an error-activated system; they are behaving exactly like the thermostat on a furnace—when it becomes too cold, on goes the heat; when it becomes too warm, it shuts off. The spouses govern each other's behavior to maintain the expected or usual emotional temperature for their relationship.

After several years, this type of behavior

pattern between two people appears to the skilled observer as constant and predictable—exactly as if it had been consciously planned and both parties were aware of it. This reciprocal behavior is to be found wherever two people have a close relationship. They may be business partners, a father and son, two homosexuals living together, two women working as nurses on the same ward, and so forth. Marriage has been studied more than other relationships and we are apt to forget it has much in common with all relationships.

We call this system of behavioral responses the *quid pro quo*. *Quid pro quo* literally means "something for something." In the marriage process, it means that if you do so-and-so, then I automatically will respond with such-and-such. It might be called "tit for tat," or "point and counterpoint," or "reciprocal behavior," but some of these names imply nasty or opprobrious responses, whereas by *quid pro quo* we imply shared, or exchanged, behavior—much of it unconscious.

Finally, if the nature of the *quid pro quo*'s is such that it seriously limits the behavior, creativity, or growth of one or both spouses, then there is a premature freezing, or jelling, of the marriage which probably will result in one or the other spouse's breaking away; or both will grow old together stuck in an emotional morass, which usually is characterized by a rigid, unchanging, negative relationship.

All of these examples demonstrate that acceptable *quid pro quo*'s can only be determined over a significant time span. *Quid pro quo*'s made within narrow temporal limits quickly become dysfunctional because they do not allow for the ever-present factor of change. Inflexible, nonutilitarian rules for the *quid pro quo* are bound to become destructive because people and marriages change in the course of time. Spouses may (and should) shift their *quid pro quo*'s as the marriage grows older, even if doing so is temporarily upsetting, instead of allowing fear of change to dominate the relationship and keep them trapped in their fixed patterns.

When the *quid pro quo* ground rules are violated by either party, trouble begins. Such violations may occur when an unexpected outside influence pressures the marriage, or when there is a change in the behavior or expectations of one of the partners. The predictable behavior pattern is no longer predictable. Confusion and discord unbalance the partnership.

If one of the spouses violates the ground rules, the other one, without knowing why, feels that he has been betrayed. He now (often unconsciously) attempts to create a new *quid pro quo* which will protect his interest. For example, if a husband comes home from a business trip and finds that his wife, without consulting him, has invited her mother to live with them for two months, and that the mother is occupying his new study, he feels betrayed. The study is *his,* and no one in the family was supposed even to enter it. A *quid pro quo* ground rule has been broken by the wife. The way the husband responds here will depend on the nature of their relationship. He may react by insisting that the newly hired maid be fired. He may be surly and rude to his wife's mother (although he agreed a long time ago to be always courteous to her even though he doesn't like her). He may start complaining about how bad business is and insist on unreasonable cuts in the household budget. He may start nagging his wife, saying that his boss is angry because he hasn't properly completed some work which he brought home. Thus he implies that he is failing at his job because his mother-in-law is in his study, and that his wife is to blame.

Diplomats recognize that the *quid pro quo* process also applies to relations between nations, as seen in the institutionalized behavioral limitation (a conscious *quid pro quo*) called protocol. Protocol may seem old-fashioned, ridiculous, or even humorous to someone outside of the diplomatic world, but it is very useful, enabling nations to observe a lawful, predictable system of behavior. Thus, as is well known in diplomatic circles, a violation of protocol conveys a significant message.

If the spouses' verbal and nonverbal behavior did not occur redundantly, forming a pattern, each individual would have to learn about the other individual (or some aspect of him) all over again every time they met. Someone who is "highly unpredictable" may be interesting for brief periods of time, but usually is not the sort of person one would choose for a spouse. Unpredictable individuals are rare in our society. People noted for their erratic behavior (such as a few famous movie actors) actually are predictably unpredictable, and therefore the label is a misnomer. Nevertheless, their notorious multiple marriages testify to the fact that such people are hard to live with.

The occurrence of the *quid pro quo* action-reaction pattern is inevitable. In these exchanges the man and woman negotiate their total conjoint behavior, and at the same time each becomes acquainted with the other's total personality. This is why a long and intimate courtship is desirable. The short or "good time" courtship, confined to wooing activities in which each attempts to appear as attractive as possible to the other, exhibits only a small percentage of the behavioral range of each. It is a common experience for someone to be shocked after marriage by the discovery that he has married a "stranger."

—From William J. Lederer and Don D. Jackson, *The Mirages of Marriage.* New York: Norton, 1968.

Commitment

Commitment must issue in action. Until something is done, commitment is not complete. Faith becomes saving only with confession and obedience; love becomes marriage only with the exchange of vows and life lived together.

Moving life in the direction of the choice is the essence of commitment. The archetype is faithful Abraham: "By faith Abraham obeyed ... sojourned ... offered" (*see* Hebrews 11:8, 9, 17). It is on the basis of faith that choice becomes commitment; by faith, decision is translated into action (see figure on p. 115).

Faith has become a fuzzy concept. It is commonly confused with a warm and possibly worshipful feeling. But biblical faith is not a feeling. It is an activity. It is a confidence that allows one to take the risk of commitment: not an unfounded confidence, it should be pointed out. For while faith is, at times, "a leap in the dark"—it is not a leap into darkness without light, nor is it essentially irrational. It is based on a reasonable assurance that what we hope for may be.

The moment of the actual exercise of faith, or making of a commitment, is a moment of intense conflict. The person who is considering the step is most aware of an overwhelming sense of risk. "If I do this, what about the other alternative that I am hereby rejecting?"

That is what the moment of commitment always feels like: the end of all that I hold dear, and the hope that it is not. The moment of commitment is always a moment when the risks appear huge. This awareness of risk may last for many months, as described by Saint Augustine in his *Confessions.* The sense of risk begins to subside at the moment at which commitment is made—never before. . . .

Every commitment is a sort of gamble. But for the person experiencing the acute sense of risk that comes at the moment of making a decisive commitment, there is a dual risk: Not only the risk of exercising faith and making a commitment, but the equally acute risk of *not* exercising faith and making a commitment. It is what Sheldon Van-

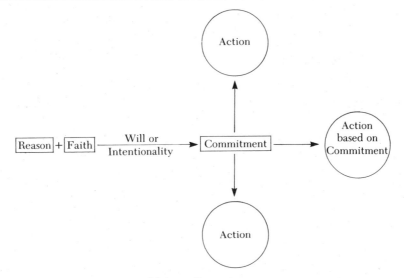

Making Commitment

auken describes so well as the "gap behind"—the sense that one cannot draw back from the risk that is to be taken, except at even greater risk. The human adult must constantly choose to take risks, for there is no risk-free living that is worthwhile.

Commitment is not irrational. It would be foolish to trust a foothold you have not properly tested, or to marry a person you have not adequately assessed, or to trust a message you have not investigated. But commitment requires more than reason. It requires the act of faith: that shifting of weight, that trusting of oneself. And then, as commitment is made —and the rope does hold on its mountain hook—the sense of risk fades and hope grows.

—From Maxine Hancock, *The Forever Principle.* Old Tappan, N.J.: Revell, 1980.

Compliments

Every couple in marriage should be growing toward personal betterment on both sides, or their union is stuck on dead center. We'll be seeing more of this when we discuss the art of disagreement and telling the truth in love. But right here it's enough to remember that varnish always melts under heat. You can only tell him he isn't wonderful where he isn't if you have told him he is wonderful where he is.

You will also be wise to *watch for signs that you aren't giving him adequate nourishment for his ego.* Most husbands now and then overpraise themselves. When yours does this too much, it may mean that he needs more of your praise. Watch for it also when you are with others. If he pushes the crowd away from the footlights and demands top billing for himself, this may be your fault. Come out of the balcony and move to the front row.

Another indicator is oversensitivity. Whenever he is ultradefensive of his own prestige, when his happiness depends entirely on the nod of a head outside your walls, you're not slipping—you've slipped.

Comes now another cue for the clever wife. *Every man has certain areas where he's particularly pleased if his woman applauds.* This can be a secret little game you play between you. If you play it well, he may grow beyond it until he doesn't need it any more. But it will be important at the outset because most every man is not as good as he would like to be at some points. Your mother was an ace at this in our early days together. As you know, I played football, baseball, basketball, and nearly every game with a ball in it. Because I was big, I got by rather well at some of these. But the truth is that I was lazy.

As I look back over the gridirons and diamonds and courts where I played, I was never as good as I would like to have been. But there *was* one spot where I was a walloping success. (Well, anyway, for a time I was!) This was in wrestling. As you know, I still hold a title back in my home state. So, what if it is the record for being thrown quicker than anyone else in the heavyweight finals? I loved wrestling, and I was right there in the thick of it. Then I met my match, and Goliath went down with a resounding thud.

Yet, you'd never have known all this from your mother. She guarded my secret until I was grown up enough to tell it myself. She skillfully cast my praises about. Then, as your husband will, her husband made it over the hump. He decided to come clean. Yours, too, will have these places of pride and places of shame. You will do well to learn them and play to the gallery. It may take time, but, as the years are sure to pass anyway, you can both have fun with this diversion. Wise wives are like that.

But having rid ourselves of this bit of chicanery, let's transfer the thought to the thing which counts most. When love is done playing, when it reaches its best, *sincerity is an absolute must for the phrases of praise.*

Some atomizerlike women go giddily spraying their vapors all over the place. Yet, though men may appear to enjoy it, most males want more than chattery flattery from the women they love. (I like this apt phrase making the rounds of our high school gang these days: "Take the roof off the greenhouse, mother! The corn is getting taller!") So be sure your words have the feel of the real. He needs the authentic from you.

—From Charlie W. Shedd, *Letters to Karen.* Nashville: Abingdon, 1965.

Courtesy

Courtesy gives an agreeable tone to the home and makes cooperation pleasant. If people are courteous to friends and strangers, is there any less reason for being so to those who are closest? Not formality, of course, but considerateness in word and action. Countess Clarita de Forceville has well said, "If love is the foundation of happy marriage good manners are the walls and roof." To use at home words or tones that would be considered uncivil elsewhere is to strike at the foundations.

Husbands and wives are known by the manners they use. This is true not only out in the world but also at home. It is a mark of a gentleman for the husband to show his wife as much courtesy as he could show to any woman. She, of course, will want always to show the high quality he desires in her.

The courteous husband will let his wife go through doorways first, will help her with her rubbers and coat, will pull out her chair, perhaps, and carry her book or package when they are together on the street. Both at home and in company the wife will want to make it evident that she appreciates his attention, just as she would if they were not yet married. Uniting two lives in courtesy is a help in keeping them united in love.

It is a part of courtesy to be more aware of virtues than of faults. Some persons wear blinders for virtues and use a microscope for faults. Criticisms must be made at times, but they should be made in private and with utmost of consideration for the other as a person. Marriage is more than friendship, but certainly it cannot thrive if it is less. It is a friendship of the most intense and satisfying sort, and like other friendships it needs the touches of exquisite care.

—From Leland Foster Wood, *Harmony in Marriage.* Old Tappan, N.J.: Revell, 1979.

Creativity

Ask me what's so special about two poached eggs on dry toast with bacon, and I'll tell you. They are giving my wife and me time to polish our friendship. Every morning at 7:00 A.M., we have breakfast at Sammy's Restaurant and talk and laugh and share what we're expecting from our day.

We stole breakfast time out of our morning sleep. The first fifteen minutes after the alarm rings are awful, but life gets better from then on. Yes, I need that sleep, but I need the talk time with my wife more. A good marriage may be built on yawns and coffee. Who cares, as long as it's being built.

Our clue that we needed talk time came as we listened to each other's phone conversations. I'd hang up after telling my friend Kent all about the artist I had lunch with and Marlene would say, "I didn't know all that." I had the same unsettling left-out feeling as I listened to her talk on the phone with Isabel. Marlene told her all about her feelings when she was called to jury duty, what the lawyers had said, why she was dismissed.

We were talking with friends about the incidents and feelings of our lives, but our best friend was getting missed as we rushed to rake the leaves, prepare the meals, and wash the spots off the bathroom mirror. It's easier to share on the phone. I say something. Then I stop and wait for my friend to say something. We fill in the holes with life. But there were no holes in my wife's and my few hours together. We had to make them.

Enter creativity!

I don't think there's another word that is more important to the life of a marriage. To me, it's the stuff that keeps our relationship growing. It's the sparkle that reminds me from time to time how very nice it is to be securely, happily married. It's the reminder that marriage is ordained by our Creator, and therefore must carry the mark of creativity on it.

When we were dating it was easier to be creative. My wife, Marlene, has said that skinned grapes were her first clue that our dating relationship was going to be special. I didn't have much money, so I invited her to the airport to watch the planes come in and eat a picnic lunch. For lunch I made a fruit salad that included skinned grapes. I stuffed the salad into pineapple halves. I borrowed linen napkins from my mother, and served my creations at the end of one of O'Hare's terminals. Chicago's airport is not only the busiest airport in the world; that night it was also one of the most romantic.

But after we were married, it seemed stupid to skin grapes for her salads. Who's got the time or energy?

And there's the problem and the first principle of adding creativity to your marriage:

1. *Prioritize your time, adding an hour here and there for the creative.* No couple has the luxury of creative time built into their relationship. But children and house and jobs excluded, you'd better work on adding that time if you want the marriage to last.

Decide together where that time will come from. For a while our decision was to make Sunday night our time. Because of my Saturday job and my week's schedule, that was the only possible time block. That's right—we cut out Sunday night church. We needed those hours for us, and for the time we did this, we felt God was pleased. We were actively working out who we were as a couple and what we needed from each other.

Now, on Sunday nights we go to a Bible study. We've moved into another phase of our lives. Those morning breakfasts provide the time together that Sunday night used to. Breakfast is the right choice for us now.

2. *Set aside some money.* Breakfast costs us $1.98 each and every day. It's the price we pay for not being able to get away from the demands of home when we are at home. It's the best money we've ever spent. Rose,

117

our morning waitress, has gotten to know us. She pours our coffee as we walk in the door or yells from wherever she is, "Want the regular?" She's making it possible for us to reorder our busy schedules and fit in that all important part—us. We tip her well.

But creativity only takes some money—not a lot of money. There are things that cost nothing and make us feel happy about our marriage and relationship. My wife enjoys it when I wash her hair. She's perfectly capable of doing it herself, of course, but it's a nice five minutes that say I care.

Perhaps as you're thinking of adding creative time to your life, you will want to add them two at a time. One might cost something and the other should be totally free, just requiring that extra push to do something together.

3. *Talk about what you're doing with your friends.* "We've decided that we're going to go to a play once every season," or "We're saving quarters this fall so that we can take one of those weekend holidays in January that we see advertised in the paper."

Talking about your creative ideas does two things. Most important, it helps you continue with your good intentions. It's embarrassing to tell everyone you're saving quarters and have them check back in three months only to find out that you banked the money and are collecting interest. (My wife tends to do this, and there's nothing wrong with saving, but sometimes it is by far better and more important to use the money on us as a couple.) People will act as your test, checking how well you did and how exciting your growth process was.

The second reason for telling is obvious. Good marriages are hard to find. If you've got an idea that is helping yours become better, it's downright selfish not to share it. Talking about your successes is a great way to share them.

Recently a couple invited us to their home

for the evening just to tell us about a weekend marriage seminar they had participated in. "You'd love it," they told us. "Why don't you do it, too?"

Marlene and I noted their enthusiasm and ever since we've been saying to each other, "Let's do it. Let's go off for a weekend and talk. What do you think we'd learn?" We're jealous, in a wholesome sense, of what our friends experienced. What a wonderful thing they've done for us simply by sharing.

4. *Come up with your ideas.* This is the hard part. So you've got an hour a week that is yours together. What will you do with it? Here are some of my wife's and my ideas. Consider them, reword them to fit your marriage, or better yet, come up with some that are totally original with you.

Idea: Do something slowly. We take walks together and talk. We start out talking about the weather and the bugs and the new additions to yards in our neighborhood. And the longer we walk, the easier it is to talk about the real stuff upon which marriages are built. "You hurt me when you didn't introduce me to your friend." "I think we're spending too much money on us and not enough on world relief." "I wish your voice sounded more excited and alive when I call on business trips. You sometimes sound bored and sleepy." And off we go. The walks toward home are always better than the walks away from home. It takes us a few blocks to get warmed up. If we didn't allow ourselves that time, the warm-up would never take place. People, even people who love each other, can't just blurt out their feelings. They sound silly without the slow warm-up.

Idea: Play games that allow talk. We get a lot discussed as we play Rummy K, our favorite game. It's easier to bring up something difficult when it's surrounded by a happy game time. Our best games are those that allow time for talking. This cuts down on our competitiveness and the importance of the game. The game just guarantees that we'll stay in one place for at least twenty minutes, long enough for the warm-up to take place.

Idea: Read the same books. We don't always discuss them together, but they give us a special world to relate to. For example, we've both been to *Dune*, and we have lived and suffered with Thomas Covenant. Often we'll read at the same time—although not the same books. It's our slow time. We try to read in a place where we can easily talk or touch. "Hey, listen to this. . . ." Just what we choose to share from our books with each other is important.

Idea: Do something dumb. We like weeds, the kind only the most ardent of weed lovers would call wildflowers. Last year we took our buckets and went out to No Man's Land to dig up wildflowers that most people dig out of the yards and burn. We brought them back to our yard and planted them. This year some came up again, and by next year we should have a real bumper crop.

One year Marlene cultivated an enormous thistle. As it flowered, she would cut the purple blossoms and make beautiful, if slightly dangerous, arrangements with them. (A few blossoms got away from her into seed, and she spent most of the summer digging unwanted thistles from our lawn.) Planting wildflowers may be dumb to others—like holding a celebration for the first dandelion of the season or raking a huge pile of leaves so we can jump in them. But it's fun for us. It's something childish and special and very conducive to a happy marriage.

Idea: Date. Just the two of you. Double dates don't count. We can be such social people. I know I've felt guilty for not inviting some of our friends along on Marlene's and my outings. They would enjoy it and there would be no extra money for gas. I stifle the urge.

Date, just the two of you. Write these dates on your calendar. This makes the time as important as time with others. And it assures that when someone calls with an invitation to a party, you can honestly say, "I'm sorry we can't come. Next time, though, we'd love to."

Idea: Take up a sport. We're still trying to get our act together here. I swim and she floats. She plays racquetball, and I freeze when I see the ball coming at me. I enjoy running, and she thinks racing from one spot to the other is silly. She roller skates, and I'm too self-conscious to make a spectacle of myself learning. But couples who have a sport say it has helped them grow together.

. . . .

Idea: And this is the most important idea of all—DO IT! Steal a little time for your creative marriage.

—BY Jack R. Risley

Forgiveness

How many times in a day we have occasion either to resent or to forgive the actions of others against us. We are especially susceptible to this problem with those whose lives touch ours most closely. Emotional health is dependent upon our attitude toward those who offend us. We grow up or wither up, depending upon our ability to forgive others and find ways of reconciliation. By living with an unforgiving spirit, we can destroy ourselves emotionally and spiritually. In our Lord's prayer (Matthew 6:12) we are taught, ". . . forgive us our debts, as we forgive our debtors." Paul admonishes, ". . . be kind to one another, tenderhearted, forgiving one another, as God in Christ forgave you" (Ephesians 4:32 RSV). There it is in a capsule, and best of all it tells us *how*—as God in Christ has forgiven us: freely, unconditionally, in costly extension of love to the undeserving.

Jesus exposed our natural inclination not only to feel resentment, but to respond vindictively toward those who hurt us. When

119

we are offended, our pride recoils only to strike back; this is the very nature of our pride system. Because we let an unforgiving spirit pervade our interpersonal relationships, we find it difficult to accept people as they really are. Surprisingly to many, this often stems from our inability to accept ourselves because we have not really accepted God's perfect forgiveness. To have received forgiveness demands that forgiveness become operative in our relationships with others. But this is resisted by the law of retaliation which roots deeply in our lives. Subtly, we retaliate by withholding forgiveness, depriving another of the healing he needs and the reconciliation we both need. This is a major block to spiritual progress, for *the one thing God cannot forgive* is an unforgiving spirit.

1. *Forgiveness is not the same as tolerance.* Tolerating an evil action is possible where there is moral neutrality—either weakness or insensitivity to the nature of the evil. If it is weakness, then tolerance is a substitute for the moral action the situation demands. It is sometimes expressed by those who shrug their shoulders in the face of an offense and say, "I prefer to forgive and forget," meaning, "I'd just as soon forget it; I'm unwilling to face the cost of true forgiveness." Tolerance of evil is itself an evil.

2. *Forgiveness is not leniency.* It is not merely a soft attitude toward a harsh fact. As Paul Tournier points out, it is morally wrong to cover up an offense with a mantle of charity; this is not God's way. When one says, "I won't hold it against him," he may mean that he himself doesn't want any further anguish over the incident. He may prefer to be relieved of any positive action in the direction of true forgiveness and reconciliation. But his charitable intent solves nothing, is completely unrealistic, and only renders forgiveness more difficult. He is saying that forgiving love is unnecessary, that the prob-

lem doesn't need to be dealt with positively and put away by the action of forgiving love. Leniency doesn't cancel the debt, nor restore the offending one, nor cleanse the heart of the offended person. And strange but true, it does nothing to change the heart of the offender. Leniency is not the Christian solution.

A further sign of weakness is indicated when the offended person does nothing but pray that God will deal with the offender, letting it go at that. God doesn't give us that option, nor is He willing that we be relieved of our responsibility and initiative. We are called to be reconcilers, even as God in Christ has reconciled us to Himself. Forgiveness is a redemptive action which every Christian should experience for himself and learn to show to others. What better school for learning forgiving love than marriage?

3. *Forgiveness is not condescension.* A husband or wife cannot effectively reconcile the other by condescending. Reconciliation makes equals of two persons; if one's response in any way lowers the self-esteem of the other, it is less than forgiving love. True forgiveness will elevate, not depress, the ego of the forgiven one. It will bring a new sense of humility to both. Forgiveness always provides a face-saving dimension and a positive creative value.

4. *Forgiveness does not demand guarantees.* Less than true forgiveness is offered whenever a husband or wife says to the other, "I'll forgive you if you promise never to do that again." That is conditional forgiveness—*a deal!*—but the forgiveness of which the New Testament speaks is never equated with driving a bargain. Christian forgiveness risks the future; *it gives and risks all!*

5. *Forgiveness has nothing to do with justice.* If a person is determined to stand on his rights, he will not forgive—he can't forgive. Neither does he see forgiveness as reason-

able; resentment and retaliation make more sense to him. Justice gives way to mercy. But the forgiveness which Jesus taught and exemplified is love going far beyond reason and justice; it is love healing, reconciling, restoring. Forgiving love is a redemptive action of the heart. It is love allowed to work its miracle in human life, creating a bond between two people stronger than anything human sinfulness might interpose to disrupt and destroy their love and trust. Love is creative power, and can use even an offense as its occasion to create a deeper relationship based on compassionate desire to meet another's need. Forgiving love is the Christian solution to conflict and hurt.

6. *Forgiveness is an empathic, felt event.* We feel genuine forgiveness, whether we're the one forgiving or forgiven. As one who receives forgiveness, we first feel the pain of what it is that must be forgiven. We feel the humiliation of our need for forgiveness, of having to be forgiven by one we've hurt. We also feel the additional anguish we cause the person who must forgive. He struggles over the need in himself to exercise forgiveness. In similar fashion, he who forgives must suffer the sense of our need for forgiveness, must enter into our humiliation and pain as a guilty offender, must share it with us. This is essential to his feeling forgiving love toward us. Empathically, he too is brought low—to the very level of our felt need.

One can't say, "I forgive you, though I don't feel forgiving love toward you," for this is a contradiction. A person doesn't truly forgive unless he *feels* forgiving love. Conversely, one can't say, "I know you forgive me, though I don't feel your forgiving love." If one knows himself to be forgiven, he will experience forgiving love—he will *feel* forgiven. In other words, perhaps there is no deeper experience of empathy between two married persons than that of giving and receiving forgiving love. This epitomizes the

incarnation of our Lord; this was the incarnation as it led to Calvary, and to the sacrifice that made forgiveness possible. Not that the sacrifice caused God to feel forgiving love; forgiving love led to Calvary's sacrifice. His forgiving love was the objective ground of forgiveness, the atoning sacrifice of the Saviour. God felt our need, entered into it, and suffered it in Himself. Thus there was far more than objective redemption on God's part; there was the divine experience of our need—*God's suffering our felt need through sin.*

Isn't this implicit in the Scripture, ". . . he hath made him to be sin for us, who knew no sin. . . ." (2 Corinthians 5:21)? Isn't this what is expressed in Hebrews 4:14, 15 (RSV)? After we read, "Since then we have a great high priest . . . Jesus, the Son of God . . . ," it continues, "For we have not a high priest who is unable to sympathize with our weaknesses, but one who in every respect has been tempted as we are, yet without sinning." The word *sympathize* in the Revised Standard and New English Versions hardly seems adequate to the full sense of the verse. In the Authorized Version it reads, "For we have not a high priest that cannot be touched with the feeling of our infirmities. . . ." Here the sense is more that of *empathy*—feeling our feelings, tempted with our temptations, sharing our suffering. Thus, as God forgave us it was a forgiveness that empathized, feeling our pain and humiliation. He shared our feeling so perfectly as to preclude any possibility of His forgiveness being purely objective. And, similarly, as we receive the reality of His forgiving love, *we feel His feeling of our feeling!*

Forgiveness given and received is mutual participation in a deeply felt event. When both forgiver and forgiven feel the common pain of the forgiving event, then they are drawn together in meaningful reconciliation. They are also bound together in a new joy, a new release, a hilarious liberty of two spirits made one again. Forgiveness cannot be less than this!

—From Dwight Hervey Small, *Your Marriage Is God's Affair.* Old Tappan, N.J.: Revell, 1979.

Friendship

Married couples today expect to be friends. This was not always the case. This expectation marks the transition from the conventional marriage—with its clearer distinctions between woman's role and man's role in marriage—toward the sense of marriage which is more prevalent today. In earlier norms a wife was not considered to be, and often was not, her husband's social equal. She was almost surely younger than he, less educated, with little experience in the world beyond the household. We know that many such conventional marriages were (and are) marked by genuine affection and care. But they lacked the base of mutuality that friendship requires. Some marriages today . . . do not carry the demand of mutuality. But more and more couples approach marriage in the conviction that they are and will continue to be friends.

These expectations of friendship correspond to some of the structural requirements of the contemporary institution of marriage. If the world of my work is a competitive and emotionally hostile environment, if geographic mobility takes me away from my extended family and disturbs my previous network of support, then I am truly fortunate that my spouse is also my friend. Without friendship as a part of our marriage, we might both be without any experience of an adult confidant—a companion who is like me in many significant ways and who can be trusted to share in some important parts of my life.

These hopes for friendship in marriage have, until recently, been most characteristic of middle-class couples. Within some working-class and ethnic groups there has been little expectation that spouses have much in common beyond their intersecting responsibilities as wife-homemaker and husband-provider. Husbands spent most of their free time (as well as work time) with other men, in taverns, social clubs, athletic events. Wives spent their time out of the house with women relatives or other married women in the neighborhood. Often these same-sex groupings provided the support and companionship that were not available or even looked for in the marriage. But in middle-class marriages (and these values are now widely accepted beyond the middle class) there has been much greater expectation that wives and husbands provide these resources of companionship to one another.

The expectation that spouses be friends, then, is an important modern alteration in the structure of marriage. This does not imply that "throughout all history until our day" married couples never were friends. But it does mean that the presence or absence of such friendship did not become a central issue in marriage until quite recently—the last generation or so. And the expectation that spouses shall be friends has contributed much to the contemporary experience of marriage. Liking each other as friends, we find that loving each other is a much richer experience. Sexuality, sensitivity and devotion overlap in a lifestyle of mutual support and challenge. Becoming friends can be a part of our movement beyond romance into the experience of committed love. The range of mutual interests and values that we share can help sustain us through the strains we experience in the family years and bring us to the mature years of our marriage with a sense of enthusiasm for this new time we shall now have together.

But this expectation that we shall be friends can make significant demands on marriage as well. Images of what constitutes friendship in marriage can vary. I may expect our friendship to mean that we will spend as much time as possible together, preferring each other's company to that of all others, as we did when we were dating. For you, our friendship may be less a question of how much time we have together and more a conviction that we are "there" for each other in times of stress or difficulty. You want to be able to count on me for solace and support at these times and you expect me to turn to you when I need this kind of help. The requirements of friendship, then, may be expressed in terms of time and presence or they may be seen as demanding that we like the same things or, especially, that we find in each other our principal source of personal support and growth. But today many married couples, as well as many students of marriage, see this emotional restrictiveness as a hindrance rather than a help to marriage for a lifetime.

That spouses should be friends is not in dispute. What is being questioned is the expectation that partners should be, or can be, each other's only significant adult relationship—each other's *only* friend. Sometimes the expectation of emotional exclusivity is related to concern for sexual or genital exclusivity. It is dangerous to make friends, at least friends of the opposite sex. These friendships will inevitably lead to trouble—an affair, even a divorce. The prevailing assumption here is that women and men are drawn together *only* through sexual attraction and that sexual attraction leads *inevitably* to genital expression. If this be the case, then it is safer to restrict my close contact with the opposite sex to my spouse.

But these assumptions are under question today, chiefly as a result of married people's actual experience of friendship. There are many factors involved in attraction between people of the same or opposite sex. Sexual attraction is part of some, but not all, friendships between people. Sexual attraction sometimes develops toward genital expression but not always and certainly not "inevitably." Within the human experience, sexual expression is much more a matter of choice and preference than it is of instinct or "need." And most extramarital affairs result from, rather than cause, marital troubles.

Friendship, a rich blessing in life, is a benefit to marriage as well. Friends can ease the strain in a marriage that comes from the unrealistic expectations that my spouse should be "all things" to me. In few marriages are the partners so similar that they share all values or interests. The pattern is rather that people marry on the basis of the similarities (and differences) they see between them at that time. Then, over the course of their years together, they learn more about both themselves and each other. They find some earlier "similarities" do not go very deep or are not as important as they once thought. They find other similarities between them which take on greater meaning. And they discover significant areas in their lives where, unexpectedly and sometimes even unhappily, they are very different. Sometimes this discovery will seem somehow unfair. I *need* you to be a certain way, to be interested in certain things that are important to me. My insistence that you be what I need (more than who you are) is likely to be intense if I have no friends who, in their range of interests and in their love for me, can complement the relationship we have together in our marriage.

In a maturing marriage the presence of friends is much more likely to contribute to than detract from a deepening of the relationship of the spouses. Friends expand the resources of support and challenge available to each of us and to us together. Our friends engage us in ongoing relationships of shared affection and mutual influence that, gifts in themselves, also teach us much about that other ongoing relationship—marriage. Our friendships exercise us in the strengths of commitment and compromise, of dependence and autonomy, that serve us as well in marriage for a lifetime. In a time of personal or marital strain, having access to a friend can serve as a safety valve, reducing the pressure without damage to the structure of commitment and confidentiality that is our marriage. For most of us our friendships and our marriage are complementary: neither replaces our need for the other; each gives us resources we bring to the other.

But, as most of us find, it is not very easy to develop friends in adult life. Friendship takes time, perhaps time that, in the face of demands of our family and work responsibilities, we feel we do not have. To develop friends I must have contact with people who share some of my values and interests. As a homemaker I may find my contact with new people especially limited. If I am working I may meet many people, but not many who see the world as I do. And even after contact is made, friendship requires the sometimes lengthy, or at least involving, process of getting to know and trust one another. But beyond these complications of time and availability, perhaps the greatest difficulty in the development of adult friendships today touches on the question of sexuality.

—From Evelyn Eaton Whitehead and James D. Whitehead, *Marrying Well*. New York: Doubleday, 1981.

Listening

A good listener recognizes his mate as a person with a right to speak and with something significant to say. What the husband or wife says may seem to be a small matter, but it has significance for both of them because of their love and concern for each other. What the speaker feels is important, the loving listener hears as significant. The careful listener will hear what is said and will retain much of it, and therefore in his reply will reflect an understanding of what he has heard. This response on the part of the listener gives dignity to the words of the other person and encourages the speaker to say more. Listening may sometimes seem like a passive experience, but the Swiss psychiatrist Paul Tournier describes it rather as an opportunity to enter into the deep and majestic experiences of another person. . . .

In the author's experimental group of neo-marrieds a guest leader pointed out a failure in communication between two persons in a role-playing experience. The reason for the failure was twofold: First, the listener was so intent on making his own point that he did not hear what was really spoken; second, even when the listener heard the words he missed the intended meaning or feeling behind the words. It is well to remember that how the speaker feels about what he says is more important than the words themselves. Therefore the listener needs to be flexible toward his mate's many moods. Sometimes a mate is like a spring from which water flows in all its richness, at other times like a mountain stream that flows in a thousand moods, and at still others like a deep well from which the water must be drawn. Whatever the mood, the wise listener can learn to hear. As the writer of the proverb would say to every would-be listener, "The purpose in a man's mind is like deep water, but a man of understanding will draw it out" (Proverbs 20:5).

Risk and Patience—Part of Listening In both speaking and listening, there is risk involved. When one speaks, he takes the risk of revealing himself and of being misunderstood. When one listens, he takes the risk of involvement in the life of the speaker. Listening also implies the risk of personal change. In fact, conversation between neo-marrieds may be so self-revealing that either person or both can be confronted with the need of changes in attitudes or actions.

A good listener is also patient, particularly if the partner is quiet. A quiet partner needs a perceptive, alert listener who can share in the silences and respond as an effective listener when the quiet person does speak. Thus, listening is a critical art that neo-marrieds can develop. It is critical because it is a major part of the communication process, and it is an art in that it can be developed. . . .

Listening is an active, total experience. Love can motivate a person to be a careful listener and to love the speaker. Risk and patience are prerequisites to good listening.

—From Howard Hovde, *The Neo-Married.* Valley Forge, Pa.: Judson, 1968.

Personal Attractiveness

That attractiveness which first won the attention and approval of the mate should be guarded and enhanced. After marriage it is no less important than before, for we all like to be happy when we look at those who are dearest to us.

While beauty of personality is of supreme importance and outward appearance is in comparison a secondary matter, yet our impression of any person, even one who is closest to us, comes partly through appearance. That part of personal attractiveness, therefore, which depends upon care and good taste deserves attention. Let the young man be proud to look well for his wife, and the wife meet her husband with something of the care for her appearance and with the gladness of heart which she showed in court-

ship days. Love is partly admiration and it is desirable to make a good bid for the continued admiration of one's mate.

Still more important than outward care are expressions of the face, for in it kindness, sincerity, and affection are expressed in many subtle ways. If you have these you will look well to your mate. While the physical appearance is worthy of careful attention the attractiveness of a love-revealing countenance with character behind it is beyond computation. A love-revealing face is a beautiful face. Outward attractiveness is a gift of nature but attractiveness of character is an expression of one's self.

If you continually wear for your mate those expressions which come from a true and loving heart, you will be constantly registering agreeably, whereas if you show irritability and unpleasantness, there is little chance for you to be attractive. Each should also make it possible for the face of the other to show pleasure and confidence. How your comrade looks is partly a matter of your own determining—happy or sad, pleased or irritated.

A writer in the field of art has said: "Art is beauty, and beauty is 'from within out,' not 'from without in.' Its quality is eternal. Beauty of mind, if it exist, may express itself unconsciously in whatever one does. Some people with very homely and ordinary features are, when thinking and acting rightly, truly beautiful."

Almost or quite as important is the habit of making the best use of our voices. When we speak of the cultivation of the voice we usually think of the singer, the public speaker, the actor, the radio, TV or screen artist. But all the joy and inspiration which come into life through such voices are slight compared with the incalculable benefits that follow when people cultivate persistently the art of using pleasant voices at home. A loving voice used with courtesy and consideration is a beautiful voice, and a mingling of such voices rings bells of joy in the heart and gives quality to any home.

—From Leland Foster Wood, *Harmony in Marriage*. Old Tappan, N.J.: Revell, 1979.

PHYSICAL ATTRACTIVENESS

Physical attractiveness is a component part of likability. If we want to be liked, we must think about how to make ourselves as honestly attractive to the one we love as we possibly can. Many Christians rebel against this concept, thinking it to be sensual or carnal. They enter a wicked circle. Certainly an overemphasis upon physical attractiveness can lead to a twisted sensuality, but that can also happen in the lives of men and women who are created to appreciate beauty but find little of it in their spouses. Rather than repudiating this need, the Christian man or woman can master it to the extent that God meant for it to play a part in our lives together.

What is beauty? I have often pondered what makes a beautiful face, for example. I am not an artist and I do not understand structure and configuration. But I do know what is pleasing to my eyes. Over the years I have come to look upon my wife as a beautiful woman. Is her beauty the result of some natural rules of form and structure, or does it rest upon the depth of my affection for her?

Thus, beauty is culturally defined; it is defined also through our appreciation of the person. But while it would be easy to say that we should always proceed on the latter of the two definitions, that is not possible. We don't possess the human willpower simply to declare something beautiful because of our love and reject the cultural criteria altogether.

Marriage partners are wise to come to terms with this fact. We are ever prone to rebel. We cannot ignore the fact that the old tendency to fit into the culture's view of beauty and attractiveness will frequently arise. Thus, a wise partner in love tries his or her best to reasonably maintain attractiveness on both levels: culturally and as an object of loving thought.

Beyond this it is worthwhile to realize that there is something beautiful about the body that God wants us to enjoy. Happy the couple who have learned the freedom to enjoy the obvious attractiveness of one another's physical appearance. They have tried their best to become physically likable.

Don't underestimate the importance of attractiveness as a reasonable deterrent in a world which overestimates the value of physical beauty. A wise husband and wife face the fact head on that others will use beauty to exploit our instincts and appetites. The more our need to enjoy physical attractiveness is satisfied in the marriage, the less vulnerability to temptation there will be outside the home. We reduce the margins of that which could appeal to our rebellious instincts; we make it easier to be liked and therefore to be loved. There is balance here: love is shaping our concept of attractiveness while our attractiveness is making it desirable to like and love.

What makes us attractive from a purely physical side? Weight, for one thing. It is sad to see a husband or wife who has become careless about weight after the courtship days are over. A cartoon shows a bride and groom in the back of a limousine driving away from church. A frightened look crosses the groom's face as his bride exclaims, "No more Weight Watchers, girdles, and cyclamates!"

A husband shares his frustration about an overweight wife. "I love her very much and she is a good wife, but I can't get my eyes off the weight and the way she eats. When we go out in public, I know people are looking at her and thinking about her weight. She knows how I feel about it, and I can't stop thinking that she doesn't love me enough to cut down on the things that make her grow fat."

This is a wife who is putting a strain on her husband's ability to love her at deeper levels. It takes greater and greater willpower for him to get past the emotional level of liking her. The less he likes her, the more he must share and serve to compensate. But the less emotional satisfaction he gets, the harder it will be to share and serve, and finally he will exhaust his capacity to keep going at such a rate.

Weight is not the only area of physical attractiveness. Even our clothing and the way we wear it is important. How does our spouse care for us to look? Standards differ from house to house. One young man likes his wife to wear slacks all the time; another prefers dresses. If she loves her husband and wishes to be likable, she dresses to meet the general dimensions of his taste. There is a sad extreme to this, of course, and that comes in the case of a man who wants his wife to dress in outlandishly sensual clothing. Then she must consider God's standards in the matter as well as the message being dispatched to other people about her.

Personal neatness and hygiene are a part of attractiveness. It does not go unnoticed that a man leaves his home in the morning shaved, smiling, and smelling like the Old Spice man. But when he returns, he is disheveled and exhausted. If he spends the evening with his wife and family in this wilted state, he seems to be saying to them, "I have taken you for granted, and I do not think that dressing for you is as important as dressing for others."

—From Gordon MacDonald, *Magnificent Marriage*. Wheaton, Ill.: Tyndale, 1976.

Sharing

Start with the idea of a willingness to share oneself. In order to communicate we may have to lead by opening ourselves up— even if it means the risk of the possibility of humiliation.

As human beings we are vast storehouses of data which have come into us through literally millions of impressions each day. We store our hurts, our defeats, our pressures, our analyses of situations where one gets into trouble. On the positive side, we stack up pleasurable memories, tremendous quantities of helpful facts and insights, and ways in which we have learned to make ourselves and other people happy. All these have gone into us; now can they come out?

Men, handcuffed by something called the masculine image, have the most trouble, as a rule, learning how to get things out. Our society has taught its men to think first before making any commitments, and this becomes true in self-expression. A man is taught *not* to show extreme emotion; he must never show pain or admit defeat. He feels that he has become less than a real man if he is laughed at, left out, or ridiculed. So in the normal run of things, he takes few risks, and reveals only that part of himself that he knows will gain approval and admiration.

If this pattern is left unchanged it creates havoc with his ability to express his authentic feelings later in life. Others find it a struggle to share themselves due to the general patterns often set in the childhood years by parents who cut them off when they expressed themselves, shamed them if they showed weakness, or welded into their souls a horrible dread of saying anything that might embarrass them or the family.

When these kinds of conditions prevail, a person often becomes an intellectual and spiritual volcano. Forces of uncommunicated and unreleased power begin to well up

127

within. If, as the years pass, there is no normal release through communication, these things may force their way out through other parts of the human system. I frequently visit with men, for example, who suffer from heart problems or ulcers. While heart problems and ulcers cannot always be traced to our present line of thinking, a significant number of these people have communication problems, and they find the ulcerated stomach and the pounding heart expressing in pain what they could not earlier put into words. Since the volcano could not erupt in the normal way, it blew sideways into the physical structure.

Part of the commitment in marriage is to overcome these communication blocks, and that begins when we turn over the key to our inner selves to our partner. It may be that what we do is to progressively give over a series of keys as layer after layer of our inner selves becomes transparent to the one whom we trust. The layers open up faster and faster if the one to whom the key has been given is wise in the way he or she handles the information we choose to share.

As we take the risk of willingness and open our lives, we place ourselves in the hands of someone who must accept the real "us." It does not mean that they cannot disagree or even place a sensitive value-judgment upon what we say, but they must be extremely careful to handle us with absolute care. It takes only a few betrayals of confidence or acceptance to erect the walls of defensiveness. Then we redeposit our fears and aches back down in our inner mental vaults where they may never be reached again.

But if we make the vital decision to take the risk and become willing, when we hand over the keys, an entire dimension of human experience begins to emerge. Now we become friends whose minds begin to weave a fabric of co-experience. . . .

But sharing ourselves takes much wisdom

and sensitivity. Having tried to make the point that we should be willing to open our lives to the one with whom we share a relationship, I come now full circle to say, be careful! There are some occasions where one might share too much, or share prematurely. For no human being is equipped to take all the real information we have to give in one sitting.

In our growing relational consciousness, there has come on the scene a tendency to want to spill everything as quickly as possible. There was an old radio game called, "Can You Top This?" Sometimes people in the freedom of a relationship can play such a game, trying to out-share each other. No! Sharing is a lifetime experience; it flows with a natural rhythm in each day as we simply concentrate in being what we are.

Perhaps there are some experiences in the past better left buried. On occasions a partner may be too deeply hurt if he or she were to become aware of events which God has already forgiven and removed. A rule is hard to devise for differentiating between things that should be revealed and those to be covered. Perhaps the answer lies somewhere in asking ourselves if the matter in question could ever come to the attention of our partner apart from our desire to make it known. Will the consequences of what we're aware of ever affect him or her in any way? Will it ever have a possibility of impairing our relationship? If the answer to any of these questions is yes, then perhaps the matter should be brought to light. We can be thankful that God's Spirit can give counsel when we are perplexed about these things.

We must also control what we share in terms of what the other person is equipped to hear. A young husband confesses to his wife that he is having overwhelming problems with sexual lust. He feels better because he has described his problem, but he may have passed his crushing burden of an uncontrolled thought life on to the shoulders of his wife. Now she becomes preoccupied with the "why's" of his problem. Does he not love her enough? Is she an inadequate sex partner? Does this mean that their relationship is threatened? In her inability to handle the information, she has sown seeds of doubt and suspicion in her heart that she may be unable to overcome. Better that he had chosen to open such struggles first to a pastor or a counselor.

—From Gordon MacDonald, *Magnificent Marriage*. Wheaton, Ill.: Tyndale, 1976.

Spiritual Life

In the past few months, we have often heard the question, "How can we grow spiritually as a couple? How can we help each other seek God?" Of course, the answers are as varied as the people who ask them. But one answer many couples have found particularly helpful is spending time *together*—as a couple—with God.

We asked several Christian couples to tell us about their devotional times as a couple. We asked each couple: *Why is it important? What do you actually do during your devotional time? How do you keep it fresh? What mistakes have you made?* We hope their answers will encourage you and your spouse to seek your own special way of expressing your devotion to God.

HOW IMPORTANT IS IT?

Most of the couples who responded to our questions said the time spent *together*—talking to each other, reading the Word, and talking to God about concerns—was very important. But the "structure" of that time varied considerably.

"For thirty-six years we have loved the 'little things' that have kept our marriage fresh and vital: tiny love notes left here and there. A cup of coffee as we sit before an open hearth. The valentines we crudely make each year. Walking in the drizzling rain. Reading aloud to each other. Candlelight at dinner time," said Rollin and Ruth Calkin from Pomona, California. "But the one great cementing force that has kept us close to each other and to God has been our devotional time together. Through the years it has been high on our priority list."

Lee and Peg Rankin from Birmingham, Minnesota, had this to say: "The consistent sharing of a devotional time has knit us together as husband and wife in a way that no other activity could do. It has been the mortar that has held our marriage together. Prayer has seen us through losing a business, seeing a parent through multiple surgeries, and a host of other problems. We believe that if a husband and wife really want to function as a victorious team, there is no better way to do so than to knit their spirits together in a regular devotional time."

Dr. and Mrs. Kevin Leman from Tucson, Arizona, said it was important for them to spend time together before God, even if it wasn't regular: "Having regular 'anything' with three small children and a terribly demanding schedule is almost impossible. For us regularity is not the key. The key is to come together as one and share our devotional time together as much as possible. *Devotion* to each other as man and wife makes *devotions* so much more fulfilling and rewarding."

Lloyd and Elsie Mattson from Duluth, Minnesota, say that their devotional time as a couple is vital to their spiritual integrity: "A couple that cannot worship together privately reveals a serious spiritual lack. This will find expression in the 'non-devotional' times of the day as well. Maybe the absence of devotions reflects the shallow perception of the Gospel often found among Christians

129

who have not been guided toward spiritual maturity. Real prayer demands honesty, a trait essential to a sound marriage."

Several couples stressed the importance of a regular prayer time in strengthening their marriage.

A pastor and his wife from Urbana, Illinois, wrote that prayer "keeps us very aware that there are three of us in the marriage. Knowing that we are including the third person, the Lord himself, means that differences and grudges need to be forgiven and resolved. By praying together every night before going to sleep, we cannot let problems carry over. Also, the prayer time—and the surrounding sharing time—is important for building and sharing in every area of our lives."

Louis and Colleen Evans from Washington, D.C., agree and emphasize the importance of spontaneity: "It's very important for us to pray together but not at a certain time or place. We have found that it is an attitude of our hearts that prompts us to pray—as we wake in the morning, at the table, in the car, with our children, 'as we walk in the way.' We both pray separately, but our times together are spontaneous, real—just part of our life."

Spending time *alone* with God was a priority for several couples. From that time alone issued meaningful sharing as a couple.

Harold and Luci Shaw from Wheaton, Illinois, said, "Because we work together as husband and wife in the same office, we felt it important to have our own individual devotions, separately, relating individually and directly to the Lord rather than sharing devotions. We share any helpful insight gained from our separate devotions."

"We think it is more important that each of us have a time with God—each alone in the Scriptures," said Keith and Gladys Hunt of Ann Arbor, Michigan. "We can't imagine not sharing what is most important to both

of us together, so we naturally want to spend time together in the Scriptures and in prayer. We began to do this together from the first day of our marriage—not a big emotional experience, just simply reading the Word of God together, talking about what it says, what it means and applying it, followed by talking to God about what we are concerned about. We do it now at breakfast. Earlier in our marriage we did it at dinner time."

Carole and Jack Mayhall from Colorado Springs, Colorado, confessed that "set time, set procedure devotions have never worked for us. We are convinced that when 'two objects draw close to a third object, they will draw closer to each other.' Through the years our concentration has been on each of us individually drawing closer to God. Our time alone with him is a priority. This has resulted in a life of sharing with each other—an openness about spiritual matters that we both value highly."

WHAT DO YOU ACTUALLY DO DURING YOUR DEVOTIONAL TIME?

For the Calkins, each day begins with a cup of coffee and a few choice morsels from the Bible. They prefer to read a few verses and then digest them, rather than a longer passage. Sometimes they read a page from a favorite devotional book by Oswald Chambers, Amy Carmichael, or Andrew Murray.

Howard and Jeanne Hendricks from Dallas, Texas, say no two devotional times are quite the same. "Sometimes it's just prayer, sometimes Bible study, sometimes discussion only—but usually some combination of the three. Usually we come together, having studied individually a Scripture passage agreed upon previously. Then we share together what we saw—that leads to discussion, questions, prayer."

"We read consecutively from the Bible,"

said the Hunts. "We choose a book, read aloud a section of the text or a chapter (depending on length and available time), and talk about it. What comes out of our discussion are answers to questions like: What does it say? What does it mean? What does it mean to me? Much of the richness of this time together comes out of our personal time with God. We don't use devotional books, because we like to cover as much of the Bible together as we can. Then we pray about what we have learned—about our family, our friends, the world."

The Evans see communication—talking to each other—as the most important element of their devotional time. "We talk to one another—and with the Lord—almost at the same time. We pray with eyes open, or when we are wrestling with a problem, we are on our knees with our eyes closed. We share 'hot' scriptures, our feelings, our fears, our joys. And we regularly pray together for each of our children and for our daily schedules."

The Mattsons claim that what they "do" during their devotional times has evolved over the years to fit their temperaments and personality as a couple. "Some would claim that our daily pre-breakfast talk-fest does not qualify as 'devotions,' for we do not always read a Bible passage, nor do we follow a devotional guide. We usually get up early, enjoy our morning coffee, and sit and chat, following no fixed agenda.

"Prayer concerns emerge from our conversation. We pray for the people in our lives, sensing that God assigns some of us in a special way. We pray for the sick and needy that are part of our broader church concern. We pray for our children, usually concentrating on one family per day (five families scattered from Texas to Alaska). We pray for each other, for the duties of the day.

"We have concluded that our conversation is just as much prayer as those sentences we utter with eyes closed and heads bowed."

HOW DO YOU KEEP YOUR DEVOTIONAL TIME FRESH AND MEANINGFUL?

Several couples cited "honesty with one another," "spontaneity in sharing spiritual insights," and "variety and imagination" as some of the elements that made their devotional time meaningful.

The Calkins pray aloud as they walk together, or while driving, sharing personal longings and needs. "We remember the time we stopped pulling weeds in our backyard and asked God to make our lives a well-watered garden. Just a sentence or two, but so often when we pull weeds we remember that."

The Mattsons say their devotional time is meaningful because of their deep involvement in the lives of others. "Our devotions relate to the life we share at the moment," they said. "Therefore our conversation and prayers are *urgent.*"

Although variety helps some couples' devotional times, the Rankins warned against using "gimmicks, innovative procedures, or 'new' devotional guides" to keep the time fresh. "We feel that anything other than the Word itself tends to get in our way. We want our communication to be direct from the Lord, so we try to eliminate all middle men. How then do we make the same old stuff meaningful? In two ways: by reading with the intent of receiving something refreshing and by bringing to the passage new insights and personal experiences."

And what if a couple's devotional time isn't always meaningful? The Hunts said they persevere anyway, because "God breaks through the pages of his Word repeatedly and says something to us that we need to hear.

"On any given morning one of us may be

131

distracted or tired, but we have built this into our lives, not as a meaningless habit, but as a discipline for building richness into our lives. We know each other better because of this—and we know God better because of it."

WHAT MISTAKES HAVE YOU MADE THAT YOU COULD SHARE WITH OTHER COUPLES?

The couples we surveyed said "being too rigid," "trying to impress each other," and "letting one person always take the lead," were common mistakes.

"Early in our marriage we felt the need to be more rigid," confessed the Evans, "and it was not as spontaneous or meaningful. A legalistic approach did not work for us. Now we pray more, not because we should, but because we know we need to pray, and we want to pray."

Early in their marriage, the Calkins were surprised by the new kind of intimacy they were experiencing, and they were hesitant about being transparent with one another.

"We had never prayed as husband or wife before," they said. "We were more intent on impressing each other spiritually. It was difficult to confess failures, mistakes, and hidden sins. Our pretense robbed us of a real sense of God's presence. We have learned (and are still learning) to pray honestly . . . to make ourselves vulnerable, even when our vulnerability attacks our pride.

"We've also learned the difference between praying *on* each other and *for* each other. To attempt to force our own way by praying *on* a mate is a subtle temptation—especially when the mate cannot come to his or her own defense. To interrupt a prayer somehow seems disrespectful."

The Mattsons' major error early in their devotional life as a couple was "the guilt we felt when we failed to live up to the stereotype of devotions established by others. Also,

periods in our life became too cluttered, robbing us of a time together. Basically, sheer spiritual immaturity kept us from disciplining our time for honest, loving conversation. The routine practice of 'devotions' has little value when people are not at ease."

Several couples warned of the danger of allowing one partner (usually the husband) to carry the burden for "leading" the devotional time.

"Early in our life together I was willing to let Keith be spiritual for both of us," said Gladys Hunt. "I was consumed with the details of homemaking and of young motherhood. Then he began to travel. It took me awhile to realize that I did not reach God through my husband. God wanted a personal relationship maintained daily with *me*—not just with *us*. Out of the riches of each of us growing in the Lord, our times together have more meaning."

The Hendricks voiced the same concern: "Early on, the 'professor' career influenced us both to assume a teacher-student profile. It didn't work. We soon learned to make a new, personal, and 'non-handicap' approach each time we came together.

"We threw away the 'duty' label. We have no one to impress. God has no brownie-point chart. We decided it's God's way to do what he wants to do with us. Besides, it's fun, it's enormously satisfying, and we can see ourselves growing in it."

Another mistake some couples made was not making their devotional time together a high priority—or depending on an emotional high to keep it going.

"Hundreds of times we haven't felt like praying," said the Calkins. "Nevertheless, we've learned the importance of praying without feeling. It's *God* we seek, with or without feeling. We've learned that five minutes spent with God daily is better than two hours once a week. However, we do not feel guilty as we once did when there are occasional interruptions. A devotional time together ought to fortify and free us—not bind us."

This seems to be a key in developing a meaningful spiritual life together as a couple—discovering individual ways to seek and worship God, remembering that the purpose is to fortify and free—not bind.

—Reprinted from *Today's Christian Woman* (Fall 1981).

Tenderness

This is the time to pose the question that actually outlines the entire spectrum of romance: How does my partner wish to be loved? To be tender is to ask that question and then to answer it in actions. Too many of us find it simple to love our spouses the way *we want to love* them. I come home for a free evening and get comfortable in the living room with a book. When I go to bed, I pride myself that I have spent an evening with Gail. But I haven't. I have loved her in a convenient way—the way I wished to love. In so doing, I failed to ask the question, first of myself, and then of her, how does she wish to be loved this evening? Perhaps she would like me to accompany her on a trip to the market. "I like to show the other women that you are mine," she says. Marketing is not my way of loving, but it may be the way she wishes to be loved that night.

Tenderness is the sensitivity one undertakes when he asks himself, "What makes her tick today?" And he launches out on a campaign of romance, loving in the way his partner wishes to experience romance.

—From Gordon MacDonald, *Magnificent Marriage*. Wheaton, Ill.: Tyndale, 1976.

Time Together

Once a couple determines to take time for communication, they must take some active steps to implement their decision. That usually means scheduling regular times during the week when they can talk.

I know that some people consider "schedule" a dirty word. They think it means all restriction and no spontaneity. I will only say that if a couple can establish adequate, regular time for communication without a schedule, they do not need one. I have seen very few such couples. Most couples I know never managed to find enough time for communication until they began to schedule it in.

A schedule is a tool which helps us assert control over the circumstances of our lives, instead of letting those circumstances control us. When we do not have a schedule, we tend to treat competing demands for time and attention on a first-come, first-served basis, rather than on the basis of their relative importance. And so the children and the relatives, the telephone and doorbell and television, all start to crowd out the time we should devote to communication.

A schedule gives us a basis for saying yes or no to conflicting demands. Suppose someone calls up to invite a couple to a bridge party on Monday night. If that time is not scheduled for communication, they will probably accept without even considering whether they should spend that evening talking. But if they had that Monday night reserved for each other, they could say, "No. We already have plans for that evening." A husband who is asked to discuss business over lunch will not be likely to turn down the invitation so that he can spontaneously take his wife out for lunch. But if he and his wife have agreed to have lunch together on that day, he can say, "Sorry, I have another appointment." Scheduling helps us implement our basic decision to give communication a high priority.

When it comes to setting up scheduled times together, the pattern of each couple's life will vary. One question is, how much time does a couple need for communication?

For most marriages, I believe that husband and wife should take at least two to five hours a week specifically to talk to each other. Some couples may want to take this all at one time once a week; others may prefer to have several hour or half-hour sessions. A couple who are still establishing basic communication may need more time; other couples, who have good communication already, may need less. But virtually all couples at all times in their relationships need to take some regular time together to communicate about their relationship and common responsibilities.

Again, this should be time in addition to the regular flow of daily conversation. Ordinary conversation is very important in itself, but it cannot substitute for time to discuss important matters seriously and at length.

Where do a husband and wife find this time to spend together? The differing circumstances of each couple's life make it impossible to give blanket rules, but I can mention some times that other couples have used successfully. Couples who have no children, or whose children have grown and left home, often find adequate time for good communication during meals. Couples with children usually have more difficulty, as they need to find times when they can be alone.

Lunchtime is one possibility. Some husbands work close enough to home to stop in for lunch several times a week while the children are at school. Some couples can arrange to meet for lunch near the husband's place of work, or near the wife's if she works outside the home.

Other couples may find the evening a better time to spend together. I know one family with six children in which the parents sit down to talk after dinner, while the older children do dishes and help the younger ones get ready for bed. Many couples are able to take one evening a week as an opportunity to talk in depth, either going out or staying at home. Some are able to get together several nights a week after putting the children to bed.

Couples who are very busy may find that even these times will not work. But I have never met any couple, no matter how busy, who could not find some regular time to spend together once they agreed to make communication a high priority and started looking for the time with determination. It may take some ingenuity, but we *can* find the time.

Once a couple has established some special time for communication, they should take care to protect it from interruption. If other activities come up for the evenings they have agreed to spend together, they should normally say no. We would not lightly break an appointment with an important business associate or with the mayor of the city, and we should not lightly break appointments with our partners in life. If changing circumstances disrupt an established schedule for communication—say the Cub Scouts meeting changes from Wednesday to Thursday, or lunch time at the office changes, or a favorite inexpensive restaurant closes—we should grab the first available time to sit down together and work out a new schedule, not letting these changes discourage us or destroy our practice of communication. Protecting time for good communication is no indulgence; it is essential to the strength of a marriage.

—From Ralph Martin, *Husbands, Wives, Parents, Children.* Ann Arbor: Servant, 1978.

Togetherness

While unity and commitment to a life together are essential in a good marriage, too much togetherness can spell disaster. Although Biblical writers refer to marriage as a relationship in which two people "become one," this should not be interpreted to mean that all individuality is lost in marriage. Nowhere is the uniqueness and worth of every human being stressed more than in the Bible.

Although the need for independence, privacy, and individuality may vary from individual to individual, a good marriage encourages the never-ending quest for self-actualization and self-realization for each partner. As paradoxical as it may sound, separateness in a relationship tends to build a desire for more togetherness; distance, a greater desire for closeness.

Although some people seem satisfied to sacrifice their personal identity, dreams, goals, and aspirations for those of their mate, most would eventually find such a relationship unbearable. When a person is called on to make such a sacrifice, it means that certain powerful and significant personal needs will forever remain unfulfilled. While marriage always demands that we give up something to get something, it is appalling to think of the price we have paid in human suffering because of our allegiance to the concept that if marriage is to succeed, one partner, usually the female, must be willing to submit to a life of self-denial.

Under such conditions even the spouse who maintains the dominant or superior position will grow to resent intrusions into his or her privacy by the weaker spouse who insists that he or she be permitted to live the life of an ever-present and compliant servant, totally dedicated to the development of the more assertive spouse.

There are those who would argue that the emphasis on personal growth and individuality in marriage is contrary to the teaching of unity and oneness in marriage. Others would argue that emphasis on personal growth and achievement for both husband and wife would play havoc with the more traditional view that the husband should be the head of the household. It is not our purpose to resolve such issues. Indeed, we are not concerned with who should be dominant or submissive, inferior or superior. We are instead concerned with the right of individuals to strive for self-realization. As stated elsewhere, it is necessary to love and respect oneself before love for another can become a reality in any true sense of the word. And one cannot learn to love and respect oneself unless encouraged to live in a manner which enables him or her to utilize God-given abilities and talents. Persons who are permitted to do so feel much better about themselves and subsequently find themselves able to enter into a close personal relationship with another human being willing to extend to them the same freedom.

For many couples, the balance between the needs for togetherness and separateness is almost impossible to assess while they are dating. This is due to the feeling shared by many couples in love: they cannot get enough of each other. Although such feelings are quite common, most couples eventually come down to earth and realize that life demands that all human beings face life first and last as individuals. No matter how close two people may become in marriage, John will always be John, and Mary will always be Mary.

While the needs for togetherness and separateness will vary from couple to couple, those contemplating marriage would do well to raise some of the following questions.

1. How much freedom am I allowed to be my own person?
2. Am I encouraged to pursue my own interests, or am I always expected to relegate my interests to a secondary position?
3. Are my needs considered important by the other person?
4. Does the other person seem threatened if I express interest in a career of my own?
5. Does the other person insist that we do everything together?

6. Does he or she get upset if I want to be alone or do things with other people sometimes?

7. Is he or she excessively possessive or jealous?

8. Are my wishes and opinions respected and given reasonable consideration?

9. Do I frequently feel smothered and stifled by the other person's presence?

10. Do I frequently resent the demands placed on me by the other person?

11. Do I feel that the other person's requests and demands on me are reasonable?

12. Has the other person made it clear what he or she expects my role in the relationship to be?

13. Would he or she be able to accept and love me if I should change my mind in the future?

14. Does the other person so completely dominate my life that I feel like a big zero when we're apart?

15. Am I dependent on the other person for meaning and purpose in life?

While it is true that expectations will vary from couple to couple as to what they expect from their mates in marriage, the need for tolerance and acceptance of the other person as a unique and worthwhile individual cannot be overemphasized. If the freedom to develop as an individual is lacking in a relationship prior to marriage, then it is apt to be lacking after marriage. It has been our observation that the absence of growth as individuals leads to an absence of growth as a couple. Although there is always the danger that a couple will grow apart if individual development is encouraged, the danger is much greater if it is not encouraged.

—From Robert L. Mason, Jr., and Caroline L. Jacobs, *How to Choose the Wrong Marriage Partner and Live Unhappily Ever After*. Atlanta: John Knox, 1979.

Touching

Romance not only feeds on physical attractiveness, appreciation, affirmation, and crazy times, but it needs a certain level of physical touching. This is not necessarily sexual contact, but movements which bring a couple into the intimate circle of proximity, a circle no one else is permitted to enter.

We need to be touched, stroked, held, kissed, and rubbed. Among the saddest moments that I face in counseling are those spent with a man or woman who is alone in a marriage—alone in the sense that the spouse has lost all desire for touch. Lionel Whiston recalls the husband who crept up behind his wife at the kitchen sink and kissed her on the back of the neck. She reacted in an irritable fashion and said angrily, "Don't kiss me while I'm in the kitchen." The husband was heard to mutter as he exited in a somewhat deflated fashion, "It will be a long time before I kiss you anywhere."

The holding of hands while walking down the street says many things. To each other it says, "I'm glad to be connected with you." To the world it says, "We belong to each other and we are proud to declare the fact." A wife sitting next to her husband in the car says by her actions, I like to be as close as I can whenever possible. The enjoyment of a morning good-bye kiss not only gets the day off to a right start, it may reaffirm for the children something they constantly need to know: mom and dad love one another, and that means everything's all right for us too.

A husband who has never quite understood the value of touching writes of his enlightenment:

"The other night we got into bed, and my wife was very nervous. You know, rolling and tossing. I don't know why, but I just started rubbing her back, and soothing her. And then I just held her face to face. I put my arms around her, and we just stayed that way. And this seemed to comfort her quite a bit, and she quieted down and had a good night. You see, I felt this might do her good and I tried it. Which I'm not sure I would have thought of six months or a year ago. In fact, I suspect a year ago I might have lain there for a while and then said, 'Well, I'm going to have a cigarette,' and gone to sleep on the couch."

—From Gordon MacDonald. *Magnificent Marriage*. Wheaton, Ill.: Tyndale, 1976.

Verbal Expression

Saying how we feel is also important to romance. Partners in romance learn how to put their feelings into words. It is as important for one to say certain things as it is for the other to hear them said. Without words, feelings are never solidified, and we are left to guess how the other one feels.

Romance depends upon the frequent and varied expression of love feelings. It was not long after my own wedding that I began to discover the excitement of creatively expressing myself to Gail, my wife. I learned, for example, that a phone call sometimes during the day that had no special purpose except to express my love was a welcome relief for both of us. Cards sent through the mail offered a surprise, and I learned to make a stop at the card store to pick out a few special verses which might share how I felt.

It was not unusual to find a note from Gail packed in a bag lunch or in a rolled-up set of underwear if I was on a trip. We developed a set of code words which said things that only the two of us understood. After reading about a man whose wife always sent him off with a special dime with which he could call home if he felt lonely, Gail began the habit of including a dime in every letter she sent. A friend of mine traveling with me in Japan

recently caught on to this particular exercise and sent Gail a card. It read, "Gordon is getting lonely; send a lot of dimes!"

If I officiate at a wedding ceremony and Gail is in the audience, we make it a point to let our eyes meet during the recessional of the bride and groom. No one notices that I am telling her with my eyes that she is far more beautiful to me than the bride. Once the head usher brought me a note from the rear of the sanctuary. I could hardly conceal my amusement when I opened up the note from Gail saying how exciting it was to be the only woman in the church that had a "thing" going on with the pastor. She was careful to sign it so that there would be no doubt as to its origin. There are the secret codes of romantic communication which refresh a relationship.

—From Gordon MacDonald, *Magnificent Marriage*. Wheaton, Ill.: Tyndale, 1976.

CONFLICT AND RESOLUTION

Conflict

Conflict is a dimension of companionship. Who said that companionship always implied that the waters of relationship would be smooth? The fact is, if there is going to be any viable sharing of minds in a relationship, there will be moments when issues and perspectives are going to be finetuned to such an extent that disagreement will be raised. Conflict is the evidence that there is some distance between the viewpoints of two partners.

Many Christians have felt that having conflict is unspiritual—that it indicates that a relationship is in trouble. On a few occasions I have met couples who claimed that they had never had a conflict. I am always reminded of the statement Dr. Leslie Weatherhead once made about such couples and which Paul Tournier quotes: "Either these people are lying, or one of them has crushed the other."

The issue of conflict has to be faced squarely. Sooner or later there is going to be conflict between two human beings because—as we have already said—we are people with rebellious and independent natures. We have some selfish impulses within us—some of which we ourselves are blind to. No matter how great our admiration and affection for one another, there are going to come from fertile minds value judgments, opinions, and observations which are going to clash. It has to happen; we are, thank God, very different people—all of us.

Take, for example, simple things like the relative value we place upon words. Early in a marriage, a husband tries to extinguish a minor disagreement with the comment, "You're being childish!" Completely missing his sense of perspective, she hits the ceiling, exploding. "Don't you call me childish!" What he has not known is that her father kept reminding her that he thought of her as a child long after she thought herself an adult. The word "child" retrieves from her memory bank all of the years spent building her self-image as a mature person. A bewildered husband raises more conflict than he is prepared to accept because a word carries different meanings.

Different backgrounds cause conflict. Our economic status as children may serve to shape our feelings about the expenditure or saving of money. If husband and wife come from two financial levels, there is sure to be conflict upon the use of the family income.

Blind spots or habit patterns which are important to one but not to another are significant sources of conflict. "I don't understand," Gail says to me, "why you cannot see that, when you say you're going to do some-

thing and you don't, it hurts me. You tell me that you'll get the letter written, and you don't. You say you'll repair the garage window by Saturday, but you probably won't. Don't tell me you're going to do something that you don't intend to do."

For Gail the conflict seems to center on my apparently deliberate unwillingness to do what I've said I was going to do. Any way you look at it, I'm wrong. But it wasn't that I lied. It was a blind spot; something at a deeper level has just blanked it out of my mind. I feel stupid standing there having been caught in the blind spot. I may even try to fight my way out of the obvious trap I'm in by manufacturing some new interpretation of what happened. But the truth is, I hit a blind spot, and there is going to be conflict about it because the truth and fact of the situation show me to be wrong.

We conflict if we have different systems of *convictions or values.* A wife believes that the family should be at worship on Sunday morning, but her husband sees nothing wrong with taking the summers away from church for times in the boat while the weather is good. There is conflict, therefore, over differing convictions. Each is frustrated because the other seems so unable to understand the opposite position.

You have to face the fact that there are numerous occasions when we simply conflict because we are operating at *different levels of reason.* Everett leaves the toilet seat up in the bathroom because he sees no need to put it down; Eileen complains because she was taught as a child that a well-mannered person always puts the seat down. The toilet seat controversy brings different images to their minds: Eileen sees her husband as a bit uncouth, and Everett sees his wife as being ridiculously picayune.

Another husband likes to think through his Christian experience with penetrating reason, always asking questions about every biblical claim, expressing doubts and even hostilities about comments which tend to oversimplify the faith. His wife conflicts with him because to her, following Christ means to simply take everything at face value and believe. She has no questions, no doubts, and no intellectual insecurities. Being a Christian is extremely simple for her. Their fellowship, therefore, is often disrupted by dispute over the very matters that should have brought them closest together.

For these and many other reasons, conflict cannot be avoided in our homes. It is a mistake to try to avoid it. I don't mean that we should necessarily welcome its arrival, but our area of concentration should be in controlling conflict—making it our servant rather than our master. If we do this, conflict helps us to grow and not to regress.

If there is an unspiritual dimension to conflict, it is in the *type* of conflict we allow to occur between us. It is speculation, but I tend to think that Adam and Eve had conflicts long before sin entered their lives. I can't imagine two people being created by the Lord without enough differences so that conflict would be a necessary part of their situation. Could Eve ever have offered some better suggestions of names for certain animals than the ones Adam had given them? As two eyes set in our heads give us depth perception, so two personalities looking at the same object or idea with different viewpoints bring dimension to its essence. Those viewpoints present conflict. Adam and Eve simply had to have it as part of their lives. The conflict was not sinful or rebellious; what would later taint it were the overtones of hidden motives, the need to dominate and prove the other one wrong—the expansive air of superiority when in the dust of the competition one has become victor leaving the other vanquished. That is when conflict becomes unspiritual.

Good conflict is *constructive;* bad conflict is *destructive.* The two words obviously explain themselves, and their differing styles are easy to identify when we see conflict's results.

I have always stepped back a little bit when someone confidently says, "I love a good argument; it makes the juices run." Well, I don't and never have. But while I don't pretend to enjoy conflict, I will not run from it if it seems necessary. But many will; they will avoid conflict at all costs—perhaps because they have been disposed of with crushing force at the hands of a ruthless warrior.

Sometimes those who run from conflict think they are doing it in love. They give in on every issue, storing up the resentments and bitternesses inside which someday may explode in an act of violence, leaving, or just getting sick. Even though they think that they are being the more mature by keeping their mouths shut, they are not that virtuous. The boiling hate that steams in their souls is no more admirable than to have let it all hang out. Call him a "clam-up"—that is until the day when he blows the lid.

The opposite extreme of the clam-up is the person we might call the "shortfuse." For Mr. Shortfuse, every little difference is a call to arms. Everything is an issue to be debated, analyzed, and sorted out. He has to win and get his jollies each time an enemy leaves the field with a white flag. Soon everyone begins to avoid Shortfuse, and if he is married, his wife may turn into Mrs. Clam-up. Need I observe that between Mrs. Clam-up and Mr. Shortfuse, companionship begins to shrivel, becoming thinner and more shallow with the passing days.

If we can see either tendency within ourselves and bring it to a resolution, we may then be able to deal wisely with the issues of constructive and destructive conflict. How can they be differentiated?

Good conflict—that which is constructive—helps clarify issues that need more than just cursory thought. In the clash of two ideas, the emotions, the intellect, and even the spiritual side of us with its conviction and values are brought to bear on the real issue. There is a grinding action which removes through conversation all the irrelevant and inaccurate pieces of data that we both thought were essential. Out of the exchange comes a single truth to which we can both agree. . . .

Constructive conflict also encourages and develops maturity. In the test of opinions we are forced to face ourselves as we really are. Gail calls me to attention about some insensitive action on my part. I listen, and perhaps I even debate the point hoping to explain my thinking. But if I am in a frame of mind to learn, I may suddenly discover in the verbal trade that she has pointed out something worth thinking about. I come out of the conflict with new insights about myself. I grow up just a bit more.

"I like fighting," someone says with a romantic air, "because when the fighting is over, the making up is fantastic." If you've heard that as many times as I have, you groan as I do. But take a second look. There may be truth to the statement after all. Constructive conflict cleans out the tubes of the relationship. Things which have been lying dormant are finally picked up and tossed in the air. If there is an ability to deal with them truthfully and bring them to resolution, the making up *will be* fantastic. It is fantastic because there is an explosion of relief. We're glad that's over with; it's been said, and now we can get on to the other business.

Take a quick look at destructive conflict. It obviously does not build relationships; it whittles them down. Conflict becomes destructive when the parties in question point their weapons at each other rather than at the issue. Note the subtle differences between the two statements, "*You* make me so mad," and "*What you have done* makes me very angry." The weapons have swiveled from one target to another.

Now we bring into view the kinds of things most people associate with conflict between husbands and wives: accusations, name-calling, strident tones, and volume heard all over the neighborhood.

This is the kind of conflict in which someone has to win. They will not call it quits until the other waves a flag of unconditional surrender. Little by little, personalities are destroyed, and one or both people come out of the relationship beaten and crushed. The relationship is cheapened, and companionship is something of the past.

Unresolved and destructive conflicts make a mess out of lives!

—From Gordon MacDonald, *Magnificent Marriage*. Wheaton, Ill.: Tyndale, 1976.

Anger

Anger . . . is really more of a symptom than the actual problem. There are three common causes for anger. The first is fear. A person experiences some type of a fear in his life, and instead of expressing it as fear, he reacts with anger. A parent may be sitting up at night waiting for his teenager to come in. First he's a half-hour late, and then an hour late. The fear response gradually begins to turn into "Why isn't that kid home?" Then to "Wait until he gets home!" The result is that instead of showing concern and relief and love when the teenager finally walks in, the parent dumps all his pent-up anger.

Another reason that we become angry is that we're frustrated because we're not getting our way. And then the third common reason is that we've been hurt in some way.

When I am counseling a client who is extremely angry and hostile, I let them pour out their feelings. But after they have done this and are a little more reasonable, I say: "I'd like to ask you three questions: Is there something that you're afraid of in your life at the present time? Are you experiencing some kind of hurt? Or, is there something that is really frustrating you?" Often it's just like seeing a balloon burst. All the leftover anger begins to dissipate. Then the person may say, "No one has ever asked those questions before, but one of them is right on the button."

I wonder what would happen in your family if, when a person is angry, you could avoid responding with your own anger, and instead begin talking about him, about his fears, frustrations, and hurts. That might show that you have a much greater sensitivity to his needs at this particular moment.

A fourth principle about conflict is that most conflict is not dealt with openly because most people have not been taught effective ways of resolving their feelings. As a result they try to run from conflict situations by whatever method they can come up with. This avoids problems, but does not solve them.

A fifth principle is that conflict provides opportunity for growth in a relationship. Now, you might not believe that at the time when you are experiencing the conflict because some pain might be involved, but conflict is often essential to growth.

The sixth principle is that unresolved conflicts interfere with growth and satisfying relationships. If you would like a different type of a Bible study, let me make a suggestion. Read through the life of Christ in the four Gospels and notice the many occasions in which He was in conflict with other people. Then study His way of resolving these conflicts. He set the example for a very healthy pattern.

—From H. Norman Wright and Rex Johnson, *Characteristics of a Caring Home.* Ventura, Calif.: Vision House, 1978.

Boredom

Boredom is an affliction that exasperates all of us throughout life, of course, which is perhaps why no one takes it very seriously—rather like the common cold; and it also resembles the common cold in being a highly visible, complex, and ill-defined phenomenon that we all thoroughly understand except for knowing exactly why we get it or how to cure it. A conscious awareness of time is always part of boredom: whenever we're bored, time stands still or drags; we have time on our hands, time to kill; whatever is boring us seems to go on forever. Under ordinary circumstances this "I-thought-it-would-never-end" feature of boredom amounts to a trivial experience of time diffusion, a mistrust of the future that lasts only until we can escape from what's boring us. But the circumstances of the crisis are not ordinary, and what is called boredom then is in most respects not identical with these other, less serious experiences. Before we can talk about this crisis malaise, though, we will first have to digress slightly to explore the nature of ennui.

Boring situations in general pose some kind of (not necessarily conscious) threat to psychological comfort and well-being; when we're bored, it's usually in self-defense. One of the most familiar boredoms, for example, is stimulus boredom: the mental restlessness and fatigue we feel after frequent repetitions of any intrinsically dull, tedious, and mechanical task such as adding columns of figures, sewing on name tapes, or driving a long stretch of superhighway. This boredom protects us against inadequate mental performance by provoking a desire for change. As a series of psychological experiments have shown, unrelieved monotony impairs normal brain activity. In one study, for instance, subjects were artificially deprived of all patterned and perceptual stimulations by being isolated in continuously lighted cubicles where airconditioning hum and specially shaped foam pillows blocked out sounds, and where, in addition, they wore translucent plastic visors, cotton gloves, and cardboard cuffs to keep other sensory impressions to a minimum. Every one of these individuals eventually developed severe mental disturbances: hallucinations, childish emotional responses, disturbed visual perceptions, and changes in brain-wave patterns, all of which persisted until the subjects returned to normal living.

As any city dweller knows, constant intense stimulation is as monotonous, tiresome, and disruptive to mental performance as lack of excitement, and we react to a continuing high level of stimulation with the same symptoms of restlessness and fatigue. Here, of course, change means withdrawal from stimuli that we perceive, once our limits of satiation have been reached, as intrusive and obnoxious—that is, boring. If physical escape from a noisy party, a too hectic schedule, an endlessly tedious anecdote, a banal movie is not possible, we simply isolate ourselves mentally by tuning out as many sensory impressions as we can and retreating with glazed eyes into contemplation.

Another psychological response, also called boredom, serves to defend us against a menacing situation that doesn't have much to do with variety. This boredom is the barrier we interpose between consciousness and unacceptable internal stimuli: when an unpleasant emotion, impulse, or desire threatens to erupt into consciousness, one way to keep it under control is to substitute for it the idea of being bored. Let us say, for instance, that you're trapped in an automobile

with your mother-in-law, a lady whom ordinarily you love dearly but whose remarks on this occasion are such that they arouse in you the primal urge to kill. There is no place you can go; you'd prefer not to admit your hostility to her or to yourself, much less implement it; so instead, you sigh and think, "What a bore she's being today," and with this for an excuse feel free to let your mind wander to other things. "Whenever I'm bored by what a patient's saying," a psychoanalyst said, "I immediately examine my own feelings to see if what he's telling me is something that's making me anxious, and I'm substituting boredom for anxiety so that I can withdraw. A lot of times patients' remarks are objectively just plain dull and truly boring, but it's always necessary to check."

Substitution boredom shades imperceptibly into alibi boredom—a maneuver by means of which we avoid the unpleasant and threatening necessity of having to admit defeat. Instead of saying we can't handle a situation or solve a problem, we save face by protesting that it's too boring to bother with, and give up trying; I've always been profoundly bored, in this sense, with the idea of even looking for, let alone finding, cube roots. There is a kind of merciful gentlemen's agreement about alibi boredom. We all resort to it so often that unless the matter is judged too important to be thus sidestepped—public opinion goes against a man who says he's too bored with the idea of working to be bothered holding down a job—the excuse is tolerated as valid.

Without question, some ... boredom is ordinary, everyday ennui applied to the special problems of a life-crisis. Indeed, judging from the number and similarity of complaints of boredom by both adolescents and middlescents, it's hard to believe either group could manage to live through their crises without these defensive maneuvers.

The adolescent cries that he's bored with life, school, parents, and family, with being lectured about the future, and with having to do what he doesn't want to and never being able to do what he does want. Forty grumbles about life, adolescents, marriage, spouse, job, housework, commuting, with routine habits and duties that've suddenly gone sour, and with having to do all these things he doesn't want to and never being able to do what he does want. Both age groups are right about how they feel—they *are* bored; and much of it is substitution or alibi ennui, being used to justify or rationalize unacceptable crisis behavior.

—From Barbara Fried, *The Middle-Age Crisis.* Rev. ed. New York: Harper & Row, 1976.

Change

Married couples grow apart for many reasons. However, one of the major reasons given for this occurrence is that of change. A woman recently said, "My husband is not the same man I married. He has changed so much that I feel as if I am married to a total stranger." The husband replied that he had not really changed that much but that his wife surely had. "In the first years of our marriage she was kind and considerate and seemed interested in building a home for me and the children. In the last few years, however, she has rebelled against everything she once stood for and seems intent on a career apart from that of wife and mother."

While they were never able to agree on who had done the changing, they were able to agree that it had occurred and that their marriage was sheer chaos as a result.

The truth is that both had changed after eight years of marriage, and neither was able to adjust to the change in the other.

If we assume that most couples marry because they love each other, then we can conclude that all marriages ending in divorce do so because of changes in the feelings of the two people involved.

Although it may seem trite to repeat that which is so obvious, we do so because many couples embark on a life together with the unspoken assumption that things will always be the same and that both parties will forever remain as they were when they were dating. It should be stressed, however, that marriage is a process, a process in which change is inevitable. While most of us strive for stability in life, there are few things in this world which are stable or permanent. Things change. People are changing all the time. No person is exactly the same today as he or she was yesterday. Consequently, all relationships are also continuously undergoing change, and all come to an end eventually. Even those marriages which are judged successful will eventually come to an end due to death.

Unfortunately, many marriages die prematurely because too many husbands and wives choose to ignore the inescapable fact that people do change.

People can grow apart even when they truly love and care for each other. For some the resistance to change is so deeply ingrained that acceptance of change, even in someone they dearly love, is almost impossible. However, since it is an indisputable fact of life that people do change, and since this is one of the major reasons listed by couples as the source of problems in marriage, couples would do well to explore in depth their ability to adjust to the many changes which are inevitable in the years after marriage.

Difficulties might be anticipated if:

1. either person seems locked into a way of thinking or behaving which allows for no difference of opinion or new ideas.
2. either has communicated to the other what he or she wants in a husband or

wife and gives the impression that he or she will not tolerate any deviation from this rigid stance, now or in the future.

3. one of the individuals demonstrates a desire to grow and improve while the other seems determined to maintain the status quo.
4. one or both shows a noticeable lack of curiosity or interest in the changes which are occurring around him or her from day to day.
5. one seems eager to experiment and try new things, while the other refuses to depart from more traditional and established ways.
6. either gets upset easily or acts as if the whole day is ruined if things do not go according to schedule or if plans are changed. The individual who is unable to adjust to change before marriage is not likely to be able to adjust to change after marriage.

—From Robert L. Mason, Jr., and Caroline L. Jacobs, *How to Choose the Wrong Marriage Partner and Live Unhappily Ever After*. Atlanta: John Knox, 1979.

Depression

Fifty thousand to seventy thousand annual suicides due to depression verify the seriousness of this problem in our culture. Any Christian counselor will testify that it is one of the most common disabilities he confronts. Because many Christians refuse to seek the aid of counselors, they try to live with the pain like a low-grade infection in the body, as if it were a necessary part of life.

Depression . . . is a result of anger, fear, and self-rejection. The many symptoms and causes are detailed in *How to Win Over Depression* which should be helpful to those who are plagued by this enemy to happy family living, for I wish to point out that a cure *does* exist. I am convinced that no Spirit-filled Christian will be depressed. In fact, depression should serve as a warning that one is not filled with God's Spirit but permeated with self.

You can actually chart your own depression, for its intensity will vary with the degree of self-pity. The time sequence is also important. Usually within one to twenty-four hours after one inaugurates the process of self-pity, he becomes aware of the depression. Those who have nurtured self-pity for years (until they are quite skilled at it) may be able to feel its effects in a matter of minutes.

Depression never starts without provocation. A happy, well-adjusted person will not suddenly become depressed, as if he were hit by a viral infection. Usually he will find that something specific happened or will remember a previous unfortunate event—perhaps rejection by someone he loves, an insult, or an injury. The following depression-producing formula should be cemented in your mind. Anytime you find yourself drifting into depression, think of this formula and then follow the steps for a cure.

Rejection
Insult $\Big\}$ SELF-PITY = DEPRESSION
Injury

THE CURE FOR DEPRESSION

1. Face self-pity as a mental sin pattern.
2. Confess this sin of the mind.
3. Ask God to take away this thought pattern.
4. Ask for the filling of the Holy Spirit.
5. Thank God in the midst of the rejection, insult, or injury that He is with you, supplying all your need.
6. Repeat this formula each time you find yourself depressed.

144

—From Tim and Bev LaHaye, *Spirit-Controlled Family Living.* Old Tappan, N.J.: Revell, 1978.

Disagreement

What can a dad teach his children on how to disagree? At home? Man and wife?

Rule 1: Expect some disagreement. Don't be ashamed of anger. It's a natural emotion. Accept it as a sign you're very much alive. If you face it honestly, you can learn to handle it.

Rule 2: As a base for healthy disagreement, skill yourself in the use of that simple little phrase "I like you because . . ." The negative always goes better against a background loaded with praise.

Rule 3: Train yourself to speak softly when you're angry. Letting it all hang out is important, but tone and volume can make a mighty difference. As the ire goes higher, lower your voice one octave instead of raising it two.

Rule 4: Keep your fusses at home. It's a good idea when you're quarreling to commit yourselves to the simple little adage, "In public we will be 100 percent loyal to each other."

Rule 5: Recognize the fact that some disagreements can go unanswered and you can still love to the maximum. You don't have to like each other 100 percent to love 100 percent.

Rule 6: Don't wait too long. Surface it as soon as you can. But be careful, you may need to postpone it overnight, or at least a few hours. So while you school yourself on getting it out of your system you must also learn to pick your times carefully.

Rule 7: Keep these two words up front— "I apologize." Who started it, who did what to whom is not as important as how can we get it back together. In our marriage we enjoy exercising together. Walking. Bicycling. Tennis. Yoga. But one of the finest exercises we ever discovered is unbending the bowed neck to say "I'm sorry."

—From Charlie W. Shedd, *The Best Dad Is a Good Lover.* Fairway, Kans.: Andrews and McMeel, 1977.

Friendship With the Opposite Sex

For a woman who is accustomed to raising children and being the wife of a husband with a career, moving outside the home offers new intellectual, cultural and social stimulation. A large part of this new experience involves relationships: boss/employee, professor/student, supervisor/clerk, peer/peer, friend/friend. And as these relationships develop, the married woman will have to decide if the edict about married men and friendship is good advice.

The woman at home raising children has little opportunity to form friendships with any man other than her husband. Even if she does know other men, she may not have much in common with them. Church functions are often segregated—couples meet with other couples, men with men, and women with women. The age-old jokes about men gathering around the fire to discuss jobs and politics while the women exchange recipes in the kitchen have not been far from the truth. In a working or school situation, however, with greater opportunities to get to know men easily, friendships can develop naturally.

A *Psychology Today* 1979 poll on friendship revealed that keeping confidences, loyalty, a sense of humor, willingness to take time, intelligence, independence and being a good conversationalist topped the list of important friendship ingredients. Those qualities are easily discovered in either sex.

C. S. Lewis wrote that friendship arises out of companionship when two discover that they have some interest, insight or taste

145

in common which others do not share. "It is when someone can say to another: 'What? You too? I thought I was the only one.' "

That commonality can be found in a book two people have read, a job, political views, mutual friends or a million other things. And it can be found as easily with men as with women.

But the same survey showed that almost three-quarters of the respondents believed friendship with the opposite sex was different than friendship with the same sex. The major reasons stated were sexual tension, societal discouragement and less things in common. Society's encouraged separateness and the idea that male/female friendships have traditionally been romantic, along with the fear of "what might happen," undoubtedly cause at least some of the tensions that make women hesitant to pursue friendships with the opposite sex.

In his book, *The Four Loves*, C. S. Lewis comments on this facet of friendship: "When two people who discover that they are on the same secret road are of different sexes, the friendship which arises between them will very easily pass—may pass in the first half hour—into erotic love. Indeed, unless they are physically repulsive to each other or unless one or both already love elsewhere, it is almost certain to do so sooner or later."

In acknowledging the problem, Lewis also gives the solution: "unless one or both already love elsewhere." Friendship with a married man, especially a Christian, is possible because he already loves.

That, of course, is the ideal. And this is where some Christians get into trouble. Because we know such emotional involvement, from God's perspective, is out of the question and because we believe it ourselves and feel immune, we wander into situations blindly, often forgetting that life, even for Christians, is not always what it should be.

A middle-aged Christian woman was be-

ginning to understand the problem when she asked: At what point am I being unfaithful to my husband? She is wise for recognizing that any eventual physical or mental unfaithfulness will have its beginning long before it actually happens.

It is important for women to understand, however, that attraction is not necessarily wrong. After all, a certain amount of attraction—be it physical, intellectual or emotional—is an ingredient of friendship, whether that friendship is with a man or a woman. The difference with male/female friendships is that the attraction may lead to something more.

One Christian single professional woman in her late twenties faced this problem in her relationship with a male associate. Her worry was not that she would be unfaithful, but that she would cause such thoughts in another: "I didn't realize I was emotionally involved until I was way beyond that line of friendship. By that time, he was there, too, and had been for a while. Then, of course, it was too late to avoid dealing with."

A married woman in her early thirties decided to back away from a friendship she sensed she could not handle, evaluated her feelings, and then went back to the friendship, confident that she had the correct motives.

Many women have faced the risks and pitfalls of male/female friendships and are still convinced that such relationships are necessary for a balanced life. Others, of course, would disagree. But it appears that maintaining a healthy friendship between sexes depends on knowing when that line between friendship and emotional involvement has become too close. And that line will be different for different people.

Five questions, drawn from women's experiences in handling male/female friendships, may be helpful in assessing danger areas in relationships.

1. What attracts you to him? Is it respect for a person successful in your career field, common interests, the way he makes you feel about yourself as a person, or as a woman?
2. Do you initiate times spent together or look for reasons to get together?
3. Do you ask him for advice you really don't need but should get from your husband, a relative or a female friend?
4. When spending time with him, do you welcome others to join you or do you want him all to yourself?
5. Is your friendship something you do not hesitate to discuss with your husband, family or other friends?

If a woman knows herself and her personality, she will also know some areas of personal weakness. Some personalities are more prone to attachments than others. If a woman always makes deep friendships quickly and naturally, she may find herself deeply attached to a male friend before she realizes it. Other women are good listeners everyone seems to seek out for a sympathetic ear. She may find married men friends coming for advice on things they should be discussing with their wives.

A woman's emotional state can also make her more vulnerable to strong attachments. Single women sometimes experience lonely times when they simply want a man to care. There are days when married women feel taken for granted or are tired of taking care of a household and long for some reprieve. The Christian woman will be wary of all these factors and watchful of how they affect her friendships—especially with men.

But it would be a grave mistake to leave the impression that every male/female friendship is fraught with sexual tension and emotional involvement. They're not. Often such a friendship becomes the best and deepest a person has known. Believing that friendship with a man is too much work or too dangerous cheats a woman out of good experiences and chances to grow as a person.

Friendships of all kinds, according to C. S. Lewis, are gifts from God. "It is not a reward for our discrimination and good taste in finding one another out. It is the instrument by which God reveals to each the beauties of all the others. They are no greater beauties than the beauties of a thousand others; by friendship God opens our eyes to them. At this feast it is He who has spread the board and it is He who has chosen the guests. It is He, we may dare to hope, who sometimes does, and always should preside."

—BY Anita M. Moreland, a freelance writer who is Director of Communications for Prison Fellowship in northern Virginia.

Guilt

We begin learning early in life through imitation and family discipline to assume responsibility for our own behavior. We recognize the command "no" before we grasp the positive side.

When we, at any age, do something we have been taught is "bad," "wrong," or "naughty" we feel guilty.

Guilt troubles all people. As Christians, we recognize the sinful condition of fallen humanity. Because of our basic problem of alienation from God, guilt troubles us all. It attacks us in many ways. We feel ashamed, unworthy, sinful, useless. Words such as *should, ought,* and *must* crop up in our conversation. "To be a better parent, I must speak up." "Because I'm a Christian, I should volunteer to sing in the choir." When those emotions stir within us, guilt results.

These "ought" voices come from many places: the church, parents, peer pressure, friends' expectations, and societal norms.

How do we cope with guilt?

1. When aware of failure of any kind, confess it. If others are involved and it will

help the situation, confess to them as well.

2. Remind yourself, "I am forgiven." God forgives us when we confess (*see* 1 John 1:9).

3. Forgive yourself. Those with perfectionist tendencies ("I ought to be better ... I ought to have known ...") especially have difficulty in self-forgiveness. If you're one of those, here's a method people have found helpful. Look at yourself in a mirror. Say aloud at least three times daily, "I am forgiven for...." Name the specific thing for which you have been unable to forgive yourself.

4. Remember, guilt comes from what we call the conscience. That's not totally God. The voice of conscience speaks from various sources such as family upbringing, and early experiences in the church.

5. You may need to remind yourself daily that God isn't like a policeman out to get you as soon as you fail. The best biblical picture is that He's a loving Father (*see* Luke 15), who takes away our sins once and for all.

—CECIL MURPHEY

Jealousy

Jealousy is resentment toward anything or anyone seen as a rival for the attention or affection of one's spouse. This gamelike power struggle emanates from an unconscious sense of inadequacy. The jealous partner can never realistically get all the attention he demands. Any rival for the spouse's attention comes to be feared as more important or more lovable in the eyes of the spouse.

For a number of years in our marriage, my husband needed time and space to be alone. That was a brand-new idea to me because my parents were (and seemed to want to be) always together. I love my husband and felt I could never have enough time with him. So for years, when he would go away or sit in his study, alone, I felt abandoned and rejected. I suspected he had found another woman who was prettier or more desirable than I. My pride, of course, would not let me tell him how ugly and unworthy I often felt. And I suspect his pride wouldn't let him admit that all the responsibilities of a wife and family seemed heavy to him.

Had he told me about the stress he endured, and explained his needs clearly, or had I been better able to clarify my worries, we would both have avoided an element of misunderstanding over a number of years. In one of the ironies of life, when I finally understood and stopped feeling threatened by his needs, my husband no longer had the craving for so much space and time of his own!

This game is over when you know that you are the best person you can be and you no longer have to try to be perfect. Furthermore, the value of yourself comes from within you and not from the opinion of anyone else. Most important, knowing that you are created in the very image of God makes you priceless in His eyes!

—From Grace H. Ketterman, M.D., *How to Teach Your Child About Sex*. Old Tappan, N.J.: Revell, 1981.

Killing Romance

I've always been amused by the bug-killer commercials on television—the ones that show a squadron of mosquitoes or flies happily on their way to a picnic, licking their lips at what is promising to be quite a banquet. Then Captain Raid appears, and the bugs' picnic is over. The expectations of a hundred insects are supposedly ended in a cloud of bug-killer.

There are several ways to kill romance in a similar lethal cloud. The brightest expectations and hopes can be extinguished in a matter of minutes if one member or the other of a marriage follows the directions in one of the following ways. I don't know how many times I've seen this happen at a social gathering, or in a conversation between a few couples—just about anywhere. Delicate feelings are smashed, and romance—at least for the moment—is over, dead.

Ridicule can kill romance. It is razor sharp, and it shatters feelings as fast as anything I can imagine. Ridicule can be sprayed on in a number of different ways. Ridiculing feelings is one way. A husband or a wife coyly confides that he or she is in a mood to do some "crazy thing," and the other person pointedly highlights the absurdity of such an idea. Besides there's work to do. How can we get away for an evening when the back door screen has to be repaired?

Ridiculing attempted affection can be devastating as. . .a person is at his most vulnerable when he reaches out to touch, only to have the partner jerk away. To be sure, we have to presuppose that there has not been some conflict which makes someone quite disinclined to be affectionate. How painful the feeling, however, of the rejection of a hug, a caress, or even a kiss. If it happens too often the person who has gone out on a limb will not return for another try.

Ridiculing a mate's attempt to please is another killer. A wife prepares herself for her husband's homecoming by honoring him with a favorite dress, a special menu, and candles. At the very best, he grunts at it all and picks up the paper. He has turned off the switch, and the chances are that his partner will wait a long time before she tries to please him in such a way again.

Ridiculing someone's dreams and aspirations can put many fires out in a relationship. A wife says to a group of couples, "Gene has the dumbest ideas. The other day he suggested that we try saving for a trip to Europe for our fifteenth anniversary. As if we don't have enough to save for. Braces for the kids, school tuition, and a new furnace this next winter—but *Gene* wants to go to Europe!" A chastened Gene sits over in one corner of the room and feels rather stupid that he dared to think out loud with his wife.

Beyond ridicule there are some other effective killers of romance. Take the *unwillingness of a person to express himself*, keeping every feeling locked up inside. No one knows how someone like this really feels; you have to drag reactions out of him with a block and tackle. You do it until you get tired of doing it and look to someone else for response. The man who feels no inclination to share himself with his wife, who never says "Thank you," or "I appreciate this," or "I'm excited to live with you," is going to kill romance in a short time.

The *selfish* person will jeopardize romance also. Thinking only of herself and what she can get out of a relationship, a selfish wife will squander all the desire her husband once had to join in the emotion of a relationship. There's no percentage; she cannot be pleased. Do something; buy something; go somewhere, and she wants to do, buy, or go more. There is no reciprocation; it's all a one-way street. Soon the husband quits trying, and his wife turns bitter. She has been let down.

Privacy together is essential to the survival of romance. A husband may spend most of his free time with his buddies. They are over at the house on Saturdays fixing cars. During the evenings, they are playing softball on the church team. On vacations, they all travel together to the beach. The husband never spends time alone with his wife. She begs her husband for some time when they can go off together, have an evening doing something by themselves. He snaps back, saying that she is always trying to separate him from his friends.

149

Romance depends upon time alone, secrets shared only with each other, and a sense that each would do anything to get away with the other to some quiet place. When a husband or wife feels as if he or she must share the partner with many others all the time, romance dies swiftly.

To complete a partial list of romance killers let me add the problem of *hyper-seriousness*. It is a mad world we live in, and many of us are caught in the closing vise of pressure from employment, taxes, inflation, uneasiness about the world stability, and a hundred other things. It is easy to become preoccupied and lose the ability to laugh. Life becomes one unchanging color: gray. Romance cannot grow in the heart of a man or a woman who cannot escape the surrounding pressures, for romance is predicated on a smile, a free spirit, and a creative drive to exult in the love of another person. And when that happens, the pipes of the relationship are cleaned out, and two people can renew the great objective of relationship: to become one flesh.

A man went into a card store to buy a birthday card for his wife. He finally found a very ornate one which carried this message: "Your love is worth the world and all its treasures." He asked the clerk how much it was. "That one is ninety-five cents," he was told. The man frowned. "Don't you have something that's a little cheaper?"

Romance is not cheap, but its price comes not in the payment of money. It only costs the giving of oneself in a relationship which says, "I really like you!"

—From Gordon MacDonald, *Magnificent Marriage*. Wheaton, Ill.: Tyndale, 1976.

Lack of Common Interests

A lack of common interests is another complaint frequently heard by marriage counselors, and it is one which seems to be high on the lists of reasons given for marital breakdowns. While it is neither possible nor desirable for couples always to share the same interests, having very little in common can lead to serious problems. When a couple finds they are doing nothing together, they will eventually raise the question "Why stay married?"

For many people the prospect of being married to someone from an entirely different background can be very exciting at first. It is not uncommon, for example, to see a gentle and sensitive woman married to a man who is both crude and cruel, or a highly educated man married to a high-school drop-out. Often a person with high moral standards ends up married to a person of questionable character, sometimes one with a long history of criminal activities. The possibilities are endless, as any marriage counselor can attest.

While there may be some truth in the belief that opposites attract, it is also important that couples have some desire to share their lives with each other. Since the tendency is to try to impress one's partner while dating, it is often difficult to determine the degree to which individuals have mutual interests.

Many people complain that before marriage their spouses gave the impression that they enjoyed certain activities. After marriage, however, there was a noticeable lack of interest in pursuing those activities shared earlier. Many women, for example, say that while dating, their husbands were very attentive, affectionate, tender, and romantic. They often went to concerts or nice restaurants and did lots of things together. After marriage, however, many wives complain that their husbands have changed, and they wonder if they were ever the way they seemed at all. Husbands likewise complain that their wives gave the impression that they were sincerely interested in sports, sex, travel, company, or myriad other activities which they seemed to have in common until the man was "hooked." When this happens, both husbands and wives end up feeling that they have been tricked or deceived.

Differences in life-styles should be considered when raising the question of compatibility with another person. Life-styles that leave little time for mutual sharing will not enhance a marriage relationship. The following are just a few of the many contrasting life-styles which can drain marriages rather than provide them with sustenance.

1. The spouse who is a "work-a-holic" vs. the spouse who likes to work from nine to five and have other activities to pursue.
2. The socialite vs. the home-body. Some people find recreation and refreshment in socializing; others find that the solitude of home enhances their emotional well-being. Both desires are normal, but they are very different.
3. The spouse who likes a predictable routine vs. the spouse who likes constant variety.
4. The spouse who wants to socialize primarily with others of the same sex vs. the spouse who enjoys doing things as a couple and with other couples.

—From Robert L. Mason, Jr., and Caroline L. Jacobs, *How to Choose the Wrong Marriage Partner and Live Unhappily Ever After.* Atlanta: John Knox, 1979.

Moods

Moods are a natural part of every personality. In my experience there are no exceptions among men. (Nor women or children either for that matter.) The only variation to the rule is one of degree or place or time or what motivates the mood. "Sometimes I'm up, sometimes I'm down" is the song of every soul. Even the saints flagged in zeal part of the time.

Come to think of it, isn't this escalator-going-both-ways a part of all life? Music has its somber fugues and gay roundelays. Nature has its cycles. History has its high times and low. It appears that all things fluctuate and husbands are no exception.

Be grateful for the blessings of contrast which these experiences provide. When our loved ones have bad moods, this may make their good stand out in bold relief after the agony has run its course. Perhaps we can appreciate our mates at their best because we are allowed to see them also at their worst.

Maybe you are asking, "But don't moods sometimes move from natural to 'sick'?" They certainly do, and one measurement is the time it takes for emerging. Any moody mind which returns rapidly to the sunshine indicates a healthy climate inside. It is good also to check for frequency. Are the morose moments coming with increasing rapidity? Another evil omen is the roller-coaster pattern—way up one day, way down the next! When these intensify at an alarming rate, you best hurry on down for advice from those who deal daily in troubled minds.

Comes now another item of real importance. *Try your best not to go down into the swamps of despair when he goes down.* This is much easier said than done, of course, and it will take some time to learn this one. It is so easy for you to become melancholy when he becomes melancholy.

Because you love him so much you want to share all things with him fully, and it may appear on the surface that you could help him best by glumming it through together! But "togetherness" of the highest kind does not mean going together to the lowest levels.

If you can keep your heart filled with high-level kindness when he is down, you will really contribute more to his recovery than by almost any other method. This may make him furious at first because most of us have never completely conquered this one subconscious little demon. I refer to the one which can't stand it for others to feel good when we feel bad.

But this initial wrath will pass if you keep calm. When it is over, he will be glad that one pair of feet remains firmly on solid ground. In time, you can work this out to a "deal" where he does his best to stay topside when it is your turn to go below.

One reason why you might be tempted to despondency when he is despondent is that you may blame yourself unduly for his bad moods. If you are at fault and you know it you will say so. But groveling in the emotional sloughs of self-criticism is strictly no good when it is *his* black mood and not your doing. You are growing up when you can honestly say, "I will remember that this is *his* problem. I will refuse to punish myself. My job is to keep calm and ready. I will prepare my heart to give him the most mature love I can manage as soon as he gives me the opening."

I have observed some skillful women doing another clever thing. *They get ready for their husband's bad moods before the low ceiling comes down.*

Maybe you can learn your man's weak points and "seed the tornado" to scatter the ugly winds. One of the most successful wives among our friends says that she asks her husband to barbecue her a steak when she feels some inner woe sneaking up on him. She testifies that the combination of a big meal and her accolades to his cooking works wonders for him.

Maybe you should go dancing. Perhaps a long drive in the moonlight is the right antidote. If he prefers to come home and glower there then put on your best, roll out your dark blue carpet, and let him work it out under his own roof. Some men I know would give their bottom dollar if they could have such a "shelter of a rock from a weary land" in their own home.

If you make enough progress at handling these things together, you might even learn to give each other warning signals. Catherine Anthony says that she and Jim have agreed to this jewel: If he's had a rough day at the office, if he's off his usual cheery base, if the stock market is down, or he lost an account he hoped to get, then Jim wears a red feather in his hat when he comes home. "Warning, dear! This is no evening to present that unexpected bill or to report the broken throttle on the mower!"

There is one thing more you can do. This is, in fact, *the* big curative! It is the one where your mother and I find our most effective remedy. You spell it with four letters: *Talk!*

—From Charlie W. Shedd, *Letters to Karen.* Nashville: Abingdon, 1965.

Quarrels

Couples about to marry seem to have as an ideal, "If we really communicate, we'll never quarrel. And if we do, we'll make up quickly." Ideally, yes; actually, it isn't likely. A quarrel may clear the air, releasing pent-up emotions in both partners. When repressed, these emotions are destructive. A quarrel also reveals how deeply each person feels about the point at issue. This is a message about a message, signaling the crisis-nature of the disagreement, and alerting the couple to the necessity of reaching an acceptable agreement rather than settling for easy appeasement. Emotional tension may cause real communication to be repressed without a couple's awareness that it is happening. Furthermore, the reasoned discussion they hope for may never materialize. Quite differently, a quarrel starts by spontaneous combustion—*but it does start!*

It may take a quarrel to meet the problem of inertia or inhibition in marital communication. The explosive crisis is the couple's means of getting through to each other in a way that counts. To disagree is not necessarily to discredit. At least the two interact and respond to each other! So, depending on its aim, a quarrel may be healthy. Some sensitive individuals refrain from open disagreement for fear they will be thought hostile. But despite such risk, and even the intensity of a disagreement, if there is acceptance of each other a couple can confirm the strength of their relationship as well as show their mutual respect for their individual differences.

Disagreements come and they must be handled in one way or another; quarreling is one way and necessary at times. We must also make the distinction that *disagreements* are one thing, *behaving disagreeably* is quite another. Disagreements simply confirm the individuality of the partners in marriage, at least insofar as they challenge their ability to manage different perceptions and convictions. A quarrel makes for good communication if it leaves both partners with the reassurance of acceptance and reciprocal love, with mutual trust in spite of all differences.

People are not changed by threats and ultimatums. Little is accomplished by duress, and all worthwhile change takes time. But a good quarrel, waged openly and fairly, is the best way in the world to get some changes started. A husband can't browbeat a wife into changing her ways, nor can a wife shame a husband into dropping his bad habits. The wife will become more resistant and stubborn; the husband will be driven deeper into his ways. If two people are bent on shaming each other into concessions, a quarrel will get nowhere. Yet annoyances and frustrations must be expressed sooner or later, and the sooner the better. The longer they are held back, the greater the possibility that only a quarrel will bring them out of concealment. A quarrel can succeed in ripping away pretenses and masks where other means fail. It reveals us as we really are, and such revelation we've seen to be necessary to full communication. As Ernest Havemann says, "It stirs the witches' brew that boils inside each one of us and lets the poisonous fumes escape." A quarrel often tells us that our overpolite, tactful conditioning borders on hypocrisy and keeps us from expressing honest emotions. Our bland pursuit of friendliness with a smile, our banality, precludes honest encounters. Our deferential way may give us pride in our civilized restraints, but hardly allows us to meet as real persons in full emotional dress. The nonquarreling couples are the inhibited, fearful people for whom honest, open communication is a threat.

Quarreling leads up a blind alley when the motivation is to change another, *or to win.* We can't remake another into something he is not, nor can we ever declare a winner in a marital quarrel. What one wins by coercion is balanced by losses of a more serious nature in terms of the ongoing relationship. But when two people in the heat of battle learn to respect each other's desires and feelings, then the late supper or the missed birthday loom less as tragedies. After the fight, when the dust settles, little allowances and adjustments seem easier to make, whereas before they were most difficult. The important thing is that two people learn to appreciate the depth of each other's feelings—something they cannot do until those feelings are adequately aired. Havemann's counsel is to the point: "If you cannot stand to have anyone cross you, disappoint you, impose on you at times, disagree with you, and pout at you, the only choice you have is to live alone."

STAYING FRIENDS WHILE FIGHTING

If quarrels are at times dangerous and unnecessary, yet are often the only way to open, honest communication, certain rules should apply if couples are to stay friends while fighting. Duvall and Hill suggest that couples spell out exactly what they don't like and how they want things changed, sticking to the point, avoiding side issues, and staying with it until things are thrashed out. A couple in conflict should especially check any inferences, assumptions, or logical fallacies that might impede communication. If they're to avoid personal rejection, they must not descend to trading insults, or using *ad hominem* arguments. Agreed-upon rules of this nature are necessary to take the acrimony out of matrimony, and to allow a couple to quarrel occasionally with profit.

Sometimes a couple will smile blandly and say to their friends, "We never disagree." Poor dears! If this is communication, how dull and unproductive life must be! Might this not be self-deception? Or flight from genuine and meaningful interaction? Or just the naïve beginning of a promising marriage? If they never disagree, then we must assume that neither are they contributing anything to the growth of their relationship. Instead, they have settled for a static relationship, a second-rate marriage. They are making allowance for a more or less permanent estrangement, without striving for solutions which would contribute to growth. As David Mace suggests, this is a rather cowardly way to give finality to failure.

POWER STRUGGLES

In a previous volume, the writer was concerned to note the following: "In every marriage there is the existence of two opposing principles: completion and competition. Completion is always imperfect at best, while conflict from competition is continually created at the deepest levels of the personal relation. Having come to marriage with faith in their love, two persons discover that each ultimately loves himself more than the other. Conflict arises between self-devo-

tion and devotion to the other. Two self-centered lives confront each other in the most self-revealing terms. Each challenges the other's self-love and freedom as they have never been challenged before. Basic conflict arises between the value of loving responsibility and the value of independence and self-desire. When the two values are at cross-purposes, how virulent can frustrated self-love show itself to be! How violently it can react! It is a rude shock to many to discover that one cannot give up an independent, self-devoted and self-directed life merely by taking a marriage vow. The love in which they placed so much faith is seen to be inadequate in itself to transform the self and resolve the tension and conflict."

Here an inherently tragic condition arises from the conjunction of two strong wills-to-power, from the clash of two free and autonomous persons. Human love is never immune from the possibility of failure and betrayal. Resident in sinful human nature is the tension between wanting to give love, and at the same time trying to possess and dominate another for one's own selfish purposes. Pride can react to the realization that one is married to a disappointingly imperfect mate, while the mate, too, is aware of being married to an equally disappointing and imperfect person.

A power struggle only inhibits the free responses of love. It is the struggle of two individuals seeking self-affirmation and recognition in the only promising relationship in a coldly impersonal world. In his Gifford Lectures, John MacMurray writes, "The conflict of ends gives rise to a struggle for power, and in this struggle the intentions of each party are perverted to securing victory over the other . . . so freedom is destroyed. For while the conflict continues, the adversaries must lay aside the hope of achieving their real intentions. Each must act for ends dictated by the other's opposition; and the victor, if there be a victor, regains his freedom of action with his resources impaired, and often reduced to a point at which they are inadequate to his original purposes." With a similar idea in mind, Havemann cautions, "Go ahead and quarrel all you like, but remember one thing. You cannot win; the best you can hope for is a tie."

The trouble with most quarrels is the wife's attempt to remake her husband and the husband's attempt to remodel his wife. A husband may never succeed in diminishing his wife's interest in late television shows, her addiction to interminable phone conversations, or her persuasion that department stores are among life's greatest pleasures. A wife may never turn her husband into a conversationalist, end his gluttony at the breakfast table, or bring him to remember little things like birthdays and anniversaries. Extracted promises are fine, except that they depend on human capacities. Similarly, sincere attempts can also fail when goals are set too high. So couples can quarrel occasionally, but not to decide a winner, to extract promises, or to "let the other have it." They quarrel successfully when they open channels of communication and bring hidden issues to light. Reuel Howe points out that some things are never settled, however good the communication may be. But mature couples understand and learn to live with them. At best, having come to an impasse despite good communicative techniques—or even by way of a quarrel—it is easier for a couple to accept the fact that the problem may never be settled, and go on to manage it with maturity and satisfaction.

If the basic approach to problem-solving is coercive, and quarreling has become the vehicle for coercion, then no facility in verbal communication can overcome the handicaps of such manipulative behavior. Coercive approaches invariably produce impasses. Tyrannical outbursts of anger, employed usually to make the other cower and give in because of fear, may succeed at the moment but will lose in the end. Sometimes, as an extreme measure, a married partner coerces with threats of legal action ("If you don't quit badgering the children, I'll go ahead with that divorce!"). This is an evasion of honest discussion, a power play, nothing more than an attempt to gain leverage.

SECRETS ISOLATE AND INSULATE

Paul Tournier stresses the role of secrets in the marriage relation. It's the secrets about ourselves (and what we think about ourselves) that isolate us from each other. Particularly in the process of disenchantment in early marriage, husband and wife see each other as they are, not as they wish they were. They see to what degree they had endowed each other with qualities they didn't have; defects they didn't see are now apparent. Each partner perceives some delusions he has created for himself, delusions he must work to resolve. So now two disenchanted persons begin to make judgments on each other, judgments they are tempted to keep secret in order not to cause a hurt or precipitate a rift. The wife now hesitates to speak of certain things for fear they will support the judgments her husband is beginning to make about her. The husband acts in the same way. Perhaps the judgment concerns a set of parents about whom there has grown some disagreement. So, in the interests of peace, they both begin to break their promise to tell each other everything. In this way they begin to become strangers to one another, and it's married strangers who quarrel most readily. Secrets do indeed isolate partners from each other.

The situation only worsens, as Tournier points out, when one says to the other, "What's the matter with you? You seem so secretive. You don't tell me anything any more." The other is quick to reply, "Oh, you're only imagining it; I'm not hiding anything from you." But the uneasiness continues. There is no longer the transparency they once knew, and now they must work strenuously to reestablish it. The insulating factor is the accumulating secrets neither partner wishes to bear alone, yet has not learned to share with any degree of security.

Good communication is an open, candid surfacing of differences, exposing even the most negative feelings. It is a meeting place for honest interaction. Married people must have the courage to believe that whatever their interaction may involve, the ultimate outcome has high promise of being well worth it all.

SCAPEGOATING

Robert W. Burns points out that a husband who says something humiliating or demeaning to his wife may merely be reflecting something in his day's work which he has suffered without opportunity to retaliate, or about which he has been unable to express himself. The etiquette of public relations and office living has required that he keep his feelings bottled up. Although his patience may have been exhausted, he dare not let it be known. He has pretended to ignore a multitude of frustrating and exasperating incidents, and has enduringly put up with a variety of distasteful personal encounters. So now he acutely needs the reassurance of his wife. If she refuses to follow what seems to be the simple and obvious logic of the moment—retaliation—and instead wisely sees his need, she can seek to understand what provoked the hostile expression aimed her way. She can give him further opportunity to express his feelings, and in this way she will have helped him. At the same time she will have demonstrated to herself that his words were merely a smoke screen and had no meaning to their relationship at all. Her spirit will rest at ease in the knowledge that her husband, quite unconsciously, was *scapegoating*, choosing her as an object on whom he could deposit the burden of his day. What the husband really was saying in his attacks was, "I need your understanding and sympathy, and I feel I can trust you even when my greatest need is to sound off, to ventilate some hostile feelings and frustrations." The husband had a deep need to communicate his feelings, and to feel accepted while doing so. If his wife truly understands this, she will respond in an appropriate manner. Her response may not be verbal, for his statements may have been largely irrational or irrelevant to their relationship. Her understanding and sympathetic response may take the form of bringing him a cup of coffee and sitting down to listen for a few moments—even though other duties are piling up in the kitchen.

Ellis and Harper touch upon another angle to situations of this kind. Our all-too-human tendency is to get irritated with others in direct proportion to our irritation with ourselves. Sometimes we may even refuse to acknowledge our own errors, and instead project them—and the blame for them—onto others with whom we intimately associate, particularly our spouses. Such inability to see ourselves clearly, or to take personal responsibility for our own behavior, is a common communication block.

Of a different nature is the situation where conflicting opinions are endlessly discussed but never resolved. This may point to something deeper than the problem under discussion. Two may have taken sides for the sole reason of expressing hostility, the focused problem being merely incidental to a struggle for dominance. It is this kind of difficulty that couples can abolish when they feel secure enough to express their negative feelings to each other openly and immediately.

THE TERRIBLE TOLL OF TRIVIA

It's been noted that the grave of love is excavated with little digs. Small hurts add up to big hurts. Minor criticisms, seemingly insignificant to the person making them, loom as major criticisms to the one receiving them. If an individual is sensitive in a certain area, even a slight remark can be taken far more seriously than intended. Maybe it's a criticism about a person's weight, or the way the house is kept. A wife dislikes her husband's habit of leaving his clothes around, or not cleaning the bowl after shaving. A husband wants more variety in the daily menu, and is unhappy with the ingenious way his wife makes use of leftovers. So one or the other skirmishes with a little dig at the other. It isn't quite so bad until there is another little dig or two—nothing big, but they hit the mark and sting. The surprise comes in the way a little barb affects the sensitive zone and inflames a whole personality. Before a couple can realize it, the whole thing is out of hand.

Innuendo, irony, and *sarcasm* make a formidable trio. They are common means to "get at" another. No one would dispute that they are sometimes highly effective, and none would deny that they have their legitimate uses. But none of these three must ever become a chronic approach to another person; they are *special devices* for *special occasions* to produce *special responses.* And along with these, we might classify *ridicule* a particularly vicious tactic. Continually resorted to, ridicule discloses the impoverishment of the one using it, while at times it's a clue to emotional illness. Never creative or beneficial, ridicule is always destructive.

The terrible toll of trivia is witnessed in the lives of couples who let other relationships so crowd their time and thought that their own relationship is reduced to exchanging only the less meaningful details of daily living. Because the more profound concerns seem elusive while their communication lines are all but overloaded with trivia, a couple begins to wonder about the meaning of their life together. If the condition remains uncorrected, it won't be long before conflict breaks out between them. Married life must assimilate a multitude of minor matters, but it's meant for more than that. The life of a successfully married couple rises above the trivia that would engulf them. They will expend every effort required to make sure the important concerns of life are shared to the fullest.

There is one thing that conflict or crisis should accomplish, and that is the fuller self-disclosure of the two people involved. For this benefit the two can be genuinely grateful. Beyond this, a conflict can accomplish just about what two people will permit. It can be the cause of bitterness and hostility, hurt pride and resentment, or it can be a challenge to the deepening of a relationship. There is no better opportunity for ingenuity to come to the fore, even in finding ways to end quarrels and make them work for a couple. One thinks of the wife who had a particular way of ending a quarrel. She deliberately made an extreme and exaggerated statement, for which she felt she could honestly apologize. Her apology started her husband apologizing, and the quarrel ended in an embrace. A little ingenuity paid off. It was clever, but did it serve the ends of honest confrontation?

The maturity of any pair will be evident in the way they manage conflict. Let each partner seek to stand outside himself in the heat of conflict and attempt two things: first, let him try what the social scientist calls "role-taking." George Mead defined it as "the ability to be the other at the same time that he is himself." In other words, let him try to empathize, to put on the other's thoughts and feelings. Let him try to state the other's position in a way that satisfies the other. Second, let him evaluate his own creativeness in the face of conflict. Can he detach himself emotionally from the problem sufficiently to work for a compromise, a mutually satisfying solution? Can he recognize his own ego-needs sufficiently to work toward higher fulfillments? And finally, can he make conflict work for better communication between himself and his partner? If he can do this, he will have added to his growth as a person, and will have helped his partner do the same.

Special problems arise out of a spiritual context. Suppose a non-Christian couple have an adequate communication system, but one in which no spiritual dimension exists. Then suppose the wife becomes a Christian. The husband senses a difference in their communication, but finds it hard to pinpoint. His wife, on the other hand, is zealous in her attempts to "bring him to see the light." He is resistant and verging on resentment because so many previously shared values are being replaced by his wife's new interests, and it seems to him that their former intimacy is threatened. His first reaction is to call some kind of moratorium on their serious communication until he can assess the situation and determine how to manage it. His wife is deeply anxious to extend their communication to include spiritual values and experiences. But if she is sensitive to interpersonal relations, she will see the need to lessen her aggressive crusade, at the same time seeking ways of bridging their differences in the myriad concerns of family living. Time will open up opportunities when spiritual concerns can be shared in a proper context. Above all, she will avoid blaming him for their inability to communicate as before, as though his lack of spiritual interest were the sole cause of their new problems. Studies beginning with Burgess and Wallin have shown that couples whose values or interests were contradictory have developed happy and well-adjusted marriages, while couples with harmonious values and interests have sometimes developed poor marriages, the difference being in the degree of their maturity and adaptability. The important thing in such situations is that whenever one partner develops a new major interest, especially as comprehensive as a spiritual experience, a new challenge to communication follows. Neither should blame the other for this, but both should explore ways to meet the challenge.

—From Dwight Hervey Small, *Your Marriage Is God's Affair.* Old Tappan, N.J.: Revell, 1979.

Self-Rejection

In recent years we have been alerted to the universal problem of self-rejection. Unlike those we have already discussed, this emotion is not always readily apparent. Instead, it may be so deeply internalized that it goes unrecognized—because it adopts so many faces, which vary with the individual and the occasion. Self-rejection can cause a person to retreat socially and vocationally, check the expression of his personality, indulge in self-depreciation, concede his inferiority, fall into depression, or succumb to a host of other misconceptions, some even quite bizarre. At best, it incites capable people to sell themselves short in life.

There are many causes for self-rejection, including temperament, but the most important are parental disapproval, criticism, and rejection. Usually the child who is given love and warmth in the home, particularly during the early stages of life, does not have a problem with self-rejection unless he has a strong Melancholy temperament. One of the weaknesses of the Melancholy is his spirit of criticism, which he often uses on himself. The Holy Spirit-filled life is the only remedy for this.

THE CURE FOR SELF-REJECTION

The self-rejecting individual must first come to realize that he is in defiance of God. When we dislike our looks, body size, temperament, or talent, who do we blame? God, of course. He is the One who arranged at conception the genes that produced us. Many people have said or implied, "I don't care what you say; if God loved me He would not have made me this way." Such thinking is not only sinful but will lead to sickness, thus compounding the problem. Only by facing their ingratitude, unbelief, and rebellion against God will such individuals learn to accept themselves. The following steps apply our method of cure to self-rejection:

1. Face and confess self-rejection as sin.
2. Ask God to take away the habit of self-rejection.
3. Ask Him for the filling of the Spirit (Luke 11:13).
4. Thank Him for who and what you are (1 Thessalonians 5:18).
5. Repeat this formula each time self-rejection occurs.
6. Look for an area to serve God and others (Romans 12:1, 2).

It is particularly important that Christian self-rejecters *formally* at least one time thank God for who and what they are. If appearance is your subject of rejection, then look at your reflection in the mirror and thank God for how you look, particularly those areas you have been rejecting. Remember, if God had wanted you to look otherwise, you would. Then thank Him for your talents and offer them to Him. Even if you consider your gifts only minimal, He is a master at taking ordinary people and doing superordinary things with them. I can certainly vouch for that. If I told you my high school and college English grades, you would probably stop reading this book immediately. If you saw my penmanship, you probably couldn't make out half the words. Our God has never been limited to talent, and since He is the Source of all power, let Him flow through you. Everyone will be amazed at the result.

You might wonder why I include self-rejection in this list of family enemies. I agree with Bill Gothard, who said, "A person's attitude toward himself will influence his attitude toward God, others, and everything he does." To function at your maximum efficiency, you must realize that you are important enough for God to let His Son die for you, and that God wants to use your life, beginning in your own home.

Many well-meaning Christians cling to the mistaken notion that self-acceptance or love for one's self is unspiritual. Admittedly, one fruit of the Spirit is "meekness," but our Lord assumed self-acceptance when He said, "Love your neighbor as yourself." God's divine order is clear—love Him supremely, then your partner and children, and finally your neighbor and yourself equally. If you depreciate yourself, it will keep you from loving your family as you should.

—From Tim and Bev LaHaye, *Spirit-Controlled Family Living.* Old Tappan, N.J.: Revell, 1978.

Selfishness

Selfishness—we are all born with it, and to one degree or another it plagues us throughout life. In our opinion, one of the chief responsibilities of parents is to train their children away from selfishness. Every baby comes home from the hospital with the self-centered attitude that he is the only child on earth. Any perceived need for food, sleep, or a diaper change will occasion a howl of protest: "I want attention now!" We accept that as normal because he is immature. But unless trained out of it through years of love and discipline, he will still be immature at twenty years of age and will serve as a bad risk for marriage. A candidate for matrimony should look carefully at the "unselfishness quotient" of the partner-to-be. If he is unselfish, his anger or fears will be kept in better check and any other undesirable characteristics will be more easily overlooked. The hardest person to love over a period of time is not one who is unattractive or possesses a zero personality, but a partner who is selfish.

An egocentric person thinks of himself first and foremost in everything. Consequently, he finds giving and sharing a difficult habit to cultivate. All temperaments have their own tendencies to be selfish, but some are by nature more easily trained out of them.

THE CURE FOR SELFISHNESS

1. Face selfishness as sin.
2. Confess it.
3. Ask God to take away this habit.
4. Ask for the filling of the Spirit.
5. Thank God for His love that is flowing through you to make you a more generous person.
6. Repeat this formula each time you do, say, or *think* anything that is selfish.

Gradually this habit pattern will begin to fade, and a mature generosity and true love for others will replace it. Your patience toward others will also be extended; you will increasingly enjoy others and they will begin enjoying you. Philippians 2:3, 4, emphasizes the words *other* and *others*. A mature, unselfish, person never lacks for friends, for he is so "others" conscious that they recognize it and feel comfortable in his presence. In the family, such a person is a delight to have around the house. Instead of being interested in his own rights or possessions, he develops "others" awareness.

—From Tim and Bev LaHaye, *Spirit-Controlled Family Living.* Old Tappan, N.J.: Revell, 1978.

Vengeance

Vengeance is getting even for hurts that have been inflicted by the partner. This game can involve the accumulation of slights, real or imagined, from many years, or only from a recent episode. The rule of this game is "Don't get mad. Get even." Getting even sexually may involve extramarital affairs as well as other conflicts.

The resolution of this game comes about through the communication of your anger or hurt at the specific incident that caused it. The sooner this hurt and anger is expressed, the sooner understanding and forgiving can be reached. Getting mad and getting over it is really much easier than getting even.

—From Grace H. Ketterman, M.D., *How to Teach Your Child About Sex.* Old Tappan, N.J.: Revell, 1981.

When the Feeling's Gone . . .

People get married for a number of reasons, but probably high on the list are the romantic feelings they have for the person they love. But what happens when the feelings are gone? Does it mean that the marriage is over? No indeed. It just means that we need to reexamine what it is that *really* holds our marriages together.

Our society often has a backward notion of love and marriage—that feelings of love come before loving behavior. At one time marriages were arranged by the families of the bride and groom. The idea was that a good match followed by acts of love would lead to happiness and longevity of marriage.

But today people "fall out of love" because the relationship is built on the notion of "falling in love." Even people who "fall in love" and live together prior to marriage to see if it's "the real thing" are no better off.

Why? Because most likely the relationship was based wholly on feelings with little or no understanding of commitment.

Commitment is a willful decision followed by loving behavior which then produces loving feelings. I don't want to sound naively simplistic about this matter of commitment, however. Sometimes the damage to a relationship is so great that a person simply cannot give the commitment necessary to make the marriage work. Whether or not the marriage is recoverable on the ground of commitment is a very personal matter between a hurting husband and wife.

If the feeling's gone in your marriage, try these practical suggestions:

1. Do not base the potential of your marriage on feelings. Determine if you both are committed to each other and to what extent you both are willing to go to *make* the marriage work.

2. Emphasize the changes in behavior that you and your spouse need to make rather than the feelings that are missing. Good feelings follow good behavior.

3. Take inventory of your marriage in terms of what *is* rewarding about it. Your spouse may be a good provider, good father, stable and easy to get along with. Your wife may be a good mother and homemaker. What are these worth to you? Remember that no matter who you might marry, the feelings of romance are going to fade and must be replaced by more durable values.

4. Don't believe all the propaganda you hear about the exciting, romantic life on the singles scene. It's lonely when you're

not dating and full of disappointments when you are. It's exhausting trying to find a person and life-style that you feel comfortable with. Your spouse may be dull, but don't think that finding a replacement is an easy matter.

5. If your spouse won't talk about your dissatisfaction with the marriage, write him/her a letter and spell out your feelings in detail. Ask for a written reply. You may find that this will break the ice and open the way for further letters or talks.

6. If you get no constructive response to your attempts to talk or write letters, and you are convinced that your marriage is over, have a trial separation to see what it really will be like to make it on your own. Most people don't separate soon enough—while there is still something to hold onto in the marriage.

—BY Andre Bustanoby

Marriage Counseling

To find a qualified counselor start calling people, perhaps from the Yellow Pages. Ask your pastor whom he might recommend. Look for someone who appears to know what he/she is doing, who is well recommended and credentialed in the state as a psychologist or a marriage and family counselor. After getting the names of three or four recommended people, take the time to call them and ask them some questions, the least of which in terms of importance is "How much do you charge?" You aren't looking for the best price for a lawn sprinkler at your local K-Mart. You are talking about someone who is going to enter your very private world, a world which is in an area that is so very vital to your being. Just be sure you find someone who is interested in helping solve your problems quickly and efficiently. Following are some of the other questions you should ask:

1. Do you have spiritual values in your own life?
2. Are you married? How long? How many times?
3. What counseling methods do you employ? Directive or non-directive techniques? Is there one particular model you adhere to?
4. Do you see couples together/individually or some of each? Do you ever see the entire family?
5. How long should we expect therapy to continue? How many sessions, roughly?
6. Will my medical insurance pay for your services? (This question should be directed to your insurance provider as well.)
7. What academic degree(s) do you have? Any postgraduate training?
8. Do you have children? If so, what are their ages?
9. What are your fees? How many minutes in a session? Do you use double sessions? (Sometimes double sessions are desirous, especially if you travel some distance to the place of the appointment.)
10. Can I make monthly payments on my account? What interest rate on the unpaid balance? (Many professionals have gone to a finance charge on the unpaid balance after 90 days.)
11. Are you certified by the State Board of Psychologist Examiners, or other appropriate boards? What are your "professional affiliations"?

Many Christians seek out only Christian professionals. In my opinion it's more important to find a counselor who is competent and able to help you and your mate.

—From Dr. Kevin Leman, *Sex Begins in the Kitchen*. Ventura, Calif.: Regal, 1981.

RENEWAL

ALL OF US MARRIED PEOPLE have to realize that time is a corrosive influence. We don't naturally drift closer together; we drift further apart. We have to fight our way back to each other, day after day, year after year, as long as we live. Across the board, in marriages that survive, the evidence seems to be that in every succeeding decade of the average marriage, the partners are less satisfied with each other and with their marriage! They no longer talk as much, interact as much. Strangers under the same roof, they live in increasing loneliness. Yet both have needs for love as great as ever—maybe greater.

But, praise God, we see lots of married couples around us who, like ourselves, are more in love, more fulfilled, more crazy about each other than they've ever been; and we know that there is this kind of marriage all around the world, too.

The two of us can look right into each other's eyes and sing, "I get no kicks from champagne (don't even touch it), but I get a kick out of you." We wouldn't dare write this book together, otherwise.

It hasn't always been easy. The thing we've got going for us has been forged and beaten out of controversy and joys and tears and fun and total misunderstandings and having a ball together. We still have irritations around the edges, and we always will, because the edges keep shifting! But the big, main hunk of our marriage is solidly in cement. You better believe it!

And there is a sense in which every time the authentic Word is proclaimed, the Word must be made flesh—backed up by a sincere attempt at obedience. If our mouths are open, our lives had better be open, too—open books, "epistles read of all men."

So what are we suggesting, you two Christian people, to put sizzle back into your marriage?

1. Hope. That must come first. A great marriage in the second half of life isn't a fuzzy pink cloud that isn't there when you reach for it; it *is* there for you. We know because ours is a great marriage.

Don't put down this book if your marriage is just on the toleration level. Pull those dreams out of your memory; all the things you longed for when love was new. Are they still available?

It all depends on how big your God is. Marriage is *His* invention, and He planned it for you long ago. Perhaps He planned that at this very time in your lives you'd come back and try it *His* way, and turn a new corner in your lives together.

You look in a mirror, and you say it's too late? Ridiculous! "Never forget," says an old philosopher friend of ours, "no matter how old you are you can still be somebody's dreamboat—even if your anchor is dragging and your cargo has shifted." One of the beautiful things about the second half of life is that there starts to be more emphasis on wisdom and less on the physique; more on know-how and less on first appearances. And this shift in emphasis benefits every area of your life, including marriage.

Consider this philosophy: Some societies allow polygamy—one husband being married to a number of wives. However, we say that in our culture we practice polygamy in a new form—one husband (wife) being married to many wives (husbands), but one at a time, through divorce and remarriage, divorce and remarriage. This system has a very strong argument in its favor: We change constantly throughout our lives, and—at any given point—we are not the same persons our partners married.

It's true!

So the two of us endorse a form of this system: Do get married, over and over through your life—but always to the same person. You have changed; she has changed. Recommit yourself to this changed person. Keep your present married status fresh and new. . . .

2. Discover renewed companionship during this period. Let the weaning away of your children from your emotional lives drive you two together again; deliberately seek each other. Go off on a honeymoon. At least increase your date life—just the two of you.

Talk! It will be embarassing, but so it was when you got acquainted the first time. When you're faced with something hard, you can't solve it by running away or pretending it isn't there. You have to plow right on through it until you come out the other side. But take it easy. Don't "talk problems" all the time. Have fun, too. . . .

3. *Discover how you can share more tasks, intermingle your roles, achieve new intimacy.* We discovered that we could spend a whole day together speed-reading for sermon material; and we do, out of town in some secluded spot, every Thursday of our lives! It's work-oriented romance. It's hearts-and-flowers in pragmatic form. Someone we know had this to say, "I saw us walking hand in hand through life, but now it's clear all we really need is two cars." (We don't agree with this.)

4. *Develop new relationships with other people.* Tenderness and "with-ness" cannot be demanded from grown children. (We must hasten to add—because our grown children will be reading this book—when you back away from them, amazingly enough, they often come freely for companionship. And how sweet it is!)

Deliberately glean new companions from among your own peers. Develop a "ministry." Have fellowship in depth. Meet the needs of others; in so doing, your own needs will be met. Serve in the church; give your gifts freely, together. . . .

5. *Discover the joy of intellectual search-*

163

ing. Read broadly and well. Make time to study the Bible together as a couple and with other couples, so that your minds grow together and you meet your friends at a high, cleansing level of communication.

"Man is the only creature," someone has said, "that is given the power to make choices, to improve thus upon yesterday, and to level the road for tomorrow. Days for men and women do not have to be the same; they can be full of innovation and exhilaration."

—From Ray and Anne Ortlund, *The Best Half of Life.* © 1976, pp. 97–102; used by permission of Word Books, Publisher, Waco, Texas 76796.

Second Honeymoon

Take a vacation without the children? I couldn't do that. At least that's what I thought until I realized how much our marriage depended on time alone, just the two of us, away from the house. Here are some things to think about as you plan your special "getaway."

1. The first two or three times you go away from your children to be alone with your spouse, expect some difficulty in adjusting. After the third time, it gets easier.
2. Make a promise to each other that you won't utter such loaded phrases as, "I wonder what the children are doing," or "I wish we'd brought the children."
3. If you can't get into the swing of vacationing as a twosome again, consider taking another couple with you next time. Start with just a weekend.
4. If you're an exceptionally anxious mama, consider spending your vacation in a hotel or motel in a nearby town or city so that you can be reached in an emergency. (Avoid calling home that first night or you'll feel as if you've never left.)
5. Get a sitter for the day and evening. Go to the city and sightsee. Have a good meal.

Take in a show. You may know each other better than in the courting days, but marital "dating" can still be a fun time of discovering new things about each other.

6. Arrange a trade with a friend. Provide the following note: This coupon entitles you to one free hideaway evening alone. At ———— o'clock a picnic hamper will appear with your intimate dinner inside. Your children will be lovingly cared for in my house between the hours of ———— and ————. Enjoy. P.S. Please pack the children's toothbrushes and a sleeping bag. (Suggestions for menu: Hot casserole, cold salad, antipasto, fresh fruit, cheeses, finger-food desserts. Tuck in a tablecloth, napkins, and if you can handle it . . . a bud in a vase. The linens will add a touch that says "It's just like dining out.")
7. Call your husband at work or tape a note to the mirror when he shaves or, if you really want to impress him, send him a telegram with the following invitation: Tonight . . . after the children are in bed, you and I are going to have a fireside picnic. Slip into something comfortable, and I'll meet you at the hearth.
8. If you think he can stand the shock, dispense with the note entirely. Let his secretary know that he needs to be home by a certain time for a top priority appointment. Arrange for a neighbor to watch the children. Put on something fresh and appealing. Spread a picnic tablecloth on the living room floor or in front of the hearth. Set out a picnic hamper with appealing goodies and a beverage served in attractive glasses. Set the mood with soft music and atmosphere lighting.

—BY Nyla Jane Witmore

Reaffirmation of Marriage Vows

Some churches regularly schedule marriage-reaffirmation services open to all couples. Other churches have such services only for those whom the pastor has married. At other times, a couple will have a reenactment of their marriage on significant anniversaries, such as their tenth, twenty-fifth or fiftieth.

While there is no standard ceremony, some pastors choose a full wedding ceremony and substitute words such as: "Will you reaffirm that you will. . . . ?

Sometimes when couples reaffirm their vows, they replace their old rings or put the original stones in new settings.

—CECIL MURPHEY

Anniversaries

Couples should not expect anniversary gifts except from each other. Of course, close friends may wish to give gifts, but cards, letters, and telegrams are usual.

Traditionally, people give gifts on major anniversaries, such as the twenty-fifth and fiftieth, although this need not be followed. These are the recognized categories of anniversary gifts.

1st-paper, plastic
2nd-cotton, china
3rd-leather (or leatherlike)
4th-linen, silk, or synthetic material
5th-wood, decorative accessories for home
6th-iron
7th-copper, brass, wool
8th-bronze or electrical appliances
9th-china, glass, pottery
10th-tin or aluminum
11th-steel
12th-linen, nylon, silk
13th-lace
14th-ivory or agate
15th-crystal or glass
20th-china or porcelain
25th-silver
30th-pearls or personal gifts
35th-coral or jade
40th-rubies or garnets
45th-sapphires
50th-gold
55th-emeralds or turquoise
60th-diamonds, diamondlike stones, gold
75th-diamonds, diamondlike stones, gold

—CECIL MURPHEY

THE MONEY TREE

An old custom for anniversaries involved the money tree. Instead of collecting gifts for people who have been married a long time, it provides a sensible alternative. They can take a trip. They can buy something special they want.

The invitation never mentions the money tree. The person sponsoring the anniversary party inserts a slip which reads something like this: "If you should wish to give a gift, we hope you will contribute to a money tree we are planning. Contributions may be sent to (sponsor and address)."

At one time people gave fifty-cent pieces and/or silver dollars, which they taped to the money tree for twenty-fifth anniversaries. Nowadays, when used, most money trees have bills taped to the branches. The tree can be real branches sprayed with gold, silver, or white paint, or an artificial tree. Sometimes people enclose bills in silver or gold envelopes; other times they roll the bills tightly like a pencil. They usually hang on the tree.

If the sponsor uses an artificial tree, bills may be taped to tree-ornament hooks so that tape won't destroy the needles.

If the couple themselves send out the invitation, they don't, of course, insert a slip suggesting a money tree. However, a friend could contact everyone on the guest list by phone or note saying that contributions to the money tree would be appreciated rather than other gifts.

—CECIL MURPHEY

LATER STAGES OF LIFE

Middle Age

DEFINITION

There is no common definition of "middle-age." One dictionary says it is "the period of human life between youth and old age sometimes considered as the years between forty-five and sixty-five." Barbara Fried, in *The Middle Age Crisis*, puts the lower limits between thirty-eight and forty-five. There are some who push it down even lower into the thirties. It obviously doesn't hit everyone at exactly the same age chronologically. Some contend that the age of one's family or vocation are factors which affect its onset. I have chosen forty-nine because, in the clergy, there is a common feeling that "no church wants to call a minister who is over fifty." Besides, *I* was forty-nine when I started this book.

Even though there is no unanimity on age, there is wide acceptance of the use of the term "crisis." Those who have the symptoms would agree with this label. The symptoms also have a commonality among writers in the field. There is a standard use of such words as: depression, emotional instability, irritability, anger, despair, anxiety, sexual problems, lack of confidence, and organic or psychosomatic illness (Barrett). One writer added "an insidious desire to destroy a way of life which took years to achieve—to move to another town, to change jobs and spouses." (*Life*)

A recent conference called by the American Medical Association composed of experts from varied fields—business, labor, education, anthropology, medicine—carried the message that this is the prime of life. However, the purpose of the conference was to discuss the *problems* of this age group. These were described as lack of identity, emotional instability, alcoholism, drug abuse, obesity and lack of physical fitness (Barrett).

"Middle-age," then, seems to be a life crisis rather than an age span.

Our purpose here is not to present a definitive study on middle-age but to assist one in identifying with the crisis, to relate some of the problems of the ministry to it, and to suggest some ways to deal creatively with it in one's own life.

—From Richard Knox Smith, *49 and Holding.* Lomita, Calif.: Morgan-Pacific, 1975.

PERILS OF MIDDLE AGE

When is middle age? To define middle age is dangerous and delicate. Someone said that you can tell you have reached it by four things: "Bifocals, baldness, bridges, and bulges." It's the age when the steps seem steeper, the cold wind stronger, and the joints stiffer. Middle age is when you get "too-itis"—You are too tired, it is too late, too far, too much, too long, too hard, too fattening, too noisy, or too loud.

Middle age starts when we begin looking at the past and we find ourselves repeating, "When I was young." It is here when we fear the future and our slogan is "Things can't continue long like this."

"Life may not begin at 40," quipped one lady, "but your life begins to show at 40." It's true. By 40 the record of our souls is now written on our faces. The record of our habits is now written on our bodies. And the record of our attitudes is written on our countenance.

Recent writings suggest that middle age, give or take a few years, goes from 40 to 65. Also it is described as a distinct period of human development—as distinct as childhood and adolescence—in which great changes take place physically, psychologically, and spiritually. This article refers particularly to the third of these changes.

Middle years—triumph and tragedy. While the dangers of youth seem obvious and center around the physical appetites and passions, the dangers of middle age are much more secret and subtle. While the more obvious sins of youth may injure fatally, the sins of middle age, usually not as open or obviously shameful, nonetheless can prove fatal. The psalmist describes this period of life as "the destruction that wastes at noonday." "In the midst of the years," says Habakkuk, God needs to revive His work and make His path known to us.

Stories of people who reached their greatest victories and then experienced their greatest defeats in the middle passage permeate the pages of history.

On the other hand, Moses led God's people out of Egypt and through the wilderness during his middle years. The mantle of Moses fell on faithful Joshua in the middle years of his life. John Wesley, at the acme of his powers in the middle years, led multitudes to the saving knowledge of Christ. John Knox and Martin Luther, in the middle of life, demonstrated the courage of clear Christian commitment. John Bunyan penned *Pilgrim's Progress* during his middle passage.

All through the centuries, in all realms of life, contributions of men and women were momentous during the middle years. Robert Weston writes, "Yet, while the middle generation is the prime mover down at the church, it is also the age group that is most taken for granted. There are the youth groups and their retreats, and young adults and their ball games, the senior citizens and their golden age clubs, but the middle generation usually has only the opportunity to foot the bill."

Calvin W. Mauser says, "Never in the history of man has any generation so taxed itself for the good of others as has the present generation in the middle."

But the opposite is also true. Middle age is also the most dangerous time of life. C. S. Lewis in the *Screwtape Letters* writes: "The long, dull, monotonous years of middle-aged prosperity or middle-aged adversity are excellent campaigning weather [for the devil]."—Letter 28.

Have you ever noticed that the most ghastly failures in the Scriptures are those who made shipwreck in the middle passage? Samson, God's strong man in his younger years, experienced his "destruction that wastes at noonday." He didn't even realize that the Lord had departed from him. Saul, the stalwart, strong young man who stood head and shoulders above his comrades, fell at the noontime of life.

Solomon, the wisest king and one who reaped the worthy honors of the world, wasted his life in the middle years. David, the great, good, and gracious young man, became lazy and lusty in middle age. He grew careless about his relationship with God and his own family. David's children hardly knew their father. He wept about Absalom—too late.

In the New Testament, Judas seemed to have come through the pitfalls and perils of youth unscathed. His character disclosed no major stain to his companions. But somehow in the middle years he allowed the corroding influence of money and the love of power to take over. And when he saw that following Christ would gratify with wealth or power, he committed the crime of the centuries, repeated again and again for the same reasons, in betraying his Lord.

Demas demonstrated and illustrated the same danger. For years he followed Christ faithfully and was a fellow-laborer with the apostle Paul. But he fell under the heat of the noonday sun. Paul writes, "Demas hath forsaken me, having loved this present world." He succumbed to the perils of the middle passage.

Recently we had a U.S. President who in his prime, along with many of his brilliant, loyal, and capable companions, made shipwreck in the middle of life.

So at every level of life, in every realm of life, the middle passage has seen great victories and great defeats.

Why so perilous? The question then arises: Why is the middle of life so perilous? Let me suggest three reasons, which pertain primarily to the spiritual.

1. *In the middle passage there is the danger that we lose our idealism.* Youth is a time of dreaming and seeing visions. Youth is a time to build gorgeous castles in the air. Early in life we cherish splendid ambitions. "Wait till I'm a man," J. M. Barrie said as a small child to his mother, "and you shall lie in feathers." He dreamed of bringing comfort to his beloved mother. The danger in middle age is that we find the ideals and comforts of life harder to achieve than we thought. They are hard to reach and realize. So, many times, in the middle years we give up on dreams. We abandon our quests. We surrender our ideals.

In Tennyson's *Idylls of the King*, Sir Gawain, like the other knights of the Round Table, sets out in search of the Holy Grail. This is another way of saying that he started with the ideal of a pure and holy life. However, he soon wearied of this quest. Soon he saw a silk pavilion in a field, full of merry maidens. Sir Gawain abandoned his quest and spent twelve months in sensuous ease and pleasure.

When Sir Gawain returns to the court, he scoffs at the idea of the quest for the Holy Grail. He now says:

But by mine eyes and by mine ears I
  swear,
I shall be deafer than the blue-eyed cat,
And thrice as blind as any noonday owl,
To holy virgins in their ecstasies,
Henceforward.

Here is the picture of a person who starts life with high ideals, but who, in time, surrenders. The aspirations of life have left and he becomes deaf and blind to the pure and holy.

"He was born a man and died a grocer" is the bitter and biting epitaph written on a gravestone in a parish churchyard. So many people begin with the vision to make a life and then settle for making a living.

When we surrender our dreams and laugh at or reason away our ideals, we commit spiritual suicide. This is the constant peril of middle age. We get settled in a groove and it becomes our grave. (These two words, by the way, come from the same original stem.) Accommodation takes the place of conviction. Compelling desire for acceptance and respect replaces the compelling witness that bears the offense of the cross. The drive for dusty gold blinds our spiritual eyes.

"We must face reality" are the words of middle age, only to lose the great realities of the Spirit. "We must be practical" are the words of the middle passage, only to forget that Jesus meant His words to be practiced. "We need to make a living" are the words of the middle generation, only to forget that before we pray, "Give us this day our daily bread," we pray, "Thy kingdom come. Thy will be done."

Middle age has the great temptation to rationalize away every wooing of the Spirit, to continually criticize the world and church, but avoid the sin in one's own life. Those in the middle of life too often look so long at the facts that they forget their walk is a walk of faith.

Middle age must guard against always

taking the easy way out. Sir Francis Bacon, the great Elizabethan philosopher and statesman, wrote: "Young men, in their conduct and manage of actions, embrace more than they can hold; stir more than they can quiet; fly to the end without consideration of the means and degrees. . . . Men of age object too much, consult too long, adventure too little, repent too soon, and seldom drive business hours to the full period, but content themselves with a mediocrity of success."

E. Stanley Jones in *Christ and Human Suffering,* page 209, has a striking paragraph: "Every man needs reconversion at forty on general principles! Because at forty we settle down, begin to lose that sense of spiritual expectancy, begin to take on protective resemblance to environment, and to play for safety. I once heard an Anglican bishop say that the period of greatest number of spiritual casualties is between forty and fifty and not between twenty and thirty, as one would expect. Why? Well, if heaven lies about us in our infancy; the world lies about us in our middle age. We come under its standards, fit into its facts, and are slowly de-Christianized."

So one of the dangers of middle age is the loss of our ideals. However, as we remain honest and open to the Holy Spirit and God's Word, the ideal of Jesus and the meaning of life as He has taught it will remain clear. These will stand the test of time and eternity. He not only sets before us the ideal of Jesus, but He stirs within us the aspirations needed for purpose and purity, and He instills within us the power for spiritual living.

2. *Another peril of the middle passage is the loss of vital faith.* Childhood is happy. Childhood looks at life through the beautiful glasses of a guile-free and trustful spirit. Old age, while not as innocently trustful as childhood, usually is more mellow and gentle in its judgments.

But between childhood and old age there is the constant danger to become hard, cynical, and scornful. Life, by middle age, has brought disappointment and disillusionment. And because we may sense that we are at our peak physically, at the job and every other way, we may let envy and jealousy take over. Resentment may run rampant.

Middle age is inclined to sit in the seat of the scornful, to make savage and sweeping judgments, and to declare with the psalmist, "All men are liars" (Psalm 116:11). Pessimism is sometimes called "the measles of middle age."

Read the literature of middle age. Every man is a scoundrel and every woman is base and soiled. Middle age produces the awful films. Middle age imagines that there are no happy marriages or peaceful homes. Middle age assumes every husband is unfaithful.

A. E. Taylor in *The Faith of a Moralist* writes: "Middle age is attended, for all of us, with the grave danger of moral stagnation." The road of middle age is crowded with moral wrecks, persons who gave up against the power of impurity and lust. Many in middle age yield to the cynicism of the disillusioned, and because we lose faith in our fellow men, we doubt God and lose contact with His Word and Spirit. The feeling of many in middle age is expressed in the words of a song, popular a few years ago, "Is that all there is?"

Dr. George Washington Truett, after 42 years as a pastor and preacher, says that throughout his ministry the "greatest downfalls have come in life's middle." Westwood Purkeiser, in an editorial, writes, "A thoughtful Christian leader in his late fifties recently commented, 'What signs there are of renewal in the church are among the young. I don't see much evidence of it in my generation.' "

One thing I learned early in my ministry throughout the church in holding revival

169

and renewal meetings is that revival starts with the young. With the exception of a few individuals here and there, it never starts with the middle-aged. Middle age, along with its inclination to react to new ideas, is cautious about making new commitments. By middle age we develop a defense mechanism that, through long practice, makes it difficult to face ourselves.

We are inclined to leave God out, especially if we are successful. We are inclined to leave prayer out, especially if we consider ourselves thoughtful persons. We are inclined to leave the Holy Spirit out and to walk by sight rather than faith.

According to one study of the religion of the middle-aged man, the man between 40 and 60 attends church less, prays less, discusses vital matters with his minister less, and says that religion has less meaning than either the older or younger persons.

Is that all there is?

The answer from the Christian is No! In Christ there is the forgetting of the past, and pressing on to that which is before, to seek to realize more fully every day the reason and purpose of Christ's calling. More spiritual treasures and joys exist ahead in Christ.

3. *A peril of the middle passage is that we can lose the sense of the eternal.* In childhood the spiritual and eternal seems strangely near. Heaven, God, the white-robed angels, are wonderfully near.

Again in old age, eternal things become vivid and clear. The mere decaying of strength reminds us that no abiding place exists here. Friends move on. And as we follow one friend after another to the grave, we find it increasingly difficult to ignore eternity.

The danger of losing the eternal perspective is the peculiar peril of the middle-aged. Middle age is a time filled with responsibility. The demands of business and the bur-

dens of life wipe out time for eternal values. As one recently said, "Scarcely can we turn aside for one brief hour of prayer."

We have no time to look to the hills and to the God who made all that abides. We materialize life and starve the soul. We struggle for bread and butter until we believe that bread and butter are the most important things in life. We lose sight of eternal riches for a few temporal toys.

Carl Jung described middle age as the time when a "man breathes his own life into things until finally they begin to live themselves and to multiply, and imperceptibly he is overgrown by them."

It was this instinct that John Bunyan had when, in *Pilgrim's Progress,* he placed Vanity Fair, not early or late in Christian's journey to glory, but near the middle. This vainglory, this avarice, this passion for money and position is more deadly than the hot passions of youth. It is the more deadly because few recognize it. It possesses no shame in the world's eyes. Success here counts to one's credit in the eyes of one's peers.

Yet it destroys the soul as surely as drunkenness. It beckons the betrayal of our Lord. It shuts out the spiritual for the satisfactions of the sensual.

No wonder Habakkuk cries, "O Lord, revive thy work in the midst of the years, . . . make [it] known."

This might be our prayer. If we make the Most High our habitation and His will our delight, if we abide in the secret place of the Most High, we will not need to be afraid of the arrow that flies by day, nor for the pestilence that walks in the darkness, nor for the destruction that wastes at noonday.

But we need God at every step. At no time do we need Him more than now, in the middle passage. And knowing Him, middle age can represent a time and chance for self-renewal and rededication, which can produce a greater stability than at any other time of life. Middle life, because it is in the middle, is capable, in Christ, of a greater depth in relationships to the young and old, to the church and world, than any other time of life.

Thank God that many of the saints of the ages experienced reconversion in the middle years. At a time when many sink in the Slough of Despond, those reconverted become increasingly aware of the presence and power of God.

—BY John M. Drescher, pastor, author, and teacher of preaching and spiritual disciplines at Eastern Mennonite Seminary, Harrisonburg, Va.

CLIMACTERIC

One of the signs of aging that may be directly related to the middle-age crisis is the climacteric. *Climacteric* is derived from the Greek word, *climakter,* "the rung of a ladder"; it is defined by Webster's as any major turning point or critical stage in a person's life, but is most often applied to the gradual loss of reproductive potential (in the grisly phrase of one authority, the "genital extinction") that overtakes us during middle age. The end of the climacteric—that is, the final loss of all capacity to reproduce—is more dramatic in women than in men because it is marked by an unequivocal signal: menstruation stops. This end point is the *menopause,* a word often but wrongly applied to the entire female climacteric; and this incorrect usage doubtless contributes to the widespread confusion about whether or not men, too, have a climacteric. They do. But, as is true of other aspects of sex also, things are just not the same for men and women, and there's no point in trying to describe what happens to one in terms of the other. Nonetheless, especially in connection with the climacteric, comparison seems to be unavoidable. The masculine wish to deny the climacteric and the diminishing potency it implies is apparently so strong that despite the cultural tradition that masculinity is the desired norm—implied in such phrases as "penis envy" and "the second sex"— men are for once more than happy to measure themselves against women. In this single special instance men are content to claim, and accurately of course, that the things that happen to women during middle age—meaning, mostly, the menopause—do not happen to them. Which leads them to the comforting, although erroneous conclusion that nothing does—or at least nothing worth mentioning.

The end point of the climacteric—the final disappearance of procreative power—doesn't have much to do with the middle-age crisis in either sex, because most women don't reach it until their late forties or early fifties, and most men until even later than that. However, the signposts pointing to sterility—the first of those many, tiny, age-related physical and mental changes whose cumulative effect after a period of years is the over-all "change of life"—may show up as early as the mid-thirties. It is these small beginnings that may play a part in the forties' troubles.

—From Barbara Fried, *The Middle-Age Crisis.* Rev. ed. New York: Harper & Row, 1976.

Empty Nest/Retirement

There is something very traumatic about having your last child leave home. Perhaps your last one is attending university but he/she is gone and you know it. And that awareness writes "finis" to a most significant period of life called parenthood. Parents continue to love their grown children and remain interested in their lives—but never again will there be that close parent-child relationship that existed in the family home.

For many couples this freedom offers one of the best times in life. Since they have prepared for it, instead of grieving they are able to enjoy the liberty to do all the things impossible before because of responsibility for children. I see many couples like this and they are a joy to watch. Usually they are people who have been working on their relationship all along. Their friendships are supportive and their activities have meaning for their lives. They are busy people who are unselfish in their relationship with one another.

For some the period immediately after the children leave is one of the most difficult times of life. This is especially true of mothers who have devoted themselves almost exclusively to "mothering" their children. Suddenly the children are gone and mother doesn't know what to do with herself. She can become depressed, bored, or even physically ill. A terrible sense of uselessness can descend on her at this time. What she's good at doesn't need doing any more.

So mother looks to her husband for sympathy and discovers that he is at the very peak of his career and is finding a great deal of fulfillment in what he is doing. Since he has not made the emotional investment in parenting which his wife has, he does not have as much sympathy for what is happening to her and her needs. This can become a really explosive situation if help is not found.

When retirement comes the roles are almost completely reversed. The wife continues doing what she had been doing with some fulfillment. This time it is the husband who is at loose ends. But with retirement come the complications of less money and failing health. All of these add pressures to the marriage relationship. There is that need to be as independent as possible, as long as possible, in as many areas as possible.

Some of the best marriages I've found have been among couples in retirement.

Nothing is more encouraging to some of us who are younger than to see people in retirement moving out with a sense of excitement into new areas of involvement and activity. Kenneth and Nelda are most representative of a host of the couples I know. We first met when I was speaking in their city and they were my hosts for lunch. Nelda was a professor at the University of Houston and Kenneth was a railroad man. Even then they were people with an interest in others. (I've decided that there's just no way people who think only of themselves can ever be happy.)

—From Kenneth Chafin, *Is There a Family in the House?* copyright © 1978, pp. 39–41; used by permission of Word Books, Publisher, Waco, Texas 76796

HELPS FOR RETIREES

Since adults can now expect to live longer and more vigorous lives than those of previous generations, here are suggestions for making those years of fulfillment.

1. Plan for your retirement by moving gradually into other forms of activity. Determine to keep yourself busy after you leave your lifetime work.
2. Divorce yourself as quickly as possible from your job. You may want to keep alive a few friendships, but don't allow yourself to continue trying to relive your former work. Stop visiting your old place of work.
3. Consider doing part-time or volunteer work. Men, too! Men are now volunteering for work in hospitals and nursing homes that previously was done only by women.
4. Consider moving to a smaller house. Look at the move as a new phase of life and an opportunity to begin an exciting challenge.
5. Have regular physical check-ups. Early

discovery and treatment of medical problems can add years to life.

6. Keep physically fit. Especially keep off weight. Older people simply do not need as many calories as they did at age thirty-five. Exercise regularly (ask your doctor how much). Get plenty of fresh air and eat nutritious foods and well-balanced meals. Get enough sleep.

7. Remain socially active. Make new friends. Most churches have golden age groups called anything from Keen-Agers, XYZ clubs, or Golden Agers. Join formal organizations such as the American Association of Retired Persons (AARP).

8. Remain active at home. Develop new skills or rediscover old hobbies. Travel, if your health and finances permit. Tackle books you've always wanted to read by setting goals for yourself.

9. Stay active in a local congregation. Don't participate only with your own group. Ask your pastor for a job you can do. Mix with younger people. How about assisting in the kindergarten class? Maybe the nursery? Many children today in our mobile society who are isolated from grandparents welcome a grandparent-type contact.

10. Use the phone. My mother, who died in her eighties, remained actively close to a dozen women her age. They belonged to the same church, and because of health, found themselves confined to home, often for days at a time. But they used the telephone. My mother spent at least two hours every morning calling her friends. My mother said, "We cheer each other up."

11. Expand yourself. Try something new. How about a "year of adventure"? One friend determined that once a week she would do something new—something she had never done before. For instance, once she visited a Quaker worship ser-vice, another week she went to an amusement center alone. Go back to college. Learn a foreign language.

—CECIL MURPHEY

Death

FEAR OF DEATH

What, specifically, do we fear in death? First, I think we fear being alone, cut off from our loved ones. I know I had to work through that fear the night I faced death. A haunting aloneness swept over me, as I pictured my parents and my husband coming in the next morning to find me—gone. And this fear stayed with me, until I became assured that beyond death I would be united with Him to whom my deepest commitments were made, united with all the family of God who had died before me, and eventually reunited with all of my loved ones who also made commitments to Jesus Christ. It was the presence of Christ Himself, made very real to me in those dark hours, that made me realize the absolute truth of His promise, "I will never leave thee, nor forsake thee."

Then, I think we are afraid of being cut off from our life work. I remember, that night, arguing intensely with God: "Lord, I've done only a little writing for You." A shiny new copy of my recently published first book sat on the windowsill of my hospital room. "If You let me live, I'll go on writing for You." Gradually, my mind was suffused with the illumination that, if I were to die, it would not be the end of my vocation, but only the beginning. All that I would ever do on this side of death would amount to nothing more than the scribbles in a student's copybook, just practicing for an eternity of glad service.

As we think of death, we are harrowed, too, with a fear of pain. "Oh joy, oh delight, should we go without dying. No sickness, no sadness, no dreading, no crying!" How beautifully the old hymn expresses the hope of being caught up to be with the Lord—a transition to eternity that one generation of the Church will indeed know. But in the meanwhile, we hope for something swift and relatively painless, while watching, numb with aching, as people we love suffer. In a culture oriented to comfort and to pleasure, the very idea of pain and discomfort is appalling. And yet, once again, we find that Christ holds out His hands to comfort. For He has taken the cup of human suffering and drunk it to the bottom. And in pain, we find Him there to sustain. The "fellowship of his sufferings" is something unknown to those who have not suffered, but it is a deep and sweet communion, known to those who have experienced pain and found that, at its worst, pain has opened out into communion. The blood He shed was for our sins, to bring about atonement. But the broken body was His total experience of our human suffering and pain. Once again, what we fear becomes something beautiful when illumined by the Presence of Our Lord.

Another element in the fear of death is the fear of dissolution, the horror of ceasing to be. We are so intensely aware of ourselves, a knit-together person of body, soul, and spirit. How can we face not being? It is only orthodox Christian doctrine, which sees the resurrection and reuniting of the whole person—body and soul and spirit—which tells us that beyond this dissolution is a new existence, that "this mortality must put on immortality." The resurrected flesh-and-bones body of Jesus Christ, recognizable, tangible, tells us that in our glorified state we will be whole—whole with a wholeness we only approximate in our short, earthly existence; whole for all eternity. What a glad hope in our calling! "Beloved, now are we the sons of God, and it doth not yet appear what we shall be: but we know that, when he shall appear, we shall be like him; for we shall see him as he is" (1 John 3:2).

There is still one fear of death. It is, perhaps, the greatest. Distasteful as the idea of nonexistence is to sentient creatures, even more fearful is the "... dread of something after death, That undiscover'd country from whose bourn no traveller returns...." Written in our hearts is the truth that, "... it is appointed unto men once to die, but after this the judgment" (Hebrews 9:27). There is both terror and hope in this truth. It is a truth which, once embraced with all its soul-searching implications, sets us free.

Solzhenitsyn chronicles the story of a little old woman being interrogated for her assistance to a church official. Despite the menace of fist-shaking jailers, she replied, "There is nothing you can do with me even if you cut me into pieces. After all, you are afraid of your bosses and you are afraid of each other ... but I am not afraid of anything. I would be glad to be judged by God right this minute."

The assurance of Christ's presence in the dark valley; of His fellowship in suffering; of ultimate wholeness and reunion with those we love in eternal, unending life of service to Our Lord; and of an ultimate righteous judgment, can give the Christian courage to live life fully and face death triumphantly.

—From Maxine Hancock, *The Forever Principle.* Old Tappan, N.J.: Revell, 1980.

COPING WITH LOSS

Couples who have lived together through the middle years will have grown increasingly dependent upon each other. After the children have grown and gone, there will have been deepening times of togetherness. Retirement brings another period of adjustment in relationships. Being around the house will fill a much larger part of life than was formerly devoted to the job. Mutual considerations are essential. The house will seem smaller and for a while you may even

STAGES OF DEATH

Those who work closely with terminal patients have defined five distinct stages of death. They do not necessarily occur in sequence. A seriously ill person may go through one stage and later revert back to it.*

1. Denial	"No, not me."	When patients first learn of their terminal condition, typically, they enter a stage of shock as they begin facing that death is inevitable.
2. Anger	"Why me?"	Resentment flares because they will die while others remain healthy and alive. Many people seem to lose faith at this stage. They also attack God whom they feel has forsaken them.
3. Bargaining	"Yes, God, but. . ."	Patients move closer to acceptance but bargain for more time with God. "I'll be a better Christian, God if only. . ." They promise to do something in exchange for more time, such as another year or month of life.
4. Depression	"Yes, me."	Once the terminally ill work through their sense of loss, right the wrongs of the past, they enter a stage of temporary grief, ready for death. They don't want visitors, and won't talk. This means that they are now ready to die.
5. Acceptance	"It's all right."	This is where patients accept that it is the end and have reconciled themselves. Some have called this victory stage—because patients sometimes are even eager to die.

* This chart drawn from *On Death and Dying* by Elisabeth Kübler-Ross (New York: Macmillan, 1969). By permission of the publisher.

get in each other's way. This time, however, can be agreeably helpful and if both husband and wife are thoughtful, there will be many opportunities to express understanding and appreciation.

But what happens when death strikes? One psychologist says flatly, "The loss of a spouse is the principal trauma of old-age." How can one prepare for this shock? How does one deal with loneliness? Henri Nouwen doesn't give a direct answer to these questions but suggests that part of being human is this yearning sense of loneliness. It haunts us at all ages of life. It can never really be satisfied through any personal relationships, however meaningful, nor through any groups, however supportive. . . .

In the aftermath of death, the sorrow will still be acutely real. Hurt will bleed into tears. But for one who has resolved estrangement, who has worked through disappointment and dealt with failure in trying to create the perfect community, there is not only power to face death, there is power to minister to life.

The deeper the love, the sharper is the pain. This is not counsel for either superficial relationships or shallow commitments. Even when two have been truly one, there can never be complete dependence for even these ties will be broken. All ties but those to Christ are passing.

—From Richard Knox Smith, *49 and Holding*. Lomita, Calif.: Morgan-Pacific, 1975.

SUPPORT FOR THE GRIEVING

All grief has common characteristics. Losing a loved one probably constitutes the greatest trauma for us. Yet other kinds of loss situations bring about many of the same kinds of reactions.

For instance, in the three months since Robb started his new job, I had seen him at church only once. As he walked into the fellowship hall for the men's meeting, I greeted him. "Hey, it's good to see you again. Guess you've been awfully busy with your new job at the bank. How's it going?"

"Oh, not so—" he stopped. "They fired me yesterday. My supervisor said I didn't have what it takes to be an executive. They—they fired me because they want to make room for up-and-coming people."

A few nights later Rosemary called me at 2:57 A.M. Their only child, Beverly, had eloped, leaving a message informing them of the fact. "She's also made it clear that she doesn't want anything to do with us," the mother cried.

In another instance, Ellen's only close friend in the church moved from Atlanta to San Diego. For three months, Ellen went through a period of deep depression. She later said, "It's been almost like—like having your twin sister die."

These people all experienced similar feelings of pain, shock, even depression—manifestations of great trauma. Naturally, one type of grief may be more intense or longer lasting than another. But grief *is* grief. In this book, I've focused on the subject of grieving over the death of a loved one, because that represents the most intense form of normal grief. What we learn from this kind of intense situation can help us in coping with lesser forms of grief.

And you *can* help people in those times of stress. By understanding what's going on inside them and by being sensitive to them, you can make a difference—more of a difference than you know! When death strikes your immediate circle, it doesn't matter how educated or experienced you are. You still feel the pain.

During my own grieving, several things helped me. These aren't gimmicks but suggestions I offer on how to do something after you've said you're sorry.

1. *Think twice before saying, "I know how you feel."* Does anyone really know how another person feels? You may have had similar experiences, but your emotional makeup differs from that of every other individual in the world. When you say, "I know how you feel," those words may circumvent the process of grief that needs to take place.

   I recall the last time I used that phrase. Judith's husband had been shot. He had walked into a grocery store, late at night, while a robbery was in progress. One of the robbers, rattled at seeing him come inside, shot him.

   Seeing Judith sitting beside the casket in the funeral home, I felt a wrench of emotion. Her husband had been a close friend. I hugged her and said quietly, "Judith, I know how you must be feeling right now."

She jerked her head back and hissed, "How can you know? You haven't lost your wife! You haven't had to try to sleep alone in a king-sized bed, knowing Tony'll never be there to share it again. You haven't stared at a closet full of clothes and realized he'll never wear them again. How can you know what I'm feeling?"

Judith cried out in pain, yet I realized that she was right: I didn't feel the things she felt. I had been thinking of his deep laugh, of his smile that showed a dimple on only one side. I really thought only of my own loss.

"You're right, Judith, I don't know. And I'm sorry for saying that. I should have said that I loved him too, and I'm already missing his friendship very much."

Then she hugged me and cried again.

2. *Don't be afraid to say what you feel.* The words you use aren't terribly important. Let the inner spirit shine through when you speak. I operate on the principle that when my feelings are genuine, my words convey the message.

For instance, two weeks ago I talked with Arnold. His father had died suddenly. Arnold had been close to his parents and idealized his father.

As we talked, I finally said, "My own father died in March. It took me a long time to get over it. Even now, I sometimes get a little teary-eyed when I think about him."

Arnold gripped my hand. "You understand, don't you? You know what it's like." Arnold said it to *me.* He recognized that we shared a common bond in our grief. I doubt he would have agreed, had I said it.

3. *Don't preach sermonettes.* One awful memory stays with me from the day of Dad's funeral. An old family friend came to the family section to offer condolences before the funeral began.

She hugged my mother and started speaking in a half-whisper, "Annie, it's hard on you now. But Jesus provides strength. He's promised to lead us through the dark valleys, and even through the fires of persecution. He has conquered death. 'The Lord is my shepherd, I shall not want.' Just think, one day we'll all be in the place where death no longer troubles us and pain no longer torments. Our bodies will be different— gloriously free of disease and age. . . ."

She kept on and on. I was sitting directly behind Mom, and even though I tried to blot out the constant chattering, I heard it all. I kept praying, "Lord, please, shut the woman up."

She went through a shorter version of her sermonette to each of us. She had not said anything wrong—nothing I could disagree with—but her timing was inappropriate. I promised myself I'd never bandy those words around at a time when people weren't ready to hear.

4. *Listen.* Let the mourner tell the story as many times as necessary and with as many details as he or she wants.

5. *Be there.* Dan and Alice have developed a unique ministry. Whenever they learn of the death of a person they've known well or who was a member of their church, they go to the funeral home that evening. They express their sympathy quietly, then sit down. Normally, they remain there until the family members all go home. Sometimes Dan and Alice hardly say anything. But they're there. And if few visitors come, they often carry on conversations with the family.

That's not everyone's type of ministry. Many of us need to be doing something. But Dan and Alice believe that their quiet presence has a calming effect on the family. They're there if needed.

"People seldom remember what everyone says to them when they're grieving," Dan once said. "But they nearly always remember who was there."

6. *Let your body speak its own language.* Clarence and my brother Ray had been best friends since both were thirteen. Ray died at fifty-one. At the funeral Clarence started crumbling emotionally. He's normally a very contained man, one who wouldn't want to cry publicly. I grabbed him by the shoulders for a minute, let go, and gripped both his hands. I held tightly. He soon regained his composure.

Holding a person's hand may help. A touch on the arm, even a hug. I recall instances when the mourner has taken my hand and gripped it. I've not been sure he or she knew what was happening. The person may have gripped so tightly that it hurt, but I didn't wince.

I like to think that body language speaks of emotional support. In traumatic times we all need people who will provide that emotional support. Having a breathing human body to grasp can be therapeutic for the griever. Perhaps taking another's hand and clutching it is what we mean when we talk about holding on. Even in that brief moment, the other person's response can communicate the offer of a relationship that won't crumple when pressure comes.

God created us to respond to other human beings. But sometimes words or actions hinder rather than help communicate. Here's a simple rule for trying to respond helpfully to a person in grief: If you don't know what to do or say, don't do or say anything. Just be there.

—From Cecil Murphey, *Comforting Those Who Grieve*. Atlanta: John Knox, 1979.

FOR FURTHER READING

Ahlem, Lloyd H. *How to Cope: With Conflict, Crisis, and Change*. Ventura, Calif.: Regal, 1980.

Augsburger, David. *Caring Enough to Confront*. Ventura, Calif.: Regal, 1978.

Bird, Joseph and Lois. *To Live As a Family*. New York: Doubleday, 1982.

Birkey, Verna. *You Are Very Special*. Old Tappan, N.J.: Revell, 1977.

Bock, Lois, and Miji Working. *Happiness Is a Family Time Together*. Old Tappan, N.J.: Revell, 1975.

Bock, Lois, and Miji Working. *Happiness Is a Family Walk With God*. Old Tappan, N.J.: Revell, 1977.

Brown, Joan Winmill, and Bill Brown. *Together Each Day*. Old Tappan, N.J.: Revell, 1980.

Burns, David. *Feeling Good: The New Mood Therapy*. New York: Morrow, 1980.

Burns, Robert W. *The Art of Staying Happily Married*. Atlanta: Christian Church Counseling, 1978.

Chafin, Kenneth. *Is There a Family in the House?* Waco, Tex.: Word Books, 1978.

Chapman, Gary. *Toward a Growing Marriage*. Chicago: Moody, 1979.

Christenson, Larry and Nordis. *The Christian Couple*. Minneapolis: Bethany House, 1977.

Collins, Gary R., ed. *Living and Growing Together*. Waco, Tex.: Word Books, 1976.

Conway, Jim. *Men in Mid-Life Crisis*. Elgin, Ill.: Cook, 1978.

Curtis, Jean. *Working Mothers*. New York: Simon & Schuster, 1977.

Davis, Drew. *On the Other Side of Anger*. Atlanta: John Knox, 1979.

DeJong, Peter, and Donald R. Wilson. *Husband and Wife: The Sexes in Scripture and Society*. Grand Rapids: Zondervan, 1979.

Dobson, James. *Hide or Seek*. Old Tappan, N.J.: Revell, 1979.

Dobson, James. *Straight Talk to Men and Their Wives*. Waco, Tex.: Word Books, 1980.

Dobson, James. *What Wives Wish Their Husbands Knew About Women*. Wheaton, Ill.: Tyndale, 1975.

Evans, Colleen Townsend. *Start Loving: The*

Miracle of Forgiving. New York: Doubleday, 1978.

Fried, Barbara. *The Middle-Age Crisis.* Rev. ed. New York: Harper & Row, 1976.

Fritze, Julius A. *The Essence of Marriage.* Grand Rapids: Zondervan, 1969.

Getz, Gene A. *The Measure of a Family.* Ventura, Calif.: Regal, 1976.

Hancock, Maxine. *The Forever Principle.* Old Tappan, N.J.: Revell, 1980.

Hart, Archibald D. *Feeling Free.* Old Tappan, N.J.: Revell, 1979.

Howe, Reuel L. *Survival Plus.* New York: Seabury, 1971.

Hubbard, David A. *Why Do I Have to Die?* Ventura, Calif.: Regal, 1978.

Jones, David and Doris. *Young Till We Die.* New York: Coward, McCann & Geohegan, 1973.

Keleman, Stanley. *Living Your Dying.* New York: Random House, 1975.

Kübler-Ross, Elisabeth. *On Death and Dying.* New York: Macmillan, 1969.

LaHaye, Tim. *How to Win Over Depression.* Grand Rapids: Zondervan, 1974.

LaHaye, Tim and Beverly. *The Act of Marriage.* Grand Rapids: Zondervan, 1976.

LaHaye, Tim and Bev. *Spirit-Controlled Family Living.* Old Tappan, N.J.: Revell, 1978.

Latesta, Robert L. *Fathers: A Fresh Start for the Christian Family.* Ann Arbor: Servant, 1980.

Lederer, William J., and Don D. Jackson. *The Mirages of Marriage.* New York: Norton, 1968.

LeShan, Eda J. *The Wonderful Crisis of Middle Age.* New York: McKay, 1973.

Leman, Dr. Kevin. *Sex Begins in the Kitchen.* Ventura, Calif.: Regal, 1981.

MacDonald, Gordon. *Magnificent Marriage.* Wheaton, Ill.: Tyndale, 1976.

Martin, Ralph. *Husbands, Wives, Parents, Children.* Ann Arbor: Servant, 1978.

Mason, Robert L., Jr. and Caroline L. Jacobs. *How to Choose the Wrong Marriage Partner and Live Unhappily Ever After.* Atlanta: John Knox, 1979.

McGinnis, Alan Loy. *The Friendship Factor.* Minneapolis: Augsburg, 1979.

Miller, William A. *You Count, You Really Do.* Minneapolis: Augsburg, 1976.

Minirth, Frank B. and States Skipper. *One Hundred Ways to Defeat Depression.* Grand Rapids: Baker Book, 1979.

Montague, Ashley. *Touching.* New York: Columbia University Press, 1971.

Morgan, Marabel. *The Total Woman.* Old Tappan, N.J.: Revell, 1973.

Murphey, Cecil. *Comforting Those Who Grieve.* Atlanta: John Knox, 1979.

Murphey, Cecil. *When in Doubt, Hug 'Em.* Atlanta: John Knox, 1978.

Narramore, Clyde M. *How to Succeed in Family Living.* Ventura, Calif.: Regal, 1968.

Narramore, Clyde and Ruth. *How to Handle Pressure.* Wheaton, Ill.: Tyndale, 1975.

Nelson, Elof G. *Your Life Together.* Atlanta: John Knox, 1967.

Norris, Gloria, and Jo Ann Miller. *The Working Mother's Complete Handbook.* New York: Dutton, 1979.

Ogilvie, Lloyd J. *Loved and Forgiven.* Ventura, Calif.: Regal, 1977.

One Plus One Equals One: Bible Discussions for Married Couples. Downers Grove, Ill.: InterVarsity, 1981.

Ortlund, Ray and Anne. *The Best Half of Life.* Waco, Tex.: Word Books, 1976.

Osborne, Cecil. *The Art of Understanding Your Mate.* Grand Rapids: Zondervan, 1970.

Powell, John, S.J. *The Secret of Staying in Love.* Allen, Tex.: Argus, 1974.

Powell, John, S.J. *Why Am I Afraid to Tell You Who I Am?* Allen, Tex.: Argus, 1970.

Renich, Fred. *The Christian Husband.* Wheaton, Ill.: Tyndale, 1976.

Scanzoni, John. *Love and Negotiate: Creative Conflict in Marriage.* Waco, Tex.: Word Books, 1979.

Schuller, Robert. *Self-Esteem.* Waco, Tex.: Word Books, 1982.

Shedd, Charlie W. *The Best Dad Is a Good Lover.* Fairway, Kans.: Andrews and McMeel, 1977.

Shedd, Charlie W. *Letters to Karen.* Nashville: Abington, 1965.

Small, Dwight Hervey. *Design for Christian Marriage.* Old Tappan, N.J.: Revell, 1959.

Small, Dwight Hervey. *Your Marriage Is God's Affair.* Old Tappan, N.J.: Revell, 1979.

Smith, Richard Knox. *49 and Holding.* Lomita, Calif.: Morgan-Pacific, 1975.

Solomon, Charles R. *Counseling With the Mind of Christ.* Old Tappan, N.J.: Revell, 1977.

Swindoll, Chuck. *For Those Who Hurt.* Portland: Multnomah, 1977.

Tournier, Paul. *Guilt and Grace.* New York: Harper & Row, 1962.

Tournier, Paul. *Learn to Grow Old.* New York: Harper & Row, 1971.

Tournier, Paul. *The Violence Within.* New York: Harper & Row, 1978.

Vernon, Bob, with C. C. Carlson. *The Married Man.* Old Tappan, N.J.: Revell, 1980.

Warner, Paul L. *Feeling Good About Feeling Bad.* Waco, Tex.: Word Books, 1979.

Welter, Paul. *How to Help a Friend.* Wheaton, Ill.: Tyndale, 1978.

Welter, Paul. *Family Problems and Predicaments: How to Respond.* Wheaton, Ill.: Tyndale, 1977.

Westburg, Granger E. *Good Grief.* Philadelphia: Fortress, 1971.

Whitehead, Evelyn Eaton and James D. Whitehead. *Marrying Well.* New York: Doubleday, 1981.

Wiese, Bennard R. and Urban G. Steinmetz. *Everything You Need to Know to Stay Married and Like It.* Grand Rapids: Zondervan, 1972.

Wood, Leland Foster. *Harmony in Marriage.* Old Tappan, N.J.: Revell, 1979.

Wright, H. Norman. *Communication: Key to Your Marriage.* Ventura, Calif.: Regal, 1974.

Wright, H. Norman. *The Christian Use of Emotional Power.* Old Tappan, N.J.: Revell, 1974.

Wright, H. Norman. *The Family That Listens.* Wheaton, Ill.: Victor Books, 1978.

Wright, H. Norman, and Rex Johnson. *Characteristics of a Caring Home.* Ventura, Calif.: Vision House, 1978.

4

Sex and Reproduction

SANCTITY OF SEX

THE ACT OF MARRIAGE is that beautiful and intimate relationship shared uniquely by a husband and wife in the privacy of their love—and it is sacred. In a real sense, God designed them for that relationship.

Proof that it is a sacred experience appears in God's first commandment to man: "Be fruitful, and multiply, and replenish the earth" (Genesis 1:28). That charge was given before sin entered the world; therefore, lovemaking and procreation were ordained and enjoyed while man continued in his original state of innocence.

This necessarily includes the strong and beautiful mating urge a husband and wife feel for each other. Doubtless Adam and Eve felt that urge in the Garden of Eden, just as God intended, and although we lack any written report for proof, it is reasonable to conclude that Adam and Eve made love before sin entered the garden (*see* Genesis 2:25).

The idea that God designed our sex organs for our enjoyment comes almost as a surprise to some people. But Dr. Henry Brandt, a Christian psychologist, reminds us, "God created all parts of the human body. He did not create some parts good and some bad; He created them all good, for when He had finished His creation, He looked at it and said, 'It is all very good' " (Genesis 1:31). Again, this occurred before sin marred the perfection of Paradise.

The Bible on Sex

Because the Bible clearly and repeatedly speaks out against the misuse or abuse of sex, labeling it "adultery" or "fornication," many people—either innocently or as a means of trying to justify their immorality—have misinterpreted the teaching and concluded that God condemns all sex. However, the contrary is true. The Bible always speaks approvingly of this relationship—as long as it is confined to married partners. The only prohibition on sex in the Scripture relates to extramarital or premarital activity. Without question, the Bible is abundantly clear on that subject, condemning all such conduct.

God is the creator of sex. He set human drives in motion, not to torture men and women, but to bring them enjoyment and fulfillment. Keep in mind how it all came about. Man was unfulfilled in the Garden of Eden. Although he lived in the world's most beautiful garden, surrounded with tame animals of every sort, he had no companionship of his own kind. God then took some flesh from Adam and performed another creative

181

miracle—woman—similar to man in every respect except her physical reproductive system. Instead of being opposites, they were complementary to each other. What kind of God would go out of His way to equip His special creatures for an activity, give them the necessary drives to consummate it, and then forbid its use? Certainly not the loving God presented so clearly in the Bible. Romans 8:32 assures us, "He that spared not his own Son, but delivered him up for us all, how shall he not with him also freely give us all things?" Looking at it objectively, sex was given at least in part for marital enjoyment.

For further proof that God approves lovemaking between married partners, consider the beautiful story which explains its origin. Of all God's creations only man was made "in the image of God" (Genesis 1:27). This in itself makes mankind the unique living creature on the earth. The next verse further states, "God *blessed them,* and God said unto them, Be fruitful, and multiply" (v. 28). Then He delivered His personal comment regarding all His creation: "God saw *everything* that he had made, and behold, it was *very good*" (v. 31).

Genesis 2 affords a more detailed description of God's creation of Adam and Eve, including the statement that God Himself brought Eve to Adam (v. 22), evidently to introduce them formally and give them the command to be fruitful. Then it beautifully describes their innocence in these words: "They were both naked, the man and his wife, and were not ashamed" (v. 25). Adam and Eve knew no embarrassment or shame on that occasion for three reasons: they were introduced by a holy and righteous God who commanded them to make love; their minds were not preconditioned to guilt, for no prohibitions concerning the act of marriage had yet been given; and no other people were around to observe their intimate relations.

ADAM "KNEW" HIS WIFE

Additional evidence of God's blessing on this sacred relationship appears in the charming expression used to describe the act of marriage between Adam and Eve in Genesis 4:1: "And Adam knew Eve his wife; and she conceived. . . ." What better way is there to describe the sublime, intimate interlocking of mind, heart, emotions, and body in a passionately eruptive climax that engulfs the participants in a wave of innocent relaxation that thoroughly expresses their love? The experience is a mutual "knowledge" of each other that is sacred, personal, and intimate. Such encounters were designed by God for mutual blessing and enjoyment.

A RAVISHING LOVER

At the risk of shocking some people, we would point out that the Bible doesn't mince any words on the subject. The Song of Solomon is notoriously frank in this respect (consider 2:3-17 and 4:1-7).

The Book of Proverbs warns against taking up with "the strange woman" (a prostitute), but by contrast challenges a husband to "*rejoice* with the wife of thy youth." How? By letting "her breasts satisfy thee at all times; and be thou ravished always with her love" (Proverbs 5:18, 19). It is obvious that this ravishing lovemaking experience should make a man rejoice, conferring upon him ecstatic pleasure. The context plainly signifies an experience intended for mutual enjoyment. This passage also indicates that such lovemaking was not designed solely for the propagation of the race, but also for sheer enjoyment by the partners. If we understand it correctly, and we think we do, it isn't to be a hurried or endured experience. Modern experts tell us that "foreplay" before entrance is essential to a mutually satisfying experience. We find no fault with that; we would, however, point out that Solomon made the same suggestion three thousand years ago.

All Bible passages should be studied in the light of their purpose in order to avoid wresting or twisting their meaning. The above concept is strong enough as we have presented it, but it becomes even more powerful when we understand its setting. The inspired words of Proverbs 1-9 record the instructions of Solomon, the world's wisest man, to his son, teaching him to handle the tremendous sex drive within himself and to avoid being tempted by its improper use. Solomon wanted his son to enjoy a lifetime of the legitimate use of that drive by confining it to the act of marriage. Since this entire passage concerns wisdom, it is obvious that enjoyable, satisfying married love is the course of wisdom. Extramarital love is presented as the way of folly, offering short-term pleasure by bringing "destruction" (heartache, guilt, sorrow) in the end.

We would be remiss if we failed to point out Proverbs 5:21: "For the ways of man are before the eyes of the Lord, and he pondereth all his goings." This text includes lovemaking: God sees the intimacy practiced by married partners and approves it. His judgment is reserved only for those who violate His plan and desecrate themselves by engaging in sex outside of marriage.

"SPORTING" IN THE OLD TESTAMENT

It may be hard for us to think of Old Testament saints as being good lovers, but they were. In fact, one may never hear a sermon on Isaac's relation with his wife, Rebekah, recorded in Genesis 26:6-11. This man, who made it into God's "Who's Who" of faith in Hebrews 11, was observed by King Abimelech "sporting with" (caressing) his wife. We are not told how far his advances went, but he obviously was sufficiently intimate to

make the king conclude that she was his wife, not his sister, as he had at first falsely declared. Isaac erred, not in engaging in foreplay with his wife, but in not restricting it to the privacy of their bedroom. The fact that he was caught, however, suggests that it was common and permissible in their day for husbands and wives to "sport." God planned it that way.

Further insight into God's approval of the act of marriage appears in the commandments and ordinances of God to Moses for the children of Israel. He instructed that a man was to be exempt from military service and all business responsibilities for one year after his marriage (Deuteronomy 24:5) so that these two people could get to "know" each other at a time when their sex drives were strongest and under circumstances that would provide ample opportunity for experimentation and enjoyment. Admittedly, this provision was also given to make it possible for a young man to "propagate" before he faced the risk of death on the battlefield. Contraceptives were not used at that time, and since the couple had so much time to be with each other, it is easy to see why children usually came early in the marriage.

Another verse displays how thoroughly God understands the sexual drive He created in mankind—1 Corinthians 7:9: "It is better to marry than to burn." Why? Because there is one legitimate, God-ordained method for releasing the natural pressure He has created in human beings—the act of marriage. It is God's primary method for release of the sex drive. He intended that husband and wife be totally dependent on each other for sexual satisfaction.

THE NEW TESTAMENT ON LOVEMAKING

The Bible comprises the best manual ever written on human behavior. It covers all kinds of interpersonal relationships, including sexual love. Some examples have already been given, but one of the most outstanding passages follows. To understand it fully, we wish to use the New American Standard translation of what is probably the clearest passage on the subject in the Bible:

> But because of immoralities, let each man have his own wife, and let each woman have her own husband. Let the husband fulfill his duty to his wife, and likewise also the wife to her husband. The wife does not have authority over her own body, but the husband does, and likewise also the husband does not have authority over his own body, but the wife does. Stop depriving one another, except by agreement for a time that you may devote yourselves to prayer, and come together again lest Satan tempt you because of your lack of self-control.   1 Corinthians 7:2-5

Here we will merely delineate the four central principles taught in this passage concerning lovemaking.

1. Both husband and wife have sexual needs and drives that should be fulfilled in marriage.
2. When one marries, he forfeits control of his body to his partner.
3. Both partners are forbidden to refuse the meeting of the mate's sexual needs.
4. The act of marriage is approved by God.

—From Tim and Beverly LaHaye, *The Act of Marriage*. Grand Rapids: Zondervan, 1976.

BIBLICAL DEFINITIONS

Cleave. God commanded the man to hold the marriage together by "cleaving" to his wife (*see* Genesis 2:24). The word *cleave* means to make one out of two or to weld inseparably so that each becomes a part of the other. This implies a total commitment by the man to his wife.

Helpmeet, Helper. The unfortunate translation of Genesis 2:18 KJV, or rather misunderstanding of a good translation, comes from the old English verb *meet.* At the time of the translation the word meant "fit" or "suited."

The intent of Genesis 2:18 was that God gave the man a helper who is fitted or suited to him. God provided the woman as a counterpart. Today's English Version reads, "I will make a suitable companion to help him."

One Flesh. In Genesis 2:24 God decreed that in marriage a man and a woman would become one flesh (Hebrew *basar*).

This not only speaks of a unique relationship but means that in the act of sexual union the two would be as one person.

God intended intercourse to be the most profound and intimate act of self-disclosure and self-committal.

—CECIL MURPHEY

SEXUAL INTERCOURSE

Female Sex Organs

EXTERNAL

Most women are vague about the appearance and function of their sexual and reproductive organs. For unlike those of a man, those of a woman are almost entirely hidden, so that in a standing position the only obvious sign is the pubic hair. Collectively the female external sex organs or genitals are known as the vulva. At the front, as if one were looking between a woman's open legs, is:

the mons veneris (mount of Venus) or mons pubis, a pad of fatty tissue over the pubic bone. From puberty this is covered with pubic hair. Extending downward and backward from the mons veneris are the

labia majora (outer lips), two folds of fatty tissue which protect the reproductive and urinary openings lying between them. These outer lips change size during a woman's life and from puberty their outer surfaces are also covered with hair. Between them lie the

labia minora (inner lips). These are delicate, hairless folds of skin quite sensitive to touch. During sexual arousal they swell and darken in color. Below the mons area the labia minora splits into two folds to form a hood under which lies the

clitoris. This is a small, bud-shaped organ and the most sensitive of the female genitals. The clitoris corresponds exactly to the male penis and like it is made up of erectile tissue. During sexual excitement the clitoris swells with blood and for most women is the center of orgasm. Just below the clitoris are the

urethra—the external opening of the urinary passage which leads direct to the bladder—and the

vaginal opening, the outside entrance to the vagina.

The hymen, or maidenhead, is a thin membrane just inside the vaginal opening. It varies greatly in shape and size, and in a virgin, it may be stretched or torn during the first experience of sexual intercourse, but quite often has already been stretched either by the use of tampons or during petting. If torn during intercourse there is usually some bleeding and possibly pain.

The Bartholin's or vestibular glands lie either side of the vaginal opening. Contrary to previous belief, these glands play little part in vaginal lubrication. They may occasionally become infected (e.g. by gonorrhea).

The *perineum* is the triangular area of skin lying between the end of the labia minora and the anus. Below its surface are muscles and fibrous tissue that are stretched during childbirth.

The *anus* lies below the perineum and is the external opening through which feces pass from the rectum.

INTERNAL

These are a woman's reproductive organs and consist of the vagina, uterus, Fallopian tubes, and ovaries.

The vagina is a muscular passage, lying between *the bladder* and *the rectum.* It leads from the vulva upward, and at an angle, to the uterus. It is about 4–5in (10–12.5cm) long and capable of great distension. Normally the vaginal walls, which are lined with folds or ridges of skin, lie close together. During sexual intercourse they stretch easily to take the male penis and extend even more considerably during labor to allow a child to be born. The vagina is usually moist, though moistness increases with sexual excitement and may also vary at different times of the menstrual cycle. A continuous secretion from the cervix and vagina of dead cells mixed with fluid lubricates the vagina, keeping it clean and free from infection. It is this self-cleansing quality that makes vaginal douching unnecessary.

The cervix is the neck or lower part of the uterus. It projects into the upper end of the vagina and can quite often be felt by sliding a finger as far back as possible into the vagina. This may not be possible at certain times during the menstrual cycle or during sexual excitement if the uterus changes position.

The os, a tiny opening through the cervix, is the entrance to the uterus. It varies in shape and size depending on whether a woman has had children, but remains very small. It cannot be penetrated by a penis, finger, or tampon.

The entire uterus (including the cervix) is a hollow, muscular, pear-shaped organ, about the size of a lemon in its non-pregnant state. Seen from the front the uterine cavity is triangular in shape and it is here that the fetus develops during pregnancy, pushing back the muscular walls in a surprising manner. During labor the fetus moves from the uterine cavity through the cervix and vagina to be delivered through the vaginal opening.

The endometrium is the mucous membrane lining the body of the uterus. Once a month it undergoes various changes as part of the menstrual cycle.

The Fallopian tubes extend outward and back from either side of the upper end of the uterus. They are about 4 inches (10cm) in length and reach outward toward the ovaries.

The ovaries are the female egg cells, equivalent to the male testes. They produce ova and also the female sex hormones, estrogen and progesterone. Once a month an ovum (egg) is released, which floats freely into the end of one of the Fallopian tubes.

—From Diagram Group, *Woman's Body*. Rev. ed. New York: Simon & Schuster, 1981.

Male Sex Organs

The male sexual system is partly visible, and partly hidden inside the body.

The visible parts are the penis, and the scrotum containing the testes.

Inside the body are the prostate gland, the seminal vesicles, and the tubes that link different parts of the system.

The two testes are the male reproductive glands. They hang in an external pouch (the scrotum), which is below and behind the penis. Each testis is a flattened oval in shape, about 1¾ inches long and 1 inch wide.

The scrotum is divided into two separate compartments (scrotal sacs), one for each testis. (Usually the left testis hangs lower than the right, and its scrotal sac is slightly larger.)

The testes make:
a male sex hormone, testosterone; and sperm cells, which are the male reproduction cells. The sperm cells are needed to fertilize the egg in the female body, if new life is to be produced.

The epididymides are found one alongside each testis. A number of small tubes lead to each epididymis from its testis. In the epididymides the young sperm cells (spermatocytes) are stored and develop into mature sperm.

The vas deferens are the two tubes—one from each testis—that carry sperm from the testes to the prostate gland. They are about 16 inches long, and wind upwards from the scrotum into the pelvic cavity. They come together and join with the urethra tube just below the bladder.

The prostate gland surrounds the junction of the vas deferens and urethra tubes. Here the sperm cells are mixed with seminal fluid: the liquid in which the sperms are carried out of the body. The resulting mixture is semen: a thick whitish fluid.

The seminal vesicles make part of the seminal fluid that the prostate gland mixes with the sperm cells. More seminal fluid is made by the prostate gland itself.

The urethra is the tube that carries urine from the bladder to the penis. It is S-shaped and about 8 inches long.

In the prostate gland it is joined by the vas deferens—so it is also the route by which the semen reaches the penis from the prostate gland.

The penis is inserted into the female body during copulation. Most of the penis is made up of spongy tissue, loosely covered with skin. The urethra tube enters the penis from the body and runs inside it to the tip of the penis. The external opening in the tip (the meatus) is where semen or urine leaves the body. In its natural state, the sides of the penis near its tip are covered by a fold of skin, called the foreskin. But this is often removed—usually because of religious or social custom, shortly after birth, but sometimes for medical reasons.

—From Diagram Group, *Man's Body*. Rev. ed. New York: Simon & Schuster, 1981.

First Intercourse and the Hymen

Often there are some problems in first sexual experiences involving the hymen. The hymen is a membrane located on the inside of the opening of the vagina. Hymens vary in thickness. Sometimes a hymen is by nature so thin and elastic that it stretches and is not broken in intercourse. The penis can enter the vaginal passage at first intercourse with only a feeling of tightness. In a few cases the hymen may be entirely absent. Also, it may have been broken by a physical accident, or by a physician for medical purposes. On the other hand, some hymens are so thick and tough that it is impossible for the couple to have intercourse. That is, the hymen so closes the opening of the vaginal passage that it is impossible for the penis to enter the opening. In our research we found that slightly over 13 percent of the brides in the sample had to have a doctor either stretch or cut the hymen before they could have intercourse. So we may say that approximately 87 percent of hymens may be broken in intercourse and that 13 percent can be broken only with difficulty, if at all.

There are two other factors involved in the success of entrance at first intercourse on the wedding night. One is the fact that the girl has a set of muscles around the opening of the vaginal passage. Tenseness at the time of first intercourse may cause these muscles to contract and partially close the vagina. A second factor involved is the size of the groom's penis. The size of the penis varies just as people vary in height and build. One cannot judge the size of the penis by the size of the man. There may be a large man with a small penis, or a small man with a large penis. Most men usually do not know whether their penis is large or small. There is no basis for a man with a large penis to feel proud or superior, or for a man with a smaller penis to feel inferior or humiliated. The fact is that the size of the penis has little to do with good sex life.

But with regard to the problem of first entrance; it is obvious that, if on the wedding night the bride has a thick hymen plus some nervous tenseness, and the groom has a rather large penis, the couple could expect some problems in first intercourse. For these reasons, marriage counselors recommend that the prospective bride go to a doctor at least two to four weeks before her wedding date and request a pelvic examination, which includes the hymen, the vagina, and the womb. If she has a thick, tight hymen, the doctor will detect it and recommend that it be stretched or cut. Only a doctor is qualified to do this.

—From Herbert J. Miles, *Sexual Happiness in Marriage*. Grand Rapids: Zondervan, 1967.

Arousal

Husband and wife are responsible to meet each other's sexual needs all of their married lives. The husband is responsible to meet his wife's sexual needs. He must regularly and lovingly arouse her to a complete sexual experience, climax or orgasm. Likewise, the wife must meet her husband's sexual needs. She must regularly and lovingly arouse him to a sexual experience, climax or orgasm. A husband should not expect his wife to meet her own sexual needs. Neither should a wife expect her husband to meet his own sexual needs. Rather, motivated by love, they will want to meet each other's sexual needs. In

187

this manner, both of their sexual needs will be met in the most satisfying and beautiful manner.

In 1 Corinthians 7:2-5 we have these words: "... each man shall have his own wife and each woman her own husband. The husband should give to his wife her conjugal rights and likewise the wife to her husband." In this passage, *conjugal* means sexual. This scripture is saying that the husband should meet his wife's sexual needs and the wife should meet her husband's sexual needs. This scripture continues, "For the wife does not rule over her own body, but the husband does; likewise the husband does not rule over his own body, but the wife does." In marriage the wife's body does not belong to her. It belongs to her husband and he rules over it. In like manner, in marriage, the husband's body does not belong to him. It belongs to his wife, and she rules over it. This passage is saying that in marriage each rules over the other's sexual life by meeting each other's sexual needs. In verse five, Paul says, "Do not refuse one another," that is, do not refuse to meet each other's sexual needs. This passage makes it clear that both husband and wife are morally responsible to meet each other's sexual needs.

There are two major problems that tend to block good sexual adjustment in marriage. To make it easy to remember these two problems, we will call them "time" and "space" and discuss them in order.

By "time," we refer to the fact that, sexually, male and female bodies are "timed" differently. Sexually, man is timed quickly. He can become aroused through sexual stimulation with his wife and usually reach an orgasm in a very short time, two minutes, one minute, or even in less time. This is normal for him. He will gradually learn to control himself, but he will always tend to be "quick on the trigger." His wife should never say to him, "You beast, why don't you con-

trol yourself?" She should understand him in terms of his quick timing sexually, and that God created him this way. She should realize that all other women's husbands are "quick on the trigger" just like her husband is quick to respond sexually. Of course, the young husband will try to control himself as much as possible, and will learn to do so.

On the other hand, sexually, a woman is timed more slowly, sometimes very slowly, as compared with a man. We can safely say that it takes the average woman ten to fifteen minutes or longer from the time she starts sexual arousal with her husband until she experiences an orgasm. This is after she is married and is experienced in regular sexual relationships. Sometimes she may have an orgasm in ten minutes, five minutes, or even less. A few women on special occasions may have an orgasm in one or two minutes. This is the exception. At other times it may take 20 or 30 minutes, or even longer. It may vary according to where she is in the menstrual cycle. Also, other circumstances such as personal, family, or community problems may affect her. A young wife will gradually learn how to move toward her orgasm a little more quickly, but she cannot change the fact that her sexual arousal nature is timed slowly. Her husband should never say to her, "You iceberg, why don't you hurry up?" He should understand her in terms of the fact that she is not responsible for being timed slowly. He should realize that all men's wives are just like his and that God created them this way. Sex in woman is as definite, as real, and as satisfying as it is in man, but it is something deep down inside of her, a spiritual gold mine. The young husband must, with patience, love, understanding, and tenderness, uncover her sexual interest, layer by layer, and gradually bring it to the surface, allowing her to express her love for him in an orgasm. This simply takes time.

When a young couple understands their

difference in sexual timing and when they accept it and cooperate with it, it is no longer a major problem, but actually may be a blessing. Let us repeat, a couple must *understand it, accept it,* and *cooperate with it* for it to be a blessing. By being a blessing, we mean that this period of sexual stimulation and arousal, whether it be 10 or 20 minutes, may become one of the sweetest, most meaningful and spiritual experiences in husband-wife relationships. It is only when a couple does not understand, or does not cooperate with their differences in sexual timing that it becomes a problem.

The second major problem that tends to block good sexual adjustment we have called "space." "Space" refers to the distance on the body of the wife between the clitoris and the vaginal passage. The clitoris is the external arousal trigger that sets off the orgasm in woman. It is made up of many nerve endings designed by the Creator to arouse a woman to an orgasm. These nerve endings must be stimulated directly by physical contact for a woman to become sexually aroused high enough to have an orgasm. The clitoris is located, somewhat out in front, at the upper meeting point of the inner lips, or labia minora. Please note that on the average sized woman the distance from the clitoris to the vaginal passage is approximately one and one-fourth inches. This is the space we are discussing.

Now, visualize the position of the vaginal passage. Note that in the process of sexual intercourse in the man-above position, the penis moves into the vagina, not from an angle above the vaginal opening, but actually from an angle slightly below it. When this fact is visualized and understood, it should be clear that in normal sexual intercourse the penis does not touch or contact the clitoris. This fact is of major importance. If the penis does not move back and forth over the clitoris in intercourse, then the wife

may not become fully aroused and thus will not have an orgasm.

The couple may use other positions for intercourse in which the penis can be forced to move back and forth over the clitoris and stimulate it directly. However, there are two problems involved in doing this. First, these positions may not be very comfortable for either the wife or her husband. Secondly, many husbands cannot control themselves for ten or fifteen minutes of this type of intercourse without reaching an orgasm before their wives are fully aroused.

Since the clitoris is the arousal trigger of the wife, and since the penis does not contact the clitoris in normal intercourse, marriage counselors recommend what is called "direct" stimulation. That is, the husband, in the process of love-play before intercourse starts, will gently stimulate his wife's clitoris with his fingers for ten or fifteen minutes, or whatever time it takes, until he is certain she is fully aroused sexually and ready for intercourse. There is nothing wrong in this procedure. A couple must do the right thing at the right time in the right attitude for full arousal and complete love harmony. It is normal in the love-play and arousal period for a couple to touch and handle each other's sexual organs. This is a pleasant and meaningful part of love expression. It was planned this way by the Creator.

The important point to remember here is that the *clitoris is the external arousal* trigger; that there must be uninterrupted stimulation of the clitoris and the area close to the clitoris for a wife to have an orgasm. The *method* of stimulation of the clitoris is not so important. Any one of several different methods may be satisfactory. The fact that the clitoris *has to be stimulated is the important thing* to remember.

—From Herbert J. Miles, *Sexual Happiness in Marriage*. Grand Rapids: Zondervan, 1967.

Increased Excitement

Following the arousal phase, a gradual and not well-defined transition into the second phase occurs. This is often called the plateau stage. After the preliminary period of stroking the entire body, the husband may enjoy fondling his wife's breasts, and she may enjoy his caresses and kisses on the nipple area. At first, the nipple becomes more firm and stands out from the breast; then as excitement increases, the nipple may appear to be somewhat hidden by the swelling of surrounding tissues. This surrounding engorgement helps guard the sensitive nipple from excessive stimulation.

A gentle caressing of the genitalia will greatly increase sexual excitement at this point. Be creative and imaginative rather than rough, blundering, or predictable in your approach. Always remember that stirring the imagination helps bring about the most response in both men and women. Anything is permissible as long as it is desired by both partners, affords mutual pleasure, and does not offend either partner. The Scriptures tell us that the joyous sexual expression of love between husband and wife is God's plan. Hebrews 13:4 proclaims the fact that the marriage union is honorable and the bed undefiled. The word translated *bed* in the Greek New Testament is actually *coitus*, the word meaning sexual intercourse.

The Song of Solomon (2:6 and 8:3) describes a position ideal for intensified love play. "Let his left hand be under my head and his right hand embrace me," the bride says. (The Hebrew word translated *embrace* usually means to embrace lovingly, to fondle or stimulate with gentle stroking.) In this position, the wife lies on her back with her legs extended, comfortably separated, and her husband lies down on her right side, placing his left arm under her neck. In this way he can kiss her lips, neck, and breasts, and at the same time his right hand is free to fondle her genitals.

As excitement continues to rise, the clitoris swells and the labia minora (inner lips) at the entrance to the vagina become two or three times enlarged. The swelling and engorgement of the lower vagina reduces the diameter of the outer one-third of the vagina as much as 50 percent, which prepares the vagina to actually grip the penis. When the inner lips change color from bright red to deep wine or from pink to bright red, this indicates that orgasm will occur within sixty to ninety seconds, if effective stimulation continues. Other responses may be tensing of muscles, increased pulse rate, a general flush of the skin, especially over the upper abdomen and the chest. There may be almost spastic contraction of some sets of muscles in the face, chest, abdomen, and buttocks. Voluntary tightening of the sphincter muscle, which holds the anus closed, and some voluntary contractions of the muscles of the buttocks may help heighten sexual tension.

While the man learns to control the timing of his response, the wife should learn to let herself go, trust her husband, trust her own body, and be as free as possible. As she concentrates on her physical feelings, she should learn to communicate her level of sexual excitement to her husband with looks, touches, and sometimes loving words. This helps the husband to properly time his lovemaking. One of the most common sources of sexual unhappiness is the failure of women to tell their husbands frankly and clearly what stimulates them and when they are ready for a particular stimulation.

While the husband's caresses of the wife's genitalia are essential to bring on the wife's orgasm, the wife's caresses of the husband's genitals do not usually speed up the male orgasm. While excitement has been building in both partners, when the wife actually touches the husband's genitals, it is soothing and comforting to him.

The wife's very light gentle caressing should center around the inner thighs, the scrotum, and the under surface of the penile shaft. Stimulation here will help maintain the husband's erection. Touching of the scrotum should be very light, since the scrotum is quite pressure sensitive. Fondling the head of the penis and the frenulum on the underside of the penile shaft will greatly increase the husband's excitement but may also trigger ejaculation more quickly than desired. By fondling and lovingly touching her husband's genitals, the wife soothes him and quiets his responses, while her own excitement builds.

The clitoris, rather than the vagina, is the center of feminine response, and its stimulation will produce orgasm in almost all women. Increase of arousal will come from manual play at and alongside the clitoris more often than from placing fingers in the vagina. As excitement progresses in the wife, the shaft of the clitoris will enlarge and become firmer. The firm clitoris usually can be felt at the peak of the surrounding lips above the vagina. Before sexual excitement, it is very difficult even to find the shaft of the clitoris, and it is important to note that in 30 percent of women there is no discernible enlargement of the clitoris during sexual arousal.

If the husband has given his wife enough stimulation to build excitement, some natural lubrication may be brought to the outside from within the vagina. A well-lubricated clitoris will be much more sexually responsive to the husband's touch. If the wife does not produce enough natural lubricant, some K-Y Jelly may be used to lubricate the clitoris and vaginal opening. (Be careful to warm the K-Y Jelly by holding the tube in warm, running water before you go to bed.) Applying the lubrication can in itself be exciting to the wife, as it shows her husband's tender care for her. Trying to stimulate a dry clitoris or inserting a penis into a dry, tense vagina indicates lack of understanding or selfishness and should be avoided. Clitoral

sensitivity in some women increases to the point where direct stimulation may become unpleasant (too much!) or even irritating. Therefore, movement of the husband's fingers should be directed to the area immediately around the clitoris. A consistent and persistent movement of the husband's fingers alongside the shaft of the clitoris is usually most effective in heightening her excitement.

When the labia minora on each side of the vaginal opening engorge or swell, the husband receives an important clue as to how far along his wife is in her arousal. These inner lips may so engorge that they protrude beyond the outer lips. The husband can only judge when this occurs by learning how to detect it with the tips of his fingers, as he stimulates his wife. This swelling of the inner lips is the most easily observable physical sign, telling the husband that his wife is ready for insertion of the penis.

Husband, although this is one sign of readiness, never insert the penis until the wife signals you to do so. Always insert the penis in the most gentle way and never follow immediately with vigorous thrusting, as this usually decreases arousal in the woman. Most couples have found that it is very useful for the wife to insert the penis. She knows exactly where it should go. This will avoid interruption at this very important time. Even after entrance of the penis, she may still need light caressing of the clitoris to increase excitement to orgasm. It is estimated that 30 percent of women always require manual stimulation of the clitoris to achieve orgasm.

Positioning of the couple's bodies should suit their own individuality. There need be no set patterns, although early in marriage, the bride, not having had her tissues stretched from childbearing, may find that some angles of penile insertion will cause discomfort. After several children have been born, the tissues around the vagina will be

191

stretched, and the wife will then be more comfortable in varied positions. Remember, changing of positions may restore interest and encourage excitement, but these new positions must be comfortable and pleasing for both husband and wife. It is worth noting that the right rhythm of movement is just as important as the right position in attaining a satisfactory response for both partners.

—From Ed Wheat, M.D., and Gaye Wheat, *Intended for Pleasure.* Rev. ed. Old Tappan, N.J.: Revell, 1981.

Positions

The *male-above position* is by far the most commonly used and gives the husband freedom of movement plus greatest control of strength and rapidity of thrusting. Many couples consider this the most satisfying of all positions. The wife lies on her back with legs extended, comfortably separated. The husband lies on top of her, supporting some of his weight on arms or elbows, his legs inside hers. After insertion of the penis her legs may be moved farther apart, closer together, inside his, or wrapped around his legs or up over his body.

To assume the *female-above position* the husband lies on his back, while the wife straddles his body and leans forward. *She* inserts the penis at about a 45-degree angle and moves back on the shaft, rather than sitting down on it. She then assumes whatever posture is most stimulating and comfortable to her. This position allows the wife by her movements to control the exact timing and degree of thrusting that affords her the most sexual response. The placement of each partner's legs will govern deeper or less deep penetration of the penis, depending on what is preferred. The female-above position gives the husband access to her breasts. He also has free use of his hands to better stimulate

the clitoris, if necessary, while they are joined in sexual intercourse. This position is often advantageous for a large husband and a small wife, and is sometimes more comfortable as the abdomen enlarges during pregnancy.

Starting intercourse in the female-above position, the *lateral,* or *side-by-side position* is assumed by the wife leaning forward and shifting her body slightly to the right, placing her right leg between her husband's legs. Her left leg is then flexed over his right leg. Advantages of the lateral position are that each partner has at least one hand free for fondling and caressing. Each is free to thrust or rotate hips. Neither has to support weight with hands and legs, and neither is being "pinned" by the body weight of the other.

The *male-behind position* seldom is used but may be tried on occasion and may also be used during late pregnancy. Both husband and wife lie on their sides facing the same direction with the husband back of the wife. The penis is placed into the vagina from the rear. Disadvantages are that the penis does not contact the clitoris and the couple cannot kiss during intercourse. This position leaves the husband's hands free to caress the body and breasts and stimulate the clitoris.

We have described the basic positions here. By all means feel free to explore the pleasure of other positions that you imagine would be exciting for you and, of course, acceptable to your mate.

It should be understood that the size of the penis has nothing to do with how much either partner enjoys intercourse, as only the outer two inches of the vagina contain tissue which is stimulated by pressure on the inside. Many men think deep penetration of the penis gives his wife greater stimulation, when it is actually better contact with the clitoris that will increase her stimulation to the point of orgasm.

—From Ed Wheat, M.D., and Gaye Wheat, *Intended for Pleasure*. Rev. ed. Old Tappan, N.J.: Revell, 1981.

Orgasm

The term orgasm comes from the Greek word *orgē* meaning *excitement*. In the woman, it has been described as a momentary feeling of suspension, followed by a sensation of warmth starting in the perineal area and pervading the entire body. Rhythmic contractions of the lower third of the vagina follow. There may be from three to ten contractions over the period of a few seconds. She can increase the intensity of the physical sensations by voluntarily strengthening her pubococcygeus muscle contractions and adding her own pelvic movements to her husband's, as she lets herself go in seeking release. As her physical movements, her response to her partner's stimulation, and her own mental concentration blend into a total reaching for satisfaction, she comes to climax—often an emotional mountain-peak experience, when the rest of the world recedes and seems to stand still—a high point of feeling, best described as *ecstasy*.

Sometimes a woman does not know if she has experienced an orgasm. If you feel your vagina contracting involuntarily, if you feel excited at first, and later feel calm and physically satisfied, you can take this as evidence that you have had an orgasm, even though perhaps a weak one.

The man's orgasm consists of involuntary muscle tension and contractions, with sensation centered specifically in the penis, prostate, and seminal vesicles. His orgasm is completed when he has expelled the semen.

Husband, there are five things that will increase the physical intensity and pleasure of your orgasm: (1) Wait at least twenty-four hours after previous orgasm to allow the body to store a larger volume of seminal fluid. (2) Lengthen the foreplay and excitement period, so that the penis can remain erect about twenty minutes. (3) Increase your imagination factor by seeing and feeling your wife's ecstatic response to your knowledgeable, skillful, physical stimulation, which brings her to the point of maximum physical pleasure. (4) Voluntarily contract your anal sphincter muscles during your orgasm. (5) Increase the force of thrusting while your orgasm is in progress.

During these few seconds of intense sensation known as orgasm, both husband and wife experience various muscular responses, even facial grimaces. As they both move in rhythm, they usually grasp one another tightly. Men and women are sometimes unaware of their extreme muscular exertions during orgasm, but it is not uncommon the next day to notice muscular aches, particularly in the back and thighs.

As soon as the husband finishes ejaculation, he should begin manual stimulation of his wife's clitoris, so that she can have repeated orgasms. This is the way the woman is designed! She should not have to ask for this, as the whole sex relationship is a pattern of pleasing each other. This means it is not desirable to change pace by having to ask for something for one's self. It should be the natural desire of the husband to provide every pleasure he knows of, and the wife may be intensely pleased by this continuing stimulation.

While arriving at orgasm at the same time may be a goal for lovers, it is not nearly as important as aiming at mutual enjoyment. Some begin to experience simultaneous orgasms as they come to understand each other more intimately. What does matter is that both partners be fully satisfied in each sexual encounter.

Time is all-essential. Take time to thoroughly arouse each other physically.

193

Take time to ensure the wife's orgasm and the husband's controlled, full response. Finally, after intercourse, take time to express your love and appreciation for each other.

—From Ed Wheat, M.D., and Gaye Wheat, *Intended for Pleasure*. Rev. ed. Old Tappan, N.J.: Revell, 1981.

Relaxation

Picture this final phase according to the poetic term one doctor has given it—*afterglow*. After intercourse is over, the fires of passion and pleasure settle down to a lovely, quiet glow. Let this be a time when the husband shows tenderness toward his wife with hugs, kisses, love pats. The couple should continue to express their appreciation as they lie close in each other's arms and just enjoy each other's presence. This ensures a smooth transition to complete relaxation together. It may be as long as fifteen minutes before all the physical signs of arousal are gone, and in a younger man it may be as long as a half hour before the erection completely disappears.

You will find a unique joy in using all the skill you possess to bring pleasure to your marriage partner. In fact, every physical union should be an exciting contest to see which partner can outplease the other. The husband should be the world's greatest authority on how to please his wife. And the wife should be able to say as joyously as the bride in The Song of Solomon—"I am my beloved's, and his desire is toward me" (7:10).

—From Ed Wheat, M.D., and Gaye Wheat, *Intended for Pleasure*. Rev. ed. Old Tappan, N.J.: Revell, 1981.

Cleaning Up

How much discharge should you expect? The man's seminal fluid will be about one teaspoonful. Women's vaginal lubrication varies considerably. We really cannot give even an approximate measure. Maybe we can picture it for you. When the man withdraws from the vagina, his penis will usually drip with the secretions. If the woman were to sit up on the sheet and let the discharge run out of her vagina, it would probably soak a spot one to five inches in diameter. This is a combination of her own vaginal lubrication and the seminal fluid that has been deposited if her husband ejaculated while in the vagina.

Is this a turn-off? Should you let your spouse see it? Most men get turned on by vaginal lubrication. It's a sign of the wife's responsiveness which many men take as a compliment. Besides, most men get turned on by a turned-on woman. They love it!

An exception to this might be some men who have extreme difficulty even touching the vaginal area. They think of it as messy and do not like messes. Some women have a similar response to the man's ejaculate. To them it is repulsive. They avoid it as if it will contaminate them. These are the exceptions rather than the norm.

For most women, the ejaculation has a positive, warm, intimate feeling. It is a symbol of the intimacy shared.

Since the usual response is positive, we encourage openness about the discharge. It is clean; it has no germs. There is nothing embarrassing or innately repulsive about it. The result of a beautiful act, it gives life. This is the way God made us and intended us to be.

If it is a turn-off to one of you, that person should talk about it and possibly even get some professional help. Removing that negative barrier from your sexual relationship could open up a whole new world of freedom for the two of you.

HOW TO HANDLE IT

There is really no prescribed, correct or proper way to take care of the sexual juices. Usually you can start by talking about what, if anything, you would like to do about it. What is comfortable for each of you?

Some couples bring a box of tissues to their lovemaking spot. Others like to have a washcloth or towel. Some have their special lovemaking sheet or blanket they put under them. Still others feel no need to take care of the discharge. If they make love in bed, the sheets absorb the discharge and that is comfortable for them.

Sometimes the cleaning up time can become a pleasant, familiar ritual. The item(s) brought to the experience can be included in the "something old" part of setting the atmosphere.

WHEN THE "NORM" VARIES

A small percentage of women experience an expulsion of fluid that is not vaginal lubrication. Robert C. Kolodny, M.D., from Masters and Johnson's Institute has researched this phenomenon. He has reported on this at a workshop and in a personal telephone call. A large amount of fluid—approximately a cup—is expelled from the urinary bladder, but it is not urine. The woman can urinate immediately before a sexual experience. She can have every drop of urine removed from the bladder with a rubber tube called a catheter. Nevertheless, if she has an orgasm within even a few minutes of having a totally empty bladder, she will expel this clear, watery fluid from the urinary bladder. This evidently happens in intensely orgasmic women. Apparently the pituitary gland causes fluid to be withdrawn from the cells of the body and fed into the blood, and from there to the bladder.

Even though this discharge is not usual for most women, it need not be a negative experience. Extra preparation will be required to protect the surface on which the sexual experience occurs. Otherwise, the area would be rather wet afterward. The fluid is clean, warm, and need not be repulsive. Some women who experience this fluid expulsion have withheld their orgasmic response because of their embarrassment. They feel as though they have lost bladder control. Getting accurate data and sharing it with each other can free the woman to make the necessary preparations before lovemaking and to allow herself to let go orgasmically. It has helped some women to think of letting themselves go with the flow of the fluid. This helps them gain a warm, positive association with their body's responses, rather than tightening up when they feel it coming. For them, this is the body's normal response. It is something to go with, not fight.

SUMMARY

The sexual organs, orifices and discharges are clean. They are free of disease-producing microorganisms. As you are able to integrate the sexual parts of yourself into your total being, you develop positive feelings toward all aspects of your sexual expression, rather than feeling hesitant toward or repulsed by them. Your positive associations contribute to natural comfort in handling the sexual dimensions of your life.

—From Clifford and Joyce Penner, *The Gift of Sex* copyright © 1981, pp. 181–83; used by permission of Word Books, Publisher, Waco, Texas 76796.

Frequency

There are no rules for frequency of intercourse that stand the test of reason. Desire is the only yardstick. Religious and secular codes from the ancient Hebrews to the present have dictated what were thought to be proper frequencies for spouses. The Talmud advised students to have coitus every night so that they might better concentrate on intellectual pursuits during the day. Medieval scholars, on the contrary, believed that all intercourse interfered with intellectual pursuits.

The frequency of desire varies with the individual. Couples will have intercourse when they feel desire, and that is all that matters. There is no such thing as sexual excess. When desire had been satisfied, there is none left for an excess of satisfaction. There may be sexual athletes who try to break records and end by exhausting themselves. But this kind of behavior is irrational and futhermore it is unlikely in marriage. Frequency of intercourse in marriage is self-regulating.

At least it should be. Since desire is not necessarily always present in both partners at the same time, there is only one way to work out such time differences, and that is by accommodation. Mature marriage partners know that, but unfortunately many arrive at their wisdom only by bitter and often thorny routes. If the relationship is a good one it is seldom a hardship for one to wait until the other's desire recurs. Impatience or recriminations over delay suggest that there is disharmony or misunderstanding in other areas of the marriage.

Occasionally, even under the best emotional conditions, a husband's urgency may become too difficult for him to manage with equanimity. Certain kinds of stress produce a clamorous, nagging sexual desire. A loving wife will assuage her husband's desire even though her own may be temporarily at a low level. It gratifies her to give him pleasure and relief. When there is a constant, unremitting disparity of desire between two partners there are other sources of trouble that should be explored.

Even when differences in frequency of desire have been successfully worked out by willing, cooperating partners, there may still be differences in the intensity of desire. Yet a strongly sexed wife who is healthy and not neurotic is thoroughly satisfied by one fulfilling orgasm. A strongly sexed husband who may require several orgasms at one encounter can be satisfied by a considerate, obliging wife. Most husbands are not ever-hungry Casanovas or tireless sexual Hercules. Few wives aspire to the appetites of Messalina, whom even a Roman brigade could not satisfy. A disparity of strength and sexual vigor is not a fatal flaw in an otherwise warm and companionable marriage.

Coitus that is serenely satisfying is no less enriching than coitus that zooms skyward. It is mostly in novels that the rockets go off. Furthermore, the great lovers of fiction are star-crossed; if they lived happily ever after there would be no story to tell. Happy lovers are not likely to read about their kind of love in books, nor do they need to. They can enjoy it in reality.

—From Jerome and Julia Rainer, *Sexual Pleasure in Marriage.* New York: Simon & Schuster, 1969.

Oral Sex

WHAT IS ORAL SEX?

Two words are used to describe oral sex. In *fellatio* the woman receives the male penis into her mouth in order to stimulate the glans penis with her lips and tongue; *cunninlingus* is the act of the male stimulating the woman with his mouth over her vulva area, usually with his tongue on her clitoris. Both forms of oral sex can bring an orgasm if prolonged.

IS IT RIGHT FOR CHRISTIANS TO PRACTICE ORAL SEX?

Almost every week we receive this question by letter or in the counseling room, especially during the last four years. Husbands tend to desire this experience more than wives, but recently, because of the many sex books on the market, there seems to be increasing curiosity on the part of women. Doubtless the practice is increasing. One author suggests that as many as 80 percent of couples have tried it. Although they may find it pleasurable, many feel guilty about it.

The Bible is completely silent on this subject, and we have encountered a wide variety of opinions. Of the Christian doctors we surveyed, 73 percent felt it was acceptable for a Christian couple as long as both partners enjoyed it; 27 percent did not approve of it. To our amazement, 77 percent of the ministers felt it was acceptable, and 23 percent did not. It is strange that many people who approach us for our opinion indicate they have already counseled with a minister who opposed it. We almost wonder if many ministers who express opposition to it to counselees (perhaps because they consider it the stand they should take) adopt a different position when reporting in an anonymous survey.

Usually one encounters strong opposition when discussing the subject; very few seem to advocate it, but who knows what people do in the privacy of their bedrooms? Some object to the practice probably because of personal prejudice for what they feel are hygienic or spiritual reasons; but doctors say it is not unhealthy, and the Bible is silent on the subject. Therefore each couple must make their own decision on the matter.

We do not personally recommend or advocate it, but we have no biblical grounds for forbidding it between two married people who mutually enjoy it. We do not think, moreover, that it should be used as a substitute for coitus; if it has a place in marriage, we would suggest it be limited to foreplay. A warning, however, should be sounded: Love would require that one partner *never demand* the experience from the other if he or she does not enjoy it or feels guilty or uncomfortable about it.

—From Tim and Beverly LaHaye, *The Act of Marriage.* Grand Rapids: Zondervan, 1976.

Enhancing the Sexual Response

KEEPING IN SHAPE

Research data to document the effects of sleep, nutrition and exercise on the sexual response is greatly needed. We are convinced that these three areas of a person's life-style are extremely important and merit more attention than has been given to them by researchers up to this point.

A woman comes to us with orgasmic difficulties. In the initial assessment and throughout the therapy process, we become increasingly aware of imbalances within her system. She has difficulty falling asleep at night, becomes depressed before her menstrual period, and starts showing signs of premature menopause. Tranquilizers are used to modify these symptoms. We refer her to an endocrinologist and a biochemist-nutritionist. The workups reveal that she is not producing adequate levels of hormones. Her estrogen level is very low. There are also indications that her body is not absorbing nutrients properly. As her diet is revised, an exercise program activated, and sleep is regulated without drugs, her system begins to show signs of clearing. Along with the clearing comes increased sexual responsiveness. We cannot prove that the increased responsiveness is caused by the changes in nutrition, exercise, and sleep. But knowledge of how our bodies work has led us to formulate some theories about this.

NUTRITION AND SLEEP

Currently there is an increased emphasis on the ways in which food affects our physical and emotional health. There has been a particular concern with sugar and its relationship to hypoglycemic depression, sleep disruption, and learning problems in children. Artificial dyes and additives in food have also received attention.

We know that carbohydrates (sugars and starches) affect our insulin production, which in turn affects our metabolism. This is directly related to our energy level.

We are also becoming more aware of the way nutrition influences hormonal production. When our bodies are not getting the nutrients they need, our sex hormones will be the first to be affected. Premature menopause can be related to reduced estrogen production due to malnutrition. This malnutrition may be caused by poor eating patterns or by malabsorption due to the body's intolerance of a particular food. Gluten is a common offender.

Many have wondered about the effect of alcohol on sexual response. Alcohol is an inhibitor. Therefore, if a person is anxious a small amount of alcohol can enhance sexual activity by reducing the anxiety. Anxiety is always a sexual inhibitor, so lowering the anxiety will allow people to get with their natural body responses. However, large amounts of alcohol will inhibit the sexual response. Many men report experiencing difficulty with erection or ejaculation after they have had too much to drink. . . .

Be alert to the way you are affected by what you take in. What do you sense about your sexual feelings after eating a heavy, starchy meal? How does such a meal affect your sleep? What about alcohol consumption for you? Does it help or hinder? Wines are usually more tolerable than distilled, hard liquors which go directly into the blood stream. Protein eaten *before* drinking slows its absorption and its effect on the body.

The area of nutrition and sexual responsiveness intrigues us. It is wide open for exploration and research. We believe that nutrition has a greater impact on us than anyone realizes at this time. . . .

Sleep research has shown that we have sleep cycles. Just as sexual responses such as vaginal lubrication and penile erections occur every eighty to ninety minutes during a normal adult's sleep, so there are other psychological and physiological involuntary processes that occur in cyclic patterns while we sleep. When sleep is disrupted, we lose more than just the actual time that we are awake. We break our body's rhythm. This can affect our energy level, emotional stability, and sexual responsiveness.

EXERCISE

We have often been asked, "Does being in good shape physically, that is, exercising regularly, increase one's sexual responsiveness?"

There are many other factors that could be influencing sexual responsiveness at the same time an exercise program is started. Thus it is difficult to be certain that the exercise has made the difference.

However, there are several ways in which exercise is helpful, and we suspect that there are even more positive effects than just these.

First, regular exercise that increases your cardiovascular functioning (heart rate, blood pressure, and so on) will enhance your circulation, increase mental alertness, reduce stress, and improve muscular tone. Since one body system cannot change without in some way affecting the other body systems, those changes will indirectly influence sexual functioning. In addition, circulation, muscular response, alertness and reduction of stress are all a direct part of sexual responsiveness.

Second, exercising often improves how people feel about their bodies. This improvement in body image will often affect general feelings of self-worth and sexuality.

Third, exercising will get people in touch with the sensations of their bodies. This inevitably increases awareness of sexual feelings. So this is another way in which exercise can enhance sexual enjoyment.

We encourage regular exercise for cardiovascular improvement—such as jogging, hiking, swimming or whatever you find works for you. In addition, we have a list of body awareness and breathing exercises used with women. All of these may also be helpful to men. We recognize that a man does not have a vagina to contract, but he does have the same pubococcygeus muscle that is used to start and stop urination. That muscle can be tightened for practice that is comparable to the exercise we call "vaginal contractions."

BODY AWARENESS AND BREATHING

Breathing:

1. Panting (increases oxygenation and energy level): Draw air into chest, above diaphragm; blow out six times, as though blowing out a candle; exhale slowly and completely. Do ten times at beginning of exercises.
2. Chest—slow, regular, smooth, relaxed breathing. This is good to do between exercises and may be helpful during intercourse.
3. Abdominal or "deep" diaphragmatic breathing: Take in maximum amount of air slowly through nose, with your chest rising first and then your abdomen. Hold breath to count of four. Exhale slowly

through slightly separated lips. Let go of all tension and let all air out.

This is done with all exercises. Try using it during intercourse.

Body Awareness and increased muscle tone in pelvic area:

1. Pelvic bounce: Lie on floor, knees slightly bent, pressure on soles of feet. Pushing with your feet, bounce buttocks up and down.
2. Pelvic rock:
   a) Get on your hands and knees.
   b) Inhale slowly through your nose as you arch your back and tense it; hold your breath in this position to count of four.
   c) Exhale slowly through parted lips as you sag back.
   d) Repeat ten times.
3. Pelvic lift (great for increasing orgasm potential).
   a) Lie on your back on a firm surface with your knees bent and feet flat on the floor.
   b) As you breathe in slowly through your nose, align your back with the floor, starting with your lowest vertebra and moving up toward your neck.
   c) As you slowly exhale through parted lips, lift your pelvis and your back off the floor, one vertebra at a time, again starting at your coccyx (tailbone) and moving toward your neck. (You may actually move to a position of resting on your feet and head, with your fists holding your heels.) Work up to this point slowly.
   d) Come back down, one vertebra at a time, from neck to coccyx.
4. Vaginal contractions (to increase friction and sensitivity during intercourse and prevent complications due to loss of pelvic muscle tone that can occur after childbirth or with aging process):

199

a) Tighten the pubococcygeus muscle, the muscle used to start and stop urination.

b) Hold as tightly as you can to count of ten.

c) Relax muscle.

d) Do a minimum of twenty-five daily (for a person with a particularly loose vagina, two hundred a day may be necessary).

e) To help you remember, connect this exercise with some other activity—driving, ironing, washing dishes, and so on.

Regular exercise, good nutrition and adequate sleep should help to banish the excessive fatigue that can block togetherness. If you get in shape but discover that you and your partner still are not getting together sexually, maybe you need to work on keeping in touch.

—From Clifford and Joyce Penner, *The Gift of Sex* copyright © 1981, pp. 185–87, 189–91; used by permission of Word Books, Publisher, Waco, Texas 76796.

APHRODISIACS

There is no scientific evidence that the ingestion of any food or combination of food extracts—animal, vegetable or mineral—serves specifically to excite the sexual appetite of man or woman. The belief that a concentrated intake of eggs, shellfish, onions, truffles, or products high in phosphorus, intensifies sexual responses has scarcely more validity than myths about the aphrodisiac powers of pigeons' blood, birds' tongues, fish roe or other fantastic elixirs, including the bark of the yohimbé tree recommended by a nationally popular sexologist.

Nothing has yet been discovered that is more consistently effective for the improvement and maintenance of sexual potency than a balanced diet, ample exercise and sleep, and a state of mind free of conflict.

—From Jerome and Julia Rainer, *Sexual Pleasure in Marriage.* New York: Simon & Schuster, 1969.

Sexual Intercourse During Menstruation

Some Christian women have said to me that they believe that intercourse during menstruation is a sin, based on certain Old Testament purification laws. Actually, these laws (*see* Leviticus 12) have to do with postnatal cleansing, not with menstruation. My counsel is that it is a matter of aesthetics rather than sin. Most men and women in our society tend to prefer to avoid intercourse during the menses, though this could be a cultural phenomenon. There are no definite medical contraindications, and it is not in any way disruptive to the cycle itself.

—From O. Quentin Hyder, M.D., *The People You Live With.* Old Tappan, N.J.: Revell, 1975.

Sexual Intercourse During Pregnancy

Coitus is a vital aid to producing a feeling of closeness between husband and wife as well as in satisfying the woman's increased need for nurturance. Many studies have indicated that the pregnant woman has a marked increase in her own dependency needs. The prohibition of coitus toward the end of pregnancy may give the woman a feeling of estrangement and also of loss of protection that she would otherwise enjoy. This must vary greatly, of course, from woman to woman. Some show little desire for intercourse at this time because of their physical discomfort or because their sex drive has decreased for other reasons. But for those who have a strong sex drive, the satisfaction of the need to be loved may depend upon consummation of the sexual act.

Although a husband may also experience a diminution in sexual desire during the late stages of his wife's pregnancy, a long period of enforced abstinence is a considerable hardship and may even represent a threat to the marriage. . . .

TRADITIONAL MEDICAL TEACHING

Present-day textbooks of obstetrics accord the subject of sexuality brief mention, stating merely that intercourse should be interdicted during episodes of threatened abortion; at all times after membranes have ruptured; if there is or has been bleeding; and—as an almost universal proscription—during the last four to six weeks of pregnancy. Although reasons for the last-mentioned prohibition are not clearly stated, it is usually conceded that it is based upon one of several unproved beliefs: the penile thrusts against the cervix or the uterine contractions or orgasm will induce labor; the membranes may rupture, heightening the probability of infection within the womb; and the sex act itself is physically uncomfortable for the majority of women during the last few weeks of their pregnancy. Following such restrictive advice, the textbooks usually add: "Intercourse may be safely resumed six weeks after delivery if no abnormalities are present."

The avoidance of intercourse following childbirth—based as it has been upon a period of time required for recovery—is far easier to comprehend than that during pregnancy, even though the genital tract of most postpartum women is well on the road to normalcy considerably before six weeks. If followed literally, this lengthy a period of abstinence—six weeks before and six weeks after childbirth—as recommended by some obstetricians for healthy, symptom-free women would disrupt coital relations for a period of three consecutive months.

CLINICAL AND RESEARCH DATA

There is scant direct and objective evidence upon which a physician may base his advice to pregnant women regarding sexual intercourse. Dr. William E. Pugh and F. L. Fernandez noted the absence of ill effects among six hundred women who had had sexual intercourse during the final weeks of pregnancy. Obstetricians who conduct large hospital services among the economically less favored and poorly educated segments of the population have been aware that intercourse takes place—without undue harmful effects—throughout pregnancy among such couples. The same has been reported by better educated and more economically favored groups.

Masters and Johnson recorded physiologic data, cinematographically and otherwise, along with the subjective responses of six pregnant women during recurrent conjugal acts of intercourse throughout pregnancy. In addition, these authors collected verbal reports regarding sexual feelings, behavior, and responses during pregnancy and the several months thereafter from 101 other women. Despite the small number of pregnant women observed or interviewed, five of the observations of these authors are of signal importance:

Contractions of the uterus like those observed to occur during orgasm in nonpregnant women occur also in pregnant women. These contractions occur regardless of what induces the orgasm—masturbation, natural coitus, or artificial coitus. Four of the women interviewed reported the onset of labor immediately after orgasm, all within eighteen or fewer days of the expected confinement.

Sexual interest was uniformly increased during the second trimester of pregnancy. This elevated sexuality, reflected in more effective performance and responsiveness, was described by the women "not only as interest in sexual encounter but also as planning for sexual encounter, fantasy of sexual encounter, and sex-dream content."

Interest in sexual intercourse waned during the last three months of pregnancy, influenced perhaps by two other factors: physicians had prohibited intercourse for some of the patients and about a fifth of the husbands lost interest, for various reasons.

Following childbirth, many women returned to coital activity within a period of three weeks. The medical prohibition to wait six weeks before resuming intercourse is evidently disregarded by those women who have healed sufficiently to be comfortable. The restoration of sexual activity took place earlier in those women who were actively nursing.

Women who were breast-feeding noted sexual stimulation during suckling by the infant. In fact, it seemed to be a source of guilt for several of the subjects.

CONCLUSIONS TO BE DRAWN FROM PRESENT DATA

On the basis of their study, Pugh and Fernandez tried to convince obstetricians that abstinence during the final weeks of pregnancy is not required except on the basis of physical discomfort. Some teachers of obstetrics have instituted programs of advice that permit intercourse when it is comfortably acceptable to both partners during all of pregnancy until labor begins, except in the presence of ruptured membranes or uterine bleeding.

According to Masters and Johnson, the prohibition of coital activity for arbitrarily established periods of time both before and after delivery has frequently done far more harm than good. They concede that there is a legitimate medical concern about intercourse at or near term, since it is probable (although definitive data are still lacking)

that the contractions of orgasm at or near term can initiate labor. However, they point out, the prohibition of intercourse during the latter part of the third trimester based only on fear of infection for mother or child is a hangover of the days before antibiotics in medicine and can largely be negated. The problem of infection, moreover, applies not just to the last few weeks, but to any stage of pregnancy, or, for that matter, to the non-pregnant state. Should infection of the vagina occur immediately before labor, it is nearly always medically controllable, with full protection for both mother and infant.

Following delivery, they say, from a purely physiologic point of view there is no reason to prohibit intercourse once the vaginal bleeding has stopped and any incisions or tears in the vaginal outlet have healed. Of course, they add, the woman should be psychologically ready to resume intercourse.

Their major suggestion is that the whole question of intercourse during the third trimester of pregnancy and the period after delivery should be considered by the doctor on an individual basis. Many women are anxious to return to sexual activity as soon as it is physically possible, and they should be encouraged to do so. In the case of those women who prefer longer periods of continence, their situation should be discussed, personal reasons examined, fears explained away, and a firm understanding between husband and wife established. A growing number of gynecologists and obstetricians are coming to accept this point of view.

On the basis of present clinical and research opinion, the following medical and counseling conclusions can be drawn concerning sexual intercourse and sexual activity during the last period of pregnancy and the period following childbirth:

Although it is not possible to state with absolute certainty that sexual intercourse will never create a hazard for any pregnant women, it is equally impossible to believe the converse—that it is inevitably dangerous. In general, sexual intercourse should be allowed at any time during pregnancy, and also for the recently delivered woman who wants it and has no significant discomfort. Just as obstetricians modify the advice they give about pregnancy generally according to the individual circumstances and characteristics of each patient, so should they modify their advice in regard to sexual intercourse.

—From Sex Information and Education Council, *Sexuality and Man.* New York: Scribner, 1970.

Sexual Interstimulation

There will come times in marriage when couples cannot have sexual intercourse. During these times they will both have their regular and normal sexual needs. Let us discuss three examples. First, we will assume, at this point, that intercourse will not take place during the menstrual period. This period involves four to six days per month. During this time a couple would normally have intercourse one or two times, but because of the menstrual period, they would have to refrain, which they could do. Let us imagine a husband and wife that normally had intercourse every three days, but because of a special set of circumstances over which they had no control, had gone five days without intercourse. By this time they would probably be very anxious. Let us assume that they had planned intercourse on the night of the fifth day, but during the afternoon the menstrual period shows up two or three days early. Suppose the period lasts for five days. This means the couple would have to wait ten days before being able to have intercourse. Normally they would have sexual intercourse two or three times during

ten days. It is true that under these circumstances a couple can refrain. However, this is not necessary.

A second example involves the time before and after a baby is born. Normally a doctor will instruct prospective parents not to have intercourse during the six weeks before a baby is born and the six weeks after it is born. The time will vary according to the condition of the prospective mother. It is well for a couple to ask the doctor for instruction about when to stop having intercourse before a baby is born, and when to start after it is born. The doctor must instruct on this matter. However, on the average, there will be a period of at least three months when it will be necessary to abstain from sexual intercourse. During this time normal sexual needs will continue. It is possible to abstain from all sexual relations during this time, but this is unrealistic and unnecessary.

A third example is when a couple wants to express their love in a sexual experience but do not have adequate contraceptives available, and feel strongly that they cannot run the risk of a pregnancy at this time. Reason would dictate that under these circumstances a couple should refrain from sexual intercourse. But it does not follow that they would avoid all sexual expression.

Marriage counselors recommend that during these and other similar times when couples cannot have intercourse, that they practice a second type of sexual experience in which they do not have intercourse and do not use the vaginal passage. This second type of sexual experience is called "sexual interstimulation." That is, husband and wife simply bring each other to orgasms through love-play and direct stimulation. The husband will stimulate the wife's clitoris with his fingers until she is aroused to experience an orgasm. At the same time, the wife will stimulate the husband's penis with her fin-

203

gers until he reaches an orgasm. Through skillful love-play, stimulation and response, the husband and wife lying in each other's arms can often have orgasms at the same time or nearly so. Let us repeat that no other type of sexual experience can take the place of sexual intercourse.

—From Herbert J. Miles, *Sexual Happiness in Marriage.* Grand Rapids: Zondervan, 1967.

Sex in Later Years

Let it be stated with finality: there is no inescapable biological event that marks the end of pleasurable sexual life excepting death itself. Neither the female menopause nor the alleged male climacteric can write the words "finis" to the sexual drama of husband and wife. There is no stage manager, charged by inexorable nature, to ring down the curtain of amorous activity, of potency and real desire, at any predestined age. The factors causing termination of activity are many, but menopause and the fictitious male climacteric are certainly not among them.

This knowledge might have dispelled the gloom of the twenty-year-old bridegroom of an earlier decade who, after enjoying coitus, sighed to his bride of equal age: "To think that we have only twenty more years of this!"

Until recently, the forties were thought to be the end of the journey, the graveyard of the sexual impulse. In fact and fiction, in popular mythology, thirty-nine was the final bastion to be grimly held against erotic oblivion. Countless women and at least one American radio comedian pinioned that year in a drowner's grasp, making it a symbol of the end to sexual capacity. They could not have been more mistaken.

They did not know what we know today about the physiology of sex, about the psychology of sex, and about the advances in health and medicine that have prolonged not only life expectancy but the span of sexual potency itself.

Male potency is at its highest point between the ages of sixteen and twenty and then diminishes in barely perceptible stages from year to year. Female potency generally attains its peak in the middle and late twenties. In Western society, the female's peak is somewhat lower than the male's, and thus her sexual decline is even more gradual, with less year-to-year difference in her desire.

But these are quantitative findings and they are misleading. They do not mirror the true erotic potential of most men and their mates. They fail to evaluate the quality of pleasure which is such a precious key to memorable human experience. Frequencies and numbers are necessary to science but they are not a way of life.

Obviously a curve for quality of pleasure cannot be drawn. However, Kinsey's records do cast a certain revealing light. By their own testimony, wives attain greater coital satisfaction with the advancing years; with experience they become more deeply eroticized and increase their orgastic capacity. Their curve of pleasure goes up as they leave youth behind them.

If wives are doing better, sensually and orgastically, husbands cannot be doing worse! Who but statisticians care to ponder that the coital frequency curve descends after youth, so long as the pleasure curve ascends?

Many a man, when he reaches the years of relatively infrequent coitus, views his youthful potency with mournful nostalgia. But against what standards is he measuring himself? The youth of eighteen, capable of many orgasms a week? The probabilities are that as a youth he did not find his mate ready or responsive to sexual marathons, and perhaps she even regarded them with a certain lack of appreciation. Those years, if he correctly recalls them, were likely to be years of flash-fire erotics. Memorable communion with his wife, enriching to the relationship, was still in the future.

Such a husband would not think to measure his business or professional powers or his value as a citizen against his eighteen-year-old self. In these respects he has accumulated maturity and wisdom, not to mention subtle skills and ingenuity. Why should he assume that in sex alone, maturity is without value? Other cultures older and in some ways more perceptive than the present one, have admired the man experienced in sex, and the woman too—*la femme intéressante.*

Generally discarded as medieval is the concept that menopause and the so-called male climacteric portend the end of erotic joy. This old wives' tale has persisted in today's society with about the same tenacity, if not the same damaging results, as the one about youthful masturbation. Let the menstrual cycle miss one beat in those late forties and certain wives sense the onset of sexual doom. Let the angle of male erectility decline by so much as a few degrees and some males foresee the end of their potency. These are the anxious spouses who suffer from baseless fears spawned by misinformation.

Menopause alters neither sexual desire nor orgastic capacity. Physiologically, menopause belongs to another department, the reproductive one. Menstruation, ovulation, and childbearing are the functions affected. The pleasure-function is left untouched. Coital pleasure continues after menopause, sometimes more keenly and enjoyably than before.

Unfortunately termed "change of life," menopause marks no erotic change. Erotically speaking, nothing has happened. In lovemaking the menopause can be entirely ignored. Only when symbolic significance is attached to it, derived from the idea of "change," are there emotional repercussions that may halt or dim the capacity for sensual pleasure or the desire for it.

—From Jerome and Julia Rainer, *Sexual Pleasure in Marriage.* New York: Simon & Schuster, 1969.

SEXUAL ADJUSTMENT

Differing Time Needs

One of the things that almost inevitably happens as a couple moves along in their marriage is that one person's time has many more demands on it than the other's. A couple was experiencing difficulty in just this area. The man was in charge of a growing business. He was earning enough money so that his wife didn't have to work outside the home, but could care for their two children. His business was expanding, so it demanded much time if he was to run it adequately. At the same time, the wife now had a great deal of time and more energy available for sexual involvement. This kind of difference in the demands on your time will often lead to stress, particularly when the one who has extra time is the one who is eager for more sexual activity. The man we just described may have been just as interested in sex as his wife was, but he had many other demands on his time. He was just not available to his wife.

It may be that the woman is loaded with time demands because she is working and has to come home and cook and clean and care for the family. The man may not feel as much concern for perfect housekeeping, so he's willing to let things go, and is certainly not willing to spend all his evenings tidying up the house. Thus this wife's available time to be together is extremely limited, and

205

usually occurs when she is most exhausted. She, then, is the one not available.

"I'm an evening person and he's a morning person" is often the way a spouse will define the sexual difficulties a couple is experiencing. Some people wake up at the crack of dawn and are ready to roar into life. By 8:00 they have been producing for three hours. We'll never forget the woman who came in at 8:00 for a psychotherapy appointment: she had already jogged her ten miles for the day. In contrast, there is the person who comes in an hour later, still trying to get her eyes open.

There is nothing right or wrong about being a morning or evening person. It only causes problems when it doesn't coincide with your partner's system. Some people are night people. They get going by about seven in the evening, and are then ready to continue until two in the morning. These are their most productive hours. We could go into all the reasons why people have various body chemistries, but the differences will still be the same. People are going to marry other people who operate on different time schedules. One of the places where this obviously causes some difficulties is in the sexual realm. Some men love to wake up in the morning and make love. If their spouse happens to be a morning person there is no problem. But the chances of that are minimal. Many women complain about husbands who wake them up in the morning to start their day with a sexual experience. Often these same men are dozing off to sleep in front of the television by 9:30. Yet this is the time when the woman may be ready for some involvement. What can a couple do about this?

SEX: A TIME PRIORITY

If the time issue is going to be resolved for a couple, both partners must be ready to make a commitment to each other that they are going to make their sexual experience a priority. It is of utmost importance that this decision should not be an edict which comes from either the man or the woman; rather it should evolve from the two of them together. It is easy to make a commitment verbally, but it is another thing entirely to make it work in day-to-day life together. What does the man do at 5:50 P.M. when he has promised to be home by six, but gets an important long-distance call that is going to take an hour? Does he say, "I've got a commitment?" Or does he stick with his business? It's easy to decide ahead of time that one is going to be committed—but it is sometimes difficult to carry out that commitment. It is the same way for the wife. She can make a time commitment, but then is she willing to let the work at the office go? Or to let the ironing pile up? Or to have the house in less than perfect order?

The man and woman have to determine a process by which they are going to make their sexual relationship a time priority, given the life-style and the time demands that exist for them. This must be a very practical kind of priority. The couple must spell out exactly how it will be worked out. Some couples choose to have brief sexual experiences at home, and then go away for a few days at a time every several weeks for more intense times together. Others find that this leaves them frustrated, or that they are unable to do it because of financial or family limitations. Each couple has to work it out in their own special way.

You might be saying, "Why all this preoccupation with time? If it's important to a couple they will get together." That may be true, and yet there are no outside pressures that demand sex. When we agree to work for a certain company we're expected to be there so many hours a week, or to complete a given project. When we work for a committee at the YMCA or at the church there are other people to whom we are responsible, and we have deadlines. If we are involved in some kind of sports activities there are practices to attend and games to play. There is no such accountability in the sexual relationship. Decisions to make this a priority have to come out of desire and the recognition that this is a crucial area of life which needs fulfilling and is not happening without a plan.

Busy life-styles may require times together "by appointment." This is true for vacation times and sexual times. First-time responses to this idea are often, "But that takes all the excitement and spontaneity out of it." This is usually said by people who have not tried it. Sexual experiences do not work simply because they are begun on a spontaneous impulse. They work because of what happens between two people once they are together, whether this is by impulse or as the result of scheduling. Normally when people begin to schedule their time together, the quality of those times and the satisfaction from those times improve measurably. We are not ruling out the possibility of spontaneous times together. Scheduling is done only to assure that there will be extensive time for the two to be involved. Spontaneous times together tend to be relatively brief. They tend to satisfy primarily the physical needs, rather than meeting all the needs present when a couple comes together. These include the need for sharing, extensive touching, enough time for arousal, for repeated arousal and release if that's what the woman desires, and a time of affirming afterwards.

One thing vital to scheduled time is that it be planned without a demand for intercourse. Of course there is the possibility that a full sexual experience can grow out of the scheduled time. But any time people approach an experience with an expectation or demand it can get in the way of their freedom in that experience. Many couples allow the possibility that they are just going to talk, particularly when one person has the need to converse and to be held. This reduces much of the pressure they would feel if they came to the experience merely with the intent to have an active sexual time together.

One other ingredient necessary in making the sexual relationship a time priority is that the times together must be free of interruptions. It is amazing how many couples report that their sexual experiences are interrupted by the ring of the doorbell, a telephone call, the cry of a child or disturbance by a pet. As much as possible, it is necessary to remove all possibilities of distractions. Taking the phone off the hook is absolutely necessary. If you live in an apartment complex where people are forever dropping by, put a "Do not disturb" note over the doorbell. Teach your children that there are times when mom and dad have to be by themselves without interruption. It is important for children to learn this in terms of respect for parents' wishes. It is even more important that they learn about a husband and a wife and the priority that their time together should have. Rather than shutting them out of your world, you are providing them with a good model on which they might choose to base their married life in the years to come.

Making sure you have time together is the responsibility of both partners. It takes forethought, planning, effort and recommitment. There is no way it will happen automatically. If there is to be time together—you will have to make it.

—From Clifford and Joyce Penner, *The Gift of Sex* copyright © 1981, pp. 215–18; used by permission of Word Books, Publisher, Waco, Texas 76796.

Impotence

. . . Impotence . . . is incapacity of the man to carry out the sexual act because he cannot get an erection when he encounters a woman and therefore cannot introduce his penis into the vagina. This sort of disorder may occur even though the man is able to have erections apart from intimacy with women, as for instance in dreams or on masturbation. There are some cases in which the man is impotent only with a certain sexual partner but not with other women. A conscious wish for an erection is as a rule a barrier to success.

—From Karl Wrage, M.D., *Man and Woman.* Philadelphia: Fortress, 1969.

Frigidity

With 3.8 billion people on the earth, over half of whom are women, no doubt *some* were born physically incapable of orgasm, but their number is so small that it is most unlikely any of them would ever read this book. Dr. David Reuben says, "There is no reason why every woman should not have regular and frequent orgasms, if she wants to." To illustrate further that the problem is emotionally caused and not physically induced, he states, "No psychiatrist has ever seen a woman with this condition who was raised by loving parents in a warm, secure family environment. Most women who suffer from orgasmic impairment suffered serious emotional deprivation during childhood and after."

One reason why we believe women raised in a Christian home enjoy the pleasures of lovemaking more than others (a belief verified by our sex survey) is because they are more likely to have experienced a warm father-daughter love relationship. One of the best things a father can do for his girls is to let them run into his heart anytime they like. He should avoid all selfish urges to shut them out or turn them off, no matter how busy he is. Frigidity is not usually a physical matter, but an emotional withdrawal from the opposite sex that can be well developed by the time a girl is six years old. Cold, selfish fathers are the greatest cause of cold, frigid women.

—From Tim and Beverly LaHaye, *The Act of Marriage.* Grand Rapids: Zondervan, 1976.

Premature Ejaculation

Here the man ejaculates either before or immediately on introducing his penis into the vagina, so that his erection subsides and his wife remains unsatisfied in her sexual excitement and expectations. Impotence and premature ejaculation are both due to neurotic disorders which in severe cases are based on erroneous sex education and failure to prepare the man for maturity; in milder cases there may be unconscious rejection of the present sexual partner with whom impotence or premature ejaculation exists. Rejection may be present in spite of conscious feelings of love. Since these disorders are emotionally caused they can be overcome only by psychotherapy. Unfortunately the area of sex is still taboo in a fair-sized proportion of the population, so that men with these disorders prefer to endanger their marriage rather than go to a doctor and obtain treatment, though the earlier treatment is begun the better the prospects of success. It should be pointed out that there are also combined disorders of potency and fertility, in which a combined drug and psychotherapeutic approach is needed.

—From Karl Wrage, M.D., *Man and Woman.* Philadelphia: Fortress, 1969.

PREMATURE EJACULATION CONTROL EXERCISES

Phase I You may both be so "gun-shy" from the husband's quick sexual release that you have been avoiding touching as much as possible. You need to take the focus off orgasm and timing and concentrate on improving nonverbal, physical communication without seeking to reach orgasm. Objective of this phase: *To improve physical communication and learn to appreciate physical closeness with your mate.*

1. Spend time touching and fondling each other.
2. Do those things which physically please your mate, such as scalp massage or stroking the back or neck, and so forth.
3. Avoid directly stimulating the genital areas.
4. Do not have intercourse, but focus on improving physical communication with your mate.
5. Learn to appreciate and enjoy physical closeness.
6. Follow this procedure for at least the first two sessions.

Phase II Objective of this phase: *For the husband to learn to recognize the physical sensation that comes just before ejaculation, so that he is able to communicate to his wife the best time to apply the squeeze.*

During this session it is vitally important that the husband concentrate completely on his own sensations. He is to block out all other thoughts, so that he will become keenly aware of the feeling that comes just prior to ejaculation. It may help if he closes his eyes. As soon as the husband feels he is nearing the point of ejaculation, he is to indicate this to his wife by some predetermined word or signal. She is then to quickly use the squeeze technique. This phase should be repeated during the daily practice sessions, until the husband can consistently recognize the sensation that occurs just before ejaculation.

1. The wife is to sit with her back against the headboard of the bed, with her legs spread comfortably apart.
2. The husband is to lie on his back, with his head toward the foot of the bed.
3. The husband positions his pelvis between his wife's legs, with his genitals close to hers. With knees bent, his feet are to be placed outside her thighs (near her buttocks).
4. The wife now lovingly and gently caresses the man's genitals, paying special attention to the underside of the shaft or the head of the penis, or wherever her husband directs, to encourage him to attain an erection.
5. As soon as the husband achieves full erection, the wife will begin the squeeze technique. She places her thumb on the underside of the penis, about one-half inch below the slit opening just where the shaft ends and the head begins. She then places the first two fingers of that hand on the opposite side of the penis, with one finger above the ridge and one finger below the ridge which distinguishes the head from the shaft.
6. She then squeezes her thumb and two fingers together with very hard pressure for about four seconds.
7. She then quickly releases the pressure.
8. After fifteen to thirty seconds, she manipulates him to full erection again and repeats the squeeze. The husband should inform his wife by word or subtle signals when he feels she needs to squeeze to delay his orgasm.
9. Repeat this procedure every four to five minutes for the entire twenty-minute session.
10. The husband may prefer to have a lubricant, such as K-Y Jelly, applied to his

penis in order to more closely simulate the sensations felt during sexual intercourse.

11. Do not have intercourse or insert the penis into the vagina.
12. At the end of the session, stimulation should be continued to ejaculation.
13. It will be desirable for the husband to use manual stimulation of the wife's clitoris to give her sexual release *after* each practice session.

Phase III   Objective of this phase: *For the erect penis to remain almost motionless in the vagina for fifteen to twenty minutes before ejaculation.*

1. The husband lies on his back, and the wife stimulates him to an erection.
2. When he feels he is nearing the point of ejaculation, he signals his wife, and she is to quickly use the squeeze technique.
3. She should repeat the stimulation almost to ejaculation, and then squeeze the penis. This should be done several times.
4. Then the wife straddles the husband in a sitting position. Leaning forward at about a 45-degree angle, she very gently and slowly inserts the erect penis into the well-lubricated vagina, then moves backward comfortably onto the shaft, not just sitting down on it.
5. She remains motionless, giving her husband a chance to achieve control. If the husband loses his erection while the penis is in the vagina, the wife should raise her body and manually restimulate him to erection.
6. If the husband becomes aware that he is nearing the point of ejaculation, he should indicate this to his wife, so that she can raise her body and repeat the squeeze procedure. Then she gently reinserts the penis.
7. Husband and wife should be able to

maintain this position with the erect penis almost motionless in the vagina for fifteen to twenty minutes before ejaculation.

Phase IV   Remember, it is important to wait at least one day before beginning a new phase. The objective of this phase: *To be able to keep the erect penis in the vagina with very gentle movements for about twenty minutes before ejaculation.*

1. Spend some time in loving foreplay.
2. Again assume the position of the wife straddling the husband and leaning forward.
3. The husband is to begin thrusting slightly, thus learning to tolerate gradually increasing amounts of movement of the penis in the vagina.
4. This gentle thrusting should be continued for fifteen to twenty minutes before ejaculation. Use the squeeze technique if necessary.
5. When this phase is mastered, the husband may now ejaculate with the penis in the vagina, but he is to continue concentrating on his own sensations, until each practice session is over and he has ejaculated. Then he is to take time to manually bring his wife to orgasm. (Remember, this is still a training session.)

Phase V   The objective of this phase: *To learn how to have comfortable sexual intercourse in the side-to-side (lateral) position.* (This position gives better control of movements by both husband and wife and allows the husband the best ejaculatory control.)

1. Spend some time in loving foreplay.
2. Again assume the position of the wife straddling the husband and leaning forward.
3. Place a pillow under the husband's head and another one along his left side.

4. The wife brings her right leg to a straight position between his legs. She leaves her left leg on the outer side of his body.

5. At the same time, the husband brings his left leg out from his body, placing it flat on the bed, with knee bent.

6. The wife is to shift her entire body slightly to the right, while leaning forward with her left breast at the level of his left breast. She will now be partially supported by the pillow at her husband's left side. Additional comfort is achieved by another pillow for her head and shoulders.

7. It will take several practice sessions to learn to change easily into this side-to-side position and arrange the arms and legs in the most comfortable manner. (Once learned, this position is used by many couples most of the time.)

8. While in the side-to-side position, the thrusting should be gentle, so that the penis can remain in the vagina for twenty minutes before ejaculation.

ESTABLISHING LASTING EJACULATORY CONTROL

1. Use the squeeze technique at least once a week for the next six months.

2. Once each month practice the squeeze technique for an entire twenty-minute session.

3. Good ejaculatory control is usually attained in three to six weeks.

4. Within six to twelve months the husband should be able to be consistently quite active in intercourse for ten to twenty minutes without ejaculation.

5. Complete control is attained when the husband does not have his orgasm until he chooses.

Prolonged emphasis on controlling orgasm in these practice sessions may sometimes cause a husband to have a temporary lack of ability to keep an erection. Do not be dismayed. It is just this portion of the husband's body demanding a brief rest.

As you read this detailed list of instructions for the practice sessions, the process may seem to be rather tedious. But any couple who recognize that premature ejaculation plays some part in their lack of maximum sexual fulfillment will find that a few weeks of mutual effort and discipline will lead to far greater sexual pleasure for the rest of their lives. It is a fact that few men possess the ability to delay their ejaculation as long as they would like. These training sessions, using the squeeze-technique procedure, can result in heightened pleasure for any couple desiring a better sexual relationship.

During the squeeze-technique sessions, the wife may discover that she is beginning to experience some new and pleasurable feelings. She begins to feel more sexual arousal. She may even experience her very first orgasm. Even if she has been able to reach orgasm before, she may now begin to enjoy multiple orgasms.

—From Ed Wheat, M.D., and Gaye Wheat, *Intended for Pleasure*. Rev. ed. Old Tappan, N.J.: Revell, 1981.

Causes of Poor Adjustment

A married woman who has not experienced a sexual orgasm wants to know, and rightly so, why she has not had the experience. What are some possible conditions which could prevent her from having orgasms? Usually it can be said that there would not be any one single cause, but rather *many small interrelated causes* working together that explain why a wife has not achieved orgasm. If a couple can locate these possible causes, understand them, and accept them as real, they are half-way to victory. These causes may be outlined as follows:

A CONFLICT RELATIONSHIP BETWEEN HUSBAND AND WIFE

1. There may have been conflicts between the husband and wife during their courtship days which have been carried over into married life. During courtship, these conflicts may be played down or ignored, but in marriage they tend to grow and become very real. They may consciously, or unconsciously, block a good love relationship.
2. There may have been conflicts or misunderstandings on the honeymoon in the initial stages of sexual intimacies. These could cause lingering emotional scars and more conflict.
3. There may be further conflicts in other areas. Five or ten years difference in age may cause unconscious disagreement and strife. If a husband feels that his mother, sisters, or relatives are better cooks or housekeepers than his wife, this could be a major source of conflict. Differences in other areas, such as education, finances, religion, social life and cultural background may cause conflict.
4. There may be secret dislikes for each other's habits, attitudes, ideas, and tastes which could tend to block an effective love relationship.
5. There may be a feeling of competition or jealousy between husband and wife, instead of a feeling of mutual reciprocal love, trust, and confidence.

PERSONAL PROBLEMS OF THE HUSBAND

1. The husband, who often has a very strong sex drive, and normally so, may tend to be selfish in seeking sexual satisfaction. It is difficult for him to comprehend the slow arousal nature of his wife. Most couples who have not developed a happy adjustment do not take enough time in the arousal period. The husband's hasty approach may unconsciously be crude, bold, and tactless, instead of an approach characterized by gentleness, kindness, patience, tenderness, understanding and humility.
2. Sometimes an insecure husband is a dominating husband. No human being likes to be dominated. If a husband tends to dominate his wife, this develops in her secret fears that may block their love relationships.
3. A few young husbands go into marriage with secret fears about their own sexual capacity, such as feeling they are undersexed, their penis is too small, or that they will not be able to satisfy their wives. Most of these fears are purely imaginary and have no basis in fact. Yet they are real in the minds of some young husbands and they may hinder a man from meeting the total sexual needs of his wife.
4. There may be strong guilt feelings about the past such as compulsive masturbation or other attempted sexual outlets.

PERSONAL PROBLEMS OF THE WIFE

1. The young wife may have developed inner fears about sex which root deep into her childhood and youth experiences. This is sometimes caused by a lack of proper parental guidance. Often, girls secretly feel they are undersexed because their sex drive is not manifested as is that of boys or some exaggerated, imaginary stories they have heard about the sex lives of some women. It is common for girls to feel that they are undersexed. Actually,

they are not. God does not create under-sexed persons.

2. Sometimes young girls enter marriage with ascetic ideas, i.e., they feel that sex is not "spiritual," that nice girls just don't "stoop to such." This *utterly false* and *unchristian* idea can easily block a woman's sexual progress in marriage. Her parents and society have failed to help her understand and distinguish between two facts: (a) sex life in marriage (monogamy) according to the plan of the Creator in nature is both moral and spiritual, and (b) only the *misuse* and *abuse* of sex is evil. (Genesis 1:27-31, Genesis 2:18-25, Mark 10:9, Proverbs 5:1-21, I Thessalonians 4:1-8, Hebrews 13:4, I Corinthians 7:1-5, and all of the Song of Solomon).

3. The rather long period of physical unpleasantness during the first days and weeks of sexual experience in marriage may condition the young wife against sex or crystallize some of her secret fears. This physical unpleasantness may include such things as failure to succeed in entering the penis into the vagina for several days, some bleeding when entrance is made, and considerable pain during the first efforts at intercourse. In our research sample 52 percent of wives indicated that they experienced slight pain at first intercourse, while 28 percent indicated considerable pain during first intercourse. Out of 151 couples, 63 couples stated that it took three to nine sexual experiences before the pain ceased. Seventeen couples stated that it took from 10 to 25 sexual experiences before this pain ceased. These are simply biological realities. Although they are unpleasant, they actually have no relation to a woman's capacity for normal sex life.

4. Some girls go into marriage with major feelings of insecurity and inferiority. These feelings tend to block sexual adjustment. Lacking self-confidence, young women are often too passive to become aroused to a full sexual experience.

5. Sometimes girls go into marriage with guilt feelings about the past. During teenage years driving curiosity leads some girls to limited experimentation. Guilt feelings about this experimentation may condition their minds against sex.

6. Sometimes a wife is simply happy with things as they are. Her main concern during courtship was marriage, a husband, a home, and a baby. Now she has them all. She is thrilled with her life situation. She enjoys meeting her husband's sexual needs. She enjoys her home, her baby, and her friends. She lives unselfishly for them and simply neglects her own sexual needs.

OTHER GENERAL PROBLEMS

1. In a few cases it may be a health problem, such as a poor diet, hormonal deficiency, or glandular disturbance. Most of these problems can be corrected by skilled medical guidance.

2. Some couples get into marriage with a simple lack of knowledge about the nature and function of the sexual organs and about normal sexual techniques. This would not be true of many college graduates or others who have had thorough pre-marital counseling by a qualified marriage counselor. Any couple which needs to improve their knowledge in these areas would profit by taking the "Sex Knowledge Inventory" tests, Form X and Form Y. Both of these tests may be secured from Family Life Publication, Inc., 6725 College Station, Durham, North Carolina.

3. One of the major hindrances to sexual adjustment in marriage is the lack of time for sexual experiences. Many couples hurry . . . hurry . . . hurry through life and

through their sexual experiences, for lack of time. It is difficult for a young wife to give herself fully to a sexual experience with her husband during hurried circumstances.

4. Equal with the lack of time is the lack of privacy, which is often experienced in the first part of married life. Unlocked doors, curtainless windows or doors, squeaking beds, and thin walls are problems. These problems can generally be solved by a couples' creative ingenuity. For example, many couples have made pallets on the floor in order to avoid squeaking beds.

5. Some couples, before marriage, assume that perfect sex adjustment in marriage would be easy, quick, and automatic. When this does not happen they develop fears, guilt feelings, and often panic. They become over anxious, are too serious, and try too hard. In their determined effort to succeed, they often antagonize each other. They need to realize that their experience is rather universal, and that it may take weeks and months to effect good adjustment. . . .

Efficient mutual sex life for husband and wife should tend to produce many positive fruits. (1) It should develop individual inner self-confidence. (2) It should release much energy to be utilized in absorbing creative projects outside of oneself, involving others in the home and community. (3) It should tend to promote security, maturity, happiness, and general personality development. (4) It should promote better physical health. (5) It should help present the right family environment for growing children, that is, a mother and father in a happy love relationship. (6) It should tend to develop the moral and social fiber of the community by decreasing extra-marital sex relationships and divorces. A community with strong family life should be able to develop an efficient social structure. (7) Last, but not least, good sexual life between husband and wife should tend to develop a close, warm, personal, spiritual relationship between them and God.

It must not be assumed that an emphasis on good sexual adjustment in marriage means that such an adjustment guarantees happiness in marriage. Every marriage counselor is acquainted with many cases where couples had good sexual adjustment but whose marriages were characterized by quarreling, conflict, emotional struggle, separation, and divorce. In order to have happiness in marriage, all of the phases of total life experience (the spiritual, the mental, the social, the emotional, the moral, the physical, and the sexual) must work as a cooperative unit. However, we must not fail to understand that in God's plan for married life good sexual adjustment is of major significance.

—From Herbert J. Miles, *Sexual Happiness in Marriage*. Grand Rapids: Zondervan, 1967.

PROBLEM AREAS

Fantasizing and Sexual Thoughts

Everyone thinks about sex because it's an important part of human nature. While some consider any thoughts about sex as immoral, evil, or impure, this isn't so. People may feel guilty and try to rid themselves of such thoughts. Yet they don't seem to disappear.

Because the sexual urge is alive within all of us, sexual thoughts, in themselves, are neither good nor evil. It's how we handle them and what we do with them that becomes good or bad.

Wrongful sexual fantasies are those in which we imagine ourselves participating in sexual conduct clearly forbidden in the Bible. It is wrong to fantasize participating in adultery, sexual relationships with animals (bestiality), homosexual activities, or orgies.

Continuous thinking or daydreaming about sexual relations with anyone other than your mate is lust, which Jesus condemned (*see* Matthew 5:28). Fantasizing can cause one to move from dreams to reality.

We curb our sexual fantasies by consciously turning our thoughts to other areas. This takes a disciplined act of the will. It may require much prayer. We can also ask one or two trusted friends to pray for us.

Many people are susceptible to outside stimuli such as movies, certain TV programs (such as R rated films on cable TV), pornography, and books. Paul told Timothy to shun evil. The advice holds true for us. We can avoid those things which turn our minds toward improper sexual fantasies.

—CECIL MURPHEY

Adultery and Fornication

Fornication (Greek *porneia*), a general word for illicit sexual intercourse, occurs in the Bible in such places as Acts 15:20, 29; 21:25; Romans 1:29; 2 Corinthians 5:1; 6:13, 18; 7:2.

Adultery (*moicheia*) appears in Matthew 15:19; Mark 7:21; Galatians 5:29.

People today often distinguish between the two English words using adultery referring to sexual acts when the person is married; with fornication limited to the unmarried. The Bible doesn't make that distinction, sometimes using the words interchangeably.

Porneia, in its widest sense, indicates immorality in general, and illicit relationships of every kind, but especially sexual intercourse (*see* John 8:41). Paul uses the word frequently (for example 2 Corinthians 12:21; Ephesians 5:3; Colossians 3:5; 2 Thessalonians 4:3). The word sometimes has a figurative meaning. In the Septuagint (Greek translation of the Old Testament), the writers used *porneia* to indicate departure from the Lord, Israel's "husband." In passages such as Hosea 6:10 (and Revelation 19:2) of the New Testament, translators have chosen words such as "whoredom" or "idolatry."

—CECIL MURPHEY

I would suggest that the basic arguments against premarital and extramarital sex are untouched by medical advances or social changes. The same questions which always needed to be asked are still basic. What values make for the growth of creative personality? What kind of homes, what patterns of values do persons need for their fulfillment as persons? What kind of person is the goal of sex, love, marriage and homemaking? What are the conditions under which sex and love remain creative for persons? The question we usually ask, but which is not really basic is: "Can a person have sexual intercourse outside of marriage without anxiety, guilt, disease, or pregnancy?" Rather, the more relevant question is: "How can sex contribute to the strength, growth, confidence, security, and identity of the person?"

With the current emphasis on individual freedom we are faced with the question of how to define the goals of a person free to choose and free to fulfill himself. It is not enough to say that freedom, or the love of persons, is the highest absolute value. A criterion of values that will keep freedom from becoming emasculated power and love from becoming self-absorption or sentimentality is also demanded. It is important to recognize that we come to know God and His will, in part, as we discover that persons cannot grow unless their beings are nourished in response to and in responsible love; and that one cannot know the full meaning or potential of their love and sexuality without marriage and a home. To be fully human, man needs and requires other human beings. There is no such individual as a "self-made" man. Therefore, no human being can or dares treat other human beings as if they were things to be used or exploited without destroying the very finest possibilities and potentials of human nature in others and in himself.

Everything we have learned from modern psychology has strengthened this ancient biblical concept. A sexual relationship can never be treated, therefore, as an individual act, for it always implicates and involves someone else in such a way that the participants can never again be as they were before coming together. Once done, it cannot be undone. Its effect, though possibly imperceptible at the moment, is indelible, and continued relationships only serve to deepen its mark made upon the personality of the persons involved, either for good or for bad. That is why it can be said with certainty that through sexual intercourse man and woman become "one flesh." They become deeply and unavoidably involved with one another in a relationship which expresses their total attitude toward each other and other persons. It may be either a self-giving love or selfish exploitation. No matter how much we may rationalize, it is not, it cannot be, a simple physical, mechanistic, biological, hedonistic, pleasure-seeking act. It is one of life's most vital and important channels of communication and it does involve the persons to the very depths of their personality so that neither can ever be as though they had never come together.

—From Bennard R. Wiese and Urban G. Steinmetz, *Everything You Need to Know to Stay Married and Like It*. Grand Rapids: Zondervan, 1972.

Homosexuality

Homosexuality seems to be the ultimate sin in the Bible that causes God to give men up, as He did in Romans 1:27, and to destroy them from the earth, as He did in the days of Sodom and Gomorrah and during the Flood in the days of Noah. Even while condemning the sin of the homosexual, a Christian should bear compassion for him as an individual and whenever possible share the gospel of Christ with him. That is the only known power available today to extricate a person from this awful vice.

The Bible is very clear on homosexuality. It is an abnormal, deviant practice according to Romans 1:27. The children of Israel were commanded by God to stone to death homosexuals (Leviticus 20:13), a severe treatment intended to keep them from becoming contagious. Every homosexual is potentially an evangelist of homosexuality, capable of perverting many young people to his sinful way of life.

WHAT CAUSES HOMOSEXUALITY?

There is no simple answer to this question, but this condition comes about from a combination of factors. One of the most common factors is an abnormal hatred toward the opposite sex aroused by a domineering mother, who "ruled the home," and a milk-toast father. This subconscious hatred of a boy for his mother spills over and makes it difficult for him to be attracted to girls his age. In the case of a lesbian, it is often the rejection of her father that prepares her for this life of perversion. Rarely does a child who is raised in a wholesome atmosphere of love from his parents develop a predisposition toward deviant sexual practices.

Another cause of homosexuality or lesbianism is an abnormal, smothering love of a child by a parent. This stifles his God-given instinctual response to the opposite sex. When a mother is not given love by her husband, she will often selfishly fill that void in her heart through an abnormal love for her son. Even though she would never think of doing anything immoral, such smothering affection sets up guilt complexes in the lad that stifle his normal reactions toward the opposite sex. Subconsciously he regards such

216

feelings as a betrayal of his love for his mother. The same thing occurs when a girl is subjected to that kind of smothering love from her father, who probably does not receive sufficient love from his wife. Dr. Howard Hendricks has made the point at many of our seminars that "children need love, but they should always realize that they are number two in the heart of their parents. If they grow up thinking they are number one, they will have a difficult time adjusting normally to the opposite sex."

Normal love responses in children are most easily fostered in a warm atmosphere of love between their parents. This is so psychically normal that they feel relaxed in their attitude toward the opposite sex. Although parents should not be indiscreet in front of their children, it is good for them to see their parents embrace and display genuine affection.

Remember also that in their early teen years, as they go from childhood to adolescence, children are commonly attracted to their own sex. Junior boys, for example, often "hate girls." And as they begin developing sexually, they may find an unexplainable attraction to another boy or man. That is why they should be well trained in their home and church in God's standards of sexuality that boy-girl impulses are right and normal and that boy-boy sexual impulses should be rejected. Such teachings guard him through this ambivalent phase of life when even he doesn't know sometimes if he is "fish or fowl," after which he develops a healthy appreciation for the opposite sex.

—From Tim and Beverly LaHaye, *The Act of Marriage*. Grand Rapids: Zondervan, 1976.

Incest

This is the practice of sexual activity of one type or another among near relatives. Commonest is that between brother and sis-

ter, but all too often it is practiced between fathers and daughters. Grandfathers, uncles and cousins are all on the list. It is extremely rare between mothers and sons.

In cases of incest, mothers are often guilty of negligence and failure to respond to the signs of, or even confessed information, about such situations. Dr. Grace has worked with many guilt-ridden adolescents and adults whose problems go directly back to incestual attacks in childhood.

When incest is suspected, Mother, please get professional counsel at once. While it is horrifying to admit and painful to deal with, it is unthinkable to ignore or wish it away! Good psychotherapy will be able to stop such practices, enable emotional healing to take place through understanding, and prevent the scars of incest from damaging your child's eventual physical and mental health.

IF A SEXUAL ENCOUNTER CAUSES PHYSICAL DAMAGE, DO NOT HESITATE, EVEN THOUGH YOU MAY FEEL ASHAMED AND AFRAID. TAKE YOUR CHILD AT ONCE TO YOUR DOCTOR OR AN EMERGENCY ROOM. THERE HAVE BEEN DEATHS FROM BLEEDING OR INFECTIONS DUE TO THE NEGLECT OF SUCH INJURIES. WHATEVER THE EMBARRASSMENT TO AN ADULT, A CHILD'S LIFE IS WORTH INFINITELY MORE. THINK AHEAD TO THE TIME OF RESTORATION AND HEALING. DO NOT GIVE IN TO THE TEMPTATION TO AVOID DEALING WITH THE ISSUE!

—From Grace H. Ketterman, M.D., and Herbert L. Ketterman, M.D., *The Complete Book of Baby and Child Care for Christian Parents*. Old Tappan, N.J.: Revell, 1982.

Masturbation

IS IT WRONG FOR A CHRISTIAN TO MASTURBATE?

There is probably no more controversial question in the field of sex than this. A few years ago every Christian would have given an unqualified yes, but that was before the sexual revolution and before doctors declared that the practice is not harmful to health. No longer can a father honestly warn his son that it will cause "brain damage, weakness, baldness, blindness, epilepsy, or insanity." Some still refer to it as "self-abuse" and "sinful behavior"; others advocate it as a necessary relief to the single man and a help for the married man whose wife is pregnant or whose business forces him to be away from home for long periods of time. . . .

Unfortunately the Bible is silent on this subject; therefore it is dangerous to be dogmatic. Although we are sympathetic with those who would remove the time-honored taboos against the practice, we would like to suggest the following reasons why we do not feel it is an acceptable practice for Christians:

1. Fantasizing and lustful thinking are usually involved in masturbation, and the Bible clearly condemns such thoughts (Matthew 5:28).
2. Sexual expression was designed by God to be performed jointly by two people of the opposite sex, resulting in a necessary and healthy dependence on each other for the experience. Masturbation frustrates that designed dependence.
3. Guilt is a nearly universal aftermath of masturbation unless one has been brainwashed by the humanistic philosophy that does not believe in a God-given conscience or, in many cases, right and wrong. Such guilt interferes with spiritual growth and produces defeat in single young people particularly. To them it is usually a self-discipline hurdle they must scale in order to grow in Christ and walk in the Spirit.
4. It violates 1 Corinthians 7:9: "For it is better to marry than to burn." If a young man practices masturbation, it tends to nullify a necessary and important motivation for marriage. There are already enough social, educational, and financial demotivators on young men now; they don't need this one.
5. It creates a habit before marriage that can easily be resorted to afterward as a cop-out when a husband and wife have conflicts that make coitus difficult.
6. It defrauds a wife (1 Corinthians 7:3–5). No married man should relieve his mounting, God-given desire for his wife except through coitus. She will feel unloved and insecure, and many little problems will unnecessarily be magnified by this artificial draining of his sex drive. This becomes increasingly true as a couple reach middle age.

—From Tim and Beverly LaHaye, *The Act of Marriage*. Grand Rapids: Zondervan, 1976.

Onanism

In Genesis 38 Onan refused to impregnate his dead brother's widow. Instead he "spilled his seed upon the ground." Some people concluded from the fact that God punished Onan for this, that any stimulation of the sex organs without the design of procreation was sinful. The proponents overlooked a Levitical marriage law that was involved.

Under the law a barren marriage could be remedied after the husband's death. The purpose was to ensure that the dead man's name and possessions stayed in the possession of the clan. Onan was expected to comply with the duty laid on him by law and give children to the widow.

Onan flouted the law, refusing the widow her rights. His punishment did not come for interrupting sexual intercourse. God's punishment came for his disobedience. His act may be called coitus interruptus or simply masturbation.

—CECIL MURPHEY

Rape

Rape needs to be discussed because it happens so often and is such a violent invasion of one's personal rights. Rape is the forceful, violent act of sexual intercourse with an unwilling partner. Usually there are threats of harm or death unless the victim submits. Rape, reported and unreported, occurs somewhere almost every day. A number of months ago, a judge was roundly condemned for blaming rape on the seductive dress and behavior of women. While such behavior may be detrimental to a person, certainly rape is not caused by women. In fact, it is often committed on helpless, elderly women, or presexual girls.

The person who commits rape is a basically angry man who feels unusually worthless. When he is angry, this kind of man can become more easily sexually aroused to the point of sexual orgasm (or climax). The rapist, either unconsciously or by effort, allows his anger to mount until it becomes a force almost beyond his control. By acting out this anger through sexual aggression, he can feel powerful for a time, and is lifted out of his inadequacy. Usually this is a recurring pattern. Often, even after imprisonment, many such people are still a danger to society. The degree of violence varies from an almost gentle persistence to extreme violence that may cause the rapist to kill the victim and grossly mutilate the body. If every boy were loved and taught respect for himself and others, if he were helped to become successful and self-confident, there would be no rape. But as long as boys are humiliated, abused, and painfully neglected, we can expect retaliation in the form of rape.

—From Grace H. Ketterman, M.D., *How to Teach Your Child About Sex.* Old Tappan, N.J.: Revell, 1981.

Venereal Disease

While sexual intercourse is a God-given function, it also causes problems, among them venereal disease (or to use a newer term—STD, sexually transmitted disease). Intercourse with a healthy person never gives anyone a sexually transmitted disease.

Some diseases are transmitted by kissing and not by actual genital contact. When two people kiss, their saliva mixes and any microorganisms present in the mouth or the bloodstream can be transmitted to the other person. Kissing can expose the other to a cold, flu, sore throat, or any of a number of viruses. Using another person's drinking glass or towel can also transmit disease.

Another type of disease, however, is almost always transmitted through genital sexual contact because germs and insects particularly adapted to living in and around the genital area spread upon contact. Diseases transmitted by having intercourse are called venereal diseases (VD), once euphemistically termed "social diseases." The most prevalent are:

Syphilis, a highly dangerous STD, is caused by a type of bacterium known as spirochete. Left untreated, it can affect many parts of the body, eventually causing heart disease, blindness, paralysis, insanity, and, ultimately, death. Large doses of penicillin (under a doctor's direction) usually cure syphilis. Trying to self-treat can be not only highly dangerous but can mask the symptoms, and the disease may not manifest itself until years later. Syphilitic women can transmit this disease to their newborn babies.

The earliest symptom of syphilis is a sore on the genitals. This usually disappears, even

219

Venereal Diseases

Disease	First Symptoms Usually Appear	Usual	Diagnosis	Complications
GONORRHEA (called dose, clap, drip) Cause: bacterial	2–10 days (up to 30 days)	White or yellow discharge from genitals or anus. Pain on urination or defecation. Pharyngeal infections are usually without symptoms. WOMEN: Low abdominal pain especially after period. May have no symptoms. MEN: May have no symptoms.	WOMEN: Culture MEN: Smear or Culture	Sterility, arthritis, endocarditis, panhepatitis, meningitis, blindness. WOMEN: Pelvic inflammatory disease. MEN: Urethral stricture, erection problems. NEWBORN: Blindness.
SYPHILIS (called syph, pox, bad blood) Cause: spirochete	10–90 days (usually 3 weeks)	1st Stage: Chancre (painless pimple, blister, or sore) where germs entered body—i.e. genitals, anus, lips, breast, etc. 2nd Stage: Rash or mucous patches (most are highly infectious), spotty hair loss, sore throat, swollen glands. Symptoms may reoccur for up to 2 years.	VDRL blood test or microscopic examination of organisms from sores	Brain damage, insanity, paralysis, heart disease, death. Also damage to skin, bones, eyes, teeth; and liver of the fetus and newborn.
HERPES SIMPLEX II (called herpes) Cause: viral	Highly variable	Cluster of tender painful blisters in the genital area. Painful urination. Swollen glands and fever.	Pap smear, culture taken when the blisters or sores are present.	May be linked with cervical cancer, severe central nervous system damage or death in infants infected during birth.

Venereal Diseases

Disease	First Symptoms Usually Appear	Usual	Diagnosis	Complications
NONSPECIFIC URETHRITIS (called NGU, NSU) Cause: bacteria, chiamydia	1–3 weeks	Slight white, yellow, or clear discharge from genitals, often only noticed in the morning. WOMEN: Usually no symptoms. MEN: Mild discomfort upon urination.	Smear or culture usually to rule out gonorrhea.	WOMEN: Pelvic inflammatory disease. NEWBORN: Pneumonia and conjunctivitis.
TRICHOMONAS VAGINALIS (called trich, TV, vaginitis) Cause: protozoan	1–4 weeks	WOMEN: Heavy, frothy discharge, intense itching, burning and redness of genitals. MEN: Slight, clear discharge from genitals and itching after urination. Usually no symptoms.	Pap smear, microscopic identification	WOMEN: Gland infection
MONILIAL VAGINITIS (called moniliasis, vaginal thrush, yeast, candidiasis) Cause: fungal	Varies	WOMEN: Thick, cheesy discharge and intense itching of genitals, also skin irritation. MEN: Usually no symptoms.	Microscopic identification	WOMEN: Secondary infections by bacteria. NEWBORN: Mouth and throat infections.
VENEREAL WARTS (called genital warts, condylomata acuminata) Cause: viral	1–3 months	Local irritation, itching, and wartlike growths usually on the genitals, anus, or throat.	Examination	Highly contagious, can spread enough to block vaginal, rectal, or throat openings.

Venereal Diseases

Disease	First Symptoms Usually Appear	Usual	Diagnosis	Complications
PEDICULOSIS PUBIS (called crabs, cooties) Cause: 6–legged louse	4–5 weeks	Intense itching, pinhead blood spots on under- wear, nits in hair	Examination	Secondary infec- tions as a result of scratching.
SCABIES (called the itch) Cause: itch mite	4–6 weeks	Severe itching at night, raised gray lines on skin where mites burrow—hands, genitals, breast, stomach, but- tocks	Examination	Secondary infec- tions as a result of scratching.

—CECIL MURPHEY

Venereal Disease National Hotline 800-227-8922
In California, 800-982-5883

without treatment. Later signs include fever, rash, and swollen glands.

Gonorrhea (clap), also highly dangerous, produces urethritis (infection of the urethra) in men. In women it causes inflammation of and scarring of the internal reproductive organs, which can lead to sterility. Treatment with proper doses of antibiotics by a physician can cure gonorrhea.

Early signs of gonorrhea are painful urination and discharge of pus from the penis. In women, there may be no early signs. Pain in the abdomen is an advanced sign in the female.

Nonspecific Urethritis (NGU) is frequently confused with gonorrhea because its symptoms in men are the same. But NGU is not caused by the gonococcus, and isn't particularly harmful. Tetracycline usually cures NGU.

Herpes. Genital herpes is a rapidly increasing STD, and a particularly resistant strain of it has no cure as yet. It causes painful blisters and sores on the penis or in the vagina and vulva. Although herpes is a family of more than fifty viruses, this particular form is causing great health concern because of its pandemic proportions.

In men, the infection usually first shows itself as tiny blisters, then crusty lesions, in places such as the penis, lower abdomen, thighs, and buttocks. In women, the fluid-filled lesions can turn to ulcers and may develop internally as well. Women reporting herpes genitalis attacks are eight times more likely to develop cancer of the cervix or of the vulva than those never infected.

Scabies. An annoying but not dangerous disease, it is caused by an infestation of small insects around pubic hair. It causes itching and red marks where the insects burrow into the skin in the pubic area. Prescribed medication and hot baths normally kills scabies.

—CECIL MURPHEY

FAMILY PLANNING

Responsible Parenthood

How many children should a couple have? No simple figure can adequately answer that question. The answer can be derived only by taking numerous factors into account and weighing them against one another. Facile reference to "population explosion" as reason for keeping families as small as possible has, at least in our country, little relevance; for the issue of overpopulation is one whose contours vary, depending on which continent or country is under consideration. Here no attempt will be made to discuss the matter on a global scale. But it is peculiar that assertions regarding threatened overpopulation in *foreign* countries are so quickly taken up as grounds for pushing unlimited reduction in the *domestic* birthrate. In truth, the average family size in this country is already too small! The massive influx of foreign laborers lends support to this thesis, completely apart from the fact that the demographic structure of many Western countries, as shown by the lopsided shape of their population pyramids, is an unhealthy one.

Each individual couple must answer the question "How many children?" in a very personal way, taking various principles into consideration and reviewing their decision from time to time in the light of their current circumstances. There is general agreement that marriage is directed toward the raising up of new life. When a couple wed and consummate their union, they thereby declare themselves ready to receive children and to do their best in rearing any children that might be conceived in the union. This duty—made manifest, after the wedding, in the marital act—can never be lost from sight, even though a couple, as is most often the case, marry primarily because they are in

love and want to belong to each other. Love, as a motive for marriage, predominates in our culture, but is not so frequent in all other countries of the world.

The desire to belong to each other in love and to assist each other in character growth is a noble motive for marriage and highlights the personal side of marriage sadly neglected in previous centuries. But it would be just as much a mistake for a couple to withdraw into themselves and completely reject the call to raise up new life. When there is a fundamental refusal to have any children, the couple's attitude must be considered morally bad and the restriction of intercourse to the infertile time morally unjustified.

There must be sound reasons to justify conscious avoidance of pregnancy at any given time. When sound reasons are present, a married couple remains within the proper moral order, even when using only the infertile time. If a couple does have sound reasons for avoiding pregnancy and decides to restrict intercourse to the infertile time, that couple is acting in a perfectly moral and responsible fashion; and we should recognize that under the circumstances there is nothing morally wrong with what they have chosen to do. The way is not easy and requires effort, self-discipline, moderation, and reflection on higher values. By that fact alone, the natural way of responsible regulation of family size towers far above all contraceptive measures, which require no effort or self-discipline, lead to immoderation, give preference to purely instinctual drive, and require only a certain technical finesse to make them halfway effective (*completely reliable* they are not).

By the time they get married, a couple should already have some idea of when they will responsibly be able to conceive their first child. It is perfectly consistent with a genuine sense of responsibility to work with nature to achieve legitimate goals rather than to drift blindly with the winds of passion. On the other hand, it would seem undesirable to plan a fixed number of children, spaced a set number of years apart, right from the beginning of the marriage. After all, the responsible bearing and rearing of children requires that after each birth, parents reassess the matter of family size, with reference to their changed circumstances. The entire marriage thereby becomes a continuous harkening to God's call regarding family size. Spouses ought to consider themselves conscience bound not to avoid the question and should remember that identifiable circumstances and alternatives available to them will point the way to a solution.

One essential factor in discerning the "right" number of children is the matter of how many children a couple can properly rear (as opposed to how many they can conceive). The strength to train and educate children for their vocations in later life is of critical importance in responsibly determining family size. The task of parenting is not fulfilled simply by giving children existence; they must be afforded intellectual, moral, and spiritual formation, as well as vocational skills. Circumstances will vary from couple to couple. Of course it should be kept in mind that couples need not be unduly anxious, for where the proper measure of generosity and Christian prudence are present, the providence of God will never leave the family at a loss. Couples also do well to keep in mind that it is more difficult to rear one child or two children than to provide several children with the experience of social grouping in the family itself, where they may to some extent educate one another.

Another essential factor to consider when making family-planning decisions is the condition of the mother's health. If another child would be a threat to her life, it is obvi-ous that no further children should be conceived. The couple should seek thorough counsel from the physician of their choice. No effort should be spared to obtain solidly based opinion, lest premature judgments be made. Occasionally a physician lightheartedly remarks that a woman should not conceive another child, because of her health. That comment, coming from the mouth of a physician, is likely to have an exaggerated impact on the couple. The couple, however, is not thereby absolved from their responsibility to obtain a well-founded opinion; they may seek another physician's opinion to help clarify the truth of the matter.

Frequently another birth would not exactly be a threat to the life of the mother, but her general physical condition is such that it would be an exhausting burden for her to bear the additional child while properly caring for the children she already has. Besides that, her husband and children have a right to a wife and mother who is as healthy and happy as possible; she should not be so bogged down in everyday chores that she threatens to collapse whenever some new difficulty presents itself. Unforeseen illnesses, too, can mean great suffering for a family and, when they occur, are to be borne as best they can, with trusting confidence in the grace of God. Afflicted families need our special compassion as well as our special assistance.

But when a couple must make a conscious, responsible decision to postpone a pregnancy for a considerable length of time or to avoid pregnancy altogether for the remainder of the marriage, the decision is best made when the possible occurrence of another pregnancy could still be accepted gladly. A woman has no obligation to bear as many children as she physically can, to the point of exhaustion. The awareness that an additional pregnancy would not represent an overbearing burden leads to a more relaxed atmosphere within the marriage. This peace enables the couple to carry out natural conception regulation all the more satisfactorily, particularly since experience shows that surprise pregnancies do not occur in such situations.

A woman's capacity to take on further burdens cannot be defined simply in terms of her health. Her condition must be assessed in relation to burdensome circumstances such as restricted social opportunities, crowded living space, tensions with relatives, employment, and so on. Without wishing to imply that a woman has no right to her own vocational or professional training and the liberty to develop her own personality, it must be emphasized that overestimating the value of employment outside the home can lead to irreparable damage to the children. The couple must carefully consider whether or not the desired additional wages of an employed mother sufficiently offset the disadvantages that accrue from her absence. All too often the assertion that a mother needs to have a "meaningful" job outside the home only conceals a flight from the proper and challenging task of being mother and teacher; this is a role in which the woman of the family cannot adequately be replaced.

Adequate living quarters are also important for the unfolding of a cultured family life and are a prerequisite for good training and solid formation of the children. Here we may include modern conveniences insofar as they make life easier, embellish it, and contribute to character formation; their service to the human person (training, education, moral and spiritual formation) should be the criterion by which to judge their acquisition and use. But any approach to material possessions that is based on a quest for self-gratification, creature comfort, and an exaggerated standard of living is unworthy of a human being and unchristian as well.

The ideal of responsible parenthood sug-

gests that married couples discern if they have a moral obligation to bring new life into the world more generously than most members of contemporary society. "Responsible parenthood" cannot be cited as an excuse for indolence or for inordinate pleasure seeking, nor can one appeal to "responsibility" (falsely understood) as justification for having as few children as possible. There must also be no denying that parents who are economically secure, healthy, and capable of rearing children have every right to have a large family if they so wish. Such parents deserve not only greater recognition and special praise; they also obviously have the special task of witnessing to society and in the church to the overflowing love of God, in that they themselves raise up new life in overflowing generosity. The government has no authority whatsoever to deny these parents the right to have children or to punish those parents in any way. There are those who have attempted to impose a mandatory limit on family size, coupled with substantial penalties for those who have more than the "permitted" number of children. But such a strategy is impermissible because it precludes legitimate diversity in family size; ultimately this kind of action will result in decline of the general level of culture, for mankind's most talented individuals frequently come from large families.

—From Josef Roetzer, M.D., *Family Planning the Natural Way*. Old Tappan, N.J.: Revell, 1981.

Methods of Birth Control

CERVICAL CAP

This device is a small cup of rubber, metal, or plastic fitted by a physician, which is placed over the mouth of the womb to prevent the sperm from entering. Many women leave it in place from the end of one menstrual cycle until the beginning of the next. Some women have difficulty in replacing it securely. Any woman using the cap should have regular checks by a physician. It has high reliability if placed securely and it has about the same problems as the diaphragm emotionally and aesthetically.

—From Bennard R. Wiese and Urban G. Steinmetz, *Everything You Need to Know to Stay Married and Like It.* Grand Rapids: Zondervan, 1972.

COITUS INTERRUPTUS (WITHDRAWAL)

The Bible story of Onan, who "spilled his seed on the ground," is generally misinterpreted as a reference to self-stimulation, and, in fact, the second meaning of onanism in the dictionary is "masturbation." In the story, however, Onan was obliged by Hebrew law to cohabit with his brother's widow so that she might bear a child in her deceased husband's name. Unwilling to father progeny for his brother, Onan practiced *coitus interruptus;* that is, he withdrew before orgasm and ejaculated apart from the woman.

The long-term misinterpretation has been used as support for judging masturbation as a sin. There is even some question in Talmudic literature whether *coitus interruptus* was Onan's sin. Some of the rabbis argued that he was punished, not for wasting his seed, but for disobeying the law and cheating his brother and his brother's widow of offspring. At least one Catholic writer, Canon de Smet, is interpreted as having concurred in this view, giving St. Augustine as his authority.

Scholarly investigators into Talmudic writings have found an occasional authority in favor of *coitus interruptus,* for example, Rabbi Eliezer who wrote picturesquely in the first century A.D. that during the twenty-four months while the mother is suckling a child, the husband "must thresh inside and winnow outside." Later rabbis have not recommended the practice, but neither have they forbidden it outright. Moslem physicians recommend withdrawal, or *coitus interruptus,* as the first of several methods when prevention of pregnancy is desired.

The anthropologists report that many primitive peoples rely on this method on ritual occasions, such as in the ceremonial defloration of virgins, and between husband and wife on the day that the infant begins to crawl and the enforced post-childbirth abstinence is ended. It is possibly the practice also among the young people who share common sleeping houses for the unmarried, in those tribes which permit premarital intercourse but frown on premarital pregnancies.

There is reason to believe that wherever the entrance of the male semen into the vagina was understood as the cause of pregnancy, *coitus interruptus* was one of the first practical—that is, nonmagical—contraceptive methods. According to one authority it is nearly as old as the group life of man. It was possibly known among the Puritan settlers of New England and has been prevalent for centuries among European working-class folk.

Medical opinion has been sharply divided on the question of whether *coitus interruptus* is harmful. A great deal has been written on the damage to the nervous system caused by withdrawal.

A rational point of view would seem to be that to rely on *coitus interruptus* as a contraceptive method adds tension and anxiety to the sexual act, that it deprives the partners of the natural gradual subsidence from climax, that it requires great skill and awareness especially in the male partner to bring the wife to orgasm and still withdraw in time to prevent ejaculation of some semen within the vagina. With the more trustworthy and more comfortable methods available today, there seems little reason to depend upon this one.

COITUS OBSTRUCTUS

By pressure of the finger on the base of the urethra, ejaculation of semen into the vagina may be prevented. The obstruction of the urethra forces the seminal fluid into the bladder, to be eliminated afterward with the urine.

As a contraceptive method this is not advised. In some early Persian and Sanscrit manuscripts it is referred to as a way of prolonging erection.

—From Jerome and Julia Rainer, *Sexual Pleasure in Marriage.* New York: Simon & Schuster, 1969.

CONDOM

A condom is a thin rubber device shaped like the finger of a glove. It is placed over the husband's penis before intercourse and prevents the sperm from escaping into the vagina. It is often called a "rubber" or "safety."

—From Eric W. Johnson, *Love and Sex in Plain Language.* Rev. ed. Philadelphia: J. B. Lippincott, 1967.

DIAPHRAGM

A diaphragm is a rubber cap, usually about three inches in diameter, which, before intercourse, the wife places in the vagina so as to wall off the lower part from the upper. It prevents the sperm from entering the cervix. It should be obtained by prescription only, and must be fitted by a doctor and used with a special kind of cream or jelly which kills sperm cells.

—From Eric W. Johnson, *Love and Sex in Plain Language.* Rev. ed. Philadelphia: J. B. Lippincott, 1967.

DOUCHING

Douching (washing out the vagina) is a nonmethod of birth control, since some sperm move from the upper vagina into the cervix where they are safe from the douche. This all happens within a matter of seconds after ejaculation.

Some have suggested that a douche, using plain tap water, may be helpful (and better than nothing!). Sperm are fragile and vulnerable to tap water. Couples should never count on douching for birth control.

—CECIL MURPHEY

HORMONAL METHODS—FEMALE (THE PILL)

Women through the centuries have swallowed all sorts of concoctions made of plant and animal materials in their attempts to prevent or terminate unwanted pregnancies. During the Middle Ages many mercury, strychnine, and lead poisonings occurred, thousands of women dying when they used these agents to try to control their fertility. With the discovery of oral contraceptives, women for the first time had a technique which, if taken as directed, was virtually 100 percent effective.

The combined oral contraceptives (estrogen plus progestin) have been in use for approximately two decades and the mini-pill (progestin alone) for more than ten years. These agents have been more widely studied than any medication in the history of mankind. At the present time it is estimated that 54 million women are using the pill, 10 million of them living in the United States. In addition, there are another 50 million women who have used an oral contraceptive at some time in the past.

The combined estrogen and progestin pills (those with dosages of 50 micrograms and above) prevent pregnancy by stopping ovulation, the monthly release of an egg by an ovary. Their use as a contraceptive method is based on the fact that during pregnancy these hormones, made by the ovaries and placenta, block the production of the hormones which are responsible for ovulation, thus preventing the establishment of an additional pregnancy. In the case of the mini-pill (progestin alone) and the low estrogen combined pills, the mechanism is somewhat more complicated. Studies have shown that not all women who use these pills stop ovulating. The mechanism (or mechanisms) of action in this instance appears to be the effects of the hormone on the cervical mucus, the lining of the uterus, and the cervix, along with certain other anatomical changes. These changes probably all combine together to block the migration of the sperm or perhaps the implantation of the fertilized ovum. While similar effects occur with the higher dose combined pills, their effectiveness is achieved mainly by the blocking of ovulation.

Major Severe Side Effects. Not long after widespread use of the pill began, it became clear that certain complications were occurring in a small number of women. Considerable unhappiness has been voiced over the years about the fact that these side effects were not recognized earlier. However, it must always be remembered that with any drug when complications are rare, say once in every quarter- to half-million users as in the case of the pill, thousands of women must be carefully followed for a number of years in order to detect those complications.

In addition, because of the complexities of civilization today, it is very difficult to be able to relate any particular adverse reaction to a particular medication. To link a given side effect with a specific drug—given the number of drugs in common use, the various food additives, and all of the other pollutants in our environment—takes wide usage of that drug over a considerable period of time.

Contraindications. At the present time the U.S. Food and Drug Administration lists a number of absolute contraindications to the use of the pill. The list is based on proven major adverse side effects, as in the case of the cardiovascular disorders, and on conditions for which a relationship is suspected, but not necessarily proven.

1. Known cardiovascular conditions or a past history of these conditions, including thrombophlebitis and thromboembolic disorders (formation of blood clots and embolisms), cerebrovascular disease (stroke), myocardial infarction (type of heart attack), or coronary artery disease.
2. Markedly impaired liver function.
3. Known or suspected carcinoma of the breast.
4. Known or suspected estrogen-dependent neoplasia (abnormal tissue growth).
5. Undiagnosed abnormal genital bleeding.
6. Known or suspected pregnancy.

Smoking, although not currently listed by the FDA, should be considered a relative contraindication. As we have mentioned, more and more evidence is being accumulated showing that the combination of increasing age and heavy smoking raises the risks of heart attack and stroke considerably higher than either age or smoking alone. In fact, current data indicate that the two factors have a synergistic effect, that is, one in the presence of the other increases the risk that each could produce separately, that their combined effect is greater than the sum of their effects simply added together.

Therefore, women of any age, but particularly those over 30 and those with additional risk factors, should be encouraged not to take the pill if they smoke or not to smoke if they take the pill. Obviously, as a general health measure, women should be encouraged not to smoke whether they take the pill or not. Indeed it has been suggested, not entirely facetiously, that, given the differences in relative risks, pills should be put in vending machines and cigarettes placed on prescription!

Minor Adverse Side Effects. There are a number of side effects which are annoying, but not serious or life-threatening. Among the most frequent of these are alterations in the menstrual flow. Most often the change is a decrease (a change considered to be desirable by many women). There may also be irregular spotting and bleeding between periods, heavier bleeding at the time of the menses, and on occasion a total absence of menses. Breast tenderness may be observed, and there is often an increase in the amount of vaginal discharge. Weight gain is noted by some women, but this is much more apt to be related to changes in dietary intake than to the pill. Pigmentation over the forehead and cheeks, the same type seen in pregnancy, may also occur with use of the oral contraceptives.

Beneficial Side Effects. Too often only the bad side effects of the pill are presented in all forms of media. The beneficial side effects of the pill are only rarely discussed in the same context.

A number of salutary changes have been noted, such as the decreases in breast and ovarian tumors. In addition, women whose cycles are extremely irregular or who have heavy menstrual bleeding resulting in anemia may be virtually assured that these problems will be solved by the use of the oral contraceptives. Premenstrual symptoms and menstrual discomfort are also often relieved,

and acne often improves markedly. One fascinating side effect which was noted in a British study is a 25 percent decrease in ear wax, although it is unclear what major advantage this may have for women.

HORMONAL METHODS—MALE

Pressure to develop male contraceptive methods has increased in recent years, particularly by activist women's groups, but even an ideal male contraceptive would in no way replace female contraception. Many women feel that men should share in the responsibility for preventing unwanted pregnancy, but at the same time they would not be willing to surrender their own fertility control to their sexual partner, even in a monogamous situation.... Although male methods would not supplant all female methods, they would certainly be an excellent addition to the total contraceptive cafeteria.

Male methods have been studied for many years. It has been much more difficult to completely block male fertility than female. There is a growing body of evidence, based on some recent studies, that a man may produce a pregnancy even though his sperm count is very low.

A number of hormonal preparations have been tested as male contraceptives. Some of the earlier studies were done with estrogens. While these agents effectively depressed the development of sperm in the male, they were quickly abandoned when it was found that they also produced a number of unfortunate side effects such as breast enlargement, impotence and the lack of desire for sex.

Research is now being done combining estrogens with progestin male hormones. These agents are either taken by mouth or given by injection. Thus far it appears that these newer techniques may be successful in reducing the sperm count to zero, while allowing the continuation of normal sexual desire and performance. It seems quite possible that some time in the next few years, after sufficient data have been collected, these agents will be approved for use by the male.

—From *Everywoman's Health* by 17 Women Doctors with D. S. Thompson, M.D., consulting editor. New York: Doubleday, 1980.

INJECTABLES

For a number of years researchers have sought a long-acting hormonal preparation which could be given by injection to block ovulation. Such a method would have its greatest application in certain areas of the world where medication is not felt to be significant or helpful unless it is given by injection, but it would also benefit any women who, because of medical, social, or psychological reasons, cannot cope with the demands of pill-taking or the use of barrier methods. Moreover, when health care personnel and facilities are limited, a technique which requires a single act of motivation on the part of the patient and infrequent professional follow-up is obviously highly desirable.

At present there is no injectable contraceptive available in the United States. A number of hormones, given once every one to six or more months, have been evaluated. One progestin preparation, Depo-Provera, has been extensively studied for more than 10 years and is currently being marketed and widely used in almost 70 other countries. Side effects of Depo-Provera include irregular bleeding, temporary stopping of menses, and in some instances a slower return to fertility. Because of concern about these effects, about laboratory tests in which beagle dogs given the drug in large doses developed breast tumors, and about the possible development of cancer of the cervix in women (which was subsequently disproved), Depo-Provera has been disapproved by the FDA for marketing in this country for purely contraceptive purposes.

—From *Everywoman's Health* by 17 Women Doctors with D. S. Thompson, M.D., consulting editor. New York: Doubleday, 1980.

INTRA-UTERINE DEVICES

These devices, called IUD's are plastic rings, coils or loops, any one of which is inserted by a doctor into the slit-like cavity of the uterus and which, by means not yet fully understood, prevent conception for as long as they are in place. The advantages of the IUD are its very low cost and the simplicity of its use, for once it has been inserted, nothing more needs to be done except for the wife to make an occasional checkup visit to the doctor. It is not as certain of success as the pill.

—From Eric W. Johnson, *Love and Sex in Plain Language*. Rev. ed. Philadelphia: J. B. Lippincott, 1967.

LACTATION

Lactation is an ancient form of family planning. Many years ago women discovered that the likelihood of their becoming pregnant was considerably less when they were nursing their children. However, it has been found that breast-feeding is only partially effective. Lactation does suppress ovulation to some degree, but the longer one goes from the time of the delivery, the more apt one is to have a return of ovulation. This can occur even before the first postpartum menses. Full lactation (nursing at all feedings with no supplementary food) suppresses ovulation and menses considerably longer than partial lactation.

—From *Everywoman's Health* by 17 Women Doctors with D. S. Thompson, M.D., consulting editor. New York: Doubleday, 1980.

"MORNING AFTER" PILL

Considerable research has been directed toward finding a substance, a so-called "morning after" pill, which will prevent pregnancy after unprotected sexual relations at the time of ovulation. It was shown many years ago in monkeys and then in the human female that the use of sufficient doses of any estrogen at this time will prevent implantation.

The major work in this area has been done using diethylstilbestrol (DES). This drug is not used in any of the oral contraceptives. At the present time DES is the only drug approved by the FDA as a morning after pill—and then only in emergency situations including rape. However, to date there is no evidence of a relationship between malignancy and DES used as a morning after pill. Research is now being undertaken to see if other estrogens will produce the same beneficial effects without producing adverse side effects.

—From *Everywoman's Health* by 17 Women Doctors with D. S. Thompson, M.D., consulting editor. New York: Doubleday, 1980.

NATURAL FAMILY PLANNING
(RHYTHM AND SYMPTO-THERMAL METHODS)

Three commonly known biological facts provide the scientific basis for natural family planning, in which pregnancy is spaced or controlled without using any of the artificial contraceptives.

1. A woman normally produces only one ovum during each menstrual cycle.

2. The ovum has an active life of only about twenty-four hours, and it is only during this twenty-four hours that it can be fertilized by the male sperm.

3. The male sperm is capable of living for only about forty-eight hours after it is released into the vagina. It is only during this two-day interval that it can fertilize the female ovum.

The conclusion from these three facts is that there are really only three days each month when intercourse can lead to pregnancy—the two days before the ovum is released and the full day afterward. If a woman could avoid having intercourse during this time, then, *theoretically*, she would be in no danger of becoming pregnant.

The idea behind all natural family planning is that a woman must simply refrain from having intercourse on the days when she can become pregnant. What makes this simple idea so difficult to put into practice, however, and what limits the effectiveness of this method, is that no fail-safe way has yet been found to determine just which days are safe for intercourse. The old **rhythm method** simply assumed that most women would be safe one week before their period, during their period, and for about five days after their period. However, the method-failure rate for the rhythm system was quite high.

Today, more and more couples are learning to use what has been called the **sympto-thermal method,** because it is far more precise in predicting the fertile period each month. Understanding and carefully charting your own monthly cycle is the key to using this method successfully. This method is equally helpful when you want to conceive a child, and even as an aid in selecting the sex of your baby through careful planning and accurate timing.

The sympto-thermal method is based on the fact that during a woman's periodic monthly cycle, certain bodily signs occur just before, during, and after the fertile phase of her cycle. The couple using this method learn to observe and interpret the signs to avoid sexual intercourse during the fertile time.

This method includes calendar calculations, daily temperature taking, cervical mucus observations, and observation of other signs that indicate the time when the woman is ovulating (releasing the ovum).

Calendar watching with daily record keeping is important, because ovulation usually takes place between twelve and sixteen days before the beginning of a woman's next menstrual flow. The problem lies in knowing for sure when the next menstrual period will begin. The number of days between periods may vary from one cycle to another, and may vary at different times of a woman's life. Irregularity in the menstrual cycle is common among very young women, and also in the years prior to menopause. Menstrual irregularities may occur when a woman experiences physical or emotional stress—or at any time.

A woman must learn just how much variation there is in the length of her own menstrual cycles. Over a period of months a pattern does emerge. With this detailed record, one can begin to predict the first day of the next menstrual bleeding, called Day 1 of the menstrual cycle. When such a record is available, she can subtract fourteen days from the next predicted date of onset of menstruation to find the day of ovulation. Then she should avoid the four days just before ovulation and the three days after it. [For details about this method, see your physician.]

—From Ed Wheat, M.D., and Gaye Wheat, *Intended for Pleasure*. Rev. ed. Old Tappan, N.J.: Revell, 1981.

VAGINAL SPERMICIDE

Spermicidal products are sometimes used by themselves as contraceptives. Available as suppositories, foam, cream, and synthetic gel, they contain chemicals which, when placed in the vagina, will kill sperm without harming vaginal tissue. Also, the foam, cream, or gel base provides a barrier over the cervix that helps prevent sperm from migrating into the uterus.

The spermicides are applied with a slim, plastic vaginal applicator, which automatically measures the proper dose. But it is important to remember that the preparation must be used before each and every act of intercourse. To allow time for all sperm to be killed, you must wait at least six hours after intercourse before douching, if you douche at all.

If you use foam, it should be deposited high up in the vagina near the cervix, not on the external vulva, and should be inserted by the wife just before lovemaking, and no more than fifteen minutes before intercourse. Shake the can or prefilled applicator twenty times before using, to make sure that the foam will have the consistency of shaving cream, and that the spermicide will be well mixed. Always keep a spare container of foam on hand.

Vaginal spermicides have been used for more than forty years and are quite safe. The foam is considered slightly more effective than the jellies or creams, and also has the advantage of being less messy. Many spermicides can now be obtained at your drugstore without a prescription, although you will need to carefully follow the labeled instructions.

Advantages of the Vaginal Spermicide Method

1. The spermicides can be bought without a prescription.
2. No fitting is necessary.
3. There is nothing to remove after intercourse.
4. No serious side effects are known.

Disadvantages of the Vaginal Spermicide Method

1. Must be used just before intercourse.
2. May occasionally cause an allergic irritation in the vagina.
3. A greater volume of discharge is present after intercourse.

Statistic: Two to twenty-nine surprise pregnancies per one hundred users per year. This user-failure-rate range indicates that this method is far less effective if used incorrectly.

—From Ed Wheat, M.D., and Gaye Wheat, *Intended for Pleasure*. Rev. ed. Old Tappan, N.J.: Revell, 1981.

STERILIZATION

Sterilization of both the male and the female is now the most frequently used method of family planning, both in the United States and around the world. There are a number of reasons for this. There is growing concern, as we have seen, about the side effects of the two most effective forms of family planning—the oral contraceptives and the IUDs. There is still considerable distaste for barrier methods. There is general disenchantment with the natural family planning techniques.

Many couples are now limiting their families to fewer children than in the past. They are tending to have only two children, fairly close together, in their mid to late twenties. This leaves them with perhaps 25 years of having to use some form of contraception, choosing among methods which are neither totally safe nor totally effective. Sterilization of either of the male or the female becomes, therefore, a reasonable and practical alternative.

Female Sterilization. Sterilization of women has been made much easier in recent years by the development of new instruments and new techniques. Prior to the last decade or so, sterilization was most often performed after delivery while the woman was still in the hospital. It was also often done immediately under the same anesthetic which was administered for the delivery of the baby. Interval sterilization (between babies) was not done very often since it meant admission to a hospital, a general anesthetic in an operating room, a major operation, a number of days in the hospital, and several weeks of recovery.

A number of techniques are used for female sterilization. The oldest of these is laparotomy, that is, the surgical opening of the abdomen. Once this has been accomplished, the fallopian tubes can be ligated in any number of ways—by tying, cutting or clipping. It makes no difference how it is done provided that a segment of each tube is blocked. The tubes can also be occluded using the vaginal route (colpotomy), and, still experimentally, via the uterine route (hysteroscopy).

With the development of the laparoscope and other more sophisticated forms of equipment, the entire scene changed radically. Procedures may now be done at any time during a woman's reproductive life. Moreover, a steadily larger percentage of these procedures are now being carried out in hospital and free-standing outpatient clinics and often under local rather than general anesthesia. Many patients come in, have their procedures done, and go home the same day or, at most, stay one night in the hospital.

Most recently, the mini-lap procedure has been developed. This method is even simpler than the laparoscopic techniques. A small incision is made near the top of the pubic hair, the tubes are grasped under direct vision and ligated. The entire procedure takes only a few minutes and the patient is able to rest for a few hours and then go home.

There has been considerable discussion

in recent years as to whether elective hysterectomy should be carried out purely for sterilization purposes, when no medical indications are present. One school of thought says it should. It cites studies which show that some women having tubal ligations later develop abnormal bleeding or cancer of the uterus. It claims that hysterectomies for sterilization would prevent both. The other school cites data showing no increased abnormal bleeding. It contends that the added risks of major surgery are not justified. The outcome of this debate awaits the results of more and better studies evaluating the situation.

While some of the new techniques are much easier, faster, and less expensive than the older ones, no method has been developed to date which is completely effective and totally safe. The failure rate in most female sterilization procedures is extremely low, being less than 1 percent. However, since the tubes are intra-abdominal organs, even the simplest procedure involves opening the abdomen. This inevitably carries with it some degree of risk, though very small, of complications such as hemorrhage and infection. The chances of repairing the tubes varies directly with the amount of the tube destroyed at the time of surgery.

—From *Everywoman's Health* by 17 Women Doctors with D. S. Thompson, M.D., consulting editor. New York: Doubleday, 1980.

Vasectomy. We have been describing the artificial methods of birth control, which can be discarded any time the couple wants to conceive. There are two surgical methods— the vasectomy for the husband and tubal ligation for the wife—which must be considered permanent and irreversible. Neither of these should be chosen, unless husband and wife are both *very* certain they will never again want to have a child.

The vasectomy involves removing a section of the tube called the vas deferens, which ordinarily carries the sperm to be stored in the seminal vesicles to await ejaculation. This prevents the sperm from leaving the scrotum, thus producing sterility. The operation is usually performed in a doctor's office, and requires only a small injection of local anesthetic to deaden a small area on the front and side of the scrotum. If a man has a desk job, he can usually return to work the next day; men whose work requires more physical exertion may need to take two or three days off. Thus, this operation is simpler, safer, and less expensive than the tubal ligation.

To prepare for the operation a man should shave the hair from the skin of the scrotum and bath before going to the doctor's office. This advance preparation helps decrease the chance for infection.

The vas deferens proceeds from the testicle upward to the seminal vesicles above and behind the prostate gland. This little tube, about the size of the lead in a pencil, can be felt by grasping the loose skin of the scrotum in the area between the testicle and the body, and rolling the tube between thumb and fingers.

The doctor begins by grasping this cordlike tube between his fingers, and then catching a loop of the tube with a sharp grasping instrument. A small incision, about one-half inch, is made in the skin of the scrotum, and a loop of the tube (the vas) is brought to the outside. This skin incision is sometimes so small that it does not even require suturing after the operation.

A section of the tube is then removed, varying from one-half inch up to two inches in length. An older man, who is absolutely certain he will never want to try to reverse the operation, may ask his doctor to take out an extra-long section of vas. The length of the section of the vas which is removed determines more than any other single factor the success rate of the operation, for the longer the section removed, the less chance there is of a new channel developing. Even the best-performed operation can fail, when a new channel develops through the scar tissue between the two cut ends. The failure rate for all vasectomies is about two per one thousand men. Therefore, you may wish to have a semen specimen checked every one or two years, if your wife desires this for her peace of mind.

The most urgent question is: *How soon after vasectomy is the risk of pregnancy no longer a problem?* This will be when there are no sperm in the fluid you ejaculate. Time is not the main factor, but the number of ejaculations is. Sterility occurs after ten or twelve ejaculations. If any sperm are then left, reexamine after five more ejaculations. It is possible to be sterile within one week, but it may take six to eight weeks, or even longer, for this to occur. Never depend on your vasectomy for conception control, until you have had at least one sperm-free specimen examined.

There is a form of microsurgery, which can possibly rejoin the cut ends of the vas, but this operation is expensive, tedious, and often fails to produce the desired results.

Probably the greatest misunderstanding about vasectomy is fear that it will adversely affect a man's sex drive. While all the possible psychological factors cannot be predicted, the vasectomy does *not* have any physical influence upon a man's sex drive or his ability to perform. The tubes which have been cut have no other function than to transport the microscopically small sperm cells from the testicles. The fluid material that is ejaculated comes from the seminal vesicles and prostate gland, so that the amount of ejaculation fluid released after the vasectomy is not visibly decreased. The physical sensations and enjoyment during orgasm will remain the same.

There is some data now to suggest that vasectomy may be a risk factor for arthritis

Summary chart of the most familiar forms of birth control*

Method	Effectiveness	Convenience
Pill	99%	Taken daily by mouth
IUD	95%	Ideal, if it stays in place
Vaginal spermicides	up to 98%	Inserted just before intercourse
Diaphragm —when combined with spermicide effectiveness estimated at 98%	up to 98%	Inserted before intercourse
Condom	up to 99%	Put on before intercourse
Symptothermal	+90%	Extensive record keeping of temperature and abstinence
Rhythm	30–40%	Requires charts and periods of abstinence
Withdrawal	low	Difficult and frustrating

* Statistics taken from information contained in the following:
  How To Teach Your Child About Sex
  Everywoman's Health
  Intended for Pleasure

and for atherosclerosis, commonly called "hardening of the arteries." We really are not sure of the long-term health effects of a vasectomy, but the question is being studied.

Advantages of Vasectomy

1. It is the simplest means of permanent sterilization for couples who definitely want no more children.
2. A couple are no longer bothered with using other methods of contraception.
3. It is relatively painless and takes only a short time to perform.

Disadvantages of Vasectomy

1. The operation required to reverse the surgery is expensive, difficult, and often unsuccessful. Permanent sterility must be expected.
2. Possibility of some adverse long-term effects to the man's health.

—From Ed Wheat, M.D., and Gaye Wheat, *Intended for Pleasure.* Rev. ed. Old Tappan, N.J.: Revell, 1981.

Abortion

ORIGIN OF THE SANCTITY OF LIFE

The sanctity of human life begins, as I see it, with the various covenants between God and man. The first of these was after Abel had been killed by Cain and Cain was cursed by God. God was very careful to point out that there was to be no blood feud and if there were, his punishment would take place sevenfold. After the flood, God spoke to Noah and told him that whoever sheds man's blood, by man shall that individual's blood be shed. Many believe that was the mandate from God for capital punishment. After that came the Ten Commandments, and one of those was, "Thou shalt not kill." It is very clear from the context that the commandment, "Thou shalt not kill," had nothing to do with capital punishment or with manslaughter, or with war, but it had to do with murder. All of these covenants, if you read them carefully, were based upon one thing: man's uniqueness in having been created in the image of God.

It was soon obvious in Judaism that life was precious to God. Christian doctrine is based upon Judaism, plus the teachings of Jesus and the apostles as recorded in the New Testament. Jesus claimed that his teachings were in harmony with the teachings of the Old Testament. He said further that the moral law was immutable and unchanging. He showed how learned men, such as the Pharisees, could misinterpret the law. In the final analysis, as a Christian, I believe in the sanctity of life because I am God's by creation and also God's by redemption through Jesus Christ and his sacrifice on the cross in my behalf.

LOGICAL AND THEOLOGICAL ARGUMENTS

The liberalization of abortion laws has brought the whole problem of the sanctity of life into focus. My reasons against abortion are logical as well as theological.

First, the logic. It is impossible for anyone to say when a developing fetus or embryo or baby becomes viable, that is, has the ability to exist on its own. The logical approach is to go back to the sperm and the egg. A sperm has twenty-three chromosomes and no matter what, even though it is alive and can fertilize an egg, it can never make another sperm. An egg also has twenty-three chromosomes and it can never make another egg. So, we have eggs that cannot reproduce and we have sperm that cannot reproduce unless

236

they get together. Once there is the union of sperm and egg, and the twenty-three chromosomes of each are brought together into one cell that has forty-six chromosomes, we have an entirely different story. That one cell with its forty-six chromosomes has all of the DNA (desoxyribonucleic acid), the whole genetic code, that will, if not interrupted, make a human being just like you, with the potential for God-consciousness. I do not know anyone among my medical confreres, no matter how pro-abortion he might be, who would kill a newborn baby the minute he was born. (He might let him starve to death. He would not kill him.) My question to my pro-abortion friend who will not kill a newborn baby is this: "Would you kill this infant a minute before he was born, or a minute before that, or a minute before that, or a minute before that?" You see what I am getting at. At what minute can one consider life to be worthless and the next minute consider that same life to be precious? So much for logic.

Although there are ample reasons for the areligious individual to be frightened about the implications of the Supreme Court's decision on abortion, I do believe that most anti-abortion individuals lean heavily upon religious convictions in coming to their pro-life position. The basis of belief may be far away in time and vague in detail but nevertheless has built into the conscience a judgment concerning right and wrong. Although I am not a theologian, I feel you should know how I have come theologically to the position I now hold. Two of the Christian doctrines which I cherish most are the sovereignty of God and the infallibility of Scripture. By sovereignty I mean that even though God has apparently given man free will, that free will is nevertheless within the sovereignty of God. How could it be otherwise if God is God? God is accountable to no one for his decisions. Even the breath that

men use to blaspheme God is a gift from God himself. As I read the Scriptures, they seem to say from cover to cover that life is precious to God. I can find no place in the Bible which clearly states when a fetus might be viable but there are some passages which are extremely significant.

In the 139th Psalm, David writing about himself says, "Yea, the darkness hideth not from thee; but the night shineth as the day: the darkness and the light are both alike to thee. For thou hast possessed my inner parts: thou hast covered me in my mother's womb. I will praise thee; for I am fearfully and wonderfully made: marvellous are thy works: and that my soul knoweth right well. My substance was not hid from thee, when I was made in secret, and curiously wrought in the lowest parts of the earth. Thine eyes did see my substance, yet being unperfect; and in thy book all my members were written, which in continuance were fashioned, when as yet there was none of them."

I am also impressed that when the Bible speaks of man in the womb, it also speaks of the whole sweep of the creation and of God's sovereignty from then until the end of time. In the 44th chapter of Isaiah we read, "Yet now hear, O Jacob my servant; and Israel, whom I have chosen: Thus saith the Lord that made thee, and formed thee from the womb, which will help thee." And then the prophet goes on to quote Jehovah in reference to the creation, the pouring out of his spirit, his blessing upon Israel, the forgiveness of their transgressions, and then he goes on to say, "Thus saith the Lord, thy redeemer, and he who formed thee from the womb, I am the Lord that maketh all things; that stretcheth forth the heavens alone; that spreadeth abroad the earth by myself." When God called Jeremiah to be a prophet, he said this: "Before I formed thee in the belly I knew thee; before thou camest forth out of the womb, I sanctified thee...."

I believe this refutes any question about a later viability of the fetus and it certainly supports the New Testament doctrine that God knew us from before the foundation of the world. Now many people will agree with these passages, but they will say, "What about the deformed baby: Don't tell me you mean the same thing about a baby who was born with some kind of a defect!" Well, God has an answer to that. You will remember that when God called Moses to serve him in Egypt, he met him at the burning bush and he said that he wanted him to go and speak to Pharaoh and after that, he would have Pharaoh let his people, Israel, go. Moses did not like that idea at all, and he protested to the Lord, "I am not eloquent, neither heretofore nor since Thou has spoken unto Thy servant, but I am slow of speech and of a slow tongue." God answered Moses, "Who hath made man's mouth or who maketh the dumb or the deaf or the seeing or the blind? Have not I, saith the Lord?" So, it seems to me that whether you like it or not, God makes what we call the perfect and the imperfect. This is a hard doctrine to accept but I think one has to agree that if God is God, if God is sovereign, then he is not able to make a mistake.

ARGUMENTS AND ANSWERS

The abortion question is argued on at least four grounds: medical, social, personal, and theological.

The three medical questions that are usually asked of someone in my position who is anti-abortion have to do with rape, suicide, and handicapped children. As horrible a bit of violence as rape is, it very seldom results in pregnancy. A study in Minneapolis of 3,500 consecutive rapes revealed not a single pregnancy. The same is true of maternal suicide. A study over seventeen years in Minneapolis revealed that suicides in reference to

pregnancy were part of generalized psychoses and in the rare instance where it did occur did so after pregnancy rather than during. In Czechoslovakia, out of 86,000 induced abortions, twenty-two were done for rape. Finally, studies on handicapped children have indicated that their frustrations are no greater than those experienced by perfectly normal children. To this latter fact I can attest. My life has been spent with children who are less than one would consider totally normal and I have considered it a privilege to be involved with extending the life of these youngsters. In the thousands of such circumstances in which I have participated, I have never had a parent ask me why I tried so hard to save the life of their defective child. Now that I am seeing children I operated upon years ago bring me their children for care, I have never had an old patient ask me why I worked so hard to save his or her life. Nor has a parent *ever* expressed to me the wish that his child had not been saved.

TECHNIQUES OF ABORTION

There are three commonly used techniques of abortion; each may have its variations. The technique that is used most commonly for early pregnancies is called the D & C, or dilation and curettage. In this technique, which is carried out between the seventh and twelfth weeks of pregnancy, the uterus is approached through the vagina. The cervix is stretched to permit the insertion of instruments. The surgeon then scrapes the wall of the uterus, cutting the baby's body to pieces and scraping the placenta from its attachments on the uterine wall. Bleeding is considerable. An alternate method to be used at the same time is called suction abortion. The principle is the same as the D & C. More than 66 percent of all abortions performed in the United States and Canada are done by this method. A powerful suction tube is inserted through the open cervix. This tears apart the body of the developing baby and his placenta, sucking them into a jar. These smaller parts of the body are recognizable as arms, legs, head, etc.

Later in pregnancy, when the D & C or suction abortion might produce too great a hemorrhage on the part of the mother, the second most common type of abortion comes into being. This is called the salt poisoning abortion, or "salting out." This method is carried out after sixteen weeks of pregnancy, when enough fluid has accumulated in the sac around the baby. A rather long needle is inserted through the mother's abdomen directly into the sac surrounding the baby and a solution of concentrated salt is injected into it. The baby breathes in and swallows the salt and is poisoned by it. There are changes in osmotic pressure; the outer layer of skin is burned off by the high concentration of the salt; brain hemorrhages are frequent. It takes about an hour to slowly kill the baby by this method. The mother usually goes into labor about a day later and delivers a dead, shriveled baby.

If abortion is decided upon too late to be accomplished by either the D & C or salting out procedures, there is left a final technique of abortion called hysterotomy. A hysterotomy is exactly the same as a cesarean section with the one difference, namely, that in a cesarean section the operation is being done to save the life of the baby whereas in the hysterotomy the operation is being done to kill the baby. These babies look very much like other babies except that they are small, weighing, for example, about two pounds at the end of a twenty-four-week pregnancy. These babies are truly alive and they are allowed to die through neglect or are deliberately killed by a variety of methods.

Hysterotomy gives the fetus the best chance, but at a very high price in morbidity and a risk of mortality for the mother fifteen times greater than that of saline infusion, the more commonly used alternative.

—From C. Everett Koop, *The Right to Live; The Right to Die.* Wheaton, Ill.: Tyndale, 1976.

INFERTILITY

UNFORTUNATELY, THERE ARE some couples in the childbearing years who have great difficulty in conceiving a baby. If having your own child is very important to you, visit a clinic or an obstetrician who can diagnose your problem and, perhaps, cure it. A blocked Fallopian tube in a wife or seminiferous tubules in a husband may be the problem. Microsurgery can correct some of these. A hormonal imbalance may prevent ovulation, or perhaps the husband's sperm count is low. It may be that the wife's time of ovulation is very short and the timing of their sexual intercourse can be adjusted by watching her basal temperature.

Fertility medication is now available to help many couples have their own children. And I use that plural term deliberately because a fairly high number of women on fertility medication do have multiple births—twins or even triplets. So be prepared!

Seek God's Will

There are times when one simply cannot have one's way. We cannot (and I think) ought not have everything we wish. Just where to draw lines, however, is hard to know. There are many families today enriched by the life of a child conceived by artificial insemination. Had they blandly as-

239

sumed their sterility to be God's will, they would have missed this joy and the opportunity to bear and train up a child—one who could better his world, as he brought happiness to them. Again, let me remind you *to seek God's will*, and then do as you feel personally guided to do.

One study showed that it was the ability of a couple to take time to work through their inability to have a child together that helped them most. In talking out their grief, understanding came to each for themselves and the other, and a mutually agreeable choice was possible. When a decision was hurried, however, and one or both failed to reveal their real feelings to the other, the decision for insemination, adoption, or no children, later resulted in misunderstandings and even divorces.

In counseling with and reading about infertile couples, we have observed the following issues to be most common.

Varying Views of Infertility

1. The one who is sterile often feels inadequate and unwomanly (or unmanly). The truth is, manliness and womanliness are qualities of being and have nothing whatever to do with bearing children.
2. Inability to conceive or bear a child is often seen as punishment for some past sin or misdeed. This is rarely true, although venereal disease (usually the result of sexual promiscuity) can cause sterility. In most cases, however, no one knows why the sterility exists, so it is not logical to assume it is God's punishment. It is simply a fact—a problem to be overcome if possible—accepted and lived with, if it is not curable.
3. Being unable to have a child may cause disapproval or some degree of rejection by others. One spouse may blame the other. Would-be grandparents may react in frustration or seem condemning. It is

important to be somewhat vulnerable if such interpersonal hurts are to be healed. The sterile person may admit his or her own sense of failure and grief with a simple explanation and statement of the heartache this has created. With honesty and dignity, a request for understanding and support may be made. In most cases, such a plea will result in just that.

—From Grace H. Ketterman, M.D., and Herbert L. Ketterman, M.D., *The Complete Book of Baby and Child Care for Christian Parents.* Old Tappan, N.J.: Revell, 1982.

Adoption

First let's discuss the possibility of adoption as an answer to your desire to have children. Adoption has made a marvelously happy family life possible for many childless people in times past. It may answer certain questions or doubts some of you experience about having children. For example, some couples who have a serious sense of responsibility about overpopulation, believe they can help other children in need of a home and parents, and fulfill their need for children at one and the same time.

The availability of children for adoption, however, has decreased dramatically in the past decade. Due to freely available contraceptives and the legalization of abortions, but mainly due to the removal of social stigma against unwed parenthood, there are few babies to be found for adoption. To be sure, there are some and, tragically, "black-marketing" (selling babies) has become all too common. But the average waiting time in this country for adopting an infant is about three and a half years.

OLDER CHILDREN

More easily found, however, are older children. Many of these were children of unwed mothers who desperately tried to care for them and couldn't. They had to give them up. Some of these babies, due to the immense stress and inexperience of their young mothers, received a less-than-ideal start in life, and thus present special needs and handicaps. Many times these can be overcome. But the first eighteen months are crucial ones in a child's habit patterning and development. We may wish that a toddler were just as easy to accept, love, and raise as an infant, but that simply is not so, especially when he has been neglected or abused. We may empathize and care about the heroic young mothers, too, but that doesn't change the facts, either. In many large cities, one out of every five births is to a teenage mother (often unmarried). Rarely have they gained the maturity and experience it takes to successfully parent a child. Every community needs to take action about such a deplorable situation.

HANDICAPPED CHILDREN

But that is not the purpose of this book. There are many adoptable children of two or three years. There are also a number who have various physical or emotional handicaps who may be adopted. Many of these require costly medical attention and certainly need parents who can manage to honestly accept and love them as they are. They demand a fine balance in empathy and concern, but firmness and consistency in expecting them to help overcome the handicap as fully as possible.

CHILDREN FROM OVERSEAS

There also are children from other countries who need parents. After the Korean War, there were many Korean children, fathered by American servicemen, who were brought to America for adoption. This has continued with full-blooded Koreans, half-American Vietnamese, as well as children from various other countries. The death rates in some impoverished countries leave a disproportionate number of orphans, and there are several adoption agencies which can help you find such children. There is, unfortunately, a great length of red tape to untangle in bringing such a child to this country.

CHILDREN OF OTHER RACES

In many communities, there is still some racial prejudice. This is tragic but true. So before you decide on adopting a child of another race, be careful that you are doing him a favor. Sound out your friends, neighbors, schools, and church. See if they will accept, love, and help you raise this special child with sincerity. If not, you may even move to a community that is more democratic. A child may be better off in poverty in his own country than to live in prosperity yet suffer the rejection of prejudice.

TELLING THE CHILD HE'S ADOPTED

If you decide to adopt a child, there are several ideas you must consider. First, how and when should you tell him he is adopted? If he is older or of another nationality, he may well know from the start that he is adopted. If not, you will want to tell him before he hears from someone else. For some reason, it is shocking to a child to learn that his parents did not give birth to him.

In a well-meant effort to save children from such a shock, adoptive parents many years ago tried very hard to keep children from finding out that they had been adopted. Fortunately, that practice gave way to a better one (in our opinion). Adoptive parents started, when the child was one year of age, to have a biological birthday celebration and an adoptive anniversary party. They would explain to this small child about their search

241

for him and how very much they loved and wanted him. This helped the child to view his adoption as a happy event. It is likely that some parents overplayed this, and perhaps a more ideal plan is to simply begin to explain as soon as the parents wish.

HAVE INFORMATION ABOUT BIOLOGICAL PARENTS

Adoptive parents need to understand their feelings about not having a child of their own. They must get over any sense of failure, inferiority, or guilt if they are to be free to be really confident parents. In the case of adoption, *it is also urgent that adoptive parents know something and feel comfortable about the child's biological parents.* Sooner or later, many adoptive children become curious about their background. They will want to know how their mothers or fathers looked, what they did for a living, what their interests were, and rarely spoken, but extremely important: *Why did they give me away?*

CURIOSITY NOT REJECTION

When adoptive parents see such interest as a rejection of themselves, they will be hurt. Often they unconsciously bristle defensively and create an unnecessary chasm between themselves and their child. This is understandable, since such questions often begin during adolescence when there will be some rebelling in any family. Please understand, however, that such curiosity is natural. You need not take it as a wish to replace you. Discuss their concerns openly, and tell them all you can about their biological parents. Tell them especially of the heroic love that prompted them to release the child to a family who could provide what they could not. Let us assure you that starting early to give as much information as is desired and

appropriate can prevent problems later. You need to find out as much as you can about the biological parents without identifying them. Any condemnation or judgment on your part—no matter how bad their behavior may have been—will be subtly but definitely conveyed to your child. And he is likely, with time, to feel that he may have inherited or acquired some of that badness. Find a way to feel loving and grateful to those people for giving you your special child. You will just as certainly convey that positive feeling to him, and he can grow in the self-esteem that is so important to healthy personality development.

SEARCH FOR "BIRTH" PARENTS

Another important issue involves the fact that it is becoming increasingly possible for adoptive children to find their "birth" parents. Courts are often willing to open records and even help trace parents once the child has reached a legal age. We believe this decision bears careful consideration. Such a search is often an outgrowth of the philosophy that one should have the right to anything he wants. We personally disagree with this idea. . . .

Perhaps a trusted intermediary could find out if the "birth" parents wish to rediscover the child. At any rate, it seems, they need a vote in the matter. If they choose to remain unknown, the adopted child and his parents will need to respect that choice and resolve their grief. It may be that this will draw them even closer to each other.

The glamorized television depiction of happily reunited families may be extremely deceptive. American people have become quite gullible and they may believe, even unconsciously, that every case will have such a happy ending. That is not true. If you were adopted and cannot find your biological parents, remember that it is not life threatening to grieve, and accept limits over which you have no power.

ADOPTIVE CHILDREN AND EMOTIONAL PROBLEMS

Still another consideration regarding the adoption of children demands a look at statistics. Significantly more adoptive children have serious emotional problems than do biological children. There are several theories but no proven facts about why this is true. It seems logical to assume that some of it comes from what we've just discussed—the unconscious rivalry of adoptive parents with the biological parents—even when the latter are unknown. Children, so prone to manipulate adults in favor of their own wishes in all circumstances, may (knowingly or not), encourage such competition and then become the victims of the outcome. Perhaps they just feel that something must have been wrong with them to make their birth parents give them away, or they may feel that they were an undue burden upon those parents. In some cases with which I have worked, all of the above factors played a role.

If you have an adopted child or plan to have one, do remember such issues. Don't worry over them, but if your child seems sad or preoccupied regarding his background, invite him to discuss it openly. Accept his feelings; comfort and reassure him. It may be useful to have a few visits with a counselor to be sure things are right, or to set them right if your own help doesn't seem to be doing the job with your adopted child.

An adoption by loving and secure parents can create a delightful family. Children need parents and a home, and if you need and want children, I hope you can find each other and live happily ever after!

—From Grace H. Ketterman, M.D., and Herbert L. Ketterman, M.D., *The Complete Book of Baby and Child Care for Christian Parents*. Old Tappan, N.J.: Revell, 1982.

Artificial Insemination

Artificial insemination has been controversial since the first known instance of it, almost 200 years ago. The latest advances and experiments in human biology are even more controversial. Do these "improved" ideas for making babies fall within the divine command to "be fruitful and multiply"? (Genesis 1:28) Are the breathtaking new lab experiments complementary to God's purposes? Could the bioscientists be going beyond what God intended, perhaps be "playing God"? Should Christians be involved? Are there dangers that man could create a race of genetically subhuman creatures? Should there be controls on experiments with human egg cells, sperm, and embryos?

Before attempting to answer these disturbing questions, we will examine the procedures now inciting so much trepidation on one hand and enthusiasm on the other. Artificial insemination (AI) is man's first successful attempt to produce children when the husband cannot fertilize his wife's ovum.

From 10 to 20 thousand AI babies are born in the U.S. each year and many times that number abroad. From one to five hundred thousand AI children are now alive in the U.S. Only a general estimate can be made because of secrecy and minimal record keeping by doctors who strive to protect the privacy of their parents.

Human AI is basically no different from the procedure long used by domestic animal breeders. Live male sperm is inseminated into the female uterus where conception occurs. About half of all U.S. dairy cows are conceived this way. Only the finest purebred bulls are used, with their sperm frozen and banked until ready for shipment to farms.

Milk yield of these scientifically bred bovines is a proven 65 percent higher than from cows conceived from uncontrolled breeding. Corresponding upgrading is noted in beef cattle, horses, and other animals.

The first authenticated successful human insemination occurred in 1790 when Dr. John Hunter so enabled the wife of a London linen merchant to have a child. The first American AI children were born in 1866. Today the procedure is routinely done by hundred of gynecologists and human fertility specialists.

The woman comes to the physician's office at her time of ovulation. He painlessly inserts part of the sperm sampling with a syringe, places a plastic pessary containing the remainder in her vagina, and instructs her to leave it there for six or eight hours. If conception results she begins her regular schedule of visits to her obstetrician. If not, she returns for another attempt. On the average about three inseminations are required for pregnancy.

1. *Husband.* AIH (artificial insemination husband) accounts for only a small percentage of AI pregnancies. The husband may have fertile sperm; yet for physical or psychological reasons, paralysis for example, he is unable to participate in normal coitus. He might be going off to war, about to have a vasectomy, or soon undergo prostate surgery which could render him sterile. Sperm can be taken by masturbation and inseminated in his wife, or frozen and kept for a later date. Or he may have a low sperm count. In this case the doctor takes several specimens which he concentrates for a successful insemination.

There are no legal questions about AIH. Only Roman Catholics and Orthodox Jews make religious objections to certain types of AIH. For most couples, it is a recommended method of having a child when the standard way is not possible.

2. *Donor.* AID (artificial insemination donor) is the same, except that a second man provides the sperm. Legal and moral complexities abound. In only 14 states is the husband recognized as the legal father of a child born from insemination of another man's seed. State courts have given contradictory opinions in cases where child custody and/or support is involved. In 1955, the Superior Court of Cook County (Chicago) ruled: "With or without the consent of the husband, 'AID' is contrary to public policy and good morals, and constitutes adultery on the part of the mother. A child so conceived is not born in wedlock and therefore is illegitimate." New York and California courts have said that where the husband gives his consent, the AID child is legitimate. Oklahoma law is considered a model by AID proponents. There a couple requesting AID simply go before a judge and sign consent papers as if they were adopting a child.

Upon learning that they cannot have children, a couple desiring AID may ask their local doctor or pastor for guidance. The counselor will refer them to a specialist who can perform the insemination. Because of feared legal problems and disapproval of the families, many couples visit out-of-town specialists surreptitiously. Then when the wife becomes pregnant, she goes to her own doctor for delivery. Unknowingly, he attests that the husband is the true father. AID practitioners admit that this is often done, but say they must respect the couple's desire for secrecy. Dr. S.J. Behrman of Royal Oak, Michigan, who has inseminated hundreds of women, says, "Laws are desperately needed to get us all—doctor, donor, patient and child—out from under a cloud."

The moral and religious questions are equally formidable.

• Is it right to parent a child whose legitimacy is in question?

- Is it proper to allow a doctor to name the husband as the father, when he is not?
- Will an AID child help or hurt a marriage?
- Is AID another form of adultery?
- Does AID fall within God-ordained procreation in marriage?
- What about the moral responsibilities of the donor and doctor?
- Would a couple be better advised to try to adopt a child?

The first question is not relevant in the 14 states where AID children are legitimate. The last question is not as pertinent as it once was. Abortions and the number of unwed mothers who now decide to keep their children have markedly reduced the chances of adoption. Unless a couple is willing to take an older child, or one that is severely handicapped, an AID baby may be their only hope.

The other questions demand thoughtful consideration. The Bible certainly forbids lying and deception. "Lying lips are an abomination to the Lord. . . . A false witness will not go unpunished" (Proverbs 12:22; 19:5). "Do not lie to one another," Paul exhorted Christians, "since you laid aside the old self with its evil practices" (Colossians 3:9).

Can a man "father" a child other than biologically? He can certainly be a father to an adopted child. Can he likewise "father" an AID child, when he has freely consented to the insemination and shared the burden and joy of developing life with his spouse? The answer to this question depends on the latitude one gives fatherhood.

The few surveys made of AID marriages indicate that such couples have a much lower divorce rate than the general population. Dr. Sheldon Payne of the Sheldon Clinic in Los Angeles has determined that only 10 percent of his patients later divorce, compared to a rate of over 50 percent in the state at large. This low rate is attributed to careful screening of applicants and the maturity of the couples when they come to the clinic.

Does AID constitute adultery? Religious leaders are greatly divided here. Catholic theologians who follow official dogma say yes. Explains Father Francis L. Filias, S.J., Chairman of the Department of Theology at Loyola University in Chicago: "It (AID) violates the marriage bond in which husband and wife have a right to each other's lifegiving powers." Father Filias believes that a husband "cannot give away his Godgiven right to his wife's procreative powers."

Conservative and Reformed Jewish rabbis and officials of the Lutheran Church of America and the United Presbyterian Church disagree with the Catholic position. A United Presbyterian committee said: "To discover in artificial insemination by an anonymous donor an act of adultery is certainly to give the word a meaning that it does not have in the New Testament" (*Time*, June 1, 1962).

Many evangelicals tend to agree. "It depends on the personal preference of the couple," says Dr. Wallace Denton, director of the Marriage Counseling Center at Purdue University and a Southern Baptist lay leader. David Mains, director of the Chapel of the Air radio ministry, does not see this as adultery. "While the husband doesn't directly participate in physical intercourse, neither does the donor. If my wife and I couldn't have children normally, I don't think I would object." "Lustful desire is the essential point of adultery," according to Dr. V. Elving Anderson, geneticist and Baptist General Conference layman. "The Old Testament Levirate marriage law provided in essence for donor insemination when it obligated a near kinsman of a deceased man to father an heir for the widow."

Of procreation in marriage, the psalmist declared, "Behold, children are a gift of the Lord; the fruit of the womb is a reward. Like arrows in the hand of a warrior, so are the children of one's youth. How blessed is the man whose quiver is full of them" (Psalms 127:3-5). Does a child conceived from another man's bequest belong in a husband's "quiver"? The Bible doesn't explicitly answer this, or many other medical-ethical dilemmas which trouble society today.

Doctors identify the typical donor as a medical student or hospital resident who is paid about $30 for his contribution. Genesis 38:9-10, which states that God was displeased when Onan spilled his seed on the ground, is sometimes applied to an AID donor. But the context indicates that God was displeased by Onan's refusal to impregnate his deceased brother's wife and "raise up seed" for him.

While many donors apparently never have second thoughts, Dr. Denton recalls one anxious Jewish student who confided that he had been asked to donate for insemination. " 'I worry,' he told me, 'about meeting children on the street and wondering if one might be mine.' "

Some doctors will not do artificial insemination. While Dr. J.J. Gold of Chicago has helped many wives become pregnant with their husbands' sperm, he declines to do AID because of the many problems involved. However, none of the doctors interviewed for this chapter think that AID is implicitly immoral.

A new cloud over AID doctors concerns insemination of single women. On March 16, 1976, The Chicago Sun-Times reported that a University of Wisconsin survey of 379 physicians administering AID turned up 47 who admitted inseminating single women, some of whom were lesbians. There are no laws to prevent this, but children born could suffer social stigma in future years. Furthermore, it is immoral for a woman to conceive a child outside of sanctioned marriage.

Where married couples are involved, AID doctors select donors to match the husband's physical appearance (hair, skin, eye color, height, build, blood type, etc.). The University of Wisconsin study also showed that some doctors even take medical histories of donor families as a precaution against inherited diseases. Other doctors do not and only 12 percent of the physicians answering the questionnaire said they did chromosome tests on donors to prevent birth of a Down's syndrome (mongoloid) child. Only 30 percent checked for traits that might result in sickle-cell anemia, diabetes, and other defects. Failure of doctors to test donors for genetic diseases borders on irresponsibility, especially when AID is sought because the husband is a carrier of a genetic affliction.

The survey revealed that over two thirds of the AID physicians were failing to keep any files on donors. Some of those who did were using the same donor for a number of pregnancies. One donor for six pregnancies was not unusual and in one instance, a single donor had "fathered" 50 children. This raises the specter of half brothers and sisters unknowingly marrying one another and possibly producing defective offspring.

Doctors with large AID practices tend to keep better records and use sperm banks. Some banks are computerized for quick screening. It is not extraordinary to use one or two-year-old sperm. Other studies have shown that sperm does not lose its potency with limited aging. A University of Arkansas researcher discovered that a group of 3000 children, conceived with thawed donor sperm, suffered only one sixth of the birth defects found in newborns as a whole.

The computerized sperm banks worry Father Filias, the Loyola University theologian quoted earlier. "The sperm bank is the scientist gone mad and the scientist gone mad plays God," he says. "This is an area that God does not intend to be in our power."

—From James C. Hefley, *Life in the Balance.* Wheaton, Ill.: Victor Books, 1980.

Test-Tube Babies

In vitro fertilization (IVF) of an egg outside the mother's body was the next logical step beyond artificial insemination.

IVF experiments date to the 1940s when Dr. John Rock of Harvard, father of the birth control pill, took eggs from female cancer patients, mixed them with sperm in a test tube, and brought them to a three-cell stage. About a decade later, Dr. Landrum Shettles of Columbia University grew fertilized embryos in a lab culture to 16 cells.

In Italy in 1959, Daniele Petrucci announced he had sustained an IVF human embryo for 29 days. He had ended the experiment because the embryo "had become deformed and enlarged, a monstrosity." Dr. Petrucci was accused of murder by some Catholic clergy and pressured by the Vatican to grow no more embryos.

Three years later English scientists removed two fertilized eggs from two English sheep, tucked them in the oviduct of a live rabbit, and shipped the hare to South Africa. There the eggs were removed and implanted in two ewes which gave birth to lambs.

More experiments followed and in 1973 International CryoBiological Services, Inc. of St. Paul, Minnesota reported "bovine ova transfer." Eggs were taken from "high quality cows," fertilized with sperm from superior bulls, and the embryos implanted in "less valuable incubator cows" for development until birth.

In 1971 Dr. Shettles removed an egg from a woman with diseased fallopian tubes, fertilized it with her husband's sperm, and implanted the embryo into the uterus of a second woman. Two days later when the recipient underwent a previously scheduled hysterectomy, the embryo was found to have multiplied into several hundred cells.

In 1974 Douglas Bevis stunned the British Medical Association by claiming the birth of three babies which he had fertilized in the lab and implanted back into their mothers' wombs. Since Bevis refused to identify the participants, doctors doubted his story.

One of the doubters was Dr. Patrick Steptoe who was then working on the process with his partner, Dr. Robert Edwards. In 1978 they presented Baby Louise Brown, "the world's first test-tube baby." The mother had previously been unable to conceive because her fallopian tubes were irreversibly blocked. A second such baby has been born in Scotland. More are on the way, with the scientists reporting a 10 percent success rate of achieving pregnancies. Enterprising businessmen are now capitalizing on the publicity. One advertises "test-tube baby plants" for sale.

Controversy in the U.S. had been building before the Steptoe-Edwards' achievement. Dr. James Watson, the U.S. Nobel Prize biologist, told a congressional subcommittee that a "test-tube" baby would be produced and warned that chaos "will break loose, politically and morally, all over the world." That didn't quite happen. Steptoe and Edwards received worldwide acclaim from their colleagues. For example, the American Fertility Society meeting in San Francisco gave Steptoe an ovation after he presented a lecture on his work.

Fears of where IVF might lead stopped U.S. grants in 1975. After the English triumph, the Ethics Advisory Board of the Department of Health, Education, and Welfare held hearings. Protestant moral theologian Paul Ramsey warned of possible physical and psychological damage to IVF children.

247

Bishop Thomas Kelly, general secretary of the National Conference of Catholic Bishops, urged that the ban be continued.

But after several scientists defended IVF, the board recommended that HEW lift the ban with certain qualifications: The public must be told of any evidence that IVF produces a higher number of abnormal fetuses. Embryos can only be formed from sperm and eggs of "lawfully married couples." Experimentation must be done only during the first 14 days after fertilization, the time required for normal implantation of an embryo in the womb.

—From James C. Hefley, *Life in the Balance.* Wheaton, Ill.: Victor Books, 1980.

Artificial Wombs

Scientists are now working on artificial wombs to aid infant "preemies" likely to die from breathing difficulties caused by hyaline membrane disease. Twenty-five thousand preemies die each year in the U.S. from this affliction. Duplicating the amniotic sac and fluid in which a baby develops in a mother's womb is enormously difficult. There are problems with exchanging gases, liquids, solids, and hormones between the fetus and its prenatal environment.

Soviet scientists are way ahead with research on an artificial womb. After the crackdown by the Vatican on his work in Italy, Dr. Petrucci gave his knowledge to the Russians. They reportedly now have about 250 human fetuses growing in artificial wombs at the Institute of Experimental Biology in Moscow. One "human" form is said to have been kept alive for six months, and a rabbit sustained all the way to birth. The Russians have declined to show even pictures of their products. Western scientists suspect gross abnormalities.

Gynecologists expect IVF to be as available in a few years for women who cannot conceive normally as AID is now for those whose husbands cannot impregnant them with potent sperm. There will likely be "host mothers" advertising their wombs for hire in classified ads. Egg banks will develop alongside sperm banks. Futurists predict that a couple or a single woman will be able to go to a "parent store" and select a frozen embryo with the genetic traits desired. Some say there will even be embryo implants in males, with babies delivered by cesarean section. Artificial wombs will be for those who want a complete laboratory product.

—From James C. Hefley, *Life in the Balance.* Wheaton, Ill.: Victor Books, 1980.

Surrogate Mothering

Television is currently bringing to every layman's attention the possibility of "surrogate mothering." This is the opposite side of artificial insemination. A husband's sperm are implanted into the womb of a volunteer mother. She provides the ovum, of course, and agrees to give the baby to the couple as soon as it is born. When a wife is sterile, she may prefer to have a child who is at least half her husband's to an adoptive child, or none at all.

—From Grace H. Ketterman, M.D., and Herbert L. Ketterman, M.D., *The Complete Book of Baby and Child Care for Christian Parents.* Old Tappan, N.J.: Revell 1982.

PREGNANCY

Conception and Pregnancy

Fertilization takes place in the shelter of a mother's oviduct, which is the tube that leads from the ovary to the womb. This is the meeting ground for the successful union of the female egg and the male sperm cell.

Egg and Sperm. The round egg of the female is the largest single human cell, yet it is smaller than a dot (·). The male spermatozoon, *sperm* for short, is similar in shape to a comma. It is much smaller than the egg, so much smaller that 2,500 would be needed to cover this comma (,)—and all the sperm needed to repopulate the world could be fitted into an aspirin tablet! The egg is so much larger because it is laden with food to sustain a growing embryo in its first few days. The relatively cumbersome egg is motionless, but the sperm is agile. With the lashing of its hair-fine tail, a sperm cell can propel itself ahead about one inch in eight minutes, which, for its size, is a much better speed than an athlete can match. At that speed, a sperm may reach the egg in an hour to an hour and a half. By way of comparison, an athlete would have to run 70 miles per hour for 250 miles to approximate the speed and distance traveled by a sperm.

Egg and sperm come together from opposite directions. At ovulation the immobile egg is thrust out of the ovary in a gently rising spring of fluids and is swept up by the fingerlike fringes (fimbria) into the oviduct opening. It must be fertilized within twenty-four hours or it will disintegrate.

During this time, the egg will be in the midportion of the oviduct. The sperm may be waiting there or may arrive after the egg. Sperm cells have a longer life span than the egg. They stay alive and vigorous for two to three days and, according to some evidence, may survive even much longer. Sperm do not have to arrive exactly at the time of ovulation. They may arrive some hours before it, or after it, providing an approximate total of three to five days in each monthly cycle during which conception can occur.

In sexual intercourse, the spermatozoa are ejected in a somewhat forceful fine stream that normally aims at the narrow entrance of the cervix and finds entry most readily at the time of ovulation, when the normally dense mucus at the entrance of the cervix is thinner and more fluid.

How Is the Egg Fertilized? Millions of sperm begin the journey, but a comparative few reach the membrane covering the tiny egg in the oviduct. Some sperm attach to the membrane and activate it, so that finally one sperm may enter and fertilize.

The one sperm that enters the egg loses its tail, which is absorbed, and its head proceeds through the food-rich substance of the egg. This one tiny sperm carries the father's threads of inheritance to the egg's center, where the mother's threads of inheritance lie. These chromosomes contain thousands of smaller units called genes that specify the inherited characteristics of the child. The male sperm carries the sex-determining chromosome. In a few hours, the threads of inheritance of the two parents become knitted together. In a few hours, the fertilized egg begins to divide and goes on to become a cluster of bubblelike cells.

The Nine Months of Pregnancy. By the end of the first week, the cell cluster comes to rest in the upper part of the uterus, where it clings and takes root. The nesting cluster finds nourishment in the lining of the uterus, prepared during the menstrual cycle. Toward the end of the second week, the cluster begins to form an embryo. Production of pituitary hormones is inhibited, so that ovulation is now suppressed, the lining of the uterus is maintained, and menstruation is postponed for the duration of the pregnancy.

During the first two months of pregnancy, the mother's breasts will enlarge and begin to be tender as a result of the change in the hormone level. Morning sickness may occur temporarily. After about the twenty-seventh day, the placenta, the so-called afterbirth, which is attached to the lining of the uterus and is linked to the embryo by the umbilical cord, starts a variety of functions necessary to maintain the pregnancy. One of these functions is the production of the hormone chorionic gonadotropin. Since chorionic gonadotropin rises to a high level for a short period of time, its detection in urine serves as a test for pregnancy. This test can be performed in a few minutes with a high degree of accuracy. (This is the simple test which you can now do yourself with a kit that may be purchased at your pharmacy.) Another function of the placenta is the production of progesterone. It takes over this important job as the ovary stops secreting progesterone. This hormone from the placenta is vitally important in maintaining the pregnant uterus and equally important in preventing the ovaries from developing another mature egg.

Quietly, a tremendous change is taking place. The whole embryo is being formed in this time from head to toe. Every feature and every vital organ is started in the first two months. The heart begins to beat on about the twenty-second day, but it is still so small that it cannot be heard easily for another four to five months. At the end of the first month, the embryo is only about the size of a small pea. By the end of the second month, it is about one inch long and so fragile that it is nearly weightless. At this time the embryo is called the fetus. It can move its arms and legs, turn the head, open and close the mouth, and swallow.

In the last three months of pregnancy the reproductive system becomes stretched to its limits in size and in capacity for supplying nourishment. The baby gains about five to six additional pounds, some of it as a padding of fat. From the maternal bloodsteam the baby also accumulates essential immunities to diseases. Its lungs mature, and its strength and coordination improve.

The uterus has now increased its capacity about five hundred times. In the ninth month a little understood chemical reaction causes profound changes in the great muscles of the uterus. This is labor. In the first stage of labor, the muscles of the uterus exert a force of about fifty pounds per square inch to push the baby out through the cervix. The narrow opening of the cervix gradually expands to let the baby's head and body pass through. Next the baby stretches the walls of the vagina and reaches the light of day.

—From Ed Wheat, M.D., and Gaye Wheat, *Intended for Pleasure.* Rev. ed. Old Tappan, N.J.: Revell, 1981.

Pregnancy in Older Women

Regarding pregnancy and birth for women over 35 and their babies, medical opinion is surprisingly un-unanimous about who or what constitutes "high risk." Beyond certain deterrents to pregnancy (diabetes, extreme obesity, breast tumor, kidney disease, epilepsy, high blood pressure, severe mental and marital problems), *age alone need not be a factor.*

The extreme conservative position, of course, says that any woman pregnant over 35 is automatically high risk to herself and baby, regardless of physical condition.

The liberal, optimistic view holds that only one in ten middle-class mothers should be considered high risk (from some already diagnosed disease or abnormality) and that 60 to 80 percent of maternal and infant complications arise during labor and delivery, regardless of age, with no prior warning. The optimistic opinion, held by enlightened physicians and most nurse-midwives, for example, emphasizes pregnancy as a normal phenomenon, not an illness, and that even high-risk patients can be adequately managed with proper diet, birth training, and attitude.

—From Carole Spearin McCauley, *Pregnancy After 35.* New York: Dutton, 1976.

CHILDBIRTH

Labor

A normal pregnancy lasts about 40 weeks from the start of the last menstrual period, although the baby may come a few weeks earlier or a few weeks later. Its impending arrival is announced by *contractions* of the uterus. These may start gently and irregularly, coming about every 15 minutes; they may not last much more than ten seconds. When they become more frequent and pronounced—at intervals of less than ten minutes and lasting half a minute—it is time to call the doctor. Labor is more rapid in the woman who has borne children before.

It happens, rarely, that labor proceeds so rapidly that there is no time to obtain expert help when it is most needed, at the moment of birth. However, babies have been known to arrive in taxis and buses and completely unexpectedly at home.

With the first baby, a woman generally feels the first mild twinges of labor some 15 or 16 hours before delivery. With later babies, it may take half this time. These are only averages, of course, and there is considerable normal variation within them. The term "labor" signifies "work"—and it is work to bring a baby into the world, although the doctor does all he can to make it easier.

Labor is usually divided into three stages.
First Stage: In this stage the cervix, or mouth of the uterus, very gradually dilates from a minute opening to about four inches, making it possible for the baby's head to pass. The contractions grow longer and more intense until each is 40 seconds or longer. The first stage lasts about nine hours, more or less.

Second Stage: The baby is born in this stage. The process may take from half an hour to two hours for a first child, 30 minutes or less for a later one. The infant passes through the cervix and the vagina. The mother bears down with her abdominal muscles to help. Usually a small incision (called an episiotomy) is made in the tissue of the vagina to make passage of the infant easier.

Third Stage: In the final stage, which lasts 10 to 15 minutes, the placenta and the rest of the afterbirth are expelled.

—From *Reader's Digest* in association with Benjamin F. Miller, M.D., *Family Health Guide and Medical Encyclopedia.* Pleasantville, N.Y.: Reader's Digest Association, 1970.

Delivery

TYPES OF DELIVERIES

Not Always Headfirst. Usually, babies are born headfirst. That makes things easier in some ways. Now and then the buttocks come first, or rarely, the feet. The problem with this is that these parts of the body are soft and the mother's openings don't always fit the later birth of the head, so it takes a bit of a beating. The doctor may have to reach in with instruments and help that head be delivered safely. Doctors use instruments only when they have to.

—From Grace H. Ketterman, M.D., and Herbert L. Ketterman, M.D., *The Complete Book of Baby and Child Care for Christian Parents.* Old Tappan, N.J.: Revell, 1982.

Breech Delivery. A birth in which the baby's buttocks (or sometimes the knees or

251

feet) are the first part of its body to come out of the mother's birth canal. About one out of twenty-five births are breech deliveries. In a normal delivery, the largest part of the baby, the head, is born first. When the head is born last, the baby runs a somewhat greater risk of being deprived of oxygen during the critical moments when breathing must start. In addition, a breech delivery is usually slower than a normal birth. It is sometimes necessary for the doctor to use instruments (such as forceps) to help the breech baby into the world. During the last week or two before the baby is due, the doctor can learn the baby's position in the womb by feeling with his hands.

Many breech deliveries proceed without trouble. However, if the baby cannot be delivered normally, the doctor may have to perform a cesarean (cesarian) section, an operation in which the child is delivered through an incision made in the mother's abdomen. If the baby is in a transverse position, that is, lying crosswise with neither its head nor its breech near the birth canal, the doctor may prefer to reach in and turn the baby to a more favorable position.

Cesarean (Cesarian) Section. Incision of the abdominal wall and the uterus to deliver a baby. This type of childbirth is practiced in cases where delivery by the birth passage presents difficulty.

Cesarean section is never performed unless it appears necessary for the well-being of mother and child. If the mother has too narrow a pelvis, if she is ill, or if there is is an abnormality of the placenta or an emergency of some kind, the attending obstetrician may recommend a cesarean delivery.

A large percentage of cesarean operations are performed on women who have already had one or more. This is because it is felt that during labor there may be a risk of rupture of the scar tissue that formed after the previous cesarean section. However, much depends on individual circumstances, and in some instances a woman who has had a cesarean delivery may have her next baby in the normal way. Quite a number of women have had three or four cesarean deliveries, and cases of women who have had even more are on record.

In the cesarean operation, the surgeon makes an incision in the abdomen. Next, inside the abdomen, he makes an incision in the wall of the uterus and lifts out the baby, the placenta, and the rest of the afterbirth. Then the uterus and abdomen are sewed up. The patient experiences some discomfort for several days, as one inevitably does after an operation. She normally leaves the hospital only a little while later than she would have if she had had a normal delivery.

—From *Reader's Digest* in association with Benjamin F. Miller, M.D., *Family Health Guide and Medical Encyclopedia.* Pleasantville, N.Y.: Reader's Digest Association, 1970.

Natural Childbirth

Natural childbirth has become quite popular in the United States over the last few years. Its popularity began after Grantley Dick-Read wrote *Childbirth Without Fear* in 1944. He wrote that labor pain could be eliminated by education in the process of labor and delivery. Despite the substantial contribution of this new theory, it soon became apparent that Dick-Read was not entirely correct, since even with the extensive knowledge about labor and delivery many women still felt pain.

The next step in the popularity of natural childbirth was the Lamaze or psychoprophylactic technique. Psychoprophylaxis is the psychological and physical preparation for childbirth. This technique originated in Russia and was brought to France by Dr.

Ferdinand Lamaze in the early 1950s. Its popularity in the United States followed the publication in 1959 of *Thank You Dr. Lamaze* by Marjorie Karmel, an American woman who became familiar with the Lamaze technique during her pregnancy in France.

The Lamaze technique combines education about labor and delivery with breathing and relaxation exercises. The exercises must be practiced in the months and weeks prior to labor. The partner has an important role as coach. Using the Lamaze breathing techniques, many women are able to go through labor needing little or no medication. Though a purist may insist that a true Lamaze birth means no medication at all, many people believe that the concept is broad enough to include the use of a small amount of medication to relieve pain.

With my observations as an obstetrician and as a woman who has experienced labor, I feel that the Lamaze technique has something to offer to every pregnant woman. I believe that the knowledge of what is happening to your body in labor and delivery can reduce your apprehension and fear and therefore reduce the pain of your labor. I also feel that the Lamaze breathing and relaxation techniques reduce, though not necessarily eliminate, the need for medication in labor.

—From *Everywoman's Health* by 17 Women Doctors with D.S. Thompson, M.D., consulting editor. New York: Doubleday, 1980.

Bonding

The doomsdayers gloomily predict an end to the family unit as such. But other souls, more cheerful, claim the American family is stronger than ever. Medical experts suggest one way to assure strengthened family ties is to better understand the biological phenomenon of bonding at birth.

Bonding, of course, is not new. Long before the days of modern scientific technology birth involved major risks. Immediately after birth the attendant placed the infant on the anxious mother's chest. No one thought twice about this first contact between mother and newborn other than to determine whether or not a healthy child had been delivered.

Today, in one of medical science's most popular areas of research, studies are proving the importance of this initial meeting between parents and child. And this years-old custom has been given a brand-new name—*bonding*.

Bonding might be thought of as a bridge—a bridge in which mother and baby continue to be kept together, only externally instead of internally. It is a bridge built in the first hour of life, and its effects can last a lifetime.

During these minutes three individuals share in the exciting transformation that has just given each of them new roles in life. In these moments of unspeakable joy, a woman becomes a mother, a man becomes a father, and as parents they embrace their new child.

These first impressions are so important and so buoyed up by the emotional high of birth itself that the time for resting can come later, say the medical experts.

Actually, bonding is but another small step in a series of giant leaps that have been taken for parenthood in recent years. In the not-too-distant past, which today's grandmothers may still remember with a shudder, medical experts were the sole voice of authority regarding childbearing.

The veil of medical mystique, if not overly popular, was certainly never questioned. For years fear of the unknown lurked in labor rooms, permeated the antiseptic atmosphere in that grimmest of all places, the delivery room, and stalked the halls of the old maternity wards. Babies were automatically whisked away to the nursery, and the drugged mother never knew until hours later whether she'd given birth to a son or a daughter.

It took nearly ten years, from 1933 to 1942, for Dr. Grantley Dick-Read to convince his colleagues that this fear created the tension that made birth a pain-filled experience.

It took World War II to trigger an experiment in a Johannesburg, South Africa, hospital that strengthened Dr. Dick-Read's theory. Right after the war, in 1948, a shortage of supplies and skilled personnel left the hospital staff with no choice but to allow mothers into the nursery to feed and care for their own babies. Fearing the worst, for germs were considered more threatening than bombs, the amazed staff found instead no increase in infection, nor did the infant mortality rate rise as the doctors grimly predicted it would.

The doomsdayers were defeated here too.

This seemingly insignificant incident in a faraway hospital reached the ears of doctors in the United States. Some of them began to agree with Dr. Dick-Read. They reasoned that if mother and baby could be kept together constantly, with no worry from germs, maybe it wasn't as necessary to put the baby in sterile isolation as they once thought. Further, if keeping mother and baby together would reduce a laboring mother's fears and tensions, then quite possibly they should reconsider Dr. Dick-Read's theory of natural childbirth.

This new thinking opened the way for Dr. Dick-Read and others to actively promote natural childbirth during the 1950s and '60s.

And then came the explosive 1970s, when the women's movement began promoting a lot of new thinking. Among other things, women started to explore new patterns in childbearing, which led to the demand for a more active and humanizing participation in the births of their children.

In response, by the mid-1970s hospitals all across the nation began converting unused labor rooms into alternative birth centers. (Quite a few hospitals use the term family birthing centers.) These cozy, homelike rooms allow the birthing couple, their relatives and friends, to stay long enough to ensure baby's safe arrival before going home (usually within twenty-four hours) with the new family member.

Birth need no longer be a solo event. Training and education during pregnancy includes both parents-to-be and family members.

That beautiful word *family* . . .

Birth need no longer be a dreaded event either. A mother-to-be tells of the eagerness she and her husband feel about finally meeting "our baby." She also quickly states, "I'm not sick. I'm pregnant." She firmly points out something else too: "I'm *giving birth*," she said, "I'm not *being delivered* of a child."

After giving birth, the next gift the parents can give their child is the lifelong *bond* of love and affection. One nurse describes the bonding ceremony this way:

"The first thing we do after the baby is born is to put that baby right on the mother's chest for a great big hug. Then the mother and father touch hands. This is called *hands on*, and the father is encouraged to touch the baby. They have a chance to meet each other, and the baby can feel the mother's presence."

These hushed and precious moments allow the new parents to cuddle, caress, and hug their newborn child *for the very first time*. The standard procedures of the weigh-in, eyedrops, and the physical exam take a momentary back seat to bonding. This is prime time. Both the parents and the baby have been waiting for this meeting for months.

During bonding communication takes place in many ways. Nature has prepared the baby splendidly for the first meeting with his parents. Studies have shown a newborn to be alert and awake, turning his head toward his parents' voices. Even before the placenta is delivered, with the infant placed face down on his mother's breast, there is immediate eye-to-eye contact. Contrary to what has been thought in the past, newborns *can* see. They can focus within a range of about eight inches, an ideal distance to clearly see the mother's face.

This touching and talking, this interfacing between three human beings, quickly establishes identity and a solid sense of belonging—all within minutes of birth. Warm hands, warm skin, warm smiles, soothing voices. Bonding forms a bridge that can never be severed and that will last a lifetime. With his safety and security thus ensured, baby can sleep, which he does, deeply, for the next three hours or so.

Modern science is discovering many benefits of bonding. Perhaps the greatest one is the strengthened relationship the baby will have with all other human beings. A curious reversal of this is true also—those present at the birth who witness the bonding become strongly attached to the baby from that moment on.

Ongoing studies reveal that bonded babies possess less anxiety as they grow and develop. Many feel that the sense of self is stronger in these children and that they tend to ask more questions and have higher IQs than children whisked away from their parents right after birth. The deep security formed from this instant and permanent attachment goes a long way toward eliminating future fears of *Who am I?* or *Who loves me?*

Thanks to today's more liberal attitudes that permit fathers to witness the birth, a bonded baby will know at once that the answer to the question of who loves him is not only his mother but his father too.

In the past, fathers haven't exactly been given star billing in the birth scene; it is only recently that his role in bonding has been understood. "We've never lost a father yet," is a tired, worn-out joke. Nurses don't quote the old line anymore. Instead they reply (a bit wearily because people keep asking the same old question), "No, the men don't faint. They're too involved." And indeed they are, often without even being aware of their involvement.

A husband who has taken required childbirth classes with his wife is trained and prepared to cope with just about everything except perhaps the depth of his own emotions. *Joy*, a word many new fathers use, is a simple yet expressive word. And that's progress, because our society had long deemed it unmanly for a male to express outwardly any deep emotion.

To *joy* can be added *wow!*—two small words that speak volumes, especially when they refer to parental bonding. One father said, "Looking back on the birth, I can still get a high on it five years later. There aren't too many times in your life you have an experience so joyous you never forget it."

New fathers have amazingly similar reactions. During the *hands on* part of the bonding ceremony one father instinctively reached for his baby's hand. He reluctantly let go even for a few seconds to allow the nurse to wrap a blanket around his new daughter. Another father could only shake his head in disbelief at the sight of tiny fingers curled tightly around his thick first finger. All he could manage to say was, "Wow!"

Obviously birth has a far more powerful impact on men than has ever been suspected. Doctors have found an almost magnetic force drawing father and newborn together at the moment of bonding. "I took one look at our new son and I left the ground—I just left the ground!" one awed father commented.

Experts agree that if more male parents experienced bonding with their newborns, the tragedies of desertion, child abuse, and incest could be lessened. At any rate today's birthing couples are sold on the strong and lasting ties formed by bonding—that unique bridge from womb to world.

—BY Carole B. Davis

"Blues" After Childbirth

In the weeks after the baby is born, it is not at all unusual for a new mother to have some days of feeling depressed and weepy. Perhaps these so-called "baby blues" are more noticed now that mothers leave the hospital so soon after the baby's birth. They're eager to get home, of course, to take charge of things. But suddenly they feel quite alone. Formerly, the "blues" hit when mother and baby were safe in the hands of experienced hospital staff.

There are many reasons why a feeling of depression is apt to occur. If you find yourself on the verge of tears for no apparent reason, you are actually being quite reasonable.

The "blues" may be no more complicated than the letdown most of us feel after any long-awaited moment has come—and gone. Christmas, for instance. Or, from your childhood, you may be able to recall the all-at-loose-ends feeling when school ended for the summer. Dreams of the vacation never quite

lived up to expectations, at first. Later on, life took shape again with the fun of going barefoot, of seemingly endless summer afternoons, of catching fireflies at dusk, of family picnics.

Physical changes within the mother's body may trigger and deepen feelings of depression, too. Since mind and body are so delicately meshed, any profound physical readjustment is bound to be reflected in our feelings and thoughts. Hormones secreted during pregnancy, for one thing, are no longer needed. Then there's the all-worn-out feeling that follows any sudden change in schedule, and the supply of available energy may not match the increased demands of the day—and night.

There are times when real problems must be faced. Sometimes it's a momentary twinge of disappointment in the sex of the baby. She's not the brown-eyed, blond boy you mentally pushed in a baby carriage during the months of pregnancy. Or the baby may not be off to a good start. He may have a physical defect which is an ever-present concern until you can take the measure of it and learn just what it will mean to you, and to the baby. If it has been necessary to leave the baby in the hospital for some time after you have come home, there is the pain of separation, even when you know the baby will be coming home eventually. The empty crib becomes a rebuke that somehow you didn't manage things better, though common sense tells you that it is not your fault. In such cases, you may find it helpful to talk with your doctor, a visiting nurse, social worker at the hospital, or counselor at your family service agency.

Sometimes new parents feel a touch of mourning or sadness. It is hard to explain the feeling of loss, after you've gained something so real, but it seems to be present for many a man and woman. Partly, it may be loss of the former husband or wife, exchanged for the mother and father you've become. Part may be loss of the freedom you felt was yours before. You haven't quite moved yet into the satisfaction of saying "Johnny already sleeps through the night" or some other conversational newsy item, but you know that the past is gone.

Probably the best way to deal with ordinary baby blues is to be reassured that many mothers have them and they are temporary. Try to keep the days as simple as possible, and ask nothing of yourself beyond the essentials. Treat yourself to all the extra help you can afford. Let thank-you notes and birth announcements wait until you have strength for them. When you can get out, indulge yourself in a trip to the beauty parlor, or whatever makes you feel fresh.

—From *Infant Care.* Washington: U.S. Department of Health, Education and Welfare, 1970.

IDEAL SPACING OF CHILDREN

THERE ARE some facts that may help you decide when to have a second or later child. It is our experience, as a family physician and former pediatrician, that about three years between children is ideal. Here are the reasons we observed and experienced that convinced us that waiting at least three years is wise:

1. By three, a child is usually toilet-trained, removing a large burden of care for the parents. Parents who have had two or more children in diapers at a time have told us this is a harrowing experience, filling life with a nightmare of changing, laundering, and feeding babies. It spoils much of the joy of both parents and children.
2. The "terrible twos" are notoriously difficult for parents and child. By three, the older child has finally accepted certain limits with much less testing, knows some of his own powers, and has moved on to a more enjoyable period of creativity.
3. Most sleep disturbances are resolved by three, and parents are able to cope with a new baby's nighttime demands without total exhaustion.
4. Language is usually fairly well developed in the three-year-old. This makes explanations easier and enables more reassurance of the older child, who will feel threatened by the new baby. A three-year-old can help the parents with a baby in many ways and may feel more important to the family instead of being a nuisance.

Perhaps you may wait longer than three years. In some ways this is easier on parents since the more independent an older child is, the easier it will be for parents to cope with a baby. An older child can also play with and enjoy a baby even more safely than a three-year-old. It is usually true, however, that when a child is much older than four at the birth of a baby, his interests are elsewhere, and he may never develop a real closeness with the younger brother or sister.

Whatever you decide (or Nature decides for you!) let us urge you to prepare your older child for the arrival of the new baby.

—From Grace H. Ketterman, M.D., and Herbert L. Ketterman, M.D., *The Complete Book of Baby and Child Care for Christian Parents.* Old Tappan, N.J.: Revell, 1982.

MENOPAUSE AND CLIMACTERIC

Premenopause

For those couples who have not "cut out" their fertility through sterilization (Dr. Paul

Marx calls this the "barnyard approach"), premenopause can be one of the most difficult times for them to live in harmony with their fertility. Only in rare cases will there be couples who may have married late and therefore seek to have children during these years.

A woman knows she has reached menopause (cessation of menses) when she has not had a menstrual period for at least a year. Before this final period, she will go through the premenopause, which is basically a period of change and is called the climacteric, or change of life. During this time, the remaining egg follicles in the ovary begin to disappear, so that the normal ovarian activity of the reproductive years unwinds gradually and becomes relatively inactive. This means that the lining of the uterus is less stimulated, which in turn causes the menstrual flow to become less regular and predictable. The controlling glands are going into low gear, as they prepare for a quieter phase of life, when the uterus is resting because its special task is completed.

This transition usually takes place between the 45th to 55th year of a woman's life. Just as each of us has a different thumbprint—unique and individual—so every woman has an individual cycle pattern. (Think of the myth of the 28-day cycle; less than 11 percent of women have 28-day cycles!) This means that her period of premenopause will also be different. Some women (probably two-thirds) won't have any difficulties at all. Others can have hot flashes, insomnia, headaches, and skin changes. Some may develop heavy bleeding episodes because of sudden surges of estrogen, followed by long intervals when the menstrual periods are absent. This time of hormonal upheaval is very similar to that which occurred at puberty.

Many women are overcome by extreme tiredness. There are three periods of life when a woman is especially tired: during puberty, during the first three months of pregnancy, and during premenopause. I recently received the following letter:

Dear Mrs. Trobisch,

. . . I have a question about the premenopause. Lately I get so tired that I can't do half as much as I used to. I felt the same way when I was a teenager. At that time, I asked my physician if there was something wrong with me. Could my present fatigue be related to what I experienced then? It would be nice if I didn't have to worry about it.

MRS. G.

Dear Mrs. G.,

The fatigue and loss of energy that you experience are definitely related to the premenopause. Try to be patient with yourself. This phase of your life won't last forever. It is important to see your physician regularly and to try to get at least an extra hour of rest each day. The premenopause is adolescence in reverse.

Think about the image used by Dr. Vollman to characterize a woman's reproductive lifetime: adolescence (a time of rising fertility), maturity (a plateau, the years of optimum fertility), the premenopause or climacteric (a time of declining fertility).

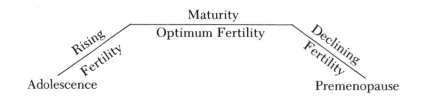

Maturity
Optimum Fertility
Rising Fertility
Declining Fertility
Adolescence
Premenopause

A woman's fertility gradually declines during the premenopause. Only about 1 in 10,000 women are able to conceive at age 47. The changes that occur during the climacteric vary from woman to woman. The mucus symptom may appear from time to time briefly and then disappear; the temperature rise may be very gradual; or there may be no temperature rise at all during the cycle. At such times, the mucus observation can be of great value. If a woman has learned to identify the sensation of true dryness, then she may consider all the truly dry and interim days, up until the first appearance of mucus, to be infertile.

INGRID TROBISCH

—From Ingrid Trobisch and Elisabeth Roetzer, *An Experience of Love.* Old Tappan, N.J.: Revell, 1981.

Menopause

Between the ages of forty-five and fifty-five the menstrual cycle ceases in most women and they can no longer have children. The ovaries not only stop releasing eggs, but produce less of the female hormones progesterone and estrogen. This hormonal reduction affects the body in various ways. Skin tone changes and wrinkles develop. The fat distribution tends to change so that a woman looks more mature and often puts on added pounds. The fat deposits tend to accumulate around the back of her neck while her hips may slim down and her breast tissue become less firm. The lining of the vagina may become thin and less able to lubricate. Some women experience hot flashes because of hormonal changes. Some women undergo emotional changes during the menopausal stage—especially if they fear growing older.

But menopause has benefits, too. It can be a highly creative and joyful period. A woman can still be attractive, especially if she keeps herself in shape. The atrophic changes in the vagina can be minimized with medical help. Women who remain sexually active continue to lubricate and respond sexually into old age.

—CECIL MURPHEY

Male Climacteric

While men do experience a climacteric which can be called menopausal, it is very different in origin and impact from that experienced by women. For men, the changes are not so related to hormonal alterations but are more psychological in nature. It is difficult for a man to face the fact that he will never reach the occupational goals that he set for himself . . . that his youth is rapidly vanishing . . . that he will soon be unattractive to the opposite sex . . . that his earlier dreams of glory and power will never be realized. Some men who have achieved less than they hoped are devastated by the realization that life is slipping away from them. This, primarily, is the male menopause. Some individuals respond to it by seeking an affair with a young girl to prove their continued virility; others work harder and longer to overcome the inevitable; others become alcoholics; others enter into dramatic periods of depression. But even when the emotional impact is extreme, it is usually motivated from the man's evaluation of his outside world. These same influences agitate a woman, but she has an additional hormonal turmoil undermining her security from within. Other things being equal, the feminine variety is more difficult to endure, particularly if it remains untreated.

—From James Dobson, *What Wives Wish Their Husbands Knew About Women.* Wheaton, Ill.: Tyndale, 1975.

GLOSSARY OF SEXUAL TERMS

Abortion: when an unborn infant is lost within the first ninety days after conception. Loss during the next ninety days is a miscarriage. Later loss is classified as stillbirth. (Most people refer to spontaneous abortion as a miscarriage.) There are two types of abortion (1) spontaneous, or natural, brought on by an accident or a defect in the fetus and (2) induced, which is brought about deliberately.

Abstinence: refraining voluntarily from sexual intercourse.

Anatomy: the structure of the body.

Amnion: a transparent membrane that lines the amniotic cavity of the fetus and secretes fluid, cushioning the fetus against outside stimuli.

Aphrodisiac: anything (usually an herb or drug) intended to stimulate or heighten sexual desire.

Areola: circular area around the nipple. In the female it is first pink and later becomes brown.

Bartholin's glands: two small glands, one on either side of the vaginal opening, which exude a lubricating fluid during sexual arousal.

Bisexuality: sexual attraction to both men and women.

Cervix: the neck of the uterus, which contains a canal opening into the vagina.

Chromosomes: microscopic parts of the reproductive cell, which contain the genes or hereditary factors.

Clitoris: the female equivalent to the penis, which is highly sensitive and erectile. Located in the vulva (female external genitals) and often called "the seat of pleasure" in intercourse.

Coitus: sexual intercourse.

Circumcision: removal of the foreskin (prepuce) of the penis.

Coitus interruptus: (sometimes called coitus abruptus) withdrawing of the penis from the vagina before climax.

Coitus reservatus: deliberately prolonging intercourse without reaching a climax (also called Karezza).

Condom: (frequently mispronounced as condrum) a rubber, skinlike sheath for the penis, a long-used method of birth control.

Contraception: the prevention of conception, usually by chemical or mechanical means.

Contraceptive pill: (or simply "the pill") taken by mouth during most of the menstrual cycle to upset the normal hormone balance and prevent conception. Probably the most reliable method of contraception yet developed.

Contractions: spasms of the uterine muscles immediately before and during labor (called labor pains) as the fetus dilates the passages through which it must go to reach the outside of the body. Contractions occur through the sending out of the afterbirth (placenta). Even later, further contractions stop the lining of the uterus from bleeding.

Copulation: sexual intercourse, coitus.

Diaphragm: a thin rubber disc used as a contraceptive.

Douche: a method of cleaning the vagina with a stream of water, usually with added chemicals.

Ejaculation: the discharge of semen during sexual excitement (the male orgasm).

Embryo: the first stage of the human being, which begins to develop immediately after conception (fertilization of an ovum by a spermatozoon). After approximately eight weeks, it is called the *fetus.*

Epididymis: tube carrying sperm from testicles; used to store spermatozoa.

Erection: fullness and firmness of the genitals

from congestion due to sexual excitement.

Erogenous zones: parts of the body where contact arouses sexual stimulation.

Estrogen: a female sex hormone.

Fallopian tubes: tubes carrying the egg (ovum) from ovary to uterus. This is where inpregnation takes place.

Fertile: fruitful.

Fertilize: to impregnate.

Fetus: the unborn child as it develops in the uterus before birth. It is usually termed *embryo* until about the eighth to twelveth week. From the third month until birth it is called *fetus*.

Frigidity: failure of a woman to respond to sexual arousal.

Genes: part of chromosomes which transmit hereditary traits and characteristics.

Glans: head of the penis (or glans penis).

Gonads: the sex glands. In men, the testicles or testes; in women, the ovaries.

Hormones: chemical substances manufactured by the endocrine glands.

Hymen: a fold of mucus membrane partially blocking entrance to vaginal canal.

Impotence: in the male, failure to achieve erection or to carry out sexual intercourse.

Impregnation: (*See* Fertilize) act of making someone pregnant.

Infertility: the inability to conceive or beget children. Research indicates that the cause in childless couples is 40 percent because of the husband's infertility, 40 percent because of the wife's, and approximately 20 percent from unknown causes.

Insemination: introduction of semen into uterus. (Artificial insemination: introduction of semen without intercourse.)

Intercourse: sexual union of male and female when the penis penetrates the vagina.

IUD: intrauterine device inserted into the uterus (a ring, bow, loop, spiral made of plastic, metal, nylon) to prevent conception.

Karezza: a system of contraception in which the male greatly prolongs intercourse without ejaculation (also called coitus reservatus).

Labia: the lips which enclose the female genitals. There are two pairs, an outer or major (labia majora) covered with pubic hair and inner (or labia minora).

Lochia: fluid discharged from the vagina in the days after giving birth.

Lactation: nursing period following pregnancy.

Membrane: a thin lining in various parts of the body.

Menarche: the onset of menstruation in adolescent girls.

Menopause: end of reproductive cycle of the female when menstruation ceases.

Menses: menstruation, the monthly discharge of blood and endometrium from the uterus between puberty and menopause, except during pregnancy.

Mucus: the secretion of the mucus membrane.

Orgasm: climax during sexual intercourse.

Ovary: female sex gland, which produces eggs (ova) and sex hormones. This pair of glands lies on either side of the uterus.

Ovulation: discharge of the ripe egg from ovary to fallopian tube. This occurs about midway between two menstrual periods.

Ovum: the female egg, or female germ cell.

Penis: the male sex organ.

Prenatal: before birth.

Premature ejaculation: ejaculation very early in sexual intercourse, sometimes before the insertion of the penis.

Prepuce: foreskin of the penis; the part removed in circumcision.

Placenta: (the afterbirth) organ consisting of maternal and fetal tissues to promote

261

exchanges of nutrients and waste matters between mother and fetus.

Prostate gland: part of the male sex system, which lies just below the urinary bladder, surrounding the urethra, and secretes fluid that helps propel semen during ejaculation.

Puberty: period when sex awakens in young people.

Reproduction: begetting of children.

Rhesus factor (RH factor) a blood factor found in rhesus monkeys and a majority of human beings. Certain combinations of its presence and absence in parents can lead to injury of fetus.

Rhythm method: a method of contraception based on the menstrual cycle either by calculating a safe period or by assessing the time of ovulation by temperature measurements.

Scrotum: pouch or bag of skin containing the testicles.

Semen: fluid discharged from the prostate gland by male at orgasm, which carries the sperm.

Seminal duct: the canal that conveys semen from the epididymis to the urethra.

Seminal vesicle: storage place for sperm, attached to the back of the bladder and opening into the seminal duct.

Smegma: cheesylike material with a foul odor that accumulates under prepuce of uncircumcised male unless carefully cleaned.

Spermatozoa: sperm, the male seed.

Sterilization: any process that either (1) removes the organs of reproduction, or (2) makes them incapable of functioning effectively (unable to reproduce or to have children).

Stillbirth: the delivery after the twentieth week of pregnancy of a fetus that shows no sign of life.

Testicle: the male sex gland, also called testis (pl. testes), which produces the male sex hormone, testosterone.

Testosterone: a male hormone.

Umbilical cord: cord attaching fetus by its navel to the placenta (afterbirth) and containing blood vessels and gelatinlike substance.

Urethra: canal from the bladder. In female only for urination. In male, seminal fluid as well as urine pass through.

Uterus: (the womb) a hollow organ which contains and nourishes the embryo before birth.

Vagina: female canal leading to uterus from vulva, which receives the penis during intercourse.

Vas deferens: duct carrying sperm from testicles to seminal vesicles.

Vulva: collective name for external female genitals.

—CECIL MURPHEY

FOR FURTHER READING

Chesser, Eustace. *Love Without Fear.* New York: New American Library, 1947.

Dennis, Muriel, ed. *Chosen Children.* Westchester, Ill.: Good News, 1978.

Everywoman's Health by 17 Women Doctors (D. S. Thompson, M.D., consulting editor). New York: Doubleday, 1980.

Family Health Guide and Medical Encyclopedia (in association with Benjamin F. Miller, M.D.). Pleasantville, N.Y.: Reader's Digest Assn., 1970.

Fix, Janet, with Zola Levitt. *For Singles Only.* Old Tappan, N.J.: Revell, 1978.

Fried, Barbara. *The Middle-Age Crisis.* Rev. ed. New York: Harper & Row, 1976.

Hambrick-Stowe, Elizabeth A. *Expecting.* Valley Forge, Pa.: Judson, 1979.

Hatch, Claudia, ed. *What You Should Know About Sex and Sexuality.* New York: Scholastic, 1969.

Hefley, James C. *Life in the Balance.* Wheaton, Ill.: Victor Books, 1980.

Johnson, Eric W. *Love and Sex in Plain Language.* Rev. ed. Philadelphia: J. B. Lippincott, 1977.

Kaplan, Helen Singer. *Making Sense of Sex.* New York: Simon & Schuster, 1979.

Ketterman, Grace H., M.D. *How to Teach Your Child About Sex.* Old Tappan, N.J.: Revell, 1981.

Ketterman, Grace H., M.D., and Herbert L. Ketterman, M.D. *The Complete Book of Baby and Child Care for Christian Parents.* Old Tappan, N.J.: Revell, 1982.

Kirk, Jerry. *The Homosexual Crisis in the Mainline Churches.* Nashville: Nelson, 1978.

Koop, C. Everett. *The Right to Live: The Right to Die.* Wheaton, Ill.: Tyndale, 1976.

LaHaye, Tim and Beverly. *The Act of Marriage.* Grand Rapids: Zondervan, 1976.

Lee, Robert, and Marjorie Casebier. *The Spouse Gap.* Nashville: Abingdon, 1971.

Leman, Dr. Kevin. *Sex Begins in the Kitchen.* Ventura, Calif.: Regal, 1981.

Lieberman, E. James, M.D., and Ellen Peck. *Sex and Birth Control: A Guide for the Young.* Rev. ed. New York: Harper & Row, 1981.

Lovelace, Richard F. *Homosexuality and the Church.* Old Tappan, N.J.: Revell, 1978.

Martin, Ralph. *Husbands, Wives, Parents, Children.* Ann Arbor: Servant, 1978.

McCauley, Carole Spearin. *Pregnancy After 35.* New York: Dutton, 1976.

Miles, Herbert J. *Sexual Happiness in Marriage.* Grand Rapids: Zondervan, 1982.

Morris, Paul D. *Shadow of Sodom.* Wheaton, Ill.: Tyndale, 1978.

Ostheimer, Nancy C., and John M. Ostheimer, eds. *Life or Death—Who Controls?* New York: Springer, 1976.

Penner, Clifford and Joyce. *The Gift of Sex.* Waco, Tex.: Word Books, 1981.

Rainer, Jerome and Julia. *Sexual Pleasure in Marriage.* New York: Simon & Schuster, 1969.

Roetzer, Josef, M.D. *Family Planning the Natural Way.* Old Tappan, N.J.: Revell, 1981.

Sex Information and Education Council. *Sexuality and Man.* New York: Charles Scribner's Sons, 1970.

Schaeffer, Francis A., and C. Everett Koop, M.D. *Whatever Happened to the Human Race?* Old Tappan, N.J.: Revell, 1979.

Shoemaker, Donald P. *Abortion, the Bible and the Christian.* Grand Rapids: Baker Book, 1977.

Small, Dwight Hervey. *Design for Christian Marriage.* Old Tappan, N.J.: Revell, 1959.

Small, Dwight Hervey. *Your Marriage Is God's Affair.* Old Tappan, N.J.: Revell, 1979.

Todd, Linda. *Labor and Birth.* Minneapolis: International Childbirth Education Association, 1981.

Trobisch, Ingrid, and Elisabeth Roetzer. *An Experience of Love.* Old Tappan, N.J.: Revell, 1981.

Wheat, Ed., M.D., and Gaye Wheat. *Intended for Pleasure.* Rev. ed. Old Tappan, N.J.: Revell, 1981.

Wiese, Bennard R., and Urban G. Steinmetz. *Everything You Need to Know to Stay Married and Like It.* Grand Rapids: Zondervan, 1972.

Wrage, Karl. *Man and Woman.* Philadelphia: Fortress, 1969.

5

Family Life and Parenting

FATHERHOOD

A CHRISTIAN FATHER is a man who has heard the call to reflect God to his family and is responding to that call. He is actively co-operating with the Holy Spirit to lead and form others into the image and likeness of the Creator. He is a man who is willing to act in God's name, trusting that Jesus can accomplish his work through him. He is a father who has accepted his role as spiritual leader of his family, a man who knows his weakness and trusts God to be God.

The ideal for Christian fatherhood is contained in Jesus' description of the Fatherhood of God. Jesus taught us four important things about God: He is a Father; he is the source of all authority; he uses his power to gather persons into unity; and that three persons make up the Godhead. In short, the nature of God is *family.* "In my Father's house there are many dwelling places; otherwise, how could I have told you that I was going to prepare a place for you" (John 14:2). Doubting his promises, as we often do, the disciples questioned him further, " 'Lord,' said Thomas, 'we do not know where you are going. How can we know the way?' Jesus told him: 'I am the way, and the truth and the life; no one comes to the Father but through me' " (John 14:5-6).

Jesus is telling us that he and he alone will lead us into knowledge of God and relationship with him. What's more, heaven is like a home and God is the Father of a family. The call to fatherhood necessitates a response to Jesus. He is the way to the Father. We have one father who is God and one teacher who is Jesus (Matthews 23:9-10). In addition to revealing God as family, Jesus shows us that we can begin to share in the fullness of God's life right now through the ministry of the Holy Spirit. His promise is unconditional: "I came that they may have life and have it to the full" (John 10:10).

A Christian father believes this good news and lives it. He is called by Jesus to be a reflection, imperfect as he may be, of the Fatherhood of God.

Another way of putting it is to say that a Christian father is a man in full relationship with the Trinity. He is an obedient son of God the Father, he is a brother to Jesus, listening to the Word and following the Way. This loving contact with the Father and the Son makes a man *teachable.* He is thus able to be led by the Spirit, who teaches him the wisdom of God.

As he grows in his identity as a son of God and brother of Jesus, the Christian father is prepared for his principal mission as spiritual leader of his home. He and his wife "enspirit" the family. Their roles in this mission are distinct yet complementary. The harmony which flows from their corporate life of grace prepares the home for change. The family is drawn deeper and deeper into the power and life of the Trinity. There is no end to this process. There is no perfection in this life—only when we reach our Father's house. Although we're always "on the way," God wants our journey to be happy and fruitful. He has provided everything we need to bring that about.

The unique gift which the Father provides for us is the grace to be priest, prophet, and kingly representative for our families. We are called to be *priest* for our home: one who offers sacrifice, labors to provide protection, and intercedes with God for our wife and children. As priest, we speak to God for our family and minister his blessings to those in our care. We provide material, spiritual, and emotional protection for them. We are called to be a *prophet:* one who speaks the word of God to others. A prophet gives testimony for God by his words and the witness of his life. He is a holy man. We also have a *kingly* role. As a son of royal blood, we are called to manage the affairs of our Father wisely. We are chief stewards of the spiritual and human resources placed in our care. As one under authority, we will be held accountable for our use of the king's gifts. "You, however, are a chosen race, a royal priesthood, a holy nation, a people he claims for his own to proclaim the glorious works of the one who called you from darkness into his marvelous light" (1 Peter 2:9).

We also share in Jesus' role of shepherd to his flock. He is the Chief Shepherd of the flock of man and the Lord of each household of the flock. But we are his assistants in this role, God's gift to our families. A father is not the Lord or the Shepherd, but rather a man who is commissioned by God to work with the Spirit in forming himself and others into images of the Almighty, reflections of his love.

The father in a Christian family also plays a critical role in God's wider plan of salvation. This plan envisions the renewal and restoration of all families and all mankind. A father's part in this overall effort begins as he takes his rightful place within the smallest unit of God's plan, the married couple. He and his wife form a pastoral team which is empowered to procreate and build the family. The family is conceived to be an earthly reflection of the unity and love which each person can look forward to in the eternal kingdom of God.

The family is a training ground, a school for shared life. The Christian home should be the place where we learn how to give of ourselves and love unconditionally. As this happens, the Christian family becomes a beacon for a dark world. It offers hope and a model for unity and peace. In fact, the family is the basic building block for the kingdom of God. It is our source of formation and strength. God's life springs forth from it. The Church has known this from the beginning and has always resisted anything which would undermine the Christian home, the basic cell of the Church.

The family is also a necessary unit in the Lord's call to evangelize the world. From healthy loving families will come the men and women who are equipped with hearts of service and a zeal for God's life. The witness of a shared life, centered on love, will draw others to Jesus and his good news. It is a vital expression of the Gospel in action.

The Christian father has a central role in this worldwide plan of evangelism. A changed father means a changed family. Changed families mean a changed, renewed Church. A renewed Church can speak with authority to a society in desperate need of truth and love. A rediscovery of the gift of Christian fatherhood will give hope to a world which is searching for truth. As the family goes, so goes the Church and the world.

—From Robert L. Latesta, *Fathers: A Fresh Start for the Christian Family*. Ann Arbor: Servant, 1980.

MOTHERHOOD

MOTHERS HAVE NEEDS

We usually think of a mother as meeting the needs of the other persons in the family because that is what she is doing most of the time. But mothers have needs which must be met if they are to continue to be effective in their role. These needs grow out of the fact that she plays many roles in the family: woman, wife, mother.

First, she is a woman. Her sense of personhood comes from this. As a woman her most basic need is for self-esteem. She needs to feel that she has worth as a person, that she is valuable, that she is special. The love, support, and appreciation she receives from her husband and children are important in relation to how she sees herself. The fatigued mother cried, "I've cooked so many meals and washed so many clothes that I wouldn't be a bit surprised to look into the mirror some morning and discover I had turned into an appliance." This is just another way of saying that she doesn't feel like a person but like a function.

All the persons in the family need an opportunity to grow and develop as persons, even mothers. The picture of a mother without interests is a picture of an uninteresting mother. The mother who does not have the opportunity to develop and grow as a person will not be able to do the best job of either nurturing her marriage or guiding the growth and development of her children.

Second, she is a wife. She became a wife

before she became a mother and those first needs do not stop once children are born and more of her time is devoted to their care. After the birth of children in some marriages the husband turns to his career to meet his needs and the wife tries to meet her needs in her children. This is not good for the children, for they deserve two parents and not one, and it will spell disaster to the marriage.

Third, she is a mother. This is not her whole identity. It is simply the name given one of her functions. In this role she has many needs. Often she has real doubts about her effectiveness. A friend whom I know to be an excellent mother told me that one of her constant frustrations as a mother had been that almost every time she picked up a magazine there would be an article in it written by some expert about what to do to be a good parent. She said the articles invariably covered a period in life which her children had already experienced. When she read the article and realized all the things she had done wrong, according to the expert, she would become depressed and feel like a failure. "One day," she said, "I made a decision about all those articles. I decided that since I was doing the very best I could and my children knew I loved them, that would just have to do."

MOTHERS MEET NEEDS

The needs which are met in a family by the mother are as diverse as life itself. Sometimes the people whose needs she meets are the least aware of all she does. An eager young mother with children in elementary school read an article which impressed upon her how important it was to spend time with her children when they came home from school. This seemed right and wise to her so to make that time she pushed herself during the day to get all the cleaning, cooking, shopping, and other responsibilities out of the way. Then she could devote herself to the children when they arrived home.

Everything went along well and she felt good about the sacrifice she was making to be available to her children. The good feeling left her completely one day when her son brought home a paper which he had written concerning what mothers do. In the paper he had said that his mother didn't do anything but watch television with him, play games, and have parties. Then and there she decided that when the children came home they would have opportunity to see her cleaning the house, cooking supper, and a few of the other things which mothers did!

A mother meets the needs of her children by modeling her role as woman and mother. To her son she begins as the most important woman in his life. A son will resist to the death any effort his mother makes to interest him in some young lady she likes and would probably resent any suggestion as to the kind of person he ought to marry. But his mother is the one by whom he judges the girl he will marry. While a son has been known to pick a wife who is the opposite of his mother, most of the time he looks for those qualities he has come to appreciate in her.

The mother plays a similarly important role with her daughter. From her mother she receives an understanding not only of what it means to be a person but to be a woman.

. . . .

Children need big ideas like love translated into terms they can understand. One of the simplest and most meaningful ways a mother does this is by being sensitive to the differences in the personalities and needs of her children. She shops with them for curtains for their room and listens as they express preferences. A mother notices the length young men are wearing their jeans and the kind of socks girls are wearing in junior high. She spends time alone with each of her children, but she is also sensitive to their need for privacy and quiet times. Every day the children are learning about a very special kind of love woven into the fabric of life by their mother. Mothers are specialists at meeting the needs of children.

Mothers play a special role in the religious development of their children. All the foundations for adult faith are laid in the simple experiences of childhood, most of which take place in the home. As the child becomes aware of himself he can be told of God's love for him which does not change. As the child becomes aware of the world with all its beauty and mystery he can learn that it is good because God made it. All the relationships which involve trust, love, and even forgiveness can give meaning to ideas which will someday equip the child for a vital faith. The words which he hears in church about God's love will only have meaning if he has had experiences which actualize it in the home.

There are certain special contributions that mothers make which enrich the larger viewpoint of the children. Mothers seem to have an elemental sense of judgment and compassion, an unusual capacity for selflessness. They can project and identify with others. Their faith in God may not be more profound than that of others but it seems more intimate. These qualities complement those of the husband and enrich the family.

—From Kenneth Chafin, *Is There a Family in the House?* copyright © 1978, pp. 101–06; used by permission of Word Books, Publisher, Waco, Texas 76796.

COMMUNICATION

Affirmation

There are several ways a father extends approval to his children. Call the first of them simply *"verbal affirmation."* Affirming others is the act of expressing how valuable we think they are as persons. We *affirm* people for what they are; we *appreciate* people for what they do. Both are quite necessary.

Affirmation seems to flow quite freely from mothers to children. Usually a child is secure about his mother's opinion of him. Unless she deliberately betrays his confidence in her, a child finds it easy to assume that his mother's love and acceptance is automatic. After all, he subconsciously reasons, she carried me within her, she bore me, and now she takes care of me. She must have positive thoughts about my value.

Not so with his father, the child thinks. Who really knows how dad feels? As far as a child can see, dad isn't really tied into the family situation—at least to the extent that mother is. Dad comes and goes, has responsibilities in other parts of the big world. How does dad feel about us anyway, the child wonders. Obviously, dad's approval will have to be earned. It cannot be assumed. His attention must be caught.

Fathers respond to their children and affirm them in all kinds of ways. Private signals such as winks, gestures, taps on the shoulders, lots of hugs and kisses, here and there a special word: they are all part of the special vocabulary of affirmation. Children learn the language quickly; they know how dad feels; it's obvious to them when he is pleased and when he's not. Once they have this system of communication figured out and know that dad is responsive to their performance as persons, they will do anything to receive a continuing flow of that affirmation.

Imagine then a child's frustration when he discovers that his father doesn't speak the language of affirmation or that the language is not consistent or discernible. It's even worse when a father's language is not marked with affirmation but rather with ridicule, sarcasm, and disgust. Disaster!

As fathers we must know not only how to affirm our children but *when* and for what purposes. Some fathers, for example, express affirmation only in response to things that are personally important to them: athletic achievements are one obvious kind of performance which might illustrate this. It is not unusual for both sons and daughters to learn that the only worthwhile things they can do as children, in terms of their father's approval, are related to winning on the sports field. The records are filled with the mistakes of fathers who made it very plain that their sons could find satisfying acceptance only as athletes. How many times has a boy donned a practice uniform and gone out on the field, but, unable to succeed, has sensed that he's not only failed to make the team but has failed his father. If his father is insensitive enough, it can be a disaster moment in their relationship, because the boy will either sink into low self-esteem or he will finally cease to care what his father thinks. The spectrum of approval has been too narrow. Sports is not enough.

Consider the son or daughter who should be affirmed for things he is genuinely capable of doing, even if they don't match a father's personal interest or expectations. The boy who is artistically inclined rather than able to throw a forty-yard pass; the girl who shows excellence in a school research laboratory, rather than being high scorer on the field hockey team. It is possible that if each senses that a father's approval is to be found only in some other area of interest, they will drop that for which they are best suited and pursue the thing that will gain a father's acceptance. Tragedy!

Herein lies a call to *sensitivity*. What does my child want to do? What does he do best? And where does he need approval? What qualities of character and personality do I see that need to be highlighted and praised so that my children can know that I consider them important? These questions need thoughtful response. . . .

It must always be remembered, however, that affirmation and appreciation must be sincere and genuine. Approval of a child's *personhood* should be automatic because they are son or daughter to a father. But approval of a child's *achievements* must be honestly earned so that the resulting endorsement will not seem phony or hypocritical. The need is for a sensitive balance.

—From Gordon MacDonald, *The Effective Father.* Wheaton, Ill.: Tyndale, 1977.

Availability

A father needs to be available and accessible to his children. Children require time with us. I have a friend who is one of the outstanding educator/counselors in the country. We were discussing the demands of our respective jobs one day and the effect this was having on our relationship with our children. He laughingly remarked to me, "Yes, Ken, I know about that. Recently I looked down at the schedule of people my secretary had made appointments for me to see and discovered my youngest son's name. When he came in I half expected him to come up with some big problem he was having which he might be reluctant to discuss at home with his mother. That wasn't it at all. He had absolutely no agenda. He just wanted to visit with me."

As I replayed the conversation with my friend, I realized that his son was really no different than any other child in his desire to be with his dad. Those of us who are fathers need to face realistically the fact that it is not possible to spend as much time with our children as we might like. But if we decide to use well the time we do have with our children, it can have a tremendous impact upon their lives. . . .

One reason we need nonstructured time with our children is that it creates a better climate for listening and talking. It would be ideal if our children would come in and ask all their difficult questions immediately after we have attended a seminar on "hard questions your children are about to ask." But it doesn't happen that way! Those moments of interest and openness and seriousness with children seem always to come in some unexpected context. And after they're over you say to yourself, "I wouldn't have missed the opportunity of that conversation for anything." Then you realize that this kind of communication takes place only when you're together.

—From Kenneth Chafin, *Is There a Family in the House?* copyright © 1978, pp. 95, 96; used by permission of Word Books, Publisher, Waco, Texas 76796.

Honesty

Honesty or truthfulness rates high on the list of personal qualities that parents want to see expressed in their own children. This characteristic is more likely to come about when two factors are present: a model of honesty and truthfulness on the part of parents, and a child who is secure in himself and in his place within the family. The Word of God has much to say concerning honesty, falsehood, and being truthful. Look at just a few of the many passages found in the Scriptures.

"He who speaks truth tells what is right, but a false witness, deceit" (Proverbs 12:17, NASB).

"Lying lips are an abomination to the Lord, but those who deal faithfully are His delight" (Proverbs 12:22, NASB).

"Righteous lips are the delight of kings, and he who speaks right is loved" (Proverbs 16:13, NASB).

"A false witness will not go unpunished, and he who tells lies will not escape" (Proverbs 19:5, NASB).

"Like a madman who throws firebrands, arrows, and death, so is the man who deceives his neighbor, and says, 'Was I not joking?'" (Proverbs 26:18-19, NASB).

"In the end, people appreciate frankness more than flattery" (Proverbs 28:33, LB).

"Do not lie to one another, since you laid aside the old self with its evil practices" (Colossians 3:9, NASB). Any kind of dishonesty, lying or deception is to be dropped from the Christian pattern of living, for all of these behaviors are associated with a non-Christian pattern of behavior.

Ephesians 4:25 and 4:15 are two other strong passages of Scripture on this subject. "Therefore, laying aside falsehood, speak truth, each one of you, with his neighbor, for we are members of one another" (NASB). "But speaking the truth in love. . . ." (NASB) This passage carries with it the dimension of tactfulness or sensitivity. One commentator suggested that a thought presented here is that when the truth is spoken, it should cement together a relationship better than it was before.

The truth should not damage or hurt others. Often under the guise of truth we hurt others. Some humiliate others and then give the excuse that what they said was true. It may be true, but should it have been said in that way? A mother notices that her son's room is messy and she goes outside where he is playing with his friends and says, "Billy! Come in here right now! Your room is a mess and you know that you cannot play until you do your job!" If a child hears this again and again, it can begin to have an effect upon him in a negative way, especially if his friends hear it. Notice the difference in this approach, which can accomplish the same goal but actually help the child by providing a model of good communication: "Billy, you forgot to clean your room. Our rule is that you need to do it before you can play. Please come in and do it now and then you can go back to playing. Thank you." Statements such as "You're too young," "You won't be able to do that," "You can't do that as well as I can," and "You look terrible the way you are dressed" may all be true, but do they need to be said in that way?

SUBTLE LIES

One of the most subtle ways of lying can be found in the questions we ask of one another. You may wonder, "How can a question be a form of lying?" Often a question is not really an honest question. We have a devious motive behind the question. We may be asking the person to build us up or we may want to hear only a positive response and not the actual truth. For example, if a wife asks her husband how he likes her new dress, does he have the freedom to give his honest (and tactful) opinion? Or is his wife really saying, "Tell me I look nice, tell me I look good, and tell me you like the dress." That is a dishonest question. He should have the freedom to express what he honestly feels and thinks. The principle here is that *all questions should be responded to at face value.* No attempt should be made to read anything into the question and try to figure out the hidden meaning.

How might we do this with our children? Did you ever ask your children how they liked the new meal or the vegetables? If you got upset when they said they didn't like it, what were you really expecting? Probably a positive response. Why get upset when they respond honestly to your question? If you ask your child, "Don't you want to go?" and he says, "no," you can still be firm and say he must go, without exploding over the fact that he responded honestly to your question.

How does your child feel when you are

going to go to a friend's for dinner and you program him ahead of time by saying, "Now be sure you tell them how good dinner was and how much you liked the meal"? How do you know that he will like it, or that you will like it for that matter? They might serve all of his unfavorite foods. What else could you suggest that he say in order to show courtesy and politeness? You can tell people that you appreciate coming to dinner or appreciate the meal, or select one item that we really did like and comment on that. This may seem like a minor point, but it is important. Your child can learn to discriminate and select an item that he does respond favorably to instead of griping about everything or lying just to please others.

It is amazing how many family members have continued certain behaviors or prepared certain dishes because they thought others really enjoyed them. Years later they discovered that the other person really didn't enjoy them but had continued to give the impression that he did. A wife one time shared what she did with her husband when she cooked him a new recipe. She asked how he liked it and when he said that he did, she then asked, "Well, do you like it enough for me to serve it a second time?" The answer she received at that moment gave her the full extent of his feelings. You need to learn to express your likes and dislikes in a positive manner so your children have a healthy pattern and model.

As parents you are concerned about truthfulness in your children. What you might see as lying on the part of another person (child or adult!) may be a matter of a difference of opinion or another point of view. Truth sometimes lies in the eye of the beholder. You want a child to be accurate. But what is accuracy? What is it to you and what is it for your child? A child will see and evaluate depending on his abilities, and he could miss some of the details. A child's feelings about

another person may influence his version of the truth. If he likes or fears another, this will have an effect. The power that parents hold over a child may force him to share partial truths, but it does not always bring out the full truth. Consider what a child thinks about when faced with telling the truth. "What will happen if I don't tell the truth? What will happen if I am found out? What will happen if I do tell the truth?" When a child tells the truth remember that he is telling it the way he saw or experienced it and not necessarily the way that you want him to tell it.

—From H. Norman Wright, *The Family That Listens.* Wheaton, Ill.: Victor Books, 1978.

Humanness

A father needs to be willing to be finite and mortal in his children's eyes. The first emotions a child feels toward a father are that he knows everything and can do anything he wants. Somehow the tiny child does not associate finiteness with either of his parents, but especially is this true of his attitude toward his father.

I remember how hard on me it was to discover that my father was like me. Our family lived on a small farm and was very poor. We had a garden for vegetables, chickens for eggs and meat, and a cow for milk. The most valuable things we owned were the two horses with which my father worked the place. One of the horses became ill and died suddenly. There was no way for me to know at such a young age what a blow this was to my father. What I remember was coming up behind him in the barn and discovering that he was crying. That's the first time I remember being aware that fathers could be hurt and not know what to do. It made me sad and I never talked to anyone about it.

Now I've come to discover how very important it is for a father to be willing to admit that he is neither omniscient nor omnipotent. This will not lessen the love or respect your children will have for you. In many cases it makes it possible for fathers and their children to be closer. The image which needs to be shattered is that fathers are the ones who know all the answers, can take charge in all situations, are always right, and never make mistakes. What needs to be communicated is that fathers *do* have great responsibility in the home but that it is possible for fathers to misunderstand a situation, to make wrong judgments, to get their own egos involved in a situation, and to need forgiveness.

There will be times when you will need the forgiveness of your child for something you've said or done. It is not an easy thing to be by yourself with a son or daughter and say, "I was wrong. I wasn't really listening and didn't understand. It was my fault and I'm sorry. I've asked God to forgive me and now I'm asking you." Knowing what kind of courage such a confession takes, a child would be very proud to have such a father.

The child who gets to know and love and respect father as a human being will have a much easier time relating honestly to his/her own children after marriage.

—From Kenneth Chafin, *Is There a Family in the House?* copyright © 1978, pp. 92–93; used by permission of Word Books, Publisher, Waco, Texas 76796.

Nagging

The pattern of communication that develops in a family depends on many factors. Your marriage is the foundation of communication for the whole family. The atmosphere you establish will determine whether communication is constructive or destructive in your family. Your communication habits as a parent are the model your children will learn from as they develop their own ways of communicating. Though the words themselves don't always explain them, emotions are one of the major elements communicated between family members. As you develop your skill and discipline in expressing yourself, communication will increasingly work for your family instead of being a source of problems.

AVOID NAGGING

One of the major communication problems in families is nagging. Often a husband comes in for counseling and says that his wife nags him. I ask what he means by nag. He replies, "Every week she asks me to clean the garage." Now this really doesn't sound much like nagging. It sounds more like reminding, especially if it is a well-expressed request. We need to note the difference between nagging and reminding.

Nagging has been defined as "a continual, persistent, critical faultfinding which creates irritation in another person." One person defined nagging as reminding a person to do something when you know he hasn't forgotten. It has also been expressed as inefficiency on our part to promote the desired behavior in another. Nagging is a negative verbal behavior that has very little communication value.

What is the difference between nagging and frequent reminders? Nagging usually continues on and on and on, but frequent reminders lead to learning. Most children when they are young need reminding because they do not have a ready-made, built-in sense of responsibility. (For that matter, many adults lack this as well!) A sense of responsibility is learned through day-by-day activities, but it is not always easy to learn. The impulses of a child are quite strong, and he needs to rely on outside controls. Couple that with a short attention span, and the tendency to become so preoccupied with what he is interested in, and it is no wonder that he needs reminding.

Husbands and wives experience nagging in terms of being continually reminded to do something. Usually the tone of voice indicates the difference between reminding and nagging. Husbands are nagged about taking out the garbage, cleaning the garage, cutting the grass, cleaning the yard, picking up the socks, etc. Wives are nagged about having dinner on time, overcooking the steak, picking up the soap and shampoo in the shower, taking clothes to the cleaners, etc. What do you think children are nagged about? Think of five or six frequent nagging behaviors.

Does nagging accomplish anything? Some say no, but this isn't true. Nagging does bring results, but they are usually negative. Nagging encourages a spouse to continue to engage in the very behavior he or she is being nagged about. This behavior leads to quarrels and resentment. It also leads the other person to develop a strange malady—a form of deafness known as tuning out the spouse. Nagging is as common as the flu and, like a communicable disease, it makes all of the family members miserable.

REASONS FOR NAGGING

What causes parents to fall into the trap of nagging? Here are several suggestions which have been given by Dr. Sven Wahlroos:

1. Parents may have unrealistic expectations concerning the abilities of a child or the amount of work that he is expected to accomplish. If this is true, then many children will not respond, since they feel they are overwhelmed or will fail the task anyway.

2. Children and parents often like to show their power, and not doing something that one is asked to do is a good way to demonstrate this.

3. A third cause concerns how parents

state rules or make requests. You need to be very clear and definitive in your statements and also expect the same from your child. When he says he will do it later, always clarify what he means by the word *later*.

4. Procrastination may develop on the part of a child because he was not informed of the consequences of not doing what he was told.

The Scriptures warn against nagging. "Love forgets mistakes; nagging about them parts the best of friends" (Proverbs 17:9, LB). "It is better to dwell in a corner of the housetop (on the flat oriental roof, exposed to all kinds of weather) than in a house shared with a nagging, quarrelsome and faultfinding woman" (Proverbs 21:9, AMP).

MINIMIZING NAGGING

Here are some steps toward minimizing nagging (if you happen to use this method), and ways to respond to one who nags you.

1. Distinguish between nagging and reminding. A reminder remains friendly, with no tone of irritation, impatience, or anger. Nagging usually involves destructive means of communication such as the use of exaggeration, sarcasm, humiliation, and playing the numbers game. "You will never do what I ask you to do!" "A moron could remember to follow instructions better than you do." "If I've told you once, I have told you a thousand times."

Although people attempt to use nagging as a means of communicating and motivating, it doesn't work. Instead of recognizing this fact and employing a different means, they intensify their efforts and nag all the more!

Nagging can become a habit. When you fail to get another person's attention before speaking to him, he will probably appear to ignore you. When you yell from one room to another without making sure the person is listening, can you blame him for lack of response? Sometimes he may hear you and sometimes not. If you allow this pattern to continue, he will soon learn that when you ask him to do something, all he needs to do is tune out, perhaps even pretend not to hear. With practice he may learn not to hear. The end result is that he learns how to control you by not listening.

2. Another reason for nagging is that we accept ambiguous answers or responses. If a child answers a request by saying, "I will do it later," tell him you don't know what he means by later; to avoid any misunderstanding, you would like to know the exact time. If remembering has been a problem for him, suggest writing a reminder note to help him remember. Always insist on clear communication and definite responses. . . .

3. One way that a family can change some of the nagging behavior that occurs is to define and clarify responsibilities for each person. Perhaps questions could be asked such as, "What are the jobs or tasks which need to be done and when should they be done and by whom?" For many couples, discussing responsibilities has helped to solve problems in areas which have been irritants for many years.

Some couples have created a chart describing the division of labor, with jobs and times when they could be done. The purpose of such a chart is to clarify individual responsibilities. Either spouse should comment on the other's failure to do his or her job.

4. Establish automatic rules which cover the subjects over which there has been nagging. When the consequences for either complying with the request or not responding to it have been spelled out, the procrastinating child will feel a greater motivation to respond. The nagging should be eliminated because if the child follows the rules there is no need for nagging or reminding, and if the child does not respond there is no need for nagging as the consequences for that behavior have been spelled out for him as well.

5. Decide if the nagging or reminding is about important or unimportant matters. Decide in your own mind which are important and concentrate upon those. For a while, at least, ignore the others. You might want to discuss the list of rules or behaviors with your child if he or she is old enough to respond.

6. Be sure that you have your child's attention. Don't do anything while you are talking that might distract his attention. You may want to place your hand gently on the child's shoulder, look into his eyes, speak in a slow distinct voice, and then ask the child to tell you what you said!

—From H. Norman Wright, *The Family That Listens*. Wheaton, Ill.: Victor Books, 1978.

Questions

Parents ask questions. Children ask questions. A question can be a rich learning experience. You can learn so much about your children by drawing out what is going on inside of them. To involve another person in a conversation, you ask a question. A question invites a reply and is a stimulus for conversation to begin. When you ask your child a question, he understands that you want to know something about what he has been doing or thinking or feeling.

What words do you use to begin your questions? Let's assume that your child has just come home from Sunday School and you would like to know what the class was about. Here are examples of the types of questions you could ask.

Did your class do anything special today, John?

What did you do in your class?

Where is your class going this Saturday?

Why did your class go into the auditorium today?

Who went with you?

How can you tell when your teacher is happy?

How do you feel when you are asked a question? What goes on inside of your mind? Take time right now and think about your response to these questions.

Some people feel threatened. They wonder what will happen if they don't know the answer. Some feel pressured. Others feel challenged. When you or your child is asked a question, you must review your experiences and organize your thoughts. That is why questions are so valuable for the mind development of a child. Questions also stimulate a child to use words more accurately and become more effective in the expression of his ideas. Your questions will help you know what your child observes, thinks, and feels.

In conversation with your child, remember to maintain a balance between questions and statements. Too many questions can overwhelm a child and threaten him. They can actually close off conversation if he becomes fearful. Too many questions may imply that the child does not have his own private world. And if the questions come faster than he can think, then frustration occurs.

KINDS OF QUESTIONS

Basically there are three types of questions: information, opinion or judgment, and feeling. An *information question* asks another person to share something about his experiences. You ask these when you want the person to share what he has learned, observed, heard or done. Unfortunately many of our information questions call for only a short-answer response, and parents have a tendency to use too many of these. This type of question skims the surface and doesn't really allow you to know the other person. If the child feels as though he is getting the third degree, or being interrogated, he may become angry, moody, or silent, and tune you out.

Information questions should ask for thoughts and an expansion on the subject. "Tell me what happened at your party." "What did you see at school today?" Both of these questions ask for information. You may receive a short or lengthy response. If you were to say, however, "Tell me the finest thing that happened at your party and describe the costumes of six of the people," or "What are ten things that you saw at school today?" you may receive a wealth of information. These last two questions may be better suited for those who are less responsive than for the talkative child. Information questions are usually the first ones you use, for they give you facts before you proceed into opinions, feelings, or emotions.

Opinion and/or judgment questions ask a child to tell what he thinks about something. You are now focusing on ideas. These questions often come from the information derived from information questions. These could also involve "what if" questions as you ask him to think about the future. Think of five different types of opinion questions that you use or could use with your child.

Do these questions call for a short or a long response? Will you ask for a yes-or-no response? For example, if you ask a person, "Is it true?" you will receive a Yes or No. If you ask, "Why do you think it is true?" or "Why is it false?" you will receive a different answer to your questions.

This category of questions is important as you are digging for the meaning and significance of things. You are also helping your child think through future consequences, to prepare him for the future. You need these questions to know what your child is learning and whether he is really in touch with reality.

The third category of questions concerns *feelings*. These questions are crucial to the emotional and mental health of your child. They deal with his fears, worries, anxieties, frustrations, joys, and delights. Many of the questions in this category include the word *feel*. "How did you feel about that?" "What do you feel about your test?"

—From H. Norman Wright, *The Family That Listens*. Wheaton, Ill.: Victor Books, 1978.

EMOTIONAL SUPPORT

Caring

The Apostle Paul referred to this motherly function. Describing his ministry to the Thessalonians he said, ". . . we were gentle among you, like a mother caring for her children. We loved you so much that we were delighted to share with you not only the gospel of God but our lives as well, because you had become so dear to us." (1 Thessalonians 2:7, 8, NIV) "Caring for" means literally "to keep warm." Figuratively, it involves cherishing and comforting. A mother instinctively longs to press her child to herself, protecting him from danger, soothing his hurts and easing his pain.

As natural as that longing may be, it is sometimes dulled by the pressures of life, by a selfish spirit, by the lack of personal security, by seething hostility, anxiety, or unresolved conflicts with others. Mother may allow herself to become irritable and sharp with the children, creating an unpleasant atmosphere of tension and discord. You see, she is the one who actually establishes the mood of the home. Father may be its head, but as many others have suggested, she is its

heart. Her emotional state will often become the condition of the entire household, and even the youngest child will absorb the effects of it. A child's mind is like a video tape recorder, carefully transcribing every word, right down to the tone of voice and facial expression. And all of it contributes to the person he will become. Some psychologists say his emotional pattern is set by the time he is two years old. That should be a sobering realization to mothers, and a challenge to examine carefully their attitudes and temperament. A change for the better will have a profitable effect whenever it comes.

Mrs. Pickit is obsessed with having a perfectly clean house. Her conversation consists of "Pick this up, put that away, straighten those things, scrub that better." Fussing has become an automatic, involuntary way of life for her. She may ultimately drive her child to the opposite extreme of sloppiness, or may produce in him the same neurotic perfectionism she has.

Mrs. Skelter is a disorganized person who is always running late. She keeps the household in a state of turmoil screaming at everyone to hurry up. A child who lives with that kind of pressure becomes tense and troubled. He does poorly in his schoolwork and finds it difficult to get along with other children.

Mrs. Wartner is overly anxious. She worries, frets, whines, and stews about every little problem, actual or potential. And every one of those fears is registering on the consciousness of the little tyke beside her, building a spirit of apprehension and anxiety that will hold him in bondage for a lifetime, but for a miracle of God's grace.

Mrs. Grumpman is unhappy and dissatisfied. She complains about her plight in life. She grumbles about the way people treat her. She gripes about the inconveniences she suffers. And little ears send impulses to little minds around her making discontentment the habitual pattern of their lives as well.

A child needs someone near him who loves him more than the house, whose heart is bubbling with the joy of Jesus Christ, who displays an inner calmness even during the trying circumstances of daily living, someone who is patient and kind, who encourages and cheers. Mother, the Spirit of God can make you that kind of person. Flee to his presence often during the day and claim his wisdom and strength.

Then spend time with your children. Read to them. Teach them the Word of God. Take casual walks with them, pointing out interesting things along the way. Play games with them. Create challenging things for them to do. Take an interest in their projects. Be available when they need you. And like the Spirit of God, be sympathetic and compassionate. Your children will someday stand up and praise you for it.

—From Richard L. Strauss, *Confident Children and How They Grow.* Wheaton, Ill.: Tyndale, 1975.

Love

And what does it mean to *receive* a child? The Greek word means "to accept" or "to take to oneself." How, then, can you receive a child and thereby make sure he feels loved? Here are seven practical suggestions:

1. *Make sure you see your children as God sees them*—as a "gift," a "reward," and as "arrows"—not as an interruption, accident, or tax break (Psalms 127:3, 4 NAS).
2. *Cultivate a childlike attitude.* Don't take yourself too seriously. Rediscover play. Walk barefoot together across the wet grass. Ride a merry-go-round. Act out a story instead of merely reading it (Matthew 18:1–4).
3. *Give your children direct eye contact.* Jesus said that "the eye is the lamp of the body . . ." (Matthew 6:22). He calls us "the apple of his eye" (Deuteronomy 32:10). The Lord said, ". . . I will counsel you with my eye upon you" (Psalms 32:8). A child has a critical need for focused attention which enables him to feel respected, important, and loved. "Daddy (or Mommy) really cares about me . . . what I say . . . what I do."

Have you ever sat in a restaurant and watched a family relating? or should I say "not relating"? How often have you observed little children bobbing in their seats while sharing some exciting news while Dad, across the table, has his eyes glued to last night's box scores or is studying the assorted ways his french fries are arranged on the plate?

Children need to know we care. Sacrificing our present activity for a minute to practically demonstrate this will insure that our children feel loved. I believe "Love that is heard but not observed is absurd!"

4. *Physically express your love.* Regular hugging, kissing, sitting close together, tousling hair, tickling, rubbing backs (my son's favorite), putting an arm on the shoulder, a playful romp (not a slugfest)—all are absolutely essential to assure a child's emotional security and to nurture his self-esteem. They communicate this thought: "I like you and enjoy being with you." These are the building blocks of a strong, healthy love bond.

. . . .

5. *Train yourself to be a good listener.* Listening requires discipline, especially with children who can tell you the same Winnie the Pooh story a hundred times. It involves the eyes, ears, mind, and heart. It means kneeling at times so as to be on their level and to communicate eye to eye. It's important that as parents we respond to our child's feelings—"Rejoice with those who rejoice, weep with those who weep" (Romans 12:15)—and not *regularly* interrupt them or cut them off.

Such statements as "Not now, I'm busy" or "Tell me later" say to a child: *I guess I'm not as important to Mommy and Daddy as other things are.*

Usually a child approaches a parent for one of four reasons: a) answers; b) affection; c) attention (to hurt or insecure feelings); d) association (companionship). We need to listen, not just to hear but also to understand and discern his or her point of need.

The moments just prior to saying goodnight are usually an excellent time to hear a child's heart. For some strange reason, this seems to be the time when many children love to open up!

My wife and I found we were able to teach Justin most of his *A B C*s and how to count to ten (before he reached three years of age) by simply lying in bed with him for a few minutes before he fell asleep. During the same time span he also committed twelve Bible verses to memory. I don't cite this to boast but merely to underscore how valuable these "retiring" moments can be when used creatively.

"Hear, O Israel: The Lord our God is one Lord: And thou shalt love the Lord thy God with all thine heart, and with all thy soul, and with all thy might. And these words, which I command thee this day, shall be in thine heart: And thou shalt teach them diligently unto thy children, and shalt talk of them when thou sittest in thine house, and when thou walkest by the way, *and when thou liest down,* and when thou risest up."

Deuteronomy 6:4–7 KJV, my italics

6. *Spend quality time together.* There simply is no substitute for regular, consistent time spent together doing ordinary things (eating, working, walking, praying, driving, swimming, shopping) or "making memories" by doing extraordinary things (visits to a zoo, pet shop, amusement park, or hospital; playing table games, attending a sandlot softball game; picnick-ing, camping, biking, hiking, building a model plane; sewing a doll's outfit; sightseeing, visiting museums, visiting your nearby fire station, and taking them for a tour of where Dad works).

A special "date" with each child on a regular basis—such as going to "Mickey D's" restaurant (McDonald's) or simply going for a walk together—is another idea.

While driving in the car, be alert to interesting sights and be flexible enough to stop. Coming upon a construction area, I often pull over for a minute so Justin and Melanie can check out the bulldozers and the dump trucks. (Isn't it amazing how bug-eyed little ones can get over the big earth-moving equipment?) Workers fixing city roads . . . men changing lamps on the streetlights . . . a homeowner chopping down a tree . . . two dogs chasing each other across the lawn, are all tailormade for a child's curiosity. Children are inquisitive. Learn to capitalize on the novel, unique discoveries of everyday life.

Susanna Wesley had more than twenty children, yet she spent one hour with each child every week—listening, encouraging, and monitoring their spiritual progress. From these Wesley children emerged two men of God, John and Charles, who shook two continents for the Lord.

Obviously, all of this requires foresight and careful scheduling. Here again, the dad has the responsibility to take the initiative and pave the way.

—From Larry Tomczak, *God, the Rod, and Your Child's Bod.* Old Tappan, N.J.: Revell, 1982.

Self-Esteem

In a very real sense, we parents are products of the society whose values I have condemned. We have systematically been taught to worship beauty and brains, as everyone else, and so have our grandmommas and grandpoppas and uncles and aunts and cousins and neighbors. We all want superchildren who will amaze the world. Let's face it, folks: we have met the enemy and it is *us!* Often the greatest damage is unintentionally inflicted right in the home, which should be the child's sanctuary and fortress. Furthermore, I have observed in working with parents that their *own* feelings of inferiority make it difficult for them to accept gross imperfections in their children. They don't intend to reject their sons and daughters and they work hard to conceal these inner thoughts. But their "damaged" child symbolizes their own personal inadequacies and failures. Thus, it takes a very mature parent to look down upon an ugly child, or one who is clearly deficient in mentality, saying, "Not only do I love you, little one, but I recognize your immeasurable worth as a human being."

The first step in building your child's esteem, then, is to examine your own feelings—even being willing to expose those guilt-laden attitudes which may have been unconscious, heretofore. Are you secretly disappointed because your child is so ordinary? Have you rejected him, at times, because of his lack of appeal and charm? Do you think he is dumb and stupid? Was he born during a difficult time, imposing financial and physical stress on the family? Did you want a girl instead of a boy? Or a boy instead of a girl? Was this child conceived out of wedlock, forcing an unwanted marriage? Do you resent the freedom you lost when he came, or the demands he places on your time and effort? Does he embarrass you by being either too loud and rambunctious or too inward and withdrawn? Quite obviously, you can't teach a child to respect himself when you dislike him for reasons of your own! By examining your innermost

feelings, perhaps with the help of an understanding counselor or doctor, you *can* make room in your heart as a loving parent for your less-than-perfect youngster. After all, what right do we have to demand superchildren when we are so ordinary ourselves?!

A sizable proportion of your child's self-concept emerges from the way he thinks you "see" him. He watches what you say and do with interest. He is more alert to your "statements" regarding his worth than any other subject, even reading your unspoken (and perhaps unconscious) attitudes. Dr. Stanley Coopersmith conducted an exhaustive study of self-esteem and concluded that parents have a tremendous influence on their child's view of himself. They can either equip him with the confidence necessary to withstand the social pressures I have described, or they can leave him virtually defenseless. The difference is in the quality of their interaction. When the child is convinced that he is greatly loved and respected by his parents, he is inclined to accept his own worth as a person.

However, I have observed that many children know intuitively that they are loved by their parents, but they do not believe they are held in high esteem by them. These seemingly contradictory attitudes are not so uncommon in human relationships. A wife can love her alcoholic husband, for example, yet disrespect him for what he has become. Thus, a child can conclude in his own mind, "Sure they love me because I'm their child—I can see that I'm important to them—but they are not proud of me as a person. I'm a disappointment to them. I've let them down. I didn't turn out like they had hoped."

At the risk of being redundant, I must emphasize the point made above: it is very easy to convey love and disrespect at the same time. A child can know that you would actually give your life for him, if required, and yet your doubts about his acceptability show through. You are tense and nervous when he starts to speak to guests or outsiders. You butt in to explain what he was trying to say or laugh nervously when his remarks sound foolish. When someone asks him a direct question, you interrupt and answer for him. You reveal your frustration when you are trying to comb his hair or make him "look nice" for an important event. He knows you think it is an impossible assignment. If he is to spend a weekend away from the family, you give him an extended lecture on how to avoid making a fool of himself. These subtle behaviors are signals to the child that you don't trust him with *your* image—that he must be supervised closely to avoid embarrassing the whole family. He reads disrespect in your manner, though it is framed in genuine love. The love is a private thing between you—whereas confidence and admiration are "other" oriented, having social implications to those outside the family.

Loving your child, therefore, is only half of the task of building self-esteem. The element of respect must be added if you are to counterbalance the insults which society will later throw at him. Unless *somebody* believes in his worth, the world can be a cold and lonely place, indeed.

There are, I believe, several common barriers which can cause your child to doubt his worth, even when he is deeply loved. I would suggest that the reader examine his own home as we discuss these pitfalls to be avoided.

1. *Parental Insensitivity.* If there is one lesson parents need to learn most urgently, it is to guard what they say in the presence of their children. How many times, following a speaking engagement, have I been consulted by a parent regarding a particular problem her child is having. As Mom describes the gritty details, I notice that the object of all this conversation is standing about a yard behind her. His ears are ten feet tall as he listens to a candid description of all his faults. I visibly flinch when I hear a parent unintentionally disassemble esteem in this fashion. Just this afternoon, for example, I took my son and daughter to a park during a break in my writing schedule. While there, an insensitive mother was talking to me about her six-year-old boy, Roger, who stood within hearing distance just a few feet away.

She spoke in Gatling-gun fashion: "He had a high fever when he was born, about 105, at least. The doctor couldn't do nothing to help him. He gave Roger the wrong kind of pills. Now Roger won't ever be the same. They say he has some brain damage now, and he don't learn too good in school."

If Roger were my boy, his mental handicap would be the very last thing I would let him hear me describe to a stranger. It was like saying, "This is my son, Roger. He's the dumb one—you know, there's something wrong with his brain." How imperceptive she was of her unfortunate son. Roger did not show shock. In fact, he didn't even look up. But you can bet he heard his mother, and his self-concept will *always* reflect what she said.

. . . .

Sensitivity is the key word. It means "tuning in" to the thoughts and feelings of our kids, listening to the cues they give us and reacting appropriately to what we detect there.

2. *Fatigue and Time Pressure.* Why do dedicated parents have to be reminded to be sensitive to the needs of their children, anyway? Shouldn't this be the natural expression of their love and concern? Yes it should, but Mom and Dad have some problems of their own. They are pushed to the limits of their endurance by the pressure of time. Dad is

holding down three jobs and he huffs and puffs to keep up with it all. Mom never has a free minute, either. Tomorrow night, for example, she is having eight guests for dinner and she only has this one evening to clean the house, go to the market, arrange the flowers for the centerpiece, and put the hem in the dress she will wear. Her "to do" list is three pages long and she already has a splitting headache from it all. She opens a can of "Spaghetti-Os" for the kids' supper and hopes the troops will stay out of her hair. About 7 P.M., little Larry tracks down his perspiring mother and says, "Look what I just drawed, Mom." She glances downward and says, "Uh huh," obviously thinking about something else.

Ten minutes later, Larry asks her to get him some juice. She complies but resents his intrusion. She is behind schedule and her tension is mounting. Five minutes later he interrupts again, this time wanting her to reach a toy that sits on the top shelf of the closet. She stands looking down at him for a moment and then hurries down the hall to meet his demand, mumbling as she goes. But as she passes his bedroom door, she notices that he has spread his toys all over the floor and made a mess with the glue. Mom explodes. She screams and threatens and shakes Larry till his teeth rattle.

Does this drama sound familiar? It should, for "routine panic" is becoming an American way of life. I recently conducted an inquiry among seventy-five middle-class married women, between twenty-five and thirty-five years of age. I asked them to indicate the sources of depression which most often send them into despair and gloom. Many common problems were revealed, including in-law conflicts, financial hardships, difficulties with children, sexual problems, and mood fluctuations associated with menstrual and physiological distress. But to my surprise, *fatigue and time pressure* was

tagged as *the* most troublesome source of depression by half the group; the other half ranked it a close second! It is obvious that many families live on this kind of last-minute, emergency schedule, making it impossible to meet the demands of their own overcommitments. Why do they do it? The women whom I surveyed admitted their dislike for the pace they kept, yet it has become a monster which defies containment. Faster and faster they run, jamming more and more activities into their hectic days. Even their recreation is marked by the same breakneck pace. There was a time when a man didn't fret if he missed a stage coach; he'd just catch it next month. Now if a fellow misses a section of a revolving door he's thrown into despair!

But guess who is the inevitable loser from this breathless lifestyle? It's the little guy who is leaning against the wall with his hands in the pockets of his blue jeans. He misses his father during the long day and tags around after him at night, saying, "Play ball, Dad!" But Dad is pooped. Besides, he has a briefcase full of work to be done. Mom had promised to take him to the park this afternoon, but then she had to go to the Women's Auxiliary meeting at the last minute. The lad gets the message—his folks are busy again. So he drifts into the family room and watches two hours of pointless cartoons and reruns on television.

Children just don't fit into a "to do" list very well. It takes time to be an effective parent when children are small. It takes time to introduce them to good books—it takes time to fly kites and play punch ball and put together jigsaw puzzles. It takes time to listen, once more, to the skinned-knee episode and talk about the bird with the broken wing. These are the building blocks of esteem, held together with the mortar of love. But they seldom materialize amidst busy timetables. Instead, crowded lives produce fatigue—and fatigue produces irritability—and irritability produces indifference—and indifference can be interpreted by the child as a lack of genuine affection and personal esteem.

As the commercial says, "Slow down, America!" What is your rush, anyway? Don't you know your children will be gone so quickly and you will have nothing but blurred memories of those years when they needed you? I'm not suggesting that we invest our entire adult lives into the next generation, nor must everyone become parents. But once those children are here, they had better fit into our schedule somewhere. This is, however, a lonely message at the present time in our society. Others are telling Mom to go to work—have a career—do her own thing—turn her babies over to employees of the state working in child-care centers. Let someone else discipline, teach, and guide her toddler. While she's at it, though, she'd better hope that her "someone else" gets across the message of esteem and worth to that pudgy little butterball who waves "good-bye" to his mommy each morning.

3. *Guilt.* In case you haven't noticed, parenthood is a very guilt-producing affair—even for the dedicated "professional." The conflict of interest between the needs of children and the demands of adult responsibilities, as described above, is only one of many inconsistencies which can strike pangs of guilt in our hearts. (It is interesting to me that the situation gradually reverses itself as we age, with our grown-up children then feeling guilty over their failures with us!) Since no one can do the job perfectly, we subject ourselves to a constant cross-examination in the courtroom of parental acceptability. Was I fair in my discipline? Did I overreact out of frustration and anger? Have I been partial to the child who is my favorite? Did I cause that illness by giving him poor care? Was the accident my fault? Have

I made the same mistakes for which I resented my own parents? 'Round and 'round go the self-doubts and recriminations.

Remember, again, that none of us can be perfect parents, any more than we can be perfect human beings. We get tired and frustrated and disappointed and irritable, affecting the way we approach those little fellows around our feet. But fortunately, we are permitted to make many mistakes through the years—provided the overall tone is somewhere near the right note.

4. *Rivals for Love.* My son arrived on the scene when his sister was five years of age. She had been the only granddaughter on either side of the family and had received all the adult attention that can be heaped upon a child. Then suddenly, her secure kingdom was invaded by a cute little fellow who captured and held the center stage. All of the relatives cuddled, cooed, rocked, bounced, and hugged baby Ryan, while Danae watched suspiciously from the wings. As we drove home from Grandmother's house on a Sunday afternoon, about a week after Ryan's arrival, my daughter suddenly said, "Daddy, you know I'm just talking. You know, I don't mean to be bad or anything, but sometimes I wish little Ryan wasn't here!"

She had given us a valuable clue to her feelings in that brief sentence, and we immediately seized the opportunity she had provided. We moved her into the front seat of the car so we could discuss what she had said. We told her we understood how she felt and assured her of our love. We also explained that a baby is completely helpless and will die if people don't take care of him—feed, clothe, change, and love him. We reminded her that she was taken care of that way when she was a baby, and explained that Ryan would soon grow up too. We were also careful in the months that followed to minimize the threat to her place in our hearts. By giving careful attention to her feelings and security, the relationship with her brother developed into a lasting friendship and love.

Danae's admission was not a typical response among children. Much more commonly, a child will be unable or unwilling to express the insecurity brought by a newborn rival, requiring his parents to read more subtle signs and cues. The most reliable symptom of the I've-been-replaced syndrome is a sudden return to infantile behavior. Obviously, "If babyhood is where it's at, then I'll be a baby again." Therefore, the child throws temper tantrums, wets the bed, sucks his thumb, holds tightly to Mamma, baby talks, etc. In this situation, the child has observed a clear and present danger and is solving it in the best way he knows.

If your firstborn child seems to feel like a has-been, I would suggest the following procedures be implemented:

1. Bring his feelings out in the open and help him verbalize them. When a child is acting silly in front of adults, trying to make them laugh or notice him, it is good to take him in your arms and say, "What's the matter, Joey? Do you need some attention today?" Gradually, a child can be taught to use similar words when he feels excluded or rejected. "I need some attention, Dad. Will you play with me?" By verbalizing his feelings, you also help him to understand himself better.

2. Don't let antisocial behavior succeed. If the child cries when the baby-sitter arrives, leave him anyway. A temper tantrum can be greeted with a firm swat, etc. However, reveal little anger and displeasure, remembering that the entire episode is motivated by a threat to your love.

3. Meet his needs in ways that grant status to him for being older. Take him to the park, making it clear that the baby is too little to go; talk "up" to him about the things he can do that the baby can't—he can use the bathroom instead of his pants, for example. Let him take care of the baby so he will feel he is part of the family process.

It is not difficult to convey love to more than one child simultaneously provided you put your mind (and heart) to it.

. . . .

Every age poses its own unique threats to self-esteem. As I will discuss, little children typically suffer a severe loss of status during the tender years of childhood. Likewise, most adults are still attempting to cope with the inferiority experienced in earlier times. And I am convinced that senility and mental deterioration at the latter end of life often result from the growing awareness by the aged that they live in the exclusive world of the young; where wrinkles, backaches, and dentures are matters of scorn; where their ideas are out-of-date and their continued existence is a burden. This feeling of uselessness is the special reward that we reserve for life's survivors, and it should not be surprising that the elderly often "disconnect" intellectually.

Thus, if inadequacy and inferiority are so universally prevalent at all ages of life at this time, we must ask ourselves "why?" Why can't our children grow up accepting themselves as they are? Why do so many feel unloved and unlovable? Why are our homes and schools more likely to produce despair and self-hatred than quiet confidence and respect? Why should each child have to bump his head on the same old rock? These questions are of major significance to every parent who would shield his child from the agony of inferiority.

The current epidemic of self-doubt has resulted from a totally unjust and unnecessary system of evaluating human worth, now prevalent in our society. Not everyone is seen as worthy; not everyone is accepted. Instead, we reserve our praise and admiration for a select few who have been blessed from birth with the characteristics we value most highly. It is a vicious system, and we, as parents, must counterbalance its impact. This book is dedicated to the proposition that all children are created worthy and must be given the right to personal respect and dignity. It can be done! . . .

The matter of personal worth is not only the concern of those who lack it. In a real sense, the health of an entire society depends on the ease with which its individual members can gain personal acceptance. *Thus, whenever the keys to self-esteem are seemingly out of reach for a large percentage of the people, as in twentieth-century America, then widespread "mental illness," neuroticism, hatred, alcoholism, drug abuse, violence, and social disorder will certainly occur. Personal worth is not something human beings are free to take or leave. We must have it, and when it is unattainable, everybody suffers.*

—From James Dobson, Ph.D. *Hide or Seek.* Rev. ed. Old Tappan, N.J.: Revell, 1979.

Adopted Children

Will it be difficult to tell a child he is adopted? Or should it be kept from him? Most adoption agencies, upon the basis of sound experience, insist that the child be told by the new parents just as soon as he is able to understand. The important thing is how the child is told. Better that he find out directly and in the proper way, than to find out through a careless relative or when the parent is caught unprepared. The wise and loving parent can make this knowledge an actual reinforcement of the child's feeling of security. He can generally explain that the child's real parents could not provide as nice

a home as they wanted him to have, and because they loved him so they were willing to give him up although it was hard for them to do so. The Christian adoptive parents can further explain that after they had prayed about God's will for their family, God chose that he should come into their home, instead of giving them their own child by birth. After praying and searching for the best child, the one who could make their home the happiest, they chose him from all the rest. So he is a very special answer to prayer and to their greatest desire!

Wayne Oates reverently calls our attention to "the Heavenly Father who adopted His own Son out to a Palestinian maid and her husband." Surely, providing a Christian home for adopted children must be very close to the heart of God!

—From Dwight Hervey Small, *Design for Christian Marriage.* Old Tappan, N.J.: Revell, 1959.

Guidelines for Pride and Approval Needs

Take the trouble to find out what each child is capable of at a given time in life. Watch his coordination, interests, and skills. Talk with other people who know and interact with him to find out how they see your child. Read about the normal capabilities of other children. Knowing what to expect of your child is essential in helping you set up goals for training and disciplining.

Take one goal at a time and explain to your child (and to yourself) just what you expect of him and how you will go about teaching him to accomplish that goal. Your best method is to go about this positively, with love and encouragement.

Follow through with firmness and patience. Correct the child when he fails and praise him sincerely when he succeeds. Now and then, in his hearing, tell someone else about his success, but be careful not to overdo it!

When he has established good habits in one area, move on to another. Not spilling milk is a major accomplishment for a two- or three-year-old. Picking up toys may be another, and going to bed without whining certainly would please many parents! Choose something the child is capable of doing, be consistent from your side of the plan, and don't go too fast.

Be alert for the time your child gets his own self-starter going. If you do your job well, at some point your child will want to get his own sense of pride and pleasure in what he does. He will always need yours to bolster him, but his real maturity will be there when *he* knows he has done well!

Understanding your child's feelings and needs can help you in preventing a troubled child. But if your son or daughter already evidences a problem, such basic understanding will also help you in the solving of that problem. Take some time and think about your child. Is she covering worry with irritation? Could she need a little more tenderness? Try a different approach, but be clear and honest with her so she will know what to expect and that she can count, absolutely, on your love!

—From Grace H. Ketterman, M.D., *You and Your Child's Problems.* Old Tappan, N.J.: Revell, 1983.

LEADERSHIP AND TRAINING

Leadership by the Father

For most men, the test will come in small doses over a long period of living. But the test comes to all, and sooner or later the judgment is rendered.

The world knows many fathers; it knows fewer fathers who are truly family leaders. Almost any man can be a father if he is capable of participating in the conception of a child. But fatherhood is more than a biological function. It is also a process of what I call effective leadership. Inside the perimeters of the family, it is the father who is required to create delicate conditions in which a child grows to be a man or woman, to attain the fullness of all that human potential that God has designed. Where those conditions do not exist, growth is retarded, and human beings fall far short of the heavenly objectives.

Families without fathers who are effective leaders face constant trouble, just like other kinds of groups where leadership is in a vacuum. We have seen leaderless situations—all of us. An athletic team lacking a leader usually loses. The business with hazy lines of authority generally goes under. A crowd which hears no charismatic spokesman becomes a mob.

. . . .

The Bible also presents a view on effective fathers when it calls a married man the leader of his home. Both the Old and the New Testaments provide descriptions and commandments which leave no questions about who is to be the head of the home and family. To be sure, the responsibility for the growth of a family is equally shared with wife and mother. But in a unique sort of way, God calls upon the man to be the family's governor, its accountable representative to make sure that God's laws are being followed, that the people in that family have every opportunity to experience all that their Creator intends for them to be.

. . . .

Perhaps the place to begin a definition of effective leadership is with the recognition that there is need for order in family relationships before God and the surrounding community. People living in proximity to one another have to be placed in some design or there will be conflict and chaos. Disordered families create disordered communities. Thus, God has sovereignly chosen one person in a family to create and maintain the needed order. There is both a positive and a negative thrust to this leadership.

In its positive sense, effective leadership is designed to bring people to maturity, to the ultimate reaches of their human potential. The leader searches out the conditions in which each person in his family can grow to be what God has made him to be. But in the negative perspective, effective leadership is the enforcement of order when there is unwillingness to fit into the process of relationships, an attitude that makes life miserable for everyone.

The head of the home—like the shepherd in Psalm 23—carries a kind of rod and staff: the staff for rescue and pointing direction, the rod for discipline and enforcement. When both are capably used, there is stability in relationships and steady process in growth. When both are unused or misused, there is drift and deterioration among the shepherd's sheep and the father's family.

If we are fully to understand the necessity of this rod and staff function, we need to take a quick glance back at some of the earliest paragraphs in the Bible.

In his original state, the Bible says, man was without sin. That is to say, he had nothing in his life that might be described as imperfection or spiritual sickness. He had an open relationship with God. His lot in life was one of discovering what God had made in the world. He was there to enjoy it, master it, and use it. The very act of discovery and mastery was pleasing and glorifying to God.

But the whole thing became derailed when man sinned. Relationship on every level was shattered. The first man fell into conflict with God, hiding from him in embarrassment and fear—in other words, guilt. He developed inner conflict, and the symptoms of an inner war—heartache, fear, worry, inner frustration—plagued him. He began to mix it up with those about him; a cruel competition sprang up. He blamed others for his misfortune. Life changed from one of basic discovery to one of domination, searching out only what was best for number one—me!

The word which seems to characterize all these ongoing relational ways which have been in motion ever since the Garden days is *rebellion*. From a relational person to a rebellious person: a bitter lifestyle and a disappointment to God. Unless those rebellious impulses are checked, there will only be exploitation and destruction. The name of the game will always be "king of the mountain." Few kings—many slaves.

We have rebellious impulses within us, and they must be restrained at all costs. A primary way in which that is done is through the structures of human community. The family is the best example. It laces people together through love, binding commitment, mutual need, and authority. In its balance of relationships, the rebellious instincts of each individual are modestly checked and various patterns of responsibility and positive behavior are developed. If the family is a group of human beings so tied together, it is the father who is the knot where the ends of the laces meet.

From the positive side of experience, the father is the head of a unit of people launched on an exploration of life and all the things God has placed in the world for us to discover and enjoy. From the negative side of experience, he is the one who quells natural rebellion and stops members of his family from hurting themselves and others. There is no greater privilege—or responsibility.

—From Gordon MacDonald, *The Effective Father.* Wheaton, Ill.: Tyndale, 1977.

Teaching

God's instruction to parents begins with a challenge for their commitment to Him:

Love the Lord your God with all your heart and with all your soul and with all your might (Deuteronomy 6:5, NASB).

Personal commitment—this is the key to being an effective Christian model and example in the home. . . .

Identification is weakened and sometimes destroyed when the parent does not fill his child's need for time and loving attention. If the parent does spend time with his children—playing with them, talking to them, reading to them, doing the things they like to do—identification will be strong and teaching effective.

Time is an expression of love that children can measure. A child thinks, "My parents must really love me. I must be important because they spend time with me." Time spent with children builds that special kind of parent-child relationship upon which identification flourishes.

The identification process is assumed in the Bible. Paul says: *As children copy their fathers you, as God's children, are to copy him* (Ephesians 5:1, PHILLIPS). This verse makes me nervous, as does all talk about modeling and being an example to my children.

Recently, I heard our three girls screaming at one another in the bedroom. I stomped in and shouted, "Would you girls stop screaming at each other! That's no way to handle things!"

They just stared at me with puzzled looks that said, "What are you talking about, Dad. That's the way you handle things."

There it was in living color. My children identifying with my actions, not my words. Once more, I had to ask God to "change my children's father!" And, in the same breath, to thank Him for His provision for forgiveness. Again I asked for help in communicating God's love and His way to our children—by my life as well as my words.

TEACH DILIGENTLY—FORMAL TEACHING

I find in Deuteronomy 6 specific instructions to *teach* our children God's Word: *And these words . . . you shall teach them diligently to your sons* (Deuteronomy 6:6,7, NASB). This says to me that God wants parents to have some definite plan for communicating His teachings to the children of the family.

Children need to see that their parents value His Word enough to share it with them regularly. Through regular family times around God's Word, children become acquainted with God, who He is, what He says, what He has done, what He is doing. Such teaching situations provide opportunities for children to discover that their parents' values are deeply rooted in Scripture.

When "teaching diligently" times are warm experiences of family sharing, they become good times that children enjoy and participate in. That, really, is what this book is all about. Much of the material is designed to help you plan teaching times that are good family times when you and your children can learn from the Bible.

TALK—INFORMAL TEACHING

Deuteronomy 6 also talks about the many informal teaching opportunities that parents have to share God's Word and His way with their children: *And these words . . . you . . . shall talk of them when you sit in your house and when you walk by the way and when you lie down and when you rise up* (Deuteronomy 6:6,7, NASB). This says that it is God's plan for parents to talk about His truths in the midst of the everyday happenings and real life situations of family life.

Each day provides parents with many opportunities to "talk about" things of God in a natural way. We need to sharpen our sensitivity to the many possible teaching situations that surround us.

God's magnificent creation furnishes us with many opportunities to talk informally with our children about His greatness, power, love, and sovereignty.

Questions our children ask about the Bible and life in general can be turned into meaningful teaching times.

By sharing family problems, blessings, and answers to prayer, we can show how God is vitally interested in our family's life.

We can guide our children toward self-discipline as we share with them what God's Word has to say about behavior.

And if we take time to get involved in the lives of our children, show interest in what they do, ask questions about school, sports, and friends, there will be many opportunities to discuss how God's Word has the answers to life's problems.

Often the contrast between the Christian life and the life-styles that our children encounter in their activities gives us a chance to teach important Christian values.

Recently, at dinner, our oldest girl, Heidi, said, "Guess what? I got to show a new girl around school today. She's nice, but she sure has got problems. The reason she had to move is that her mom can't keep her any longer, and she doesn't even know why. She has to live with her dad and stepmother. She sure is mixed up about it."

This conversation gave us the chance to explain, once again, God's ideal for marriage—one woman and one man for one life. We asked such questions as: "How do you think your friend feels?" "How would you feel?" "How can you show your new friend special love?" And our three girls were soon involved in caring about someone else's needs.

Informal teaching should never be "preachy." Encourage conversation with questions like: "What do you think? How do

you feel about it? What would you do?" And, then, as you talk, help your children think through problems and apply biblical principles as you share your own feelings, thoughts and biblical insights.

My wife and I find that it helps us to be aware of teaching opportunities when we:

- Talk about times during the past few weeks when we used an opportunity to comment on God's greatness, His love or some Bible truth with the children.
- Try to remember situations when we missed a chance to relate an everyday happening to God's love and His presence.
- Count the times that we spent with each child alone, talking and sharing needs and interests.
- Think specifically about *today.* What opportunities did we use? What ones did we miss?

WHY DOES GOD WANT PARENTS TO MODEL, TEACH, TALK?

There are good reasons why God chose the home as an important place for the teaching and learning of His truth.

- When we teach God's Word at home it becomes obvious to us that our actions must match our words or very little learning will take place. Therefore we must start with ourselves.
- If we are to teach our children well, we must be able to talk about our faith. This causes us to study and apply God's Word.
- As we spend time and teach our children we become better acquainted with their real needs.
- We know and love our children as no one else possibly can. This allows us to understand and touch sensitive areas of our children's lives.
- The home is where the action is! The very best teaching is life-linked. We can teach in real life situations.

• Teaching at home increases communication at the deepest level—at the spiritual level.

When we teach at home, our children have everyday opportunities to know that Christianity is our way of life. As we teach from day-to-day situations we help our children discover that God is involved in everything we do.

—From Wayne E. Rickerson, *Good Times for Your Family.* Ventura, Calif.: Regal, 1976.

Being an Example

Involved in fatherhood is the awesome responsibility of providing for our children a climate conducive to growth. There needs to be a realistic example of those values, behavior patterns, and interpersonal relationships which Scripture, reason and conscience affirm to be desirable. It is not enough for you to tell your children how you want them to act, or even to enforce your teaching by a variety of excellent family rules.

They must see dad demonstrate in his own life what he teaches.

"Do as I say but not as I do" may serve as an easy attitude to get dad off the hook, but it's both wrong and destructive to have a double standard in the home. Children learn most of what they really know through observation, and they imitate what they see in their parents. They will tend to do what *you do* rather than what you say.

Most of us are quite careful about *what we believe* about life, but all too frequently are casual about *how we live it.*

One day I began to realize how careful I was to insist on the children being frugal in their use of money, while I found myself spending quite easily for a cup of coffee or other incidentals whenever I felt like it.

We had a rule about food: "You don't have to like it; you just have to eat it." But I could weasel out of the rule by clueing my wife ahead of time not to prepare dishes I didn't like!

The Holy Spirit began to check me in many "little" areas where I, as dad, was frightfully inconsistent.

Like—

—I was very glad my wife stayed positive and encouraged me when I made mistakes or failed. But it seemed I was miserably critical when the children didn't measure up to my expectations.
—It was easy for me to insist the children learn self-discipline, but how slow I was to practice it for myself.

An effective way to remain up-to-date on your being an example is periodically to have a family conference. Include everyone and as a group agree on a number of important points:

1. That all of you—including dad—need God's continual motivation and enablement to live as you should.
2. For this reason you will pray regularly for each other, especially that God will undertake for specific needs, weaknesses and sins.
3. That you will maintain a policy of openness and loving honesty with each other, sharing with each other those areas where each of you needs specific prayer.
4. That you will discuss as a family your standards and how well you are living up to them.

If you as a parent will be honest, open and free in sharing with the children your need for God's grace and their help in being the person and parent you should be, it's amazing how honest and helpful the children will be toward you. Even small children have a keen sense of justice. They will respond with openness and honesty when treated fairly by elders.

Part of being fair is to admit when you are wrong and to ask for forgiveness. This is a very important part of being an example to your children.

Your example must demonstrate what you hold to be right and appropriate in three areas:

—Values
—Behavior patterns (life-style)
—Interpersonal relationships

—From Fred Renich, *The Christian Husband.* Wheaton, Ill.: Tyndale, 1976.

Boundaries

Another thing a father needs to do for his children is to define the boundaries for their young lives. Children need limits. These boundaries need to be arrived at with wisdom and they need to be communicated with love and firmness. Children are not simply shorter adults. They are children. If they are to know who they are, feel loved, and learn how to function, they need a sense of stability and security. Once the structures are established and the child understands them, he feels more secure.

Firmness is not the same as rigidity, and exercising authority is not the same as being authoritarian. Most of us have heard some version of the story about the man who came out of the army after a highly successful career. He married and decided the best way to "run" his family was according to the military system. His children were awakened by reveille and before breakfast were lined up to stand inspection. After one particularly complicated explanation of the "orders for the day" the father asked, "Are there any questions?" His youngest son's reply was, "Yes, how does one transfer out of this chicken outfit?"

While there is a great difference between a family and a military unit, a family does need rules. All families have them. Sometimes they're verbalized and sometimes they aren't. Certain families have too many rules and some too few. These rules set the boundaries. They have to do with everything: how people are treated, behavior at meal time, use of the car, when to come in at night, and a host of other things. Rules are absolutely essential if a family is to function efficiently.

While a family requires a great deal of flexibility, at the core there need to be some rules which are not negotiable. These need to be understood and enforced. Another group of rules should be negotiated as ages change and growth and maturity take place. A father who is fair and firm in defining and applying the rules of the family will be meeting a real need in his children.

—From Kenneth Chafin, *Is There a Family in the House?* copyright © 1978, pp. 89–90; used by permission of Word Books, Publisher, Waco, Texas 76796.

Discipline

Two unbiblical extremes of loving correction are the *disciplinarian* and *libertarian* approaches.

The disciplinarian approach is an overreaction to balanced discipline. It is militaristic. Cold. Stern. Catch-phrases like the following may be heard: "Spare the rod and spoil the child." "Children should be seen, not heard." "Do as I say, not as I do." "If you don't like it, there's the door." The rod or hand is quickly used by an angry parent for anything, anytime, anywhere. If no rod or hairbrush is available, a slap across the face or smack to the head will do. Usually the blowup stems from fatigue and/or frustration and often ends with, "Now get to your room!" (NOTE: Reports of child abuse spring from this approach carried to its extreme, not from loving correction applied in the spirit of Christ.)

Many of us grew up with some form of the disciplinarian approach to correction, and hence we recoil whenever we hear terms like *child discipline* or *the rod*. Besides, we recall those rat-maze studies in school which "proved" that punishment doesn't really influence human behavior. Noted child psychologists have given us a more sophisticated way to bring up our children in the twentieth century.

The libertarian approach stresses the inherent goodness of the child. Never repress. Never frustrate. Allow the child to express his feelings honestly and openly. Temper tantrums will be outgrown if ignored. Never spank a child, for it inhibits growth, bruises the ego, threatens security, and contributes to violence in society. Spanking is an assault on the dignity of a child. It is dehumanizing. Give rewards and incentives but never impose your values upon him. Let him develop naturally into his full personhood.

Last week I was finishing up some grocery shopping when, upon leaving the checkout line, I saw a freckled two-year-old begin to assert himself. Beneath his I'M GRANDMA'S BOY tee shirt was a superstrong self-will.

"Come here, please. It's time to go," beckoned the young, tanned mommy.

"No," junior defied, adjusting his Yankee cap firmly in place.

"Oh, come on," she coaxed.

Throwing himself down on the tiled floor, he cranked up the tears, stomped his feet, and made sure she knew he wasn't budging.

Gritting her teeth, she stiffened her torso, spun around, and walked out of the store.

As she vanished from sight, the toddler (whose outburst was now at the wailing stage) jumped up and ran, terrified, after his disappearing mom. I ran right behind him lest he dart into the stream of oncoming cars beyond the exit doors. Turning the corner, his mother picked him up like a sack of charcoal and steamed off to the car. Feet flying, arms waving, head jerking, "Grandma's boy" continued to "express his feelings honestly and openly" while "developing naturally into his full personhood."

In the Bible is a verse which comes to mind: "Claiming to be wise, they became fools" (Romans 1:22).

Both of these approaches are counterfeits and extremes. Everywhere people are realizing that yesterday's permissive parental attitudes have produced the rebellion evidenced in the younger generation today. Moreover, many of us are victims of our own parents' style of discipline (although many did the best they could, having only what was passed on to them).

On certain products you'll find the label: "For best results follow the instructions of the manufacturer." And for best results in marriage and rearing children, we must follow the instructions of the One who created us and ordained the family unit.

Whether His instructions please our intellect or emotions is beside the point. We must move ahead in obedience and faith (not an "Okay, I'll try it and see if it works" attitude). *All progress in the Christian life is by faith.* "And without faith it is impossible to please him [God]" (Hebrews 11:6).

"All scripture is inspired by God and profitable for teaching, for reproof, for correction, and for training in righteousness" (2 Timothy 3:16).

Notice the words *correction* and *training in righteousness*. The Lord wouldn't have put them there if there wasn't a need for them.

Loving correction is the biblical procedure for training children in righteousness so that they will become self-disciplined individuals. It is educating a child and overseeing his choices in an atmosphere of unconditional love, until he can make wise choices of his own. In doing so, we help him become self-disciplined. "Listen to counsel and accept discipline, That you may be wise the rest of your days" (Proverbs 19:20 NAS).

The primary goal of loving correction is to produce godly character in our children so that God will be glorified. Our goal is not merely to find a little peace in troubled times at home. We are participating in shaping lives so that our children's character will reflect God's glory (His manifest presence) for all eternity.

Loving correction (child discipline) means far more than punishing. Punishment is what you do *to* a child. Discipline is what you do *for* a child. Punishment, a part of loving correction, is derived from a Latin word meaning "pain." It is inflicting pain on a person for misbehavior.

Discipline comes from the same root as *disciple*, meaning "to learn." In rearing children, we want them to *learn* self-control; in other words, initial parental control gives way to self-control. The Bible speaks of a father who "manages his own household well, keeping his children under control . . ." (1 Timothy 3:4 NAS). If God says so, He must know that children have a need to be controlled.

Scripture not only teaches corporal punishment for disobedience and wrong attitudes in children but it commands it as well. *Consistent correction is not an elective but a directive from Almighty God.* Unless you establish this fact in your heart, you'll be tempted—when it's inconvenient (you're on the phone, in a supermarket, or eating dinner) or when such thoughts arise as "My child is different" . . . "It's probably too late"—to compromise or "cop out." But let us emphasize this right from the onset: *The rod of correction will only bring true success when administered in the context of a strong, healthy, love bond between parents and child.*

Now let's examine what God's Word says about loving correction.

"Foolishness is bound in the heart of a child; but the rod of correction shall drive it far from him" (Proverbs 22:15 KJV).

Contrary to modern, humanistic thinking concerning the "inherent goodness of a child," the Bible makes it clear that "foolishness" (literal Hebrew, "waywardness") is bound up in a child's heart (the center of his being). No one has to teach him to be selfish, to lie, steal, or disobey; yet one must teach him to share, be honest, truthful, kind, and obedient. "His royal majesty, the baby," has a self-centered nature regardless of how cute and innocent he may look.

The word *foolishness* comes from "fool," and Psalms 14:1 says, "The fool says in his heart, 'There is no God' " Or to paraphrase it, "I'll run my own life . . . do my own thing . . . be my own God." So Scripture says that when (not if) a child manifests this attitude of self-will, the rod of correction is applied to "drive it far from him." Remove the *nt* from parent and you get "pare" which means to remove or cut away.

In writing a book like this, it was important for me to remind myself of my children's foolish bent. That way I wouldn't have to feel as though my family must maintain some sort of image of perfection. My children do disobey—often! Yet of one thing you can be sure: I'll deal with such disobedience biblically, and sooner or later see the fruit. The mistakes I've made have been many, but I pray my experiences will now benefit you.

Here are two important points before we survey the basic elements of correction.

First, loving correction will involve an investment of time. Larry Christenson, in his book *The Christian Family*, cites a Christian parent as declaring that "spanking is an event." In other words, a parent does not simply haul off and "nail" a child because of reaching the breaking point. Loving correction has nothing to do with this quick and easy, yet cruel and unbiblical approach.

Second, loving correction should be started early. It may not be full-blown initially (using a simple finger flick when anger or rebellion is discerned), but wise parents will not procrastinate. The reason parents experience the so-called Terrible Twos is that attitudes which were never dealt with before now surface.

"Discipline your son in his early years while there is hope. If you don't you will ruin his life" (Proverbs 19:18 TLB). "When I was a son with my father, tender, the only one in the sight of my mother, he taught me . . ." (Proverbs 4:3, 4).

Setting an arbitrary age for beginning isn't my intention. I would suggest you ask the Lord to alert you when the time has come.

Couples in our Christian fellowship, and numerous others I have taught in, usually begin somewhere between nine and eighteen months. It may sound early, but over the years we've seen the positive results with scores of children. (Remember we are talking of dealing with *discerned rebellion,* not crying due to gas, sickness, hunger, discomfort, and so forth.)

—From Larry Tomczak, *God, the Rod, and Your Child's Bod.* Old Tappan, N.J.: Revell, 1982.

AT WHAT AGE?

Many parents shy away from disciplining either a very small child or a teenager. They are sure that the one is too young to understand correction and the other too old for physical indignity. I myself would not necessarily recommend spanking infants or sixteen-year-olds, but neither would I set an arbitrary cut-off date for any type of discipline.

In general, I believe that some form of discipline should start at an early age. The proverb, "Discipline your son while there is hope" (Proverbs 19:18), speaks of a critical formation period in children's lives that parents must take advantage of. The smallest infant is already learning how to respond to parents, to other children, to the world outside. As soon as a child is able to understand what the parents want, the need for discipline appears.

What age might this be? Nine months, a year, thirteen months, fourteen? The actual age varies with each child, but somewhere around that age children can understand that their parents don't want them to throw food on the floor or pull over the lamp. Once the child can understand that, the parents' authority is on trial.

"Susie, don't throw your food on the floor." Susie throws her food down, and nothing happens except that mom or dad picks it up. Susie tries again, and again nothing happens. At this point Susie decides that mom and dad don't really mean what they say. If she wants to throw her food around, she can do it.

From a very early age, then, children are learning whether they really have to obey their parents. The discipline, or lack of discipline, they get is what teaches them. This is not to say that a nine-month-old girl should get a full-fledged spanking every time she throws her food around: often a slap on the hand or some type of consequential discipline, like taking the food away, is very effective. Nor should parents expect children of this age to obey automatically even after they are corrected. If little Jonathan starts to pull the lamp over, he may need to have his hand slapped, but he should also be removed from the lamp.

I would certainly not want to rule out spankings for younger children. I know one woman who spanked her seven-month-old daughter for crying and fighting when her diaper was changed. First, the mother checked to make sure that she was not hurting the baby in any way. Once she was sure the crying was unnecessary, she spent several days communicating that she wanted this behavior to stop by gently restraining her squirming daughter and saying no. When she was sure her daughter understood what she wanted, she began to spank her—giving her a few slaps on the bottom—whenever she fought. Within a couple of weeks, the problem was gone.

As a child grows older, the need for physical discipline usually diminishes. If parents have administered discipline while the children are young, their authority will be well established. Children will continue to need discipline as they go through adolescence, but if they already have a good basic relationship with their parents' authority, they will usually need only some type of consequential discipline rather than a spanking. As children grow up, the parents will finally stop using physical discipline completely.

Yet parents should not attempt to set an arbitrary age limit for physical discipline. I was recently talking with the principal of a Christian school. A seventeen-year-old girl who had just become a dedicated Christian began attending this school and was giving her teachers a hard time. One day when she was acting particularly badly, the principal felt that he should spank her, a discipline which the school policies permitted. He explained the policy of the school to her, took her to his office, and spanked her. The girl let out a big shriek and bawled her head off. But as she left his office, she told the secretary, "Did I ever need that!" From that day, her whole attitude toward her teachers changed for the better.

I do not propose this example as a helpful way to deal with all seventeen-year-olds. But I think the story shows that there are no hard and fast rules for when children become too old to be spanked. Some children reach a point where they no longer need much physical discipline when they are as young as nine or ten. Others don't reach that point until much later. The parents need to judge carefully what discipline is right for each child.

Parents who have not been disciplining their children as they grow up should be especially cautious about suddenly introducing physical discipline when the children are older. This is a very difficult situation in which the parents need special discernment and sensitivity to decide on a discipline that helps their children obey.

—From Ralph Martin, *Husbands, Wives, Parents, Children.* Ann Arbor: Servant, 1978.

SPANKING

Spanking, once universally accepted as an appropriate disciplinary measure, ran into trouble by the 1960s. Many people confused spanking with beating or child abuse. When a parent spanks a child, it hurts. It's supposed to hurt! But not hurt enough so that it leaves physical scars or emotional trauma.

Scripture gives many statements about discipline, which includes spanking, such as Proverbs 13:24, "He who spares the rod hates his son."

When I've heard people speak about spanking, they've generally been highly permissive people who don't want to curb or thwart their child's growth (another modern fallacy). But, mostly, such people confuse discipline with the stern, unloving beatings of pioustype parents. If spanking were the only contact between the two, I would probably agree. But in the design of God, parents are also expected to love and nurture their children. Good parents respect their children as persons in their own right. They don't belittle, embarrass, or insult. They encourage the development of self-esteem in their offspring, helping them feel worthy and loved.

When spanking, or other forms of discipline such as withholding privileges, is done in the context of a loving relationship between parents and children, it can be an expression of love. The child realizes the parent cares and wants only the best for him/her.

During the early years of our marriage, Shirley and I first attended a church where George and Edna were members. Parents of eight children, they had the most beautifully behaved family I'd ever seen—with no evidence of suppression of their personalities. Once, his then-seven-year-old disobeyed, and George said, "Dawn, I'm going to spank you, but before I do, sit down here with me." He placed her on his knee and talked softly. "Dawn, I want to make sure you understand why I'm doing this." George told me that even when the children were small and he wasn't sure they understood his words, he felt they did understand his attitude.

Then he spanked Dawn and waited until the crying stopped before he picked her up again, held her in his arms, and kissed her. "I love you very much," he said.

By his example, I saw spanking as a loving form of discipline.

I believe in spanking as one form of discipline. The older children get the less they need spankings, and other means can be used.

When spanking children, there are a few things to keep in mind.

1. *Never spank in anger.* When that happens, you are alleviating your anger, but you are not helping the child. Spanking in anger may even make the child fear you.
2. *Keep your voice calm.* Tell the child what you are going to do and why. No lectures, threats of future punishment, or moralizing. Explain that he/she disobeyed and this is the result.
3. *Spank in private.* Public spanking, even of preschool children, is embarrassing and a form of ridicule. Spanking is a private matter.
4. *Afterward, hold the child and express your love.* Explain once more the behavior you expect from then on.
5. *No threats.* Don't say, "If you do this again, I'll . . ." Instead, simply explain the expected form of behavior.
6. *Set the boundaries in advance.* Don't punish children for accidents or for doing what they're not aware is wrong. (Even in law courts, people can't be punished for committing a crime before it's established as a crime!) Disciplining the child depends upon the child knowing the expected behavior. Once the child knows what's expected, the discipline can be meted out fairly.
7. *Be consistent.* Once children know the boundaries, hold firm to the standards. Follow through every time the child disobeys.

ALTERNATIVES TO SPANKING

Cecile, our second child, did not respond to spanking. If anything, she became even more stubborn. I discovered that other forms of punishment worked more effectively on her. The older children grow, the less effective spanking becomes. Here are alternatives.

1. *Losing a privilege.* Not being able to play outside affected Cecile more than anything else. As children get older, this form of discipline seems one of the best ways of coping with discipline problems.
2. *Send the child to his/her room.* "Go in there and sit on your bed and think about

what you have done. You may not lie down." After five or ten minutes, go into the room, talk it over, pray with your child, asking God to help him/her. Love the child so that he/she knows you mean it. Then ask, "Do you understand now what you did wrong?" If the child understands, then this is the end. No future reminders or nagging.

3. *Some parents use the old method of putting the child in the corner, facing the walls for five minutes.* Five minutes, for a child, is a very, very long time. I wouldn't make a child stay in the corner for any longer.

4. *Help your child overcome problems before they happen.* If the child gets in trouble because of a wild temper, help decide on ways to deal with the temper before it erupts again (it also helps if mother and father have dealt with their own temper problem!).

5. *Make sure your children know you understand their problems and that you love them.* If it's a serious and ongoing problem, make it a matter of daily prayer for and with the child.

6. *Reward good behavior.* Rewards don't have to be material. A sincere compliment, a hug, even a smile, let children know they've done well. "You made your bed this morning, son. That's three mornings this week. I'm proud of you." This works better than on the fourth day saying. "You didn't make your bed today. You didn't make it one day last week either." Even worse, "Be sure and make your bed. I'll have to punish you if you don't make it."

7. *Spot potential problem areas.* Pray for wisdom for both you and your child in coping.

8. *Set the example.* Many of our offsprings' behavioral problems are learned experiences—learned from observing parents in action. For instance, don't expect truthful children if they hear you saying when the phone rings, "If that's Mrs. Little, tell her I'm not in."

—CECIL MURPHEY

LIMITATIONS OF SPANKING

Punishment by itself will not always resolve a child's behavior problems. While parents should normally punish wrong behavior under any circumstances, they may also need to deal with other factors if they want the problem fully resolved. For example, small children sometimes become so over-tired that they lose the ability to control their behavior. At such times, they may need to go to bed more than they need a spanking, and the parents' rules should allow enough freedom for this to happen.

Misbehavior may also signal some frustration or anxiety in a child's life. The wrong behavior itself should be punished, but the parents must also help the child deal with the frustration at its source.

We used to live near a Christian family with a nine-year-old son, Jeffrey. Our son John played with Jeffrey a lot, and despite their age difference, the two boys got along very well. At one point, however, both sets of parents noticed that Jeffrey was testing John and treating him badly. Since he was disobeying his parents' rules for how to treat younger children, he was spanked.

After the spanking, however, Jeffrey's parents noticed that he seemed to be feeling some kind of frustration. A little probing revealed that he was having problems in school; his frustration there had provoked the mistreatment of John. This didn't excuse Jeffrey, but it did show his parents how to get to the root of his bad behavior. They talked to their son and his teacher to help clear up the school situation, and then John and Jeffrey were back on good terms.

Parents whose child has a physical, emotional or mental handicap must also take this factor into account when dealing with misbehavior. They should expect obedience and good behavior from their child, but they will need to make adjustments in their goals and means of communication according to the child's abilities.

Today parents worry so much about children's psyches that we are sometimes paralyzed by the fear of making a mistake that might damage their self-esteem or give them some kind of complex. But children are not too fragile to survive an occasional mistake. Any parent is going to end up giving an undeserved spanking or laying down a rule that proves to be unjust. In these cases, the parent should be willing to admit the mistake and ask the child's forgiveness, but they need not get excessively worried by the slip. Children will not be warped for life just because they had parents with human limitations.

—From Ralph Martin, *Husbands, Wives, Parents, Children.* Ann Arbor: Servant, 1978.

Obedience

The object of training children is not to teach them to be blindly obedient to their parents. I know that obedience to parents is a very necessary factor in raising children. The Scriptures say so: "Children, obey your parents in the Lord, for this is right" (Ephesians 6:1). It is part of the proper process. But if our concept of obedience is that parents are to make the decisions for their children up until the time they leave home, we will produce ill-formed, distorted, helpless, overly dependent children. The goal, then, is not to train them to a blind obedience; the goal is to transfer their obedience, as quickly as possible, *from parent to God.* And though obedience is required, it must not be a blind obedience to the authority of parents.

The reason for this, of course, is that par-

ents make mistakes. If I were to make my children obey blindly everything I say, I would make them obey my mistakes and they would suffer for it. Rather, as quickly as possible, I need to make clear to my children that *I* am capable of making mistakes and that I, too, must be subject to the authority of the Word of God. Thus they will learn that the ultimate authority is not their parents; the ultimate authority in life is God.

We often speak of the "chain of command," referring to the line of authority reaching from God to the husband and through him to the wife and children. But this phrase can easily be misunderstood to mean that children are bound into an authority-link with their parents as long as they are at home. I would prefer the term "the chain of *guidance.*" It is true that parents have ultimate authority over young children and are to command them. But, as rapidly as possible, that command ought to be merged into a chain of counsel in which the parent allows the decision-making to rest more and more in the child's hands. And as he is able to handle it, the parent becomes a counselor instead of a commander. This is the picture that Scripture gives. We are to transfer their obedience, as rapidly as possible and in as many areas as we can, from ourselves to God.

—From Ray C. Stedman, David H. Roper, et al., *Family Life* copyright © 1976, pp. 70–71; used by permission of Word Books, Publisher, Waco, Texas 76796.

Growth Guidelines

Since limit setting can provoke considerable conflict, consider these guidelines to help you choose the limits you will set for your teenagers.

1. *Recognize that every person is different.* What was right for you when you were a

teen, or what is right for one teen is not necessarily suitable for another.

2. *Discuss the possible limits with your teenager before making a decision.* If your mind is already made up and you don't really listen to your son or daughter's perspective, he or she will know you are simply defending your position, rather than really looking at the situation with an open mind.

3. *Differentiate between a biblical absolute and your personal preference.* Sometimes we parents just naturally assume that our way of looking at things is the biblical way. Whether it is hair length, clothing styles, or forms of entertainment, we conclude that we have the final word on the issue. Many teenagers have been turned off by parents who thought they were being helpful by claiming that certain forms of dress or certain social activities were obviously sinful and out of God's will. If we are convinced that a certain style of dress or an activity like movies or dancing is not helpful, we should tell our teenagers why we think so. And we can share with them our reasons. But we must take great care not to tell them the Bible clearly supports our position, unless God has in fact clearly spelled it out in Scripture. Our teens can read for themselves and are likely to be very resentful, when they start reading the Bible for themselves and find out we have been putting words in God's mouth!

4. *Be flexible.* There are reasonable exceptions to most rules. A special situation with proper safeguards may call for revised limits.

5. *Compare your standards to those of a variety of other parents.* This can help avoid narrow decisions. It can also help see where we may want to set limits that other parents haven't.

6. *Work toward cooperative development of standards.* Don't get in the position of being a policeman or a judge. You are a loving, caring parent, who wants to work together with your teenager for his good.

7. *Allow increased freedom and responsibility with age.* Sixteen-year-olds can generally make better decisions than they could at fourteen, and their responsible choices are encouraged by growing freedom to form decisions.

8. *Never set a limit without giving a good reason.* "Because I said so!" is a frustrating reason to growing, fair-minded teenagers. They are bright enough to understand our reasons even if they don't agree. We will develop their abilities to make decisions by giving a clear answer to their question *Why?*

A frequent temptation is to impose a rule or regulation to attempt to control teenagers *after* a problem has arisen. Let's say, for example, that you find out your teenage daughter has become involved in heavy petting or premarital sexual encounters. The immediate tendency is to find a rule or regulation that will limit this behavior. You might forbid her to date the offending boy, or set a very early curfew. Such limits are very unlikely to solve the problem. Premarital sexual experiences reflect a combination of forces including biological urges, desire for warmth, peer pressure, personal values, and family communication. None of these qualities are significantly affected by rules set up after a problem has arisen.

The need here is for improved parent-teen communication that will allow us to understand our teenager and her struggles, so that we can help her with the underlying problems. Rules and regulations are a cheap substitute for this type of understanding and are often imposed as a last-ditch sort of effort, when we think all else has failed. But instead of helping, they only stir up more resentment. Teenagers who are violating curfew, involved in premarital sex, or using drugs and alcohol are crying out for understanding. They are telling us they have a need and want us to understand and listen. To throw another rule at them in this situation is to give them one clear message. "We do not understand and we have given up being parents. All we know how to do now is try to control you like a warden does a prisoner."

This is certainly not to say that rules are unnecessary for our teens. The issue, however, is the sequence and the attitude. Before we establish any rule, we first take time to understand, to listen sympathetically, and to think through the issue, so that any decisions or regulations will grow out of a deep and sensitive caring for the welfare of each member of the family. In other words we should never attempt to establish rules apart from personal relationships. And if our relationships are so ruptured that we cannot work out agreeable guidelines, we should probably look for a professional counselor, or a third party, who can help us solve the underlying conflicts that are causing the heated debates about behavior.

—From Bruce Narramore, Ph.D. *Adolescence Is Not an Illness.* Old Tappan, N.J.: Revell, 1980.

Maturity

The process of emotional development and maturity attainment takes a long time. Even in middle age, many men and women are still immature in some areas. Therefore, it is hard to evaluate the maturity of someone of student age. What is often diagnosed by psychiatrists as a personality disorder or an adolescent-adjustment reaction in a young person is really immaturity as measured by a comparison of his behavior with that of other people his own age.

A patient I saw recently, a sophomore in college, manifested his immaturity by *narcissism* (a condition named after Narcissus,

the handsome young man in Greek mythology who fell in love with his own reflection in a pool of water). His parents had smothered him with love and generosity. He was constantly the center of attention at home, a state that he had found most pleasing. At school he was always showing off, to hold the interest of others. Lack of imposed discipline at home led to a lack of self-discipline in his personal life. He was dependent on frequent praise and verbal approval, encouragement, and congratulations of others. He had no confidence in his own worth or abilities because all his life he had relied on the reassurance of others as to the quality of his performance. He was supremely selfish, even to the point of overt antisocial behavior, and was constantly striving to gratify his wants at the expense of others.

He had come into treatment when he realized that the adult world was not accepting of his behavior. Competition was tougher than he had been prepared to handle with his own abilities. Because of poorly disciplined study habits, he was beginning to fail academically and his social life was nonexistent since he had not developed any close relationships. Unhappily, his motivation for treatment was also immature. He wanted me to help him to regain popularity so that he could continue his egocentric life-style. When I pointed out that more healthy goals in treatment would be directed towards a mature integration into responsible adult society, he failed to show up for another session.

The young child is a good example of immaturity and selfishness. He cries if he wants something and goes on crying until he gets what he wants or his attention is diverted. He has little understanding or concern for anyone but himself and has a minimal ability to postpone his gratification. To describe a child as immature and demanding is not derogatory. It is normal, indeed sometimes necessary, for him to be the way he is; but some adults are like that: selfish to the point of complete rejection of the needs and interests of others and totally unable to postpone the satisfaction of their supposedly urgent needs.

Maturity is the acquisition of all those virtues which enhance the full healthy development of the adult personality and is measured by the individual's ability to respond appropriately to the various pressures and difficulties of life. No one can achieve absolute maturity any more than one can achieve sinless perfection in this life. The two are relative rather than absolute, and to some extent, are related. It is not that the mature adult is free of sin, but rather that the sanctified Christian who has victory over sin by God's power is better able to adapt to stress and change in a mature way.

Some of the characteristics of maturity are:

1. Self-understanding of one's abilities and limitations
2. Unselfish willingness to give rather than receive
3. Ability to learn by one's mistakes and experiences
4. Formation of satisfying relationships and permanent loyalties
5. Freedom from anxiety, depression, dependency, and insecurity
6. Showing love, sympathy, understanding, generosity to others
7. Determination to change what can and should be changed
8. Serenity to accept the unchangeable, trusting God's control
9. Intelligent application of sanctified common sense
10. Self-control to postpone gratification of desires and needs when necessary
11. Willingness to take responsibility and accept calls to leadership
12. Having the grace to be humble before God and man.

The test of maturity in a person is the way he responds to adversity or disappointment. The mature person will not wallow in self-pity, but will have the courage of his convictions, self-discipline and a steadfast determination to pursue what seems to be the right course, in spite of all difficulties and setbacks.

The true Christian has both the obligation and the resources to achieve maturity. He is obliged to achieve it if he is concerned with the fulfillment of his spiritual duties. He needs to be a well-integrated person, both for the maintenance of a deep, obedient relationship with his Lord, and also for his effective witness of the Gospel to others in an enthusiastic and attractive way. His main resource consists of the changing power of the Holy Spirit which can help him to grow to maturity. This power is available through regular and systematic devotional prayer and Bible study and a moment-by-moment appropriation of it by faith.

The acquisition of the qualities of maturity requires hard work, effort, and willingness to grow. No one becomes mature by drifting through life like a leaf being carried downstream. We have to fight the upstream battle continuously, and the hardest part of the battle is combating the greatest enemy of maturity—selfishness. God wants to give us this victory, however, and we need to appropriate unto ourselves both the cleansing power of the shed blood of Christ and the power of the Holy Spirit to resist our continuing carnal nature. In this way we gradually become transformed into the image of God that He desires us to be. He promises to change us so long as we continue, in sincere repentance, to live by faith.

Evaluation of maturity in the Christian is the measure of the extent to which he is living in conformity with the will of God for him. "Prayer changes things," we often hear people say. I would prefer to say, "Prayer changes *me*." This is what the prayer of supplication should be. I tend to ask God to change *things*. He usually replies by changing *me*. I can then change what I must or He can help me to accept what cannot be changed and adapt myself accordingly. *Things* can sometimes mean circumstances, and God can and does change circumstances for my benefit, but only if I myself am willing to be changed. Sometimes these very circumstances become the means which God actually uses to effect changes in me.

Thus, Christian maturity is the experience of bringing my will into conformity with God's will for me through prayer. He either gives me what I have asked for or alters my desire into the direction that He knows is best. In this way I cannot lose as long as I continue to desire God's will. David said: "Delight thyself also in the Lord; and he shall give thee the desires of thine heart. Commit thy way unto the Lord; trust also in him; and he shall bring it to pass" (Psalms 37:4, 5).

Believing that His will is the best in the light of eternity, the mature Christian not only permits but actually *wants* his own will to be made to coincide with God's. When this can become his attitude in all things he will have attained a maturity in Christ which is his ultimate goal in this life.

—From O. Quentin Hyder, M.D., *The People You Live With*. Old Tappan, N.J.: Revell, 1975.

Financial Training

ALLOWANCES

A primary means of teaching children the responsibilities of handling money is to give them an allowance. This should be done as soon as a child is ready for school.

The philosophy behind the allowance is two-fold. As a family member: 1) The child is entitled to a certain amount each week as his share of the family income; 2) He is responsible for routine chores without pay as his share of the family work—washing the dishes, etc.

The amount of the allowance will vary, of course, according to such factors as the child's age, his financial needs, and the financial circumstances of the family.

However, the amount of the allowance is not as important as the responsibility of handling money. It is a new experience, and the child will make many mistakes. Don't hesitate to let the "law of natural consequences" run its course. You're going to be tempted to help little Johnny when he gets his quarter and spends it all the first day on candy. You won't like the fact that he has to live the rest of the week without all the other things he wants and maybe needs. Don't bail him out. His mistakes will be his best teacher.

Parents should offer advice on how to spend money, but your child must have the responsibility of freedom of choice. Excess restrictions will only reduce his opportunities to learn by experience.

The first few pennies and nickels will make a lasting impression. Every Saturday morning I used to walk to the corner store with my son Matthew to buy him a "special treat," a pack of his favorite gum. Despite my persistent advice, the entire pack would be consumed that first day.

When we started to give him an allowance, we decided that Matthew would have to buy his own gum. I will never forget the pained look on his face as he came out of the store with his first purchase that cost him two weeks allowance. "Daddy, this gum costed me all my money!" he blurted. That pack was rationed with tender care and lasted more than a week.

Parents should slowly increase the allowance as the child grows in his ability to handle additional purchases. The father of a close friend used to periodically test his three children. He would give each child money for their clothes. If they were conscientious in the spending of the money, shopping for the best values, the father knew they were prepared for greater responsibilities and a larger allowance. But if any of the children would spend the money frivolously, the father knew that child needed to mature before his allowance was increased.

—From Howard L. Dayton, Jr., *Your Money: Frustration or Freedom?* Wheaton, Ill.: Tyndale, 1979.

STEWARDSHIP

Children should have an opportunity to learn effective use of money at an early age, realizing that possession of money necessitates choice—whether to save or spend and on what to spend. Children who learn good stewardship of money in the years of dependency will show more responsibility when they become independent. At an early age they should learn to take care of themselves and their possessions as a trust from God and to protect property and to respect the rights of other individuals. They should learn to share gladly their gifts and abilities and to be aware of and to meet the needs of others. Progressively they should participate in planning with the family in the Christian use of money, abilities, and possessions.

Children should be given allowances both because they have needs to be met and because they must learn how to handle money. They need to learn the difference between short-term and long-term objectives and how to evaluate the many different items for which they can spend their incomes. The amount of money that children receive should be related to their needs and maturity.

Even though parents can afford to give everything to their children, they should not do so, for children need to learn some degree of independence and gain a sense of personal achievement. Allowances should not be given as rewards or as payment for doing chores, nor should they be withheld for poor grades in school, bad behavior, or a similar reason. Children should seek to do commendable work at home and school because of the responsibility involved. One is not paid for doing or being good, nor can money purchase the affection or approval of others. Work is a given, a fact of life, and there is no such thing as "no work" on the part of any healthy family member.

Careful thought should be given to financial arrangements with children because they become conditioned to a pattern of events which they expect to continue and which creates certain behavior habits. Children who are conditioned to gratification expect things to be acquired without effort on their part by making a demand or creating a "scene." Children need a sense and dignity of achievement, but too much pressure for achievement beyond ability puts too much strain on them, which has a destructive effect and causes anxiety, tension, and aggressive behavior.

Teens have trouble spending wisely. The Rand Youth Poll reported in *Youth Today* that 38 percent say they buy ridiculous products to satisfy their egos and frustrations, that two-thirds think their friends are making foolish purchases, and that teenage savings are short term.

As children and youth earn money, they can be helped to set up spending plans and records of their own which are simple at first and then expanded to suit their growing earning power. Setting financial priorities, including offerings to our Savior, should be learned.

Parents need to set clearly defined standards and limits. Properly administered, these guides are a sign of loving children enough to care about their well-being by defining limits and holding to them, including handling money. All should realize that the use of money is a revealing index to their character and to their heart's attitude and commitment to Christ.

—From Waldo J. Werning, "Family Financial Planning" in *Living and Growing Together*, Gary R. Collins, ed, copyright © 1976, pp. 70–72; used by permission of Word Books, Publisher, Waco, Texas 76796.

Sex Education

Probably the most basic factor of all in sex education in the home is that dad and mom love one another and that the kids are aware that this strong love exists; also, that dad and mom communicate about their own sexuality and attempt to work out the problems that are plaguing them, and that the kids know that these problems are being worked out. Love is basic. Parents who are seeking a sound approach to sex education need to know that, first of all, there is no single approach or method that is always right for all children. Yet the core of any approach or method that is always right for all children is a continued, reassuring love between parents and between parents and children. In a home where love exists and radiates, the young child learns how to give love in return and a mature love develops as he first loves his parents, then playmates, teachers, special friends, and finally that love that leads to marriage and family. But if the child is not loved, it will be all but impossible for him to learn how to give love.

Love must be communicated and it can be in so many ways. Affection must be demonstrated. Companionship, attention, comfort, happy sharing of joy and enthusiasm, all help to communicate love in the home. All youngsters must know they are loved, wanted, and appreciated at home because if they do not have this assurance, some young people become deeply unhappy, some become emotionally disturbed, some become rebellious non-conformists, or some even become mentally ill. Some young people seek almost exclusive acceptance in their peer groups and often engage in a good deal of unhealthy sexual experimentation as they seek to establish a close relationship with some person of the opposite sex, a kind of relationship they never experienced at home.

Many parents feel anxious about their own ability to show affection to their children and to other young persons. There is no real need for concern if the anxiety is sincere. The need for concern arises when it is but a rationalization to escape responsibility and involvement with their children. If affection and love are sincere, the children will quickly recognize it and they will feel the genuine liking and concern and will respond accordingly. A genuine love in the home makes it possible to make the story of the passing of life from one generation to another full of wonder and beauty which helps to create sound attitudes of dignity and self-respect which in turn help to bring good health and happiness in marriage and family life.

A second important concept regarding sex education in the home is that sex education comes through many experiences which begin at birth and continue throughout life. Since sex is more than a physical act or expression, rather a major aspect of one's personality, it is intimately related to the person's emotional and social development as well as the person's physical development.

The importance of human sexuality can be fully understood only by relating it to the total adjustment of the person in his home, family, and society. Parental attention needs to be directed to a very important fact which is often overlooked and minimized at most. The fact is that whether adults give sex education or information or withhold it from the child, his experience of life itself begins his sex education at a very early age. We need to rid ourselves of the naive assumption that in the absence of direct instruction, no sex education takes place. The fact that sex education does take place continuously cannot be escaped by any parent. Parents cannot choose whether or not they will give their children sex education; they can only choose whether they will do something negative or positive about it, or whether they will accept or deny their parental responsibility.

. . . .

What then are some objectives of sex education in the home? The following positive and functional goals will be beneficial for self-evaluation and helpful for implementation of sex education in the home that really works.

1. To provide for the individual an adequate knowledge of his own physical, mental, and emotional processes as related to sex.
2. To eliminate fears and anxieties relative to individual sexual development and adjustments.
3. To develop objective and understanding attitudes toward sex in all of its various manifestations—in the individual and in others.
4. To give the individual insight concerning his relationships to members of both sexes and to help him understand his obligations and responsibilities to others.
5. To provide an appreciation of the positive satisfaction that wholesome human relations can bring in both individual and family living.

6. To build an understanding of the need for the moral values that are essential to provide rational bases for making decisions.
7. To provide enough knowledge about the misuses and aberrations of sex to enable the individual to protect himself against exploitations and against injury to his physical and mental health.
8. To provide an incentive to work for a society in which such evils as prostitution and illegitimacy, archaic sex laws, irrational fears of sex and sexual exploitation are non-existent.
9. To provide the understanding and conditioning that will enable each individual to utilize his sexuality effectively and creatively in his several roles, e.g., as spouse, parent, community member, and citizen.

This is a big order. It can be adequately accomplished in the home through example and teaching by encouraging free and open communication. Since sex education is a function of the total personality, it must be broadly conceived and concerned with the biological, psychological, spiritual, and social factors involved in personality and interpersonal relationships both ideally and actually.

—From Bennard R. Wiese and Urban G. Steinmetz, *Everything You Need to Know to Stay Married and Like It.* Grand Rapids: Zondervan, 1972.

Problem Areas

CHILD ABUSE

With almost daily headlines revealing the tragedy of child abuse, we think it is a new phenomenon. It has, however, always existed, and seems to be a part of the condition of mankind. It is not easy to define child abuse because a practice some people believe to be good discipline is the very thing others see as abuse.

Definition of Child Abuse. A definition we personally find helpful is this: "Child abuse is any treatment of a child that threatens his safety, or leaves physical or emotional scars." If your methods of punishment leave such marks on your child, please commit yourself to changing.

Description of a Child Abuser. There are several *common denominators of people who abuse their children:*

1. *They are lonely* and usually emotionally or physically far from their families. They are often afraid or suspicious of people, so they become "stuck" in their isolation.
2. *There often is conflict* in their marriages, or they are divorced.
3. *They are people who live under great stress,* such as financial, job-related pressure, trouble with neighbors, or housing.
4. They are *parents who were abused* by their own parents in childhood.

One abusive mother recently told us about the cruelty of her own mother. She said, "But, you know, I wish I could go back to her even now, I miss her so much!" She was explaining, a little bit, how it is that being abused creates habits of abusing. When this mother abuses her children, she is unconsciously being like her mother, and can momentarily feel the old closeness.

Strangely enough, the abusive parent really loves his child. More often than not, we have seen abused children preferring their own parents to the safest of foster care. Partly this is due to the love—strangely as it is expressed—of those parents. Abusive parents also generally are energetic people, and children tend to be attracted to people of high energy.

Qualities of the Abusive Parent. On a personal level, there are several qualities of the abusive parent that we feel need to be understood.

1. *Lack of self-control.* Abusive adults often act like spoiled children. They actually have a temper tantrum, and at that moment they feel powerful.
2. *Lack of self-confidence.* Parents who do not know their true wisdom and strength go to great lengths to try to prove themselves. Such people overreact to fairly normal situations with extreme rage.
3. *Lack of trust in their parents.* While they usually loved their parents, they were also put down by those parents. They usually felt either extremely intimidated by, or extremely powerful with, their parents.
4. *Seeing in the child some negative quality* that was present in their parents, in each other, or themselves. Unconsciously, such parents take out, on the helpless child, vengeful feelings that really belong elsewhere.
5. *Lack of sense of self-worth.* Because they basically feel so unworthy, abusive parents find it impossible to ask for help. They don't want anyone to know how bad they are, and feel if anyone knew, they would be even more rejected.
6. *Child learns to fit into the pattern.* Children quickly learn how to get a parent's attention. They may even sense that they are meeting a need in that parent by evoking the abuse. So the child forms the very habits that fit into the vicious cycle.

Treatment of Child Abuse. Obviously the best treatment of child abuse is the prevention of it. The following ideas will help in that prevention as well as contribute to a cure.

First of all, if you even suspect that you

are an abusive parent, do something! Do not wait for the next explosive episode to happen. It could be the time when you might lose control and seriously hurt your child. Talk with your minister, some trusted friend, or a professional counselor.

If you can't bring yourself to talk to someone you know, *call your local child-welfare agency.* You need not identify yourself until you feel more comfortable. Ask for any help you need.

Find a "Parents Anonymous" group. They are parents who are or have been abusive themselves, and they will fully understand your feelings. The national headquarters are:

Parents Anonymous
2930 West Imperial Highway
Suite 332
Inglewood, California 90303
or
Parents Anonymous
250 West 57th Street, Rm. 1901
New York, NY 10019

They will help you find or organize a group in your own vicinity.

Reread the above paragraphs and *try to identify your deep needs and feelings.* By knowing them and admitting them, you are well on your way to finding real solutions.

Dealing With Potentially Abusive Situations. In dealing with such situations, try one or more of these suggestions:

1. Get in touch with your earliest feelings of desperation and rage—before they take your self-control away from you.
2. Remove yourself from your child and that explosive situation at once!
3. Talk with Jesus Christ. Close your eyes and imagine He is present with you—as He said He is. Tell Him how you feel and ask Him for whatever you need—love, guidance, tenderness, or whatever.
4. Call a friend, if you can. Talk over your problem and ask specifically for what you need. Plan together how you can safely discipline this child, or handle a touchy situation.
5. With courage and caution, go to the waiting child and put your disciplinary plan into effect.
6. Remember your own childhood. By recapturing your experiences of fear and anger, you may understand your child and learn to treat him better.
7. Learn to love yourself and treat yourself kindly, even in your deepest emotional being.

If you have ever been an abusive parent, you probably should religiously avoid all physical punishment of a child. Just as one drink can revive an alcoholic's old habits, one such punishment can trigger a chain reaction of abuse. *Avoid it like the plague!*

Counseling. For some people, the best answer to child abuse is professional counseling. If you are an abusive parent, swallow your pride and go for it! It may save your child's life. It will certainly improve yours. You may learn how to understand and accept yourself as a whole person, as well as how to deal with your child. As you discover your strengths and weaknesses, you may find they balance out better than you feared. Learning to truly love yourself will inevitably teach you how to love others—including your child.

—From Grace H. Ketterman, M.D., and Herbert L. Ketterman, M.D., *The Complete Book of Baby and Child Care for Christian Parents.* Old Tappan, N.J.: Revell, 1982.

DRUGS

People resort to drugs for a number of reasons, and it is not surprising that the greatest attraction of these agents is to young people in the midst of adolescence with all its turmoil. It would be wrong to say that there is one single answer to the question of why adolescents are attracted to drugs, but some reasons stand out more than others. Basically, the abuse of any kind of drug, whether it is legal or illegal, is an admission of failure to cope with one's internal anxiety and with the world as it is. Some of the commonest reasons for drug abuse that I have seen in my clinical practice with adolescents are as follows.

Experimentation. Many young people experiment with drugs as a response to peer pressure. Fortunately, many of them never repeat the process. Those who become chronic users of a drug tend to have more than the usual degree of adolescent problems and they seem to be desperately trying to establish some form of psychological homeostasis.

Identification. The process of identification may be one of two sorts. It may be an identification with peers and with the peer group as a means of separating from the parents, or it may be a negative identification in which the adolescent becomes as unlike the parents and their values as possible. If the family beliefs and the family value systems have been very much against drugs, the adolescent may choose drugs as a means of demonstrating individuality, difference, and his or her own identification. Similarly, it may not be so much an antiparental maneuver as part of an initiation fee one pays to be fully accepted in the peer group.

Alleviation from anxiety of any cause. Adolescence is one of the most anxiety-ridden periods in life, and a very common reason for taking drugs at this stage is to treat the anxiety by self-medication. Since anxiety is the outstanding characteristic of this age, it should not surprise us that adolescents are especially afflicted with this malady. Nor should it surprise us that the adolescent should use a variety of pills or alcohol to treat this anxiety when, in effect, although perhaps legally, his or her parents may be doing exactly the same thing.

Mystical Preoccupation. It would be very wrong to imagine that the present generation of young people has turned away completely from inner spiritual experience. I believe that, indeed, just the opposite is the case and that adolescents today appear to be searching for authentic religious experience more than at any other time in history. In adolescence the religious and spiritual needs of a person are perhaps more acutely felt because one has not yet gained the calloused quality that so often goes with maturity in the world today. A common story in the American family today is that as our standards of living have gone up our standards of loving have gone down, and no adequate value system will be formulated outside of a milieu of love in the family. When parents try to supply the needs of the growing adolescent with dollars rather than love and compassion, that value will very rapidly be found to be self-destructive.

Spiritual Vacuum. By far the most important cause of drug abuse seen in my clinical practice is the existence of a spiritual, religious, and existential vacuum. It seems that young people today, lacking foundational value systems from stable family units, are constantly looking for meaningful models of identification in other places in society. When they fail to find them, they are left to struggle on their own with an increasing sense of frustration, lack of purpose, and meaninglessness. As materialism has become a god, there has been a simultaneous humanization of God. Experience has shown that when such an "adamification" of God occurs there always is a corresponding deification of man. Such a human production of God, however, will always fail to fill a sense of emptiness and to infuse any sense of value, hope, or meaning in the existence of the young person. Thus, again, adolescents become likely prospects for the psychochemical experience, fascination with the occult, and have all the prerequisites for the development of antiestablishment delinquent activities.

—From Basil Jackson, "Drugs, Adolescence, and the Family," in *Living and Growing Together.* Gary R. Collins, ed., copyright © 1976, pp. 115–16; Used by permission of Word Books, Publisher, Waco, Texas 76796.

PEER PRESSURE

[Peer pressure] is a normal phenomenon, influenced by our teenagers' needs for love and acceptance and their desires to begin breaking the ties of childhood and finding new sources of support. Now we will look at specific guidelines for helping our teenagers benefit from, rather than be harmed by their peer relationships.

The starting place is to realize peer influences do not have to be negative and harmful. A Proverb says, "He who walks with the wise grows wise, but a companion of fools suffers harm" (13:20). Many teenagers are helped immensely by their friends, and all learn some important lessons in interacting with their peers. Recently the teenage son of some acquaintances of ours came home from a party, drunk. It was the first time this had happened, and the parents were shocked. To their surprise, a few days later, they discovered that their son's teenage friends had already talked straight with him about the harm he could suffer if he continued drinking!

During adolescence, our teenagers try out new social roles. They are learning what it is like to choose friends and build relationships. These skills are essential in later life, and adolescence is the place to learn them. Without growing experiences in adolescence, our children will enter marriage and other adult relationships seriously deficient.

Sometimes our teenagers' friends can help them overcome potentially serious problems. They hear out our troubled offspring when we are too busy or otherwise are unable to listen. Sympathetically they encourage and even offer wise guidance. Sometimes our teenagers' peer relationships help correct or overcome negative attitudes they have learned from us. A teenage girl, whose father is a hard-driving, demanding and perfectionistic person, for example, may be under constant pressure to perform in order to gain her father's approval. A good relationship with a boyfriend may for the first time give her a glimpse of the fact that she can be accepted exactly as she is.

A teenage boy, whose mother has been controlling or overprotective, may have a distorted image of all women. A healthy relationship with a girl friend may help him see it is possible to relate to the opposite sex in an open, mutually rewarding manner. He can begin to alter his perception that all women are controlling, and he can begin to feel more at ease and less threatened when with the opposite sex. These changes will serve him well when he marries.

Even in families with good relationships, adolescents need peer friendships for the give-and-take between "equals" that is critical for normal growth. For these reasons, *we need to affirm the value of our adolescents' friends and encourage our teenagers to bring their friends to our house or have them "drop by" for visits.* Parents who know and like their adolescents' friends, and are comfortable having them around, are much less likely to have problems with negative peer influence.

One parent offered this advice: "Be prepared for an ever-changing cast of characters—friends of all sizes, talents, and dispositions. One by one they will file through your home and your life. Their ultimate destination will be your heart and your refrigerator!"

By being hospitable to our son's and daughter's friends, we are demonstrating the value of friendships. We are also avoiding much anxiety that accompanies our teens' associations with friends little known to us. One of the main reasons we are so afraid of negative peer influence is that we generally don't know much about the people our teens are running with. We get an outward glance or a quick impression, but we seldom take time to sit and chat and really get acquainted.

Hopefully, we have started valuing our children's friends long before they reach the age of adolescence. If not, we need to make up for lost time. We can open our home for a party. We can bring out a snack when friends drop by. We can invite a friend for a weekend visit. We can pay a friend's way to a parent-teen outing or give a welcome to a family activity. There are endless ways of cultivating our teen's friends and of working out enjoyable times together.

These attentions tell our teenagers that they and their friends are important to us, and that helps make us more important to them. Encouraged by our acceptance, our teens will be more inclined to be discriminating in their choice of friends.

Attitudes toward our teenagers' friends are as important as our actions. Teenagers tend to be intensely loyal. To disparage a friend is to insult your teen. We should think twice before we dispense criticisms of our adolescents' friends. Even when we have some serious questions about our adolescents' friends, it is best to refrain from criticism. Instead, we can ask our adolescents how *they* feel about the friend in question. Quite often you will find your son or daughter has some of the same reservations you do. If we take time to listen and don't jump in too soon, we may find that they are pretty good judges of character themselves!

If our teenagers don't perceive some potential problem that we observe, we can raise our concern in a nonjudgmental way. We might say, "What do you think about Tom's drinking?" Or "I wonder why Tom has trouble getting along with his teachers?" These questions or other concerned comments express concern over Tom's well-being. They also encourage discussion that is instantly cancelled by accusatory statements like: "I don't want you running around with that alcoholic!" or "Your friend has a terrible attitude!"

If our teenagers join the wrong crowd, or we sense they are headed for trouble because of the friends they keep, we need to explore the underlying causes. Chances are we won't have to search far. The single most important reason children from "good families" choose the wrong crowd is the lack of a warm and sustaining relationship at home. In fact, psychological research indicates the lack of family unity and communication is one of the three major causes of susceptibility to negative peer pressure. The other two are low self-esteem and the presence of a very strong and homogeneous peer pressure. Sometimes we fathers are just too busy to spend a lot of time with our adolescents. We leave early for work and come home late. By the time they finish supper, someone is off to another activity or meeting that shrinks family time together and divides interests. When this is the case, we had better reevaluate work and family priorities. Too many families are becoming strangers to one another from lack of quality time together.

I am one of those parents who had to learn to relax and enjoy my family. I grew up on a small farm in Arizona, where a high value was accorded to hard work, and little time given to family play. After our own children were born, I began to realize I was following the same pattern with our children. I was among the first to arrive at work and one of the last to leave. I arrived home tired and didn't feel like playing with the kids. Gradually I began to realize Dickie and Debbie needed more of my time—and that I needed to learn to relax and enjoy them! I had to face the fact that it was easier writing about rearing children than doing it! And I had to admit that I was a workaholic and would neglect my family, if I wasn't careful! As I changed my schedule and spent more time with my children, I began to learn the meaning of fatherhood. We played games, surfed, shopped, and did all kinds of enjoyable things. My kids showed me I had been missing a lot of living.

If you are a bit this way, let me encourage you to step up your family fun. Go to your teens' athletic contest this week. Take your son fishing, biking, or skiing. Work on his car together. Have a lunch date with your daughter, or go window shopping. The "right" activities are not as important as the doing. Learn how to enjoy your adolescents. If they are happy with you and your spouse, they will not seek out undesirable companions to make up for lack of love and approval at home.

Another suggestion for coping with the possible negative effect of peer pressure is to *see that we attend a church that has a youth group that appeals to our teenagers.* We may need to seriously consider changing churches, so our teenagers will have an opportunity to fellowship with Christian young people they enjoy and serve in challenging ministries. . . . Here I simply want to point out that one reason for church attendance is personal encouragement, and it is hard for a teenager to be encouraged by a group of adolescents he finds incompatible, or among adults who seem out of touch with teenagers. The author of Hebrews tells Christians to "encourage one another daily, as long as it is called Today, so that none of you may be hardened by sin's deceitfulness" (3:13). Support by Christian friends helps us avoid sin. If we want to help our teenagers avoid sin, fellowship with encouraging friends should be a high priority.

Sometimes teenagers turn excessively to their friends, because they feel overprotected or restrained at home. If we supervise details and regularly impose our decisions, they instinctively retreat toward breathing space. Like us, they want freedom from pressure, coercion, and criticism, and they know it's available with their friends.

Other times teens turn to questionable peers with their problems instead of to parents because of low self-esteem. Most of us choose friends that match the mental picture we have of ourselves. If this is a problem with our teens, we may need to seek skilled professional help. We may need assistance in overcoming some destructive parental habits and in building up our adolescents' sense of self-esteem and self-reliance.

Ask yourself what your teenagers' friends reveal about their relationship with you. Do their choices reflect an acceptance of you and your values? Do they reflect hidden (or not so hidden) resentments? Are there signs of self-rejection in undesirable choices of friends? Or are the signs largely positive? As we understand the meanings of our adolescents' choices of friends, we are in a position to influence them constructively in further growth.

—From Bruce Narramore, Ph.D., *Adolescence Is Not an Illness.* Old Tappan, N.J.: Revell, 1980.

FAMILY LIFE

Busyness

How can you beat the battle of busyness? Take a leaf from successful management:

1. Set aside time for a realistic evaluation of your family situation as it is.
2. List all the activities in which you and your family are involved. What are the time and frequency factors of these activities?
3. Set aside an evening for a family conference on this general subject.
4. Map out your "activity profile" on a calendar so you can see where you are doubled up or where you may have free time of which you were unaware.
5. List your priorities and evaluate them.
6. Discuss as a family some practical steps for reducing the feeling of hurry and pressure in your home.
7. Place high on your priority list having time to be together as a family and/or as a couple.
8. Plan "family times" and put them into your date book.

—From Fred Renich, *The Christian Husband.* Wheaton, Ill.: Tyndale, 1976.

Consideration

The very heart of the home is consideration for its members. The day to day expression of your consideration for your family will be determined by the practical value you attach to the many material things which are so much a part of life as we know it today.

What can you do about this?

1. Ask some honest questions:
   a. Are you more committed to your work than you are to the total well-being of your family?
   b. What is your *real* purpose for living?
   c. Would you be content with a less demanding job with a smaller income, if by this you could have a more satisfying family life?
   d. Do you feel driven by your work?
   e. Are you uptight over financial pressures created by unwise and perhaps unnecessary buying?
   f. Have you subconsciously substituted providing a nice home and all that goes with it for the day to day development of wholesome, happy people-relationships in your family?
2. Evaluate your personal and family lifestyle. Is it centered in things or in people? Are you so committed to obtaining and maintaining things that there is little time or heart for the individuals in your family?

. . . .

It is the being *burdened* about many things, that so subtly kills the graciousness of consideration in a family.

3. Discuss with your family the subject of materialism as it affects your family relationships. Come up with practical suggestions for guarding against being corrupted by too great an attachment to things and adding more.
4. Face honestly the fact, clearly stated in the Bible, that all we are and have is really God's and is only loaned to us as a sacred trust. What a tragedy if the gifts on loan to us become the cause of our own corruption. To pursue this further look at I Chronicles 29:11-17; Psalm 24:1; Matthew 25:14-30; Ephesians 4:28; Luke 12:13-21.
5. Think of ways you could use your possessions for the blessing of others. In this way you will become a channel for good, and God's gifts to you will not harm you. A lake with no outlet becomes stagnant and foul. The same lake used as a source for

irrigation becomes a reservoir of life. Study Luke 3:11; Matthew 25:31-46; Acts 10:1-4; Proverbs 11:24-26; II Corinthians 9:6-11.

There are many other causes contributing to the lack of true consideration in our homes, but most of them stem from the basic causes mentioned above. Be aware that life will get more hectic, not less. Our society is moving steadily toward greater depersonalization, less need for people around us, greater mechanization, increasing living and job transience. There is an accelerated disappearance of the ideals of chivalry, with the marked erasure of the finer distinctions between men and women. You and I will have to live in the world as it is, regardless of what we would like it to be. It is important, therefore, that we take positive steps to develop genuine consideration in our family relationships.

Here are several suggestions:

1. Identify the areas where your consideration of your wife and children needs to be improved. Look at your daily habits. In what ways do you seek to conform your habits to the convenience of others?
   a. List some things you do which indicate you are sensitive to the needs of your wife and children.
   b. Note three instances this week showing you are alert to opportunities to help them or make life easier or more enjoyable for them.
   c. How do *they* know that you are interested in the things that concern them, or that they are interested in?
   d. What indicates that you understand and appreciate their sense of values?
   e. Make a list of their hopes, fears, and aspirations.
2. Check your speech and communication patterns. Recall the past week.
   a. How many times have you monopolized the conversation?
   b. How often have you clammed up in rude silence?
   c. In how many conversations did you participate freely even though the subject didn't particularly interest you?
   d. How did you disagree? Can you present differing views without having to prove your point or make others feel threatened or belittled?
   e. Is your language courteous, clean and gracious? What is your tone of voice like?
   f. Do you speak at the age-level and emotional response of each member?
3. List areas you want to improve.

Now look honestly and objectively at the list. Take only one or two of those areas and write down some practical steps that you can take to realize improvement. It might help to talk these over with your wife or possibly have a family conference on the subject—depending on the nature of the issues and the ages of your children.

—From Fred Renich, *The Christian Husband*. Wheaton, Ill.: Tyndale, 1976.

Fun Times

EATING

There are many areas of family life that can make ordinary living together more fun: mealtime, snacktime, bedtime, household pets, music, books, games, hobbies.

What is it that a family does every day together more often than anything else? Eat. In our modern culture probably most families do not eat, *all members together,* three times a day. Breakfasts are staggered according to the individual's time of departure. The head of the house and perhaps some of the children, may not come home for lunch.

So dinner becomes the best opportunity for enjoying the family—as well as the food—around the table.

Probably most families gather at a dinner table because of hunger for food rather than for the sake of each other's company. And the meal is often eaten in this spirit. We have found that it may require real effort to make our dinnertime more than that, and sometimes we don't succeed. But the effort can be rewarding, with the appointment becoming a pleasure rather than a mere satisfying of the appetite and refueling of the body.

In "Make Dinner a Family Meal," Angelo Patri, in the *Chicago Daily News* said, "The members of a family need each other.... But unless Mother arranges the scheme of living so as to bring the family together at least once a day, the precious family unity will not be created.... The only possible way to get the family together is the evening dinner hour.... Set the dinner hour and insist that every member of the family be at the table freshened up and present in spirit as well as in body.

"This family rule must be put in force early in the life of the household group. The children, from childhood on, must be held to the rule: Everybody in his place on the hour, by the clock, and no excuse accepted. Then this meal must be planned, prepared, and cooked with consideration for the family's pleasure in it. It must be served with grace and dignity even though it is as simple as bread and cheese.

"The second rule, which strengthens the first, is that only pleasant conversation is allowed at the table. It is no place for corrections or complaints. It is the place for evidence of family unity and affection."

There are probably no "methods" that could rescue some dinnertable situations from disaster, but it *is* possible to improve the whole tone of eating together. Start when your children are young.

Don't forget that the atmosphere the table itself creates is an important factor. A colorful cloth, a pert centerpiece, an attractively arranged salad, and candles (at least on occasion), can help set the stage for a pleasant experience. And a touch of grace and simple loveliness makes learning manners seem more reasonable.

Even plastic tablecloths can be pretty. Centerpieces don't need to be expensive. I've used those lovely, bumpy (the dictionary calls them "warty"!) gay green hedge apples, otherwise called Osage oranges, or dried grasses and flowers, or pine cones—and, of course, the wonderful artificial flowers that can be washed, rearranged, and used for years.

Let your children arrange a centerpiece—anything they want. It may not always be altogether appetizing (Lorraine once included a scrubby old pair of her baby shoes—*un*bronzed) but it will seem glamorous to them, and it does open the door to creativity.

The absence of milk bottles, cereal boxes, breadwrappers, and other unnecessary commercial clutter on the table will make a big difference. And the presence of some evidence that Mother cared about dinner's being a happy occasion is bound to be at least subconsciously appreciated.

A real table discovery for my family was found in a florist shop—tall, wrought iron candle holders, high enough so that I could use in them all the colorful candle stubs left over from my more formal entertaining. But don't try to eat with less than four candle flames to light your table. It will be so dim that your family may rebel, and you may not be able to determine how much Junior eats from his sister's plate.

Eat in different places. Try the porch (Who has one?) or the back yard, eat in front of the fireplace or even in the bedroom. When a member of our small family is ill, and his ailment is not too contagious, we sometimes set up a folding table by the side of the patient's bed. He sits on the edge of the bed and dangles his feet, while we surround the table. We may even have a lighted candle in the center, or some other necessarily small centerpiece, and the whole performance is so ridiculous that it's automatically fun.

Once, when for some practical reason our dining area couldn't be used, we had a winter picnic on the living room floor. It's fun! Put a blanket down, and pillows if you want them. Use paper plates and cups, and follow your traditional family picnic pattern for equipment and menu. You may want to prepare food on your barbecue. A few extra props like the popular and successfully repulsive foam-rubberish insects—spiders, bugs, worms, and even a lovely green snake—will give your picnic an authentic touch. I haven't seen any fake ants yet, but they would be a fine addition.

Eat cafeteria style once in a while. Children love it, and they can carry their trays to whatever place you elect. We children in the home in which I grew up, were allowed to fix such a meal ourselves, usually on a Sunday night.

One family I know give their children two dollars every so often to take to the store and buy for dinner whatever they want (and can afford). They bring the food home, prepare it themselves, and serve it to the family. The first time they tried it the children served pizza (frozen variety) and fruit salad. It's easy on Mother and fun for the children.

There are children's cook books (like Betty Crocker's) that whet the appetites of the small fry for participating in the romance of meal-getting. The eating will be "fun" whether the cooking turns out to be good or bad! And don't forget to be creative yourself in the food you serve. New recipes, family favorites, and considered color combinations in the food, as well as in its setting, add sparkle to a meal.

Years ago we had to get a barbecue because Lorraine would come home from a neighbor's and report wistfully, "The Wilsons are barbecuing!" You don't need elaborate barbecue equipment, and the results can be as delicious as the process is fun. If you don't know how to proceed with your barbecuing, just ask someone who does. They'll enjoy advising you as much as they enjoy barbecuing. Current periodicals are full of practical help and new ideas.

BEDTIME

Putting the children to bed at night can fall into the category of being a chore, but it can also be a shining togetherness. The most important thing is to start at an early enough hour so that you are not hurried. That won't be possible some evenings, but it can usually be arranged if the experience is highly valued.

The hardest hurdle to get over is the late homecoming of a commuting husband, which makes dinner necessarily late. During the years when the children have to go to bed early, including Daddy in the bedtime fun may have to be confined largely to weekends, but a little careful planning may work out the problem for weekdays too. Small tykes can be bathed and put into their night clothes before dinner, so that there is time for play with Daddy after the meal. It isn't easy to feed a baby just before the family meal, but there was a time in our family when Lorraine ate better that way, and we ate with more pleasure afterwards.

If the father works locally and can get home for an early dinner, say at 5:30, then there will be room for playtime after dessert. This won't interfere with evening appointments at 8:00 o'clock or even at 7:30.

Whatever else you do or don't do with your children, make a practice of reading to them often at bedtime. It is a cuddly time, a time to get close physically, emotionally, and spiritually. The youngsters are tired after an active day and are more ready to settle down and listen. If possible read aloud a book the whole family will enjoy together. Or read the bedtime story individually with smaller members of the family.

But sometimes children want to do something else. I can remember our playing hide-and-seek when Lorraine was small and in a two bedroom ranch house with no basement! We knew all the places to hide in, and she knew we did, but we all pretended we didn't, and it was hilarious. You have to be a good enough sport not to find the child too soon, even when you know where he is. Talk aloud about the hunt as you go along, so he can relish your not finding him in some possible places.

I agree with the advice of one child specialist who insists that every father should put his children to bed at least twice a week if he has any desire to establish the closeness that ultimately wins and keeps their confidence. I am sure most mothers would agree! Intelligent fathers will view this as a privilege rather than a chore.

HOBBIES

Hobbies offer another interesting area of enjoyable family activity. You can collect something, or make something, or learn to do something, and share your enthusiasm, acquisitions, and achievements with the rest of the family.

Among one writer's listed incentives for pursuing a hobby are relaxation, pleasure, new friends and social contacts. I would em-phasize rewarding contacts with members of your own family also, for here too hobbies enrich the relationship.

Collecting stamps (or coins) has become almost a science, so extensive is the information and the number of countries and issues involved. You may do better to specialize in one era or country—for example, United States stamps from the latter part of the twentieth century. Or you may collect stamps around a special theme, such as transportation, famous people, plants, animals, music, flags, or industry. An album for mounting and a catalog for classifying are essential.

Stamp collecting is a hobby almost anyone can undertake, regardless of age, state of health, geographical location, or financial resources. Many cancelled stamps can be bought for a cent or less, though it is true that some rarer varieties cost a small fortune.

These rather exacting hobbies intrigue some children more than others, but whatever hobby suits your child, it becomes an opportunity for you to enter into his enthusiasm. Give as much help as is welcome, and occasionally contribute to the collection as a seal of your genuine interest.

Collections that require less technical know-how and a smaller investment of time may feature anything from sugar envelopes or matchbooks from different restaurants to old shaving mugs. Especially popular with children is the collecting of miniature animals—cats, dogs, horses, rabbits, giraffes, or what-have-you. Our daughter inherited a collection of miniature skunks from one of my nieces!

TELEVISION

Here are a few suggestions for the parent who has problems with children in the area of television. Most of these solutions have come from others, since we ourselves have never had to deal with the problem.

1. Make a list each week of approved programs. One family draws up this list as a group.
2. Set up priorities, listing what children must do before they may view TV—for example, homework, music practice, household chores.
3. Set time limits. Some permit only an hour a day; one family none at all except on weekends. The average adult spends four hours a day in front of a television set, and preschoolers six hours!
4. Teach children *how* to decide for themselves which programs are acceptable.
5. Don't let television interfere with meals, bedtime, or church appointments. We watch the *Today* show while we eat breakfast, for my usually charming husband is at that hour a wordless lump, and our daughter—so soon out of bed—is inclined to be edgy. The arrangement has been a relief as well as often educationally rewarding.
6. Avoid overstimulating programs.
7. Integrate available programs, where possible, with your child's current classroom interests.
8. Write to television stations and sponsors, approving or disapproving their programs.
9. Ask local stations for advice about suitable programs, or write the National Association for Better TV & Radio, 882 Victoria Ave., Los Angeles, Calif.
10. *Maintain the rules you have made.* The most common failure, on the part of parents, is to make rules and set up wise safeguards and then fail to carry out the arrangements.

PETS

For many adults, some of the happiest associations of their early years revolve around childhood pets. Some memories are gay, some sad, and some hilariously funny. But, whatever they are, they usually reflect a vital part of family living, experiences that are richer because they were shared.

If you are going to get a pet, or even if you already have one, it is good to think clearly about *why* you have it. Perhaps it is to satisfy the intense, insistent craving of a child. To some youngsters, coming into possession of a pet is, for one of several possible reasons, of crucial importance. Since your children probably have other urgent desires you cannot satisfy, be sure you have sufficient reason before you unnecessarily deny this one.

Perhaps the best reason for owning a pet is the togetherness of the experience, whether it be good or bad. The whole family is (or *should* be) interested in the project, concerned about the health and happiness of the creature, amused at its antics, and proud of its successful training and development.

It is true that caring for pets provides a natural channel for the teaching and learning of responsibility. It is also an aid to sex education.

SPECIAL DAYS

We make it our business to be at home on *Halloween* night to greet the young people who come to our door. If we *have* to be away, we import someone to answer the doorbell and distribute the goodies. Our daughter sometimes found it hard to decide which was more fun—going from house to house or staying at home to answer the bell and enjoy the costumed creatures who rang it.

Don't turn *Valentine's Day* over completely to children and young people. It is another chance to communicate warm feelings of affection, spiced with a bit of fun and nonsense, to loved ones at home and away from home. You can tactfully encourage your children to build the habit of giving valentines to Mother and Father and Grandparents on this occasion. And, if possible, do something extra to make the day special at home. A heart-shaped cake, bought or home-made, will please everyone at the dinner table and remind them that Mom isn't too old or stuffy for fun.

We still like to use the old-fashioned Valentine candy hearts with a word or two of sentiment on top. Pass them around the group in a container in which they can't be easily read. Each person, before he takes one out, says, "This is how I feel about   ," naming someone present or absent and known to all. Then he reads aloud the candy sentiment he draws out—"sugar baby," or "go away," or "nice guy," or "real square."

The *Fourth of July* has become one of our favorite holidays. We are really disgruntled if we can't spend it at home, for we love the holiday features our community offers. We personally start the day with blueberry pancakes for breakfast. In the afternoon we go to the parade—determined to enjoy it with enthusiasm, especially if it isn't quite as good as the year before.

After dinner, and just before dark, we—along with several thousand other inhabitants of our area—trek to our North Side Park, loaded with a blanket for the children and folding chaises for the adults. We have discovered that there's no way to enjoy fireworks so comfortably as stretched out on a chaise with its back let down. You literally face the sky and avoid even the threat of a stiff neck.

—From Marion Leach Jacobsen, *How to Keep Your Family Together and Still Have Fun.* Grand Rapids: Zondervan, 1969.

Vacations

As valuable as days off and "minute vacations" can be, there is a crucial need for *concentrated* periods of time when families can get away from the usual routine and enjoy new places, new people, and new experiences. A vacation for a family is a time when everyone can do together things which are not normally possible with the day-to-day demands of pressured schedules and responsibilities. These diversions will express themselves in different ways with different families.

Whereas my work has been highly demanding in the summer, as a family we have faithfully taken time, even when we haven't had it, during the winter, sometimes taking the children out of school, to have special outings as a family. I only wish there could have been more such times and that they could have been longer. So soon our children are gone, as depicted in the songs "Sunrise, Sunset" from *Fiddler on the Roof* and "Turn Around." Whatever could have been more important than the cherished memories of shared travel and adventure together?

Unquestionably the greater value of vacations is "clearing the cobwebs," taking a fresh look at life—its purpose and your goals—in a new and different environment. But also of great value is the opportunity to chisel rough edges from another (and parents come in for their share). The most crucial ingredients of life for any human being to survive happily—acceptance, recognition, and self-worth—can all be infused in steady amounts in a vacation atmosphere. Respecting another's viewpoint, complimenting him or her for an expression or act, inviting interaction from the more reserved ones through good questions, and apologizing and forgiving especially after hard encounters all go far toward building up one another. We learned early in our trip that no one could survive in an atmosphere filled with the "put-downs" so common in routine family life, but we needed constantly to watch our stance toward one another. We could not afford to be careless in this when each day was full of so much pressure. It finally dawned on

318

us it shouldn't happen at home either, unless carefully pondered so as to be "speaking the truth in love."

It has been my observation through twenty-five years of counseling young people that few concerns have made them more bitter toward their parents or their parents' jobs or churches or other Christian involvements than the failure of many parents to give vacation experiences high priority each year. There is no way to justify the oft-heard statement, "We haven't had a vacation, at least away from here, for nearly ten years now." That's dedication, all right, but to the wrong thing.

—From William D. Gwinn, "Leisure, Vacations, and the Family," in *Living and Growing Together*, Gary R. Collins, ed., copyright © 1976, pp. 79–80, 82–83; used by permission of Word Books, publisher, Waco, Texas 76796.

Building Happy Memories

"I remember . . . it was during the depression years of the thirties. Our family didn't have much money at all. Dimes were precious items, but my father had given me one to go swimming. I was so happy! I knew it was a sacrifice. On my way to the pool, I lost the dime. Sad and crying, I started back home: no dime, no swimming. Just then, my father, who was a traveling salesman, came by, listened to my story, was touched by my feelings, and reached deep into his pocket to replace my lost dime. I remember he spoke so kindly as he dried my tears."

My friend's story goes back four decades, but the precious memory is preserved in her adult mind, and the recall of it warms her heart with the knowledge, "I was loved!"

Everyone needs a storehouse of precious memories that enhance a sense of belonging, a sense of being loved, a sense of worth, a sense of competence. A memory becomes

valuable as it relates to one's needs being met. The opposite is also true—unpleasant memories are the product of situations when one's basic needs were not being met.

Parents, teachers, friends, sisters, aunts, uncles, and grandparents have the joyous privilege of helping children, young people, and other adults build happy memories that can feed their souls' needs. This can be an instrument for developing a whole person, building character, and reproducing happy memories in others.

A memory is a legacy—something special, handed down from one generation to another. It can be much more than a material object. In fact, the best memories are often stored only in the mind, not in the cedar chest or the far corner of the attic.

Family togetherness is a memory. Sometimes it involves doing the same thing in the same way enough times, until it becomes a tradition. "That's the way we do it at our house. It's always been that way. That's what makes birthdays special!" "It wouldn't be Christmas without it." Sometimes it's a surprise that will never be forgotten, but probably never repeated. Sometimes it's, "That's just the way my mother was!"

CHRISTMAS THANKFULNESS

In our family, we developed a special custom for Christmas Eve. With a desire to honor the Christ of Christmas and build in our children a spirit of thankfulness and appreciation for each gift received, when the children were tiny, we began the custom of sitting around the Christmas tree, all holding hands. Each one prays, remembering God's gift to us in the gift of His Son and praying for those who brought gifts to us and for those receiving gifts from us. This sets the tone and takes the frantic excitement out of tearing into the gifts. Each card is read, and gifts are opened one at a time. This taught appreciation of both the gift and the giver. Our children still practice this custom in their own homes.

A FAMILY TREE

Through the years we have established a family Christmas tree. Every Christmas a new ornament, containing the child's picture, is added to the tree. This year our son will have nineteen and our daughter fourteen! It has become a conversation piece, and our children are so proud of it. Needless to say, it's also a special time of reminiscing for parents! This year our nineteen-year-old son wants his picture on top of the tree. Guess where his picture is going to be? You're right: on top of the tree!

ANNUAL CHRISTMAS-TREE-CUTTING TRIP

Eighteen years ago we started taking an annual Christmas-tree-cutting trip—our four children and Dad and I. This December there were twelve of us. We have doubled in number, with the addition of two sons-in-law and two girl friends and two grandsons. We all look for the right tree, cut it down together, and then go have a big Italian dinner together. My children loved running through the trees, and this year our grandsons took the place of our boys, running through the trees. It's a great together time for the family.

A LOVE GIFT

I give each one in my family a Love Gift at Christmastime. After carefully listening to my husband and two boys (fourteen and seventeen), I determine what my Love Gift to each should be. It may not be a big thing: One was to change the sheets each week for a year, on the youngest one's bed. But as I carry out my gift of love through the year, it brings me closer to that member of the family. As I do it, the Lord gives me such joy and blessing and puts a prayer in my heart for that one, as I'm giving his gift of love. I am learning that as I take on a servant's attitude, this is freeing them to give of themselves in areas that were battlegrounds before.

CHRISTMAS THANKSGIVING

At Christmastime we have a Tree of Thanksgiving. At Thanksgiving I pick a small branch off a tree and mount it. Then each day between Thanksgiving and Christmas, we write a thank-you for something that day. I make up colored papers in shapes of bells, snowmen, and stars for each thank-you. We have great fun with this, and it has become a traditional Christmas activity for our family.

BIRTHDAY TIARA

We didn't realize until recently that what we did to honor the birthday child in our home was a big thing for our daughters (now twenty and twenty-three). When they were young, we had a jeweled tiara (crown), which they wore all day on their birthday. Also, they didn't have to do any work on their birthday, and I put out the flag for their day, just as we do for presidents' birthdays. As they reminisced at their last birthday dinner, I realized that this made them feel a very special and loved member of the family.

TEENAGE CELEBRATION

Our children are all over twenty years old now. Since they were teenagers, in addition to celebrating on their day, we have celebrated all of our birthdays together, by spending a night or a weekend together at a motel. The children loved the swimming pool and the game room, and being together brought much harmony to our family. One person was honored at each meal. It was always a fantastic time!

TENTH BIRTHDAY WITH DADDY

On each child's tenth birthday, he or she had a special day alone with Daddy. With some guidelines as to cost and distance, they could choose what they would like to do with their daddy for one whole day. Since my husband travels a great deal and is gone quite a bit, this has offered both children an opportunity to feel special and to get better acquainted with their dad. Their tenth birthdays have now come and gone, so we periodically announce that one of the children will have another special day with Dad. Last year, our son chose to go fishing. As we eat the fish that we put in the freezer when they returned, Keith is again reminded of and relives his fishing day with Dad. This had been a very positive thing in building relationships and happy memories in our family.

GIFTS FOR GRANDCHILDREN

At the beginning of the year, each of our six grandchildren can request something he or she wants my husband or me to make for him during the year—such as a quilt, a giant-sized cushion, a chair, a desk. This then becomes that year's Christmas present.

This gives them the joy of choosing and also keeps them from asking for things too often. No one is jealous of what the other receives, since it has been his own choice to receive something else. It also gives my husband and me something to work on and plan during the year. We do it joyfully, with love, knowing it is something that will please that grandchild.

LITTLE SIS

There were nine years between my younger sister and me. The age gap made her feel left out of a lot of things my older sister and I enjoyed, with our two-year age difference. Sensing her loneliness, I would ask her to go for an Adventure Walk (we lived in the country). I would summon her secretly, by a nickname that signaled the purpose of the walk was for sharing—not just a hurried trip to the mailbox or the neighborhood store.

We agreed on the nicknames Kiddo for her and Butch for me. When she sensed a need to share in private, she would use my nickname, and we would go for an Adventure Walk. First we would notice several things in nature that had changed since our last walk, and eventually the problem would come up. We found we shared better by taking this approach.

Another sister was born nine years later. Since I had left home by then, she became Butch. A special bond is still felt when one of us is addressed by this "signal" nickname. It's still the signal to find a quiet place to talk or to go for an Adventure Walk.

LOVE SITTING

In three years of marriage, my daughter-in-law has had three children. Though she is an excellent and loving mother, she has mentioned that it's easier to stay home than take the children anywhere alone.

So that I could get better acquainted with my grandchildren and also share love with my daughter-in-law, I have begun Love Sitting with my grandchildren one day a week, all day. The children and I have a delightful time enjoying one another, and it gives their mother a chance to be an adult for a few hours. I also prepare dinner for them, if she is gone till late in the afternoon.

I'm growing in love and appreciation for

my daughter-in-law's many abilities and loving attitudes.

THANK YOU, MOM

Last year I sent a dozen red carnations to my husband's mother on *my husband's birthday,* with a note: "Thank you, Mom, for Charlie!"

She is still talking about it to everyone.

P.S. We used to have mother-in-law problems. They are no more!

GRANDMA'S BOX

When our mother-in-law passed away, my sister-in-law and I were trying to decide what to do with her meager worldly goods. She didn't really have anything that was of great monetary value, but there was a lot of sentiment wrapped up in her possessions. However, neither my sister-in-law nor I had room in our homes for some of her dishes, linens, jewelry, and other whatnots. Finally, we decided to make a special box for each of the grandchildren to open on his or her seventeenth birthday. We divided the different types of items up as evenly as possible and simply stored the boxes and picked one at random on each child's seventeenth birthday, marking one box for the only grandson.

After we all sing "Happy Birthday," the teenager very carefully opens his or her special box, slowly takes out each item, and passes it around the table. There are a lot of memories shared, as we each recall when Grandma used this item or that. We made this decision before the nostalgia craze hit, and we never anticipated the intense delight each child would have with the old items. Just this year, my niece was absolutely delighted to find an antique stickpin in her box. Each teenager looks forward eagerly to his

seventeenth birthday, when Grandma's Box makes them feel very special.

MEMORY QUILT

Sixteen years ago, a little girl blessed our home. I was delighted, of course, and being fond of sewing, I was especially happy to have a daughter. I have saved material from everything I ever made for her and plan to give her a quilt made from years of memories, for her wedding. With each piece I attach a note: "Birthday-party dress, three-years-old," or, "Christmas, 1979," and so forth. I have such joy, cutting this material in the old "flat-iron" pattern, tucking away the pieces, and planning in years to come to sew them together.

I shed a few tears when I think of giving her the quilt, because it ends a period of time that she radiated so much sunshine under our roof. Even though the children are off my lap, they are never off my heart. This is one way I plan to show my daughter what a joy she has been to us through the years.

—From Verna Birkey and Jeanette Turnquist, *Building Happy Memories and Family Traditions.* Old Tappan, N.J.: Revell, 1980.

Health

Some families undergo more than their share of illnesses. Others enjoy robust health, with the members seldom even catching as much as a cold. Doctors as well as laymen used to speak of family differences in "constitution" and susceptibilities which "run in the family." Then, some forty years or more ago, medicine began to look at the emotional psychological components of physical health and illness. In doing so, the health professionals were rediscovering what the fathers of medicine, all the way back to Galen and Hippocrates had taught: that mind and body cannot be separated, and that what affects one affects the other. Even the new word given to this interaction, *psychosomatic*, implied some sort of dichotomy, but it did, nevertheless, reintroduce an important way of viewing the human being as a total person which had been virtually lost in the mechanistic approaches of previous centuries. . . .

We probably all have evidence to support this hypothesis. Let's take, as examples, two families. Family A—mother, father, two children—average about nine illnesses per family member each year. Most are minor (upper respiratory, influenza, gastrointestinal, etc.), but some may be chronic (migraine headaches, colitis, asthma) and in rare cases one or two might even be life-threatening. (Incidentally, nine illnesses per family member is approximately what some studies have reported as average.) Thus for Family A, illness occurs on the average of thirty-six times per year! Family B, the next-door neighbors, also including father, mother, and two children, average only four illnesses per year for the entire family. Can we come up with a plausible explanation for these differences?

The first possibility: Family B may be "just naturally" healthier than Family A. Perhaps genetics favor them. Perhaps some people are born of "good stock" while others are not. This is a difficult hypothesis to test. Less difficult is a second possibility: that the members of Family A receives a less nutritious diet, engage in less exercise, have fewer vitamin pills, or less frequent medical checkups. Perhaps the members of Family A live in a more germ-ridden environment. This hypothesis is easier to test. But if we cannot explain the differences by our first two hypotheses, it makes sense to at least entertain the third, that the psychological ambience of the respective homes may differ significantly, and that this variable is more important than the others.

Increasingly, physicians and psychotherapists have found evidence that psychosocial factors in the cause and progress of disease have been given less importance than they merit. Medicine can now cite substantial clinical evidence to support the position that a happy, emotionally sound home environment is also the healthiest physical environment. The family members get sick less, and recover from illnesses more rapidly.

That we feel better when we are in "good spirits" is self-evident. We can all draw upon personal experience to affirm it. The physiological mechanisms through which we ward off disease, and how these mechanisms are affected and/or controlled, by our intellectual/emotional states are still not fully understood. We have learned a great deal in the last thirty years but we still have much to learn.

ILLNESS

Reactions to the illness of a family member are almost always ambiguous. Often, they are love/hate reactions, and they are affected by whether or not the illness is acute and short-lived, such as a severe cold, or long-lasting or chronic. The latter may, obviously, produce the more profound effects—whether positive or negative. Whatever the severity or duration of the illness, the reaction of other family members may be as follows:

Compassion. This is a feeling of deep sympathy and sorrow for another's suffering or misfortune, accompanied by a desire to alleviate the pain or remove its cause. It is the reaction we expect from concerned, loving persons. But what if our desire to alleviate their pain or remove its cause is frustrated? What if there is nothing we can do? The compassionate feelings may center solely on sympathy. In fact, sympathy (rather than remedial action) becomes the primary focus. Unfortunately, it often tends to be overdone.

Excessive sympathy is never helpful, and it can be harmful. Nevertheless, if we feel we have nothing more to offer, we may layer on sympathy to an inordinate degree.

Compassion is, of course, an emotion we want to encourage. We also want to encourage our children to engage in the actions which are motivated by the emotion. We hope they will learn the meaning of charity. Sympathy, however, especially when it is excessive and borders on pity, is seldom of much help to the patient. The relationships no longer remain the same. Patients are often heard complaining, "Everyone acts so different; why can't they just be natural?" There are some individuals, however, who seemingly soak up all the sympathy they can get. They are the types who seek a lot of attention at all times, and sympathy provides attention. How the compassionate impulses of the family members are expressed must, therefore, like all interactions within the home, be monitored by the parents. It is the parents who must encourage charity while at the same time set the limits on sympathy. People may not be killed with kindness, but if it is expressed in the wrong ways, they can be kept sick.

Withdrawal. Young children are often baffled and frightened by illness in the family, especially illness which strikes down a parent. When mother is confined to bed it is more than an inconvenience to the child, it is a threat to his or her security. To the child, parents simply do not get sick; parents don't die; parents always are and always will be. They are the Rock of Gibraltar. To a lesser degree this is true of their siblings. Any serious illness affecting any family member unsettles the child's world. The illness need not be life-threatening to have this effect. When a family member is confined to bed, everyone speaks in whispers. This is unnatural. They don't laugh as much. Equally unnatural. And everyone pays particular attention to the sick one. The well child may respond by withdrawing into himself. He may talk less and spend more time alone. His withdrawal may reflect fear (of the unknown: outcome of the disease, changes in the family), feelings of rejection due to the nursing demands of the ill member, suppressed hostility—often followed by guilt toward the "privileged" sick one, feelings of impotence ("No, there's nothing you can do to help"), and vague anxiety.

Denial. In reacting as if nothing has happened and nothing has changed, the child constructs a shield against the painful reality. Parents may attempt to explain that Jimmy is very ill and may be in the hospital several days or even weeks, but brother Chris may, no more than an hour later, ask if Jimmy can go to the track meet with him the following day. Chris denies Jimmy's illness. The more unacceptable and fearful the reality, the more the defensive denial is apt to be employed.

These reactions, and others as well, may also be expressed by the parents. If the wife and children have seen the husband as the strength of the family, unflappable and stoic, his illness may create severe stress in all family relationships as they struggle to find new sources of strength and self-sufficiency. The mother may have to take over roles with which she is unfamiliar. She may feel overwhelmed, frightened, and resentful. She may in turn make additional, even excessive, demands on her children. Her stoic pillar-of-strength husband may seem to revert to childhood, a frightened, complaining, and demanding little boy in pain. She then finds herself nursing a stranger, reacting to her own fatigue and/or resentment. If she is the one to become ill, her husband may be the one cast in the roles for which he feels totally unprepared. Ironing a little girl's dress or doing the weekly grocery shopping may be baffling. The specific chores and roles are not important. In most young families today, traditional household chore designations of "men's work" and "women's work" is seldom heard (a very positive move toward egalitarianism and common sense), yet nevertheless, husband and wife will almost invariably have developed proprietary roles. Whether for reasons of convenience, talents, or interests they will have fallen into patterns which result in their performing separate and very distinct functions within the home, roles with which they have become familiar and comfortable. With illness, then, the roles the indisposed spouse has regularly assumed will be thrust upon the other family members. Often these roles will not be assumed with the same expertise, and frustration for everyone will be the result. The newly assumed roles can, of course, be accepted as challenges, but the frustrations will usually lurk there as at least a potential danger. With the illness of any family member, especially a parent, the family members can, with help, pull together. They can assume the new roles and take on additional tasks. They can adjust to their altered life-styles, whether for a few days or for many months, and they can do so with equanimity and love.

—From Joseph W. Bird and Lois Bird, *To Live As a Family*. New York: Doubleday, 1982.

WEIGHT CONTROL

It came as a shock to me to realize that the Apostle Paul calls the body the temple of the Holy Spirit. His recorders of the first century would have understood that much more clearly than we. They thought of the tabernacle or the temple as that special place where God dwelt. They kept it clean; they followed minute instructions in its maintenance. Certainly, then, Paul is saying that we're to give care to our body.

This is not only to please God. It's also for our own benefit. Obesity is a definite health hazard. Somehow we tend to think of obese people as jolly, always full of life. Often that's only a cover-up. Obesity walks hand in hand with chronic diseases and early death. The burden of extra weight we haul around every minute takes its toll. Countless studies have proven that fat people are more likely to develop degenerative diseases and to die at younger ages than those of normal weight. Overweight people are more prone to cancer, diabetes, strokes, heart attacks, high blood pressure, and kidney diseases.

The knowledge that my body is God's holy temple and his dwelling-place encourages me to keep the rules—that is, to watch the way I eat, to be a slimmer me. The more seriously I believe in Jesus Christ and observe his commandments, the more faithfully I watch what I eat and count the calories.

SELF-HELP REMINDERS FOR CALORIE COUNTERS

1. No fad diet or pill can alter overweight eating habits. Only *I* can change them.
2. I am setting an eating style *for the rest of my life.* I am not going to quit when I reach my desired weight. I'll always be conscious of what I eat.
3. The faster I lose weight, the more likely I am to regain it unless I alter my long-term eating habits. Weight control requires effort and a change of life-style.
4. Most overweight people eat too fast. There is a lag between the time food enters the mouth and travels to the stomach and the signal reaches the brain. Quick eating won't satisfy me until after my stomach has received more food than I need. I will consciously learn to slow down my eating time.
5. Some foods help me slow up my eating such as cauliflower, lettuce, celery, cu-

cumbers, broccoli, and cabbage. They also have negligible calories, and I can eat them in almost unlimited amounts.

6. Bay windows are out of style. I will work toward trim lines.

7. The best exercise: pushing myself away from the table. The next best: running, because it's inexpensive, can be done almost anywhere at any season, and provides one of the best, all-around exercise programs.

8. In addition to a sensible diet, I can help my weight-loss program by daily exercise. If I expend more energy than I take in through food, I lose weight. Many people feel they have less appetite and actually consume less food after exercising.

9. If I take in only one hundred extra calories every day, I will gain ten pounds in one year. If I eat one hundred calories less every day than I need, I can lose ten pounds a year.

10. I will not eat only one meal a day. It's more fattening. When I eat a large meal, my body secretes more digestive juices and I actually digest the food faster. Consequently, I become hungry soon after a meal. It's easier and healthier to digest smaller meals. My body also needs nourishment more than once a day. I can divide up my total calories for the day into six meals instead of three.

11. Negative emotions cause me to overeat. When I become aware of anger, anxiety, sadness, or loneliness, I will find corrective ways of dealing with that emotion rather than by eating.

12. As I achieve goals in my weight-loss program, I will celebrate through buying or doing something nice for myself (but not by eating).

13. I will remind myself regularly that I am beautiful, acceptable, and lovable to God, no matter what my weight.

14. I will remind myself that this body I live in is also God's house.

15. I want to lose weight. I will be less prone to diseases such as diabetes, heart conditions, and high blood pressure.

16. Because God wants me at my best, he will help me in my calorie counting.

—From Cecil B. Murphey, *Devotions for Calorie Counters*. Old Tappan, N.J.: Revell, 1982.

Hospitality

"We're having a family party," David said. "Each of our four kids is allowed to invite a couple or single. You and your husband were our teenagers' choice." He laughed. "Of course, we tried our hardest to talk them out of their suggestions, but they stood firm!"

His children, Randy and Missy, are in our high school Sunday School class, and in spite of their father's teasing, we were thrilled that they liked their teachers well enough to invite us as their guests. We were even more impressed with the idea of a family party. Their parents were making a creative effort to involve their children in hospitality.

Why not? We train the children God gives us in stewardship, discipline, and Bible study. Why shouldn't we use our homes as training grounds for Christian hospitality? Why shouldn't they grow up learning to say, "This is my home, open to you to enjoy and laugh and share and cry. You are welcome here."

You can get started involving your whole family in hospitality by talking together about why Christians open their homes to each other, and often to strangers. Search out what the Bible says about hospitality. Discuss what makes a guest comfortable or uncomfortable in your home.

Next, with your youngsters, pick a hospitality idea that seems like it will work in your home situation. You may start with something simple like inviting another family to lunch. Or, it may be an elaborate yard party designed to help your family get to know the neighbors or people at your church better. The key thing is to involve the kids from the very beginning. The whole family plays important parts—developing the guest lists and party ideas, cleaning the house, preparing the food, and talking with the guests.

The ideas you use in your hospitality event are very important. You'll want to pick activities that both youngsters and adults will enjoy. For part of the evening your kids will probably play with their younger guests, and the adults will have time to share with the adults, but in order for a family hospitality function to be a success, the two age groups must mix at some points.

If you have teenagers, this mixing may be doubly important. Young people are establishing who they are apart from their parents, and quite often they will, for a time, need to shut their parents out of their lives and begin to share ideas, secrets, dreams, and doubts with others instead. They are wise parents who provide opportunities for Christian friendship between mature adults and their teenagers. Those adults could become the teenagers' confidants, their models of growing adult Christianity.

I'm big at setting goals for any planned hospitality event. A goal is a statement of what you want to happen at your party. The best goals can be measured, so the family can say for sure at the end of the evening, "Yes, that happened," or "We missed that goal." Here's a goal example: *My goal is to have each child get to know three adults well enough to consider them friends.* Once the goal is set, the family can pick games and arrange seating to help the goal be realized.

Idea-Starters for Family Hospitality Times

That's right—just starters. These aren't complete hospitality ideas, but they will get you started. Read them, and wait for one to hit you with the feeling, "Hey, that's it!" Then, with your family, develop the idea into a complete party. You'll have a great time showing God's love to others and enlarging your children's circle of Christian supporters.

CHRISTIAN HOLIDAY SHOW OR TELL

Ask each guest and family member to be prepared to show or tell something that points to the Christian meaning of the holiday. You might pick Easter, Christmas, and perhaps even Thanksgiving or a national holiday.

Encourage everyone to strike a balance between light and heavy responses. Caution adults to pick things that everyone in the group, even the five-year-old child, will understand.

For example, I might play an Easter song on my violin. I'm terrible on the violin even after years of lessons. My best friends don't know of my attempts to play. But for such an occasion, I just might drag out my lack of talent. My husband could bring a picture that is important to him and tell how God touched him through it. Our five-year-old nephew could master several sets of rhyming couplets—and the party is on its way.

POLAROID PICTURE PARTY

Divide the guests into two or more teams, giving a Polaroid camera to each team. Divide the teams so an equal number of children and adults are on each.

Give each team the same list of pictures to take. The first team back with all the pictures wins. Create lists that make sense in your area and that fit the season or theme of your party. For example, if the party is in the spring, you might include items like these:

- A bird building its nest.
- Two people who look like they are in love.
- A man in a spring-colored suit.
- A picture of something that wasn't here last spring. Strike a balance between easy and difficult pictures. When all teams return, make a picture display and award prizes.

BET I CAN BEAT YOU

For this game evening, all the games should be suited to the abilities of the children, not the adults. The competition is between adults and kids. Each child will play against a different adult for three ten-minute games. Blow a whistle when time is up and the person who is ahead at that time wins fifty points. At the end of the evening, add all the children's scores together and all the adults' scores. The team with the fewer points has to wash dishes that evening—or some other terrible thing.

Games could include pickup sticks, jacks, two-person board games, or tiddlywinks. In order for this game evening to be successful, children should be nine years or older.

MUNCH A BUNCH

It's a cookie making and eating party. It could be an all-female event, but that certainly isn't necessary. Almost all of my husband's male friends are great cooks and their children—boys and girls—would enjoy playing in dough and chocolate chips.

Each adult brings his favorite cookie or candy recipe. A youngster is assigned to an adult partner (not a parent) and together they mix up a batch.

This idea could easily grow into a service project. When the cookies are made, half could be eaten and the other half beautifully wrapped and delivered to someone in the church who might need a cookie lift.

SUMMER SHOW

Invite people who hate winter to come and build summer snowmen with you. Use Styrofoam balls and toothpicks to make the men. Then have children and adult partners decorate their snowmen with material scraps, construction paper, and glitter.

Give prizes for the funniest, ugliest, or most original.

And, of course, serve nothing less than ice cream balls for dessert. You could even roll them in chocolate and coconut.

COME-AS-YOU-ARE PARTY

Everyone has heard of this type of party and even seen situation comedies on television developed around them. But I've never been invited to a come-as-you-are party. Have you?

Let guests know that within the next ten days, your family is having a come-as-you-are party. The exact date and time are surprises. When the time arrives, let the children call each person invited to announce, "It's now. Come exactly the way you are."

Once the guests arrive, you might plan do-it-yourself costume competitions. For example, have partners use newspaper, pins, and tape to make great-people-in-history costumes. Or perhaps, great-people-in-the-Bible costumes.

'SORT OF' RELATIVE PICNIC

Many families live far away from their blood relatives. So why not make some adoptions? Ask your family to choose who they would pick for relatives in your area.

Invite these "sort of" grandparents, aunts, uncles, or cousins to a picnic. Make a relative button for each guest that identifies who that person is: "Grandmother for the Day."

Ask adults to come prepared to share some stories from their childhoods, and perhaps the stories surrounding how they came to accept Christ.

PROJECT-PLANNING PARTY

Decide on a family who has children about the same ages as yours. Meet together to pick a special project your families could do for God. Pray about it together. Plan ways the families can earn money necessary to complete the project. Make certain every child has his part.

Project ideas are limited only by your imagination. How about earning money to get something the church or a missionary needs? Or, could you sponsor a refugee family? Is there something you could do to help a third family in need?

How do you earn money? The way doesn't matter as long as each child has a part. You could have a car wash, print a neighborhood newspaper and sell it, or bake goodies to sell. Or do something unusual like starting a special-day reminder service. You'll call people who subscribe two days before special events that they might otherwise forget. Your families provide phone reminders of birthdays, anniversaries, etc.

TREASURE HUNT

Invite several families to a Treasure Hunt that your family plans. This hunt can be done in a neighborhood, park, or even throughout a city if you decide to have parents drive.

Remember—in a treasure hunt, one clue leads to another. The final clue points to the treasure which is usually dessert. The first group finished wins.

Here are a couple of clues to show you how a Treasure Hunt might work:

Clue 1: Go to the split tree at the end of Market Street. On the lowest branch, you will find the clue.

Clue 2: (On the branch) Climb this tree and look north. Go to the door of the church with the highest steeple. Under the third step is the next clue.

Each group can have a different set of clues, as long as the last clue tells them where to return for food. Or, you can start groups at fifteen-minute intervals, and keep track of time. The group that comes back in the shortest time wins.

LIVE A BIBLE STORY

Younger elementary children enjoy impromptu drama. To help them visualize Bible stories, plan a living drama with another Christian family with children about the same age as yours.

Before the drama, both sets of parents should read the story to the children. At the site for acting out the story, children should have first crack at choosing their characters. Some good stories to play in a park include selected stories from Joshua's life, Paul's second missionary journey, the last week in Jesus' life.

Actually, this idea will work with high school-age kids and adults who are interested in serious Bible study. The enactment could cover, for example, the wandering in the wilderness or the complete ministry of Jesus. This walk-through drama helps geography become real. The events fall into order. The implications of the Scripture to us today might even become easier to understand and put into practice.

YOUR FAMILY'S OWN ORIGINAL
NEVER-BEEN-DONE-BEFORE IDEA

This is the best hospitality idea of all. It's the one that usually begins with someone excitedly saying, "Quiet, everybody. I just had the most terrific idea." Then you know the seeds of hospitality have taken root. With God's help and your loving care, those children will continue practicing true hospitality and expanding its definition far beyond food and parties and laughing conversation. And that expansion will last the rest of their lives.

—BY Marlene LeFever.

In-laws

"In-law" can mean a given husband and wife as one distinct emotionally fused subcultural unit and the families of both husband and wife as the other unit regardless of their form.

In-laws can be a source of trouble. My clinical experience indicates that in the early years of marriage problems are caused in about 40 percent of the cases by in-laws. As the marriage grows and improves this decreases to an average of about 10 percent after twenty years or so of marriage. In-laws thus become less important to a given marriage as time goes on.

There are two major causes for in-law problems. One results when the parents do not emotionally release their child. The second is caused by the child not emotionally breaking away from the parent.

The causation really depends on the total personality structure of the people involved. Here, maturity plays the major role. A mature marriage is not childishly dependent and can break away from its parents. A mature parent is not possessive and can release the child. If neither can function maturely,

then we really have no "in-law" problem. Rather we have people with problems which affect their interrelationship with other people.

We think we are actively involved in three areas of time—past, present, and future. This is a delusion. The present is merely a fraction of a second. No one is emotionally capable of dealing with fractions of seconds in his daily routine of living. This leaves only two areas of time—past and future. Look at all creation, everything is geared for forward (futureward) moving action. Generations are born, they live, they die. The next generation takes over. Time marches on. This forward motion is *natural law.* We cannot live in the past, for we will be frustrated because it violates this natural law. This is the order of creation.

This same law applies to a marriage. The marriage of the man and wife is one unit. The children of this unit are the future, and the "in-laws" of this unit are the past. We human beings are so constructed in accord with this natural law that none of us is emotionally capable of coping with all three generations. We are capable, because of the order of creation, of successfully fulfilling the demands of our "present unit," the marriage, and to perform for the future of our children. The past must be released. The Biblical exhortation validates this with the words, "A man should leave his father and his mother."

Many husbands and wives become disturbed over the "obligations" they have toward their respective parents. This is too often exaggerated by the uncanny techniques of parents in instilling a false guilt in their children. No child asks to be born. Responsibility and obligation do not rest on the children to "lay up for the parents, but on the parents for the child." However, if the parents (not necessarily all in-laws) become irresponsible in either health or money, out of respect and honor the husband and wife (children) assume an area of responsibility. This involves the condition when both parents are bedfast or if their finances are depleted.

This does not necessarily mean that the past is brought in to live with the present, or the present takes leave to live with the past. This responsibility can be operative by proxy. For example, money can be sent to take care of financial hardship, or nursing care can be employed to take care of the sick.

These, plus other such practical aspects as living with parents, or parents living with their children, cannot be governed by any rule of thumb beside that which is determined by the maturity rank of all involved. One cardinal rule must be adopted: the marriage must be protected. Creation orders it.

A practical violation of this relationship with in-laws is often committed by many spouses. When the husband and wife are in the company of in-laws (or friends) the act of open disagreement takes place. Be careful, especially with in-laws. Always present a united front to all concerned even if you disagree with your spouse. When you get home you can register your opinions. Your spouse is grateful for this backing in public (I am assuming you have a mature marriage).

Remember, when you marry you do marry into another family. It cannot be ignored or maliciously discarded. To be a better in-law means to be a better person within yourself. This calls for employment of acceptance of yourself and mutual respect for each other's identities. No in-law relationship is always acceptable, it has its "ups" and "downs." Keep yourself emotionally well and spiritually upgraded and you won't be the butt of the manifold in-law jokes.

—From Julius A. Fritze, *The Essence of Marriage.* Grand Rapids: Zondervan, 1969.

Aging Parents

. . . . While the debate on so-called "old folks homes" rages, another argument ensues over aging parents living with their children. While seventy-five percent of the elderly people in our country still head their own households, many of them live in a house they can't keep up, that's underoccupied, and often in a deteriorating neighborhood with a rising crime rate.

Care for aging parents has more impact on women, because, studies show, they generally feel greater responsibility than men for the emotional well-being of people. And since the life expectancy of women exceeds that of men, it's more likely to be a mother or mother-in-law who needs care.

Sooner or later most women are confronted with the problem and have to make a choice with their parents about how they will live out their years. While there are no easy answers, there are some guidelines that can help:

1. *Recognize and own your needs.* Like the answer to "the greatest of all commandments" question (Love the Lord your God . . . and your neighbor as yourself), our relationships to others depend on our relationship to self. Our true acceptance of others, even our parents, starts with self-acceptance. This includes an awareness of who we are and what our needs are. But beyond that, we have to own our needs and realize that it is legitimate to see that those needs are met. If you attempt to care for an aging parent or anyone else at the expense of meeting your own essential needs, anger, guilt and sickness can often result.

2. *Examine your view of aging.* Our society measures the worth of a person by his or her ability to produce and consume. Lacking that ability means not having a valued social function to perform, and thus makes one worthless. However, the Bible

teaches that our worth comes not from what we do, but from who we are—beings made in the image of God. One's worth does not depend upon one's usefulness to others, but upon God's unmerited and unmeritable love.

The theoretical perspectives concerning aging include two very different approaches. Activity theory suggests that the key to successful living is to remain active. On the other hand, disengagement theory suggests that aging involves inevitable mutual withdrawal. Whatever one's theoretical approach to aging, it does involve change and, frequently, loss. But a biblical perspective would be that life is a continuing opportunity to grow into the full stature of Christ. Even loss can be seen as spiritually significant in the "emptying" and "letting go" process. Not only will your attitude toward aging greatly influence your experience of aging, but it will affect your response to your aging parents.

3. *Accept your own aging.* The mid-life crisis, an increasingly discussed concept, is a painfully real experience for many. Part of the mid-life crisis involves coming to grips with the significance of one's own life. Just as we begin to face up to our own aging, we are confronted by aging parents who force us to "pre-live" our own aging. Aging parents remind us that the greater part of our earthly pilgrimage is past. As grandparents and then parents decline and die, we are pushed to the "front line" of mortality. This can result in a good deal of emotional stress.

4. *Strive for an acceptance of your parents' aging.* To see parents who were once strong, healthy, independent, and in control over us, become weak, dependent and looking to us to take charge, is a frightening experience. Rather than relating to our parents as parents or as dependent children, we should strive for "filial maturity": Adult children relating to parents as adults.

5. *Assess your feelings about your aging*

parents. Formed in childhood, our feelings toward our parents generally establish a pattern which we carry throughout life. Because no parents are perfect, children often grow up feeling they were never completely accepted by one or both parents, that a brother or sister was more loved or favored, that they were not given needed emotional or financial support, or that they were generally manipulated or restricted. As adults, our feelings toward our parents tend to be the same ones we had toward them as children. Added to that are feelings and attitudes toward our parents developed from our adult experiences. These feelings may not be "acceptable" ones, and we try to avoid dealing with them. But ignoring them won't make them go away. Instead, unresolved or unrecognized feelings are oppressive and hinder us from being truly helpful. Indeed, they often catapult us into unwise decisions.

6. *Finish any "unfinished" business.* Remember that your parents were once someone else's children, and they probably did as good a job of parenting as they were capable of. Our job now is to develop a relationship with them that permits us to relate to them—not out of anger, guilt, or fear, but out of love, care, and concern as adult children. Coming to grips with our own feelings helps to develop a filial maturity which respects both the strengths and weaknesses of our parents. Forgiving their past mistakes, we can accept them as human beings who are our parents. If you need to ask forgiveness or to help them say, "I'm sorry," do it now. Don't put it off until the day when you will say, "I wish I had." Tell them how much you love them, rather than trying to prove it after it's too late.

7. *Plan with your parents.* Letting your parents know that they can depend on you when they need you is important. However, it is equally important that they know you

love and respect them and will not make plans *for* them, but *with* them. Assuming it is possible, find out what your parents perceive their needs to be and how they would prefer those needs be met.

Admittedly, the abilities, desires, goals, health, economic resources, and other personal characteristics of both parents and children will influence your plans. However, because each person in each family is different, there isn't one general solution which is always the best. Most would agree that it is desirable for older couples to remain independent as long as possible. An environment which is overly supportive robs an individual of his adaptive capacity; however, a situation which provides the needed support for one elderly person might be constraining to another.

For example, in a home for the aged, Mrs. Smith may feel reassured by a staff member's nightly check, but Mrs. Jones may regard it as snooping or patronizing. Whatever the plan, it needs to allow for as much independence and individual choice as possible.

8. *Share the caretaking responsibilities.* Changing parents' living arrangements or lifestyles is a difficult decision. The parents and ideally all the family members should be involved, and perhaps even a doctor or other professional. Even in a large family, the responsibility for being "caretaker" frequently falls on one person. While that one person may not have been chosen, or did not volunteer for the wrong reason (for example, being a martyr, the family scapegoat, the only single child), it is frequently a female who bears the load.

It is unfair to assume that one child should be more responsible than another. Caretaking should involve *all* the family members according to some equitable plan. For parents who prefer to go on living in their own home, the family may need to make a list of exactly what is required for that to work, and then, in a family meeting, decide who will do what and when. Or, if the parents go to live with one of the children, the other family members will work out how each can help. If you are an only child, or the only child living in an area where the parents live, you may need to involve "surrogate family"—neighbors, friends, volunteers, paid helpers. This is an area where the church family could and should be actively involved. The apostle Paul commands us to "bear one another's burdens," but we must always remember that it's a two-way street: bearing implies sharing.

9. *Minister to your parents' emotional needs.* Because of the personal, social, physical, and financial losses of old age, emotional needs are perhaps greater than at any other time in life. As people get older they tend to feel less attractive and therefore less lovable, so they are especially in need of physical contact. So touch, kiss, or embrace your parents if you can do it sincerely. Even a parent who has been undemonstrative will frequently treasure a pat on the back, an arm being stroked, or a hand being held. In a poignant poem entitled "Minnie Remembers," an elderly woman speaks about kids who do their duty, pay their respects, chatter brightly and reminisce, but never touch her.

Aged adults are still sexual human beings. "Because there's snow on the roof doesn't mean there's no fire in the furnace," a friend assured me. For adults who have been sexually active, sex continues to be important. Do what you can to insure that your parents have the privacy necessary for meeting their sexual needs.

10. *Respect the dignity of your parents.* Encourage them to take an active part in the community in which they live. If they are unable to do that, do what you can to bring as much of the community to them as possible. Put them in touch with whatever resources are available, but don't allow that to be the substitute for what you can provide.

As they age and lose ground, it is especially important to provide help in a way which undermines their independence as little as possible. Find ways of letting them know that they are really worthwhile people— even if they can't do everything for themselves.

Whatever form your care for your aging parents takes, your relationship can be enriched by observing the following:

1. Thou shalt maintain regular contact by phone or mail or in person with thy parents.
2. Thou shalt include thy parents and family in holiday celebrations.
3. Thou shalt be imaginative in thy gift giving (perfume is better than liniment).
4. Thou shalt listen to thy parents' reminiscences thoughtfully, for life review is a necessary and healthy process.
5. Thou shalt not gloss over thy parents' complaints and worries with cheerful clichés and patronizing reassurances.
6. Thou shalt not make thy parents speak about matters which are embarrassing or distressing to them.
7. Thou shalt not in any way undermine thy parents' self-regard or assurance.
8. Thou shalt let thy parents know that thou art on their side.
9. Thou shalt try looking at thy parents' situation through their eyes.
10. Thou shalt not lose the ability to laugh at thyself, nor the ability to encourage thy parents to do likewise.

—BY Dorothy J. Gish, Ph.D.

CARE OF THE AGING

If at all possible, an elderly person should be allowed to stay at home. A terminal nursing home is a very impersonal place where individual privacy is almost nonexistent. An elderly couple, in particular, should at the very minimum have the dignity of their own bedroom. It is both common and healthy for sexual interest and some measure of potency to be maintained even into the eighties and nineties in both men and women. Even if they are no longer capable of orgasm, an elderly couple can derive much pleasure and comfort from sleeping together and this should never be denied them by consigning them to custodial care simply for the convenience of the junior generation. Young people often find that the thought of sexual activity in old people is distasteful. By contrast, studies have shown that sex not only can continue into late age, but also that some couples have actually experienced increased activity after retirement; many women, it was found, become orgastic for the first time in their sixties.

Eventually the time will come when, with great age, a person can no longer continue the interesting pursuits of the early retirement years. At this point his family, personal physician, and friends have special responsibilities, especially if the patient becomes a shut-in. "I was sick and ye visited me" (see Matthew 25:36). This saying of Jesus compels us to a personal ministry of visitation of the sick and infirm. As visitors, our task is to help mobilize the life-force and arouse the will to live within the sick one. Elderly people especially enjoy visits from their grandchildren. The carefree joy of youth is good therapy for one sinking into despair and hopelessness. We need to be good listeners, patient to hear even that which is repeated several times. The obligation to help someone to live "in the truth" is important to the Christian but this has to be balanced by the factor of the shut-in's measure of contact with reality.

Our visits should be brief if he is tired, longer if he is anxious to communicate. We should keep away from negative subjects such as illness or the death of others. At all times we should be cheerful and optimistic, always mentioning something, however trivial, that the shut-in has to look forward to. If possible, the occasion can be not only social but spiritual. "Is any sick among you? let him call for the elders of the church; and let them pray over him, anointing him with oil in the name of the Lord: And the prayer of faith shall save the sick, and the Lord shall raise him up; and if he have committed sins, they shall be forgiven him" (James 5:14, 15). The verbalizing of a brief prayer can be very therapeutic. In this we can invoke God's help to relieve discomfort and pain, to direct doctors and nurses caring for him, to bring healing if it be His will, to watch over the needs of loved ones, and to draw closer to the patient with strengthening assurance and love. The reading of short passages of Scripture can bring added peace. Especially remember the beautiful promise in Isaiah: "And even to your old age I am he; and even to hoar hairs will I carry you: I have made, and I will bear; even I will carry, and will deliver you" (Isaiah 46:4).

—From O. Quentin Hyder, M.D., *The People You Live With*. Old Tappan, N.J.: Revell, 1975.

SPIRITUAL LIFE

Dedicating of Children

A husband and wife ought to give their child to God even before he is born. And they should pray together after the birth of the child, willingly dedicating themselves to train him as God directs. Some churches conduct public child dedication services. In others, the pastor participates in a quiet act of dedication in the home. The important thing is that the parents themselves covenant with God to handle their children as a sacred trust, arrows to be shaped for God's glory.

Raising children is obviously a serious responsibility. And isn't it strange—for almost any other job we are required to take some specialized training first. But for the most important business in life, the shaping of young lives for God's glory, we can get away with none at all if we want to. For that reason some people have drawn the erroneous conclusion that being a good parent comes naturally. On the contrary, it takes a great deal of study and continuous attention to the assignment. But God's guidebook is available, and we are going to search it for the help we need. Since this is one job we can't quit, we might as well press on together and learn what God has to say about being a better parent.

—From Richard L. Strauss, *Confident Children and How They Grow*. Wheaton, Ill.: Tyndale, 1975.

Dedicating the Home

When a family cares enough about spiritual things to incorporate them in its life the home will gain a sense of high fellowship. A daily recognition of the spiritual is like looking up at the stars. Each family will shape its own program of religious expression, probably with some elements adapted from the childhood homes of the two, and others worked out in their own experience.

The new custom of dedicating homes places an emphasis on the sacredness of the home and on the distinctness of the new family.

The dedication service offered here can be conducted by homemakers, either by themselves or with any others they may desire to have present. Parts of it may be assigned to the pastor or others. The parts are here divided between the husband and wife.

DEDICATION SERVICE

Musical Prelude. (Optional)

Recognition

Husband: "Behold I stand at the door and knock; if any man hear my voice and open the door, I will come in."

Wife: We recognize Christ as the head of this house, its Guest and also its Lord.

A Beatitude for the Family

Happy is the family that has a true home built by loyal hearts,

For home is not a dwelling but a living fellowship,

In love and understanding.

And happy is the family whose members find a deeper unity

In sharing truth and beauty and devotion to the good.

Their love shall be an altar fire

Burning in the temple of the Highest.

Prayer

O God our Father, and our eternal Friend, we recognize with joy that Thou art the Source and Giver of the love that draws us together. We pray that Thou wilt be present in this home, that Thy love may enrich its fellowships, Thy wisdom be its guide, Thy truth its light and Thy peace its benediction, through Jesus Christ our Lord.

House Blessing. (May be repeated in unison, or responsively.)

[Select a favorite prayer, poem or hymn.]

Scripture

A new commandment I give to you, that you love one another; even as I have loved you, that you also love one another. By this all men will know that you are my disciples, if you have love for one another. (John 13:34, 35 RSV)

Love is patient and kind; love is not jealous or boastful; it is not arrogant or rude. Love does not insist on its own way; it is not irritable or resentful; it does not rejoice at wrong, but rejoices in the right. Love bears all things, believes all things, hopes all things, endures all things. (1 Corinthians 13:4-7. RSV)

Hymn. "For the Beauty of the Earth."

For the beauty of the earth,
For the beauty of the skies,
For the love which from our birth
Over and around us lies,
    Lord of All, to Thee we raise
    This our hymn of grateful praise.

For the joy of human love,
Brother, sister, parent, child,
Friends on earth and friends above,
For all gentle thoughts and mild,
    Lord of All, to Thee we raise
    This our hymn of grateful praise.
                    —CONRAD KOCHER

[Other hymns may be chosen as desired.]

Declaration

Husband: We who make up this family believe that God has brought us together and that He is our Helper.

Wife: We agree to work and pray that our home may be a source of strength to its members and a place of warmth and fellowship to all who come into it.

Dedication and Candle-Lighting Ceremony (Parts divided as desired.)

We dedicate our home to love and understanding. May its joys and sorrows be shared and the individuality of each member appreciated.

We light a candle to FAMILY LOVE

We dedicate our home to work and leisure. May it have gaiety and high fellowship, with kindness in its voices and laughter ringing within its walls.

We light a candle to HAPPINESS.

We dedicate our home to a friendly life. May its doors open in hospitality and its windows look out with kindness toward other homes.

We light a candle to FRIENDSHIP

We dedicate our home to cooperation. May its duties be performed in love, its furnishings bear witness that the work of others ministers to our comfort and its table remind us that the work of many people helps supply our needs.

We light a candle to COOPERATION

We dedicate our home to the appreciation of all things true and good. May our books bring wisdom, our pictures symbolize things beautiful and our music bring joy and inspiration.

We light a candle to APPRECIATION

We dedicate our time and talents to live for one another, to serve our generation and to help build a world in which every family may have a home of comfort and fellowship.

We light a candle to UNSELFISH SERVICE

We dedicate our home as a unit in the church universal, an instrument of the kingdom of God, a place of worship and Christian training and a threshold to the life eternal.

We light a candle to SPIRITUAL ENRICHMENT

If there is a fireplace the husband may light a fire and all present throw twigs on it.

Husband: As the flames point upward so our thoughts rise in gratitude to God for this home, and in prayer for His blessing upon it.

Prayer of Dedication. (Followed by the Lord's Prayer, all uniting.)

O God, our Father, we thank Thee for this home, and for those other homes whose good influences remain with us. Help us so to live together here that Thy blessing may rest upon us and Thy joy be in our hearts. As we grow in love and comradeship may our thoughts go out in good will to our neighbors and to all mankind, and more and more may we know Thy love which passes all understanding.

As we dedicate this home we pray that Thou wilt consecrate it by Thine own indwelling, that its light may so shine before men that they shall glorify Thee, through Jesus Christ our Lord who taught us to pray:

Our Father—

Solo or Reading, "Bless This House" by Helen Taylor.

[another hymn may be chosen if desired]

Benediction

"The Lord bless us and keep us, the Lord make His face to shine upon us and be gracious unto us, the Lord lift up His countenance upon us and give us peace. Amen."

Closing Moment of Silent Prayer. (Soft music if desired.)

If guests are present the occasion should now lose all formality and everyone should be made to feel very much at home. A song fest of old favorites would be in order, if desired; or one or more solos if persons present are prepared for them. When the two are alone they will express their love to each other with joy and gaiety, for the home is their honeymoon continued.

GRACE AT TABLE

At meals together in the cozy intimacy of the new home, there is no finer custom than grace at table. It will be most natural for the husband and wife partaking of their daily food at their own table to look to God in gratitude. Then later when children have come into the family a little circle joining hands and bowing around the table will be a pleasing sight.

The following forms of grace are offered by way of suggestion:

We give thanks to Thee, our Father, for this food provided for our returning needs, and for all the hands that have helped to prepare it for our table. Bless them and us, in Jesus' name. Amen.

For what we are about to receive may the Lord make us truly thankful, through Jesus Christ our Lord. Amen.

God bless thy gifts to our use and us in thy service, through Christ our Lord. Amen.

Give us grateful hearts, our Father, for all thy gifts to us, and make us thoughtful of the needs of others. Amen.

PRAYER IN THE HOME

Prayers for the home should enter into its hopes, joys, sorrows, struggles and triumphs. On occasion the members will pray wholeheartedly in connection with some special need. The pair who pray will lay hold on sources of power and of understanding greater than their own, and will gain for their home something of the strength and serenity of God, Himself.

—From Leland Foster Wood, *Harmony in Marriage*. Old Tappan, N.J.: Revell, 1979.

Biblical Goals for Parents

Here is a basic list of biblical goals we want to accomplish with our children.

1. *To lead them to a saving knowledge of Jesus Christ.* It must be in his own perfect time, but we cannot really expect them to be all that God wants them to be until they have a new nature imparted from above.
2. *To lead them to a total commitment of their lives to Christ.* We want them to make their decisions in accord with his will, share every detail of life with him in prayer, and learn to trust him in every experience they face. Asking first what God wants us to do is a habit pattern that must be cultivated. The time to begin is very early in a child's life.
3. *To build the Word of God into their lives.* We will endeavor to teach it to them faithfully, relate it to the circumstances of life, and set an example of conformity to it.
4. *To teach them prompt and cheerful obedience, and respect for authority.* By developing their willing submission to our authority, we seek to instill a respect for all duly constituted authority, such as public school, Sunday school, government, and ultimately, the authority of God himself. Submission to authority is the basis for a happy and peaceful life in our society.
5. *To teach them self-discipline.* The hap-

piest life is the controlled life, particularly in areas such as eating, sleeping, sex, care of the body, use of time and money, and desire for material things.

6. *To teach them to accept responsibility*—responsibility for happily and efficiently accomplishing the tasks assigned to them, responsibility for the proper care of their belongings, and responsibility for the consequences of their actions.

7. *To teach them the basic traits of Christian character,* such as honesty, diligence, truthfulness, righteousness, unselfishness, kindness, courtesy, consideration, friendliness, generosity, justice, patience, and gratitude.

Now we know where we're going. But remember, our purpose is not just to insist on these things while our children are under our care. It is to make this whole package such a part of their lives that when they leave our care it will continue to guide them. That seems to be what Solomon had in mind when he wrote, "Young man, obey your father and mother. Tie their instructions around your finger so you won't forget. Take to heart all of their advice. Every day and all night long their counsel will lead you and save you from harm; when you wake up in the morning, let their instructions guide you into the new day. For their advice is a beam of light directed into the dark corners of your mind to warn you of danger and to give you a good life" (Proverbs 6:20-23, TLB).

Internalizing these standards, that is, making them an integral part of the child's life, seems to be indicated in the second word Paul used in Ephesians 6:4 to describe the training God gives which we are to emulate, the word *instruction.* This word means literally, "to place in the mind." The emphasis is on verbal training—warning, admonishing, encouraging, instructing, or reproving. But it goes far beyond the famous parental lecture. It pictures the faithful parent tenderly planting the principles of God's Word deep down in the very soul of the child so that they become a vital part of his being. The standard is no longer the parent's alone. It now belongs to the child as well. He is ready to move out into the world, independent of his parent's control, with the principles of God's Word so woven into the fiber of his life that he finds delight and success in doing the will of God, even when nobody is watching him. Maybe this explains why some parents are reluctant to let go of their children when they should. If parents suspect they have not successfully instilled God's way of life into their children, they may hesitate to break their emotional ties with them, but seek to influence and manipulate them in various ways long after they have married and left home. God wants us to begin building toward independence from the time our children are born.

Parental rules, regulations, and restrictions are only temporary. Their purpose is to prepare the child for freedom, the only kind of freedom that can bring him real satisfaction, the freedom to live in harmony and happiness with his Maker and Lord. As he learns and matures, the restraints are decreased and the independence increased until he leaves our care to establish a home of his own, a self-disciplined, Spirit-directed adult, capable of assuming his God-given responsibilities in life.

—From Richard L. Strauss, *Confident Children and How They Grow.* Wheaton, Ill.: Tyndale, 1975.

Prayer

Prayer is not something we do for God. It is something God does through the Spirit who dwells within us. It is through the action of God that our relationship with him grows. The Father must have time to teach us who we really are as sons of God. Our identity in the Kingdom begins to unfold as we become men of prayer. A man must know "who he is" and only his father can explain that to him.

Prayer is also essential if we are to serve God rightly. Too often we try to serve him in the wrong ways and with the wrong motives. We need to see our service from God's perspective, as a joy and not drudgery. The attitude of willing service is nurtured in prayer. Our service for God makes little sense unless we understand his mind about it.

We also need a rich prayer life if we are to experience some form of community or shared life. Efforts to form community without a firm grounding in the discipline of personal prayer usually fail. Meaningful shared life can only flow from shared prayer among individuals who are experiencing a deep personal union with God.

Prayer is critical if we are to have something of value for others. We cannot rely just on our gifts, resources, and ideas. Those around us need to receive God's word through us. They will not receive it unless we seek that word in prayer.

Personal prayer is essential for renewed corporate prayer. When our liturgy and other worship services seem to be dull, the solution is not to be found just in renewed rites, but also in the renewal of personal piety.

For Christian fathers, prayer is absolutely central. Fatherhood is difficult without the revelation and direction which comes through prayer. God wants to unfold his plan for our lives and our families; we need to take the time to listen to him. Could you imagine trying to train one of your children if he wouldn't sit still and listen to your instruction? We must *decide* to sit and be taught by God. Otherwise we will stumble around in confusion and darkness. As we grow in relationship with the Father through our prayer, we can be taught everything we need to know. The wisdom we need to shepherd our flocks is provided freely to a man who seeks.

I realized how freely the Spirit had taught me only when I began to write this book. I spent days and weeks going through my personal journals and found that God had taught me in prayer most of what I had to know. I later did research to give a solid base to my work. This was a joy because it simply confirmed what God had already revealed. I have been frankly amazed at how much we are taught through diligent listening to God.

We need personal union with the Father in prayer to expand our vision. We don't understand the power and the grace of fatherhood; so God must explain it to us. He must broaden our horizons and show us our place in his plan. Consider how God dealt with Abraham, our father in faith.

"When Abram was ninety-nine years old, the Lord appeared to him and said: 'I am God the Almighty. Walk in my presence and be blameless. Between you and me I will establish my covenant, and I will multiply you exceedingly.' When Abram prostrated himself, God continued to speak to him: 'My covenant with you is this: you are to become the father of a host of nations' " (Genesis 17:1-4).

Imagine yourself childless at ninety-nine. Would you have a vision of fatherhood? God gave Abram a vision beyond his wildest imagination: he became the father of a nation, and God worked a miracle of life and salvation for all men through his obedient heart. God wants to work miracles; he needs men who will agree to be his instruments.

A Daily Discipline.   To learn about prayer, we should look to the example of Jesus. He prayed to establish communion with the Father and to provide strength for a full immersion into life, not an escape from it. His is the perfect example for the Christian man who must draw courage and vision in prayer to live the gospel in his everyday life. Jesus' public ministry drained him as our work drains us; the source of his replenishment is the same as ours. I would like to highlight just a few characteristics of the prayer of Jesus which can serve as inspiration and instruction for us.

The prayer of Jesus is *simple and to the point*. "In your prayer do not rattle on like the pagans. They think they will win a hearing by the sheer multiplication of words. Do not imitate them. Your Father knows what you need before you ask him" (Matthew 6: 7-8).

The man of prayer must find the *right place and the right time* to be alone with God. "Rising early the next morning, he went off to a lonely place in the desert; there he was absorbed in prayer" (Mark 1:35). "Whenever you pray, go to your room, close your door, and pray to your Father in private" (Matthew 6:6). "Then he went to the mountain to pray, spending the night in communion with God" (Luke 6:12).

Our prayer must be *honest*. "Then Jesus went to a place called Gethsemane. . . . He said to them [his followers], 'My heart is nearly broken with sorrow. Remain here and stay awake with me.' He advanced a little and fell prostrate in prayer. 'My Father, if it is possible, let this cup pass me by'" (Matthew 26:36, 38, 39).

The prayer of *forgiveness and abandonment* is always heard by the Father. "When they came to Skull Place, as it was called, they crucified him there. . . . Jesus said, 'Father, forgive them, they do not know what they are doing'. . . . It was now around midday and darkness came over the whole land. . . . Jesus uttered a loud cry and said, 'Father, into your hands I commend my spirit.' After he said this he expired" (Luke 23:33, 34, 44, 46).

By the example of his life, his words, and his prayer, Jesus taught simple men how to relate to God and each other. He spent time, even through the night, to gain the wisdom and power he needed to serve the Father and the people of God. He taught his followers to be men of prayer. He did not leave us with a list of formal prayers, but rather with the example of a life spent in prayer.

Throughout Church history, Christians have followed Jesus' example. The apostle Paul called for constant prayer. "Rejoice always, never cease praying, render constant thanks; such is God's will for you in Christ Jesus" (1 Thessalonians 5:16-17). The prayer life of the Church is constant; we are called to join with that, in some way. For me, the experience of praying at regular intervals during the day has become a real treat. All of us can "rejoice always" by stopping periodically to renew our communion with the Father. "No matter where we happen to be, by prayer we can set up an altar to God in our heart" (St. John Chrysostom).

A technique which can help us pray constantly is the "Jesus prayer," one of the earliest prayer forms of the Christian church. The Jesus prayer has its origins among the early Christians and the monastic orders. Its shortest form has two parts: First, "Lord Jesus Christ"; the second, "have mercy on me." Simply repeating and meditating on the meaning of those seven words can draw us closer to God and strengthen our daily relationship with him. The Jesus prayer illustrates a principle: As we become more disciplined in prayer, we should be able to pray in simple and more direct ways.

Developing this kind of daily discipline will help us avoid the pitfall of praying only when we need something. God does not want our prayer to be crisis-oriented, but a regular part of our day. I think it is also true that regular prayer—like good habits of eating, rest, and exercise—will help us physically and emotionally as well as spiritually.

—From Robert L. Latesta, *Fathers: A Fresh Start for the Christian Family.* Ann Arbor: Servant, 1980.

Family Evangelism

In the Bible, evangelism is very much a family affair. Salvation itself is family-oriented. The living God (and the Trinity is in a very real sense a family!) has made himself known to us as Father. The best definition I know of a Christian is one who through the new birth has God as his Father. Adoption into God's family is the highest blessing of the gospel! By faith we are justified; justification is a *legal* idea and sees God (correctly) as *judge.* But adoption is a *family* idea and sees God as Father! This is especially exciting to me because I myself am an adopted child, I have always been thankful that my parents chose me to be their own; they didn't *have* to, but they did, and God has done the same.

British theologian J. I. Packer points out that being God's adopted children should control our whole life-style. We are to imitate the Father, Jesus said, loving our enemies as our Father in heaven does (Matthew 5:44). We pray to "Our Father in heaven," knowing he is always available (Matthew 6:9). We walk by faith because we believe our Father anticipates our needs and will supply them (Matthew 6:25). Earth is the place where God wants us to bear the family likeness of his Son (Romans 8:28). And heaven will be a grand family reunion!

Through evangelism we want people everywhere to be able to say, "I am a child of God. God is my Father. Heaven is my home. Jesus is my brother, and so is every Christian!"

The family was a high priority in God's purpose as it unfolded. In the Old Testament the family head would pledge allegiance to the Lord for his household: "As for me and my house, we will serve the Lord" (Joshua 24:15). The Jewish family was a kind of visual aid to demonstrate God's grace. Many Gentiles became proselytes because the spiritual solidarity of the Jewish family made a tremendous impact on them.

Through Jesus, God zeroed in on the family. Scan the Gospel of Luke, and you'll see how true this is. The Savior came to bless the world and was introduced through two faithful families (Luke 1,2). Jesus and his disciples used homes—Levi's and Martha and Mary's and Zacchaeus's—as headquarters to reach and teach (Luke 5:29, 10:38, 9:12, 10:5, 19:5). A dinner party was often the setting for Jesus' message (Luke 5:29, 7:36, 14:1). He helped families and widows in trouble, healing Peter's mother and Jairus's daughter, bringing back to life the widow of Nain's son (Luke 4:38, 8:41, 7:11). Home life gave him many of his best illustrations—his parables of the friend who comes at midnight (Luke 11:5), the wedding feast (Luke 14:1), the prodigal son (Luke 15:1). Concern for family life comes through clearly in what Jesus teaches about divorce (Luke 16:18) and about blessing children (Luke 18:15) or causing them to stumble (Luke 17:1).

Yet Jesus also makes clear that there is a higher allegiance, that loyalty to the Father takes first place even over family ties! His Father's business was top priority in his own life, though he willingly submitted to his parents (Luke 2:41). His family was made up, not just of his mother and brothers in the flesh, but of all those who do God's will (Luke 8:31). When he called disciples, he spelled out that it might involve a break with their families (Luke 9:58, 14:26). But any sacrifice they might make in leaving home would be repaid; God would give them a hundred homes in his wider family (Luke 18:28)!

A STRATEGY OF FAMILY EVANGELISM

A strategy of family evangelism must have at least three parts: (1) leading members of Christian families to personal faith; (2) evangelizing non-Christian families; (3) developing Christian families as a base for evangelism.

Evangelism in the Christian Family How can believing spouses and children best lead their non-Christian partners or parents to the Lord? That is a large and important question, but an even more important question is, How are we to evangelize the children of Christian parents so they can be Christ-bearers to their peers?

The problem of the "second generation" has been recognized, and I hope the research results will give us valuable insights. Nominal, hand-me-down Christianity has plagued every age (for example, the great debate over that Half Way Covenant in colonial New England), every church (whether they practice infant or believer's baptism), and every part of the Christian world. And it touches every parent! Many of us have ached when our children seemed indifferent or rebellious to the Lord we love. And many of us have praised God when we saw them begin to show signs of their own precious faith!

Theologian Henri Blocher suggests that the Bible sets forth three basic positions relevant to the evangelism of our children: (1) faith is *not hereditary;* (2) there is a *spiritual* solidarity to the family; (3) the child is not already a responsible person; he *becomes* one.

Discipleship involves a personal faith and commitment. As Corrie ten Boom says, "God has no grandchildren!" The problem is shared by the Christian home and the Christian church. It's easy enough to get children or church members to *comply* with the words we ask them to say or the rituals in which we ask them to take part. It's also fairly simple to get children or church members to *identify* with the faith of their parents or some person they admire. But what God desires and what we seek are children and church members who will *internalize* their faith until it's really theirs. What we want is not just proselytes or semiconverts but *disciples* who follow Jesus as Lord!

To this cause the "spiritual solidarity of the family" is an ally, not an enemy. "The promise is unto you, and to your children," said Peter (Acts 2:39). As a Christian parent, I can claim God's promise on behalf of my children, believing, even when the blossoms or fruit haven't yet appeared, that God intends to call my children to himself! But this faith is meant to spur me as a parent to my spiritual responsibility, not to leave it to God or others.

—From Leighton Ford, "The Family," in *Living and Growing Together,* Gary R. Collins, ed., copyright © 1976, pp. 143–46; used by permission of Word Books, Publisher, Waco, Texas 76796.

Choosing a Church

Where do you go to church? At the church where you were brought up? A church of your parents' denomination? One where all your friends go? The most prestigious church in town? Or perhaps the smallest, newest, or most unconventional?

There are few institutions that come in so many varieties as the local church. But whether large or small, liturgical or avant-garde, the local church plays an important role in most Christians' lives. It provides supplementary training for children, opportunities for service, social contacts, and most importantly, spiritual training and guidance.

Questions about finding the church that is "just right" often don't arise until a person's living situation changes. It can be something as drastic as a job transfer to another part of the country, or as simple as wanting to get away from the church of one's childhood.

No matter what the reason for church hunting, the task is an elusive one. Yet many experts agree that along with the family doctor, a friendly neighborhood, and familiar stores, a church helps people most in feeling secure in a community.

But the question remains, how does one actually find that church?

Surrounded by the unfamiliar, one family may be drawn to a church that uses familiar hymns, the same order of worship, or a familiar mode of celebrating communion.

Others might gravitate toward the church where the people are the friendliest, or where the pastor is the most colorful. A single woman who had just moved to a new city waited until she met some people she wanted to get to know and then visited their churches.

But beyond familiarity and friendliness, there are other important factors to consider when choosing "your" church:

1. What are your particular needs at this time in your life?

One couple who had moved to Boston decided against joining a very friendly, active church, because they felt there would be too much pressure, to "get involved." The husband was in a very intensive doctoral program at a local seminary. The wife taught school full time. During that particular period of their lives, they didn't have the time or energy to spend on "reaching out" as the church seemed to demand.

Are you at a point where your need to "be fed" and nurtured is greater than your need to minister to others? Or are you looking for an opportunity to discover and use your gifts to the fullest? Or are you concerned that your children get involved in an active youth program? How you evaluate your (and your family's) needs will help you match them to the particular style and program of a church.

2. Are the church's pastor and staff guided and directed by biblical principles?

It might not be as important that every sermon be spellbinding as it is that they be biblical. One couple who joined a large, well-respected church in their new community found that during the year prior to a national election, their pastor only preached on acceptable political positions for Christians to take—never from the Bible. Although they kept attending themselves, many others left, disappointed at the lack of spiritual training offered.

On the other hand, some may choose to stay at a church that lacks a sound biblical base so they can be a catalyst for renewal. A pastor of a large church in Maryland recalled how he and his family were influenced by a "turned-on" Christian couple in a "sleepy, liberal church." "If it wasn't for that couple," he said, "we wouldn't have discovered what it means to have a personal relationship with God."

Being a catalyst, however, is not for everyone. A more ideal choice would be a church where you can receive biblical teaching *and* be a catalyst. If you have questions about where a pastor stands on certain issues that are important to you—e.g., his view of Scripture, the deity of Christ, or the meaning of the atonement, baptism, etc.—set up an appointment to ask him. Or ask for the church's doctrinal statement.

3. What are the church's priorities as they relate to ministry?

One way to judge a church's concerns is by the programs offered—youth groups, prayer meetings, Bible studies, evangelism, shut-in visitation, choirs, singles ministry, etc. Another way is to discover what ministries the church supports—both in the community and overseas.

Perhaps the most important indicator of the church's priorities is how its people are ministering between Sundays. Is the Sunday service merely an in-grown group meeting or are people being challenged and rejuvenated to be "salt" and "light" wherever they are during the week? Talk to members about their jobs and how they see God using them during the week. Notice how many lay people are involved in the various church and non-church ministries.

4. Do you feel comfortable at this church?

A church often provides a Christian's major social activities, so it is important to feel comfortable with the people in the church and to want to get to know them better. Unfortunately, some churches seem cold and less enthusiastic about accepting newcomers. One couple attending a church for the first time was surprised—shocked, really—when *no* one spoke to them during or after the service. They didn't return for several months.

Other factors contribute to a feeling of comfort and belonging in a church—such as style of worship. Perhaps your thoughts turn toward God more easily in an informal service. Or maybe a structured liturgy is more your style. Of course, the attitude of the worshipper on a given Sunday can determine his or her ability to worship. But be aware of the kinds of things that help you forget your concerns for a time and redirect your attention to God.

5. What can I contribute to others through this church?

In this search for a church that fulfills needs and wants, it's easy to forget about what each member contributes to a church. A vital facet of every Christian's church involvement is the role he or she plays in the life of that church. The writer of Hebrews gives a glimpse of the divine perspective on

the local church: "Let us hold unswervingly to the hope we profess, for he who promised is faithful. And let us consider how we may spur one another on toward love and good deeds. Let us not give up meeting together, as some are in the habit of doing, but let us encourage one another—and all the more as you see the Day approaching." (Hebrews 10:23–25 NIV)

Those who never get involved in a church because they find none perfect enough, or enough "like the church back home," deprive themselves of the kind of fellowship with other Christians that enables spiritual growth. No church will be perfect enough to fulfill all your wants and needs.

But if you're willing to give of yourself to others as much as you are able, you'll find yourself receiving much more in return.

What church is right for you? Everyone will have a different list of priorities. None is right or wrong. "God isn't against thirty-one flavors in ice cream or in churches," says one pastor. "The important thing is finding the flavor you like."

—BY Anita M. Moreland, a freelance writer who is Director of Communications for Prison Fellowship in northern Virginia.

The Church Family and the Covenant

The church is primarily concerned with the lordship of Jesus Christ. The church serves as a constant reminder to the family that its highest loyalties belong not to husband, wife, parents, or children but to Jesus Christ. The church, with Christ as Lord, also serves as a reminder that his lordship creates a family described as the body of Christ and that this family is of equal importance with the individual family unit because both are under his lordship.

The church under the lordship of Christ also reminds the neo-married of their wedding vows. Remember that the covenant made at the altar was first of all made with God revealed in Jesus Christ and therefore the homes which the neo-marrieds are establishing are under his lordship as surely as the church is. The vows which were spoken in the wedding ceremony were a shared verification of the previous vows which the neo-marrieds, if Christians, made when they were initiated into the church family through believers' baptism or confirmation. Those earlier vows, though actually made in some local church, were also made as a part of the church universal, to which all Christians belong and for which Jesus Christ gave his life. . . .

THE HOME AS THE CHURCH IN MINIATURE

The most important manifestation of the church is the home. In other words, the home is the church in miniature. The Old Testament family had many rituals with religious significance over which the father was the family priest. Today the home should be the place where the family worships most regularly, proclaims the gospel most clearly, teaches the truth about God most fully, and serves the world most heartily. . . . If the church is truly to be found in miniature in the home, the home will be involved in worshiping, teaching, proclaiming, and serving.

Many probably think of worship mainly in terms of going to church, reading the Bible, and saying grace at meals. But true worship is more than these formal observances. The word "worship" means "*worth*ship"; everything the family does in recognition of God's worth is worship. What papers and magazines the couple reads, what pictures they hang in their home, and how they work and play, can all be forms of worship. Such practices as saying grace at meals, praying before sleep, and reading the Bible are important to

every Christian neo-married, of course, but worship of God in one's home is more inclusive than these facets. It includes one's whole life.

Teaching the things of God in the home is another task of the family that offers many possibilities. Study of the Bible is one important practice in the learning family. Likewise, a book chosen with Christ's lordship in mind can give to a neo-married a friendship with the finest lives and best minds our world has known. What a neo-married reads is important in the light of his primary commitment to Jesus Christ. Disciples are learners, and the home is one of the most important places where learning about the things of God should take place.

The proclamation of the gospel in the home is a natural outgrowth of the couple's primary commitment. The early Christians lived in such a way as to prompt observers to say that Christ's followers were turning the world upside down. These same observers noticed how much the Christians loved each other. As a result of the unique quality of their lives, men asked the Christians why they lived as they did, and the Christians responded with the good news of Jesus Christ. Many Christians today feel a similar commitment to demonstrate their faith. Some couples invite families to their homes through a loving desire to share the good news of Jesus Christ. The home can be a powerful instrument of proclaiming God's love and care for all.

Another way in which the home can be the church in miniature is by serving. The home is not an end in itself; too strong an emphasis on the home can lead to a kind of home idolatry. Rather, the home is the place where neo-marrieds get strength and grace to go out and serve mankind.

—From Howard Hovde, *The Neo-Married*. Valley Forge, Pa.: Judson, 1968.

FOR FURTHER READING

Anderson, Margaret J. *Your Aging Parents*. St. Louis: Concordia, 1979.

Baker, Yvonne. *From God's Natural Storehouse*. Elgin, Ill.: Cook, 1980.

Bird, Joseph W. and Lois Bird. *To Live As a Family*. New York: Doubleday, 1982.

Birkey, Verna, and Jeanette Turnquist. *Building Happy Memories and Family Traditions*. Old Tappan, N.J.: Revell, 1981.

Birkey, Verna. *You Are Very Special*. Old Tappan, N.J.: Revell, 1977.

Bock, Lois, and Miji Working. *Happiness Is a Family Time Together*. Old Tappan, N.J.: Revell, 1975.

Bock, Lois, and Miji Working. *Happiness Is a Family Walk With God*. Old Tappan, N.J.: Revell, 1977.

Bush, Barbara. *Successful Motherhood*. Grand Rapids: Zondervan, 1981.

Carey, Ruth Little, Irma Bachmann Vymeister, and Jennie Hudson. *Commonsense Nutrition*. Mountain View, Calif.: Pacific Press, 1971.

Chafin, Kenneth. *Is There A Family in the House?* Waco, Tex.: Word Books, 1978.

Collins, Gary R., ed. *Living and Growing Together*. Waco, Tex.: Word Books, 1976.

Dayton, Howard L., Jr. *Your Money: Frustration or Freedom?* Wheaton, Ill.: Tyndale, 1979.

Dennis, Muriel, ed. *Chosen Children*. Westchester, Ill.: Good News, 1978.

Dobson, James, *Dare to Discipline*. Wheaton, Ill.: Tyndale, 1970.

Dobson, James, *Hide or Seek*. Old Tappan, N.J.: Revell, 1974.

Fritze, Julius A. *The Essence of Marriage*. Grand Rapids: Zondervan, 1969.

Hovde, Howard. *The Neo-Married*. Valley Forge, Pa.: Judson, 1968.

Howard, Linda. *Mothers Are People, Too*. Plainfield, N.J.: Logos, 1976.

Howell, John C. *Teaching Your Children About Sex*. Nashville: Broadman, 1973.

Hunt, Gladys M. *Focus on Family Life*. Grand Rapids: Baker Book, 1970.

Hyder, O. Quentin, M.D. *The People You Live With*. Old Tappan, N.J.: Revell, 1975.

Jacobsen, Marion Leach. *How to Keep Your Family Together and Still Have Fun*. Grand Rapids: Zondervan, 1972.

Ketterman, Grace H., M.D. *How to Teach Your Child About Sex*. Old Tappan, N.J.: Revell, 1981.

Ketterman, Grace H., M.D., and Herbert L. Ketterman, M.D. *The Complete Book of Baby and Child Care for Christian Parents*. Old Tappan, N.J.: Revell, 1982.

Kounovsky, Nicholas. *The Joy of Feeling Fit*. New York: Dutton, 1971.

LaHaye, Tim and Bev. *Spirit-Controlled Family Living*. Old Tappan, N.J.: Revell, 1978.

LaHaye, Beverly. *I Am a Woman by God's Design*. Old Tappan, N.J.: Revell, 1980.

Latesta, Robert L. *Fathers: A Fresh Start for the Christian Family*. Ann Arbor: Servant, 1980.

Leman, Kevin. *Parenthood Without Hassles (Well Almost)*. Eugene, Ore.: Harvest House, 1979.

LeShan, Eda J. *Winning the Losing Battle: Why I Will Never Be Fat Again*. New York: Thomas Y. Crowell, 1979.

Lessin, Roy. *Spanking: Why? When? How?* Minneapolis: Bethany House, 1979.

Little, Paul E. *How to Give Away Your Faith*. Downers Grove, Ill.: Inter-Varsity, 1966.

MacDonald, Gordon. *The Effective Father*. Wheaton, Ill.: Tyndale, 1977.

Martin, Ralph. *Husbands, Wives, Parents, Children*. Ann Arbor: Servant, 1978.

Miller, William A. *You Count, You Really Do!* Minneapolis: Augsburg, 1976.

Morehouse, Laurence E., and Leonard Gross. *Total Fitness in 30 Minutes a Week*. New York: Simon & Schuster, 1975.

Murphey, Cecil B. *Devotions for Calorie Counters*. Old Tappan, N.J.: Revell, 1982.

Murphey, Cecil B. *Prayerobics*. Waco, Tex.: Word Books, 1979.

Narramore, Bruce, Ph.D. *Adolescence Is Not an Illness*. Old Tappan, N.J.: Revell, 1980.

Preston, William H., ed. *Fathers Are Special.* Nashville: Broadman, 1977.

Powell, John, S.J. *Unconditional Love.* Allen, Tex.: Argus, 1978.

Renich, Fred. *The Christian Husband.* Wheaton, Ill.: Tyndale, 1976.

Rickerson, Wayne E. *Good Times for Your Family.* Ventura, Calif.: Regal, 1976.

Rohrer, Virginia, and Norman. *How to Eat Right and Feel Great.* Wheaton, Ill.: Tyndale, 1977.

Schuller, Robert. *Self-Esteem.* Waco, Tex.: Word Books, 1982.

Shedd, Charlie W. *Letters to Philip.* New York: Doubleday, 1968.

Shoemaker, Helen S. *Prayer and Evangelism.* Waco, Tex.: Word Books, 1974.

Small, Dwight Hervey. *Design for Christian Marriage.* Old Tappan, N.J.: Revell, 1959.

Stedman, Ray C., David H. Roper et al. *Family Life.* Waco, Tex.: Word Books, 1976.

Strauss, Richard L. *Confident Children and How They Grow.* Wheaton, Ill.: Tyndale, 1975.

Tomczak, Larry. *God, the Rod, and Your Child's Bod.* Old Tappan, N.J.: Revell, 1982.

Ulene, Art. *Feeling Fine.* Los Angeles; J. P. Tarcher, 1977.

Vernon, Bob, with C. C. Carlson. *The Married Man.* Old Tappan, N.J.: Revell, 1980.

Welter, Paul. *How to Help a Friend.* Wheaton, Ill.: Tyndale, 1978.

Wright, H. Norman. *The Family That Listens.* Wheaton, Ill.: Victor Books, 1978.

Wright, H. Norman, and Rex Johnson. *Characteristics of a Caring Home.* Ventura, Calif.: Vision House, 1978.

Wright, H. Norman. *In-Laws, Outlaws.* Eugene, Ore.: Harvest House, 1977.

6

Finances

BUDGET

What Is a Budget?

. . . A budget is—a plan for spending money.

Actually it is simple and easy when you understand its purpose, follow a workable plan, and use it to maximize your income.

Why Budget?

Budgeting Makes Your Money Go Further. When the bank notified the depositor of her overdraft she replied in disbelief, "I must have more money left in my account. I still have six checks in my checkbook!"

Like the surpised depositor, if you do not have a written budget chances are that you are flying by the seat of your financial pants.

Budgeting is not always fun, but it is the only way to follow through and apply what has been learned about getting out of debt, saving, and sharing and still meet basic needs. Regardless of the income, most families have difficulty making ends meet unless there is a plan for spending. As someone has said, "Expenses will always tend to rise just a little higher than income."

I have seen countless examples of this. In-variably, whether a family earns $8,000 or $80,000 a year, it probably will have too much month at the end of the money unless there is a carefully planned and disciplined approach to spending.

Using a budget introduces an attitude of control in spending that is needed to reach financial objectives.

Budgeting Provides an Opportunity to Work and Pray Through Spending Decisions as a Family. This is important because 48 percent of the most serious marital problems are financial, according to a recent survey of young husbands. In fact, one judge has said, "Quarreling about money is the major reason for America's unprecedented divorce rate." I seldom see a family with financial problems where there is not real tension within the marriage.

A successful budget should be a "team effort." Budgeting can help each member of the family participate in deciding what should be purchased and what the goals of the family should be. It is a good tool for the husband and wife to use for communicating together.

A budget can also help a family get full value for its money without losing sight of the things its members want most. A family in our neighborhood is committed to sending

349

their children to camp each summer for two weeks. Several years ago as they were planning their annual budget in January, it became apparent that there would not be enough money for the children to go to camp.

The family then agreed each member would "contribute" to summer camp by making a sacrifice: the father gave up his golf game once a month, the mother did not join her summer bowling league, and the children received no birthday presents. By using a budget, the family was able to anticipate a problem and make adjustments in their spending to enable the members to get what they wanted most—in this case, summer camp.

How to Budget

No one I have known to be in financial difficulty used a budget. Some had made a budget and then promptly filed it away. Others had made an unrealistic budget that provided nothing for such items as clothing or medical care. A budget is useful only if it is used. It should be a plan tailor-made for managing *your* finances, not someone else's.

To set up your budget, you need only a simple inexpensive notebook of accounting paper that can be bought in most bookstores. Then follow these three steps:

Step 1—Where We Are Today. Developing a budget must begin with the current situation. Determine precisely how much money is earned and spent.

In my experience spending tends to be significantly underestimated, particularly in the areas of food, clothing, transportation, and the "miscellaneous" expenses. For this reason it is essential for the family to keep a strict accounting of every penny for a month to get an accurate picture of what they are actually spending.

The most efficient way to accomplish this is to pay for all large purchases by check. Then, have each family member carry a small notebook or a three-by-five card to record all cash purchases. In the evening record the check and cash purchases under the appropriate category on the Monthly Budget Form.

The Monthly Budget Form on p. 351 is a guide that you can alter to fit your situation.

If your wages are not the same each month (like the income of a commissioned salesman), make a conservative estimate of your annual income and divide by twelve to determine your monthly income.

Then complete the Annual Expense Form (p. 352) for those expenses that do not occur each month. Examples are real estate taxes and homeowner's insurance which are paid annually. Divide the yearly premium by twelve to arrive at the monthly expense. This Annual Expense Form will also be helpful in reminding you when to anticipate these periodic expenses.

Some expenses, such as vacations and auto repairs, do not come due every month. Estimate how much you spend for these on a yearly basis, divide that amount by twelve, and fill in the appropriate categories on the Monthly Budget Form.

Armed with this information you can construct an accurate budget of what you are actually spending and earning today. Do not be discouraged! Almost every budget I have seen starts out with expenditures in excess of income. But there is a solution.

Step 2—The Solution—Where We Want To Be. To solve the problem of spending more than you earn, you must either increase your income to the level of your expenditures or decrease your expenditures to the level of your income.

It's that simple—either earn more or spend less. There are no other alternatives.

MONTHLY BUDGET FORM

INCOME PER MONTH   EXPENSES PER MONTH

Income		Expenses	
Salary	_____	1. Sharing	_____
Interest Income	_____	2. Taxes	
Dividends	_____	(a) Income taxes	
Rental Income	_____	(b) Social Security	_____
Other Income	_____	(c) Other taxes	_____
Total Income	_____		
		3. Saving	_____
		4. Housing	
		(a) Payments	_____
		(b) Insurance	_____
		(c) Taxes	_____
		(d) Maintenance	_____
		(e) Telephone	_____
		(f) Utilities	_____
		(g) Other	_____
		5. Food	
		(a) Eating at home	
		(b) Eating out	_____
		6. Clothing	_____
		7. Transportation	
		(a) Payments	_____
		(b) Gasoline	_____
		(c) Maintenance	_____
		(d) Other	_____
		8. Insurance	
		(a) Automobile	_____
		(b) Life	_____
		(c) Health	_____
		9. Miscellaneous	
		(a) Medical/Health	_____
		(b) Education	_____
		(c) Gifts	_____
		(d) Vacations	_____
		(e) Recreation	_____
		(f) Personal allowance	_____
		(g) Other	_____
		10. Debt Reduction	
		(a) Credit card	_____
		(b) Installment	_____
		(c) Other	_____
		Total Expenses	_____

ANNUAL EXPENSE FORM 19____

ITEM	JAN	FEB	MAR	APR	MAY	JUN	JUL	AUG	SEP	OCT	NOV	DEC
real estate taxes											$300	
home owner's insurance					$225							

Adding to Your Income. A part-time job, or better yet a family project that would involve the whole family, are ways of increasing your income. The ever-present danger of increasing income is the tendency for expenses also to rise. The key for eliminating this problem is to agree ahead of time to apply any extra income to balancing the budget.

Another potential problem is to sacrifice family relationships in order to earn extra money. Extra income is valuable only as it helps the family get more of what it wants out of life.

Reducing Expenses. My father was in the hotel business as I was growing up. He owned a resort in Florida that catered to tourists. Business was seasonal—during the winter it flourished, in the summer it practically withered and died.

He tells me that just the thought of summer sent chills down his spine, but after the lean months he was always grateful. Summer taught him the habit of asking these questions about his expenses: Which are absolutely necessary? Which can I do without? Which can I reduce?

You can ask these same questions of your personal budget as you work to reduce spending.

On p. 353 are some guidelines to help you evaluate your major expenses. When you exceed the upper range in any category, this should warn you to carefully evaluate your expenditures.

The best way to reduce spending is to plan ahead. Decide in advance what you need and make a list. By using the "need list," you will be able to shop more wisely and avoid impulse spending. Consider these suggestions:

Shelter:
1. Purchase an older house that you can improve with your own labor, or buy a modest-size house suitable to your needs today with a design that can be expanded should you need more space in the future.
2. Consider apartment living. It is less

CATEGORY	PERCENT OF INCOME (after sharing and taxes)
Shelter	20–35%
Food	15–25%
Transportation	10–15%
Clothing	4– 8%
Insurance	3– 5%
Health	3– 5%
Entertainment & Recreation	3– 5%
Debts	0–10%
Saving	5–10%
Miscellaneous	3– 5%

expensive and without the responsibilities—lawn care, maintenance, etc.

3. If you can do repair and maintenance work such as lawn spraying, pest control, painting, and carpet cleaning, you 'll save a substantial amount.

4. Lower the cost of utilities by limiting the use of heating, air conditioning, lights, and appliances.

5. Shop carefully for furniture and appliances. Garage sales are a good source for reasonably priced household goods.

Food:

1. Prepare a menu for the week. Then list the ingredients from the menu and shop according to the list. This will help you plan a nutritionally balanced diet. Avoid impulse shopping, and eliminate waste.

2. Shop once a week. Each time we go shopping for "some little thing," we always buy "some other little thing" as well.

3. Cut out the ready-to-eat food which has expensive labor added to the price.

4. Leave children and hungry husbands home. The fewer distractions from the list the better.

5. The husband's lunches are often budget breakers. A lunch prepared at home and taken to work will help the budget and the waistline.

6. Reduce the use of paper products—paper plates, cups, and napkins are expensive to use.

Transportation:

1. If it is possible to get by with one car, this will be the biggest transportation savings.

2. Purchase a low-cost used car and drive it until repairs become too expensive.

3. The smaller the car, the more economical to operate. You pay an estimated 35¢ a pound each year to operate an automobile.

4. Perform routine maintenance yourself—oil changes, lubrication, etc. Regular maintenance will prolong the life of your car.

5. If purchasing a new car, wait until new models are introduced in September. You can save 5 to 35 percent during these year-end sales.

Clothing:

1. Make a written list of yearly clothing needs. Shop from the list during the off-season sales, at economical clothing stores and at garage sales.

2. A wife who uses a sewing machine can cut the cost of garments in half.

3. Purchase simple basic fashions that stay in style longer than faddish clothes.

4. Do not purchase a lot of clothing. Select one or two basic colors for your ward-

robe, and buy outfits that you can wear in combination with others.

5. Purchase home-washable fabrics. Clothes that must be commercially cleaned are expensive to maintain.

Insurance:

1. Select insurance based on your *need* and budget, and secure estimates from three major insurance companies.
2. Exercising the deductible features will substantially reduce premiums.
3. Seek the recommendation of friends for a skilled insurance agent. A good agent can save you money.

Health:

1. Practice preventive medicine. Your body will stay healthier when you get the proper amount of sleep, exercise, and nutrition.
2. Also practice proper oral hygiene for healthy teeth and to reduce dental bills.
3. Obtain the recommendation of friends for reasonable and competent physicians and dentists.

Entertainment and Recreation:

1. Time your vacation for the off-season and select destinations near home.
2. Rather than expensive entertainment, seek creative alternatives such as family picnics or exploring free state parks.

FIVE BUDGETING HINTS

1. Reconcile your checkbook each month.
2. It is helpful to have a special savings account, in which to put aside the monthly allotment for the bills that do not come due each month. For example, if your annual insurance premium is $240, each month deposit twenty dollars in this savings account. This method will insure that the money will be available when these payments come due.
3. We are trained to think monthly. To better understand the impact of an expense, extend it to a yearly cost. For example, if the husband spends $2.50 for lunch each working day, multiply $2.50 by five days a week by fifty-two weeks a year. It totals $650 for lunches. This will help you give proper attention to the seemingly inconsequential expenses.
4. Control impulse-spending. Impulse-spending ranges from buying automobiles to snacks. Here is a suggestion on how to control such spending. Each time you have the urge to spend for something not planned, post it to an "impulse list" and date it. Then wait thirty days and pray about buying the item. If you're like me, I guarantee that you will not purchase at least half of the items, because impulses do not last. If you don't believe me, just look at the garage sales in your neighborhood.
5. It is wise for the husband and wife to include personal allowances in the budget. Each should be given an allowance to spend as they please. The wife can go to the beauty shop and the husband can play golf as often as they like, so long as the allowance holds out. This will eliminate many arguments.

Step 3—Do Not Stop! The most common temptation is to stop budgeting. Don't do it!

Remember, a budget is simply a plan for spending your money. It will not work by itself. Every area of your budget should be regularly reviewed to keep a rein on spending. "Any enterprise is built by wise planning, becomes strong through common sense, and profits wonderfully by keeping abreast of the facts" (Proverbs 24:3, 4).

To help us "keep abreast of the facts," at the middle of each month Bev and I compare our actual income and expenses with the amounts budgeted. If we find ourselves overspending, we make mid-month adjustments by cutting back on our spending plans for the rest of the month. You need to maintain adequate records to compare the money actually spent with your budget.

Through the years there will be frustrations, but a budget, if properly used, will save you thousands of dollars. It will help you accumulate the savings for your children's education and your retirement. It will help you stay out of debt. More important, it will help the husband and wife communicate together in an area that is a leading cause of marital conflict.

COMMITMENT

Keep a strict accounting of all expenditures for thirty days to determine your current situation. After that, plan a budget suited to your income and personal objectives. Finally, use it.

—From Howard L. Dayton, Jr., *Your Money: Frustration or Freedom?* Wheaton, Ill.: Tyndale, 1979.

SAVING

A SKILLFUL STEWARD divides his income among sharing, spending, and saving. "The wise man saves for the future but the foolish man spends whatever he gets" (Proverbs 21:20).

Because of their instinct for saving, the ants in Proverbs 30:24 are commended for their wisdom: "There are . . . things that are small but usually wise: Ants aren't strong, but store up food for the winter." They put aside and save from the summer's plenty to meet a future need.

Another example is Joseph, the faithful steward, who saved from the seven years of plenty to insure that there would be food enough to eat during the seven years of famine.

I call saving the "Joseph Principle." Saving means to forego an expenditure today so that you will have something to spend in the future. Perhaps this is why most people never save; it requires a denial of something that you want today, and our culture is not a culture of denial. Because it is a culture of instant gratification, most people spend their entire income.

Saving is important in faithful financial planning for three reasons. First, saving provides a cushion to meet unexpected events—loss of employment, major repair bills, and sudden illness. Second, savings should be accumulated to enable you to purchase your car, furniture, etc., without having to use credit. And third, accumulated savings provide a pool of resources for investing.

How to Save

The essential rule for saving is to make yourself your number one creditor after the Lord. Habitually save a portion of your income, putting it into a savings account or savings program. The percentage of your income that you save does not matter. What is important is that you establish a pattern of regular savings.

To develop this habit you can use several different methods. For example, before we spend anything Bev and I set aside a certain percent of our income each month in a savings account. It might be easier for you to use one of the compulsory savings plans that are available through most banks, or an employee payroll plan. Here is a maxim for saving: If the money budgeted for saving is deducted directly from your paycheck, you will save more.

As you begin to save, you will discover what bankers have known for a long time—the benefits of interest, money working for you, not against you.

MONEY WORKING FOR YOU AT 8 PERCENT INTEREST

Year	Amount Saved	Interest Earned	Ending Balance
1	$ 1,200	$ 45	$ 1,245
2	1,200	200	2,600
3	1,200	450	4,050
4	1,200	850	5,650
5	1,200	1,350	7,350
6	1,200	2,000	9,200
7	1,200	2,800	11,200
8	1,200	3,800	13,400
9	1,200	5,000	15,750
10	1,200	6,300	18,300
10 year Subtotal	12,000	6,300	18,300
15	1,200	16,600	34,600
20	1,200	34,900	58,900
25	1,200	65,100	95,100
Total	$30,000	$65,100	$95,100

Let us examine how money works for the family that saves. Assume saving $100 a month and receiving 8 percent interest, compounded monthly for twenty-five years.

At the end of twenty-five years the family will be earning $635 each month in interest alone! What an incentive to begin saving.

For an even greater incentive to save, compare the results of spending $100 more than you earn each month for 10 years with spending $100 less than you earn each month. Should you spend $100 more each month you will *owe* $23,000; spend $100 less and you will *own* $18,300—a staggering difference of $41,300 at the end of ten years!

The difference between overspending $100 and saving $100 a month is $6.50 a day.

This illustrates the importance of a disciplined commitment to save. The difference between sinking in debt and walking on the firm ground of savings is a matter of a few cents each day.

The biggest enemy of saving is *procrastination.* For instance, if you plan to save $100 a month for 25 years at 8 percent, you will accumulate more than $95,000. However, look what happens if you decide to delay such a program by one year. Although you will have an extra $100 a month to spend for one year, it will cost you $8,500 in accumulated savings on the other end. Do not wait—begin to save now!

—From Howard L. Dayton, *Your Money: Frustration or Freedom?* Wheaton, Ill.: Tyndale, 1979.

INVESTING

INVESTMENTS DIFFER from saving in that they are not always quickly convertible to cash, and they represent a conscious effort to provide for specific future events or as a hedge to beat inflation. For example, college for children and funding for retirement represent future expenditures that may be planned and financed from current income.

How Should We Invest?

There is no investment without risk, and Scripture does not recommend any specific investments. I prefer to spread the risk by diversifying according to these priorities: 1) life insurance, 2) vocation, 3) home, and 4) other investments.

George Fooshee in his excellent book, *You Can Be Financially Free*, says, "The first priority is life insurance because that's the only way for most of us to provide for our families in the event of our own death. Whether you buy term insurance or whole-life insurance should depend upon your own analysis of the costs and the benefits of each kind. An excellent article on the subject is 'Term Insurance vs. Whole Life' (*Forbes*, March 15, 1975). What is right for one person may be wrong for another.

"Your vocation should rank next as an investment. Your own education is an investment that should pay excellent returns during your working years. A principle in Scripture is to invest in your business, which will be productive, then build your house: 'Develop your business first before building your house' (Proverbs 24:27). Many people today reverse this order. The large house, purchased early in life, tends to involve so much of their money that investing in their vocation is out of the question.

"The home is the third priority. During the last few decades, the home has been one of the steadiest profitable investments for the average family.

"Other investments (fourth priority) are almost as varied as the imagination. Real estate, oil, commodities, stocks, bonds, antiques, coins, and virtually anything people collect can be considered investments. Some of these, such as stocks, bonds, and real estate, pay a return on an annual basis. Others are held with the expectation that they will increase in value as time goes by.

"Your investments beyond life insurance, vocation, and house should be matched with your own interests and personality. If you were raised on a farm and have knowledge of agricultural products and enjoy keeping abreast of the farm situation, then you might pursue a lifelong interest in agricultural investments. These could include everything from commodity purchases to owning and acquiring farmland. If common stocks are your interest, you might specialize in a study of those companies that are primarily agriculturally oriented.

"All these investments that have been discussed are the kind that lend themselves to systematic investing. The regular monthly payment on the home for a twenty-year mortgage results in having a home completely paid for. Yearly whole-life insurance premiums not only provide insurance in case of death, but also add up to retirement values. Steady hard work in your own business often results in a substantial salable asset. The key to most investments is to set aside regular amounts for systematic investing. 'Steady plodding brings prosperity; hasty speculation brings poverty' (Proverbs 21:5)."

The Danger of Saving and Investing

As you are successful in accumulating your "nest egg," it is easy to transfer your trust and affection from the invisible living Lord to your tangible assets. Money will certainly compete for your trust and attention. It has so much power that it is easy to be fooled into thinking that it is money which provides our needs and is our security. Money can become our first love. Paul warned Timothy of this temptation in 1 Timothy 6:10, 11.

For the love of money is the first step toward all kinds of sin. Some people have even

357

turned away from God because of their love for it. . . . Run from all these evil things.

I would like to suggest a radical antidote for the potential disease of loving money: determine a maximum amount of savings and investments that you will accumulate.

The amount will vary from individual to individual. If you are single without any dependents, the amount may be modest. If you have a family with educational needs, it may be more substantial. If you are the owner of a sizable business that requires large amounts of capital, the amount may be in the millions.

Each person should decide before God what amount will be his maximum. After you have reached your maximum goal, begin to *share* the portion of your income that used to be allocated to savings and investments.

Avoid Risky Investments

The desire to secure large, quick, and effortless returns is the primary reason for losing money through speculative investments.

There is another serious problem I [Solomon] have seen everywhere—savings are put into risky investments that turn sour, and soon there is nothing left to pass on to one's son. The man who speculates is soon back to where he began—with nothing. This, as I said, is a very serious problem, for all his hard work has been for nothing; he has been working for the wind. It is all swept away.

Ecclesiastes 5:13–15

Scripture clearly warns of avoiding risky investments; yet each year thousands of people lose money in highly speculative and sometimes fraudulent investments. How many times have you heard of "little old ladies" losing their life's savings on a get-rich-quick scheme? It is not uncommon.

To help you identify a potentially risky investment, I have listed eight benefits that often appear in such schemes.

1. The prospect of a large profit is "practically guaranteed."
2. The decision to invest must be made quickly. There will be no opportunity to thoroughly investigate the investment or the promoter who is selling the investment.
3. The promoter will have an "excellent track record," and he is doing you a "favor" by allowing you to invest with him.
4. The investment often will offer attractive tax deductions as an incentive.
5. You will know little or nothing about the particular investment.
6. Very little will be said about the risks of losing money.
7. The investment will require no effort on your part.
8. You are going to make a "handsome profit" quickly.

If any potential investment has one or more of these "benefits," it should trigger a red warning light in your mind and alert you to carefully and thoroughly investigate the investment before risking your money.

Before you participate in any investment, seek the wise counsel of those experienced in that particular investment media.

Be patient! I have never known anyone who made money in a hurry. Diligence, study, and counsel are prerequisites for improving your chances for successful investments and for avoiding risky ones.

—From Howard L. Dayton, Jr., *Your Money: Frustration or Freedom?* Wheaton, Ill.: Tyndale, 1979.

CREDIT

YOUR INCOME should be the basis for all financial planning. This does not mean that occasionally you cannot go into debt for essential items necessary for your family. If you plan for the debt you are about to incur, you will have no great difficulty meeting the credit payments when they are due. Authorities on family finances say people who get overextended on credit purchases are usually those who buy on impulse rather than by careful planning. These authorities use a number of guidelines in discussing how much debt a family can afford. Let's look at some of these:

1. Use installment credit, but learn to use it wisely. Before you take on debts, figure out what you can afford as monthly payments. A good general rule is never to go into debt more than one month's salary on a loan repayable in one year.
2. Every family should have a reserve fund, preferably one month's pay, before buying on the installment plan.
3. When you buy on credit, shop carefully for your goods and your credit. This will result in savings for you. Become a comparison shopper, know prices and interest rates.
4. Consider your repayments as a form of saving and budgeting, but also build a saving's nest egg by continuing to put aside some cash from each paycheck, even though it may be very small.
5. Plan your major installment purchases together so you both know exactly what you are taking on and what responsibilities you are accepting for payment.

When you are shopping for items in your home, watch with great care the advertising slogans that remind you of Easy credit! Quick credit! Nothing down! Payments begin next year! and so on. Remember that credit costs money. Not only will you be required to pay for the items you purchase or the money you borrow—these payments include a charge for the credit service. Maximum charges are usually determined by state law, but be sure you understand just how much you are paying for the privilege of purchasing on credit.

Used wisely, credit is a help to family living. Things purchased on credit can, in the long run, make possible better management of living expenses. A television set may mean less money spent on outside amusements, and a washing machine may mean a savings on what is usually spent at the laundromat.

Credit is a budgeting medium. It assists families by permitting the cost of major purchases to be budgeted out of several month's income. In so doing, it permits greater freedom in family economics, allowing for a more stable and rewarding family life.

—From Elof G. Nelson, *Your Life Together*. Atlanta: John Knox, 1967.

Credit Cards

1. Is it wrong to use credit cards? I hope not, since I carry many of them when I travel. There's a big difference between using a credit card for *credit* and using it for *debt*. The user for credit is not overspending, and he knows it. Funds are available to pay each bill when the statement arrives. No finance charges are ever paid.

The user for debt is overspending, and he knows it. When the statement arrives, he'll be fortunate to have the money to pay the minimum amount due. So he'll pay the maximum interest.

One man in a California seminar told the audience that he "hadn't used his credit cards since Christmas."

"Has that been a help?" I asked.

"Golly, yes," he replied. "Otherwise I'd owe at least one thousand dollars."

2. What do you think of credit cards for most people? Since Americans owed $50 billion to credit-card companies in October 1979, I think that the cards were too great a temptation for most people to handle.

—From George and Marjean Fooshee, *You Can Beat the Money Squeeze.* Old Tappan, N.J.: Revell, 1980.

DEBT

1. Is there a time in your early life when you will be more in debt? My experience is that debt becomes a habit. The choice is between debt and no debt. Once the line is crossed from no debt to debt, people seldom pay off their charge accounts. The minute the car is paid off, the question is, "What can we buy with those payments we've been making?"

A friend of mine was given a bottle of champagne for his wedding. With it came a card that read, "Don't open this until you are out of debt." My friend laughingly told me that, after fifteen years of marriage, the champagne was still unopened.

2. How can a person in a low-income bracket ($10,000), with two or three children, provide the necessities of living without going into debt? The question includes part of the answer. With or without debt, persons of very low incomes will probably provide only the *necessities* of living and not the *niceties* of living. To borrow to provide such necessities only means less money in the future, when payments and interest come due.

3. Would a debt-free population cause an economic depression in the country? Most certainly! If our government quit overspending its income by the average $54 billion it has gone into debt during each of the last three years, the economy would certainly suffer. And if consumers began to pay off the $256 billion in consumer debt, while not adding the 1978 increase of $40 billion, the economic ripples would be felt throughout the world. But don't hold your breath! It's almost like saying, "If every Christian tithed. . . ."

4. What do you think about the national debt? I think that, corporately, we're violating biblical principles. Someday we'll reap what we've sown for our greed. "So each of us shall give account of himself to God" (Romans 14:12 RSV).

5. Do you recommend debt-consolidation loans to pay off your bills, if you also change your spending habits? I do not recommend borrowing as a way of getting out of debt. You just can't borrow your way out of debt. Transferring debt from high interest to lower interest may make sense. If a person owed on several accounts charging 18% interest, I've seen cases in which borrowing from his credit union at 12% to pay off the 18% accounts made sense. Most credit unions maintain insurance which pays off the credit-union loan in case the borrower dies or becomes disabled.

6. Aren't you overlooking two factors in counseling people to keep out of debt? By being in debt, but paying regularly, I keep a good credit rating, in case of emergencies. In addition, the interest I pay really costs a lot less, since it is deductible from my income tax. I prefer to be prepared for emergencies with savings rather than credit. Does the Bible glorify the ant (Proverbs 30:24, 25) because it has good credit? No! The ant stores up food for the winter. The ant is a saver.

As for those tax deductions, I prefer to list

giving deductions rather than interest deductions. If Marjean and I had paid interest on our cars and major purchases for those twenty-five years of marriage, our giving to the Lord's work would have been thousands of dollars less.

—From George and Marjean Fooshee, *You Can Beat the Money Squeeze*. Old Tappan, N.J.: Revell, 1980.

HOUSING

THE HOUSING area has produced the most questions by seminar participants. The most-often-asked question concerns whether a home mortgage violates the scriptural principle of keeping out of debt. The answer is found in this chapter on housing, which shows the difference between overspending and making a well-planned monthly payment that fits within your budget. Overspending results in debt. The house payment results in building an equity in your home, which becomes an asset—just the opposite of debt.

1. What about going into debt for a house, as against renting an apartment? It all depends. You'll have to weigh all the factors, seek the Lord's direction, then act.

Here's an illustration that will help you calculate your own situation. A friend of mine and his wife rent a nice two-bedroom house for $160, an unheard-of rent, at this time, in our town. The house came as the result of specific prayer. Since they are renting, their only additional shelter expenses are for utilities, which are averaging $70, making the total expenses $230 a month. What can they buy?

With a house payment only making up about 60% of shelter costs, their house payment could total $138 a month for principal and interest (60% of the $230 they spend now). Such a payment will support a 30-year, 10¾% mortgage of approximately $14,800. With a down payment of $1,600 added to the mortgage, the house they could buy for their present expenses could cost $16,400. Since the house they live in is valued at $20,000, they couldn't afford to buy it, unless they could increase their budget for housing by $48 a month, or increase their down payment by $3,600.

By continuing to rent, they'll accumulate the difference between the rent they pay and the amount they can save through not having higher housing costs. They'll also not have to fix the leaky roof, the crumbling foundation, or paint the outside of the house.

By buying, if the house appreciates, they'll accumulate the equity they build as the mortgage is reduced *and* the additional amount the house may sell for several years later. As they invest time in fixing up the house, they'll add additional value which may be gained when they sell.

If the past trend of inflation on real-estate property continues, the house purchase should work out to be the better plan. They should pray over such a decision and seek counsel from others.

2. What about debts for houses? This decision will depend on your goals. Many Christians today have the long-term goal of becoming debt free to the glory of God.

Long-term financial planning should certainly include a debt-free home. In our own case we applied some of our annual savings to our mortgage payment. Since each annual additional payment applied to the principal only, each extra annual payment reduced, by over two years, the number of years we had left to pay. It was a lot of fun to cross out those payments on that long chart and to have the mortgage paid off in half the time.

Savings money paid on your mortgage is not readily available, except at great cost and inconvenience. I'd seldom recommend that anyone put *all* their savings into paying off their home loan. But if you are saving regularly, and if your long-term goal is to have a mortgage-free house, then a regular, annual, additional loan payment will greatly reduce the length of your mortgage.

Beware! Some loans contain a penalty provision for prepayment. You may be penalized for additional payments or for payments beyond a certain percentage of your loan. Check this provision before you sign any home loan or before you attempt prepayment.

—From George and Marjean Fooshee, *You Can Beat the Money Squeeze.* Old Tappan, N.J.: Revell, 1980.

AUTOMOBILES

1. If you find the car you own is costing you too much money, what is the best thing to do? Mine is only one year old. The writer of Proverbs had the answer for you, centuries ago:

You may have trapped yourself by your agreement. Quick! Get out of it if you possibly can! Swallow your pride; don't let embarrassment stand in the way. Go and beg to have your name erased. Don't put it off. Do it now. Don't rest until you do. If you can get out of this trap you have saved yourself like a deer that escapes from a hunter, or a bird from the net.

Proverbs 6:2–5 LB

2. You talk about old cars being economical. A young single woman is thinking about purchasing her first car. Is it practical *for her to buy an "old clunker" when she is not a mechanic?* There is a lot of difference between a new car and an old clunker, both in price and in age, and most of us who drive cars are not mechanics. My mother is still driving her eighteen-year-old Ford, which causes her no more trouble than some of the new cars a few of her friends drive. There's also a lot of difference in price between a new car and a two- or three-year-old car, but not that much difference in utility.

3. If you can afford to buy new cars, is it wrong to drive nice cars, have nice clothes, and other luxuries, especially if you are tithing? The real question concerns whether you have the nice cars, clothes, and things or whether these things have you. Do you love to give or do you love to get?

Faithful tithing is not automatic license for you to buy whatever you want. In our own situation, the way the Lord has blessed us, a tithe would be stingy. Our own giving goal is to have our giving exceed our living expenses. To do this, we must do without many of the "nice things we want." For Marjean and me, part of that doing without has included new cars.

4. In a business, do you recommend leasing a new car? My own company buys used cars. If you lease a car, you're paying for a new one, plus interest on the money, plus a profit for the leasing company. We buy two- to three-year-old cars with 20,000 to 30,000 miles on them, so we save the interest and leasing company's profit, as well as the difference between the price of the new car and the price of the used one.

5. How do you know how much to figure for transportation per mile? The best way is to gather your own figures.

. . . .

This is really an important question. My experience has proved that few people plan to spend what it really costs to run their car(s).

One day I was speaking in an upper-level business class in a Christian college. For starters, I asked how many of the twelve students had cars there at college. Ten students replied affirmatively.

Next I asked them to tell me how much a month it was costing them to drive their cars. Silence!

As I went to the chalkboard, I began to ask them some questions. I discovered they were driving everything from an old clunker to a $10,000 'vette.

When we had finished, they had proved to me and to themselves that it was costing them an average of $150 per month to drive each of those cars. And they didn't even know it!

6. What's the best way to buy a used car? Decide how you will use the car. Decide what size and what kind of car will meet those needs. Decide how much money you want to spend. Read the latest annual auto issue of *Consumer Reports*, which usually comes out in April. You may get it from your local library or subscribe to it directly (Orangeburg, New York 10962). Study it carefully. Decide what make, model, and year of car will meet your needs. Pray for the Lord to supply the exact car to meet your needs. Then do as He leads you.

When we look for a new car for our company salesmen, we ask God to provide a two-year-old model of a Ford or Chevrolet, with the best repair record, with less than 30,000 miles on it, with one owner with whom we can talk, and for a selling price that is at least 35% below a new car of the same make. And He always has.

—George and Marjean Fooshee, *You Can Beat the Money Squeeze*. Old Tappan, N.J.: Revell, 1980.

INSURANCE

1. If we are to trust God to supply our every need, does it show a lack of trust to put money into such things as life and health insurance, instead of putting that money into Christian charities and programs? The Bible does say that God will supply our needs. There's no reason that supply can't come through various kinds of insurance, however.

Solomon said, "A prudent man foresees the difficulties ahead and prepares for them; the simpleton goes blindly on and suffers the consequences" (Proverbs 22:3 LB).

God's Word never tells us we won't be sick or suffer from disease. Medical insurance provides a plan for the prudent man to pay for illness. By making a monthly premium payment, a person is budgeting for future medical expenses. I carry medical insurance and also provide part of the premium for my co-workers to obtain good major-medical coverage at the lowest group rates.

Life insurance is a way to make provision for your family in case of the death of the wage earner. The person who cares enough for his family to purchase life insurance is expressing a unique brand of love.

One woman who came to me for financial counseling told me this story. At the time her daughter was preparing to leave for college, her husband died. His life insurance made it possible for the woman to buy a house in the college town, where she and her daughter could live together. Since the woman had eye trouble and couldn't work, the life insurance made the difference between a poverty existence and continuing a life-style similar to their past one. I've never seen anyone who was collecting life-insurance proceeds who could be anything but thankful for the unselfishness of the deceased loved one.

Disability insurance can be equally important. A far better name for it is income-protection insurance. When the wage earner becomes unable to work, due to sickness or accident, after a waiting period of several days to several months, the insurance begins to provide income payments.

My own company carries such insurance for our company family. Scripturally I have a responsibility to them to meet their needs in times of crisis. What a blessing to know that the incomes of several disabled employees have continued long after they were unable to work.

—From George and Marjean Fooshee, *You Can Beat the Money Squeeze.* Old Tappan, N.J.: Revell, 1980.

GIVING

YOU AND I, who are God's people, are to be funnels for God's flow of resources. The Bible says, "Give, and it will be given to you . . ." (Luke 6:38 RSV). When the spout is blocked at the bottom, because of our stinginess, God can put nothing else in at the top.

Young couples often feel that they just don't have enough to give now. With their incomes low and their desires for furniture and stuff to fill the place where they live, there's just no money to give to the Lord. Such an analysis will prove that there's not enough to give and buy all those other things.

Giving to the Lord is not so much a matter of money as it is trusting God. When we give to the Lord first, we are really telling Him that we have the faith that He will replace it with more than enough to meet our needs. As our needs are met, we'll continue to be His channel for giving resources to others.

Are you trustworthy with what God has given you? Do you acknowledge that everything you have has come because God has made it possible?

A first-off-the-top-of-your-income tithe is the best way I know to prove to yourself and to demonstrate to God that you trust Him. One of my friends says that God is the only business manager in the world who can make 90% go farther than 100%.

Start your marriage as tithers. Know the joy and blessing of giving to others as you start your life learning to give to each other in marriage. The outflow of money from your new marriage will add to your relationship a certain rare quality that will be meaningful to you and attractive to others.

—From George and Marjean Fooshee, *You Can Beat the Money Squeeze.* Old Tappan, N.J.: Revell, 1980.

CONTENTMENT

1. If you are content with what you have, how do you get ahead? Why work if you are content? We are told in the Bible to be content with what we *have*, not what we are (*see* Hebrews 13:5). Our task is to work heartily, as serving the Lord and not men. With a servant attitude toward our employers, we can expect to receive promotions to greater responsibilities.

2. Can a young person who feels a call to the Christian ministry be content with less than an optimum education, because of financial limitations? Paul instructs us by example to be content ". . . in every situation, whether it be a full stomach or hunger, plenty or want" (Philippians 4:12 LB). Can you imagine Paul's feeling limited because he didn't have a graduate degree from the top Christian seminary?

3. Does being content with what you have mean that we are wrong in trying to improve our present financial standing? The biblical principle is that we reap what we sow. Work is often equated with prosperity in the Bible (*see* Proverbs 14:23; 28:19). If the Lord wants to entrust you with more money, He'll most often do it through your efforts at work.

4. How do you balance being content with having a drive to do better in life and being a success at business? What is your goal? Jesus said that if you ". . . seek first his kingdom and his righteousness . . . all these things shall be yours as well" (Matthew 6:33 RSV). Obey God and obey your employer. Serve God and serve your customers. That's the formula for success.

—George and Marjean Fooshee, *You Can Beat the Money Squeeze.* Old Tappan, N.J.: Revell, 1980.

WORKING WIVES

Going Back to Work

Two-thirds of *Today's Christian Woman* readers who responded to a recent survey were working at least part-time outside the home. For many it was a matter of necessity: one income was simply not enough to make ends meet under present economic conditions. Others went back to work so they could more fully develop their gifts and talents and enrich their lives.

For whatever reason, reentering the work world is an exciting experience, but not without a degree of frustration and adjustment. "I knew I wanted to go back to work," one thirty-five-year-old woman said, "but I had no idea that the transition from home to the office would be so difficult. I wish I had been more prepared." You won't be able to anticipate all the changes that will occur if you decide to seek a job outside the home. That's part of the fun—and the risk, too. But if you feel God is guiding you in this direction consider these questions:

1. Why do you want to work? Are you dissatisfied? Bored? Feeling useless? Although a new job can help you find fulfilling outlets for your energies, it isn't a cure-all for unresolved conflicts within or with your family. In fact, your new job may create all kinds of new tensions and frustrations.

Do you need the extra money? Be sure to sit down with your husband and figure out exactly *how much* you need. The extra expenses of gasoline, work clothes, and baby sitters could eat up the extra money you thought you'd be contributing to the family income.

2. Have you discussed with your family the implications of your working? Your new job will affect your family and your home. Long-standing patterns about who does what will have to be reevaluated and changed to fit the new demands on your time. Unless you, your husband, and/or kids are willing to be flexible, you may be up against more resentment and conflict than you can handle. Talk it all out as completely as possible and write down your joint conclusions. Be open about *why* it's important to you to work (money needs, fulfillment, using your gifts).

3. What kind of career do you want? Many women feel the urge to "go back to work," but have only a vague idea of what type of job they would be good at and would enjoy. Take some time to assess yourself—your personality, your skills, your past experience. What were your most significant accomplishments? What do you value most in life? (Don't discount your accomplishments as a mother and homemaker. Your nurturing and organizational skills may apply in a number of other situations.) A career counselor may be able to help you discover your strengths.

4. Do you know the job market? It may have been awhile since you looked carefully at the possible careers open to you. Check the library for the U.S. Department of Labor's Dictionary of Occupational Titles which contains a listing of 20,000 jobs. If you've narrowed your interest down to a particular area, consult people in this field concerning job opportunities, credentials needed, and how to land a job. Inform your friends, relatives, and church members of your desire to go back to work. More jobs are found through personal contacts than through any other source.

5. Will you need further training? You may discover through research that you'll need additional training or schooling to get the job you want. You may be able to take a night course, or a short-term workshop in which you sharpen your skills or develop new ones. Should you pursue a master's program? Perhaps. But assess your needs carefully before undertaking a long-term educational program.

6. Are you willing to spend some time and energy in an extensive job search? Once you're ready to go back to work, the hard part begins: contacting prospective employers, sending out resumes, checking employment agencies and want ads regularly for possibilities.

When you're called for an interview, be prepared to answer questions about why you want the particular job, what skills you have, etc. And ask your own questions about the company and the job. Remember, you must determine if you want the job as much as they must determine if they want you. Be confident. You are a person with gifts and

skills, and even if you don't get a particular job, you'll gain valuable experience in the process.

—Kelsey Menehan, "Back to Work," *Today's Christian Woman*, Summer 1981.

Consequences

The Consequences for the Child. Do the children of working mothers perform more poorly in school than those of nonworking mothers? Is maternal employment related to juvenile delinquency? Does it affect the mental stability of children?

Research does not show sizable differences in academic performance between the children of working mothers and the children of nonworking mothers. Certain studies have shown a slight but not significant tendency for the children of working mothers in the middle class to obtain higher grades, but the opposite appears true in the lower class. Given the present state of research, these can be accepted only as very tentative conclusions.

It has often been argued that because working mothers are absent from the home more than nonworking mothers, their children are less supervised and hence more prone to delinquency. The data do not bear out this argument. As with academic achievement, there are small differences by social class. Sons of working mothers in the middle class appear to be slightly more delinquent than sons of nonworking mothers, but in the lower class there is no difference. The lack of significant differences here is understandable when one considers the fact that children old enough to commit delinquent acts are already of school age. If their mothers are employed, those mothers are likely to be working while the children are under the supervision of school personnel.

People reared in American society, where

the traditional pattern has been for infants and young children to be cared for primarily by a single maternal figure, are likely to think that alternatives to this pattern may well damage a child's emotional development, even to the point of precipitating mental illness. Those who think this are not without their professional supporters. Yet family sociologists Nye and Berardo state, "None of the current research found any measurable differences in symptoms of poor mental health in the children of employed and nonemployed mothers." What seem to be crucial for the mental development of a child are such things as warmth, affection, stimulation, and adequate food. In other words, the data suggest that the more important factor here is quality of care, not who performs that care.

Another concern about working mothers is the effect on the mother's emotional state and hence on her adequacy as a mother when she does have contact with her children. It has been suggested that working outside the home may drain the mother physically and emotionally to the extent that she has little left to give to her children when she does return home.

Research, however, finds a number of mediating factors. One is whether or not a woman is satisfied with her lot of working or not working. Researchers studying mothers of elementary school children divided the women into four groups: satisfied working mothers, dissatisfied working mothers, satisfied nonworking mothers, and dissatisfied nonworking mothers. On a scale designed to measure adequacy of mothering, satisfied nonworking women scored the highest, dissatisfied nonworking women the lowest, while the two categories of working women fell in between. Since satisfied working women scored lower on adequate parenting than satisfied nonworking women but higher than dissatisfied nonworking women, the

crucial question becomes: Would a working mother who enjoys her occupation be dissatisfied as a full-time homemaker? The answer appears to be yes. Data on professionally employed mothers and mothers who graduated from college with exceptionally high records but had chosen to become full-time homemakers showed that the homemakers in this case were lower in morale, self-esteem, and feelings of personal competence (even in regard to child rearing) and showed a greater concern about personal-identity issues. When questioned about what they felt was most notably absent from their lives, the professional women responded that they lacked "time"; the full-time homemakers most often mentioned the lack of "challenge and creative involvement."

Another mediating factor is the extent to which the working mother feels guilty for not being a full-time housewife-mother. There is evidence that employed women do feel guilty about being absent from home. Even the relatively happy professional women in the research just mentioned indicated that they frequently felt anxious and guilty about their employment and its effects on their children. This is hardly surprising in a society that has traditionally looked askance at working mothers. The implications of these feelings of anxiety for the children of working mothers are not fully known. But if any reasonably clear pattern has emerged from the research in this area, it is that mothers who feel very guilty about working tend to overcompensate by being overindulgent and overprotective toward their children. As it becomes more and more culturally acceptable for mothers to work, the guilt feelings and their results are likely to diminish.

One last mediating factor involved in the mother's emotional state is the degree of role strain she experiences. Common sense would have it that working part-time may place little strain on a mother and indirectly her children but working full-time creates a lot more strain and more adverse effects. Research evidence simply does not permit this blanket contention. What appears to be crucial here is whether or not the woman feels her child-care and household-care arrangements are adequate, not whether she works full- or part-time. If she feels that the arrangements are acceptable, strain is minimized, and her emotional state and indirectly her children are not threatened by this source of anxiety.

In summarizing the evidence on the effect of working on a mother's emotional state, Lois Wladis Hoffman, an acknowledged expert in this area, states: "The working mother who obtains satisfaction from her work, who has adequate arrangements so that her dual role does not involve undue strain, and who does not feel so guilty that she overcompensates is likely to do quite well and, under certain conditions, better than the non-working mother." Moreover, for mothers who wish to work, "the job often seems to act as a 'safety valve' . . . , reducing nervousness and frustration."

A final area of research concerning the effects on children of a mother's employment has to do with the sort of role model she is presenting to them. Some are concerned that a working mother presents a role model that, because it is different from the one that mothers have traditionally presented, serves to confuse the children's role perceptions. They fear that such role ambiguity places undue strain on the child and hinders the child's identification with the parent.

Research does not substantiate such fears. Boys in the middle class tend to identify with their fathers and accept them as role models as frequently when their mothers are employed as when they are not. However, this is not as true of sons in the lower class. A probable reason for this difference is that lower-class fathers are less frequently adequate providers and hence mothers are pressured to take jobs. Given present cultural values, in such cases it seems reasonable to presume that often someone other than the father who is inadequately providing would be selected as a role model.

Daughters at all social-class levels are more likely to select a mother who works as a role model than one who does not. The reason why working mothers are more attractive role models to their daughters is so far an unresearched question. However, there has been considerable research on the consequences for daughters of having a working mother rather than a nonworking mother as a model, and from the perspective of moving toward a society more completely characterized by stewardship of talents and by task flexibility for women and men, those consequences are laudable. For instance, research indicates that among girls of elementary school age, daughters of working mothers have a less stereotyped view of the world than daughters of nonworking mothers. The former were more likely to say that both men and women engage in a wide variety of activities, such as using guns, choosing home furnishings, and climbing mountains. The daughters of working women were also more likely to perceive women as being active in the world outside the home.

Another body of findings closely related to the idea of role modeling has to do with how the children of employed versus nonemployed women perceive role attributes for men and women. In a recent study of college-age students, the investigators found that children of both working and nonworking mothers tend to stereotype men as more competent and effective and women as more warm and expressive. However, this tendency was significantly more decided for the children of nonworking women. The authors conclude that maternal employment tends to soften sex-role stereotyping in children.

Maternal employment also appears to have an effect on daughters' evaluation of female competence. [Earlier] we looked at research by Goldberg in which he found that college women tended to view scholarly articles as less competently done if attributed to female rather than male authors. Later research, using the same research techniques but dividing the college women by the employment status of their mothers, found that the daughters of working women were much less likely to downgrade the competence of female authors than the daughters of nonworking women. Apparently, maternal employment helps daughters develop a more realistic view of the talents of women.

The Consequences for the Husband. A wife's employment has certain consequences for her husband and for their relationship. One of the more predictable ones is the effect on the division of labor in the home. As the wife moves into the provider role, the husband tends to get more involved in traditional female tasks. The evidence clearly shows that husbands of working women engage in more "homemaker tasks" like cleaning the house, caring for the children, doing dishes, and shopping for groceries than husbands of nonworking women. But they by no means come to share these tasks equally with their wives. Whether she works part-time or full-time, household care generally remains the wife's responsibility.

The relative contributions of husband and wife to family decision making are also affected by the wife's employment. Working wives have more influence than nonworking wives in decisions on such matters as borrowing money, paying bills, and determining what job the husband should take. An important question about these findings is this: Do wives who were more influential in the first place tend to be the wives who get jobs, or does entering paid employment actually result in increased influence? Research comparing the influence of wives before and after employment indicates that the latter is more often the case. Generally speaking, if a wife enters the labor force, her husband can expect to share influence in the family decision-making process more than he did before. This is hardly surprising, since she has now taken on an additional role that is highly valued in society. The change in the wife's influence is likely to be greater in the case of a lower-class than a middle-class family, because the lower-class family is usually less egalitarian to begin with.

A frequently recurring argument against the wife's employment involves the possible threat to the husband's ego. By moving into the traditionally accepted husband's domain of family providing, it is said, the wife may create feelings of inadequacy or hostility in the husband. There is not a great deal of evidence that husbands, at least at present, are particularly threatened by their wives' employment. The proportion of husbands who disapprove of their wives' work is very small and has been decreasing. The most common interpretation offered here is that husbands are not threatened because the jobs their wives hold are usually of lower status than their own.

However, if the task flexibility and stewardship of talents argued for .... becomes more of a reality, the status of working women will eventually become more comparable to that of their husbands. If this happens, traditionally oriented husbands may come to feel more threatened by their wives' employment. But the problem then for Christians will be not the wife's employment but the husband's response. If a husband feels inadequate because his wife shares in the responsibilities of family providing, he is basing his identity and establishing his self-worth on something other than the biblical attributes for Christians.

Marriages in which the wife works have more conflict between spouses than those in which the wife does not work. This holds true regardless of the family's size or social class or the educational level of the spouses. Although the difference in conflict level is not particularly large, it is significant enough that social scientists have tried to find out why it exists.

They have advanced a number of possible explanations. One is that marriages involving working wives were more conflict-ridden to start with and this is what prompted wives to work. A second suggests that working wives, being less financially dependent on their husbands, are more likely to state their opinions when they disagree with their husbands and so contribute to a higher level of conflict. The third explanation is called the "increased interaction hypothesis." This maintains that with the wife-mother's employment, an additional dimension is added to the family's day-to-day life. The activities of all family members must be adjusted to the demands of the mother's job. This raises additional possibilities for disagreement and conflict. All three of these explanations have some empirical support and, depending on the family involved, can account for increased conflict in families with working wives.

A question closely allied to that of conflict in the marriages of working wives is whether the rise in the employment rate of wives has contributed to the increase in the divorce rate. While it is true that a disproportionate number of women who are divorced are also employed, it is common knowledge that many of these women work simply because for economic reasons they must. Comparisons of working and nonworking women reveal that a similar portion of each group were in their second or subsequent marriage.

Although not definitive, this evidence does suggest that "it is more likely that divorced women get jobs than that women get divorces because they have jobs."

There is one more facet to the relation between wives' employment and marital conflict. While it is true that working wives experience more conflict with their husbands than do nonworking wives, this does not mean that working wives are less satisfied with their marriages. The evidence is that they do not report any less satisfaction than nonworking wives. In fact, if they take jobs voluntarily, their satisfaction with marriage increases. Apparently, if a wife enters the labor force because she wishes to, she can generally expect a higher standard of living, more influence in family decision making, and additional social relationships—that is, with people at her place of work. While her job tends to result in more conflict with her husband, it also adds satisfaction to her life. That satisfaction seemingly extends to her assessment of her marriage.

The Consequences for the Working Wife-Mother. When married women significantly increased their participation in the labor force after World War II, they were accused of possibly harming not only their children but also themselves. Although there has been less research in this area than into the consequences for children and the husband-wife relationship, there are enough data to dismiss some of the more common myths about working mothers.

One such myth is that taking on the additional role of paid employee negatively affects a mother's physical health. According to research evidence, employed mothers as a category apparently are healthier than nonemployed mothers; they report considerably fewer symptoms of poor health. Whether working improves the health of the mother or healthier mothers tend to be the ones working is an unanswered question. Before-and-after research is needed in this area. At any rate, the finding that working mothers are generally healthier than nonworking mothers is sufficient reason to dismiss the assumption that employment is necessarily a detriment to the mother's physical health.

Although nonworking mothers also have doubts about their adequacy as mothers and wives, more working mothers experience these doubts. The working mothers who are most subject to feelings of guilt and anxiety are those who are not satisfied with their substitute child-care arrangements and those whose own parents are very traditionally oriented toward the mother's role.

Working mothers' feelings of guilt and anxiety about their mother-wife roles, however, do not seem to get transferred into psychosomatic symptoms of mental illness. For instance, one major study measured ten psychosomatic symptoms, including shortness of breath, nightmares, nervousness, insomnia, and dizziness. No significant differences were found between working and nonworking mothers. In fact, the minor differences were on the side of more symptoms among the nonworking mothers.

Perhaps part of the reason why working mothers' anxiety about how well they are fulfilling traditional female role expectations does not get transformed into psychosomatic symptoms is that working mothers tend to feel better about themselves than nonworking mothers. In studies of self-concept, working mothers are more likely to mention positive things about themselves and to show self-acceptance than nonworking mothers.

Other consequences of employment for working married women are quite predictable. For instance, they spend less time at recreational pursuits. Interestingly, the recreational activities reduced are watching television, visiting neighbors, and entertaining formally. There is no reduction in recreation involving the husband or the family as a whole. Employed mothers are also less likely to take positions of responsibility in voluntary organizations, but they are as likely as nonemployed mothers to belong to such organizations and attend the meetings.

Much argument over married women's employment centers on whether it increases or decreases happiness. Some argue that it brings fulfillment, others that it produces more conflict and tension in the family and hence unhappiness. Researcher F. Ivan Nye asked two thousand mothers to indicate the degree of their satisfaction or dissatisfaction with several areas of their lives. These areas included such things as daily work, income, relationship with their children, and their community as a place to live. Overall, working mothers, whether employed part-time or full-time, showed more satisfaction with their lives than nonworking mothers. Interestingly, the differences between the two groups were greatest in two nonmaterial areas: relationship with their children and how they viewed their community as a place to live. In both, working mothers were found to be more satisfied than nonworking mothers. Whatever the perceived costs of employment for working mothers, these costs do not appear sufficient to give the women a negative assessment of their lot in life. If anything, such women are more likely to feel positive about their lives.

Conclusion. From a sociological perspective, there do not appear to be significant negative social consequences associated with the employment of mothers and wives. Working mothers experience more feelings of guilt and anxiety about their adequacy as mothers, but this does not get transformed into negative consequences for their children. They also experience similar doubts regarding their adequacy as wives, but these feelings do not lead to greater dissatisfaction with their marriages or more symptoms of physical or mental illness. Nor does the greater amount of conflict in the marriages of working wives seem to result in higher divorce rates or less satisfaction with their marriages. All this is not to say that taking on an additional role is not difficult or does not create strain; what the evidence does suggest is that working women and their families have found ways to cope with that strain fairly effectively.

From the point of view that it is desirable for society to move more toward sex-role task flexibility and less sex stereotyping of attributes so that stewardship of gifts can be more fully realized, the increased participation of married women in the labor force seems to have many positive consequences. Their children are less likely to stereotype roles for women and men. Their daughters evaluate the competence of women more highly. Their children and husbands share more in day-to-day household tasks. Their husbands are likely to share family decision making with them. And their self-images are higher.

Although extensive, the research about the consequences of married women's employment is not as complete as we would like. Of primary concern to Christian parents, for instance, is the spiritual growth of their children. With so many non-Christian influences at work in society, they are rightfully concerned with anything that might hinder this aspect of their children's development. Although the sociological evidence on married women's employment does not directly address this concern, it does indirectly offer some reassurance by suggesting that working mothers are as influential in their children's lives as nonworking mothers. Quality of child care appears more important than the absolute amount of time spent with the child or who offers the care. Chil-

dren of working mothers identify with their parents as readily as children of nonworking mothers. Once employed, mothers do not reduce recreational time spent with their children. Working mothers are as satisfied with their relationship to their children as nonworking mothers.

In the end, it must be remembered that these sociological statements are generalizations, or statements of probability; they must not be indiscriminately applied to particular families. Decisions about how a given wife and husband will responsibly provide for their family must depend upon their particular situation. However, these generalizations surely should be sufficient to reassure the Christian community that the trend toward married women's employment has not ushered in the negative results for the family that were predicted.

Throughout this section we have compared working and nonworking women in order to reach some conclusion about the consequences of women's taking on a share of the family providing role. Does this mean that if the consequences on balance had been found to be negative, we would be saying that responsible Christians ought to speak out against married women's employment? No. The way in which the issue was handled here was merely a reflection of the way in which previous social scientists have conceptualized the issue and collected relevant data. Regardless of whether the consequences proved to be decidedly negative or decidedly positive, the basic question for each Christian husband and wife would remain the same: how can they fulfill family responsibilities and at the same time make optimum use of their talents in their roles of Christian servanthood? Since each marriage represents a unique combination of talents and conditions, practicing such an orientation will mean that some Christian families look quite traditional in their structure for accomplishing family tasks while others appear non-traditional (e.g., husband and wife share equally in family providing and child rearing, or the wife as the primary provider and the husband the main child rearer).

—From Peter DeJong and Donald R. Wilson, *Husband and Wife: The Sexes in Scripture and Society.* Grand Rapids: Zondervan, 1979.

ESTATES

Wills

God does take care of His own, yes, but He also has directed us to do some things for ourselves. One Bible verse says to those who have families,

". . . if any provide not for his own, and specially for those of his own house, he hath denied the faith, and is worse than an infidel."

Sue and Richard had five children and a very happy home. Richard was working on a scaffolding one day on a tall building in a large city. The scaffolding broke and Richard fell to his death. Sue and the children bore it bravely, their deep faith giving them strength. They continued to attend church regularly and the two children who had not professed their faith in Christ did so publicly and were baptized.

A few months later, Sue, while crossing a street, was killed too. The children felt strongly that their mother was with their daddy in heaven, and those with whom they went to live supported that belief. Not only did the children have the legacy of their faith to support them, and a good home to go into, but because of advance planning on the part of Sue and Richard, they were left well cared for financially from provisions in their wills and life insurance.

I Don't Have Enough to Bother With A pastor friend of mine was almost dragged into my office by his little wife, Jan. His first statement was, "George, I just don't have very much. To tell you the truth, the only things I have that are worthwhile are my wife and six children." As we added it up, however, Pastor Willis was surprised as many are, at how much in the way of material possessions he did have. Although they had no insurance, and he had no retirement program except for social security, they did own a little home and a car. Before we were finished planning, we had done the following:

1. Changed the deed on their home and the title to the car so as to avoid probate (court involvement), in the event one spouse survives.
2. Prepared a will for both Willis and Jan, with a contingent trust to take care of those six p.k.'s (preacher's kids) in case of the death of both parents.
3. Funded the contingent trust with low-cost term life insurance. (The insurance is payable to the wife if living and if not living, directly to the trust, thus avoiding probate of the insurance proceeds.)
4. Suggested the pastor have the trustees of his church consider funding a modest retirement program for him at the church's next annual business budget meeting, so as to supplement his Social Security.

Pastor Willis and Jan are delighted with the results, and the nagging thought of going on welfare or being forced to go out and find a job in case of Willis' death, while the children are still small, no longer bothers Jan.

. . . .

Choosing the people who will carry out the provisions of your will must not be a

373

game of chance, either. Executor, Trustee, Guardian, Attorney, all may play an important role in your future.

Although sometimes their duties overlap, we'll try to give a definition of each one plus some idea of the services they perform.

EXECUTOR

The *executor* is the person or institution named in a person's will who carries out the terms of the will. Traditionally, the word has referred to the male, and *executrix* to the female, but this distinction is rapidly disappearing.

When a person dies, the executor's job starts at once. The executor must carry on for the dead person, usually making the funeral arrangements, presenting the will to the Court, gathering the estate, continuing a business, paying bills, canceling magazine subscriptions, collecting insurance and other benefits, selling all or portions of the estate property, if necessary, completing tax reports as required, paying taxes, accounting to the Probate Court and governmental agencies, distributing what's left of the estate in accordance with the will, paying for the support of any dependents from the estate, suing, if need be, if the deceased died from an accident where another is liable, etc.

If there is no trust, and the estate is to go to minor children, the executor distributes what is left—after bills, taxes, and other costs are paid—to a *guardian*. If there is a trust to care for the estate and a guardian to care for the children, then the executor distributes to the *trustee*.

The executor's job may take a few months or longer, depending upon the problems in the estate. When the required work is completed, the executor is discharged by the Court.

The executor is *paid a fee*, but the method of determining that fee will differ from state to state, so check your local law. If you name a spouse or relative, often that person will waive his or her fee, thus reducing the amount in settlement costs.

Who? Generally a husband names his wife, and a wife her husband, as executor, and then they name one or more alternates. It need *not* be a spouse. It can be a relative or friend, a business associate, a bank or trust company, or an attorney. A beneficiary named in the will *may* serve as executor.

NOTE: Where there is an estate to be administered and there is no will or the deceased leaves a will but fails to name an executor, the Court appoints an administrator to do the job, with the law specifying who is entitled to be appointed.

TRUSTEE

The *trustee* is the person or institution named by a person making the trust, or appointed by the Court, to carry out the terms of the trust.

When the executor's job is finished, the trustee's job begins, assuming a trust has been set up through a will.

The trustee takes the property and administers it as instructed by the trust instrument (the person's written instructions) and as required by law. Normally the trustee is given *wide* discretion in this administration of the estate property, as to how it is to be used for the benefit of the person's loved ones. For example, the trustee takes care of it, pays support to the guardian for the children from it, and makes decisions which the trustee considers best.

This is why your choice of trustee is *very important.* You not only want the trustee to make decisions somewhat like you would make and which would be best for your loved ones under constantly changing circumstances, but you want the trustee's philosophy of rearing children and views on life to agree with yours!

The trustee and the guardian should be able to work together for the benefit of those little ones you would rather rear yourself.

The trustee is *paid a fee* which will vary in different areas and which depends upon services rendered. A typical annual fee will be from $5/10$ to $7/10$ of 1 percent of the value of the trust assets. As with the executor, if the trustee is a relative, the fee may be waived.

Who? The guardian and trustee can be the same, but we recommend they *not* be because of a possible conflict of interests.

A beneficiary in the will may serve as trustee, if the beneficiary has legal capacity to receive and hold property. A minor doesn't have that capacity nor does an incompetent person. If the beneficiary is the sole beneficiary and sole trustee of a trust, the trust ceases to exist.

The choice you make should depend upon the ability of the trustee to not only serve your purposes but do a good businesslike job of managing and working with your assets. As we mentioned before, the trustee has *wide* discretion in deciding what is best regarding your properties and your children, so your choice is of *vital importance.*

In case of death of both parents, the trustee can be a relative (parent, brother, sister, uncle, aunt, etc.), a business associate, a bank, or an organization authorized by law to serve as trustee. Attorneys often serve as trustees as well as executors.

In the case of a trust set up for children which is contingent upon the parents both dying, then a third party must be named trustee.

With some living trusts, the one who makes the trust often serves as trustee.

When it comes to tax-savings trusts, the surviving spouse often serves as sole trustee even when the trust provides for invasion of principal of the trust to satisfy the needs of the surviving spouse. But special care should be taken, by the one who drafts the document, to include ascertainable standard provisions in order to satisfy the requirements of the Internal Revenue Service and assure that the assets of the tax-savings trust are not included in the estate of the surviving spouse on the death of the surviving spouse. Otherwise, the estate on the second to die may be taxed heavily.

In the case of tax saving trusts for a surviving spouse where the children are adult, the trustee or co-trustee can be chosen from among the adult children. Be careful with this choice, however, as it may carry with it possible problems and conflicts. Further, if you choose an adult child as trustee, don't permit the trust principal to be used by the child for the child's own health or maintenance, or for the child's dependents, for, if you do, the income from the trust may be taxable to the trustee personally.

GUARDIAN

The *guardian* is the person who is appointed by the Court to care for the person and/or estate of a minor child or incompetent person. One can nominate a guardian in a will, and though normally the Court will honor that nomination, the Court has the right to agree or disagree. That is, the judge can appoint a guardian who the judge feels will better serve the interests of the minor or the person who is incompetent. The Court's intervention is useful, of course, if conditions are different when you die than when you made out your will.

The guardian steps into your shoes, so to speak, so far as the responsibility for your child is concerned, except that the guardian need only look to the provision you left for the child in caring for that child. The guardian has no obligation to use personal funds.

The guardian may resign, should he or she be discontent with the arrangements, so it is very important that you set up a mechanism by contingent trust in your will or by living trust, or other means, prior to your death, to see that the guardian has sufficient funds available to care adequately for your child's needs.

The guardian is entitled to be paid a court-approved fee but it is nominal and most people do not accept the job with the fee as motivation.

Who? Naturally, if only one parent has died, the surviving spouse is responsible for the child or children. In preparing for the possibility that both of you may be dead, you can name relatives or friends as guardians. We suggest you choose a couple who agree with your views on rearing children and who, if you wish, have children about the age of yours so there will be companionship. If you can find that combination among relatives, you are blessed, but if not, you should nominate friends who meet your requirements. Whatever you consider important (the arts, the out of doors, learning the value of a dollar, spiritual growth) should be considered when making this choice.

You will want a first choice and at least one alternate.

A bank or trust department usually *cannot* be guardian of the *person* of your child, but it can be guardian of the child's estate.

ATTORNEY

The *attorney* (or lawyer) is a person licensed by the state to practice law and is hired to represent and assist the executor, trustee, and guardian. It is conceivable that each could hire a separate attorney, but usually one attorney represents all three.

The attorney assists the other three in completing their duties and responsibilities both in and out of the Court.

It is possible that one person could be executor, trustee, and guardian and do everything without an attorney, but I've never known anyone who attempted this.

The attorney is paid a fee for representing the executor. The amount of the fee and the method of computing same will depend upon the laws and practices in your state. The attorney's fees for representing the guardian and trustee are most often based upon the reasonable value of services rendered. . . . All fees in court-supervised matters are subject to review by the Court and, except for fees set by the legislature, all fees in matters with or without supervision, can be challenged in court, by or on behalf of all interested persons.

Who? The executor hires the attorney, and that choice can be the same attorney who prepared the will (which is usually the case) or it can be someone else.

Should I choose guardians, a trustee, or executor who reside out of state?

Yes, if they best serve your purposes, are willing to serve you, and there is nothing in your local law restricting your choice.

As a practical matter, though, your executor will need to do a lot of things with your property and affairs that require the executor's presence where the property is located. Your trustee can do a much better job with the funds and property to be administered as it relates to your loved ones if distance isn't a factor.

Keeping Them Honest. Must my executor, trustee, and guardian be bonded?

Generally, before the Court will appoint a fiduciary (executor, trustee, or guardian) of an estate, the fiduciary must be bonded to insure faithful performance of the fiduciary's duties. The bond is an indemnity bond—similar to an insurance policy which pays the estate in case there is loss caused by default or fraud by the fiduciary. If you trust your fiduciary, your will or trust should waive the bond: that is, direct that a bond is not required, thus saving your estate the cost of the bond premium.

Probate

Probate is the legal process of proving a will, appointing an executor, and settling an estate; but by custom, it has come to be understood as the legal process whereby a dead person's estate is administered and distributed.

Built around it is a system of checks and balances, put there by the legislature (your duly elected representatives) to see that the estate is administered and distributed properly. In addition to the checks and balances of the law, the Court and agencies of the Court review and screen what has been done to see that it has been done properly, and in some instances have to pass on an act *before* it is done. Anyone interested in the estate has a right to seek redress from the Court, in case he believes something has not been handled correctly. Even the fees charged for the services of the executor and attorney are set by law and/or must be approved by the Court.

Yes, where people are involved, there are bound to be abuses, but the process of probate is widely used, seldom abused, and is constantly being improved upon in areas where abuse does occur.

SOME ADVANTAGES OF PROBATE

1. It sets rules for the *orderly passing* of property, free of lien or cloud (when others claim they have a right to your money or debts incurred by you or others):
2. It designates *who* is to wind up your affairs;
3. *It provides powers and rules* for the gathering and disposition of your assets;
4. *It provides a forum* or place where questions, claims, and disputes can be settled;
5. It provides for a special and in most states a shortened time within which creditors can make a claim against your estate, after which time the claim is barred;
6. It can provide *tax advantages* in certain cases, and it provides a convenient method of estate splitting for tax savings;
7. In some states, it *sets rigid limits on fees* to be charged for professional help that may be rendered. For instance, an attorney is usually needed in helping to wind up the affairs of a deceased person. That service, outside of probate, is normally charged at an hourly rate, which could result in a fee in excess of the probate fee set by law.

SOME DISADVANTAGES OF PROBATE

1. *Publicity.* Sometimes a person who is in the public eye prefers to keep the public from knowing what is going to be done with his or her estate, or what the estate consists of, so avoids probate for these reasons.

   Publicity is not totally a disadvantage for the average person, however, for few seem to read these published notices, and many times the publication is in a local trade paper which has limited circulation. Also, that publication satisfies the legal requirements of notice to creditors and begins a new and usually short period for creditors to make a claim against your property. (After that period, creditors' claims are cut off forever.) This, in turn, allows your estate representative to proceed in a timely and orderly manner to make distribution of your property, free of cloud or threatened lien (debts by creditors).

2. *Costs* for professional help. This seems to receive the loudest complaints. (As stated before, this burden can be greatly reduced by having a relative serve your estate in a representative capacity.)
3. It can result in *delays* in winding up a person's estate if those handling the probate procrastinate, but we've found people procrastinate in or out of probate.

Let's take a look at some examples of those who have seen the wisdom of using probate in the settling of their affairs, following death.

These people generally will fall into one of three categories:

1. Persons needing only a simple will.
2. Persons needing no tax saving trusts, but needing a will with trusts for care of children, and/or others.
3. Persons who need a will and estate splitting, tax saving trust.

Intestacy

If the deceased (the one who dies) leaves no instructions, the State *gives* the instructions, based on laws decided upon by lawmakers. These instructions from the State Legislature are known as *laws of intestacy, laws of intestate succession,* or *laws of descent and distribution.*

Sometimes these legislative directions will give a result you *would* have wanted anyway, but often that is not the case. It is not unusual for very unexpected and unfair results to occur. . . .

You may agree or disagree with the result, but that is really not the point. The point is, do you want to be the one to decide where your property is to go at your death, or in the case of small children without parents, who will rear them? Or do you want that decision to be made by someone for you? . . . .

Some undesirable results of intestate succession laws are as follows:

1. Your surviving spouse and children may have to share ownership of your estate;
2. You lose the opportunity of specifying who or what will receive any of your property or specific items of your property;
3. You lose the opportunity of waiving bond for both guardian and executor;
4. You lose the opportunity of setting up a trust for care of your children;
5. You lose the opportunity of choosing a trustee and guardian who will be sympathetic to the spiritual as well as the physical needs of your children;
6. You lose the opportunity of planning your estate so as to minimize tax and administration expense;
7. These laws make no allowance for you to fulfill your obligations of charitable stewardship (giving to charities);
8. They include no allowance for friends.

There are many other negatives and very few positives to a course of no planning.

—From George and Margaret Hardisty, *Successful Financial Planning.* Old Tappan, N.J.: Revell, 1978.

FOR FURTHER READING

Burkett, Larry. *What Husbands Wish Their Wives Knew About Money.* Wheaton, Ill.: Victor Books, 1977.

Burkett, Larry. *Your Finances in Changing Times.* Chicago: Moody, 1982.

Dayton, Howard L., Jr. *Your Money: Frustration or Freedom?* Wheaton, Ill.: Tyndale, 1979.

Fooshee, George and Marjean. *You Can Beat the Money Squeeze.* Old Tappan, N.J.: Revell, 1980.

Gallagher, Neil. *How to Save Money on Almost Everything.* Minneapolis: Bethany House, 1978.

Hardisty, George and Margaret. *Successful Financial Planning.* Old Tappan, N.J.: Revell, 1978.

Juroe, David. *Money.* Old Tappan, N.J.: Revell, 1981.

Thomason, James C. *Common Sense About Your Family Dollars.* Wheaton, Ill.: Victor Books, 1979.

7

Divorce

LEGAL ASPECTS

Contest Divorce?

If your mate demands divorce there is little if anything to be gained by contesting such action. There was a time when most states required evidence of efforts at conciliation before a divorce would be granted. At this writing, only two states still compel the parties to try for a reconciliation when the ground for divorce is "irreconcilable differences." Forced efforts of reconciliation profit very little, because the blending of lives requires choice, not coercion. Divorce laws in most states are very liberal, and efforts at contesting the divorce result in little except expensive legal fees.

Contesting the divorce is simply a legal step in which one party seeks to prove that the other does not have grounds for divorce. That was feasible when state laws allowed for divorce only on the grounds of insanity, adultery, or abandonment. Today, however, with virtually all states having some form of no fault divorce laws, such action at most only slows the process a bit. You may ask for time, and some states even require a separation of some months before divorce, but to seek to thwart divorce is futile.

It may seem unfair that if your spouse demands a divorce you have little choice except to go along with that choice, but such is the nature of human relationships. We cannot force anyone to be our friend. Friendship is a mutual choice between two people. If one chooses to dissolve the friendship, the other is helpless to keep it alive. Marriage is the most intimate of all friendships, and it too requires reciprocal action.

You cannot force reconciliation, because by its very nature reconciliation requires two people. Divorce, however, which literally means "to disunite," requires only the action of one. If one person desires union and the other disunion, the one who desires disunion holds the upper hand, for union is impossible without his or her acquiescence.

Do I Need A Lawyer?

Divorce not only severs an emotional and physical relationship, but also a legal contract. Each state has its own laws and regulations regarding the dissolution of a marital contract. In most cases a lawyer will be needed to interpret the laws and guide in the process. California has recently initiated a no-attorney, no-court process for childless couples with no real estate, less than $5,000 in personal property, and less than $2,000 in debt. That streamlined divorce procedure costs only forty to fifty dollars in court fees. Other states may follow California's example, but for most couples a lawyer would be a necessity.

Do spouses need separate lawyers? If your spouse is divorcing you, his or her lawyer will be representing your spouse's interests. If you have had problems agreeing on finances, property, and child-related issues, then you will definitely need a lawyer to represent your interests. If you and your spouse can agree on an equitable settlement, then one attorney can represent both of you. Before you agree on one attorney, however, you should make a trip to the public library and read some of the many books and pamphlets on the legal aspects of divorce. You may also want to talk with several friends who have experienced divorce. That will give you a more realistic idea of what is involved in an equitable settlement.

—From Gary Chapman, *Hope for the Separated,* copyright ©1982, Moody Bible Institute, Moody Press, pp. 98–100.

ASSUMING RESPONSIBILITY

PEOPLE OFTEN MARRY other people with the assumption that the person they are marrying will make them happy. What an awesome responsibility is placed upon that person's shoulders. What if they fail? Who gets the blame? Where can other happiness be found? A marriage built upon that premise often leads to a divorce and unless the lesson is learned, the hunt is on for another person to provide happiness.

Many divorced persons feel that the answer to all their problems will be found in finding the right person. I call this the "abdication of responsibility syndrome." It often leads to a quick second, third, fourth, etc. marriage.

Divorce can be a teacher if you let it. It will teach you how, as an adult, you can assume responsibility for yourself, your thoughts and your actions. Persons who GROW through divorce experience this. They can go from a marriage that was a total dependency into a divorce that teaches personal responsibility.

A child learns very young that he is spared punishment and responsibility if he can blame his actions or deeds on someone else. We begin to build a pattern in youth that affects our later years. It is easy to come to the place where we always blame someone else for our situation, misdeeds, problems, struggles, lack of growth, or misfortunes. I listen to many people say "If only I would have . . . we would not be divorced today." Assuming responsibility for yourself may be a new discovery for you. It begins in the following areas.

1. I ASSUME RESPONSIBILITY FOR MY PART OF THE FAILURE OF MY MARRIAGE. One of the insidious traps that divorced persons get caught in, is playing the blame game. One or more can play the game but no one ever wins. Every action in a marriage draws a reaction. Actions and reactions build for years, one person explodes and leaves and the blame game starts. No one can relive the years of a marriage and change what is history. But accepting responsibility for *your* part of the failure can certainly change your future. PEOPLE DON'T DIVORCE SITUATIONS, THEY DIVORCE PEOPLE WHO CREATE SITUATIONS AND FAIL TO TAKE RESPONSIBILITY FOR THOSE SITUATIONS.

In a divorce, assuming responsibility for yourself does not start with your future, it starts with your past and putting that in perspective. It means expressing *your* responsibility for the failure in your marriage to your ex-spouse. If both parties do this, the blame game will come to an end and postmarital relationships will not be warring ones.

2. I ASSUME RESPONSIBILITY FOR MY PRESENT SITUATION. I frequently hear people blame their present situation, whether it is housing, lack of money, job, etc. on their past. It is easy to say everything is bad because of what I have just gone through. This kind of situation is known as the "Woe Me's." Many get caught in the routine of wishing things were different. They are hooked on extracting pity from others that will reinforce for them the fact that they are merely the victim of circumstances and powerless to handle or change their present situation.

If you do not assume responsibility for your present situation, who will? Part of being an adult is accepting responsibility. If you are a single parent with children at home, a house to maintain, money to earn, a job to pursue, you will not get the job done by endless television watching, bar hopping, chain smoking and retreating from life because it has given you a raw deal. Being responsible says you need to assess your present situation and the needs you have. Make a list with the heading at the top reading I AM RESPONSIBLE FOR: Be honest and don't pass the buck. Then draw a line down the center of the page. At the head of the second column write I WILL FULFILL THIS RESPONSIBILITY BY: Spend some time on this. Share it with a friend for further input. In effect you are accepting and articulating your responsibilities for right now and setting goals to achieve their fulfillment. Things that are frightening in our mind usually become obtainable realities when placed on paper.

3. I ASSUME RESPONSIBILITY FOR MY FUTURE. There are many people who live their entire lives with contingency goals. These are not real goals but negative goals that are based upon circumstances and other people. They change constantly as people come and go in our lives. Examples are:

I won't go to work because I might remarry.

I won't go back to school because I might fail.

I won't date because I might get hurt again.

I won't move because I might not get as good a situation as I have.

I'll do this until something better comes along.

I won't set goals because they might interfere with someone I'll meet.

I could add numerous other statements I hear people make every day. Instead of securing their own future with constructive plans and growth producing goals, they make no moves for fear they will make the wrong ones.

Many people are divorcing today after twenty and thirty years of marriage. When I ask these people what goals they have set for themselves, they often respond by saying its too late or that their goal is just to survive each day. Someone has said, "Shoot at nothing and that is what you will hit."

No one else is responsible for your future but you. You have to live in it. Accept responsibility for it. Make the best plans for you. Whether you remain single or remarry should not affect your present planning. You do not have to be married to be headed somewhere in life.

4. I ASSUME RESPONSIBILITY FOR MYSELF. During college, we often discussed whether environment or heredity played the biggest part in our personality development. The arguments were good but no one ever seemed to prove one or the other. A fitting conclusion would be that both play a great deal in who we are today. If we are successful today, we can attribute it to our successful influences. Determining causes does not change present realities. Each of us is responsible for ourselves. We cannot renege that responsibility. Three basic areas in self-responsibility are: thoughts, feelings and actions.

THOUGHTS

What does a divorced person think about?

Why has this happened to me?

What went wrong?

What will I do now?

Can I make it on my own?

How long will I hurt?

Can I ever be happy again?

TEN COMMANDMENTS FOR FORMERLY MARRIEDS

1. THOU SHALT NOT LIVE IN THY PAST.
2. THOU SHALT BE RESPONSIBLE FOR THY PRESENT AND NOT BLAME THY PAST FOR IT.
3. THOU SHALT NOT FEEL SORRY FOR THYSELF INDEFINITELY.
4. THOU SHALT ASSUME THY END OF THE BLAME FOR THY MARRIAGE DISSOLVEMENT.
5. THOU SHALT NOT TRY TO RECONCILE THY PAST AND RECONSTRUCT THY FUTURE BY A QUICK, NEW MARRIAGE.
6. THOU SHALT NOT MAKE THY CHILDREN THE VICTIMS OF THY PAST MARRIAGE.
7. THOU SHALT NOT SPEND ALL THY TIME TRYING TO CONVINCE THY CHILDREN HOW TERRIBLE AND EVIL THEIR DEPARTED PARENT IS.
8. THOU SHALT LEARN ALL THOU CAN ABOUT BEING A ONE PARENT FAMILY AND GET ON WITH IT.
9. THOU SHALT ASK OTHERS FOR HELP WHEN THOU NEEDEST IT.
10. THOU SHALT ASK GOD FOR THE WISDOM TO BURY YESTERDAY, CREATE TODAY AND PLAN FOR TOMORROW.

—From Jim Smoke, *Growing Through Divorce.* Eugene, Ore.: Harvest House, 1976.

LONELINESS

ROBERT S. WEISS, professor of sociology at the University of Massachusetts, who has pioneered in the exploration of loneliness, identifies two forms of loneliness—emotional and social. Although the symptoms differ, the cause of both types of loneliness remains the same: the inability to satisfy the need to form meaningful attachments.

Emotional loneliness springs from the need for intimacy with a spouse or a best friend. A person who is emotionally lonely feels that there is no one he can absolutely count on. Symptoms include feelings of tension, vigilance against possible threat, restlessness, loss of appetite, an inability to fall asleep, and a pervasive low-level anxiety.

In social loneliness the individual experiences a sense of detachment from the community at large. He experiences the feeling that "what matters is taking place elsewhere." Often the divisions of the day become meaningless to the socially lonely. They may doze in the middle of the day and awake in the middle of the night. Social loneliness is especially pronounced among individuals who have no significant vocation. They sense that their lives are not accomplishing anything worthwhile.

The separated are likely to experience both kinds of loneliness. That is especially true when one does not have a social support system outside the marriage. The wife who has been at home through the years will likely feel cut off not only from her husband but from the whole world when separation occurs.

Loneliness is sometimes mistaken for depression. Though lonely people may eventually become depressed out of frustration at their inability to dispel loneliness, the two are very different states: depression resists change; loneliness produces pressure to change. Depression renders one immobile, whereas loneliness will press one to move in any direction that offers hope. That is why many lonely people move toward singles bars, feeling all the while that they should not go. Depression keeps one at home with all the shades drawn in self-pity.

Emotional Loneliness

The ultimate answer to emotional loneliness, the lack of an intimate relationship with another person, is to reach out and establish wholesome contact with yourself, God, and others. . . . You have the capacity to be your own best friend. You spend more time with yourself than anyone else. Why not make the time pleasant? Learn to like yourself and create an atmosphere in which you can enjoy life. You need not destroy yourself because of what has happened. You have admitted your failures—now get up and do something today that will make you feel pleased with yourself.

The church can greatly assist you in making meaningful contact with God and others. It is a joy to observe what happens when a lonely separated person enters the life of our church. In the sermon he hears hope, which he has not heard for many weeks. In the informal study groups he meets people who are finding that hope for themselves. He discovers people who are not perfect, but forgiven, who reach out to him in love. Week by week, little by little, a person comes to respond to God and to those hands of hope. He learns to talk to God and to hear His word for him. He learns to share himself with others who genuinely care. In time the loneliness fades, and the beauty of that once dejected individual begins to unfold like a fragrant rose. Few things are more rewarding for those of us who minister in the fellowship of a local church.

—From Gary Chapman, *Hope for the Separated*, copyright © 1982, Moody Bible Institute, Moody Press, pp. 73–74, 76–77.

SEX

ATTITUDE ONE. Sex is okay—anytime, anyplace, with anyone who is a consenting adult and of legal age. Does that sound a little like the last television show you watched? Probably! This attitude is held by a large segment of the singles world today. It follows the slogan "If it feels good, do it." We could probably call this sexual liberty or sexual freedom. We forget that freedom always comes with responsibilities attached. In the world of sexual license, there are seldom thoughts of responsibilities. This is, at best, random sex.

Attitude two. Sex is okay—anytime, anyplace, with anyone of legal age, but only if you have a "meaningful relationship" with the person. The question that arises here is,

385

"What does meaningful mean?" It is a relative term. If I said I had a meaningful breakfast this morning, would you know what I had? It could be two vitamins and a glass of juice, or the whole breakfast special at my neighborhood restaurant. What is known as meaningful to one person may lack meaning to another person.

Meaningful in the above context could mean you have had three dates with the same person before you engage in sex. It could mean sixty dates. It could mean engagement.

Some people would call this selective sex. Many singles find themselves in this situation. They don't want to be known as bed hoppers, so they opt for a smattering of involvement to justify a sexual relationship.

Attitude three. Sex is a gift from God, and it comes with great responsibilities to the participants. It is best enjoyed to its fullest within the context of a marital relationship. Sounds rather restrictive, doesn't it? You might wonder if anyone in today's world really believes this. Contrary to what you might think, there are many single-again persons who believe that this attitude is the right one for them and seek to live by it.

These three attitudes are widely scattered throughout the singles community. Let me ask you several questions to help you sharpen your own focus:

1. Which one of the three attitudes describes where you are in your own thinking right now? Be honest.
2. How did you arrive at that attitude? What led you to it and what or who influenced you?
3. Is it the best and right place for you to be? Why?
4. Where do you think God wants you to be? Why?

What I have discovered from talking to thousands of single people about this subject is that many of them have never really thought much about where they stand. They have developed a conditional stand, a sort of "We'll see what happens and what kind of opportunities come up, then decide." Living by situation ethics is always precarious. You never have a solid foundation under you. You are totally subject to your emotions of the moment. It's a little like standing on a cloud.

I believe that people with well-thought-through convictions draw respect. People who live in the cracks of life are never taken too seriously.

The above questions will provide you with a lot of homework. If you do it, you will find your struggles in this area greatly reduced.

What Does God Think About Sex and Singleness?

That's a good question, and many people don't want to know. If you have decided to follow God, then you need to know and wrestle with the implications.

The Scriptures talk about a general principle for all our behavior in 1 Corinthians 10:31: "So, whether you eat or drink, or whatever you do, do all to the glory of God." The "whatever" is pretty comprehensive. It includes relating sexually in your life. Most people would not think that. They would look at the obvious things like fun, hobbies, conversation, and jobs. Paul put the *all* in there for our own safety in making decisions.

—From Jim Smoke, *Suddenly Single.* Old Tappan, N.J.: Revell, 1982.

REBUILDING

THERE ARE THREE STAGES most people have to work through as they rebuild their lives as single-again men and women.

The first stage involves looking back on the yesterday of your life and saying, "If I'd only...." You don't have to think too long or too hard to come up with an immediate list of things you wish you had done differently. The truth is that you cannot change history or memories. You can only learn from them. Looking back with regret only dulls your hope for today.

In my work, I often refer to what the Bible tells us about situations we may face. The Apostle Paul said, "... forgetting what lies behind and straining forward to what lies ahead, I press on toward the goal for the prize of the upward call of God in Christ Jesus" (Philippians 3:13, 14). Paul had some things in his yesterdays that he wanted to forget. He knew that the only way this could happen was to live today, with his eyes open toward tomorrow.

Thinking in reverse only keeps you from moving forward. Many single-again people are still living in yesterday. Put all your yesterdays in your file drawer and concentrate on building today.

A second stage in rebuilding is known as forward-fear projection. It simply means you look at tomorrow and say to yourself, "What if ...?" What if you run out of money? What if you never remarry? What if you get sick and have no one to look after you? What if the stock market crashes and the gasoline supply dries up? What if your children become delinquents? The list could go on and on.

Fear of the future can immobilize you in the present and keep you from making the plans that will help you rebuild your life. Your future is a trust that is best handled by placing it in God's hands. Writing to the Early Christians at Philippi, Paul said, "Don't worry over anything whatever ... tell God every detail of your needs in thankful prayer ..." (Philippians 4:6 PHIL-LIPS).

The future can be frightening, not just for those who are single again but for all of us. Only God can translate that fear into trust.

The third stage deals with living in the present. At the conclusion of a divorce-recovery workshop, a lady presented me with a gift. When I opened it, I found it was a blue T-shirt with the words I CAN DO emblazoned across the front in large, bold letters. Those words translate what living in the present is all about. They stand in direct contrast to the first two attitudes. They plant you in the present with the challenge to accept responsibility for your life and to start your renewal.

The *I can dos* usually start with small things: small plans, small challenges, small triumphs. As these build in your life, you begin to feel good about yourself and your progress. A man in a workshop recently summed it up. He said, "The road back is full of potholes and mountains. It is definitely more fun climbing mountains than falling into potholes."

Paul's *I can do* statement is found in Philippians 4:13. He said, "I can do all things in him who strengthens me." Paul was a rebuilder. He was a "right now" liver infused with God's strength.

What are your *I can dos?* Have you taken time lately to write them down? Are you saying, "I can go back to school; find a new career; do a good job of single parenting; be responsible for myself; rebuild and go on with my life"?

No one else can do your rebuilding for you. Sometimes the temptation is to go hunting for that special someone who can do the work for you or who already has a game plan going in his or her own life. If you were a dependent person in your past marriage, the tendency will be to search for a person who will continue to do everything for you. Many second marriages are started on this premise, and many of them fail. Healthy marriages are ones in which an interdependent relationship exists.

The Different Levels of Relationships

Relationships are built on many different levels. Most of us are inhibited just enough to want others to do all the reaching out toward us. That's usually safe, for it puts us in charge of the response we choose to make. When we reach out to others first, we run the risk of their rejection, and that puts them in charge. Here are several types of relationships we all encounter.

1. *Random relationships.* There are a great number of come-and-go relationships drifting through most of our lives. There is the clerk at the supermarket who bags our groceries and exchanges small talk. There is the service-station mechanic we see every three months for car maintenance. The list also includes the mailman, the paperboy, the friends at our church, and our children's friends' parents. You could add a whole lot more to your own list.

These are the surface people in our lives. Our conversations usually consist of "Hi, how are you?" "Fine, how are you?" These people serve our own needs at an operational level. We don't want to know how they are. We don't have time to find out. Even worse, we really don't care, because we have no real involvement with them. They are merely our "maintenance people." We know their names and faces, but not their lives and struggles. We choose no deeper involvement than we have.

2. *Social relationships.* There are people in our lives whom we socialize with. We bowl, party, picnic, vacation, and camp with them. We invest ourselves recreationally with this group, but we rarely relate on a deep emotional level.

Many of you single-again people have had the experience of going to a social event attended by couples who were once a part of your world. It doesn't take long for you to feel very out of place. The visible togetherness of others just accentuates your aloneness. That special someone is no longer with you. Some singles have shared with me how they have run teary eyed from these kinds of events.

3. *Deep relationships.* Sometimes in my seminars, I ask the question "How many of you have a deep, intimate relationship with someone other than your spouse; a relationship of over ten years' endurance?" Usually not many hands are raised, but most people express the honest desire for this in their lives.

In the Bible, David and Jonathan had a deep friendship. It did not come about overnight. It took time to grow into an enduring relationship.

Few of us have the time to invest in more than one or two deep relationships. Our busy schedules push us toward an "instant intimacy" with other people. Our cry is, "Bare your soul. Tell me your history, and let's have a deep relationship." The problem with this is that friendships of lasting and enduring quality do not happen this way. Our world is in a hurry, but you can't rush the growth of a significant relationship.

Deep relationships involve listening, sharing, caring, and a great deal of personal commitment. A relationship with depth is always an investment.

We could call these three levels of relationship building "stepping-stones." All relationships begin on a random or casual level. We decide whether or not we will elevate them from there to the social level. Once at the social level, we decide whether we will move toward intimacy or depth with that person. All the while, we look for a commonality that draws us to another person. There is a certain chemistry in all relationships. Both people have to invest equal energy in the relationship. One person alone cannot make it happen. Sometimes our most meaningful relationships begin in strange ways. You can't plan them any more than you can set aside a day to go shopping for a new spouse. Relationships begin when we are available to them. That essentially means they will not happen if you are hiding in your closet or stuck in your rocker looking out the window at life passing by.

I meet some people who try to spiritualize their lack of good relationships by stating that God will send friends to them when He is ready. I deeply believe in God's direction in our lives. I also believe that we have to take the initiative and push ourselves out into the mainstream of life. Fishing in the bathtub can be a frustrating experience.

Let me clarify here that in talking about relationship building in this chapter we are not talking about finding a husband or wife. We are talking about finding friends of both sexes. It is possible, though, that a relationship can bloom into a marriage. That would be serendipity.

Building relationships means bringing meaningful people into your life at many different levels. Many single-again people have only one objective in mind: Find a person to marry as soon as possible. The pressure and panic that results from this kind of pursuit is enormous. An alternate response to the marriage-partner search is to see how many relationships you can sustain while "playing the field." The "one-night stand" is sometimes synonymous with this kind of behavior. People are used and discarded for self-gratification rather than relationship building.

When two people marry, they already have a relationship with each other. In-laws and relatives on both sides of the family form an instant circle of additional accepted relationships. Divorce and death can strip away this close circle and leave a person standing alone. Looking into the world of singleness

means restructuring and building new and meaningful relationships.

Jesus' Circles of Relationships

A model in relationship building is Jesus. We will gain more from looking at how He built and needed relationships than "how He survived as a single." Relationships were important to Him, and He gave quality time to them. The closest and most intimate relationship Jesus had on earth appears to have been with John, the beloved disciple. Beyond His immediate family, John was a relationship priority with Jesus. We are not sure about the "why" in this relationship, but the Scriptures portray the deep love and intimacy between Jesus and John. It was a special friendship.

On another level, Peter, James, and John seemed to form the inner circle that Jesus counted close to Himself. He confided in them. He asked special support from them. They were near Him in His moments of triumph and agony. They were as different from each other as night from day. Yet their friendship with Jesus was deep.

On other levels of relationships with Jesus, we have the 12 disciples; after that, the 70, the 120, and the 500. Beyond all of these were the crowds that followed Jesus everywhere. They reached out to touch Him, and He touched them back. They went their way, and He went His.

As you explore the Scriptures, you can quickly see where Jesus spent most of His time. The disciples were His inner circle. They shared in His life. Jesus knew that He could not give quality time to everyone.

At yet another place in Jesus' friendship circle stood Mary, Martha, and Lazarus. Scripture indicates that it was to their home Jesus went for refuge, renewal, and rest. All of us need a center like that to retreat to— away from the demands of life—distant from the reaching hands of others and their constant expectancies. We need a place and a circle of friends in which to let down our guard and be ourselves in a relaxed way. This is a very important part of relationship building. Where is your special place to rest and be renewed while the world races by?

The Value of Deep Relationships

Perhaps we should take a look at the value of those relationships we need and what they will add to our lives.

1. *Acceptance.* We all have that basic human need to be accepted by others as we are—warts and all. We generally only reveal little bits and pieces of ourselves as we get to know others. We are really testing them to see if there is a point of nonacceptance where they will cut us off and the relationship will go no further. Sometimes this is done very adeptly in the dating process. Hours are spent in prepping for a date so that someone will see us as we would like them to see us. Only as our acceptance level with the other person climbs do we lower our preparation time. After marriage, we seldom give much thought to how we look to the other person.

As children, we are told to make a good impression on people. We will be liked and accepted if we do. One day my doorbell rang, and I raced through the house from my back yard gardening to answer it. As the sweat and dirt ran down my face, I opened the door, only to stand nose to nose with one of the most immaculately dressed women I had ever known. She was in my singles group and was dropping off some fliers.

Standing there in my cutoffs, shirtless and dripping, I certainly did not look like anything close to a senior staff minister at a large church. Her comment was, *"Jim,"* with what seemed to have a large question mark behind it. I found myself racing through an apology

for the way I looked, explaining that I was knee-deep in gardening. I was desperately concerned about her continued acceptance of me as her pastor, even though I did not appear pastorly looking.

From time to time, we all get caught when we are not looking the way we would like to look. Life seems to be one long prep course in acceptance.

2. *Trust.* A deep relationship with another person has trust as one of its root ingredients. Without trust, there can be no depth in a relationship.

I speak with many people in divorce counseling who have had their trust violated. Perhaps their husbands or wives ran off with another person after an affair was discovered. They wonder if they will ever be able to trust another person again.

Trust is an earned commodity as a relationship or friendship grows. When a friend says he will pick you up at eight, you place trust in his promise. If it is constantly violated and he is habitually late, the trust level goes down. Building trust is believing promises as you see them lived out.

God has placed an infinite amount of trust in you and me as His creative work. We return that trust by believing His Word and accepting the promises it contains. Our trust level in God grows as we watch those promises being fulfilled in our lives. When He says He is with us—*He is really with us!* A deep relationship with a friend says, "I literally trust you with my life." A deep relationship with God says the same thing.

3. *Lack of jealousy.* Can you have a deep and meaningful relationship with someone of whom you are very jealous? I don't believe you can. Jealousy becomes a noose around a relationship that strangles the life from it. Jealousy ran rampant in the Early Church in the Bible. Paul constantly spoke about it in his letters. Even the disciples had to deal with it as they struggled for the highest posi-

tion in the kingdom they thought Jesus was setting up on earth.

Jealousy is a part of our human situation, but it destroys relationships. Celebration replaces jealousy. Instead of being jealous of my friends' gifts, talents, promotions, success, and wealth, I can choose to celebrate them. If I want the best for them, I will realize that I am not in competition with them. I am in friendship with them.

4. *Honesty.* When faced with a conflict or a decision, it's so easy to go from friend to friend collecting opinions. We call this a "pooling of ignorance." What we are doing most of the time is listening for only what we want to hear. Too few of us tell the truth to others. We are afraid that if we do, our relationships with them will falter and end. It is always interesting to me that the scriptural directive is to "speak the truth in love" (Ephesians 4:15 PHILLIPS). Truth, when spoken, demands a gentle handling. It is not something that we throw at people and hope they will catch. It is fragile and demands a loving touch. Only those who are our real friends and love us most will tell us the truth. Honesty will always hurt a lot less when it comes from someone who loves us and whom we love in return.

5. *Loyalty.* Loyalty in relationships says, "I will stand with you no matter what. If you do something I disagree with, I will tell you, but I will still be loyal to you with my friendship." Some of the best visual expressions of loyalty seem to come from animals. The world could certainly use a few more Lassies, Silvers, or Old Paints. Loyalty is the cement of friendship. The one thing Jesus' disciples had a difficult time with was loyalty. They enjoyed recognition when the miracles were happening, but when the clouds of the Crucifixion hung over them, they wanted to hide.

6. *Being there.* Single-again people have often shared with me that the toughest part of their day is coming home from work when they know that no one will be there to greet them. Loneliness is intensified at that point.

God has created us with a burning need to have people around us who are significant to us and care for us. This doesn't mean you need a party every day when you come home from work so that the house won't be empty. It does mean that you need to have special people in your life who will be there for you when you need them.

Hospital calling has always been uncomfortable for me. I feel pretty helpless and realize I can do little to enhance a person's healing process. I pray, encourage, make small talk, smile, and leave. Later people thank me for the visit. I wonder why. Then they say something like, "Thanks for just being there." Building relationships helps us learn that there are people who will be there for us when we need them.

7. *Spiritual resources.* Have you ever had a time in your life when a crisis hit you full force? I have. The shock and hurt were so great that it seemed my faith in God and His promises had gone on vacation.

It's a time like this that a trusted friend can offer his or her spiritual resources and strength to you. I recently called a friend in the midst of one of my chaos times. It was reassuring to know that someone on the other end of the phone, over two thousand miles away, listened intently as I shared my struggle. The simple words, "We will have faith for you," were what I really needed to hear. I am not always strong enough to have the faith I need in troubled times. I need my friends and their spiritual aid.

The years of developing deep relationships with people take on more meaning as we get older. There is a richness in friendships that gives our lives meaning and continuity. Our spiritual growth is not a solo flight. It is a shared journey.

One of the ongoing struggles in the world

of singleness centers around the intensity of relationships. The priority of many singles is finding the ultimate person for them—a potential mate. There is nothing wrong with this unless it becomes a pursuit that denies the building of other healthy relationships.

I have suggested to many singles across the country that they would experience less pressure if they built more brother-sister relationships.

—From Jim Smoke, *Suddenly Single*. Old Tappan, N.J.: Revell, 1982.

FORGIVENESS

I BELIEVE that one of the greatest therapies that God ever gave to man was the therapy of forgiveness. Without it, we would live in a constant state of guilt that could never be removed. Jesus set the stage for this in the scriptures. In the Gospel of John, chapter 8, Jesus is confronted with some religious leaders of His day who have brought a woman to him. The charge is that she was caught in the act of adultery. You will not read very far in this chapter before you will decide that the religious leaders were bent upon exacting punishment while Jesus was concerned about enacting forgiveness to the woman. In the last verse of this biblical incident, Jesus speaks to the woman with these words, "Neither do I condemn you; go your way; from now on sin no more."

What I see happening here sets an example of how we can look at other people's mistakes and how God deals with those mistakes. Jesus did not penalize the woman. He forgave her and encouraged her to begin living a new kind of life.

The religious leaders would have made an example of her to others. Jesus understood man's humanity and imperfections far better than those who were supposed to be the priests to men.

The scriptures contain numerous accounts of how Jesus dealt with human weakness. He expressed disappointment at it many times but he never condemned it. He was in the forgiveness business. In response to the disciples' request for an example of prayer, Jesus included the words "Forgive us our trespasses as we forgive those who trespass against us." Forgiveness is reciprocal. In the First Epistle of John, chapter 1, verse 9, we read, "If we confess our sin, He is faithful and righteous to forgive us our sins and to cleanse us from all unrighteousness." This verse is a promise that lets us know we can be forgiven if we admit our sin.

I believe divorce is a sin. It was not a part of God's perfect plan for man. But man in his weakness and humanity cannot always live up to God's ideal. The standards for man are set by God. When man breaks the standard, he must have a way to experience God's forgiveness and be restored to fellowship with God.

Dr. Dwight Small in an article entitled, "Divorce and Remarriage: A Fresh Biblical Perspective" states: "All divorce is failure to meet God's standard and hence it is sin; all parties alike need God's grace. But to all divorced Christians, guilty as well as innocent, renewing grace is available. The sole condition is true penitence, confession, and the sincere desire to go on to fulfill God's purpose."

Experiencing God's forgiveness begins by confession of our weakness and wrongdoing.

Remember when you were a child and you disobeyed your parents. Perhaps you covered it up for a time and they did not know about it. But you knew and you lived with the threat of being discovered and punished. Added to that was the weight of a guilty conscience. When you finally confessed your wrongdoing, you experienced a great sense of relief and the good feeling that everything was all right again between you and your parents.

The same good feeling prevails when we make things right with God. Here is a simple prayer that may express how you feel. Take a moment and share it with God.

> God, I know that divorce is wrong.
> I know it was not your ideal for me.
> God, I confess to you my weaknesses and human failings that contributed knowingly and unknowingly to my divorce.
> God, I ask your forgiveness for my divorce.
> Help me to know and experience your love through your forgiveness.
> Lead me to new growth and new beginnings in my life.
> Thank you, Lord! Amen.

I Forgive Me!

The second part of experiencing forgiveness is the most difficult for many people. It is easier to confess our humanity before God than it is to admit it to ourselves. We live by the motto: "I'M NOT PERFECT, BUT JUST DON'T REMIND ME OF IT." It is extremely hard to admit your own weaknesses and shortcomings.

The finest court in the land could not examine all the intricacies that combined to cause a marriage to fail. Few counselors are skilled enough to assess who or what caused the marriage to disintegrate. Lacking a pronouncement of some form that would place the blame, many people who go through a divorce take the blame upon themselves. Others might tend to absolve themselves of all blame.

Many people who experience divorce cannot forgive themselves for whatever part they played in the process. They end up playing the game of "IF ONLY I'D. . . ." There is no way you can win this game because you can't change anything. What has happened is history.

Forgiving yourself means:

> I ACCEPT MY HUMANITY AS A HUMAN BEING
> I HAVE THE FREEDOM TO FAIL
> I ACCEPT RESPONSIBILITY FOR MY FAILURES
> I CAN FORGIVE MYSELF FOR MY FAILURES
> I ACCEPT GOD'S FORGIVENESS
> I CAN BEGIN AGAIN

Many people live under the yoke of self-imposed guilt. They are unable to accept the fact that to be human means you will make mistakes. Until they can experience the refreshing climate of self-forgiveness, they will not enjoy their humanity.

I Forgive My Ex-Spouse

I can hear you saying, "Now that's carrying things too far! After all that he or she has done to me, I will never forgive them."

When a person is caught in the heat of argument and emotional combat, forgiveness is usually the very last thing to come to mind. Be aware that forgiveness is not an instant thing but a process that you grow into. Few people that I have shared these thoughts with in Divorce Growth Seminars have raced out of the class to see if they work. Forgiveness from God comes easiest and is the first step. Self-forgiveness is second and is a little harder. Forgiveness in the ex-spouse realm is usually a long way down the recovery road and can only happen when the fires of divorce cool long enough to let sound thinking take over.

A person asked me recently what to say to an ex-spouse in this area. You might start by saying, "I'm sorry. I ask your forgiveness for all my mistakes and whatever part I might have played in contributing to our divorce." Sounds hard doesn't it?

—From Jim Smoke, *Growing Through Divorce.* Eugene, Ore.: Harvest House, 1976.

EFFECT ON CHILDREN

I LEARNED SOMETHING recently from a knowledgeable children's worker: often a child gets the feeling that he or she caused the divorce. He may have overheard one of his parents when they were arguing say, "If it weren't for the children I'd get a divorce." The child is not able to understand this completely, but he does put together the emotion of anger and the words "children" and "divorce." He may even feel that something he did or didn't do was responsible. The guilt which a child can accumulate from assuming the responsibility for the breakup of the family can be terribly destructive.

There is no way to predict how a child will react to a divorce and the prospect of not living with both parents. It would depend upon the individual child and the family. Some anxiety can be alleviated if the parents communicate with the children about what is about to happen. Children need to be reassured by their parents that they are loved and will be cared for. They need to be reassured of their worth by the parents. It is sometimes hard for them to grasp the idea that though the marriage is dead the family continues to exist. The adjustment the children have to make is not merely to living with just one parent. It is an adjustment to having two parents who don't live together any more. While this is not easy, with some added effort on the part of both parents and help from friends, the children can have most of their needs met as they grow to adulthood.

There are two major problems which must be dealt with concerning the children, and

this can only be done by their parents. First, the parents must make an effort not to let the children become the extended battleground of their own difficulties. It is important for the children to respect and love both parents. This is made difficult when parents ask the child to take sides or share bad stories about the other parent. Some parents even interrogate the child about what was said, done, and observed at the other's house. The natural tendency of those going through a divorce is to divide up the furniture and children. I'm not too worried about the furniture but the children deserve better treatment.

The second problem is to find constructive ways to meet the needs of the children which were usually met by the absent partner. There's always the tendency, or at least the temptation, on the part of the parent in the home to be overprotective and overindulgent. The parent who has the children only occasionally is tempted to buy gifts for the children and make all the visits fun and games. Neither of these situations is what the child needs. The needs of children have not changed basically. It's just the means of meeting those needs.

The children of a divorce, both young and old, have the same needs as their parents. They need love and care and assurance. These needs can be met by all the members of the family and extended family plus a host of friends. Don't forget the children. Jesus said, "For the kingdom of God belongs to such as these" (Mark 10:14).

—From Kenneth Chafin, *Is There a Family in the House?* copyright © 1978, pp. 143–45; used by permission of Word Books, Publisher, Waco, Texas 76796.

Child Custody Arrangements

Courts are now much more willing to consider awarding custody to fathers. This doesn't mean it's easy. As Robert K. Moffett and Jack F. Scherer point out in their book *Dealing with Divorce:* "Some fathers have always received custody and what we may be seeing at present is no more than a statistical 'blip' with no real significance." Mothers who want custody "still have all the odds in their favor when it comes to a custody fight." However, "the best interests of the child" is becoming the increasingly accepted norm by which custody cases are decided. Moffett and Scherer point out that the most comprehensive act to be passed into law is the Michigan Child Custody Act of 1970 which declares that in awarding custody, the court should consider:

(a) The love, affection, and other emotional ties existing between the competing parties and the child.

(b) The capacities and dispositions of the competing parties to give the child love, affection, and guidance and continuation of the educating and raising of the child in its religion or creed, if any.

(c) The capacities and dispositions of the competing parties to provide the child with food, clothing, medical care, or other remedial care recognized and permitted under the laws of this state in lieu of medical care, and other material needs.

(d) The length of time the child has lived in a stable, satisfactory environment and the desirability of maintaining continuity.

(e) The permanence, as a family unit, of the existing or proposed custodial home.

(f) The moral fitness of the competing parties.

(g) The mental and physical health of the competing parties.

(h) The home, school, and community record of the child.

(i) The reasonable preference of the child, if the court deems the child to be of sufficient age to express preference.

(j) Any other factor considered by the court to be relevant to a particular child custody dispute.

The law specifically states that a judge *"must* take these factors into consideration in determining which parent gets custody." And with Michigan's "no fault" divorce law, the sole ground for divorce is "irretrievable breakdown" of the marriage. With fathers generally taking a more active interest in their roles as fathers, it seems fair to assume that more flexible custody laws eventually will be adopted by other states.

The June 3, 1979, issue of *Suffolk Life,* a weekly newspaper, carried an article entitled "Parent Custody Groups Speak Out" that began: "In what has been labelled the International Year of the Child, about 150 groups throughout the United States have become increasingly vocal about the laws which they feel are a violation of a fundamental human right—the right of a divorced parent to share the custody of his or her children."

Joint Custody. I interviewed Dr. Radh Achuthan, an activist in the joint-custody movement and President of the League for Human Rights in Divorce, at his home in Southhampton, New York. Dr. Achuthan, who is a physics professor at Southhampton College, made the point that individuals should divorce as "spouses not as parents. The present setup creates divorce between parent and child." He also believes that in 99% of divorce situations, both parents are fit custodians. What he would like to see is a custody situation in which joint custody was awarded as the norm and it would take a special legal process to prove that single custody was in the best interests of the child. He sees the only exception to joint legal and alternating physical custody occurring "where one or both parents can be proven to be grossly unfit. . . . The physical residence

395

of the children should be left to pragmatic decisions based upon the individual situations."

I sympathize deeply with fathers who are cut off from their children due to custody battles. It does seem that in theory, joint custody is fairest. And certainly flexible visiting arrangements that allow children stress-free time with both parents are desirable. However, I can see that joint custody which is legally mandated could create problems. What happens if one parent moves to a distant location and still insists on a 50-50 division of children's time? Or does joint custody merely imply that both parents have an equal say in the training and schooling of the children?

The most successful arrangements seem to be those that are worked out between the parents, as the situation grows and develops, regardless of what's down on that legal agreement. . . .

In terms of the suggestion about child support and/or alimony enforcement, most experts agree that enactment of the proposed Uniform Child Custody Act would be a great help in enforcing these payments and in preventing childnapping incidents. Thirty-three states already have reciprocal agreements that prevent a delinquent parent from taking shelter in those states. But the problem is still acute.

In an interview, three school specialists— a teacher, a school nurse and a school social worker (all of whom are single parents themselves)—stated that they were in favor of joint custody. They also listed these objectives:

- Attain universal understanding that not every child has two parents, and if he doesn't, that does not necessarily mean that he is a troubled child.
- Establish more support systems: "In light of my professional experience [as a social worker], more community support systems are needed to assist single parents—men and women—make the transition. Also, older single parents need a vehicle to meet one another."
- Pass no-fault divorce legislation in every state, with divorce counseling by accredited professional required, in order that children will not be so hurt.
- Make child-support laws tougher by stiffening up penalties for evading them and providing more personnel for tracing the evaders.
- Provide more day-care centers for working single parents (both male and female).
- Give homemakers social security credit.

—From Carol V. Murdock, *Single Parents Are People, Too!* Piscataway, N.J.: New Century, 1980.

Child Support

Child-support payments differ from alimony in that they are for the benefit of the child, not for the support of the former wife. If you and your former marriage partner have worked out an agreement concerning the support of your child, the court probably will approve that agreement provided, in the judgment of the court, the provision is adequate. The court has a great deal of power when dealing with children, however. Even if you and your former spouse have agreed on what is to be paid for child support, the court may either increase or decrease the amount. If you have not come to some agreement, the court will determine on its own what is to be done. Furthermore, the court can make changes at any time until the child legally becomes an adult.

The payment of child support is not tied in with the question of whether a woman can support her child alone. Whatever her circumstances, the child's father has responsibilities which he cannot evade. He cannot plead insufficient income as an excuse for not helping support his child. The amount of his income is a factor in determining *how much* he may be required to pay, but not a factor in determining *whether* he is to pay anything. Support is his obligation.

The amount of support that a man must pay will be determined on the basis of the same factors considered in deciding the amount of alimony. As always, the court will be primarily concerned with the welfare of the child. And realistically, the court is not likely to require more than the man is capable of paying.

The person who pays the required child support is not entitled to receive an accounting of how the money is spent. A woman who has custody of her child is presumed to be capable of fulfilling her obligations properly. If it can be demonstrated that she is not doing so, and that the child is suffering some kind of neglect, she may lose custody. But so long as she has custody, she alone determines how best to care for the child.

For many women, one of the most serious problems after divorce is the collection of the child-support payments which her former husband was ordered to make. It is not unusual for a man to skip payments from time to time, or to make payments of less than the specified amount. If he does so, the courts may take action against him. His property and/or wages can be attached. He can even be sent to jail for his refusal to pay. The difficulty with these procedures, however, is that he may have no property to attach, and he may quit his job and move elsewhere.

In dealing with the question of the support of your child, whether you have custody or whether he is under the custody of his other parent, you must put first the needs of your child. Unless you are better off financially than most divorced parents, you will have a difficult time of it. A family income that was perhaps barely adequate before your divorce now has to be stretched somewhat to support two households. If there was only one income, the mother may now have to go to work outside the home. That will involve added expense for child care. If both husband and wife worked before their divorce, there is little likelihood that their income can now be increased. The only alternative seems to be to find some way of cutting down on expenses. That is not impossible, for most of us have a rather high standard of living. It will be difficult, however, for most of us have become accustomed to and enjoy that high standard. The facts being what they are, however, there seems no other alternative.

—From Roger H. Crook, *An Open Book to the Christian Divorcee*. Nashville: Broadman, 1974.

Visitation Rights

Traditionally the courts have awarded the mother custody of children unless there was some specific reason for doing otherwise. That tradition is changing, however, and increasingly the courts are giving equal consideration to the rights and claims of the father. In a sense this is a real plus, for the decision is then based more upon what is best for the child in each situation.

In most instances, again unless there is reason to do otherwise, the courts grant "reasonable visiting rights" to the parent who does not get custody of the child. Whether such an arrangement is really in the best interest of the child is not at all certain. It often results in each parent trying to alienate the child from the other. In such case, the child is the innocent victim of a continuing battle between his parents. Yet it does seem needlessly cruel not only to the child but also to the parent to cut off all contact even though visits are quite possible.

Since visitation rights usually are granted, however, and since absent parents usually exercise those rights, you should do all within your power to make those visits happy experiences for your child. If you have custody, your former mate probably has worked out plans for having the child at regular intervals. As the two of you implement these arrangements, your paramount concern cannot be your own happiness but the welfare of your child. The two of you will therefore have to cooperate much more closely than apparently was possible for you as husband and wife.

You should make every effort not to spoil the occasion for your child or for his other parent. Issue no warnings—to your child or to his father (mother). Lay down no ultimatum. Cooperate with their plans. Have your child ready on time. If his father (mother) is late arriving, make no snide remarks. Give to your child no hint of your resentment at what is happening. Since you and your former partner are mature adults, you can at least be polite and considerate. In so doing you will ease things for your child.

Your child probably will appreciate it if you can arrange for his other parent to participate in events of special significance to him. Programs at school, birthdays, holidays—these are usually family events. Because of your divorce they cannot be so for your child in the same way as they are for most other children. Yet if they can be so at all your child will be happier. . . .

If you do not have custody of your child, but instead have only the right of visiting him from time to time, you are at something of a disadvantage. You live away from him, perhaps in an apartment with no arrangements for children. You have had to rearrange your life—your home routine, your work patterns, your social activities. If you

have remarried, your new husband or wife complicates your relationship with your child. If your new mate has children, the problem becomes even more complex. You have to work out your visit with your child in terms of convenience to yourself in your new situation, and your former mate in his (her) situation. With it all you will be trying to make the visit a happy experience for your child.

If you genuinely love your child, you will not try to buy his affection. Because you have little contact with him, you may try to load him down with gifts, or to spend all your time together in "fun and games." You may try desperately to convince him that you are in fact a good and loving parent— even that he would be better off with you. Although you may not intend it as such, these efforts may be your attempt to win your child away from your former mate. You cannot reverse the court's decision, however. All that you will succeed in doing is to confuse your child and make him even more dissatisfied with his lot in life.

"Fun and games," in fact, is a most abnormal situation. Your child needs not your gifts but you. He needs to learn from you. He needs to be disciplined by you. He needs to be with you at work as well as at play. He needs your counsel and advice. He needs your interest in his activities. He needs your example. He needs, in short, those things which you would supply if you were still living at home with him. Although you cannot supply them in the same way and to the same extent, you may be able to do something. If your child is not better off because of your visits with him, you would do well to forego those visits no matter how much they mean to you.

Your continuing interest in your child should not be confined to those weekly or monthly visits. No matter what has happened between you and your former mate, your child is a part of your life. You have a continuing responsibility to him and for him. You may succeed in separating yourself from an unhappy marriage. You cannot succeed in severing your relationship with your child. His physical well-being is in part your responsibility, no matter what happens. His emotional health and development are in part your responsibility. Perhaps the most painful aspect of your divorce is not being able to be with your child every day and in not being able to play that part in his life which you feel you should play. You will do well, therefore, to make special arrangements for special occasions, to keep in touch by telephone, to anticipate developing needs and provide for them.

All that has been said about visitation rights presumes a cooperative if not a cordial relationship between you and your former marriage partner. If you do not have that kind of relationship, you are the one who will suffer most. The parent who has custody of the child has the upper hand. One way or another, he calls the shots about when and under what circumstances you can see your child. As we have indicated, your child needs you. Your meeting that need demands that you do everything within your power to get the cooperation of your former partner.

It may develop that your child would be better off if he had only minimal contact with you. If your relationships with your child were stormy before you were divorced, they are not likely to be better now. If you were a poor parent then, your divorce does not make you a better one. A violent temper is not healed by a divorce. Neither is alcoholism or indifference or suspicion or self-centeredness or any of the other things that trouble a family. Occasionally a divorce will bring a person to his senses, make him take stock of himself, and effect a change in his character or personality. More often, however, it only adds failure in marriage to an already long list of personal problems. If that is what has happened in your case, you will do well to consider whether in fact you should exercise your right of visitation!

What I am saying to a parent who does not have custody of his child is simple: What you do now should be whatever is in the best interest of your child. I am not indifferent to your wants and needs. It will be well if they can be supplied. But at this stage, your dominant consideration must be the interest of your child. He is the innocent victim of what is happening. He stands in the position of greatest danger in this whole affair. His character and personality are still in the formative stage. Nothing can prevent his being hurt by what has transpired. Every possible effort must be made to minimize the hurt, however, and to make it possible for him to develop into a normal, healthy, mature adult.

—From Roger H. Crook, *An Open Book to the Christian Divorcee.* Nashville: Broadman, 1974.

SINGLE PARENTING

As a divorced parent with custody of your child, can you give your child a normal home-life?

"A normal homelife" is generally assumed to be essential to the healthiest emotional development of a child. In our minds "normal homelife" means two parents and their children living in a community where most of the neighbors are also two parents and their children.

One-parent families, however, have always been a part of the American scene. During periods of war, by the tens of thousands men have been taken away from their families for indefinite periods of time. In war and peace, young widows and widowers by the thousands rear their children alone. In smaller numbers, but significant nevertheless, unmarried mothers rear their own children. With the rising divorce rate, formerly married parents are becoming, if not commonplace at least not unusual.

How do the children of such one-parent homes fare? Specifically, how do the children of divorced parents fare? Are the chances increased that the child of divorced parents will become a problem to society?

A clue to the answer to this question can be found in the area of juvenile delinquency. One study of approximately eighteen thousand juvenile delinquents revealed that only about 10 percent of the delinquent boys and 20 percent of the girls were children of divorced parents. These figures do not tell the whole story. Obviously the best environment in which a child can grow up is a happy home with two parents present. Yet "the largest proportion of these children who fall foul of the law come from families which are emotionally broken. . . ."

—From Roger H. Crook, *An Open Book to the Christian Divorcee.* Nashville: Broadman, 1974.

Single Mothers

Divorce is one of the great tragedies of our times, but it is very much with us and ignoring it will not make it go away. In many cases children are involved, producing a large corps of single parents. Add to their ranks the widows, widowers, and unwed mothers and their number is enormous. The vast majority of these single parents are women, and so we direct a brief word to their plight here. The comments we make should be equally applicable to single fathers, however.

Not long ago I had the opportunity of addressing several questions to a group of Christian singles about their parental problems. Most of them were divorced. When I asked what advice they would give to someone who had just become a single parent, one woman wrote, "If possible, don't become one." That's the best advice I know. God has the solution to every marital problem. If there is any hope at all of a reconciliation, seek it diligently whether or not the divorce is final. With godly counsel and a willingness to work at the marriage there is hope for success.

For the widowed, that advice is meaningless. And for many of the divorced, it's too late. What then are the problems of single parenthood? One recurring theme was *loneliness*. "Eight or nine P.M. comes, your child is in bed, and you are alone. There's no one to share burdens and joys with. You have the responsibility of rearing a child. But that child cannot meet you at your level of communication. Often that loneliness turns to self-pity."

What is the answer to this gnawing empty aloneness? Another single writes, "Join a caring group of single parents who are interested in the welfare of the children in addition to their own social needs, especially a Christian group." Family outings with such groups will expose your children to adults of the opposite sex and help fill the void in their life. More important for you personally, it will provide opportunities for fellowship with adults. Contact with adults who have similar problems to yours will meet some of the needs in your life and will help you relate better to your children when you are with them. But the best remedy for loneliness is to cultivate a growing relationship with the Lord. He has promised never to leave you nor forsake you (*see* Hebrews 13:5).

A second common problem was *having the time, energy, and patience to meet the needs of the children.* A woman writes, "Often it seems there is never enough time in the day just to be Mama. For example, having just finished a hard and hectic day at the office, now it's time to pick up my daughter from nursery school. She's been playing and learning happily all day and is unaware of my frustrations (as she should be). She's so excited to see her Mama. She wants Mama all to herself. But Mama is tired. And it's time to make supper, wash dishes, do some cleaning. Then it's time to get her ready for bed. Where has the time gone? A single parent has to do the work of two. Yet her child needs the love and reassurance that only she can give. Is there time?"

The same single mother answers her own question. Mark it well! "Your child needs you, his parent, *now*—not when you have the time, but now. Therefore, you must make the time. Share your activities with the child, let him be your helper. It's not easy, for sure, but so very necessary."

The third most frequent problem cited by divorced parents relates to their ex-mates and the *bitterness* that remains between them. There always seems to be a temptation to put the blame for your troubles on your former mate and make that one look bad in the child's eyes. A single dad offers some good advice: "Don't criticize the 'ex.' Encourage the children to love and respect the other parent. And do everything you can to make it clear that the children are not responsible for the breakup." One divorcee told me that every night when she prayed with her son at bedtime, she assured him that God loved him, she loved him, and daddy loved him. In spite of the calamity of divorce, that little fellow enjoyed a healthy relationship with his father.

There is only one way to reduce the lingering pain of divorce and to heal some of the wounds that endure. "Get rid of all bitterness, rage and anger, brawling and slander, along with every form of malice. Be kind and compassionate to one another, forgiving each other, just as in Christ God forgave you" (Ephesians 4:31, 32, NIV).

Single parents and their children are needy people. It would be to the credit of every complete Christian family to reach out with Christ-like love to help meet those needs. Some children of divorce have never seen a happy marital relationship. We can invite them to our homes and show them that marriage can be a wonderful experience. God may use us to help build successful homes in years to come.

—From Richard L. Strauss, *Confident Children and How They Grow.* Wheaton, Ill.: Tyndale, 1975.

Support Groups

Parenting responsibility is essentially the same whether a couple or just one parent is involved. An increasing number of families have but one parent in the home. This situation presents a difficult but not impossible task. Many single-parent families are doing well. Without exception, the ones I am aware of are making up for the absent mate by plugging into a network of support groups which become allies of the parent and the children. A father or mother with sole responsibility for children will find immeasurable help from Sunday school teachers, scouting, choirs, camps, grandparents, and close adult friends. The basic needs of children and the goals of parenting are the same whether done alone or with help from a mate.

—From Kenneth Chafin, *Is There a Family in the House?* copyright © 1978, p. 68; used by permission of Word Books, Publisher, Waco, Texas 76796.

THEOLOGICAL ASPECTS

1. It has been God's divine provision from the beginning that marriage be a perma-

nent, lifelong union between one man and one woman.

2. From the Genesis passage and Christ's affirmation of the creation account, the "putting asunder" of the marriage union is against God's plan and the contracting of another marriage is a breach of God's unconditional will.

3. The Deuteronomic code which allows divorce does so only as a concession to man's sinfulness, and is not God's answer to marital problems.

4. When approached by the Pharisees regarding Mosaic legislation, Jesus allows for a dissolution of the marriage union when there is fornication or adultery on the part of one of the spouses, and the "innocent" partner may remarry.

5. The destructiveness of adultery, however, is not imperative to dissolution, but the divine ideal is that there be repentance, forgiveness, reconciliation, and renewal rather than separation, divorce, and remarriage.

6. Adultery can be interpreted from the original as an act of sin rather than as a continuing state of sinfulness. Therefore, the hostile feelings and acts which wedged the two partners from each other, including adultery with another party, can be repented of and forgiven. If reconciliation with the married partner cannot be achieved, remarriage is a possibility.

7. The Apostle Paul, confronted with a Corinthian problem, granted permission for dissolution of the marriage vows when an unbelieving partner deserted his/her spouse. The believer may contract another marriage, but the new union must only be with a Christian.

Our careful examination and exegesis of the pertinent biblical passages has suggested some basic principles we as Christians need to keep in mind in our specific dealings with persons who are personally facing these issues. How do these principles apply to the church today? It is my conviction that where divorce and remarriage have already occurred, the church must be a discerning, compassionate, and forgiving body. On the one hand it must avoid condoning and minimizing unrepentant sin, but on the other hand it must be an agent of Christ's deliverance from condemnation and sin. Both pastoral leadership and laity must search together for the will of Christ in individual cases, attempting to discern through Holy Spirit wisdom what the Scriptures are saying to us and how we can apply them to situations so that persons are lifted up and assisted on the road that leads to God.

Approaches of Churches

Even though it is true that all Christian denominations use the Bible as their basis for guiding denominational polity, divergent beliefs on the divorce-remarriage question have abounded through church history. In the first place, the existence of numerous denominations points out that scriptural interpretation on various issues, from modes of baptism to what denotes worldliness, differs widely. . . .

THE LAISSEZ-FAIRE APPROACH

This approach involves two extremes. The first is typified by the "marrying parson" who agrees to perform the ceremony for any couple who asks for his services whether previously married or not. The preacher in this case does not consider seriously the possible degree of success or failure of the marriage. He feels that by performing the ceremony, he has at least been in contact with the couple. Possibly their exposure to a short sermon and the sharing of Christian vows will be of some spiritual help to them. At least they will be exposed to more scriptural teaching than if they had settled for a civil wedding.

The other expression of the laissez-faire approach is the legalist kind of minister who says he will have nothing to do with any divorced person. He does not even suggest counseling sessions in order to ascertain the situation. Instead, he holds high the institutional part of his ministry and does not relate at all in this case to the needs of his community, and in some cases, even his church. Concerning one case I personally am acquainted with, the ruling body of the church would not allow the pastor to respond in any way to a couple, both partners previously divorced, who had asked that pastor to marry them. Pastors caught in this narrow bind, impeded by their own stringent convictions or those of the denomination or local congregation, seem to look on divorce as "those peoples' problem."

In either of these cases—marrying anyone who comes along or never getting involved—pastors seem to be either ignorant of the causes and unique problems related to divorce or they do not understand the deep personal needs of the divorced. John R. Martin, in treating this laissez-faire approach, says, "In either case, the approach is basically the same, namely, I will do anything asked of me by a divorced person seeking remarriage or I will do nothing asked of me by a divorced person seeking remarriage."

THE IDEALISTIC APPROACH

The approach taken here by denominations or churches contends that Scripture does not allow for the remarriage of divorcees. Even the "exception clause" in Matthew 5:32 and 19:9 does not justify remarriage. In fact, marriage, ordained by God, is indissoluble. However, separation from bed and board is allowed.

Very briefly here, the position of the Anglican Church is set forth as an example.

. . . .

The Lambeth Conference of 1930 saw the marriage union as dissoluble only by death. Remarriage during the lifetime of a former partner is unbiblical. The church cannot remarry anyone while a former partner is still living.

As a general rule, however members within the church are not rejected by the Anglicans because they are caught in this type of a marital situation. Instead, the pastor counsels with the couple seeking marriage. Pertinent information about the couple is given to the bishop for his evaluation. If the bishop feels that each of the members in this proposed new marital union is living in good faith with the church, the marriage is given his approval. However, at this point, the couple is married not by the church, but by the civil authorities, and the church recognizes the validity of the marriage. By remaining aloof from the actual ceremony, the church is demonstrating its stand, and it also feels that it is keeping the biblical standard clear.

The Roman Catholic Church, as we shall see, takes the idealistic approach without the step in the direction of redemptiveness for the remarried couple.

THE FORENSIC APPROACH

This approach regards the biblical teachings on divorce as applicable only to a Christian marriage, but not to marriage in general. In this case, the church sits in judgment on the first marriage to determine whether it was a true Christian marriage: hence the term forensic approach.

In this approach, the Roman Catholic sacramental view of marriage comes into focus. Marriage is looked upon as a sacrament for those who are baptized.

. . . .

Churches holding this view need to ask these various questions if confronted with a request for remarriage: Was the previous marriage a Christian marriage? Were the persons seeking remarriage professing Christians and members of the church at the time of their first marriage? Since the time of divorce, have the persons become Christians? What about the new union—is it going to be composed of Christians or not?

Two of the problems in this approach are, "How will the theological condition of the previous marriage be determined?" and, "Is true marriage limited only to a covenant between Christians?"

THE CONFRONTATIONAL AND THERAPEUTIC APPROACH

This is the least judgmental and the most holistic of all the approaches presented. No effort is made to determine whether there is a guilty or innocent party, because rarely is this possible. In a marriage that has broken up, who can say that one is innocent and the other guilty? Everyone involved in a divorce is, to some extent, responsible. In fact, if the partners to this new union were from a church background, most likely the church must share corporately in the sin. Either it provided inadequate preparation for marriage, failed to provide good pastoral follow-up, or lost contact and caring by congregational members when separation took place. Or the breakdown could well be a combination of all three of these.

In the therapeutic approach, the church family attempts to be redemptive by extending itself in any way possible to provide a healing ministry where there are still hurts. This caring relationship which the couple feels from the church goes a long way in aiding each of them in developing a good relationship with the other.

—From G. Edwin Bontrager, *Divorce and the Faithful Church*. Scottdale, Pa.: Herald Press, 1978.

FOR FURTHER READING

Bontrager, G. Edwin. *Divorce and the Faithful Church*. Scottdale, Pa.: Herald Press, 1978.

Chafin, Kenneth. *Is There a Family in the House?* Waco, Tex.: Word Books, 1978.

Chapman, Gary. *Hope for the Separated*. Chicago: Moody, 1982.

Crook, Roger H. *An Open Book to the Christian Divorcee*. Nashville: Broadman, 1974.

Dahl, Gerald L. *Why Christian Marriages Are Breaking Up*. Nashville: Nelson, 1979.

Duty, Guy. *Divorce and Remarriage*. Minneapolis: Bethany House, 1967.

Fix, Janet, with Zola Levitt. *For Singles Only*. Old Tappan, N.J.: Revell, 1978.

Galloway, Dale E. *Dream a New Dream*. Wheaton, Ill.: Tyndale, 1975.

Hensley, J. Clark. *Coping With Being Single Again*. Nashville: Broadman, 1978.

Hunt, Morton. *The World of the Formerly Married*. New York: McGraw-Hill, 1965.

Hunter, Brenda. *Beyond Divorce: A Personal Journey*. Old Tappan, N.J.: Revell, 1978.

Johnson, James. *Loneliness Is Not Forever*. Chicago: Moody, 1979.

Kysar, Myrna and Robert. *The Asundered*. Atlanta: John Knox, 1978.

Murdock, Carol V. *Single Parents Are People Too!* Piscataway, N.J.: New Century, 1980.

Richards, Larry. *Remarriage: A Healing Gift from God*. Waco, Tex.: Word Books, 1981.

Schuller, Robert. *You Can Become the Person You Want to Be*. New York: Hawthorn, 1973.

Smith, Virginia Watts. *The Single Parent*. Rev. ed. Old Tappan, N.J.: Revell, 1983.

Smoke, Jim. *Growing Through Divorce*. Eugene, Ore.: Harvest House, 1976.

Smoke, Jim. *Suddenly Single*. Old Tappan, N.J.: Revell, 1982.

Stewart, Suzanne. *Parent Alone*. Waco, Tex.: Word Books, 1978.

Strauss, Richard L. *Confident Children and How They Grow*. Wheaton, Ill.: Tyndale, 1975.

Index